Crimetown U.S.A.

The History of the Mahoning Valley Mafia

Organized Crime Activity in Ohio's Steel Valley 1933 - 1963

Allan R. May

ConAllan Press, Cleveland, OH

Published by ConAllan Press, LLC
Cleveland, Ohio, USA

Library of Congress Cataloging-in-Publication Data

May, Allan R.
Crimetown U.S.A.: the history of the Mahoning Valley Mafia / by Allan R. May.
- 1st ed.
p. cm.
Includes bibliographical reference and index.
ISBN 9780983703754
Library of Congress Control Number: 2013939304
1. Mafia—Youngstown—Mahoning County—History
2. Youngstown—Ohio—Biography
3. Gangsters—Youngstown—Biography
4. Organized Crime—Youngstown—Mahoning County—Ohio
5. Murders—Youngstown—Ohio—Biography

Cover Art and Interior Design by Lynn Duchez Bycko, Commoner Company
Cover photograph of Youngstown courtesy of Jason Sforza

First published 2013

In taking on a project of this proportion - working with newspaper articles, police reports and conducting interviews - it is possible for mistakes to be made. Names, dates and locations could be incorrect. If the reader comes across any, the author would appreciate being contacted so corrections may be announced on his website. Also, if family members or friends of the people mentioned in this book would like to contribute additional information, we would be happy to share these on the website www.AllanRMay.com. Mr. May can be contacted at Allan@AllanRMay.com

This book is dedicated to the memory of

William E. Gruver

One of the Good Guys

and

To all the law enforcement
officers that serve and have served
in the Mahoning Valley
with honesty, integrity and courage.

Table of Contents

Acknowledgments

The writing of *Crimetown U.S.A.* is the end of a long journey that began well over a decade ago. In January 1999, I was working with Jerry Capeci, the dean of organized crime writers, on his popular *Gangland News* website. Around this time, Cleveland Heights native Rick Porrello launched AmericanMafia.com and approached me about writing a column for the website. This opportunity allowed me to write my own stories, giving me a little more creative freedom. Sometime during the summer of that year, Rick, who had already written two books about organized crime in Cleveland, asked me about co-authoring a book about the history of organized crime in Pittsburgh and Youngstown. Rick would handle Pittsburgh and Western Pennsylvania, and I would take on Youngstown and the Mahoning Valley.

Taking on Youngstown was not as easy as it sounded. Soon, I was spending weeks at a time in the city, meeting and interviewing people and camping out at the Youngstown Public Library on Wick Avenue. My travels also took me to Warren, Akron, Ashtabula, Canton, Toledo, Beaver Falls, Pennsylvania and Wheeling, West Virginia. Everywhere I went I was fortunate to meet and work with many kind and wonderful people, developing friendships that still exist today. Sadly, more than a dozen of the people I interviewed and became friends with have passed away.

As I began writing the book, it became apparent to both Rick and myself that there was too much material for just one volume. We soon decided to do two books. Then, after finding a whole new cast of characters in Warren and Trumbull County, I decided there was enough material there alone to produce another book. In November 2011 – with the support of Rick Porrello and the help of Lynn Duchez Bycko – my wife Connie and I self-published *Welcome to the Jungle Inn: The Story of the Mafia's Most Infamous Gambling Den.* The book was received well in the Mahoning Valley and we sold out the first printing and did a second run, which also sold out. At our first book signing and lecture, at the Warren-Trumbull County Library, we had a standing room only crowd, estimated at 250 people.

In deciding upon a publishing strategy for the Youngstown portion of the research, I finally decided to break it into three parts. This portion, titled *Crimetown U.S.A.*, is actually the middle of the story. Named after the John Kobler Saturday Evening Post article of the same name, it covers the years 1933 to 1963. The thinking here, as you will read in the Prologue, is that the underworld figures in Youngstown, who made the headlines during Prohibition, were not the major organized crime figures in the city after Repeal in 1933. This book covers the infamous lottery houses, the introduction of the "bug," and the bombings of the late 1950s and early 1960s. Youngstown received its notorious moniker "Crimetown U.S.A." following the tragic bombing murder of nine-year-old Tommy

Cavallaro in November 1962. After that, there was a relative easing of gang warfare in the Valley until the early 1970s.

A separate book will cover the earlier years and will discuss Black Hand activity in the Valley during the first two decades of the 20th Century. This volume will also include the Prohibition years and the highlights of that era – the Ohio liquor permit scandal, the corruption trial of David J. Scott and the murder of Youngstown's first Mafia boss, "Big Jim" Falconi. In addition, all the publicized bootlegging murders of the "Dry Years" will be discussed.

The last book of this Youngstown saga will begin where *Crimetown U.S.A.* leaves off. The 1970s saw the Carabbia-Naples War; an escalation of the division spoils between the Cleveland and Pittsburgh Mafia Families; a Cleveland gang war that utilized hoods from the valley; rampant corruption in both the city and county government; and the rise and fall of a brash local football hero, who went from county sheriff to United States Congressman to Federal prisoner. The corruption in the Valley had its beginning of the end in the mid-1990s, led by Cleveland-based Assistant U.S. Attorney Craig S. Morford.

As mentioned, I met a lot of wonderful people during my time in Youngstown and Warren. At the Youngstown Public Library the staff was friendly and extremely helpful. Two employees in particular were especially helpful to me, Carole Anderson and Theresa Cousins. The two always took care of all my technical problems, and their kindness made me look forward to my trips down there. We had many pleasant conversations during my long hours upstairs in the research section. At Warren-Trumbull County Library I met the incredible Carol Bell, who was responsible for providing the depth of information that made me comfortable in doing a book about that area. Sadly, Carol passed away before that book was published. After her passing Carol Genova provided me with great support.

It was while I was doing research in Warren that I met Jan Vaughn. As program director at Warren-Trumbull County Library, she scheduled me as a speaker numerous times and through her programs I was blessed with a faithful following among the citizens of there. During this time Jan was promoted to Assistant Director of the library. She became my biggest supporter and a dear friend to me and Connie; so much so that I dedicated *Welcome to the Jungle Inn* to her.

In addition to the folks at the libraries in Warren and Youngstown, I received assistance from the following library people: Pete Ewell, Ryan Jaenke and Melinda Schafer at Cleveland Public Library; Betty L. Conner at Beaver County Research Center, Beaver Falls, Pennsylvania; Audrey John, Niles Historical Society; and Lynn Duchez Bycko at Cleveland State University Special Collections.

Many authors will agree with me that when taking on a project of this nature you are sometimes blessed by connecting with that certain person who is willing to go the extra distance in providing you with the help you need to make the end project extremely special. In the case of *Crimetown U.S.A.* this individual was Officer Nick Marciano of the Youngstown Police Department. Working in the records department, Nick provided much of the technical material, along with the majority of the mug shot photos used in this book. The best part was sitting in the station listening to the stories police officers are famous for telling. Nick and I became friends and he introduced me to several of the fine Italian restaurants in the city; further endearing himself to me. He was a regular at my talks at the Warren-Trumbull County Library. Nick retired after 32 years of service in 2009.

During my years of research in the area, I also had the help of many members of law enforcement. Among them, Ray Bagaglia and the late Albert Timko, Sr., (Warren Police Department); Carl Frost (Beaver Township Police Chief); John J. Gocala (Youngstown State University Police Chief); the late John M. Mandopoulos (former Police Chief, Warren Police Department); the late John Terlesky (former Police Chief, Youngstown Police Department); Captain Michael Cannon and Sergeant Arthur Lichtinger - retired (Cleveland Heights Police Department). The following FBI agents, all now retired, were also extremely helpful and supportive: John Kane, Robert G. Kroner, Lawrence L. Lynch, Michael D. "Mickey" Roberts and Mark S. Swanger.

I want to offer a very special thank you to three of Youngstown's former finest. Captain Donald Komara, who as a young patrolman appeared at the murder scene of Sandy Naples and his girlfriend; and at the home of Charles Cavallaro after the tragic bombing. Komara was invaluable in discussing the activities that took place in the city during the turbulent early 1960s.

Randall "Duke" Wellington, who, next to Eddie Allen is probably the Mahoning Valley's most famous law enforcement officer. Wellington is the only man to serve as both Chief of Police of Youngstown and Mahoning County Sheriff. He was a living legend by the time I met him.

The last is Officer William Gruver. Bill became a dear friend of mine. My wife Connie and I would often have dinner with Bill and his wife Donna up until his passing in 2008. He was one of the kindest individuals I have ever met and was always so full of life even when he was ill during his final years. He provided me with many photographs and stories from his years on the police force, most spent with his famous partner "Duke" Wellington. My greatest regret is that he didn't survive to see this book. I miss him dearly.

Mahoning Valley residents that I would like to single out are Thomas Micklas, the nephew of Dominic Caputo. I spent several pleasant evenings with Tom, who provided photographs and stories about his notorious uncle and his friends. He is a fine gentleman. The late Joseph F. Fortine took time to help me. Finally, Anthony Misik from Calvary Cemetery was a tremendous help in directing me to all the gravesites at the cemetery. Also a special mention of the late Donald Hanni.

Is there anyone in the Valley who isn't familiar with him? More about him in the next volume.

Outside of the Valley, I want to extend a very special thank you to Michael A. Tona – the most knowledgeable man on the history of the Buffalo underworld. Mike was a big help in allowing me to understand the Buffalo angle and its characters, most notably Joseph DiCarlo.

Sylvia Lewis introduced me to some of the characters in the Valley. She and I became good friends and we spent a lot of time together at many of Youngstown's great restaurants – mostly Italian. She introduced me to Marino's on Mahoning Avenue, a fine restaurant which I still frequent. Sylvia was a special friend through my many years of research.

The three people who made the most significant personal contributions to this project were Lynn Duchez Bycko, Charles R. Molino and Connie May. Lynn was the key person in helping me to self-publish *Welcome to the Jungle Inn.* For more than a decade Lynn has served as an advisor, counselor and therapist to me, and has become one of my best friends. She was invaluable to me in finally getting this much awaited project to market. I can't thank her enough for all that she has done to make *Crimetown U.S.A.* possible.

During the brief time I worked for Jerry Capeci, he introduced me to Charlie Molino. When I purchase Charlie's headstone it's going to proclaim: "The most knowledgeable man on the history of organized crime in America." I've spent more time with "Charlie Moose" than any other person in the Valley. He drove me to many of the sites mentioned throughout the book; helped me find grave stones at the cemetery; provided me with endless articles and research data and became my top confidant. In addition, he has read tirelessly everything I have ever written, whether it be about Youngstown, Warren, Cleveland, New York, Chicago and even the tiny village of Iron River, Michigan. He's a constant source of information, but more importantly has been my best friend for the past fourteen years. During my weeks in the city, which spanned several years, his wife Barbara invited me for her famous baked Ziti and other wonderful Italian meals. Her kindness and hospitality has extended to Connie as well. Charlie, stay well my friend, we still have much work to do.

My wife Connie has been a constant moral support for me since we met in the early 2000s. During our time together, although battling a serious illness, she never waived in her love for me and the support of the work I was doing. During my time writing columns for AmericanMafia.com, she has taken phone calls from mob figures, ex-girlfriends of gangsters and the occasional former Mafia boss – all in good spirit. My life has been much enriched over the years because of her. As time goes by she has become more and more involved in helping me promote and market my work. This takes time away from the things she loves, but allows us to spend even more time together on road trips for lectures and book signings throughout northeastern Ohio. For all her hard work

I have rewarded her again with helping me to promote this book. God knows I couldn't do it without her.

I also want to spend some time talking about the premier newspaper in the Mahoning Valley. I could not have written, let alone researched, this book without the use of the Youngstown *Vindicator* and two of their key personnel – Martha Clonis and Neva Yaist. These two wonderful women were a tremendous help in getting me the information I needed to focus in on all the people and events I wanted to research. Without their invaluable assistance, I would have been reduced to sitting in front of a newspaper reel viewing machine at the Youngstown library for years on end, searching page by page for the information I needed.

The *Vindicator* played a very power role in keeping the exploits of these criminals on the front pages. Whenever the police or the prosecutors or the judges failed in their duties, it was always the *Vindicator* that brought the stories to light and refused to allow these underworld figures to avoid exposure or walk away unscathed. The reader will surely recognize the wonderful work of these reporters through the decades in *Crimetown U.S.A.* as they kept these hoodlum activities in the headlines, and the corruptness of individuals from law enforcement, the justice system and local politicians on the public hot seat.

As always, a very special thank you to the following family members, friends and supporters. Charlotte M. Versagi, who provided me with encouragement and support for my writing for the past decade and a half. She and her father Frank Versagi have provided technical support, advice, counsel and guidance since the day I began writing.

A special thank you and good luck to Youngstown native John Chechitelli, who directed the *Youngstown Still Standing* documentary. He is working hard in Hollywood pursuing a film adaptation of this work.

In closing, I list these folks as the usual suspects. James Barber, Patrick Downey, Abby Goldberg, Robert Gross, Jerry Kovar, Tom Leahy, Fred Merrick, Biagio Morgano, John Murray, David Pastor, James Trueman, and Fred Wolking. And a special thanks to family members: Tammy Cabot, Gary May, and the Vaciks – Nelda, Bob, Melanie and Robbie.

I hope you enjoy *Crimetown U.S.A.*

Prologue

There's no way John Young could have foreseen how the city of Youngstown would turn out when he arrived in the early 1800s after purchasing some 15,000 acres of land in the Western Reserve from the Connecticut Land Company. In fact, neither could the Mahoning Valley's next generation of wealthy landowners – the Butlers, the Stambaughs, the Tods and the Wicks; nor the prominent families that followed them.

Mr. Young and the others would be as hard pressed back then, as well we are today, to explain how Youngstown, with a beginning based on so much abundance, could have turned into a city whose very name conjures up visions of car bombings, political corruption and rampant crime to the outside world. Most citizens of Youngstown hold in disdain the nicknames the city has had to endure over the decades; forced upon it by the outside media – Bomb Town, Murder Town and Crimetown, USA.

Many people, both inside and outside the area, wonder "why Youngstown?" What makes this city so unique when it comes to organized crime and corruption? One of the answers to that question is Youngstown's size. No other American city with a prolonged history of organized crime is as small as Youngstown. Because of that simple factor, most residents of the city, even the "average Joe" on the street, knows the participants. And everyone seems to have a personal story about them...or, at the very least, an opinion.

Another factor in Youngstown's crime heritage is its resilience to change. With the exception of New York City and Chicago, no other city has had such a long history of organized crime tied to political corruption like Youngstown. Most residents today don't even know when this reputation began. Did it start with the numerous bombings of the 1950s? Was it due to the violent killing spree in the early 1960s? Most younger residents can only point back to the Carabbia / Naples War of the late 1970s and early 1980s. Try again! Here's a quote from Youngstown Mayor Fred J. Warnock as he addressed his officers on the eve of Prohibition, January 16, 1920:

> "Youngstown has the reputation in the outside world of being one of the worst cities morally in the country. There is not any reason for this, except for the fact that a mere handful of people, possibly 300 to 400, openly defy law and decency."

This alone proves that even city officials were keenly aware more than 90 years ago that there was something wrong with Youngstown.

Another characteristic unique to the Valley is that never before in one city had efforts been so concentrated at the citizens to help clean up the criminal element and help run them out of town. This effort – by churches, schools, social clubs, politicians and police – was focused on the "bug" players and those who frequented the gambling houses, brothels and bookie joints throughout the county.

Fueling the fire, adding to the negative reputation of the city, have been the jokes about Youngstown. What other city in the country has its name attached to the description of a car bombing – the "Youngstown tune up?" Then there's the famous joke, "In Youngstown the barber will charge you two bucks to give you a haircut, but he'll charge you three bucks to start your car."

The corruption here has led to what people call the "Youngstown mentality." A young lady who had moved here from Texas explained this to me. She said, "When people from where I come from get a speeding ticket, they go to the courthouse or police station and pay the damn thing. In Youngstown, they find a crooked lawyer who knows a crooked judge and they get the thing fixed."

One morning, a few years ago, I was driving to Youngstown to appear on the Louie Free Radio Show. Louie was quite aware of the "mentality." As I was nearing the station, Louie was on with a guest and they had just finished listening to a song by performer Jackie Wilson; the popular singer suffered a heart attack while performing in 1975, which resulted in brain damage and death some nine years later. The question came up, "What a great singer he was, what ever happened to him?" To which Louie answered, "I think someone murdered him." I poked fun at Louie when I arrived. "So, Louie, just because the guy died before his time, doesn't mean someone murdered him. That's just your Youngstown mentality!"

During my research the name of a *Vindicator* photographer named Ed Shuba came up. My partner in crime, Charlie Molino questioned if he might have been related to George Shuba, a professional baseball player. I entered George Shuba's name into the Internet search engine and his professional and biographical record came up. Sure enough, it stated Shuba was from Youngstown. As I looked at the information about him it listed his nickname – Shotgun! What better nickname to come out of a city known as Crimetown USA.

As cute and witty as these tales might sound, the truth is they are based on a very long history of tragic and senseless loss of lives – some totally innocent. The victims include fathers, husbands, sons – in some cases, very young sons and in one instance a devoted daughter.

What is the reason for the slaughter? Simple greed!

In my classes on the History of Organized Crime, I provided an elementary formula:

Organized Crime / Mafia = Greed

The greed comes in two forms – money and power.

Murder in the underworld normally comes in two forms also: competition murders and revenge killings. Sometimes murders are committed as punishment. In several Youngstown cases, the killings were accidental. Whatever the reason for the murders, in the end they all proved to be quite senseless. The competition murders during the Prohibition years, liquor is now legal; the battle for control of the "bug," we now have state controlled lotteries; the war to see who controlled gambling, Ohio now has legalized gambling and casinos, plus people can drive into neighboring states and do it without fear of raids or arrest.

All those senseless murders destroyed families. Do family members recover? Sometimes. Some relatives never do. Children are raised without fathers, wives are left without husbands and forced to be the family breadwinners. Parents are forced to live out their lives in neighborhoods many times in shame and humiliation due to the deaths of sons. Some young women carry the stigma of being a "mob widow" to the grave, never remarrying.

In writing this book I had hoped to receive more participation from family members of the individuals involved. During radio interviews and lectures I never failed to mention that I would love to speak to relatives and let them share their views. But sadly, few did. Some who were interviewed unfortunately passed away before the book was published including John Terlesky, William Gruver and Donald Hanni. I especially wanted to meet Billy Naples' widow, Enez. But, those who cooperated will be happy with the result.

The progression of crime in the 20th Century in Youngstown was not unlike that of any other city. With the influx of Italians flooding in during the last decade of the 19th Century and for the first two decades of the 20th Century, a small portion of that population were criminals who continued their trade here in the new world – mostly against their fellow countrymen. The most popular crime was Black Hand extortion, which for the most part ended with the dawn of Prohibition. Bootlegging, the cash cow of the underworld from 1920 to 1933, replaced the extortion rackets. After Repeal, organized crime focused on gambling, sports betting and, later, the playing of numbers, also known as policy, clearing house, the lottery or the "bug" as it was called in Youngstown. Toward the end of the century the selling of drugs was the number one moneymaker of organized crime. Throughout the century, prostitution prospered as one of the staples of the underworld.

Another thing unique to Youngstown in its underworld history is that the hoodlums who made their names during Prohibition did not dominate the illegal activities during the decades that followed Repeal. Nearly every city with a reputation for organized crime was dominated by mobsters who had "made their bones" during the 14 years of the "Noble Experiment."

That being said, the focus of *Crimetown USA* begins with Repeal. It discusses the characters of Mid-West Crime Wave fame whose movements brought them into the Mahoning Valley; covers the notorious Lottery Houses of the late 1930s and early 1940s; talks about the "Smash Rackets Rule" initiative by Mayor Charles Henderson and his famed Police Chief, Eddie Allen; showcases the "bug" and bombing activities of the 1950s; and ends with the vicious murder spree of the early 1960s.

The book also focuses on the noted personalities of these eras with in-depth coverage of the following individuals – Joseph "Fats" Aiello, Frank and Joseph Budak, Dominic "Moosey" Caputo, Joseph DiCarlo, Vincent DeNiro, Frank and Peter Fetchet, Baxter Lee Harrell, George, James and Nick Limberopoulos, Roy "Happy" Marino, Billy and Sandy Naples, and Jerry Pascarella. These men are from many nationalities; this book is not about Italian criminals. Few of the early lottery house operators were Italian. There was a strong Greek presence in organized crime in the Valley, as well as Irish, German, Syrian and Croatian. Too many times books on organized crime single out just the Italian element. Youngstown has an incredibly strong Italian community with a miniscule proportion involved in crime. A look at the books by Tony Trolio about Brier Hill, point out the incredible heritage of one Italian neighborhood and many of its accomplished residents.

One thing this book is not is a study of the politics and politicians of that day. That would require another book...or two, or three...to cover. Governors, mayors and councilman are mentioned only as they relate to certain individuals or events. I also refrained from comment on local politics – Democrat or Republican – as it pertains to the belief that corrupt politicians helped organized crime to exist in the Mahoning Valley.

This book is about the who, what, when and where of the history of organized crime in Youngstown and the Mahoning Valley. The why and how are seldom explained by its participants.

What I would like the reader to keep in mind is that this book is not just a story of the hoodlum element of the Mahoning Valley, but rather a history of how it was dealt with by law enforcement. All too often with the image of the valley of its organized crime and political corruption comes questions about crooked law enforcement officials and cops on the take. While this certainly took place, it was never as widespread as the rumors would have you believe.

During the years covered in this book no police officers were ever brought to trial for corruption. Were policemen on the take? Yes. We know that from the comments of other officers on the force. As mentioned before, with the small size of Youngstown everyone seemed to know someone in this underworld fraternity. With there being different factions – police, prosecutors and judges were in a position to favor one side or another and sometimes both.

So how did this corruption take place? Keep in mind, as far as the vice squad was concerned, for years officers were selected to this squad through their Ward councilman. Because of this, many of these officers were indebted to the politician and kept them abreast of what police actions were being planned inside their wards. When raids or arrests were scheduled, officers could tip off the intended targets or individuals, or pass along the word to others who would. A lot of underworld money was spent to get this type of service from the cops on the beat to the judges on the bench.

A judge in the pocket of an area racketeer could tip off the criminal after a warrant was approved. Officers in authority who were "on the take," such as captains, lieutenants and sergeants directed the men under them to "lay off" certain bug men while they conducted their lottery business, or not to harass specific after-hours establishments. One policeman told me his captain transferred him to different beats three nights in a row because he was not willing to "play ball" with the illegal establishments operating on those beats.

Payoffs from policy chieftains allowed them to run their operations without their bug writers being harassed and let proprietors of houses of prostitution and after hours joints run unobstructed. The payoffs were normally made in the bars and nightclubs the hoodlums operated. When the police were being paid by a certain faction – for instance the Naples or DeNiro – those operators instructed the police which opposition places to raid.

These payoffs didn't mean that the officers were totally corrupt. By backing off the "victimless crime" activity it certainly didn't mean they were negligent in their other duties – chasing robbers, burglars, bank robbers, rapists and traffic violators. This also didn't mean the entire department was on the take. By an insider's estimate only fifteen percent of the force accepted money "to look the other way."

On the other hand, when the police had their hands free, they delighted in "giving the racketeers hell," and were encouraged to do so by their superiors. During every "harassment" campaign the officers went out of their way to make life miserable on these underworld characters. One of their favorite tricks was to enter an establishment like the Purple Cow or the Tropics Night Club after 4:00 p.m. on a Friday afternoon and arrest a hood for suspicion. With the judges gone for the weekend, they would then be thrown into lockup until Monday morning at which time they were released before arraignment. The police also enjoyed finding any cars belonging to racket figures illegally parked. They would arrest the owner and impound the vehicle. All these things pissed off the hoods to no end, but they accepted it as being part of the life they chose to live.

As you read this history I hope what will come through as a lasting memory will be the efforts of the honest law enforcement officers on both the city and county level, and the work of dedicated prosecutors and judges in their attempt to put these hoodlums away. I tried my best to highlight the efforts of these individuals as they battled the evils of the underworld and their lawyers who fought so hard to keep their clients free, many times leaving the reader to wonder just who the real criminal was.

Was the Mafia involved in the Steel Valley? Yes. Even though no reliable informant or government witness ever came forward from this period to confirm that any Youngstown area hoods were inducted members of the "secret society." Men from outside the valley such as Joe DiCarlo and Jack Licavoli were no doubt initiates members. Rumors had Sandy Naples becoming a made member of the Pittsburgh Mafia Family after befriending several such figures while serving a prison term in Pennsylvania. Some allegations were made to the effect that Naples was "sent back" to Youngstown as an overseer for the Pittsburgh mob. Vince DeNiro, on the other hand, was known to be close with men who had connections with the Cleveland Mafia Family. Men such as Calgora Malfitano, said to be DeNiro's mentor, "Cadillac Charlie" Cavallaro and Anthony "Tony Dope" Delsanter.

It easily becomes confusing when we try to pigeonhole the players in the Cleveland-Pittsburgh struggle – if indeed there even was one prior to the 1970s. Certainly one must consider the role of the Buffalo and Detroit Families also. By most accounts the Buffalo-Cleveland-Detroit hoodlums drew the line at Trumbull County, while there is no indication of any infiltration by the Pittsburgh Mafia there. That still leaves DeNiro with his Cleveland connections operating in Youngstown. Making this pigeonholing process even murkier is the role then of "Fats" Aiello, due to his connections with members of both camps. Sandy Naples was obviously with him, as was seen in the Purple Cow shooting incident on New Years Eve 1946. But Aiello's "partnership" with DiCarlo placed him squarely with the Buffalo-Cleveland-Detroit faction.

The Pittsburgh and Cleveland Mafia Family's involvement in the Mahoning Valley would become clearly defined in the decades after Youngstown was dubbed "Crimetown USA."

Section I

The 1930s

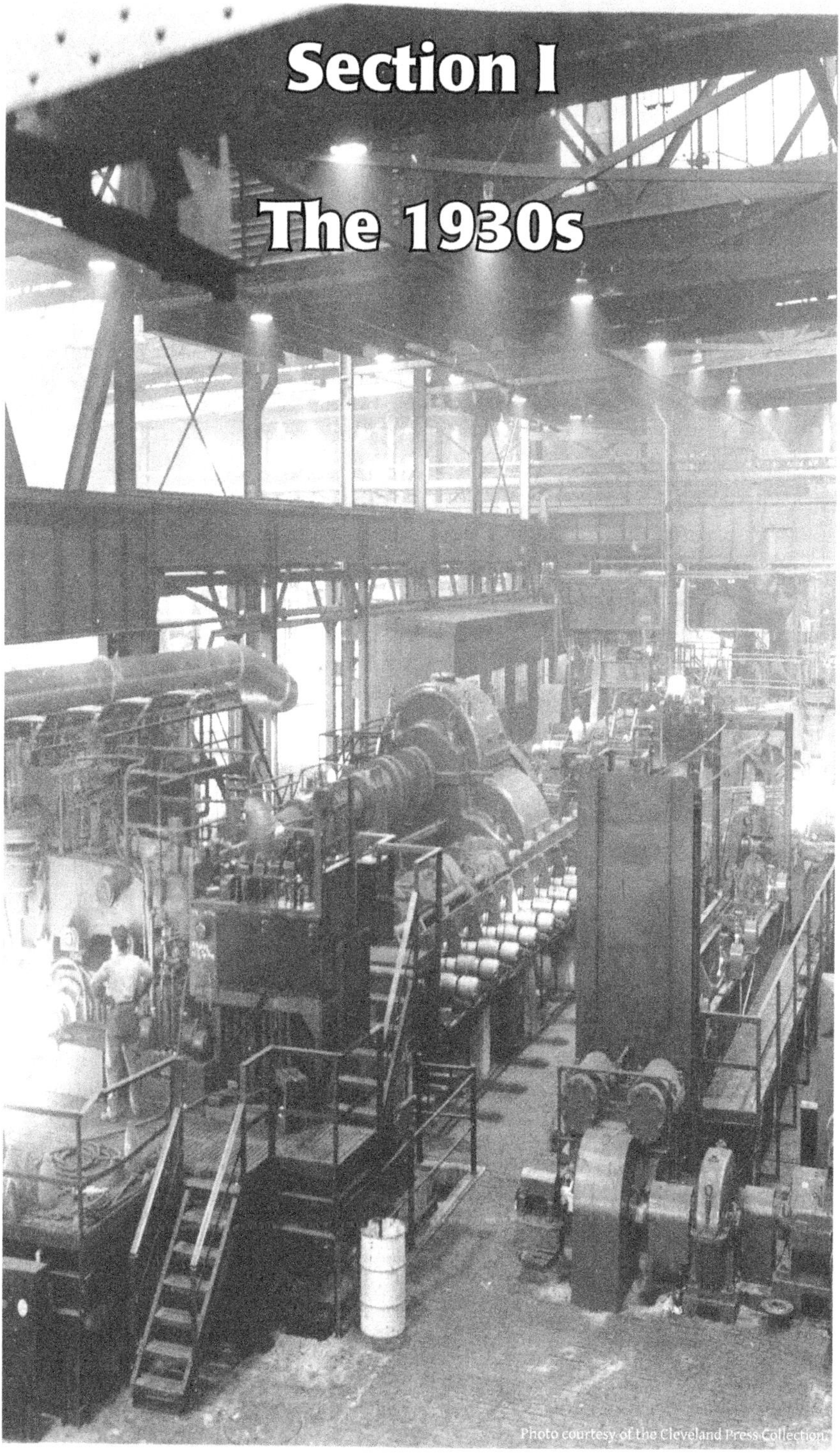

Photo courtesy of the Cleveland Press Collection.

1

Aftermath of Repeal

After the tremendous profits realized during Prohibition dried up, gambling became the main staple of organized crime in the Mahoning Valley. It remains so to this day. Gangsters, whose craving for fast easy money was provided by bootlegging's non-stop lawlessness for the past 14 years, also moved full time into narcotics, labor racketeering and prostitution. No illegal opportunity to make money was passed over.

The advent of the 21st Amendment created the establishment of state liquor control boards. Despite the new chapter in the legislation of alcohol, the government was kept busy for decades to come regulating and policing bars, restaurants, nightclubs, inns and taverns for liquor violations such as underaged drinking, Sunday sales, the serving alcohol after the legal closing time, allowing prostitution to run, and operating as gambling dens and numbers establishments. In addition, many operations, which had once flourished with the sale of illegally produced alcohol, continued to either make their own product or purchase bootleg alcohol to avoid having to pay taxes.

Places wishing to serve alcohol had to purchase a state liquor permit. Any infraction of state law could result in the permit being revoked. Later in the decade, new regulations were passed regarding the sanitation of beer equipment and signage by the establishment. State liquor agents were kept busy policing the hundreds of permit holders throughout the Valley. Raids and arrests were frequent and always made for front-page newspaper stories. "Clean up" campaigns occurred often, especially around election time, and most liquor busts usually involved arrests for gambling on the premises.

Illegal gambling dens offered a wide variety of game options for people to spend their money. These games included poker, dice, bingo, keno, roulette, chuck-a-luck, black jack, faro, and a popular Greek dice game called barbut. In addition, the most popular form of gambling at the close of the "Dry Era" was the playing of slot machines. The seemingly omni-present "one-armed bandits," were always available to take the players loose change. New devices called pinball machines, but more popularly known as marble boards, were considered gambling devices because of the playback features the user enjoyed.

Just days after national Prohibition went into effect, Youngstown Mayor Fred J. Warnock spoke to a group of citizens at the Central Christian Church. His address focused on the "epidemic of gambling sweeping over the cities." Before the disaster of Prohibition became painfully apparent, Warnock warned his audience:

> "Now that John Barleycorn is legally dead at least, gambling is here and threatens to take the place of intemperance. In the estimation of many, the slick gambler, who plies his low profession and robs the weak, is worse than the drunkard."

2

Mid-West Crime Wave 1933-34

If the Prohibition years gave birth to organized crime in America then the criminal era that succeeded it should be acknowledged for establishing this country's greatest law enforcement agency – the Federal Bureau of Investigation. The Mid-West Crime Wave of 1933-1934 spawned a group of bank robbing criminals, sensationalized by the media and Hollywood, who still remain household names 75 years after their demise. John Dillinger, Charles Arthur "Pretty Boy" Floyd, "Baby Face" Nelson, Ma Barker and her sons, George "Machine Gun" Kelly, Alvin "Creepy" Karpis and Bonnie and Clyde were the marquis names during this colorful, yet short-lived era. Their criminal activities helped establish the FBI as the premier law enforcement agency in the United States and catapulted its director, the self-promoting J. Edgar Hoover, into the limelight as America's Number One crime fighter.

Demise of Charles Arthur "Pretty Boy" Floyd

The Mid-West Crime Wave figure to have the biggest impact on the Valley was Charles Arthur "Pretty Boy" Floyd, who met his demise here. Floyd was second only to Dillinger, as far as the media-hype, during this lawless period. A bank robber who took on a folklore mystique and Robin Hood image, Floyd was arguably the best liked of the era's outlaws until the Kansas City Union Station Massacre. The tragic event, to this day, has crime experts on both sides of the issue, arguing the validity of "Pretty Boy's" participation.

The infamous shootout occurred on June 17, 1933, as FBI agents were returning Frank "Jelly" Nash, a prison escapee, to Leavenworth Penitentiary. The FBI was involved not because Nash was a bank robber – bank robbery was not yet a Federal crime – but because he escaped from a Federal prison, where he was serving time for mail robbery, which was a Federal offense. Nash was captured in Hot Springs, Arkansas and was being transferred through Kansas City by train on his way back to Leavenworth on this warm Saturday morning. After exiting the station, where the group was met by two Kansas City police detectives and another FBI agent, Nash and his escorts had just climbed into an agent's automobile when they found themselves face-to-face with an armed rescue squad consisting of two machine-gunners and Vernon C. "Verne" Miller, a former war hero-turned sheriff-turned bank robber from South Dakota.

For some never explained reason, the authorities opened fire and the slaughter was on. When it was over, Nash and four law enforcement officers – Raymond J. Caffrey of the FBI, Orrin Reed, police chief of McAlester, Oklahoma, and

William J. Grooms and Frank Hermanson of the Kansas City Police Department – lay dead in the parking lot. The country was outraged by the senseless murders.

Floyd and his current bank-robbing companion, Adam Richetti, were in the Kansas City area the day before and were immediately considered suspects even though none of the eyewitness descriptions of the machine-gunners fit either man. In addition, none of the surviving law enforcement officers could offer any description of the two machine-gunners. Miller, however, was identified almost immediately, and when his home was searched the FBI found a beer bottle in the basement with a "single fingerprint" on it belonging to Richetti. Based solely on this fingerprint, Floyd and Richetti remained high on the list of suspects who were believed have wielded the Thompson sub-machineguns that day.

With one of his agents murdered, Hoover used Floyd's notoriety and milked the situation to get concessions for his fledgling crime bureau from Congress. Floyd biographer Michael Wallis wrote in *Pretty Boy: The Life and Times of Charles Arthur Floyd*:

> "Over the next year, a host of legislative measures was passed by Congress to increase the bureau's jurisdiction and broaden its authority. At last, agents would be permitted to carry firearms. They were granted the power of arrest anywhere in the country. They were also allowed to investigate certain cases of stolen property, bank robbery, racketeering, or flight to avoid prosecution. This momentous legislation, signed into law by Roosevelt in the late spring of 1934, sounded the death knell for Depression-era outlaws and gave rise to the modern Federal Bureau of Investigation, as the agency became known in 1935."

Other suspects in the Kansas City Massacre were falling by the wayside – either being arrested for other crimes or being eliminated by gunfire from law enforcement officers or other underworld figures. On November 29, 1933, the badly mutilated body of Verne Miller was found in a ditch on the outskirts of Detroit. Since the massacre, Miller knew he was living on borrowed time and conducted his life that way falling deeper and deeper into the bottle. His months on the lam brought him in contact with New York/New Jersey racketeers Louis "Lepke" Buchalter and Abner "Longie" Zwillman. By the time he was murdered, the underworld had a multitude of reasons for wanting it done.

On December 30, the last prime suspect, Wilbur Underhill was shot down in Shawnee, Oklahoma. Known as the "mad dog of the underworld," Underhill died a week later in a state prison hospital facility. His last words were, "Tell the boys I'm coming home." With the death of the "mad dog," the FBI's focus switched to Floyd and Richetti. The following month "the biggest single manhunt in the nation's history" failed to turn up the two outlaws in the Cookson Hills of Eastern Oklahoma.

Floyd and Richetti had fled the area months earlier, leaving that September with "Pretty Boy's" girlfriend Beulah Baird and her sister Rose. Several newspaper editorials stated Floyd was the ghost of Jesse James. Floyd was flattered by the comparison and during a stopover in Canfield, Ohio, a town southwest of Youngstown, he sent a letter of thanks to a local newspaper that published an article with several sketches comparing the career of the infamous western outlaw to that of Floyd.

On September 21, 1933, Floyd and his three companions rented an apartment in Buffalo, New York, where they would live – and go stir crazy – over the next 13 months. It was during this time that the other suspects in the Kansas City Massacre met their demise, as did several marquis names of the Mid-West Crime Wave. Clyde Barrow and Bonnie Parker were shot to death near Arcadia, Louisiana on May 23, 1934, and on July 22, agents led by Melvin Purvis killed John Dillinger outside the Biograph Theater in Chicago. Just twelve days earlier, Kansas City mob boss John Lazia was machine-gunned to death in front of his wife outside the hotel where they resided. Ballistics later showed that the bullets that killed Lazia came from one of the Thompson sub-machineguns used in the Kansas City Massacre.

On October 11, Michael James "Jimmy Needles" LaCapra, a government witness whose testimony helped convict several peripheral participants in the Union Station killings, claimed that on the eve of the massacre Lazia convened a meeting of Miller, Floyd and Richetti after the mob boss ordered Miller not to use any "local muscle" in his efforts to spring Nash. LaCapra claimed that Floyd was wounded in the left shoulder during the shootout and that he and Richetti left town the next day. With this information Hoover and the FBI claimed they had solved the murders outside Union Station and newspapers across the country printed the story. In Buffalo, Floyd read the story in the *Courier-Express*. The headlines boasted:

U.S. Men Solve Massacre Of 5 In Kansas City
Pretty Boy Floyd, Two Others Named By Federal Agents In Railway Station Tragedy

Author Michael Wallis wrote, "The story read like a death notice to Charley Floyd. He knew that Hoover's G-men would be relentless. Charley felt compelled to make a move. Oklahoma's familiar hills and prairies beckoned."

On October 18, 1934, Floyd gave Rose Baird $600 from his dwindling cash supply to purchase a Ford automobile, the choice vehicle of bank robbers. At 3:00 a.m. the next morning the two couples left Buffalo heading for a place on the eastern border of Ohio, known to Floyd as "Hell's Half-Acre," near East Liverpool. Just south of there, near Steubenville, Richetti had relatives that the group hoped they could stay with. On Friday, October 19, a bank was robbed in Tiltonsville, Ohio, south of Steubenville, which was later blamed on Floyd and Richetti, despite eyewitness descriptions that failed to match either man.

Early on the morning of Saturday, October 20, the group was travelling south on Ohio Route 7, just north of the Wellsville city limit. Driving was a little treacherous, as it was foggy and the roads were rain-covered. Suddenly the automobile left the highway and hit a telephone pole near a closed brickyard in an area the locals referred to as the "Silver Switch." The men were able to get the car back on the road, but Floyd insisted that the women take the car into town and have a mechanic look it over. Floyd and Richetti grabbed the weapons and some blankets and headed up a hill to await the return of the sisters. While they waited, the two men started a small fire to keep warm. Neighbors noticed the two men and soon called Wellsville Police Chief John H. Fultz to report the presence of two "shady characters." Fultz deputized two locals as "special patrolmen" and the three went out to the "Silver Switch." Only Fultz was armed.

On the hillside the three men encountered Floyd. Suspecting that they were law enforcement officers, he escorted them to where Richetti was waiting. According to Fultz, when they reached this area Floyd yelled out to his partner, "Stop him, shoot him! Don't let him kid you, he's an officer!"

A gun battle ensued between Fultz and Floyd and Richetti, while the unarmed "special patrolmen" ran for safety to the nearest home. When Richetti's gun jammed he discarded it and took off for a nearby house, hobbling from an ankle wound. Richetti could not get inside the home and quickly surrendered to the pursuing Fultz.

The "special patrolmen," who by now had retrieved two shotguns from a nearby home, began a running gun battle with "Pretty Boy." Floyd ran to the blankets, grabbed his machinegun and got off a short burst before the gun jammed. Floyd escaped, making it to a home where he enticed one of the occupants with $10 to drive him to Youngstown, some thirty miles to the north. Once in the car, Floyd produced two .45s and informed the driver not to be scared, just stick to the back roads and "don't stop for anything." Minutes later the car sputtered to a halt; it had run out of gas.

Floyd appropriated the vehicle of a nearby florist and with two hostages headed toward Lisbon, Ohio. By now law enforcement officers had identified Richetti and figured the man on the run must be Floyd. All local police agencies were warned to be on the lookout. On Route 30 outside of Lisbon, the Floyd party spotted a roadblock and turned around. The quick action caught the attention of deputies, who started after them. Floyd chose to pull the car off the road and shoot it out with his pursers. In the ensuing gunfight one of the hostages was wounded in the leg and Floyd escaped into the forest. For the remainder of that Saturday afternoon and night posses spread out across Columbiana County searching for Floyd while a steady rain fell.

By late Sunday morning, Melvin Purvis, who was in Cincinnati working on a kidnapping case, received word through the local FBI office that Richetti was arrested the day before. Purvis "got Washington on the telephone" and advised them that he believed Floyd must be in the vicinity of Wellsville and got authorization to fly there immediately. In addition to the men who came with Purvis from Cincinnati, other agents arrived from Cleveland, Detroit, Louisville and Pittsburgh. Even legendary lawman Tom Bash arrived from Kansas City to support the effort. Problems soon arose between law enforcement personalities as Michael Wallis writes:

> "The ace federal agent, however, ran into problems with Chief Fultz, who had grown somewhat cocky after surviving his duel with Pretty Boy Floyd. Enjoying the limelight, Fultz decided to keep Richetti in Wellsville to face Ohio charges and not to release him to the bureau. Purvis fussed and fumed. Fultz told him to get a federal warrant."

Purvis released a press statement late Sunday night claiming that the bureau had "definite proof" that Floyd and Richetti were involved in the massacre and made note that the Wellsville police chief was refusing to turn Richetti over.

By 2:00 a.m. Monday morning, fearing that posse members might become targets of Floyd in the darkness, the manhunt was called off until daylight arrived. In *Pretty Boy* Wallis writes:

> "Lights burned in farmhouses throughout the night. Men leaned shotguns or rifles on the walls next to their beds. Some folks locked their front doors for the first time in memory. There had not been so much excitement in Columbiana County since the summer of 1863, seventy-one years earlier, when John Hunt Morgan, a daring cavalry officer, had surrendered his exhausted raiders there after making the Confederacy's deepest thrust into Union territory."

On Monday morning, October 22, there were no new official reports of Floyd's whereabouts. Unconfirmed sightings, however, continued to flow into overworked police personnel throughout the area and the rumor mill was running rampant. One report claimed that Floyd was shot in the stomach during his shootout with Fultz and his men and that he was dead or dying in the woods. Referring to this rumor in his autobiography, *American Agent*, Purvis wrote:

> "Any person shot in the abdomen at the point indicated by [Fultz] certainly could not have lived long alone without medical aid. We therefore began checking every hospital, every clinic and every doctor in the vicinity. We checked taxicab drivers, the rented-car agencies. We had stops placed at all bridges across the Ohio River. We conducted raids on the homes of the relatives of Richetti, who resided in that district – all without results."

Around noon, Floyd appeared at a farmhouse and was given something to eat. Agents checking the area arrived an hour and a half later and the farmer identified Floyd from a photograph. Several other farmers had spotted a man walking through fields ten miles north of East Liverpool. After informing Washington that they had a promising lead, Purvis and three agents were soon on their way into the area. Purvis commented in his book:

> "Previous to this, every bit of information we had been able to gather indicated that Floyd was trying to go to Youngstown to seek refuge with a friend, and so during our search of this section I stopped at a farmhouse and called the chief of police of Youngstown, Ohio, and requested that he dispatch squads of his own men along the highways and into the woods and farmlands near the highways. The chief at Youngstown offered us every co-operation."

Once in the section where Floyd was seen, Purvis and his agents encountered the chief of police from East Liverpool, who was also searching for Pretty Boy with three of his own men including Chester C. Smith, a former sharpshooter in the "Great War." The two cars formed a caravan, stopping at every farmhouse they passed. They searched abandoned houses and every barn and shed in sight. At one farmhouse Purvis was nearly chased off the property by a ram.

At approximately 3:00 p.m., Floyd arrived at the farm of Ellen Conkle, a widow. Floyd told her, "Lady, I'm lost and I want something to eat. Can you help me out with some food? I'll pay you."

Despite the wild look of the man, who claimed he was out squirrel hunting in a business suit, Conkle later recalled, "I couldn't refuse him food."

After finishing the last meal of his life, Floyd paid Mrs. Conkle a dollar and asked if she could help him get to the bus station in Youngstown. Conkle told Floyd that her brother, Stewart Dyke, and his wife would soon return from husking corn in the field and might be willing to take him. When the two appeared at 4:00 p.m., Floyd was told by Dyke that Youngstown was "too far," but they would take him to Clarkson.

The three went to a Ford Model A parked outside. Floyd climbed into the backseat and they all waved goodbye to Mrs. Conkle. The car traveled just a few feet before they noticed two automobiles full of men fast approaching. Melvin Purvis had arrived at the Conkle farm.

Dyke recalled what happened next:

> "When Floyd saw them, his face paled and he ordered me to drive to the back of the corncrib. After I backed up he said, 'Get going!' and called me a nasty name. He pulled out his gun and jumped out of the car and crawled under the corncrib. An instant later, he darted out and came toward the car. Then he started across a pasture."

Eight men alighted from the two cars; they realized immediately that they were in the presence of their adversary. Sporting a .32 Winchester rifle was Chester Smith, who recalled what happened next as Floyd started up a hill behind the farmhouse:

> "We stopped and I jumped out with my rifle and ran toward the shed. I saw the man running up a hill in the rear, and shouted to him to halt. He kept going, darting to the left and right, trying to make the crest of the hill. I'd had a good

> look at him, and was sure it was Floyd. I called again, but he wouldn't stop. Then I knelt down and took aim at him. My first shot hit him in the arm above the elbow and knocked the .45 out of his right hand. I didn't want to kill him, just bring him down. My second shot hit him in the side above the shoulder blade and brought him down."

As Purvis and the lawmen surrounded the wounded Floyd on the hill, legend has the following exchange taking place.

"You're Pretty Boy Floyd," stated Purvis

"I'm Charles Arthur Floyd," he replied. "Pretty Boy" then passed into eternity at the age of 30.

The autopsy report showed that there was no wound to Floyd's left shoulder as Jimmy LaCapra had told the FBI.[1] But there was something mysterious in the report. In addition to noting the wounds Smith said he made with his rifle, the autopsy noted: "4 wounds, shot in stomach."

In 1979, Chester Smith, then 84 years old and a retired police captain, revealed another version of events that day on the Conkle farm. Smith told reporters, 45 years after the death of the outlaw, that Floyd was sitting upright in the field as lawmen surrounded him. Purvis called out to his men, "Back away from that man. I want to talk to him."

"Were you in on the Kansas City Massacre?" asked Purvis.

"I wouldn't tell you son of a bitch anything," Floyd answered.

With that, Smith recalled, Purvis ordered an agent to, "Fire into him." The story varied over the years as to whether Floyd was finished off with a revolver or a machinegun. "It all happened very quickly," Smith told reporters. Later Smith said he asked Purvis about the "execution."

"Mr. Hoover, my boss, told me to bring him in dead," Smith claims Purvis replied. In *American Agent*, Purvis seems to support this point himself when he reveals: "True, we were looking for Floyd and hoped to find him, but somehow I dreaded the encounter. Floyd was a killer; I knew he wasn't to be taken alive."

Smith later explained, according to Michael Wallis, "that he felt compelled to clear the air since he was the last of the eight lawmen in the celebrated deed." Wallis points out, however, that Smith, who died one day after the 50th anniversary of Floyd's death in 1984, had forgotten about one FBI agent who was still alive. W. E. "Bud" Hopton was not only alive, he was livid over the accusations made by Smith. He denied that Purvis had ordered another agent to finish off the wounded outlaw, claiming that the agent Smith accused of carrying out the "execution" was not even at the farm. Hopton contended it was FBI bullets that downed Floyd to begin with, not those fired by Smith.

While details of Floyd's demise remain murky to this day, one thing is clear. Hoover had used Floyd's notoriety to help the bureau gain concessions from Congress. But, with Floyd alive, Hoover would have to prove in court that the famed outlaw had pulled a trigger in the infamous massacre and his only piece of evidence was the sole fingerprint of Adam Richetti from a beer bottle. Hoover couldn't even rely on the testimony of his star witness Jimmy LaCapra since the autopsy revealed no wound to Floyd's left shoulder existed. To this day the debate rages on among crime historians as to whether Floyd ever participated in the Kansas City Massacre. Many believe that from the day Hoover pegged him as one of the participants in the shooting that "Pretty Boy" would never see the inside of a courtroom to deny it.

One man who did live to deny his participation in a courtroom was Adam Richetti. On June 17, 1935 – exactly two years to the day after the massacre – Richetti was found guilty. During the trial, three FBI agents, who could offer no description of the gunmen after the shooting, positively identified Richetti and Floyd as part of the gun-squad outside the Union Station. Richetti was sentenced to death by hanging.

Richetti protested his innocence until October 7, 1938 when he became the first person to be strapped into the chair inside the new gas chamber at the Missouri State Penitentiary in Jefferson City. Richetti's last words to one of the guards securing him were, "What have I done to deserve this?"

Minutes later the 28 year-old Richetti was pronounced dead.[2]

"It's a bum rap. I can prove I was home asleep when the holdup took place. Every time anything happens within 100 miles of Youngstown local detectives try to pin it on me." – Roy "Happy" Marino after being charged with being one of four men who carried out the $11,000 robbery of the George D. Harter Bank in Louisville, Ohio on June 10, 1933.

3

Murder of Roy "Happy" Marino

The life of Roy "Happy" Marino, described as "one of the best known underworld characters" in the Valley, came to a brutal end on September 10, 1937. His murder investigation proved to be one of the Valley's most bizarre. Whether this was due to overzealous law enforcement officials seeking a speedy solution, or shoddy reporting and interference by newspaper people is open to debate. With the information the *Vindicator* presented during the days after Marino's murder, even a seasoned crime investigator would have needed a flow chart to understand all of the theories, connections and non-connections being offered about the Valley's latest murder mystery.

Background

Marino was born on March 4, 1904, in Youngstown, where he lived his entire life. He was one of seven children – six of them boys – of Charles and Marie Giadullo Marino. At the age of 19 Marino married Helen Foley. The couple had a daughter named Mary. A *Vindicator* article claimed Marino "earned his sobriquet of 'Happy' because of his reckless abandonment of worry."

It was never clear what Marino's activities were during the Prohibition years in Youngstown. One of his first publicized crimes, which didn't even take place in the Valley, was the hold up of "an exclusive club" in Pittsburgh. The Metro Club, formerly known as the Danny Winters Memorial Club, was robbed of $2,000 in February 1932. Pittsburgh detectives, believing Marino was a participant, made 18 trips to Youngstown in an effort to extradite him, which Judge J.H.C. Lyon refused to allow. Lyon ruled "there was no evidence to prove Marino was a fugitive from justice," this despite one of his young accomplices, Donald "Porky" Joyce pleading guilty to the robbery.

On June 10, 1933, four men carried out a plan to rob the George D. Harter Bank in Louisville, Ohio, a rural town east of Canton. With one bandit waiting at the wheel, the others, dressed in overalls, entered the bank with sawed-off shotguns hidden in a basket. While holding five employees at gunpoint, the men proceeded to rob the bank of an estimated $11,000.

Police suspected Marino's participation in the holdup after they learned he "had been spending money lavishly – $800 within a few days" of the robbery.

Detectives devised a clever plan to allow bank employees to get close enough to Marino to identify him. They donned disguises and then visited The Town Club, a nightclub operated by Marino, on Coitsville Road, just outside Youngstown proper. A police department official revealed, "They definitely identified him as one of the three men who came into the bank during the robbery." Marino and his two accomplices were then secretly indicted by the grand jury.

Youngstown detectives arrested Marino on a downtown street and booked him on a "suspicion" charge on July 10. The other men could not be located. Police refused to allow his attorney, Dominic Rendinell, to see him. At 4:30 the next morning Marino was taken to the Stark County jail in Canton. When Rendinell returned to the Youngstown Police Department to speak with his client he was informed Marino was no longer there. Claiming that his client knew he was going to be arrested, Rendinell told reporters Marino had nothing to do with the robbery. "Every time something happens they try to blame 'Happy,'" he complained.

After being arraigned, Marino was released on a $10,000 bond on July 15. The next day he told reporters, "It's a bum rap. I can prove I was home asleep when the holdup took place." In words echoing his attorney's comment, he said, "Every time anything happens within 100 miles of Youngstown local detectives try to pin it on me." When confronted with the detective's allegations that he was throwing around a lot of cash, Marino replied, "I paid for my car and bought a suit on June 9, a day before the holdup."

The time until Marino's trial did not pass uneventfully. On August 2, Marino was arrested in the tourist town of Geneva-on-the-Lake, located on the shores of Lake Erie, in the company of John "Pinky" Walsh, a Valley criminal whose career lasted into the 1960s. Walsh was wanted for questioning by the Columbus police about several robberies in the capital city. Marino was picked up simply because he was with the wrong hood at the wrong time. He was soon released.

On November 14, Marino failed to appear for trial in Canton. The judge immediately ordered his $10,000 bond forfeited. The order was rescinded when Marino appeared the next day claiming he thought the trial was postponed, however, the judge ordered Marino remanded to the Stark County jail.

The bank robbery trial of Roy Marino began on November 23, 1933. Witnesses for the prosecution included the bank's branch manager and a teller. A local farmer, who was conducting business in the bank, testified that Marino had shoved a shotgun against his stomach and told him to "get going." Defense witnesses included Helen Marino, who testified that her husband was home the morning of the robbery; a maid who backed up the story, and a contractor who claimed he went to the Marino home that morning to pay a bill.

The next day, a jury of six men and six women found Marino guilty, but recommended mercy. The judge sentenced "Happy" to 20 years in the Ohio Penitentiary. Marino was carted off under heavy guard to Columbus to begin his sentence, despite a plea by Rendinell for his release on bond while a motion for a new trial was pending.

Marino had hardly settled in his prison environment before being named in another bank robbery. On December 9, Angelo Ferruccio of Canton testified that Marino was a participant in the October 18 holdup of the First National Bank of Fredonia, Pennsylvania, a small town about 25-miles northeast of Youngstown. During the hearing, Angelo, in trying to protect his 16 year-old brother Pat, implicated another man, but witnesses were unable to identify him as one of the robbers. Ferruccio then named Marino as an accomplice. Days later Angelo Ferruccio changed his story. (Pat Ferruccio later became a member of the Pittsburgh Mafia Family and remained active into the late 1990s, he passed away in 2006.)

Despite tireless work by Rendinell, on March 28, 1934, the Ohio Supreme Court refused to review Marino's appeal and declared he must serve his sentence. This decision did not deter his brothers Andrew, Anthony and Rocco, who were hard at work trying to clear him. Two of the brothers were successful businessmen in the city; Andrew ran an automobile dealership, while Rocco operated the DeLuxe Cab Company. Andrew and Rocco traveled to Salem, New Jersey, where a former Canton man, Charles Kent, was serving a 15-year term for robbery. On April 4, Kent suddenly confessed he was involved in the Louisville bank robbery and that Marino did not participate. Despite Kent's confession the Stark County prosecutor refused to recommend Marino's release. There were, however, other forces at work inside the Ohio Penitentiary helping Marino.

On January 12, 1935, outgoing-Governor George White commuted the sentence of Roy Marino. White was commuting sentences on a wholesale basis, which caused a highly publicized scandal in the state parole office. Marino was the governor's 51st commutation since December 1, 1934. In releasing Marino, Governor White declared, "Since his imprisonment in the penitentiary, certain circumstances have arisen which lead the Governor to believe there is grave doubt as to the guilt of this man. A complete investigation was ordered in the entire matter and the investigation also bears out this fact."

Marino's family was elated. Anthony Marino told reporters, "The Governor reviewed the facts and took into consideration the confession made by Charles Kent...We had never given up hope. We were certain Roy was innocent and would be freed. Two other men, indicted with my brother...were never tried after Kent made his confession."

Marino's pardon was made possible by corrupt forces at work inside the Ohio Penitentiary led by Arch W. "Stub" Naylor, known as a "parole and pardon broker." While in prison, Marino became a friend of Thomas "Yonnie" Licavoli, who was serving a life sentence for the murder of popular Toledo bootlegger Jackie Kennedy and three others. Licavoli, described as one of the most influential prisoners in the "Ohio Pen," introduced Naylor to Marino. Naylor had another influential friend, Leland S. "Jim" Dougan, the chairman of the Ohio Board of Parole. With Naylor's help, within fourteen months Marino was able to buy his way out of prison for $2,500.

Ten days after Marino obtained his release he had a new houseguest – "Stub" Naylor. The two were planning to go into business together. But Naylor soon realized the toll that the Great Depression had taken on the Mahoning Valley. He wrote a friend, "There is no money here just now, people have been out of work too long. Happy was offered a big night club, but says there is no money in night clubs." Whatever business deal the two talked about never materialized and "Stub" Naylor soon moved out of Marino's life.

Two and a half years after his release from prison, the *Vindicator* reported that Marino had purchased his freedom from the Ohio Penitentiary. The roles of Naylor and Dougan in the parole scandal were exposed in a Cleveland Press article on July 10:

> "The closing months of the administration of Governor George White were marked by such wholesale paroles and commutations that the newspapers began to raise a storm of protest all over the state. Likewise, prosecutors and trial judges registered their protests that gangsters...supposed to be safely behind the bars were home again and doing business at the old stands."

The expose by Scripps-Howard reporter James T. Keenan revealed:

> "Naylor and the Marinos had another mutual friend for whom they all had a high regard. He was Charles Kent...notorious bank robber.
>
> "Kent stayed with Naylor at the Flory Hotel in Canton early in 1934. In February of that year, however, he had the bad luck to be caught, with three others, in the $130,000 robbery of the Penns Grove National Bank of Penns Grove, N. J.
>
> "When he was arrested in Camden, N. J., Kent had $36,346 of the loot on his person. He was sentenced to 15 years in the New Jersey State Prison at Trenton.
>
> "Almost immediately after he was 'settled' in Trenton, Kent had a flock of visitors. They were A. R. Marino, R. E. Marino, Mrs. Charles Marino and Helen Marino, all of Youngstown."

A little over a year after "Happy" was released he was back on the front page. On March 3, 1936, Marino, James "Lulu" Lallo and another man traveled to Brier Hill, the Italian section of Youngstown, and entered the beer garden of Paul Gorvanec looking for Mike Locke, a pick-up man for the "Big House" lottery gang. Marino and his companions were trying to muscle in on the lottery racket on the city's West Side and Brier Hill. They demanded that the lottery slips Locke was turning over to the "Big House" be handed over to them instead. Locke told the men that when he returned that afternoon he would hand the daily slips over to them. When Locke failed to return, Marino and Lallo robbed Gorvanec of $2 in front of witnesses. Gorvanec went to the police and had arrest warrants sworn out against the pair.

On August 22, 1936, Youngstown detectives raided Marino's newly opened horse-race bookie joint, the Hazel Smoke Shop on South Hazel Street. Officers recovered betting slips, racing forms and $60 in cash. The place was equipped with wire service to receive the latest race results. During a trial, held just six days later, Marino was found guilty on the strength of a new law in which prosecutors needed only to present physical evidence – racing forms and rundown sheets – to obtain a conviction. Marino was fined $100.

In the years after his release from prison the newspapers labeled Marino, "One of the best known underworld characters" in the Valley. Just what Marino accomplished to earn that accolade is lost to history. By most published accounts Marino had become a bookie and degenerate gambler. His efforts to come to the forefront of organized crime in the Valley were not succeeding. Perhaps nothing bore this out more than Marino having to seek the help of the Youngstown Police Department when his car was stolen from a parking lot near his Hazel Smoke Shop in December 1936. A Girard, Ohio, police officer with the unlikely name of Barney Mushrush found the automobile abandoned on South State Street at 4:00 a.m. with stolen plates on it.

Murderous Week

During the second week of September 1937, Youngstown served host to two vicious murders in three days. The armed holdup of beer garden owner James Tisone was well planned, but its execution was brutal and deadly. Tisone was born in Italy in 1885 and came to Youngstown with his family as a young boy. He went back to his homeland in 1906 and returned to the Mahoning Valley with a wife, who bore him six children. Tisone settled into the city's ethnic makeup and in 1933 opened Tesone's Tavern[3] at 1810 Wilson Avenue.

On Wednesday, September 8, as was his routine, Tisone went to the Dollar Bank where he withdrew over $9,000 so he could cash the pay checks of the local railroad workers. On his way back to the cafe he stopped and picked up several cases of liquor at a downtown state store. When he arrived in front of his establishment, armed robbers awaited him. Tisone was confronted by a gunman who leapt onto the running board of his automobile and demanded the money. Two other armed bandits were close by; one on the passenger side of the car to ward off passersby, and the other outside the front door of the café. A fourth man waited in a getaway car parked nearby.

Witnesses said Tisone exited the car, but refused to give up the money when the gunman grabbed for it. Shots were fired and Tisone fell, mortally wounded. Tisone's daughter, Mrs. Ruby Policy, grabbed a revolver her father kept under the counter. She was about to shoot when the gunman standing out front stuck his pistol inside and ordered her to drop it. An employee ran to a store next door, got a gun from the proprietor and fired at the fleeing automobile. Another man recorded the license plate number of the getaway car. Several people helped Tisone into an automobile which raced to St. Elizabeth's Hospital; he died enroute.

Police were focusing on members of the "notorious Al Brady gang" as the killers of Tisone. The gang members, "listed as public enemies, and other desperados," were alleged to have been seen in the area around the time of the ill-fated robbery. This theory was later abandoned. In a strange turn of events it was originally reported that the gunmen who confronted Tisone on the driver's side fired both of the fatal shots. This changed when the Mahoning County coroner reported that the two bullets were recovered and one was a .45 slug, the other a .22. Before the week was out David Cowles, a renowned ballistics expert with the Cleveland Police Department identified the bullets as a .38 and a .41.

The day after Tisone's murder, Marino left the Hazel Smoke Shop late in the afternoon and gave one of his employees a ride home. At his parents' North Side home, Marino was enjoying dinner with his family when someone stopped their vehicle outside and sounded the horn. Little Mary Marino and her cousin stepped outside to see who was there and then informed Roy that a man in a "big new black sedan" wished to speak with him. Marino went outside and a few minutes later returned to the house and informed his family "he had to meet some fellows." He left quickly. It was the last time his family saw "Happy" alive.

Marino drove to the Youngstown Hotel, arriving about 7:30 p.m., and went to the room of Miss Elizabeth "Betty" Jaynes, an attractive, blonde ex-chorus girl from Cleveland, with whom he was having an affair over the past two years. While visiting his paramour, he received a telephone call from a man who asked if he could meet with Marino in New Castle, Pennsylvania, just across the state border. Instead, the two men agreed to meet at Chick's Café, a beer garden, located at Wilson and Forrest Avenues, just down the street from Tesone's Tavern. Jaynes told police, "He didn't say who the fellow was."

Marino and Jaynes jumped into his new blue coupe and drove to the beer garden, parking across the street from the establishment. As he exited the vehicle, he told Jaynes, "I won't be gone long." It was 8:20 p.m. While waiting for Marino to return, Jaynes observed an automobile, one matching a description of the vehicle that had visited the Marino home earlier that evening, parked on Forest Avenue. The car left within fifteen minutes of the couple's arrival.

Strange as it may seem, Jaynes reportedly remained in the automobile until 1:00 the next morning. At that time John Chick, the son of the beer garden's owner, came out and asked her who she was waiting for. After she described Marino to him, Chick informed her that no one matching that description was in the place. Chick then called a taxi for Jaynes, as she did not want to drive Marino's car back to the hotel. A waitress at Chick's Café later told police she remembered Marino arriving. She said he "walked into the place hurriedly, had a drink of expensive whiskey, and walked out."

When police interviewed Jaynes, she came across as a typical "gangster's moll." She certainly had the lingo down:

> "For the past year, as far as I know, he had gone straight." He had an interest in the bookie shop, got about $125 a week. I don't know of any enemies he had.
>
> "He was in a particularly good humor when he left me, and I know he didn't think he was on the spot."

Miss Betty Jaynes quickly packed her bags and left the Youngstown Hotel, leaving no forwarding address. She returned to her East Cleveland home and was never heard from in the case again.

Around 4:00 o'clock on the morning of September 10, farmer J. C. Ashford awoke to the sound of five gun shots. Soon afterwards a truck driver discovered a body lying beside Route 7 in Columbiana County, Ohio, a mile south of the town of Rogers. The truck driver drove to Rogers where he notified the authorities.

The Investigation

Authorities contacted the office of Mahoning County Prosecutor William A. Ambrose and county investigator John A. Callan was requested. Ambrose, after being elected prosecutor, had made Callan one of his first appointments. Callan, born in Pennsylvania, spent most of his life in Youngstown. A sports enthusiast, he was an outstanding lightweight boxer as a youth and later became a referee. In the early and mid-1940s he officiated many of the area's top bouts. In addition, he was a highly respected local baseball umpire.

Callan and two of his four brothers were active in local Democratic politics. One brother, Eugene, ran for state senator in 1938. Another, Harry J. Callan served as fire chief of Youngstown. He later served as the Ohio State Fire Marshall and had a significant role in the closing of the Jungle Inn after a raid in August 1949. Before becoming county investigator, John Callan was named to a position in the city water department by Mayor Mark E. Moore. Callan played a pivotal role in the murder investigation of Roy Marino, pursuing the case to its completion. His involvement began shortly before noon on September 10 when he and two Youngstown detectives were called on to identify Marino's body in an East Liverpool morgue.

Shortly after the body was identified, George Case, a deputy sheriff in Lisbon, Ohio, received a strange telephone call. The voice on the other end stated, "This is Marino. Have they identified that man who was murdered down there?" When Case replied that the murder victim was Happy Marino the caller replied, "Thank God for that," and hung up.

Case traced the call to the DeLuxe Cab Company owned by Rocco Marino. Shortly after completing the trace Case received a second phone call. He recognized the voice as that of the previous caller. This time the man identified himself as Rocco Marino and asked where his brother's body was taken.

From the moment the body was identified, strange tales and murder theories filled the *Vindicator*. The first reporting of the murder stated that Marino's body was "punctured by 18 slugs," leading to speculation that a machinegun was used in the slaying. An autopsy revealed that only five bullets from a .38 caliber weapon were fired into his body, "but 16 wounds were noted." Autopsy surgeons said the various wounds were caused by "muscle, ribs and bones deflecting the bullets." Also, entrance and exit wounds caused by the same bullet were listed as multiple wounds. Due to brush burns found on his head and leg, they concluded that Marino was thrown from an automobile. The crime scene indicated that after the initial fall he arose and "staggered 10 feet along the rim of the highway before he fell dead over an embankment." He lay in the Ashford farm field until the truck driver's discovery. The explanation of the multiple wounds cleared up the rumor of a machinegun being used in the slaying, but many more rumors were to come.

Based solely on the fact that a .38 was used in the murder of James Tisone, detectives said the two murders were linked. On September 11, the *Vindicator* presented the various murder theories:

> "The theory in the minds of Youngstown police and Columbiana County authorities is that Marino may have been killed by the gang which executed the $9,300 holdup murder of Jim Tisone Wednesday. Authorities are working on the theory Marino helped arrange the Tisone stickup. Wishing to obliterate all possible clues the gunmen bumped off the 'fingerman,' police reason.
>
> "Police also are investigating the possibility that Marino, who is said to have been 'broke,' learned who executed the Tisone robbery and tried to shake them down. Following this theory, police reason Marino was killed during the shakedown process.
>
> "Another theory in which police officials place credence is that Marino encountered trouble at the greyhound track at Fowler. It was learned last night that Marino tried to 'muscle in' on 'something pretty good' when the plant opened a month ago, but that he withdrew when he was told he wasn't wanted to help run the plant.
>
> "Marino, however, had been a frequent visitor at the track sometimes winning and sometimes losing. It was reported that about 10 days ago he 'hocked' a ring and mortgaged his auto to meet gambling obligations."

In addition to local law enforcement investigating the murder, a state probe was underway spearheaded by Ohio State Attorney General Herbert S. Duffy. It was announced that Marino "was one of the key figures in the disclosures which led to Duffy's inquiry of parole board operators." The investigation of the parole board was initiated after the murder of two police officers from Springfield,

Ohio, in early September by several paroled convicts, one of whom was killed in the shootout.

On September 12, the most bizarre piece of the murder investigation was reported in a front-page *Vindicator* story. Two reporters for the newspaper, attempting to trace Marino's movements after he left Miss Jaynes outside Chick's Café, discovered that Marino was spotted in a Vienna roadhouse, north of Youngstown, with two male companions less than an hour after he abandoned his girlfriend. The article quoted the roadhouse operator's conversation with Marino after he learned the trio was headed to the Fowler track for the dog races. "I kidded Marino about losing on the dogs. He said he would win some of it back that night," stated the proprietor. The revelations sent investigators rushing into Trumbull County to track down Marino's two companions. Later, when John Callan questioned the roadhouse proprietor, he was now unsure if Marino was there the night of his disappearance or the night before.

The busy Callan also cleared up another mystery. The black sedan spotted outside Chick's Café was traced and it was determined that the owner had no connection with the events. There were more mysteries to come.

On the same day the *Vindicator* reported the bogus Marino sighting at the Vienna roadhouse, prosecutor Ambrose made an ambitious statement. Hinting at possible arrests in the next few days, he told reporters, "We have developed some good leads. Anything may happen." He indicated that the county's investigation of Marino's murder may rip Mahoning Valley's gangland "wide open."

While new theories were being offered, one of the earlier ones fell to the wayside. The newspaper reported, "State officials today virtually eliminated Marino's death from the state-wide investigation of penitentiary paroles in which Marino was a leading figure, and threw the murder mystery back into gangland's lap. Although the *United Press* reported [Asst. Attorney General George] Hurley as saying the killing was timed 24 to 36 hours before planned arrests in an investigation of an Ohio parole scandal. Hurley denied here that he had made such a statement."

The next allegation to run the rumor mill was that Toledo gangsters were trying to muscle their way into the lucrative Mahoning Valley number's racket. It was said that in local gambling circles there was a recent tale of a "big, tall" Toledo gangster snatching lottery slips from "Big House" operators. Marino was somehow tied to this due to his "outside connections." Perhaps his prior association with "Yonnie" Licavoli from Toledo led to this belief.

On September 13, a new "solid theory" and an old "solid theory" were again reported on the front page. The article's opening line was "The fatal gangland 'ride' of Roy "Happy" Marino...was definitely linked to the Ohio prison parole scandal and the gang killing of Mike Russell, Wheeling, West Virginia number's king, two weeks ago."

The newspaper announced that, "Bullets removed from Marino's body were fired from the same pistols that mowed down Russell as he stepped from his automobile to become, apparently, the victim of a numbers lottery double-crossing." Marino and Russell were said to have been underworld friends. The "similarity" of the bullets was announced by State Attorney General Duffy in Columbus at the same time he "definitely linked" Marino's murder to the parole scandal. Duffy, however, refused to discuss the connection. State investigators and assistant attorney generals were being "reached" around the state to investigate each new allegation that surfaced during the case.

Yet, still another mystery was unfolding. This was at the Schultz & Son Funeral Home where Marino's body was laid out. Roy's brother, Rocco was told by the funeral home owner that around 1:00 o'clock Sunday morning "three well-dressed middle-aged men" knocked on the door of the funeral home and insisted on seeing Marino's body. They claimed they were relatives of Marino from Cleveland and they couldn't view the body during the daytime. One man was described as being "dressed in a dark blue, double-breasted suit, had protruding eyes which bulged out from his eye sockets." Approximately an hour later, a tall inebriated man, with "two black eyes" arrived and demanded to see the body. He was refused entry.

It was estimated that 12,000 people viewed the body at the funeral home on Saturday and Sunday. Funeral services were held for 33 year-old Roy Marino on Monday, September 13 at St. Rocco's Church in Brier Hill. Callan and several investigators attended the funeral mass. Traffic police were on hand to direct the crowds.

The next day, while promising a "speedy solution" to the Marino murder, Attorney General Duffy abandoned the case and pulled his investigators off the murder probe. He now declared the killings of Marino and Russell were not connected.[4]

On September 15, Columbiana County Prosecutor Karl T. Stouffer reported that Marino was seen in Salem, Ohio an hour and a half after he had left Betty Jaynes outside of Chick's Café. During Stouffer's investigation it was reported that he received a threatening letter from members of "the notorious 'Purple Gang' of Detroit." When advised to "get two bodyguards" Stouffer improvised and got two guns.

Some of the investigators strongly believed that Marino's murder was tied to Mike Russell's. That theory was shelved after it was revealed that no bullets were recovered from the body of Russell. Duffy had announced earlier that bullets from Marino and Russell's bodies matched.

Edward Schrector, a special state investigator, believed that Marino was murdered because he knew who Russell's killers were. The two men were reported in each other's company shortly before Russell's death. In 1936, Marino was linked to an alleged jewelry robbery at the home of William Lias. The Wheeling racket's boss believed his cousin, Russell, was behind the theft.

Suspects Arrested

The Marino murder investigation sputtered on for seven months. Then on April 8, 1938 the Valley was informed that five men were indicted for the murder. Three were quickly arrested:

Solly Hart – was described as a "notorious Cleveland gangster." His career in the Cleveland underworld began in 1924 when he was just 18 years old. He was convicted of "driving a car without the owner's consent." Hart was fined $50 and sentenced to 90 days in the workhouse. This was later reduced to just a $25 fine. In 1925, he was arrested for carrying a concealed weapon – the case was "no-billed" by the grand jury. In 1927 he had a repeat of his 1925 arrest. The next year he was arrested on a suspicious person's charge, but his sentence to the workhouse was overturned by an appeals court.

In 1930, Hart's name came up during the murder investigation of Morris Komisarow. The two men were allegedly involved in a rum-running operation on Lake Erie. Several weeks after a boat exploded in the Rocky River lagoon, Komisarow's body, despite being tied to a 50-pound anchor, was found floating in the lake. The prime suspect in the murder was Cleveland Syndicate bigwig Moe Dalitz. In 1931, Hart was arrested and held for questioning in the sensational murder of former Cleveland City Councilman William E. Potter, which gained national media coverage. Hart was a friend of "Pittsburgh Hymie" Martin, who was convicted, and later acquitted in a retrial, of murdering Potter. Hart was "tentatively identified" as having entered the apartment in which Potter was found murdered, prior to the killing. Ironically, two other leaders of the Cleveland Syndicate, Morris Kleinman and Louis Rothkopf, were also suspects in the murder. Police "revived" the concealed weapons charges against Hart and he received a term in the Ohio Penitentiary, serving there from November 1931 until September 1934. Hart was one of the 50-plus inmates released by outgoing-Governor George White.

Hart returned to Cleveland and in 1937 was identified by Ardell Quinn, an infamous Cleveland madam, as the man who shot one of her "guests" during a robbery. The grand jury "no-billed" the case when a witness from New York refused to return to testify. After the robbery at Quinn's establishment, Hart left for the Youngstown-East Liverpool-Steubenville area where he allegedly became involved in the slot machine racket.

John Anthoulis – was the "reputed czar of the Steubenville lottery, slot machine and vice rackets." During a vice cleanup in January 1938 he paid a $500 fine for a slot machine infraction.

Herbert Ross – was an "alleged henchmen" of both Hart and Anthoulis. Some reports referred to him as Hart's "bodyguard." In 1929 he was convicted of carrying a concealed weapon. Sent to prison, he was paroled a year later. Ross was connected to underworld activity in Steubenville since 1936. He and Hart reportedly helped Anthoulis muscle in on the gambling there.

On the day of the arrests, Ross was nabbed at the garage/headquarters of the Novelty Amusement Company in Steubenville. The garage warehoused jukeboxes and slot machines distributed by the gang. An hour after his arrest, John Callan led a team of men to the offices of Steubenville political boss, attorney John F. Nolan. Hart and Anthoulis, who were tipped off to the indictments, were there seeking legal advice. On the advice of Nolan, the two surrendered without incident. While the three men were being booked at the Steubenville city jail, a reporter asked Hart if he had retained Nolan as counsel. "What the hell do I need counsel for?" Hart replied. After a brief stay at the Steubenville jail the men were transferred to the Mahoning County jail where they were housed on three separate levels to prevent them from communicating.

In addition to the three arrested, the indictment also named Thomas Galati and John A. O'Boyle of Cleveland. Galati's criminal record consisted of an arrest for carrying a concealed weapon and a conviction for picking the pocket of a Michigan man. Galati, whose automobile was identified as being parked outside Chick's Café the night Marino disappeared, turned himself into Cleveland police in January 1938 after hearing he was wanted for questioning. Brought to Youngstown, he was interrogated by Callan, but released due to lack of evidence.

John O'Boyle was the brother of Cleveland underworld figure Martin O'Boyle, described as a former "King-Pin Bootlegger." During the Prohibition years the brothers were associated with members of the Cleveland Syndicate and Irish underworld power Thomas J. McGinty.

Law enforcement officials still believed there was a tie-in between the Marino murder and that of Mike Russell. When police went to search the home of Anthoulis they found Elsa Russell, the attractive widow of Mike Russell, which only strengthened their belief. In addition, they believed these same men "held the key" to the James Tisone murder. Cleveland Press staff writer A.C. DeCola reported rumors from the Mahoning County jail indicated that Ross had cracked under the pressure of being grilled and named Hart as the triggerman in the murder. The alleged motive for the killing was that Marino "knew too much" about the Mike Russell murder.

On April 11, the three men were arraigned before Judge Erskine Maiden, Jr. They pled not guilty to first-degree murder and were held without bond. After a meeting between defense attorneys and Assistant County Prosecutor Harold H. Hull, dates were set for three separate trials; the first to be held on May 16.

The next day DeCola reported that he had interviewed Andrew Marino. The brother of Roy revealed:

> "My brother was in my office at Christmas time a year ago. He told me that he had gotten a job working as a bodyguard for a racketeer in Steubenville.
> "I asked my brother what kind of protection he could give this man. He told me the racketeer told him he had been threatened and wanted someone with him.
> "Sometime later my brother came back. He told me the man for whom he was acting as bodyguard paid him $1,600 for the work.
> "Happy told me that he had been asked to kill a fellow in Steubenville. I told my brother that if he had anything to do with a killing I would be the first man to turn him into the police. My brother told me he would not do the work and said he was only 'pulling the guy's leg' for some money."

DeCola claimed the man Roy Marino was asked to murder was Mike Russell. The *Cleveland Press* also reported that on the night of Roy's murder, Marino was "invited" by someone he met inside Chick's Café to come outside to the Galati automobile. It was alleged that John O'Boyle was behind the wheel of Galati's car and the two passengers were Hart and Ross.

One of the technicalities involved in the trial was the actual location of the murder. Authorities claimed Marino was apprehended and shot in Mahoning County before being dumped in Columbiana County, thus making Mahoning County the jurisdiction where the trial should be held.

The Trials

The first trial held was for John Anthoulis, which began in mid-May. Counsel for the Steubenville vice boss were John Nolan, his law partner Hugo F. Chestosky, and Youngstown attorney James S. Cooper, a former assistant Mahoning County prosecutor. One of the pre-trial squabbles was over a defense motion to depose Edward F. Hegert, a handyman working at Anthoulis' garage who helped collect money from the slot machines. He was the state's star witness. Mahoning County prosecutor, William A. Ambrose, went as far as to remove Hegert from the county jail to keep defense lawyers from interviewing him while Judge Maiden considered the motion. He was taken to Beaver Falls, Pennsylvania and later moved to the Struther's city jail. Another area of dispute involved the prosecution's failure to "file a bill of particulars establishing the time of the killing." Defense attorneys needed this so they could prepare alibis for their clients.

On May 17, a jury of eight men and four women were seated. They were selected from a special panel gathered for the three trials. During opening statements John Nolan told jurors that the defense, "welcomes this opportunity to meet the attempt of the state to show that Anthoulis had any connection with the crime. The testimony will show the defendant knows nothing about this crime...that Anthoulis never saw Marino...that he was never in Youngstown since 1925, and that he had no connection with the death of Marino."

The first witness was Columbiana County Coroner Arnold Devan who testified that at the death scene "a trail of blood along the road indicated the victim had dragged himself about 14 feet to the spot where the body was found." Dr. Roy C. Costello, who performed the autopsy, said that Marino's body had suffered 12 wounds from five bullets. Costello said any one of three wounds – to the head, chest or abdomen – could have caused his death. The fact that there was vomit at the scene confirmed that Marino was alive after being dumped out of the car.

The next morning, Edward Hegert was scheduled as the government's first witness. Three defense motions were overruled in an attempt to suppress his testimony. First, Chestosky was denied an interview with Hegert before he took the stand; second, an attempt to block Hegert's testimony regarding conversations that took place in Jefferson County was denied (defense counsel claimed this testimony should not be allowed because the alleged conspiracy took place in Mahoning County); and third, the defense objected to Hegert being allowed to testify as to what took place after Marino was murdered. Chestosky claimed a "conspiracy ends when a crime is committed." Ambrose and Hull argued that "a conspiracy does not end until all elements in the case are abandoned." Hull claimed that "efforts to cover the alleged crime were part of the conspiracy."

Hegert testified that he was introduced to Anthoulis by Clevelander John O'Boyle. Hegert started working for Anthoulis at his Steubenville home, where his employment began with repairing slot machines in a combination garage/office. Two weeks into the job, he met Solly Hart, and later Ross and Galati, who were described as associates or lieutenants of Anthoulis. Hegert soon inherited new duties – retrieving the coinage deposited each day by the players at the various locations where the machines were placed. While making his daily rounds, it was normal for at least two of Anthoulis' lieutenants to accompany him.

Hegert said that one day in late August 1937, while he was repairing one of the slot machines, he overheard Anthoulis tell Hart, Ross and Galati that Roy Marino was "a double-crosser and as long as he lives we will have trouble with him." Anthoulis, according to Hegert, made several attempts to reach Marino in Youngstown by phone, although telephone company records did not bear this out. Hegert then said he heard Anthoulis issue the orders, "go and take care of him." A week later, Hegert said he overheard Hart remark, "Tommy, Herb and I have a date with Marino on Thursday." Hegert then told the jury, "A few days later I read in the newspapers where a bullet-ridden body was found along the highway near East Liverpool. Later I learned it was Marino."

A few days after the murder, O'Boyle drove Galati's automobile to Anthoulis' Steubenville garage. Inside the vehicle was bloodstained upholstery which,

Hegert testified, he was asked to replace with upholstery from another automobile. While removing the upholstery, he said he noticed a bullet hole in the car's roof. When O'Boyle noticed the hole, he took a hammer and wedge and proceeded to pound a dent into the metal to disguise it. Hegert testified that while he was working on the car, Anthoulis arrived and ordered O'Boyle to "get this car out of here. The police are on the corner." The car was moved to a farm owned by Anthoulis, located about 20 minutes outside of Steubenville. The next day, Hegert went to the farm where he finished replacing the upholstery. Later, a piece of upholstery from the Galati car, found by a Steubenville police officer at the farm and identified by Hegert, was introduced as an exhibit. Also placed into evidence, was a door panel that Hegert removed from the vehicle and threw into a nearby creek.

Hegert told the court that O'Boyle was forced out of the Steubenville slot machine business by Hart, Ross and Galati, who believed that he was helping himself to some of the proceeds of the slot machines. Hegert was told by Ross, in an accusatory tone, "You're going to get $35 a week and there won't be any more pockets full of nickels going home after work." Hegert was told if that arrangement wasn't satisfactory that he could quit. Then Ross warned him if he had any notion of going to the authorities, "We have ways of stopping that."

Worried that he might be the next victim of a "ride," Hegert quit his job in late October and went to work for a relative. Hegert said he was so concerned for his safety that, "I intended to get out of the country." Instead, he made it back to Cleveland where he was arrested on February 26 and held at the request of Mahoning County officials. Scared that he was in danger even in jail, he asked the police to book him under the name Arthur Snyder. Hegert remained in jail until the trial because he felt safe there.

Charles Calaris, described as "an acquaintance of Marino and former associate of Anthoulis," followed Hegert to the stand. He claimed that Marino was one of three men accused by Mike Russell of taking part in a $35,000 jewel robbery at his home. The next witness was Jack Sperry, an ex-employee of Anthoulis, who testified that John Murphy, one of Anthoulis' associates, brought a large automobile to his garage and asked if he could store it there. Sperry stated, "It was a big car with only one Michigan license tag. I noticed there was no upholstery on the seat. Murphy said the car had been burned, I told him there was no odor of fire and he told me I was getting too inquisitive."

The prosecution then attempted to track Marino's movements the night before his murder. His brother Andrew testified that Roy was home having dinner when an automobile arrived and sounded its horn. "Roy seemed to be expecting the call," Andrew Marino testified.

The next witness then testified that Marino entered a drug store on Wilson Avenue near where he left Betty Jaynes. He purchased a pack of cigarettes, made a telephone call and left. John Chick was then called to tell the court that

Marino walked into his beer garden and remained there for five minutes before leaving. When he left, Chick stated, a "stranger" followed him.

Two students from East High School told of seeing an automobile parked in a "dark spot" in front of one the student's homes on Forest Avenue, a short distance from Chick's beer garden. The one youth became suspicious because "the two men in the front seat tried to cover their faces with their arms," when people walked past. He wrote down the license plate number of the car.

Next the prosecutor traced the second car which was purchased solely for its upholstery. According to the Michigan Department of Motor Vehicles in Lansing, the automobile was sold to John Navin of Detroit on September 22, 1937. The prosecution then had an official of Ohio Bell Telephone produce phone records from Anthoulis' office showing fourteen calls to Detroit between September 21 and 23.

Ambrose and Hull closed out the first week of the trial by presenting corroborating testimony on the gang's movements in Detroit. A room clerk at the Book-Cadillac Hotel identified hotel registry records showing that a Herbert Ross and Sol C. Hart checked into the hotel on September 20 and left on September 24. During that period Ross made two long distance phone calls to Steubenville. Then a Western Union office manager in Steubenville testified that two telegraphic money orders, one for $100 on September 21 and a second for $775 the next day, were wired from John O'Boyle to Herb Ross in Detroit. This was followed by the manager from the Detroit office verifying that the drafts from Steubenville were received and that Ross was paid the two amounts.

When court resumed on Monday morning prosecutors called their final two witnesses. Ancil Smith, a Detroit automobile salesman, identified Ross as the man who purchased a new Packard and drove it away. The upholstery from this car was used to replace the bloodstained material in the Galati automobile. Before resting their case, the state had 32 exhibits entered and information was read into the record that traced the death car to Thomas Galati.

Just before noon, attorney Chestosky asked for a directed verdict of acquittal from Judge Maiden. The *Vindicator* reported that in addition, Chestosky "wants part of the testimony of Edward F. Hegert and 11 other state witnesses excluded as incompetent because it related to incidents [that occurred] after Marino's murder, and he wants the 32 exhibits, admitted by the state, excluded." The judge excused the jury for the day while motions were argued.

On the afternoon of Tuesday, May 24, the wives of Solly Hart and Herbert Ross took the stand. Mrs. Hart testified that her husband worked the previous summer as a "special policeman" at Thistledown Race Track, located in suburban Cleveland. When the season ended on August 28, 1937, he left for Steubenville. Asked to explain her husband's work at the track, she stated, "He would watch people making side-bets other than at the windows, and was supposed to get them to place their bets at the mutual windows." Mrs. Ross said her husband worked at the racetrack also. After the season he went to Steubenville where he was interested in a juke box company. She claimed she never questioned her husband about his business.

The defense went out of its way to produce witnesses and testimony – in all three trials – to show that Ross and Hart were in Cleveland as employees of Thistledown Race Track until the end of the summer "race meeting" in late August and not in Steubenville. This was to contest Edward Hegert's testimony that during a "late August" meeting he had overheard Anthoulis's conversation with them when he made his "double-crosser" statement about Marino. However, "late August" certainly includes August 31, the day in which the defense itself proved Ross and Hart checked into the Fort Steuben Hotel. Anthoulis could have been waiting for the race season to end before hatching his scheme to have Marino killed. During Hart's trial, when he took the stand in his own defense, he widened the window by stating he hadn't been in Steubenville before August 27.

The last defense witness that day was Matt Brock, an ex-boxer who fought Johnny Kilbane for the featherweight championship in 1917. Brock, who worked as a mutual clerk for several Ohio race tracks, claimed he saw Hart and Ross everyday during the summer racing season at Thistledown.

The next day defense attorneys put John Anthoulis on the stand. The "vice king" of Steubenville denied all the allegations that were made against him during the previous week's testimony. The fall guy in the defense's strategy was clearly John O'Boyle. Anthoulis claimed he started out in the juke box business after he went into partnership with Mike Russell in 1936. The next year, he was told by Russell and O'Boyle that they were going into the slot machine business. After Russell's murder his wife went to Anthoulis and sold her husband's interest in the Steubenville slots. Anthoulis then went into business with O'Boyle on a 50/50 basis. It was O'Boyle who brought Hart and Ross into the business at the end of August 1937.

Anthoulis testified that O'Boyle called him on October 15 from the Fort Steuben Hotel. "I am in very bad shape. I'm very hot. They accuse me of the $35,000 robbery at Wheeling," Anthoulis claimed he was told by O'Boyle. Anthoulis said he purchased O'Boyle's interest in the slot machine business for $3,000 – agreeing to $600 up front and weekly payments of $100 to be sent to an address provided to him by O'Boyle. Anthoulis claimed he hadn't seen O'Boyle since he left town and no additional monies were paid.

As for Hegert, Anthoulis declared he was stealing nickels from the slot machines he was servicing and was given a warning. A week later, after an argument between the two, Hegert was fired. Anthoulis said Hegert called five times requesting his job back. When questioned about Marino, the vice boss said he "never knew Marino, never had any business with him or spoke about him."

Closing arguments by defense attorneys and prosecutors provided a spirited ending to a somewhat uneventful trial. Attorney John Nolan attacked the prosecution's star witness saying he was "convinced the state refused to show Hegert's statement because it would conflict with the testimony given by Hegert on the witness stand." Nolan discounted the entire testimony of Hegert claiming he lied to avoid prosecution.

Nolan's message to the jury was that the prosecution failed to present a motive for Marino's murder. "The state has even failed to prove that Anthoulis was acquainted with Marino, that Marino was ever in Steubenville, or that Marino had attempted to 'muscle in' on the slot machine business," Nolan contended. Defense attorney Cooper summed up his argument by stating that the evidence "had shown nothing, there is nothing to show a conspiracy was formed between the five men to kill Marino."

Assistant Prosecutor Hull told the jury the state had proved the essential elements of a conspiracy. "The proof of a motive is not necessary in homicide cases where guilt is clearly established," he stated. Mahoning County Prosecutor William Ambrose gave a caustic closing argument. "Don't show him any more mercy than was shown Marino in the back seat of that car when he was filled with gaping holes and thrown in the muck to die like a dog," he said. Turning to face Anthoulis, Ambrose barked, "It may be news to your unwilling ears, but you could have been in Bellaire, Ohio, taking lessons for your second citizenship papers, Mr. Anthoulis, and still be guilty. You directed this whole thing."

On the morning of May 26, after final instructions from Judge Maiden, the jury retired at 11:53 to begin deliberations. They could deliver one of three verdicts. The *Vindicator* wrote, "The jury may find Anthoulis guilty without mercy, which automatically will mean the death penalty; guilty with mercy, which will save him from the chair, but automatically means life imprisonment, or not guilty."

The jury deliberated for 6 hours and 12 minutes before coming to a unanimous decision. Court personnel quickly rounded up the principals, but only a handful of spectators were present when Anthoulis arrived from his county jail cell at 9:00 p.m. The jury found Anthoulis guilty, but recommended mercy. The defendant listened to the verdict with no outward show of emotion. Judge Maiden decided to defer the final say on the sentencing until the other cases were heard.

Returned to the Mahoning County jail, Anthoulis had a brief reunion with Ross and Hart. "Can you believe it?" Ross remarked dejectedly. "They want you to put your life in the hands of 12 people who don't know what's going on in this world. What just happened is the eighth wonder of the world. My wife, I won't be able to look her in the face tomorrow. This will break her heart."

In his small cell Anthoulis paced and puffed on a large cigar. "Sure they give me a break – they give me mercy. Well, I know I'm innocent and my conscience no bother me. I hope their conscience no bother them."

Hart sat and chuckled at the remarks of his companions. "Well, this thing is far from over yet," he stated.

Ross's trial was scheduled for May 30. The judge pushed it back until June 6 to give both sides a rest. Two days before the trial, deputies at the county jail recovered a pulp magazine left by three visitors containing ten "coded" messages for Ross. It appeared from the content of the notes that there was some fear in the underworld that Ross might talk. One note addressed Ross as "you sweet little singer of songs." Two other notes said, "Thirty days in the electric chair," and "Don't forget that doorman job next week." The intercepted magazine never made it to Ross.

The prospective jurors came from the special panel selected prior to the Anthoulis trial. Potential jurors were screened more thoroughly for the Ross trial as they now had to be questioned regarding their knowledge of the Anthoulis trial, as well as to what they had read about the attempt to "smuggle coded messages" to the defendant in jail. Special precautions were maintained inside the courtroom and each day Ross entered surrounded by five deputy sheriffs. Jury selection took less than two days and opening statements were made on the morning of June 8. The prosecutors and defense attorneys remained the same throughout the three trials. In asking for the death penalty, Ambrose told the jury that Ross "plotted, aided and helped in the murder of Marino. We shall ask at your hand, the extreme penalty."

The line up of prosecution and defense witnesses was basically the same as in the Anthoulis trial, with Coroner Devin and Dr. Roy Costello leading off. Edward Hegert, the state's star witness, again provided the damaging evidence. But it was the testimony of Ancil Smith, the Detroit auto salesman, which caused the greatest stir. When Smith repeated his account of Ross being with John Navin when the car was purchased in Detroit – for the purpose of exchanging the upholstery – and then driving the automobile away, Ross jumped to his feet and screamed, "You never saw me before in your life." He returned to his seat uttering profanity until being calmed by attorney James Cooper.

The testimony of another defense witness, a Detroit automobile firm official, helped tighten the noose on Thomas Galati, who was still in hiding. The man testified that an automobile purchased in July 1936 by the fugitive, which the state contends was the death car, had the identical upholstery as the Packard purchased by Ross in September 1937.

During the Ross trial, Marino's girlfriend, Betty Jaynes, was supposed to testify. Instead, county detective John Callan was called to the stand to admit he was unable to locate her. Callan said that after giving Ambrose a statement regarding her and Marino's activities on the evening of September 9, Jaynes was released "on the promise she would return to testify if we wanted her." A check of an East Cleveland address proved fruitless.

The state rested its case on Friday afternoon June 10, at which time Judge Maiden overruled a defense motion for a directed verdict. There were no surprise witnesses for the defense. Both Ross and his wife Roselynde took the stand. Roselynde testified her husband was in Detroit during September 1937, but had gone there to purchase slot machines. She claimed the deal was never consummated.

The jury received the case to begin deliberations at 3:30 on the afternoon of June 14. The nine women and three men deliberated for just over 14 hours before arriving at a verdict around 5:30 a.m. the next morning. The *Vindicator* wrote, "The jurors, who had upset precedent during the deliberations by asking to be allowed to remain out until they agreed, instead of going to bed, looked weary and drawn as they marched to the jury box. Each looked tired and pale, but all answered clearly and without hesitation while being polled."

Ross was pronounced guilty with a recommendation for mercy at 6:15 a.m. by Judge Maiden. As with Anthoulis, Maiden reserved sentencing pending the outcome of the last trial.

The trial of Solly Hart was scheduled to begin the day after Herb Ross was found guilty. Attorneys for both sides called Judge Maiden at home that evening and requested a delay. Maiden rescheduled the trial for June 27. On the day the trial was to begin, Hart filed a pleading in the clerk's office to waive a trial by jury and requested that a three-judge panel try him. With the same result in the first two trials there was some belief that Hart must have figured he was in for the same fate and decided to roll the dice and take his chances with the judges. In granting the request Judge Maiden announced, "Having tried the two previous cases, I do not consider it proper to sit as a trier of the fact in the Hart trial."

The three-judge panel consisted of George H. Gessner, the presiding criminal judge, Fred H. Wolf, of Wauseon, Ohio, and J.H.C. Lyon. Ohio Supreme Court Justice Carl V. Weygandt appointed the latter two to the case. It was Judge Lyon who denied the extradition of Roy Marino in 1932 to Pittsburgh when he was accused of a country club robbery there. The trial began on July 11. While the lineup of witnesses remained the same attorneys on both sides agreed to speed up the process by allowing much of the testimony to be read from the previous two trials. At 10:00 a.m. on the fourth day of the trial the state rested its case.

Taking the witness stand, Hart's explanation for being in Detroit was to accompany Ross, who traveled there "to take care of some business" for Mrs. Mike Russell, the widow of the late Wheeling mobster. The money wired to Ross by O'Boyle was to "take care of salaries" and for the purchase of slot machines. When the machines were found to be "no good," they gave the money back to O'Boyle after their return to Steubenville. Hart denied being involved in any automobile transactions while in the Motor City.

On Friday, July 22 at 10:00 a.m. Solly Hart stood before Judge George Gessner to hear the panel's decision. The *Vindicator* reported that, "the three-judge court overruled the defense contentions that testimony regarding events after the date of the murder was incompetent, and that Mahoning County was not the proper venue for the case." Neither Hart nor his lawyer had any comments before the nine-page opinion of the three-judge panel was read pronouncing the defendant guilty. The judges deemed that Hart was entitled to mercy like Anthoulis and Ross and sentenced him to life in prison. After Hart's sentencing, Judge Maiden overruled motions for new trials for John Anthoulis and Herb Ross. At 10:55 Anthoulis was sentenced to life in prison. Thirteen minutes later Ross received the same sentence. Commenting on the sentence for Hart a *Cleveland Press* editorial said (in part):

"Life" for Solly Hart

"Solly Hart, the Cleveland gangster who so often has escaped punishment because he had the right contacts, has been found guilty of first-degree murder and sentenced to life imprisonment in the Ohio Penitentiary.

"Decent citizens will approve this verdict. If some skeptically wonder how long a life term will really mean in Hart's case it is only because of a system which has permitted Hart to sneer at the law for so many years.

"Law-abiding citizens will feel that justice will be served if Hart is kept behind prison bars for the rest of his life. He will not be unless they are on guard. Even before the penitentiary gates close behind Hart, sinister influences will be at work to obtain the release of Cleveland's No. 1 gangster, if past performances prove anything."

A couple of hours after the sentences were handed down, Hart, Anthoulis and Ross were manacled – by their wrist and ankles – and placed in Mahoning County Sheriff Ralph Elser's car to be driven to the Ohio Penitentiary in Columbus to begin their life terms. They were followed by a second car, where one of three deputies was armed with a Thompson submachine-gun. The convicted men arrived at the grim prison that evening.

The next day one of their partners-in-crime, Thomas Galati was arrested in Marion, Ohio. A fugitive for the past three and a half months, Galati was asleep in his brother-in-law's home when a squad of eight law-enforcement officers surrounded the house. Galati surrendered without a fight. John Callan and a pair of Youngstown detectives were sent to retrieve him.

More than six weeks after his arrest Galati was still without counsel. Due to his association with O'Boyle, and O'Boyle's alleged split from the others after the murder of Marino, there was speculation that Galati was "abandoned" by lawyers for the gang. Attorney Chestosky had met with Galati several times, but made no arrangements to represent him. Galati was reported to be "financially ruined." He was finally arraigned on September 14, 1938 and pleaded not guilty before Judge David G. Jenkins. He informed the judge that he was unable to afford an attorney and didn't know when he could. Jenkins assigned Clyde W. Osborne to represent him.

Osborne decided on a jury trial and on October 19 the case got underway. The prosecution's case was basically the same as it had been in the three previous trials. In Osborne's opening statement he told jurors, "he had no doubt that a car bearing Galati's license plates was here September 9 and that if such a car were here with Galati's plates, Galati never knew it and there was no proof that Galati did know it." During the afternoon session Edward Hegert was on the stand. Osborne had just begun his cross-examination of the witness when he suddenly said to Judge Jenkins, "I ask for an adjournment." The *Vindicator* reported, Osborne "slumped into his chair and did not seem to be aware of his surroundings. He was taken home, where the attending physician said that complications resulting from a leg injury last winter and nervous exhaustion from the trial had caused his collapse."

The trial resumed on Monday, October 24. Near the end of the week Galati took the stand in his own defense to refute the testimony of some eleven prosecution witnesses. Galati's only connection to the crime was his automobile. He told the court, I have never seen my car since two days before Marino was killed. I owed Johnny O'Boyle $300 and I gave my car to him as security. He got it on September 7 and that's the last I ever saw of him or the car."

The jury got the case on Tuesday, November 1 at 11:45 p.m. They deliberated until 4:45 a.m. Wednesday before resting. They resumed deliberating at 1:00 pm. that afternoon, and reached a verdict nine hours later after a total of twenty-one and a half-hours of work, the longest period of time a jury was out for any of the trials. At 11:00 p.m. Wednesday Judge Jenkins read the guilty verdict from the panel of seven women and five men. They recommended mercy. Jenkins sentenced Galati to life in prison at the Ohio Penitentiary.

On April 21, 1939, the Seventh District Court of Appeals upheld all the verdicts. The four men had appealed based on the grounds "that since Marino was found slain in Columbiana County and there was no evidence he was killed in Mahoning County, the court had no jurisdiction over the cases." In their decision the three-judge panel claimed, "the defendants should feel quite satisfied that they were not asked to pay the extreme penalty." A month later the decision was appealed to the Ohio Supreme Court. They too turned it down.

Just days after the appellate court decision, Solly Hart was named in a massive indictment in Cleveland after a policy probe headed by famed Cleveland Safety Director Eliot Ness. Among the 23 indicted were mobsters who had already made their names during the Prohibition Era – George and John Angersola and Albert Polizzi – as well as men who made their mark in later years – Alex "Shondor" Birns, Frank Hoge, Angelo Lonardo, John DeMarco and Milton "Maische" Rockman. These indictments, which resulted in the fleeing of many of those named, effectively brought to an end what was known as the Mayfield Road Mob. With Hart in prison serving a life term the charges against him were dropped in July 1942.

Aftermath

In December 1941, Ohio Penitentiary Warden Frank D. Henderson announced that Hart was a trusty and one of three "life-termers" who were given special duties at the prison. Hart drove a pick-up truck and was allowed to perform errands around the Columbus area. Ironically, the other two "lifer-termers" were Sarantino "Wop English" Sinatra and Jacob "Firetop" Sulkin, who were initially condemned to death for their role in the murder of Jackie Kennedy. It was Kennedy's murder that Thomas "Yonnie" Licavoli was serving life for when he befriended Happy Marino in 1934.

There was a tragic note to the story. During the pre-dawn hours of February 24, 1944, county investigator John Callan was killed in an automobile accident. Callan was on his way home from Warren, where he was investigating a case, when his speeding automobile skidded out of control on an icy stretch of Market Street at Wayne Avenue in Youngstown. Callan's car hit a steel utility pole broadside killing him instantly. Callan left behind a wife and two daughters.

With four of the five indicted men serving life sentences for the murder of Marino only one remained on the run. John O'Boyle continued to be a fugitive until the spring of 1945 when the FBI arrested him in Los Angeles in connection with the theft of $100,000 worth of homeowner's bonds from the Bank of America. By that time he was wanted in five cities on bank theft charges, in addition to the murder charge in Youngstown. When there was insufficient evidence for the West Coast authorities to hold him, Prosecutor Ambrose began the process of preparing extradition papers to have him returned to Youngstown. O'Boyle was indicted, however, by a federal grand jury in Chicago for illegally possessing gasoline coupons. The charges arose from a December 6, 1944, robbery at an Ashland, Kentucky, rationing board. When O'Boyle was arrested in Los Angeles he was in possession of "$1,900 in cash, coupons worth 1,400 gallons of gasoline, and a ration check for 4,000 gallons of gas" from the robbery. His wife Kitty Kelly O'Boyle was apprehended in Toledo on January 9, 1945. She pled guilty to possession of stolen coupons and was given a two-year federal prison sentence.

Ambrose forwarded a "hold order" to Chicago for the federal marshals to return O'Boyle to Youngstown once the government's case was completed. Instead, O'Boyle was brought directly to Youngstown from California in July 1945 to stand trial. O'Boyle pled not guilty to first-degree murder charges before Judge Maiden on September 10.

O'Boyle was represented by three local attorneys, including Clyde Osborne. The trial was scheduled for December 17, but prosecutors told the judge that two of their key witnesses, the former high school friends who had testified to seeing Galati's car parked outside Chick's Café, were serving in the Army Air Force outside the United States. Ambrose told the judge, "Without the testimony of these boys, the state can't show jurisdiction in this court." Maiden set a new trial date for February 18, 1946.

Ambrose was still having trouble rounding up witnesses and the case suffered another delay. On April 27, 1946, O'Boyle walked out of the county jail a free man. The *Vindicator* reported the state was "unable to locate a number of key witnesses needed in the case and felt a successful case could not be prosecuted without their testimony." The newspaper also pointed out that because Ambrose "nolled" the case it was possible that a future grand jury could re-indict O'Boyle. The one-time Cleveland bootlegger was not completely in the clear. He was ordered to return to Chicago to face charges from the robbery of the gasoline coupons in Kentucky.

Hart and the others languished in prison, their appeals and motions for new trials denied over the years. On January 8, 1949, Hart got a break when outgoing-Governor Thomas J. Herbert, in the closing days of his term, commuted his first-degree murder conviction to second-degree. Hart, who had become a respected trusty and was given driving privileges outside the prison seven years earlier, served as a chauffeur to Warden Henderson, as well as his replacement Ralph W. Alvis. Herbert's commutation meant that Hart could receive immediate consideration for parole, which he requested. It was reported that, "Letters to Governor Herbert from leading penologists in the state expressed 'grave doubt' as to Hart's guilt in Marino's death. Some said they believed he was 'framed.'" Ambrose, who heard about the commutation by Governor Herbert in the newspapers, was incensed. In addressing the "leading penologists" he fired off a letter to the State Pardon & Parole Commission questioning, "Where or when and in what manner testimony was addressed or any situation as shown by a record of the testimony that would justify the belief that Hart had been framed is beyond me.

"It seems improbable that 13 judges [the 3-judge panel who tried Hart and 10 jurists in the court of appeals and the Ohio State Supreme Court] with their legally trained minds would overlook testimony tending to show that Hart had been framed."

The efforts to get Hart released drew headlines and brought back stories of the parole scandal exposed in 1937. An editorial in the *Vindicator* on January 10 called Governor Herbert's action a "disservice" to the state. The newspaper was of the opinion that Marino's murder was some how still connected to the scandal:

> "Now Hart apparently is a beneficiary of the parole abuse which he sought to protect by killing Marino.
>
> "If Hart has made a good chauffeur for prison wardens, that's fine; he ought to be kept doing this work, the first useful thing he has done in his life. But the underhand means he and his pals have used to make him eligible for parole indicate that the leopard hasn't changed his spots, and can't be trusted outside a cage. The legality of the commutation should be examined; if it stands up, then Hart's application for release should be strongly opposed when it comes before the parole board."

The State Pardon & Parole Commission announced it would hear Hart's petition for parole at its regularly scheduled meeting. When the hearing took place on February 8 the three-member commission refused Hart a parole, but continued his case until June. On July 11, 1949 the parole commission issued the following statement:

> "This commission has carefully considered the case of Solly Hart, whose commutation [from first to second-degree murder] was based solely on the possibility of his innocence.
>
> "Following as thorough an investigation as possible after a passage of years, we are not convinced of his innocence and can see nothing to distinguish his case from those of his accomplices whose commutations we are unwilling to recommend.
>
> "Some people have voiced sincere doubt of Hart's guilt and have pointed out his fine institutional record. We believe something more than this is necessary and have discovered no convincing proof of his innocence, although it has not been possible to convict one man at least equally guilty with those now serving time.
>
> "His case now stands continued until such time as we are required to hear his accomplices for clemency. If, in the meantime, the lack of guilt of these men is affirmatively established, we will act accordingly."

More than seven years passed before any of Marino's murderers were heard from again. On October 9, 1956, John Anthoulis died in the Ohio Penitentiary hospital of "pulmonary thrombosis with heart disease contributing." Two months later, on December 15, 1956 the *Vindicator* reported: "Hart, once dubbed Cleveland's Public Enemy No. 1, is being considered along with several other prison inmates for Christmas clemency. The governor [Frank J. Lausche] could commute Hart's sentence to expire at once or commute his second degree murder charge to manslaughter, permitting the State Pardon & Parole Commission to take up the case for possible parole."

Hart's full term, due to Governor Herbert's commutation, would expire in July 1958. At that time he could leave prison with no parole supervision. On January 3, 1957, in one of his last official acts as governor, Lausche commuted the now second-degree murder conviction to manslaughter. Hart immediately appealed to the State Pardon & Parole Commission and his case was set to be heard the following month. On February 14, Hart was again denied parole.

All of the articles about Hart since the early 1940s had referred to him as being the trusty chauffeur of two different wardens. Both men had gone to bat as "penologists" in hopes of getting him an early release. On January 29, 1958, however, it was Warden Alvis who was chauffeuring Hart when both men nearly lost their lives. The driver of a dump truck was making a left turn as Alvis, driving his own convertible, tried to pass him. In the collision Hart was thrown from the vehicle. He was rushed to a local hospital in critical condition with back, chest and internal injuries. He was later required to wear a steel back brace. Warden Alvis lost his right eye in the accident, for which police cited him.

On July 22, 1958, twenty years to the day after he was convicted, Solly Hart was released from the Ohio Penitentiary. He was 52 years old. Hart went back to Cleveland, still in his back brace, to continue his recovery at the home of his sister. In April 1959, the State Sundry Claims Board recommended that Hart be paid $8,600 for his injuries. The recommendation was passed by the state house in July that year, but was still being held up a month later by Governor Michael V. DiSalle after an informant told him that "Hart is not so badly off financially as he has maintained." Hart was granted $5,150 up front with the balance to be paid in 23 monthly payments of $150.

In September 1960, Governor DiSalle, acting on the advice of the State Pardon & Parole Commission, commuted Herbert Ross' sentence to second degree murder. Ross had spent most of his prison time at the Ohio Penitentiary, but in the past few years was relocated to the London Prison Farm. A trusty, he made daily trips to Columbus delivering legal documents to state penal officers. After Hart's parole there was bitterness on the part of Ross and Galati. They claimed to have become "forgotten prisoners," and Ross declared that he and Galati were convicted because of Hart's reputation as "Cleveland's No. 1 underworld boss." On November 23, 1960, after serving more than 22 years in prison, the 57 year-old Ross was released. The parole commission called Ross "fully rehabilitated" and reported that he had secured work at an optical company outside Columbus. Ross died in December 1982, at the age of 79.

In January 1963, in his last days in office, Governor DiSalle commuted Thomas Galati's sentence from first to second-degree murder. In April, Galati was paroled from the Marion Correctional Institution. At 54 years of age Galati had spent over 24 years of his life behind bars for the Marino killing. Galati died in Cleveland on June 15, 1968 at the age of 59.

Did 20 years in prison rehabilitate Solly Hart? Apparently not. Hart eventually got back together with surviving members of the Cleveland Syndicate, but long after they had left the city by the lake. By the mid-1960s, Hart was living in Miami, Florida where, according to Hank Messick in *The Silent Syndicate*, one of the people he was associated with was Jake Lansky, the older, less infamous, brother of Meyer. In late June 1966, Hart was arrested in Miami for leaving the scene of an accident after his car struck a fence. Police charged him with drunken driving. While making a routine search of his automobile police found betting slips and a .38 caliber revolver under the front seat. Hart was then charged with these violations.

In November, Hart appeared in Dade County Criminal Court and, just like he had done back in 1938, waived a jury trial. The case was not heard until June 1967. Hart was found guilty on two bookmaking charges. The judge, however, delayed sentencing pending a Supreme Court ruling. The newspapers reported a decision was to be made on "whether testimony from Internal Revenue Service agents can be used in local gambling cases. Testimony from IRS agents on Hart's acquisition of the federal gambling stamp was introduced during the trial. The Supreme Court has under consideration complaints from gamblers that it is unfair for the government to require them to purchase the gambling stamp and then to use the stamp as evidence of guilt in local cases. In federal cases, such testimony is not being used."

Hart's name last appeared in the *Vindicator* on November 30, 1969. A small article announced that the 64 year-old former "gangland" figure was released recently from a Miami hospital where he was being treated for emphysema. Hart died in October 1976, at the age of 71.

The murder of Roy "Happy" Marino remains one of the few mob killings in the Mahoning Valley ever to be successfully prosecuted. Between the time of his murder and the capture of his killers, Marino's status in the underworld, at least in the eyes of the newspapers, had changed drastically. Marino went from "one of the best known underworld characters" in the Valley, to "petty local racketeer." In the reporting of Solly Hart's activities during the mid-1960s, however, Marino seemed to have reacquired some level of importance. He was then referred to as the area's "slot machine baron."

"This is a dastardly thing. Such gangsterism must be stamped out. We are going to get to the bottom of it, and not rest until we do." – Youngstown Mayor William A. Spagnola commenting on the attempted murder of attorney Dominic F. Rendinell, a political enemy, on January 23, 1941.

4

Rise of the Lottery Houses

Introducing the "Bug"

In the Valley the term "bug" is synonymous with lottery, numbers and policy. The game of policy made its way to many northern industrial cities during World War I, brought here from the south by black migrants who were needed to take the place of factory workers sent off to war. The bug became popular in the Valley in the late 1920s while bootlegging was still the main source of illegal income. In the gambling world the bug took a backseat to bookmaking and the profits being made from slot machines. Before the decade of the 1930s was over, however, the profits from the bug surpassed all other gambling operations. What made playing the bug so popular was the simple fact that, "no bet was too small." The wagers included pennies, nickels, dimes and quarters. Anyone could play and everyone did.

The *Vindicator* outlined the basic operations of the lottery games in the first of a seven part series on local gambling that appeared in June 1938:

> "Lottery banks have very efficient organizations which compare favorably with those of any large concern. They hire a small army of workers here – "writers," who take the bets; pickup men who gather the slips on regular routes, and cashiers and bookkeepers who handle the cash and pay out the 'hits.'
>
> "When the racket first took root here, it was confined to one group of operators who reportedly made a small fortune during the several years they held control. Operations then were far less extensive than now. Selling of numbers usually was done at the corner cigar stand, newsstand, grocery or drug store.
>
> "About 1933, control of the racket reportedly changed hands. The story was that original operators sold their business but the rumor also went the rounds that they were 'frozen out' by the new combine which has come to be known as the 'Youngstown Bank' and 'Big House.'"

The "Banks" or "Houses" were split along ethnic lines in the Valley. By the mid-to-late 1930s four major "Houses" were operating throughout the Youngstown area. They were identified as the Big House, also known as the "Youngstown Bank" (Greek); the American House (Irish); the Campbell House (Croatian); and the South Side House (Italian).

Law enforcement's first major offensive against the lottery houses came on June 12, 1935. Mahoning County Sheriff Ralph Elser celebrated his 24th wedding anniversary by conducting two raids in downtown Youngstown. The first was at an operation on South Watt Street. The second was at 315 West Federal Street at a pool hall, which operated at the time under the name Recreation Billiard Parlor, but became infamous as the Liberty Pool Room.

By the time Elser had his prisoners ready to be arraigned the municipal court was closed. Squire Robert W. Raymond agreed to go to the county jail and arraign the men there. One of the prisoners brought before Raymond stated, "I write my own numbers. I have five children and a wife. If I go to jail they go on relief. And I can't raise a bond." This confession was in line with problems Elser confronted on a daily basis with America still in the throes of the Depression. In pointing out the real devastation caused by playing the bug the sheriff related, "Just last week a woman told one of my deputies she hadn't anything to eat. Yet a bug man said her husband was a regular 50-cent customer." Sheriff Elser told reporters, "The good people of the city want these bug places driven from the city, judging by the way we receive calls from taxpayers and mothers of boys and girls who play the bug. These bug places can be driven out if only the law enforcement officers of the city get busy."

Apprehended during the raids were Nick Brown and Peter Rigas. They were the first two major players to face arrest once the bug craze got underway in the Valley. Neither man was at a shortage of words for reporters. Brown talked candidly about the "trials and tribulations" of a numbers man. "I suppose we have about 75 writers working for us. We [the partners in the operation] only make money on good days – and we've only had a lot of bad numbers [winners] lately," he claimed. In explaining the day-to-day operations he said that a writer, the employee who meets with the players and takes the bets, receives 30 percent of the money he collects. The net profits are then shared by the three partners.

"We pay 500 to 1 on all [winning] numbers," Brown explained, "and we pay our winners." This seemed to indicate that there were other operators who didn't pay off if a heavily played number turned out to be the day's winner. It was these operators who were giving the bug business a bad name. "There are too many small numbers banks in Youngstown. That's why business is not so good," he said. Brown disclosed that the city had between 10 and 15 "numbers banks," but most of them were small. The New York bank, which Brown said he worked for, operated at approximately 100 "pickup" stations throughout the city. The "pickup" stations were magazine stores, poolrooms, drug stores, newspaper stands – just about anywhere that a customer could place his money down discreetly. Brown finished with reporters stating, "And don't forget to put in your story that there are a lot of good church people who play the numbers every day – probably more people of this type then people like you and me," he advised.

Peter Rigas expressed surprise at his arrest, "I've been in Youngstown 20 years, and this is the first time I've been in jail. I've been in the racket about one and a half years." Rigas stated that on good days the South Watt Street location grossed $1,000 in bug sales. Both he and Brown denied having to pay protection money to local officials to remain in operation.

As Elser continued to make raids, accusations of preferential treatment were being raised by some of the lottery house operators. The Big House, sometimes referred to as the "Youngstown Bank," was the prominent lottery house in the Valley. In December 1935, the frequently raided and harassed American House, or "American Bank," operating out of the Steel City Club on Central Square, began to complain that the Big House "operated virtually unmolested." On December 7, Elser's raiders used sledgehammers for the second time in a week to smash open the doors at an American House location on Mahoning Avenue. After deputies arrested five men and two women and carted them off to jail, bug salesmen, not captured in the raid, returned to the house. "What a hell of a note this is! We no sooner get straightened around than they raid us again," one bug writer complained. In the crowd watching the raid were several American House workers. Once the raiders cleared out, someone opened a second floor window and shouted, "It's all right to come up now." It was soon business as usual.

Two years later it was the South Side House, with its headquarters in the Radio Athletic Club on Market Street, crying foul. On December 29, 1937, Judge Harry C. Hoffman was about to bring down a heavy fine on three bug men from the South Side. The men were in Hoffman's courtroom before and the judge promised them "the limit" if they returned. "I am going to force you out of the business," Hoffman told the trio. "I told you what I would do when you were here before. I don't blame you much either. I blame the jacklegs who hired you."

One of the men was defended by Clyde W. Osborne. The noted defense attorney informed Hoffman that since August, 80 of the 119 bug arrests were of men associated with the South Side bank, while only five were connected with the Big House. Osborne pointed out that the detectives who made the arrests drew salaries that totaled $990 a month. With that Osborne's co-counsel remarked, "The citizens of Youngstown actually are paying $1,000 a month to assist the Big House."

After an argument over not being able to "clean out" the bug because so many people play it, Hoffman stated, "I have no intention of reforming the bug, but I do know if the good people would quit patronizing it we wouldn't have it."

Osborne replied, "If this city and the police department were trying to break up the bug, the court would be justified in imposing a sentence which would break up the practice. But where it is made to appear to the court that the plan is to break up the practice in favor of one bank against the other, I say the court has the right to know and have those facts brought before him before imposing sentence."

Police Prosecutor David Neiman objected to Osborne's argument calling it irrelevant. "Mr. Osborne has no right to air his views of the police department in this court room. Any judge who listens to a lawyer who...brings this kind of thing into the court room is not true to his office."

After listening to both arguments, Hoffman suspended the $500 fines he imposed on the three men. Instead, he ordered them to be photographed and fingerprinted, then placed them on probation for one year, warning them that if they were arrested again the $500 fine would be re-imposed.

Earlier that week Hoffman had fined 16 men $15 each after they had pled guilty to selling bug tickets. At that time Osborne had asked the judge for a light sentence for the men. "There must be some intelligence in the back of the system which forces 106 men from other bug fraternities to be brought in as against only five men of the Big House," Osborne stated. "If you are going to make fish of one and foul of the other, make the sentence light on the fish." Included in the 16 were Louis Tiberio, Frank Fetchet, Joseph Russo and Frank Gioia.

On May 23, 1938, Daniel Shovlin and Anthony DeCarlo, the latter one of the three men who appeared before Judge Hoffman the previous December, swore out an affidavit before Innocenzo Vagnozzi, a Youngstown councilman and notary public. Below are some of the key points of their statement, which alleged police discrimination in the bug racket

◊ Both men claimed they earned their livelihood by collecting lottery slips.

◊ Six members of the Youngstown Police Department discriminated against them and their employer – the South Side House.[5]

◊ Both men worked for the American House for two years during which time they operated unmolested.

◊ In the last ten months, as an employee of the South Side House, DeCarlo was arrested nine times. In addition to the arrests, both men were "molested, warned and threatened by police officers at the average rate of four times a week, sometimes to the extent of being followed all day."

◊ The men claimed they were told by the officers that they "were dancing with the wrong orchestra and that unless they turned their slips and collections into some other lottery organization other than the South Side Bank they would be arrested and interfered with daily."

◊ Both men claimed that on various occasions "these officers, pursuing them in the streets, blocked their car during the hour period when the slips must be turned in to be of account in the lottery. At the same time these officers ignored the operations of pickup men connected with rival lottery banks, signaling the rival pickup men to be on their way to turn the slips in while they detained DeCarlo and Shovlin."

◊ On May 20, 1938, police protected pickup men from the American House as they collected slips from a Midlothian Boulevard location they had recently muscled away from the South Side House.

The affidavit was presented at a Youngstown City Council meeting that afternoon where DeCarlo and several others were on hand to provide additional information. DeCarlo claimed that the lottery houses were bringing in $8.0 million annually and that between 4,000 and 4,500 men and women were engaged in some phase of the lottery rackets locally, either 'writing' numbers, picking them up or working in the several lottery headquarters and sub-headquarters." DeCarlo also revealed that he picked up the daily numbers from 60 to 65 writers and turned the slips into the main lottery headquarters around 1:00 p.m. His daily earnings were "normally" between $16 and $20. DeCarlo claimed that "police interference" had cut his daily income down to $6.

The council seemed split on what action to take. Some requested that a grand jury investigate the allegations, others wanted the information turned over to Mayor Lionel Evans, Police Chief Carl L. Olson and members of the civil service commission. Mayor Evans was quick to respond, telling reporters, "I don't know whether the charges made at the hearing are true, but I do know that I don't want anyone to have any basis for making such charges in the future. As far as I am concerned, no one is getting any police protection, or paying for it." He then ordered Chief Olson to beef up the vice squad and warned him, "Unless these charges of discrimination are stopped, I will consider some very drastic changes in the police department." Olson responded by adding four police officers to Detective Chief William W. Reed's vice squad and stated that Evan's orders would be "complied with to the fullest extent."

The affidavit from DeCarlo and Shovlin didn't seem to cause a let-up on the attack on the South Side operators. On July 11 vice squad officers entered a poolroom at 1603 Market Street. Inside was Louis Tiberio, a South Side lottery agent. When he saw the officers enter he placed several "bug" slips in his mouth. Tiberio later claimed Vice Squad Officer Joseph Lepo grabbed him by the throat and choked him until he coughed up the slips.

Tiberio stated, "Lepo then punched me in the mouth and face although I had my glasses on. He didn't hit me while I was in the billiard room, but took me into a backroom to do that. Some vice squad men visit the poolroom every other day in an effort to put the screws on me and my boys. They started to get sore today when the boys started to ask, 'Why don't you raid the Big House places some time?'

"The detectives say I was resisting arrest. Now I have been arrested enough times by them to know it wouldn't be of any use to resist a big policeman with a badge and gun."

The police report told a different story. Officers wrote that Tiberio "made several attempts to hit Lepo," and that he "swung at officers and used vile and insulting names while the poolroom was being searched." At one point he attempted to throw billiard balls at the officers. Tiberio pled not guilty to charges of possession of betting slips and resisting arrest before Judge Hoffman.

The alleged partiality by police in favoring the Big House led to the sidetracking of a city ordinance that would have provided a 90-day jail sentence for those convicted on lottery charges. In June 1939, Councilman Carl Fisher stated he had no confidence that police were enforcing existing lottery laws impartially. He then declared he was opposed to the measure and would not "be a party to persecuting one bug outfit and helping another."

Evans and everyone else knew that the bug's popularity would never allow the police to eradicate it from the city, but he stated, "All lotteries must be treated alike." The mayor also made a declaration that any city employee found playing the bug would be discharged. Evans had apparently initiated this action after the lead of the Strouss-Hirshberg Company, a major downtown department store, which threatened to fire its employees if they were found to be playing the bug.

As was normally the case, when such matters flooded the headlines, police action in the form of raids followed. It was a typical vice drive where, in addition to arresting numbers men, others were taken in for prostitution, illegal liquor and unlicensed pinball machines. Sheriff Elser's men were helping out by visiting a dozen places in the county and seizing "marble boards," the popular name for pinball machines. After destroying six machines found during raids, the sheriff commented, "And that is my answer to any form of gambling in the county. Any operators who would like to see a lot of expensive marble boards smashed to bits can do so by following their boards back to the jail after we've seized them. There can't and won't be any marble boards or slot machines operating in the county as long as I have any say in the matter."

Not to be outdone, Chief Olson announced, "I'm going to smash the bug. If police work can do it, we are going to clean it out." This followed three raids in two days on Big House lottery operations in the city. Places hit were the South Watt Street substation run by the Rigas brothers, another substation at 552 West Federal Street and the Recreation/Liberty Pool Room at 315 West Federal Street. Raiders confiscated lottery slip pads, adding machine tape and other paraphernalia, but none of the key operators were arrested.

On the first weekend after Mayor Evans' cleanup orders police arrested 24 individuals bringing the total to 46 for the week. The raid at the Recreation/Liberty Pool Room during the week did not prevent the Big House headquarters from operating in a "business as usual" manner that weekend. The *Vindicator* pointed out, "One man, usually an unimportant clerk, is arrested when a raid is made. Since the stations have been raided 15 or 20 minutes before the daily deadline for turning in slips with the current day's numbers, very few pickup men with the current day's slips are present as the raid is made. The raiders seize slips, most of them dated several days prior to the raid, but get very few current slips. Pickup men, especially of the Big House, rush into headquarters during the last five or ten minutes before deadline."

On May 31, Chief Olson issued the following decree:

> "To all members of this department:
>
> "While we have a vice squad assigned to vice daily, it is the duty of every member of this department to do everything possible to clean up gambling and all forms of vice and make arrests wherever possible. All officers in charge will see that this order is carried out."

That afternoon four employees of the South Side House, including Frank "Frankie Joy" Gioia were arrested. Gioia was arrested for reckless driving as he apparently tried to elude police on Rayen Avenue. The vice squad made a second arrest at an American House station on Mahoning Avenue and another at a Big House substation on East Federal Street. Still, none of the major operators were brought in.

Over the next two days four more South Side House employees were arrested and jailed. One of the men was James "Brier Hill Lulu" Montello, a former associate of Roy "Happy" Marino. Another man was arrested at the Press Club on South Phelps Street. Initially he gave his name as James Costinee and said the bug slips he was caught with were to be turned over to the Big House. At the police station he gave his correct name, Constantino and admitted he was associated with the South Side House.

As the vice drive continued into its second week the police found their efforts being aided by citizens supplying information on bug sellers. The mayor and police chief were also getting strong support from local business leaders who announced a stand against the sale and playing of bug numbers by their employees during business hours. Prominent among these businesses was the aforementioned Strouss-Hirshberg Company, G.M. McKelvey Company, and the Stambaugh-Thompson Company. In mid-July city religious leaders and heads of local women's organizations stood united behind the mayor's efforts and condemned Councilman Anthony T. Kryzan's attempt to have the city's bug ordinance repealed.

Marble Board Craze and the Rendinell Shooting

While the lottery rackets continued going strong into the war years, the marble board, or pinball, craze was reaching a peak in 1940 and 1941, as well as the efforts to regulate it locally. The city passed an ordinance, which licensed pinball machines and collected an annual fee from the establishments that displayed them. On May 29, 1940, attorney Dominic F. Rendinell filed a lawsuit on behalf of Joseph Sergi, a West Side tavern owner, for an injunction to restrain the further issuance of pinball machine licenses declaring that the city ordinance was illegal. The suit, which was upheld by both the common pleas court and the court of appeals, forced the city to quit selling licenses.

When Democratic candidate William B. Spagnola was campaigning for mayor, in the fall of 1939, one of his supporters was attorney Rendinell. In addition to stumping for Spagnola, the lawyer contributed $100 to the campaign fund. After Spagnola won it was reported that Rendinell "had been slated for the law directorship, or some other important post in the city government, but he was not included in the appointments." Whatever caused the rift in the relationship never came to light, but future events clearly showed that Rendinell had a bitter split with Spagnola and the administration.

During the first week of 1941, Rendinell filed a contempt of court proceeding against Mayor William Spagnola and two members of his staff after discovering that several licenses were issued by the administration violating the court order. Judge David Jenkins dismissed the charges, but advised the administration that no more licenses were to be issued. Mayor Spagnola's reaction was to issue an order banning all pinball machines in the city and on January 13 Judge Jenkins affirmed its legality. While the city faced losing between $13,000 and $15,000 in annual licensing fees, it was predicted that the cost to the operators would be $300,000. Vice squad chief Captain Charles N. Richmond warned all locations possessing the machines that they had to be removed by the deadline the mayor set or face having them confiscated. In areas of the county outside the city Sheriff Elser had already begun a successful campaign to remove the machines a month earlier.

After Spagnola's order, other cities throughout the county gave consideration to a similar move. Mayor William A. Strain of Struthers took a "look and see" approach, waiting to see if Youngstown could be successful with their effort. When Strain made his decision to ban the machines he gave operators just 24 hours to have them removed, instead of the four-day warning Spagnola had allowed.

Two days before the deadline set by the mayor, police found 359 pinball machines in operation at 195 places throughout the city. Captain Richmond was willing to work with proprietors who had unplugged their machines and were waiting for the owners to come and remove them. Richmond had a real concern as to where he was going to store all the machines if the mayor's order was defied. The police property room was already filled with other confiscated gambling devices. Consideration was given to City Hall, as the machines would have to remain intact until the courts decided how they would be disposed of.

After the order going into effect on January 13, police seized ten machines from six locations and arrested two men. Spagnola felt more arrests were necessary and declared, "Arrests will be made in every case where boards are confiscated." In spite of the mayor's efforts, one councilman criticized Spagnola for not "extending the cleanup to penny slots machines, punch boards and penny gumball machines."

Despite Jenkin's ruling, the mayor's decision to outlaw the city's pinball ordinance was meeting with some legal opposition. The city law director was concerned that the city would face an injunction against making any more arrests or seizing additional machines. While Spagnola was willing to "sit tight" and allow those willing to press the matter to do so in the courts, he was worried that attorney Rendinell would "prosper" because of his opposition to the ordinance. The *Vindicator* reported, "Attorney Rendinell, it is known, is not on good terms with the mayor."

On January 23, the first case came to court where a defendant was charged with operating a pinball machine as a gambling device. City Prosecutor Forrest Cavalier brought two pinball machines to the court room where he attempted to show that by achieving a certain score the machine returned a free game to the player thus, under law, labeling it a "gambling device." The city seemed to be in a "catch 22" over the matter. The newspaper explained, "If the city wins this case and proves that the boards are gambling devices, it will not be able to license them. On the other hand, if it loses the case, it may be able to license the boards, resulting in about $15,000 income annually to the city."

The person Prosecutor Cavalier selected to play the pinball game was unable to achieve the desired score that produced the free game. The *Vindicator* reported, "Bells rang, lights flashed and pretty maidens danced across a dial in Municipal Judge Robert B. Nevin's court," but no winning score was rung up. Defense attorneys argued the machines would not produce a free game and objected when vice squad members testified that they saw "similar boards" in other establishments do so. One lawyer removed the glass covering from the pinball machine and manipulated the bumpers to run the score as high as it would go, and still no free game was given. When Captain Richmond[6] took the stand he introduced a device called a "jack," which the operators used on the pinball machine to trigger the free game option.

Meanwhile, Rendinell's injunction, leading to the banishment of the pinball machines, incensed store proprietors and bar owners who profited from the play of the machines, as well as the producers of the board games. Many blamed the mayor's decree on Rendinell and it was alleged that the attorney was given a beating just after police began confiscating the machines. Rendinell denied the attack. But the attorney couldn't deny what happened next.

On the night of January 23, Rendinell, as was his habit, was playing solitaire in the sunroom of his Fairgreen Avenue home. Around 9:20 the attorney heard a pop and felt something hit him in the back. Rendinell turned to his wife, who was seated nearby reading, and stated, "That lamp bulb must have exploded and hit me in the back." Mrs. Rendinell walked behind her husband and saw blood beginning to stain through his jacket. You're bleeding, Dom," she screamed. In a panic she ran out of the house to the garage where she unsuccessfully tried to start the car. She quickly returned to the house and called police, who took Rendinell to St. Elizabeth's Hospital.

In minutes police and detectives were on the scene looking for evidence. At the hospital doctors discovered that a flattened .38 slug had hit Rendinell in the back and, while not piercing his clothes, pushed the fabric of his coat, shirt and undershirt into the wound. Police determined that the bullet, fired from 35 feet away in a neighbor's backyard, had lost its velocity after passing through a thick, plate glass window in the sunroom.

Detectives questioned Rendinell the next morning. "My activities in fighting the licensing of marble boards in the city are the only motive I can give for the attempt on my life," the attorney stated. Later, a reporter asked him about an allegation that he was on the payroll of the Acme Appliance Company, reputed to be "one of the largest marble board syndicates in the city." Rendinell scoffed at the accusation stating, "It is silly to think of such a thing. The facts show that. Why would I be fighting the marble boards and then turn around and draw pay from the people I have publicly denounced?"

At the same time Acme officials were responding to the accusation in a statement of their own:

> "We, the Acme Appliance Co., a group of local citizens who own a large number of marble boards and other amusement devices join with the other citizens of this community in condemning the cowardly act perpetrated upon our attorney, Mr. D.F. Rendinell.
>
> "Since our inception in July of 1940, when we retained D.F. Rendinell as our attorney, he has been of invaluable aid in the growth of our organization."
>
> "His relationship even extended beyond the bounds of attorney and client. We pray for his speedy recovery."

It was learned that back in July 1940, Roy Silvestri, one of "a half dozen independent operators that made up Acme," had approached Rendinell about handling the firm's legal matters. Rendinell agreed and was put on a retainer of $75 a month. Rendinell had to launch some immediate damage control. Mrs. Rendinell was told to call the reporter who had interviewed her husband and say that he had "suddenly remembered" several cases he handled for Acme. Still denying that he was ever on the company's payroll, Rendinell claimed he handled a number of legal matters for the firm, but he believed Acme to be in the business of "selling radios, washing machines, electrical appliances and mechanical devices."

Two days after these embarrassing revelations, an official of Acme Appliance announced that the company was being dissolved; not because of the Rendinell incident, but because of Spagnola's recent order to ban pinball machines.

Runaway Grand Jury

On the night of February 18, 1942, a killing took place at the corner of Madison and Fifth Avenues. The death of William "Billy the Greek" Scodras was accidental. He was actually sent into a coffee shop at that location to draw out the intended victim, Jerry "the Sledgehammer" Pascarella. (Complete details in next section on Pascarella and this shooting) The resulting investigation led to the end of the lottery houses.

The murder of "Billy the Greek" touched off a week of turmoil in the Youngstown Police Department and proved the old underworld adage, "murder is bad for business." First, a disgruntled police officer told reporters that, "Youngstown's vice squad is controlled by a slot machine racketeer, not by Chief John W. Turnbull." The officer went on to state, "Why are the racket leaders – the so-called big shots in charge of the 'bug,' bookie joints, marble boards, slot machines, and prostitution – never arrested? Almost every policeman knows these men by sight and it would not be difficult to obtain evidence for an arrest." It was common knowledge, even among top police brass, that many officers were employed part time by various racketeers in the area. The garrulous policeman, who asked not to be identified, defended his fellow officers saying, "You can't blame the cops, because they're human and they don't get very good salaries." He finished his assessment by claiming the department has been thoroughly "demoralized" by conditions and by lack of discipline.

The accusations enraged Turnbull and he responded by shaking up the department. In addressing the comments made in the press the chief acknowledged that there was a certain amount of demoralization, which resulted from a long period of no pay increases. Despite a lack of police cars and an undermanned staff Turnbull promised, "The lid will be clamped down and will stay down."

Prompted by the killing of Scodras, Mayor Spagnola ordered Turnbull "to rid the city of gangdom." While these statements were normally issued to show voters the mayor was not sitting idly by, this time there was a little bit of bite to the command – members of city council's finance committee had submitted an ordinance enabling police to seize any type of gambling device. With the machinations in progress to put in place an anti-gambling device ordinance, the police were off in pursuit of the gamblers. Horse-betting rooms, which had flourished for nearly a decade without being hindered, were suddenly being told to suspend operations. Downtown bookie joints and lottery operators were ordered to close down. Four lottery employees were quickly arrested.

While most citizens applauded the efforts of the mayor and police chief, one local minister spoke despairingly about the situation. Dr. Donald P. Montgomery, pastor of Pleasant Grove United Presbyterian Church complained, "This is a Christian nation and yet we must wait until gangsters shoot down their fellow gangsters [Scodras] in our streets before the mayor of the city does anything about it."

Surprisingly, Youngstown City Council moved quickly to push the ordinance through to support the new effort. During the council session in which the vote was being taken there was a large delegation of church and civic representatives present. Many rose and spoke in favor of the new ordinance. Councilman Benjamin Ross, who sponsored the ordinance, stated, "It is tragic that council had to wait until there was almost a breakdown in law and order in the city to adopt such a ban on gambling." One week after the killing of Scodras the *Vindicator* announced, "Youngstown racketeers suffered another severe blow...when city council unanimously passed the most dramatic anti-gambling ordinance in the city's history." The ordinance, which took 30 days before going into effect, gave the police department the power to confiscate any gambling device. The newspaper printed the penalty clause section of the new ordinance:

> "Whoever permits a game to be played for gain upon or by means of a device or a machine upon the premises of which he has the care or possession, shall be fined not less than $50 or more than $100.
>
> "Whoever permits the use of a gambling table, a device or machine or a billiard table for gambling, shall be fined not less than $50 nor more than $500, or sentenced to jail for a term of not less than 10 days or more than 90 days, or both.
>
> "The ordinance includes 'any machine, device or instrument, whether or not it purports to vend or distribute merchandise or furnish recreation for amusement, which is caused to operate by insertion of any token, slug, disc, or coin'"

While critics claimed the ordinance would "die" in the Ohio Supreme Court, the police were already off and running. Sergeant William Davis was placed in charge of a "special" vice detail on February 20 by Mayor Spagnola and given orders to clean up all vice in the city. He quickly handed out warnings to bug operators and raided bookie joints. On February 24 police arrested 18 men during raids in the downtown area. Davis noted that even though his special squad didn't have an automobile at their disposal, they raided, on foot, ten bookie joints in the city including the One-Eleven Club on Commerce Street and Ray's Smoke Shop on Champion. The next day Davis raided the T.C.A. Club on Mahoning Avenue and arrested four bug men in possession of gambling slips. This was followed a day later by raids on a gambling club and two disorderly houses where seven men and a woman were apprehended. On February 26, police hauled in 21 more people in vice raids in the city.

Throughout March 1942, Sergeant Davis and his special vice squad continued their raids. Then, during the first week of April, under orders from Spagnola, Chief Turnbull appointed Andrew P. Przelomski, a traffic patrolman, chief of the department's regular vice squad. The "special" vice squad was disbanded without any public explanation, and Davis was ordered to return to uniform duty. Despite the transfers, Davis and a few of his former vice crew, including future vice squad chief George Krispli, continued to carry out raids on their own. In mid-April, they raided four bookie joints in the downtown area that Przelomski had claimed were closed. Davis and his men found the joints "doing business as usual" with the race wire service and racing forms still in use. At one of these locations, 15 East Commerce Street, the raiding crew arrested Leo Manley, the joint's operator; at the Erie Terminal Building they apprehended Phil Rose, alias Ross.

On Sunday, April 19, Davis was winding up a few days of vacation where he had performed spring cleaning chores on his South Avenue home. This day was spent painting cupboards and woodwork in the kitchen. He left home at 11:15 p.m. and reported to work. Around 1:10 Monday morning a bomb went off near the basement wall at the rear of the Davis home. The explosion, heard by Mayor Spagnola who lived several blocks away, wrecked the basement wall, ripped shingles from the roof and shattered virtually every window in the house. Davis' handiwork was nearly destroyed and the carpets and furniture throughout the home were covered with dust and glass fragments.[7] Fortunately, neither Davis' wife nor the couple's 16 year-old son were injured.

Informed of the explosion at work by his wife, Davis and a squad of police raced to the South Avenue residence to investigate. Although they believed the explosive to be made from dynamite, it was reported that, "The only clue to the nature of the bomb was several pieces of finely shredded newspaper, some of them bearing a foreign language."

Davis was incensed by the attack on his home and family. "This is what you get for doing your duty," he barked in anger. "The dirty cowards! If that's the way they want it, that's the way they'll get it. And, by God, I'm telling them now they can start closing up tomorrow." Davis didn't even wait until "tomorrow." Two hours after the bomb went off he and his old crew raided a brothel on East Federal Street and arrested four people.

The response to the bombing by public officials was immediate. Chief Turnbull, who arrived at the bombing scene and helped direct the investigation, told reporters, "If this was caused by Davis's police work, that was no fault of his. These raids are being conducted under my instructions and they are going to be continued. Rackets are out."

Mayor Spagnola notified Davis in a letter: "I was horrified to learn of the outrageous act perpetrated at your home and you and your family have my sympathies. You are hereby assigned the case." Spagnola was emphatic about giving Davis free reign in the case. He told Davis that there "absolutely are no strings." The letter informed him to, "Call on the chief of police, the police department, any of its members or me for any assistance. The sky is the limit." In addition, the mayor called on Youngstown Fire Chief Michael J. Melillo to conduct an independent investigation.

The bombing also incensed Judge J.H.C. Lyon, who reacted on Tuesday morning by recalling the Mahoning County grand jury and ordering them to investigate the incident. He told the 15-member panel, "This is still America, and hoodlums should not be allowed to run over our community." Lyon then ordered the grand jury to investigate the bombing and find out, among other things, why was Davis relieved of his job as head of the city's special vice squad?

Finally, Mahoning County Prosecutor William A. Ambrose "wrathfully" stated, "something will have to be done. I'm not the police department, but I can be, and will be if I have to." The prosecutor blamed the current rash of problems on outsiders who were coming into the Valley to organize gambling. Ambrose claimed, "There is no doubt that this is the work of outside gangsters imported into the city by someone. There'll be no fooling around about this investigation by this office. We've been threatened before, but we're not worried about threats."

On April 21, the *Vindicator* was quick to report that, "Most of the city's rackets apparently went into hiding again Monday after the Davis bombing. There was little activity in lottery houses and other rackets seemed to be comparatively quiet." The next day Chief Turnbull placed a letter on the roll call bulletin board which read:

> "An attempt has been made to not only destroy the home of a brother officer but to kill or injure his family. This is a challenge to every member of this department. I expect everyone of you to take up this challenge and to rid this city once and for all of undesirables as well as individuals whom in your opinion would be guilty of such a dastardly act.
>
> "I want you to cooperate with one another to the end desired. You must be on the lookout for law violations of all kinds and I charge you with the rigid enforcement of these laws."

Prosecutor Ambrose seemed to throw himself into his grand jury work with a fiery passion: "Things have gone too far in this city and it is time we put a stop to it. No stone will be left unturned until we apprehend the responsible parties." This attitude stood in stark contrast to his position at the end of the grand jury session. Ambrose asked veteran Assistant County Prosecutor Harold H. Hull to assist him. In announcing that Davis was the grand jury's first witness, Ambrose stated that the sergeant "will lay the groundwork and the basis for an investigation so intensive that if it is humanly possible we will ferret out the gangsters or hoodlums who perpetrated the bombing."

On Monday morning, April 27, a week after the bombing, the grand jury began hearing testimony in the case. Monday's slate of witnesses included Davis; patrolman and future police chief William R. Golden, the past president of the Youngstown Fraternal Order of Police; Andrew Przelomski; Thomas Bowser, a city detective selected by Davis to help in the investigation; and Jerry Pascarella. The next day the grand jury questioned Rocco E. Marino, brother of the murdered Roy "Happy" Marino and owner of De Luxe Sales Company, a pinball machine concern; Frank Budak operator of the Poland Country Club and leader of the Campbell House lottery; H. M. Horowitz a former punch board operator; Chief Turnbull; and Mayor Spagnola. The grand jury spent little time questioning the witnesses. Davis was questioned from approximately one hour while the rest of the witnesses were questioned from 10 to 30 minutes.

Early on the afternoon of Tuesday, April 28, a bizarre incident took place as Mayor Spagnola was walking to the courthouse to be questioned. Accompanying the mayor was his bodyguard Jack Palermo. As the two men passed the entrance of the police garage on West Federal Street, Dominic Rendinell appeared, fully recovered from his wound. The attorney, according to witnesses, greeted Spagnola with, "Hi ya, Number One racketeer." He then referred to Palermo as the "Number One collector." Palermo responded by punching Rendinell in the mouth, knocking him to the pavement. The dazed lawyer struggled to his feet only to be followed into the garage by Palermo and struck again. The bloodied attorney cried out to several nearby police officers, including Sergeant Davis, to have Palermo arrested, but to no avail. Both men quickly filed charges of assault and battery against one another. Rendinell pled not guilty and was released without having to post bond, while Palermo had to post $200.

The trials for both men took place on May 15 with Judge Nevin deciding the case instead of a jury. Palermo's trial was first and Rendinell testified that his comment to the mayor was preceded by Spagnola calling him "vicious names." After calling out "Hi ya, Number One racketeer," the attorney claimed he was punched in the mouth by Palermo. When asked why he didn't defend himself, Rendinell replied, "I was in no condition to." The attorney explained that he had purchased a new set of teeth recently. After the assault he claimed he spent two hours in the dentist chair for treatment. That night and the next day he stayed in bed suffering "severe and excruciating pain." He told the court, "I hollered for help and nobody came to my assistance."

During the afternoon trial of Rendinell, the courtroom was packed with a number of attorneys as spectators. Palermo took the stand and claimed that during the confrontation Rendinell struck him first. "He shoved me and hurt my nose," Palermo stated.

On May 20, Judge Nevin announced his decision:

> "The first thing that appealed to me in both of the cases was that this was the action of assault and battery, and being such this court was not called upon to determine the truth or falsity of any of the remarks said each to the other.
>
> "The paramount duty in arriving at a just decision is to determine who the aggressor was. After carefully considering the evidence...I could not in all fairness arrive at but one decision, and that was that you, Mr. Palermo, were the aggressor in this matter."

Nevin scolded both men telling Palermo, "Your grievance should have been taken to civil court." Then, turning to the attorney he stated, "It was childish of you, Mr. Rendinell, to make remarks of that kind to either of these gentlemen." The judge fined Palermo $100 and sentenced him to ten days in the county jail.[8]

Meanwhile, after Spagnola's brief appearance before the grand jury on the afternoon of April 28, the panel adjourned. The adjournment came as surprise because many expected more witnesses to be called throughout the week. The grand jury indicated that they would return on Friday morning, but instead met secretly that night without Ambrose, or any other members of the prosecutor's office present. Ambrose had gone to work immediately compiling a written report for Judge Lyon based on the conclusions he had drawn from the testimony of witnesses. In part, his text to Lyon read:

> "According to the evidence, Sergeant Davis was removed from his special detail as chief of an independent vice squad because the purpose for which he had been appointed, to wit: a clean-up of the city, and vice and rackets of all kind, had been accomplished, and the interest of the public would better be served by again placing him in uniform in his former position as sergeant at the head of his shift.
>
> "It is the opinion of this grand jury, gathered from all the evidence, that racketeering and vice conditions of all sorts could perhaps be eliminated, or certainly reduced to a minimum, if that job were left in the hands of a capable chief of police, such as John W. Turnbull...To bring this change about would require only that the mayor attend strictly to the administrative phase of his job and place the full responsibility in the hands of his chief of police, without meddling with, or in the slightest, interfering with his judgement as to the appointment of a head of the vice squad...
>
> "We believe, if this recommendation is followed, that outrages such as bombings, and other acts of violence, now before this body, will be eliminated."

Wednesday morning Ambrose presented his work to the men and women who comprised the grand jury. To his surprise, every member of the panel refused to sign the document. The grand jury members, under the leadership of foreman Ira E. Christman of Canfield, had drawn their own conclusions and prepared their own statement for Judge Lyon. On Thursday afternoon, in the grand jury room located on the third floor of the county courthouse where all the testimony was heard, the panel presented their findings to the judge without any member of Ambrose's office in attendance. The conclusions of the grand jury members, and their recommendations, showed such a vast disparity from those of the prosecutor's office that one was left to wonder if both groups were listening to the same testimony. The following is what the panel members submitted to Judge Lyon:

A Resolution

WHEREAS we, the members of the grand jury of Mahoning County, are charged with the duty of inquiring into criminal offenses against the State of Ohio and its citizens and

WHEREAS, from evidence obtained from witnesses and from information otherwise obtained we are convinced that there has been a breakdown in law enforcement in Mahoning County to the extent that organized criminals have openly and flagrantly killed a citizen, they have bombed the home of a police officer who attempted to do his duty, they have attempted murder against others; gambling, prostitution and other forms of vice go on without apparent interference by the constituted authorities and

WHEREAS, this grand jury has been unable to obtain the necessary co-operation in the preparation and presentation of evidence or in its inquiries and has been hindered in its efforts;

THEREFORE this body, in the interest of the proper administration of justice and in the interest of public welfare, peace, safety and suppression of crime hereby recommends to the judges of the court of common pleas of Mahoning County the following measures to correct this evil:

1. The immediate appointment of a new grand jury and the appointment of a special prosecuting attorney with sufficient aids to obtain necessary evidence to indict and prosecute these offenders if such appointment of a special prosecutor and necessary assistants can legally be made.
2. From the investigation and evidence we have received we are convinced that crime is prevalent in Mahoning County and law enforcement has completely broken down; therefore the governor of the State of Ohio should be requested and urged to have the attorney general or an assistant, with the aid of a special grand jury, make a complete investigation of vice and rackets in Mahoning County.
3. Sufficient funds should be appropriated to conduct a full investigation and prosecution of crime in Mahoning County.

It is the consensus of opinion of this body that because of these facts it is useless to make further inquiry under existing circumstances and therefore we ask to be discharged.

Ambrose considered the grand jury's conclusion an affront to his character and blamed foreman Ira Christman for instigating it. The prosecutor told reporters, "The report is so misleading that I as a prosecutor should pay no attention to the illogical drools of a neophyte in law enforcement." Without using Christman's name, Ambrose claimed, "the arrogance and egotism of one man had 14 honest jurors so confused that they didn't know what they were doing." Commenting on the panel's recommendation for a "special prosecuting attorney" to be called, Ambrose declared, "I'll never agree to step aside under these circumstances."

After reviewing the grand jury report, Judge Lyon claimed, "this presents a pitiable spectacle of law enforcement in our community. It is indeed a revelation to our citizens. You have saved the taxpayers considerable money by showing that conditions exist making it useless to spend further time and money."

Lyon must have felt some degree of redemption as the *Vindicator* reported that the judge "said he resented keenly the attitude of the public as brought out in a remark in last Sunday's paper that people on the street were betting 9 to 1 that the grand jury's investigation would end in a 'whitewash.'"

Mayor Spagnola, while denying that law enforcement had broken down, made the following comments to reporters on the findings:

> "The grand jury has made a good start. I certainly would be willing, if it were my choosing, to divorce myself completely from the police department after having appointed a chief, but this is not possible under the city charter, which places all responsibility in the mayor, who in turn is responsible to the people.
>
> "If the police chief were placed under permanent civil service, by charter amendment, I would be relieved of this responsibility."

Spagnola took his stand a step further by making a public declaration that a new "hands off" policy was in effect and that Chief Turnbull was not to tolerate any interference in the performance of his duties by anyone including the mayor. In an order read aloud at roll-call, Spagnola stated:

> "Reserving to myself only those powers and responsibilities specifically imposed on the mayor by the charter provisions, I hereby call upon you to exercise to the full the duties of your office, free of interference by me, by political friends, white collar boys with a pull, and any and all who pretend to have the mayor's ear.
>
> "In short, you are the boss of the police department. Operate it."

Police Chief Turnbull accepted the new "full responsibility" and told reporters, "the next time any politician or man who thinks he has a 'pull' tries to advise me how to run the police force, I am going to tell him very bluntly to go to hell."

Strange as it may seem, one of Turnbull's first decisions was to "re-create" the special vice squad and place Traffic Commissioner Clarence W. Coppersmith in charge. Coppersmith, who was chief of the regular vice squad in 1933, continued in his position as traffic commissioner. The order given to Coppersmith by the chief was "if you think any person should be in jail, into jail he goes, regardless of race, creed or political affiliation." Turnbull told reporters, "The purpose of this vice squad is to verify the fact that Youngstown is closed – that vice has been eliminated. It is for my own satisfaction to make sure vice conditions do not exist in Youngstown. Coppersmith will make a report to me everyday and if it is found that vice still does exist, he can draw on the whole department for cooperation." The chief then stated that the creation of the squad was in no way a reflection on the work of Przelomski and his men, whom Turnbull pointed out, had "done a damn fine job."

Apparently lost in all the hoopla of the grand jury's decision and the changes made by the mayor was who was responsible for the bombing of Sergeant Davis's home.

Meanwhile, citizens' committees and religious organizations were quick to support the grand jury's recommendations and sent resolutions to Judge Lyon. A new group formed calling itself the Council for Civic Action. At their initial meeting, Ludwig "Wally" Pascarella spoke out about his brother Jerry. The killing of William Scodras was the spark that ignited the current vice campaign. Wally Pascarella, while denying that his brother was involved with slot machines, claimed Jerry had "been pushed out in front by the real racketeers." The *Vindicator* reported Wally Pascarella's comments in a May 2 article:

> "He said Jerry first became associated with rackets when Jerry worked for Rocco Marino, marble board operator, who recently appeared before the grand jury.
>
> "He said Jerry left Marino's employ and 'Caputo and another fellow wanted him to work for them.' Wally asserted that Jerry's new employers asked Jerry to smash Marino's machines but Jerry refused.
>
> "'Jerry is not a petty racketeer and he is taking the blame for a lot of things he is not doing,' the brother said."

Jerry Pascarella was making a name for himself in the community as a do-gooder. The reason for this was he had found himself pushed out of the slot machine business by Dominic "Moosey" Caputo, an up and coming underworld figure in the valley. He saw his new role as a vice-crusader as a way of getting even with his underworld enemies.

On Saturday afternoon, May 3, after conferring with other members of the bench, Judge Lyon sent a letter to Ohio Governor John W. Bricker asking him to grant the grand jury's request for the state attorney general and a special prosecutor to conduct a special grand jury investigation of criminal activity in Mahoning County. Due to Ambrose's strong position in the matter, the newspaper speculated that the judges, "shied from taking necessary steps" to make the appointment themselves because it "probably would involve a prolonged court fight to disqualify Ambrose."

Days later, Youngstown leaders of the League of Woman Voters, Better Government League, Federation of Woman's Clubs and Council of Jewish Women met with Governor Bricker to encourage him to go along with the request for a special grand jury investigation in Mahoning County. With the exception of Ambrose and the county prosecutor's office, everyone seemed united in the effort to attack the organized crime problem in the area.

On May 7, the Council for Civic Action held another "indignation" meeting, where they adopted a resolution and started a petition drive to show the governor their support for a special grand jury. Appearing at this second meeting was Jerry Pascarella, along with his brother Ludwig, his mother and two sisters. "Sledgehammer Jerry" walked in with two bodyguards. The *Vindicator* reported:

> "Jerry arrived at the meeting a few minutes after it began, accompanied by Carl Venzeio, alias Joe Marko, alias 'Lucky,' who early in 1941 set records month after month for traffic tickets fixed by Municipal Court Judge Peter B. Mulholland, and another man.
>
> "'He's my bodyguard,' Jerry beamed after the meeting. 'The mayor has one.'
>
> "Jerry's other companion was not identified."

Pascarella spoke briefly to the group and talked about his "campaign" against slot and pinball machines, telling the audience, "I tried to do alone what you people are trying to do together. Why doesn't the governor come in here right away?" Pascarella questioned, "Hasn't there been enough filth so far? I think there has."

Claiming he is now employed as a painter, Pascarella described himself as a "reformed racketeer turned vice crusader" who spent weekends in jail for his efforts. He failed to explain why a painter needed the presence of two bodyguards. Pascarella's talk was brief as the newspaper explained, "Jerry and his two companions left hurriedly a short time later when it was announced that Jerry's car and another were blocking a driveway."

After Pascarella's departure the council adopted a mission statement promising to "promote honest and efficient government...by encouraging the observance of a decent moral code by all, and by encouraging public interest and participation in civic affairs."

On May 8, Governor Bricker announced that he would order State Attorney General Thomas J. Herbert to launch an investigation into the vice and rackets operating in Mahoning County. Within a week it was reported that the special assistant prosecutor of Hamilton County, in which the city of Cincinnati is located, was appointed to conduct the investigation. Simon R. Leis,[9] a 45 year-old father of five, was with the Hamilton County prosecutor's office for eleven years. The newspaper reported, "Leis is known among attorneys as an excellent trial lawyer and as special counsel to the attorney general and aided in investigations of Pike County election conditions and dog track operations in Steubenville and Portage County."

Leis, who was prosecuting a murder case, when asked about the appointment by reporters stole a line from Will Rogers and responded, "All I know is what I read in the newspapers." He then made a surprise visit to the city on May 15 to "make a preliminary study of the situation." The media was unaware of the visit and didn't catch up to him until after he had returned to Cincinnati. Leis refused to divulge the names of anyone he had met with. Several months passed before anything more came about.

A *Vindicator* editorial the next day expressed that neither the governor nor a special prosecutor could clean up the Valley and keep it clean, that it was "Youngstown's Responsibility." The following are a few key comments from the editorial:

> "Governor Bricker's decision to appoint a special prosecutor, probably Simon Leis of Cincinnati, is a long step toward clean government in Youngstown and Mahoning County. Even before Mr. Leis begins his investigation, however, it should be recognized that neither he nor the governor can bestow good government on Youngstown; it must be wanted and built by the city's own people, with time and toil and trouble.
>
> "The fact that the citizens have had to go outside for help in running their own affairs is a confession that they have failed in their duty heretofore.
>
> "This point was brought out in Governor Bricker's remarks to the delegation of Youngstown women. Suppose the state comes in and cleans up the existing situation, he said, what guarantee is there that it will stay cleaned up? Ohio cannot assume the responsibility for repeated cleanups for a citizenry which does not help itself.
>
> "In addition to co-operating with the investigation so that it will result in a thorough cleanup of the present situation, the citizens can do two things to keep it cleaned up. The first is to be more active in politics. The second...is to quit supporting the rackets.
>
> "All the elements that can be mustered are needed; plenty of heat behind the law enforcement, citizen activity in politics, abstention from playing the bug and the slots. The investigation cannot provide them all. Now that Governor Bricker has furnished the necessary first step, the electorate which asked his help should keep in mind its own responsibility for carrying through."

A week later a public appeal was made "that the investigation be the real McCoy and not just a sham." Shortly after this, the investigation disappeared from the front pages and was out of the public eye until January 1943.

During the April/May clean-up drive, as dozens of "bug men" came pouring through the courtrooms many of them tried to conceal their true identities to avoid the higher fines as repeat offenders, which could reach a maximum of $500. The city ordinance didn't call for any jail time for the defendants so the only way the judges could punish the men was to hit them where it hurt – in their wallets. To counter the defendant's effort to be charged and sentenced under a fictitious name, thus avoiding the higher fine, Judge Robert B. Nevin kept his own index card file on every policy violator who appeared before him. Nevin demanded that when the men appeared in court they have their draft registration cards with them as proof of their identity. The judge urged that, "Police should insist on right names and addresses. In fact, these men should be fingerprinted so they can't change their names between arrests." The numbers men then began coming into court and demanding a jury trial. This clogged up the court calendar and slowed down the conviction process. Nevin responded by boosting their bails to $2,000 and demanding that property put up for their bonds be free and clear of encumbrances before it was accepted as security. Many times property presented had already been pledged in other cases.

Police were also stepping up their efforts against brothel operators. After Police Prosecutor Forrest Cavalier compiled a listing of properties where suspected brothels were operating, the owners were notified and called in for a meeting. On May 15, six targeted property owners met with Chief Turnbull and his staff. The owners were given a 10-day grace period to notify their tenants to cease and desist in their "unlawful enterprises," or face immediate padlocking procedures. A state "nuisance" statute allowed the police to padlock any property used for "lewdness, assignation or prostitution," for one year. After a few objections were cleared up, the owners agreed to hand out eviction notices. "We'll give them 30 days after you notify them. If they fail to follow your eviction orders within a reasonable time, write a letter of notification to me. From then on it will be my job," the chief assured them.

From May until the end of July the "lid" appeared to have been closed on Youngstown's rackets. During this same period, however, there were rumors about unrest in the leadership of the police department. The situation came to a head on July 29 when Mayor Spagnola received the following note:

> "It is my wish to resume duties as captain of police under authority of your appointment of me as such, dated Aug. 24, 1941.
>
> "Therefore I hereby tender my resignation as chief of police to take effect at midnight Aug. 15, 1942, with the request that you accept it. I shall report for duty as captain of police on Thursday, Aug. 16, 1942."
>
> "Respectfully yours,
> JOHN W. TURNBULL

Turnbull was already chief of police when he passed the civil service examination to become a captain in August 1941. As in many police departments the position of police chief is a political appointment, not a civil service post. The position of chief normally changes with each new administration – or in Youngstown's case could change several times within an administration.

The *Vindicator* was kind to Chief Turnbull, stating in one editorial:

> "The police department's general operation has improved under Chief Turnbull. As to rackets, in recent months the city has been closed up tighter than for a long time. Organized, commercialized prostitution has been driven underground if not entirely eliminated. Bookie joints have been closed most of the time; slot machines have been confined to a few private clubs. The record has one flaw: Youngstown's major racket, the 'bug' or numbers lottery, is being carried on about as usual."

The newspaper claimed that Turnbull "gave no explanation" for his decision. They reported, "Rumors have been rife for months. Many sources say Turnbull was 'forced out' of his job by the administration. It also has been said the chief desired to run for sheriff at the next election and did not want to do so from the position of city police chief."

Possible names for Turnbull's replacement were floating around weeks before his resignation as chief. The top contenders, according to the rumor mill, were Sergeant William Davis, Detective William T. "Buck" Lally, at one time chief of detectives, and Joseph Lepo, a long time member of the vice squad. Mayor Spagnola surprised nearly everyone by naming Andrew Przelomski as his new chief.

Mayor Spagnola was quick to address all the rumors and allegations put forth by the newspaper. He denied that anyone other than Przelomski was considered for the position and that "rumors purporting any strained relations" between himself and Chief Turnbull were "out of the question." In appointing Przelomski chief, Spagnola issued the following order, which sounded like a repeat of a similar one made to Turnbull back in May:

> "This is one order, direct, explicit and absolute. Under Turnbull the town was closed. To those spectators and wisecrackers insofar as these orders are concerned, I want to say that you are to be absolute boss of the police department and are to keep the town closed for the balance of my administration.
>
> "In the performance of your duties I will not interfere because I know your mettle and makeup, and by all means take good care of the self-seekers when they pester and bother you.
>
> "Insofar as your duties are concerned, permit no member of this administration or anyone else to interfere with your duties. I have faith and confidence in you and know you will put some discipline in the department.
>
> "You may depend on me, but only when you feel it absolutely necessary. You are the boss of the police department."

To call the *Vindicator's* reaction to Przelomski being named police chief a disappointment would be an understatement as was revealed by a scathing editorial that appeared on July 30:

> "Mayor Spagnola's position before the public has been weakened by the mysterious change in the police department under which a competent and honest chief has been edged out or persuaded out of office, and replaced by a traffic patrolman who is amiable and well liked, but lacks the training and experience of other officers eligible for the post.
>
> "No reason is given for Chief Turnbull's resignation, and no good reason appears for Andrew Przelomski's appointment to his place. This mystery lends force to rumors that have been in circulation for months to the effect that the city administration was fixing to pay its debt to the underworld.
>
> "The mayor cannot complain if 'speculators and wisecrackers' draw unfavorable conclusions; he has laid himself wide open to adverse speculation."

Przelomski's first decision as the new chief of police was to dissolve the "special vice squad," headed by Traffic Commissioner Clarence Coppersmith, and reassign the four men under him. One returned to traffic duties under Coppersmith, two were assigned to the regular vice squad. The fourth officer, Joseph Lepo, who was rumored to be in the running for the chief's job, was told to report to the detective bureau, "to help bolster vacation-depleted forces."

Przelomski was told by Spagnola to appoint a new vice squad chief "who can and will execute his order." For whatever reason, the new chief left the position vacant and instead appointed as "acting vice squad chief" his former vice squad secretary, William Miglets, who was a member of the police force for only one year. Miglets set out to make a splash by immediately raiding two Big House lottery stations, including the headquarters at the Recreation/Liberty Pool Room where the Limberopoulos brothers held sway.

During the frenzy that followed the bombing of Sergeant Davis' home and the subsequent grand jury investigation, Przelomski, then the vice squad chief, boasted of the number of vice arrests being made by his men, including 124 busts during a four-week period beginning April 3. But by late summer gambling and numbers activity were beginning to pickup. By the last quarter of 1942 bug arrests were down to average of five per week. In addition, slot machine activity was increasing. Private clubs, like the Poland Country Club, had the bigger versions of the machines while a new, smaller counter-sized model was becoming popular and appearing throughout the Valley in drug stores, gasoline stations and small shops. Gambling joints and after hours spots were also on the rise. Despite the obvious increase in the illegal activities, when Chief Przelomski ordered a cleanup of punch boards in the city all his men could find were three.

Meanwhile, Special Prosecutor Simon Leis and his staff were busy secretly investigating underworld gambling and lottery operations in Youngstown since September 1942. Their work came to light after carefully planned raids were executed on Thursday, January 21, 1943. The next day *Vindicator* headlines screamed:

5 "Bug" Offices Raided at Once
Mayor Threatens to Dismiss Chief as Special Prosecutor Strikes;
Davis Heads Squad

> After five months of secret investigation of Youngstown's gambling, vice and crime, Attorney General Thomas J. Herbert's probe is out in the open, swinging hard. Here are the first day's results:
>
> RAIDS by state men and Sheriff Ralph Elser's deputies on four headquarters of the "Big House" lottery in Youngstown and a big lottery office in Campbell.
>
> ORDERS from Mayor William B. Spagnola to Police Chief Andrew P. Przelomski: "Clean up the town or resign."

SERGT. WILLIAM J. DAVIS, former head of a special vice squad, who was taken off that assignment April 1, is appointed head of the vice squad, a post which has been vacant since Przelomski left it to become police chief, July 29.

Davis Is Pleased

NEW VICE SQUAD appointed immediately by Davis, who greeted his assignment with "That's right up my alley."

ORDERS by Przelomski to patrolmen to clean up their beats or face suspension.

COMMENT by Sheriff Elser: "If they clean up the city we won't have to. That's what they should have done long ago."

The timing of the raids was imperative to their success; however, they almost didn't get off the ground. The raids were scheduled for 2:30 p.m. when the number's headquarters were at their peak activity just prior to the day's winning number being announced. The search warrants authorizing the raids had to be signed by Attorney General Herbert, who was in Cleveland that morning. Due to a mysterious "unavoidable delay" they were late in getting to the Attorney General. Realizing the importance of the timing, Herbert, after signing the warrants, called the Cleveland airport and requested that a Youngstown-bound flight be delayed until the documents could be brought aboard. When the plane arrived in Youngstown, one of Leis' men met the aircraft and received the warrants. He then raced to a "secret" gathering place on North Lima Road, where the warrants were distributed to the raiding teams comprised of 25 deputies from Sheriff Elser's office.

Divided into five squads, the deputies were given the addresses of the bug houses they were assigned to raid with orders to enter the premises at 2:30 p.m. and keep everyone there until a state investigator arrived. The first state official went to work in a poolroom at 22 South Phelps Street, right next to the Youngstown Police Department. Ten minutes later, one of the investigators entered 106 South Avenue where, the *Vindicator* reported, "deputies had upset the composure of the bug men." The newspaper gave a detailed account of the day's raiding activity. "The bug room is in the very back, reached through a dilapidated but thickly populated poolroom, across a large, dark store room and through a narrow, cold back hall. The room was heated by a pot-bellied stove and there must have been about 25 disgruntled-looking operators and pickup men milling about. There were six adding machines, used for counting the day's receipts, nine unopened cartons of new bug slips and six cartons crammed with old ones. The investigators worked smoothly and quickly, prying into corners, closets and drawers. Deputies remained behind to keep the customers until transportation to headquarters could be arranged."

Next on the list was the headquarters of the Big House lottery operation run by the Limberopoulos brothers at 315 West Federal Street – Recreation/Liberty Pool Room – and a second office operating at 552 West Federal Street. The newspaper reported, "Almost 100 persons, most of them waiting for the bug number to be announced, and a few playing pool, were locked in the place during the investigation. Two city detectives walked into the pool room during the raid and were kept there along with others found in the place... 'You fellows just beat us to it. We came in to raid the place.' The officers [without a warrant in hand] offered to aid in the raid but their offer was ignored... Raiders were surprised here to see the large amount of stored new numbers slips. In the basement near a little room in which there was a dilapidated but professional crap table, there were stored many large cardboard cartons of slips. They were stashed as high as a man's head in one spot."

The Campbell House operation, located on Wilson Avenue, was the last to be visited. "Money was piled on a long table, which also held four electric adding machines. There were new steel cabinets, strong boxes and even a small safe which was found fitted into a suitcase. Telephones jangled incessantly with people calling for Mr. Big and asking: 'What's the number today?' There probably were more confused bug customers in Campbell and Youngstown Thursday than ever before in history. The state officer got tired of the constant jingling and posted a deputy on an extension to 'give 'em a number, any number.' He did just that."

"The Campbell office was on the second floor of a shabby building facing railroad tracks. The main offices were in a suite of rooms which had a doctor's name and his office hours marked on the door. As soon as a *Vindicator* photographer appeared, Mr. Big grew militant. 'If you take a picture of me, whether it's for the newspaper or otherwise, 'I'll fight right here and now,' he said. As he got out of his chair and headed for the cameraman. [While "Mr. Big" was never identified in the story, it is believed it was Frank Budak due to the fact he was the owner of the Campbell House lottery and, as will be seen from a future incident, had little tolerance for newspaper photographers.] The photographer had previous orders not to take pictures of the principals and was merely focusing his camera on large sacks of money being piled on the desk by raiders. These piles were so heavy that the men strained to lift them from the strong boxes. The man in charge of this place at first told deputies that he didn't know where the key was to one of the larger strong boxes. When the state man promptly ordered it smashed, the bug big shot said 'I suddenly remembered where the key is' and produced it.

"So complete was the raid that if 'substitutes' should want to run the outfits today, they would have to get new equipment, even down to the tables and chairs in a couple of places."

The raids were a complete success and Prosecutor Leis spoke to the media while those who were detained were still being questioned. He explained that the people brought in for interrogation were not under arrest and were not charged with any crimes. After being interviewed each one was released. Leis told reporters, "I cannot praise the sheriff and his men too much in their work."

The prosecutor was quick to point out, however, this was only the beginning of their work.

The next day, in what seemed like an attempt to jump on the bandwagon – even after it had passed through town – Mayor Spagnola issued his fourth cleanup statement in a year's time. This one was his shortest on record as he warned Chief Przelomski to, "Clean up the town or resign!" Apparently shaken by the ultimatum, the chief told members of the force that if they did not "clean up their beats and rid them of vice and crime" they faced suspensions or firings.

The *Vindicator* reported, "three different times...Mayor Spagnola has come out in public statements saying he would take 'full responsibility' for vice cleanups and was giving the 'go' to his police chiefs for a complete cleanup." Little had changed.

Przelomski quickly appointed Sergeant Davis to the long vacant position of chief of the vice squad, which by now was reduced to a two-man operation. Davis was told he had a free hand in selecting new squad members. Some wondered how "free" a hand Davis exercised as one of the men named to the squad was Przelomski's younger brother. Davis was given a written command "to clean up all vice in Youngstown. This does not mean one type of vice or gambling only, but all types."

Sergeant Davis' vice squad had an inauspicious debut. The newspaper pointed out that the squad didn't even make a "token" raid on its first day. Perhaps this alerted gamblers that something was planned for the second day. Davis and his raiders made four stops the next night. Although the *Vindicator* titled their article "Vice Squad Chief Nabs 6 in Clubs," the facts were that five of the "nabs" were on a charge of not having their draft registration cards on them. After the raids Davis declared, "Bingo games are out! All bingo games must cease. It's my intention to close them – and that means all of them, not just a few." The following night managers of the Disabled American Veterans Hall defied Davis' ban order. When asked why the establishment was not raided Davis replied my men have "a pile of work to do. We can't clean the city in one day or even a week; it takes a little time."

Three days later Davis led a well-planned raid on the A. A. Social Club on West Rayen Avenue. Formerly known as the West End Smoke Shop, an oft-raided gambling joint, raiders found nearly 40 people gambling at card and dice tables around 5:00 p.m. on a Thursday afternoon. Davis correctly suspected that the place, protected with electronic security devices, was packed with a payday crowd.

On January 23, Carl V. Weygandt, Chief Justice of the Ohio Supreme Court, assigned Adrian G. Newcomb, a Cuyahoga County common pleas court judge, to oversee the special grand jury assigned to investigate crime in Mahoning County. The 61 year-old Newcomb, a successful trial lawyer who Clevelanders recently elected to a six-year term on the bench, was a veteran of both the Spanish-American War and World War I. Newcomb and Judge Lyon were friends from years back when Lyon handled special assignments on the Cuyahoga County bench.

Assigned to aid Leis in the questioning of witnesses was Colonel G.L. Yearick, an assistant state attorney general. Yearick's first name was not a military rank but actually the birth name bestowed upon him by his parents. Leis and Yearick began questioning witnesses before Judge Newcomb on January 26. Some of the witnesses were those detained during the raids. The witnesses, as well as the nature of the questions were kept strictly confidential. Raids, conducted at the request of Leis, continued to be carried out as the special prosecutor built his case. Dozens of individuals were brought before the special grand jury for questioning. Leis' efforts and those of the grand jury culminated in a massive indictment on June 16, 1943, that put an end to Youngstown's infamous lottery houses forever.

"And don't forget to put in your story that there are a lot of good church people who play the numbers every day - probably more people of this type than people like you and me." – Lottery operator Nick Brown speaking to a Vindicator reporter following a raid at the Recreation Billiard Parlor on June 13, 1935.

5

Lottery House Operators

To make it less convoluted to the reader we have decided to break each of the lottery house stories into separate segments and tell the full story of their members from beginning to end.

While the hey-day of the Lottery Houses was from 1935 until June 1943, the activities of some of these operators lasted well into the 1960s.

"Big House" (Greek)

Nicholas Limberopoulos (aka Limbert)
James G. Limberopoulos (aka Limbert)
George Limberopoulos (aka Limberty)
Louis Metro
Sam Metro
George Rigas
Peter Rigas
Sam Rigas
George Chukas

"American House" (Irish)

Patrick J. "Pack" Scanlon
Peter J. Higgins

"Campbell House" (Croatian)

Frank Budak
Joseph Budak

"South Side House" (Italian)

Dominic "Big Dom" Mallamo
Joseph Fezzuogho (aka Joe Peppe)
Frank Gioia (aka Frankie Joy)

Big House Lottery

The Big House was said to be one of the "largest lottery syndicates" in Ohio, taking in, at peak times, $8,000 to $10,000 per day. All nine members were from Greece. Court records later revealed that the Big House organization "hired an average of 80 pick-up men and that eight to ten men daily worked in the two main counting stations at South Watt Street and the pool room on West Federal Street, to say nothing of the several sub-stations in the various parts of the city."

Limberopoulos Family – consisted of three brothers, Nicholas, George and James, all born in Asea, Greece. While their names appeared as Lambert, Limbwert, Limbert and Limberty in newspapers over the years, two of the brothers appeared to have changed their last name legally to Limbert, while a third, George, changed it to Limberty. (As to not confuse the reader we will use to the Limberopoulos name).

The brothers immigrated to America between the years of 1907 and 1915, while other siblings stayed behind including a brother, Christ, who became a prominent doctor in Athens. Nicholas, the oldest of the three, was born on March 25, 1891. In Greece he left school after the fourth grade. At the age of 16 he came to the United States and found a home in Chicago where he shined shoes and worked as a fruit peddler. In 1909, he moved to Youngstown and worked as a waiter and later established a shoe shine stand and a cigar shop on West Federal Street. Around 1912, Nicholas opened the Liberty Pool Room at 315 West Federal Street. The "notorious" poolroom became the center of the brother's lottery operations. In 1920, Nicholas became a United States citizen. In 1935 he was arrested for operating a lottery; he pled guilty and was fined $300 and sentenced to a 30-day jail term.

George was born in 1894. Of the three brothers, George spent the most time in school leaving after the eighth grade. When he was 15 he joined Nicholas in Chicago where he was employed by Sears, Roebuck and Company. Instead of following his older brother to Youngstown, George returned to Greece in 1912 to serve as a volunteer in the Greek army during the Balkan Wars. After a year George was honorably discharged and came back to the United States and Youngstown to join Nicholas again. Instead of remaining in the Valley, George traveled around working at jobs in Minneapolis and in Detroit's automobile industry. During World War I, George served again and was honorably discharged. After returning to Youngstown after the war, George attended night school and became a United States citizen in 1918. Prior to his arrest in 1943 he had no criminal record.

James, the youngest of the three brothers, was born on March 15, 1899. He quit school after the third grade and when he was 16 he arrived in Youngstown. James became a citizen in 1928 and, like George, had no criminal record until 1943.

The family got its first public exposure during April 1939 when a member of Youngstown's vice squad attempted to capitalize on the Big House lottery members using a little known law of the Ohio code. The filing of the lawsuit touched off a major crackdown on the numbers operators resulting in three Big House members announcing that they were leaving the business. According to a *Vindicator* report, Herbert F. Bodine filed the suit using the law, "which holds that one losing money to a gambling house may recover the money, and that anyone may sue for the money lost by others, provided the actual losers fail to sue within six months of the time of the loss." Bodine's suit asked for $400,000, an amount he claimed represented the losses by bug players between April and October 1938.

In his original filing there were 29 defendants. Bodine named all of the Big House operators, their wives, family members, banks and brokerage houses. Bodine won an early motion to tie up all of the assets of the lottery leaders. Later, all of the restraining injunctions were dropped as well as all the defendants except the actual Big House operators, but not before "scores of bug writers, pickup men, bank and brokerage officials were called to testify," which provided weeks of "sensational" testimony.

The case pitted two of the Valley's most noted trial lawyers at the time against each other. Clyde W. Osborne represented Bodine, while Russell Mock was counsel for the Big House operators. During the trial, held in June 1939 before Judge Erskine Maiden, Jr., Frank Fetchet testified that he was employed by Limberopoulos, as a numbers writer and pickup man, working for the Big House during the mid-1930s. Fetchet and several other "number runners" testified about the money they helped generate. Fetchet claimed that his daily take was between $75 and $100, of which he paid the "writers," the people who actually took the bets from the players, 30 to 35 percent, while his own commission was 5 percent. The figures were the same as those testified to by Louis Tiberio, another former Big House worker, who claimed he had 30 to 40 pick up locations that he serviced. In a bizarre explanation of how Tiberio operated, the *Vindicator* reported the following:

> "Tiberio...said that two men, whose names he did not know, got him a job as a pickup man with a lottery outfit whose name he didn't know, run by men he didn't know, and that he turned in money to men he didn't know, out of which he deducted a certain commission, the percentage of which he couldn't remember."

After getting his start with the Big House, Tiberio began his own operation, but soon went broke. The reason, he claimed, was because his operation was frequently raided while the authorities didn't touch his competition. He was soon back at work with a new employer – the South Side House.

The case dragged on until March 1940 when Judge Maiden dismissed it on the grounds that Bodine "failed to show a cause of action." In explaining the decision the newspaper reported, "Judge Maiden ruled the suit failed to contain the 'special matter' constituting the cause of the action. Such information consisted of the names of those who lost money in the lottery, the amounts lost, the time the money was lost, and other pertinent data concerning each separate claim."

James Limberopoulos was back in the news in November 1940, amid rumors that "friction" between the Big House and the South Side House had resulted in policy slips being "hijacked" and destroyed. During this "friction" Limberopoulos was seen nursing a black eye. Rumor had it that he received the "shiner" in one of two ways. First that he was waylaid by a group from the South Side House in the Liberty Pool Room. Another tale was that James was "blackjacked and beaten" after a profitable night at the Jungle Inn.

This incident was the first report of violence between the numbers operators in two years. In this latest tiff, the rumor was the South Side operators were ready to close their "house" and be satisfied with a "monthly cut" of the spoils. There was some dispute over how much of a "monthly cut" was fair. Supposedly the beating of James and the destroying of the bug tickets was an effort to move the negotiations along.

The Limberopoulos brothers' position as leaders of the most prosperous lottery house in the city provided them little respect in the criminal community. In April 1941, Nick Limberopoulos had his pocket picked clean of $112 while standing in the crowded lobby of a downtown theatre. A week before Christmas 1941, three thugs waited for James outside the garage of his home. When James arrived he was relieved of $37 and his automobile, which was later found abandoned in the city. A partner in the Big House, George Chukas, experienced a similar experience in December 1940, when thieves broke into his home and stole $420.

Through the late 1930s and early 1940s the Liberty Pool Room was the site of numerous raids and arrests involving policy activities. In February 1943, Peter Limberopoulos, a cousin, was arrested after vice squad detectives seized a man with lottery slips, which he claimed came from the poolroom. In court, Peter's attorney, Russell Mock claimed his client was arrested without due process because there was no warrant, nor had detectives seen the violation take place. The judge didn't buy the argument and Peter was fined $25 and court costs. Two months after this conviction, Peter was at the Liberty Pool Room when raiders swooped in on May 28 and uncovered a pack of lottery slips that he had just hidden in a backroom.

On June 16, 1943, law enforcement in the Valley enjoyed one of their greatest victories over the lottery leaders. Simon L. Leis, the special appointed prosecutor, working with Cleveland Judge Adrian G. Newcomb, who was assigned to handle the grand jury judicial work, announced a 58-count indictment against 15 men, all known leaders of the four lottery houses in the Valley. The investigation was launched in May 1942, by the "runaway" grand jury, which was attempting to deal with rampant vice and crime in Mahoning County. In January 1943, Nick Limberopoulos and Sam Metro were called before the grand jury and promised immunity if they testified. The men testified, however, but they were both named in the indictment because they continued their activity in the policy rackets.

Despite the well-publicized raid on January 21, 1943, and several after it, nothing seemed to stop the continuing operations. The headquarters, or "banks," were moved to different locations including private homes. In late April, over a month and a half before the indictments, the nine members of the Big House moved their entire operation to New Castle, Pennsylvania, where they set up shop in a hotel. They continued the operation using telephones and associates until the June indictments. At this time the operators fled – to locations as far east as the Atlantic Coast and west to Chicago – on the advice of their attorney, Russell Mock.

When the indictments were first announced, only one of the operators was arrested; but soon four others turned themselves in and quickly posted bail – none of them Big House operators. A week after the indictments, Louis Limberopoulos, a cousin of the three brothers, was arrested as a material witness. He was released on a $1,000 bond and told he must appear and testify, if and when his cousins appeared for trial, or he forfeited his bond. It was soon discovered that the remaining ten were in hiding and not about to turn themselves in until certain conditions were met. Russell Mock, the attorney for the indicted men announced that the surrenders would occur "when the time came."

Six months passed before any of the Big House lottery leaders were arrested. Ironically, two were captured on the same day in different cities. On December 17, Nick Limberopoulos was arrested in a "dingy" Chicago rooming house by local police and officers sent from the Ohio State attorney general's office. A few hours later, George Limberopoulos was captured at his home. Sheriff Ralph E. Elser's deputies were keeping a watch on George's Southern Boulevard dwelling. On this night, as they made their usual inspection, they discovered a light on in the rear of the home. Deputies surrounded the house and state law officers were called in. After authorities knocked, George answered the door calmly. Standing there with his shirt sleeves rolled up, he announced that he was glad the ordeal was over and that he was trying to get back to town for some time to surrender. George's wife reportedly spoke "quite freely" with law enforcement officials claiming her husband was negotiating for a lower bond. In a statement untypical of a mobster's wife she related, "He was only in the business two years and only received two percent."

In June, at the time of the indictments, Judge Newcomb had provided for bonds to be set at $2,000 when the defendants appeared for arraignment. When none of the Big House leaders came in, Newcomb doubled the bond and later cancelled it completely. George was forced to stay in jail until a bond hearing was held before Newcomb on December 20. That same day, the other two Georges – Rigas and Chukas – also surrendered and were in court. The judge was not in the holiday spirit while setting bond. Limberopoulos's new attorney, John P. Barrett, told the judge his client had received "bad legal advice" from previous counsel, Russell Mock, who had informed George and the others to "stay away." Barrett claimed that his client had wanted to surrender all along. Newcomb responded that while Barrett's client's "intentions might have been good the fact is he didn't surrender." Newcomb reminded the attorney that his client was not "above the law," and set his bond at $9,000.

James Limberopoulos and the four remaining Big House leaders surrendered on January 3, 1944, and pleaded not guilty. They were all represented by William R. Fairgrieve, an attorney from Cleveland. Fairgrieve also entered a not guilty plea for Nick Limberopoulos, who was still in Chicago, unable to travel due to health problems (he returned nine days later). Fairgrieve announced that in a short time all the men would be negotiating guilty pleas with the court.

On January 25 the Limberopoulos brothers and the six other leaders of the Big House, appeared in court all represented by Fairgrieve and Neil W. McGill, a former Cuyahoga County common pleas judge. The men pled guilty to a total of 164 lottery and gambling related charges. Before the judge set a February sentencing date, McGill asked Newcomb to consider probation for the nine men.

At the sentencing hearing on February 8, Fairgrieve and McGill put up a commendable effort on the part of their clients. In asking for clemency and probation the lawyers made the following arguments:

◊ The men were not involved in robbery or any violent crimes. The bug was "voluntary with the public."

◊ The state was saved "much expense" by the men pleading guilty and not going to trial.

◊ The men have no interest of ever starting in the numbers game or anything like it again, but merely want to go back to peaceful lives in a legitimate business.

◊ The profits were overstated by prosecutors. In 1933, when they began the profit was only $300 to $400 per day. At one point the nine partners "were forced to mortgage their personal properties to pay off large hits and added that only in the last few years had they got into the big money."

◊ The newspapers, which printed the stock market totals from which the winning lottery numbers were determined, could cease printing these figures.

◊ The men had increased the city's income by $12,000 between 1939 and 1942 by paying fines for the bug writers and pick-up men who were arrested by the police.

The attorneys then made two ridiculous points on their client's behalf:

◊ "These men were divided into three groups in the numbers business and then consolidated. It is commendable that the three groups did consolidate so that they could better pay off on big hits. If there is such a good thing as a good motive in a bad business these men had that good motive."

◊ The men, in a patriotic move, wanted the adding machines, which the state confiscated, donated to the Army.

Judge Newcomb then handed down the following fines and sentences:

Nicholas Limberopoulos	$2,000	150 days
James Limberopoulos	$7,700	150 days
George Limberopoulos	$5,500	150 days
Louis Metro	$7,700	240 days
Sam Metro	$2,000	150 days
George Rigas	$7,700	240 days
Peter Rigas	$7,700	150 days
Sam Rigas	$6,600	150 days
George Chukas	$7,700	240 days

Of the 31 sentences handed down since the indictments were announced in June 1943, these were the most severe. The men were given a week to get their personal affairs in order. On February 14, all nine Big House operators arrived at the Mahoning County jail to begin serving their sentences.

George Limberopoulos was the first of the Big House operators to be released, serving just 68 days of his 150-day term. After Judge Newcomb reduced his fine to $2,000, George paid it by mid-April. He then secured a job in the defense industry and was placed under the jurisdiction of George Hadnett the Adult Probation officer in the area.

After paying their fines and serving their sentences the Limberopoulos brothers stayed out of trouble until October 21, 1945. This time it was the Liberty Pool Room that was under fire. "Clean house or we'll clean house for you!" That was the order given by Juvenile Court Judge Henry P. Beckenbach. The judge issued this order after reports that young men, 16 and 17 years of age, were frequenting the West Federal Street location and getting involved in illegal activities there. A youth who patronized the place was recently involved in a racial disturbance at a local high school.

Exactly two months later the poolroom was back in the news after the filing of a lawsuit seeking $21,700 in gambling losses by an unlucky gambler. After racking up the huge loss over a five-month period, the man chose to sue under an Ohio law which holds that "owners of premises being sued for gambling are liable for gambling losses if they know the property is being used for that purpose." The lawsuit was eventually dismissed.

By the mid-1940s, a new underworld force was making it presence known in the Valley. Its members were not afraid to throw their weight around. Shortly after noon on February 14, 1946, four gunmen entered the West Federal Street poolroom with plans to destroy it. Two gunmen went to the large back room where they ordered 40 men, who were playing or watching pool, down to the basement where they were locked in. The men were soon joined by Nick Limberopoulos. While one man watched the front door, the other three took turns with sledgehammers in smashing the furniture and equipment in the place. A barbut table, wall partitions, lighting fixtures, pop bottles and adding machines were smashed or splintered. Cue sticks and billiard balls were then tossed about the room. While this was going on, a small crowd gathered on the sidewalk outside to watch. The four men left behind a mess that Carrie Nation would have been proud of, smashing out the front plate glass window as their final act of destruction. An interesting side note to the attack was that the gunmen didn't touch several hundred dollars in bug receipts that were on a table in the front room.

While bystanders viewed the damage, the telephone rang. The caller wanted to speak to Nick Limberopoulos. When told Nick was indisposed, the caller said, "Well, tell him they're out to wreck the joint."

"You're late by five minutes," the caller was informed.

"Oh, hell!" the caller said as he hung up.

As the year 1948 rolled around, and with it the new administration of Mayor Charles Henderson, the city began another crack down on the lottery operators. Leading this early effort was Youngstown Police Sergeant Charles Bush. The dedicated officer had already been involved in a number of raids and arrests at the West Federal Street location. Bush's latest visit to the Liberty Pool Room on January 5 proved no different.

Bush and his partner executed a two-man raid in the middle of a cold Monday afternoon. They entered through the front part of the establishment, which housed a shoeshine parlor where most of the bug transactions took place. Numbers slips were seized and Peter Limberopoulos, who was racking balls in the poolroom, was arrested. Peter reached into his pocket and pulled out an envelope full of policy slips. As he attempted to tear them up Bush wrestled them away from him. To add insult to injury, when his brother Nick showed up to post the $50 bail, he was $4 short. In court, at the end of the month, Judge Frank P. Anzellotti reminded Peter it was his third bug arrest since July 1942 before fining him $100 and placing him on probation for two years.

The Youngstown police were cracking down not only on the lottery sales, but also on cleaning up the poolrooms. They began enforcing an old billiard parlor ordinance that made it illegal to have a partition in a poolroom because it could conceal operations such as the selling lottery tickets. On February 13, 1948, Sergeant Bush arrested Nick Limberopoulos for violating the city's ordinance by having a partition. The following month Nick pled guilty and was fined $10. Despite the best efforts of police, like Sergeant Bush, once these operators went to court there were seldom any heavy penalties to pay. Most fines handed down usually had all but a small portion suspended, and probation instead of prison time was normal. In Nick's case a meaningless $10 fine was the penalty even after Limberopoulos was given a warning about the partition.

As the decade of the 1940s was winding down the moneymaking days of the Limberopoulos brothers, and their Big House lottery, were in the past. A *Vindicator* article discussed their demise:

Once Powerful Group

> "The Limberopoulos name (of late changed to Limbert) has for a long time been synonymous with bug operations in Youngstown. The brothers, cousins and friends, who made up the nine partners of the Big House in the late '30s and early '40s were powerful in gambling circles.
>
> "After most of them were jailed in the state investigation of '42 and '43, and during the war, their monopoly on the numbers racket was broken up.
>
> "They are said to be only one of the larger of 20 or 25 bug outfits working Youngstown and Campbell areas."

The brothers failed to realize this, or accept it, and apparently the sledgehammer raid in February 1946 failed to confirm it. On July 9, 1949, the mob decided to put an exclamation point on their message in the form of a bomb tossed into the doorway of the Limberopoulos' new operation, Federal Billiards, located next door to its infamous predecessor the Liberty Pool Room. All of the front windows were destroyed by the blast, which rocked buildings for several blocks. No one was hurt.

On November 24, 1950, George Limberopoulos was arrested with 17 lottery slips in his coat pocket inside the repaired Federal Billiards parlor. Despite having been arrested, fined and imprisoned in 1943, vice squad officers told Judge Robert B. Nevin that this was George's first bug offense. Because of this, Nevin suspended $350 of a $500 fine and placed Limberopoulos on probation for two years.

It was nearly a decade since James had last been in the news. During this period the crime fighting duo of Henderson / Allen was largely responsible for keeping the lottery houses out of business. On September 9, 1955, a vice squad raid was conducted in the middle of the afternoon to break up a floating dice game being played in Federal Billiards. James was taken into custody, but later released. On October 2, 1956, James was again in trouble with the law as he was jailed after police uncovered a stack of lottery slips in a cigar box at a cigar counter in Federal Billiards. He pled not guilty to possession of gambling equipment before Municipal Judge Frank R. Franko.

A few days later the city law department filed a padlock action against Federal Billiards, as well as two other lottery locations, which were referred to as "common nuisances" – Sportsman's Barbecue (Foster Street) and Carlyle Grocery (High Street). Listed as defendants in the Federal Billiards suit were the owners of record, Viola Limberty and Mary, Melopomens and Nicholas Limberopoulos.

The trial for James Limberopoulos didn't take place until March 1957. It was a colorful one. Under questioning from future judge, then Assistant Mahoning County Prosecutor John Leskovyansky, the two arresting officers testified that a "stranger," later identified as a porter in the poolroom, showed them the bug slips in the cigar box. When confronted, James told the officers to arrest the porter instead of him. The officers told the court that if they did as James had asked, he said, "I'll fix you up."

James Limberopoulos was represented by another future judge, who became the long-time chairman of the Mahoning County Democratic Party, Donald Hanni. James took the stand and denied the officer's testimony, claiming he was in the backroom shooting pool when he was called to the front and told he was under arrest. Taken to the city jail, James said he was locked up in the "bull pen" and at 10:00 that night was approached by Youngstown Police Chief Paul H. Cress. Limberopoulos testified that Cress promised, "He would turn me loose if I said they [the bug slips] were mine." The prosecution objected when Hanni referred to the "bull pen" as the "Black Hole of Calcutta."

At the end of the trial, held before Judge Franko, the future mayor found Limberopoulos not guilty stating, "the city failed to prove the charge beyond a reasonable doubt." He also questioned why police did not arrest the porter who had brought the lottery slips to their attention.

The move to padlock Federal Billiards was dropped when James announced he was no longer connected with the business. The padlock threat was raised again a year later when James was arrested on another gambling charge. The decision to padlock was delayed by a first assistant law director who later made national headlines as a federal judge in Cleveland – Frank J. Battisti.

On February 11, 1958, police officers arrested James Limberopoulos at Federal Billiards once more for possession of gambling equipment. The case was tried before Municipal Judge Forest J. Cavalier. Police had seized seven pages containing names of basketball teams, along with the betting odds. In addition, police confiscated a list of first names with dollar figures and $320. During the trial in March, James testified that the list was of loans he made to borrowers whom he only knew by their first names. On May 2, well over a month after the trial had ended, Judge Cavalier ruled that there was "not enough evidence presented to warrant a finding of guilty."

James Limberopoulos stayed out of the news until June 22, 1963, when he was one of four men arrested on a gambling warrant. The arrest made sensational headlines due to the work of an undercover rookie police officer (more on this in Section IV on the 1960s). A few days later George Limberopoulos, who was also named in the warrant, turned himself in. Both brothers pleaded not guilty. Because the men were arrested on a "complaint," City Prosecutor William Green decided it was better to have the charges dismissed and then have evidence presented to the Mahoning County grand jury in order for indictments to be issued. On September 11, the grand jury issued a 33-count indictment for nine men, including the Limberopoulos brothers, on felony charges of booking numbers. On September 21, George and James pled not guilty to several counts of "promoting the numbers game" and were released on $2,500 bonds.

Also in October 1962, Federal Billiards came to an official end. After one of the raids over the summer, Dan Maggianetti, chief of police intelligence, lifted the poolroom's operating permit. A city license was issued to McCullough Williams, Sr., a former parking lot owner, to operate Town Shoe Shine & Billiards at the West Federal Street location. In an article announcing the new ownership the newspaper referred to the Liberty Pool Room / Federal Billiards site as the former "center of gambling activity in the city." Before the week was out the city "pulled" the soft drink and shoe shine parlor license for the new operation.

On October 4 George and James changed their pleas and pled guilty to three and two counts, respectively, of promoting a numbers game before Common Pleas Judge John W. Ford. Both brothers asked for probation. They remained free on bond while a probation officer was assigned to review their case and report back to Judge Ford. The criminal careers of the Limberopoulos brothers came to an end on October 9, 1962. George, now 68 and James 64 were fined $1,500 and $1,000 and given six months probation. Judge Ford declined to send the men to the penitentiary claiming that since they had sold the West Federal Street pool hall, prison "did not seem called for."

James Limberopoulos died before the year was over. On December 14, he passed away after an illness of two months in North Side Hospital. The newspaper said, "His most recent occupation has been in real estate investment." Six months later Nicholas, the oldest of the three, died of a heart attack on June 12, 1963, in South Side Hospital. Finally, on February 19, 1964, after an eight-inch snowfall in the city, George suffered a heart attack while shoveling his driveway. The 70 year-old was under a doctor's care for a heart ailment. He was pronounced dead at South Side Hospital. The funerals for all three brothers were held at St. John's Greek Orthodox Church.

Rigas Brothers – The Rigas brothers, Sam, George and Peter, were born in Corinth Greece. Sam, the oldest and most prominent, was born on September 1, 1888. Sam attended school until his junior high school years and in 1906 arrived in the United States. He first moved to Butler, Pennsylvania where he was employed by the Standard Steel Company. From 1909 to 1912 he worked in a bed factory where he helped manufacture metal bed frames. Like George Limberopoulos, Sam Rigas returned to Greece during the Balkan Wars and served in the Greek army for 16 months. Returning to Butler after the war he suffered an injury to his hand which ended his days as a factory worker. Sam soon found work in the poolroom and billiards business. In 1920, he arrived in Youngstown and opened a restaurant on Watt Street. Two years later he opened a combination restaurant-poolroom on Phelps Street. In addition, he acquired the Champion Recreation center at Champion and Commerce Streets in downtown Youngstown, which he operated for half a century. Sam's first arrest came in 1935 for operating a lottery. He was fined $100.

Peter Rigas was born on August 15, 1893. He attended schools in Greece until after the seventh grade, and then moved to Butler to join his brother Sam. Peter worked in the steel mills and in a munitions factory during World War I. In 1920, he moved to Youngstown and went to work with Sam. Until 1935 he had no criminal record.

George, the youngest of the Rigas brothers, was born on March 5, 1895. Quitting school after the seventh grade he joined his brothers in Butler in 1912 and found work in the local steel mills. During World War I, like Peter, he worked in a munitions factory. George became a citizen in 1918, and the next year moved to Youngstown and worked for Sam in his restaurant business.

On July 1, 1935 Peter Rigas and Nick Brown pled guilty to operating and promoting a game of chance and were fined $200. George Rigas was arrested the next month on a charge of "conducting a house for gambling purposes." A disgruntled lottery player retained an attorney and swore out a warrant claiming Rigas "failed to pay off a four-cent 'hit' which would have returned $20." The "hit" was later made good and the charges were dropped. Sam Rigas, the president of the Youngstown Bowling & Recreation Company, had his first arrest in December 1935. Sheriff Elser raided the combination bowling alley / poolroom / bug operation, which was called a "sub-headquarters for the Big House lottery, and Rigas was charged with possessing lottery slips. It was obvious that Sam was not familiar with jail protocol. First, he tried to give $62 to a friend there for holding; he then tried to walk out 20 minutes after he arrived. Rigas insisted his bond was paid and was on his way out when deputies stopped him. He was placed behind bars until his $100 bond was met. In February 1936 he paid a $100 fine.

The Rigas brothers were in the news again at the end of July 1937. Another suit was filed against them for not paying off on a 'hit.' This time the owner of the Press Club, a beer garden on South Phelps, filed a lawsuit to recover $940 after placing a bet of $1.88 on number 188 earlier that month. The suit named five men – Sam and George Rigas, Louis Metro, James Limberopoulos and George Chukas – all of whom were arrested for belonging to "an association engaged in operating a numbers business."

Winning policy numbers were not the only debts Sam Rigas wasn't paying. Earlier that year he announced he was ready to "sell out" his poolroom equipment after he was sued for non-payment by the manufacturer. The judgement, awarded to the Brunswick-Balke-Collender Company, was $9,788 for equipment that was purchased in 1930.

Despite his involvement in the numbers racket, George Rigas was looked on with high regards in his church and community. Early in 1939 he was installed as the new president of the executive committee of St. John's Greek Orthodox Church.

In April 1939, the $400,000 lawsuit filed against James Limberopoulos resulted in a vice crackdown being ordered throughout the city by Mayor Lionel Evans. The mayor issued an ultimatum that all bug operators were to be out of the city by high noon on April 26. The mayor's position was supported by Police Chief Carl L. Olson, who "launched a city-wide campaign on all forms of vice."

The crackdown was successful – for a short while, as all crusades of this type were in the city. When Olson began his tour of 20 downtown bookie and policy establishments, he found everyone closed. It was rumored that the bug operators would either shift their downtown operations around or would flee outside the city into the nearby city of Campbell or to Trumbull County.

The highlight of the mayor's order was a response by George Rigas, who promised Chief Olson, "We won't operate. We got our orders and we are through forever." The "we," according to the *Vindicator* was George and Sam Rigas and Louis Metro of the Big House's South Watt Street operation.

The day after Mayor Evan's ultimatum, police found 12 numbers joints and 13 bookie operations closed, as well as all of the "temporary stations to which Big House business" had been transferred the previous day. After nine lottery suspects were arrested – and met the $50 bail – authorities agreed quickly to double all bond requests.

Over the next few years the Rigas brothers stayed out of trouble as it pertained to the numbers business. Sam, however, was gaining a reputation of being one of the Valley's biggest cheapskates. On June 30, 1939, he ran a stop sign at the corner of Dewey and South Avenues. The result was six people, four of them teenagers, being seriously injured and three automobiles heavily damaged. Rigas was cut over the left eye and on both legs. At South Side Hospital, Rigas told a traffic officer that he drove through the stop sign. In a municipal court hearing on August 2, judge and future mayor William B. Spagnola fined Rigas $25 for reckless driving and suspended his driver's license for 90 days.

Despite the testimony of witnesses, and Rigas's own admission, his attorney James A. Modarelli said he would appeal the decision. A motion for a new trial was filed and the fine was stayed. On December 14, 1939, Spagnola overruled the motion before he left the municipal bench. Fifteen days later Municipal Judge Peter B. Mulholland granted a new trial claiming that he "acted because of the length of time Spagnola took before denying the request." There was some "legal conflict" with Judge Mulholland's "entry" to retry the case, thus causing the case to be continued after it was scheduled for retrial on March 5, 1940. The case dragged on another year, with judges and prosecutors arguing points of law, before the *Vindicator* pointed out in a front-page article on March 3, 1941, that 20 months passed since the accident and the fine handed down, by now Mayor Spagnola, and had not been paid. The newspaper pointed out the real reason for the delay by quoting attorney Modarelli from an appeal where he stated that Spagnola's decision was the "foundation for four or five civil actions" for damages against Rigas.

Judge Mulholland drew the wrath of the *Vindicator* in a scathing editorial that appeared on March 8, 1941:

Mulholland and the Rigas Case

"Judge Mulholland of the municipal court does not come up for re-election for two years, but the voters should keep his action in the Sam Rigas case in mind as a good reason for opposing any candidates with whom the judge "makes book" in next fall's election.

"Judge Mulholland wants to be presiding judge of the municipal court. Two places on the bench are to be filled next fall. It is to be expected that he will make a deal with two candidates, throwing his political influence to them in return for their promise to make him a presiding judge.

"Judge Mulholland's flagrant record in ticket-fixing has been thoroughly aired recently. The Rigas case is another black mark on his record. Rigas, active in one of the 'bug' rackets here, was convicted of reckless driving after an accident in which six persons were injured and three cars damaged. A motion for a new trial was denied by Judge Spagnola.

"If the verdict stands it will do Rigas no good in any civil cases for damages that may be filed against him. Obviously it would be nice for him if someone should rescue him from the criminal charge. Whatever Judge Mulholland's motive, that is what he achieved by stepping into the case, reversing the court's previous action, and granting a new trial.

"The legality of this remarkable action has been questioned. There ought to be some way to test it. At any rate, the case is further reason for mistrusting Judge Mulholland's activities on the bench. He should not be the presiding judge, and electors should resolve to vote for no one whom he supports next autumn."

Mulholland was not due to assume his seat on the criminal bench until July 1. On March 11, he told Police Prosecutor Forrest Cavalier that "he would not hear the case at the present time." He offered no explanation for his decision, but instead told Cavalier that the reckless driving case was "initiated to provide a basis for the damage cases."

The day Mulholland took the criminal bench on July 1, 1941, exactly two years and a day after the accident, he dismissed the case. The newspaper stated, "He gave no reason in his entry for his action, and could not be reached ...for a statement."

It was over a year before Sam Rigas was in the news and again it was due to not meeting a legal obligation and the efforts he expended to avoid it. An employee who worked for Sam was injured on the job in June 1933. He filed a claim for damages in July 1939 and was awarded a $900 judgement in May 1941. In between, Sam transferred the assets of his bowling alley and billiard parlor to a new corporation called the Champion Recreation Center and now claimed that the company the employee had previously worked for was non-existent. In August 1942, the former employee filed a suit against Sam Rigas for the fraudulent transfer of his business assets.

In early 1943, as the state lottery probe spearheaded by Special Prosecutor Simon L. Leis was gaining momentum, all of the lottery house operators were relocating in and out of Youngstown. On March 30, the investigators conducted their most spectacular raid. The Rigas brothers were operating out of the basement of Peter's LaClede Avenue home. Lookouts in "bug scout cars" cruised the quiet residential neighborhood watching for any signs of the state raiders who were making their lives miserable. Not far away seven deputy sheriffs and two state investigators were hidden in the back of a large yellow moving van. Shortly after 3:00 p.m., the van pulled to a stop a few houses from the Rigas home. Once the driver determined that the "bug scouts" were not suspicious of the van, he pulled in front of Peter's house. A signal was given and the raiders leaped from the back of the van and headed for the side door of the home. The men learned a quick lesson that the Hollywood method of shooting out the lock was just that – Hollywood. They then used a length of heavy steel piping to batter in the door.

The *Vindicator* reported, "Deputies spread to every corner of the house so fast that Chief Deputy Otis Heldman was able to catch Peter Rigas, who tried to climb from a cellar window when he sensed that the pounding on his side door was anything but a social call. For his trouble, Pete only got his suit dirty." Caught by the raiders, in addition to Peter, were George Rigas and three assistants. The men were pushed back down the stairs into the cellar where they were searched. The raiders seized money, lottery slips and adding machines.

As one of the investigators announced he was going to conduct a room-by-room search of the house, Peter Rigas told him that the operation was confined only to the basement. When the belligerent homeowner refused to allow the raider entrance to the first floor, deputies smashed through an inner door leading to a breakfast nook and a back hallway. Nothing was recovered from the other floors in the house.

George Rigas, who had once told Police Chief Olson that he and his brothers were quitting the numbers game for good, told an investigator, "I'd of quit the bug before if Leis had told me to the last time I was down there [at the headquarters of the special prosecutor]."

The newspaper stated, "All the operators and other bug employees were taken to state headquarters for questioning and further investigation. No arrests were made."

An editorial in the *Vindicator* on April 2 was mild in its attack on the Rigas brothers and pointed elsewhere to the problems of the bug:

> "It illustrates anew the brazen persistence of the racketeers, the curious inability of a succession of police chiefs to discover rackets though the state and county men find them readily – and the continued existence of a large crop of suckers who are still willing to pour their money into a game that is stacked against them.
>
> "The continued readiness of a large section of the public to line the racketeers' pockets is worth attention. It is only by the suckers' continued cooperation in fleecing themselves that the lottery operators can keep on enjoying ill-gotten wealth and debauching law-enforcement agencies. An effective remedy lies in the hands of the people themselves."

The Rigas brothers were already in hiding by the time the June 16 indictments were announced. The next month Sam was named in another lawsuit, this one asking for $40,000 in damages, by a man who caught his hand in a ventilating fan with blades exposed and uncovered. In February 1943, the incident resulted in the injured man losing his index finger and the use of his entire hand. The suit involved other members of the Rigas family as defendants and also exposed some apparent illegal maneuvers that took place in setting up two "dummy corporations" by Sam Rigas involving his Champion Recreation Center.

The first Rigas brother to come out of hiding and turn himself in was George. He and fellow Big House operator George Chukas appeared before Judge Newcomb with their attorney William Fairgrieve on December 22, 1943. Newcomb quickly advised the attorney, "In my opinion, these men, by staying away from the court for six months, have waived any right to expect much courtesy and consideration of this court."

Of course the fall guy for Fairgrieve was attorney Russell Mock, who had advised the policy men to stay away. Coincidentally, Mock happened to be in the courthouse that morning apparently unaware that two of his former clients were on their way in. When asked the whereabouts of the men Mock boldly announced, "None of the men is in town and they won't be back today or this week." When Rigas and Chukas suddenly appeared Mock hustled out of the courthouse without replying to reporter's questions.

On February 15, all of the Big House men had turned themselves in at the Mahoning County jail to begin their prison sentences. By June 10, all but George Rigas were released. All the men had paid their fines except one – Sam Rigas.

George suffered a nervous breakdown shortly after entering the county jail and was transferred to St. Elizabeth's Hospital to recover. One report said that Rigas had lost 36 pounds since entering the county jail and that he had internal bleeding. When he was well enough to leave, his doctor requested two weeks off for him and Judge Newcomb granted the release on June 22. After what the newspaper called a "two week vacation," George reported back to the jail on July 16, but was released five days later "to regain his health." Due to report back on September 9, George was unable to make it. On September 21 Judge Newcomb placed George on six months probation.

Over the next three and half years the Rigas brothers were out of the public eye except for one incident where 25 pin boys from the Champion Bowling Alley picketed Sam's operation demanding "a pay increase from six to eight cents per line." The increase was granted.

On February 16, 1948, George Rigas was sitting in the Piccadilly Café on South Avenue watching a card game. At 1:30 in the afternoon Frank Bartolec, a 34 year-old acquaintance of George, entered and asked if he could speak to Rigas in private. The two walked to a room in the rear of the café, where Bartolec suddenly drew a gun and said, "This is it, Rigas." Rigas was shot twice, in the groin and hip, after which Bartolec fled from the restaurant. He went to the home of a friend where he asked if he could borrow an overcoat. He announced, "I just shot a man and I've got to get going." Rigas was rushed to St. Elizabeth's Hospital's emergency room. After a two-week recovery period he was released. Police quickly arrested Bartolec and the case was turned over to the grand jury. On May 30, the *Vindicator* reported, "Bartolec, who later told police he had no motive for shooting Rigas except that he just wanted to shoot someone, was believed by the grand jury to have a possible mental ailment. As a result Judge Maiden committed him to Lima [state mental hospital] for examination. Hospital officials, however, reported Bartolec sane and the man pleaded guilty, asking for probation..." Judge Maiden sentenced Bartolec to a term of one to twenty years in the Ohio Penitentiary. After just six months in prison Maiden granted Bartolec a rehearing and placed him on three years probation.

The underworld powers that were seizing control in the valley and pushing the Big House lottery operators out of business in the late 1940s were successful in ousting the Rigas brothers from the policy business. Although Sam Rigas continued to build his legitimate businesses, the brothers' names only appeared in print when there was a death or tragedy.

In 1953, Peter's wife died in the Cleveland Clinic after a two-week illness. In January 1954, Sam's house caught fire and burned. No one was home at the time. During October 1956, the church-going Sam brought down the wrath of several clergymen when he and his son sought an application to extend the liquor hours at their Champion Bar & Restaurant from 1:00 a.m. until 2:30 a.m. The local church leaders, who met with an officer from the Ohio Liquor Control Board, indicated that there was already a problem in the area with the earlier closing time.

In September 1958, George's wife Katherine passed away. The family's property, which was placed mostly in her name, was later valued at more than $173,000. George died of cancer at the age of 68 in St. Elizabeth's Hospital on October 9, 1963. His obituary said he was a retired restaurant owner.

Fire again struck the Sam Rigas home in March 1969. The family had left days earlier for a Florida vacation. The $20,000 blaze gutted the house.

Peter remarried in 1960 and moved to Florida. On July 19, 1982, after a two-month illness, he died at the age of 88.

By 1970, Sam had retired as president of the Champion Recreation Center, an operation he had overseen for 50 years. His wife Penelope died in October 1982 just over a month shy of the couple's 68th wedding anniversary. Sam, now in his 90s, moved to the Maplecrest Nursing Home in Struthers to live out his final months. On April 11, 1984, Sam Rigas died of pneumonia at the ripe old age of 95.

Metro Brothers – The last set of brothers that made up the Big House were the Metro brothers – Sam and Louis B. Their last name was a shortened version of Papademitriou. Both brothers were born in Corinth, Greece – Sam in 1893 and Louis 1896 – and moved to America when they were in their late teens, settling in Butler, Pennsylvania, as did the Rigas brothers. During World War I the two worked in a munitions factory. In 1919, Louis moved to Youngstown and was employed by the Truscon Steel Company for about nine months. After Sam arrived the next year they both began working with the Rigas brothers. The Metro's sister was married to Sam Rigas. In 1924, Sam became a naturalized citizen and was joined five years later by Louis.

Sam Metro worked with Sam Rigas in the operation of the latter's Champion Street bowling alley in the early 1930s. Up until the Leis led probe the only criminal act between the Metro brothers was an arrest involving Sam in 1935 for "operating a lottery." He was fined $300 and given 90 days in jail.

On the afternoon of March 26, 1943, eight deputy sheriffs and a state investigator raided the home of Paul Domer, described as an "important pick up man" for the Big House. Inside the home, cranking out the day's receipts on an adding machine, were Louis Metro and two others. All the men were hauled before Special Prosecutor Leis for questioning.

When the June indictments came down the Metros, like the rest of the Big House leaders, had left town on the advice of attorney Mock. After their surrender, guilty plea and sentencing Louis was looking at 240 days and Sam 150. Sam was given 48 hours off for the Greek Easter holiday in mid-April 1944.

After their release from prison there was no indication that the brothers were ever involved in anything illegal again. In September 1948, they purchased a half interest in the Tod Hotel from the Petrakos family for a reputed $182,000. The brothers stayed involved with the operation of the popular hotel for the next 20 years.

On May 11, 1979, Sam died of "infirmities" at the age of 86 in the Monterey Nursing Home in Columbus. His wife of 52 years Mary, the sister of Peter Rigas' first wife, died in July 1976. Louis passed away four years later on June 25, 1983, also at the age of 86. He died in South Side Hospital of a heart ailment after a two-week illness. At the time he had been married for 54 years.

George Chukas – The final member of the Greek Big House lottery was George Chukas. Born in Greece, he arrived in America at the age of 12 in 1908 with his father. They settled in Harrisburg, Pennsylvania, where his father worked for the railroad and George shined shoes. Around 1910, George and his father moved to Youngstown. The father remained for six months before returning to Greece. George continued to shine shoes to support himself and soon met Nick Limberopoulos.

The two men opened their own shoe shine parlor in 1914 on West Federal Street and applied their trade for the next four years. After working as a taxi driver for the next three years, Chukas met Sam Rigas and worked in a Phelps Street poolroom until 1928. In 1933, he opened a restaurant on Fifth Avenue. He saved enough money to finance a trip back to Greece for a year in 1936. After returning, he opened his own poolroom on Phelps. Chukas, who had become a citizen in 1928, had never been in trouble with the law until the time of his indictment in 1943.

On May 17, 1944 Chukas, who was sentenced to 240 days and a fine of $7,700, was ordered released on probation after serving just 94 days. No explanation was given in the newspaper for the early release by Judge Newcomb.

In early July, a *Vindicator* article claimed Big House operators were "reported to have itchy fingers again and are trying to edge back into the racket." A few days later Chukas, acting as a spokesman for the Big House, issued a statement saying, "None of them are interested in or participating in any 'bug' operations."

Being part of the Big House paid off for Chukas. In July 1947, he paid an estimated $100,000 for the property at 22 South Phelps Street. The building included a billiard parlor, bowling alley, sporting goods shop and the Youngstown Commercial Club. Ironically, the basement of the property was home to the Big House lottery operation that was the first to be hit by raiders back in January 1943. A little over a year later, in September 1948, police raided the Youngstown Billiard Parlor and arrested Chukas, who was booked under a fictitious name for several hours. After this incident Chukas faded from the public eye.

Campbell House

Of all the lottery house operators Frank Budak, of the Campbell House, had the longest and most publicly scrutinized career. Born in Lika, Croatia on December 15, 1899, Budak, his brother Joseph and their family arrived in the United States in 1912 and settled in the Youngstown area.

An uncle of the Budak brothers, Milan Budak, was active in the Croatian independence movement since before the First World War, when the country was still part of the Austrian-Hungary Empire. Milan Budak was a reputed lieutenant of Dr. Anton Pavelich, leader of the Ustachi, a secret Croat extremist organization. The group was credited with the October 1934 assassination of King

Alexander while he was on a visit to Marseilles, France, after which Milan became an exile. In February 1940, Milan was captured by secret police in Zagreb, Yugoslavia, and charged with "plotting to breakup the country."

Frank Budak remained active in Croatian fraternities all his life. Just prior to World War II, Budak served as treasurer of "Domobran," the Home Defenders of the Croatian National Representation for the Independence of Croatia. The organization was composed of naturalized American citizens of Croatian descent. In the years leading up to America's entry into the war the group's news letter slanted its editorial content from pro-Nazism to pro-Americanism. When Croatia became a Nazi puppet state, Justice Department officials believed that some Croatian societies in the United States became sources for Nazi propaganda. The organization disbanded on a national level on May 30, 1941, issuing a statement that they were firmly behind President Franklin D. Roosevelt. After the bombing of Pearl Harbor on December 7, 1941, the FBI got involved in rounding up the records of the organization. Lee V. Boardman, special agent in charge of the Cleveland FBI Office, subpoenaed Budak as records were seized from the Campbell, Warren and Youngstown chapters of the group. Nothing to indicate that Budak, or any of the organization's local members, were involved in any illegal activities was uncovered.

Frank Budak's earliest involvement in crime in the Mahoning Valley came in January 1932, when he was convicted on a numbers charge. He was fined $150 and sentenced to ten days in jail. He never served the jail time. Representing Budak at that time was future Mahoning County Prosecutor William A. Ambrose. Practically all of Budak's criminal activities, up until the late 1950s, were tied to his connections with the Poland Country Club. The property, which seemed to pass in ownership between family members at will, was located in Boardman Township on the Youngstown-Poland Road, bordering the city of Struthers. The country club became infamous due to the number of vice raids conducted there over the years.

In March 1937, title to the Poland Country Club passed from Dollar Savings and Trust Bank to Agnes Budak, Frank's first wife. It remained in her name until 1940, when title transferred to Frank's mother, Mary. The price of the 80-plus acres of land was $20,000. In April 1939, an attorney for the Budaks filed a petition with Struthers City Council to have them annex the property. The paperwork claimed the Budaks were offering Struthers the opportunity to have its own golf course. Others believed the motive behind the proposal lay in the fact that Boardman Township had voted to go "dry" in the 1938 fall election. The Poland Country Club would be able to regain its liquor license if the annexation were approved.

During this period Sheriff Elser conducted a number of raids at the country club for illegal gambling and assorted liquor violations. Seldom was the name "Poland Country Club" mentioned without the following four words – "target of numerous raids." In late 1938, an Elser raid closed Budak's operation for more than a year. In December 1939, the country club reopened and the Purple Heart, a veteran's benevolent association, began conducting benefit bingo games there.

Around 1:45 a.m. on January 6, 1940, a bomb exploded ripping apart an enclosed porch that was used as an entranceway to the rear of the club. Frank Budak and his parents were there but no one was injured. Early speculation behind the explosion was laid to the mayoral change in Campbell. Budak, a longtime resident of Campbell, was involved in local politics and had supported the candidacy of former Mayor T. Roy Gordon in the late 1930s. When John J. Borak won election, many believed that Budak lost his political muscle in the city.

A year after the country club bombing, Budak opened a gambling room in the Jennings Night Club, owned by the Jennings (nee DeJaniro) brothers, in Niles. On January 15, 1941, a man tossed a bomb from an automobile into the building. Part of the club served as a home to James Infante, his wife and four children. Years earlier, in September 1936, a bomb blew the front porch off the Infante's home. Infante was allegedly involved in the numbers racket. In 1939, Marty Flask, a Jennings relative, was murdered in front of the club.

On July 15, 1941, after state liquor agents purchased drinks at the Poland Country Club, the bartender was arrested and charged with serving liquor at a premise without a permit. Frank Budak was arrested for being the owner of the establishment. After two delays in a Struthers court, overseen by Mayor William A. Strain, Budak claimed he wanted a trial. His position was that he was arrested because he was believed to be the proprietor of the country club. At a hearing in late August, Budak's attorney filed an affidavit claiming Mary Budak was the owner and requested that Mayor Strain be removed from the case because he was "fanatically opposed to liquor and gambling." Just days before the hearing, another raid took place at the club and liquor and slot machines were seized.

Sometime around late 1941 or early 1942, Budak established a numbers operation, which became known as the Campbell House. In early 1943, Ohio State Attorney General Thomas J. Herbert began to make raids to bolster the information being presented to a secret Mahoning County grand jury to indict the lottery house operators. On January 21, Budak's Campbell operation was the first to be raided. Three weeks later, on February 10, state raiders backed by Sheriff Elser smashed down a door at the Poland Country Club in the middle of the afternoon. Budak and Elser got into a heated exchange over opening a steel case that contained slot machines. Budak refused to unlock the case and Elser's men were about to swing away with a sledgehammer before a key was finally produced. In addition to three slot machines, deputies confiscated a race horse bookie board. A further search of the premises revealed "an adding machine, 35 to 40 cartons of new policy slips, more than $1,000 in cash and a mass of assorted gambling equipment." Budak, his wife Irene, and their son maintained a "most luxurious" living quarters at the Poland Country Club. Budak was questioned there by Special Prosecutor Simon Leis.

On June 4, a Frank Budak operation was raided for the third time in less than five months. This time state investigators were in for a big surprise. The raid took place at Jack DeNiro's roadhouse on Jacobs Road in Trumbull County. As the raiders entered the room Budak and another man were busy cranking away at adding machines counting the day's numbers take. Mixed in with Budak's Campbell House bug tickets were policy slips from both the Big House and the American House lottery operations, clearly indicating that some type of merger had taken place. The newspaper reported that Budak "admitted to state agents that the merger had come about and [Budak] was especially peeved that the raid came on the first day of business as a three-way combine."

Among the four men found with Budak were Bruce Davidson, a man described as Budak's right-hand who had also been caught in the previous two raids, and Pat Bucilli, a former Campbell city councilman described as the "final pickup man, the fellow who carries the bundle." In the upstairs rooms of DeNiro's roadhouse investigators found two slot machines and three "well-furnished" card rooms.

On June 16, Budak was arrested in the massive indictment which named the other fourteen members of the four lottery houses. Budak was being taken to the Mahoning County jail to be photographed and fingerprinted when Lloyd S. Jones, a *Vindicator* photographer, snapped his picture making Budak furious. The next day Jones was on his way to an assignment and was sitting in traffic on Commerce Street in front of the Erie Terminal Building. Budak, on foot, saw Jones and jumped on the running board of his automobile. The driver's side door was locked and after failing to pull Jones out through the window, Budak pummeled the photographer about the face and left side of his body. A brave pedestrian pulled the enraged lottery operator off the automobile. As Jones drove off, Budak continued his cursing and repeated, "I'll get you for taking that picture." (During the famous Jungle Inn raid of August 1949, Lloyd Jones was again the target of angry gamblers).

Jones went to the police station and swore out an assault and battery warrant and later that afternoon Budak was arrested. The next day he pled not guilty to the charges before Judge Mulholland and a hearing was set for the following month.

In July, Budak was involved in some political controversy during a Croatian picnic held in Campbell. Anthony F. Pacella, a former mayor of Campbell, got into a discussion regarding comments made by Budak. Pacella's side of the story was, "As I walked away from him he hit me, knocking my glasses off. I hit him on the nose and his nose bled." Reports from other witnesses claim Pacella simply knocked Budak down and broke his nose. Pacella was running against incumbent mayor Andrew J. Hamrock, who Budak strongly supported. Budak had talked another candidate into entering the race to take votes away from Pacella.

Also making news during the summer of 1943, was Frank's older brother Joseph Budak. In June, Joe got drunk and insulted a waitress at Clark's Restaurant in downtown Youngstown. Police were called to calm the situation and were told to "go to hell," by Budak. The officers arrested him and he was later given a suspended fine of five dollars. Joseph, who was the owner of Club 22 on South Phelps Street, was arrested again in September after a disturbance downtown in which he again was intoxicated. This time Joseph forfeited a $13 bond when he failed to appear for court the next day.

Frank Budak pled guilty to June's nine-count indictment on October 6 and was the first lottery house leader to be sentenced. Two of the counts carried a 90-day jail sentence and Judge Newcomb decided that Budak should serve the terms consecutively. Budak's attorney announced immediately that he would appeal the sentence, which included a fine of $3,510 and seven separate suspended terms of 30 days each on the remaining counts. Budak's bond was increased to $4,000, which he paid thinking he would be free until his appeal was settled. Judge Newcomb, however, filed an order on October 14 that Budak was to report to the Mahoning County jail on November 5. This allowed Budak, who was deeply involved in Campbell politics, to participate in the upcoming election.

Controversy was already brewing in the local Campbell election, which pitted Democratic incumbent-mayor Andrew J. Hamrock against two Republican challengers - former Campbell Mayor Joseph E. Julius and T. Roy Gordon. Two weeks before the election Julius dropped out of the race throwing his support to Gordon. Julius said his decision to drop out was because, "Frank Budak is the real mayor of Campbell and Andrew J. Hamrock only a puppet." Hamrock won by a two-to-one margin.

On November 5, Budak turned himself in at the county jail six hours early to begin his sentence. Before the month was out Budak, while still in jail, was front-page news again as federal authorities filed tax liens totaling $160,000 against him and other family members. The liens were for unpaid additional taxes owed by the Budak brothers for the years 1940 and 1941. Judge Newcomb released Frank Budak for 60 hours on March 11, 1944, to attend to these legal matters. The newspaper reported that the release was to allow him "to make tax returns, unemployment compensation forms, and social security returns for the federal government." Budak was given an additional three and a half days off in April to observe the Greek Orthodox Easter (Byzantine rite) and "take care of business matters." On April 30, Budak was released from jail after serving 178 days of his 180 day sentence.

Over the next year and a half Budak busied himself with Campbell politics - his tax problems looming in the background. On October 26, 1945, a federal grand jury in Cleveland indicted Frank and Joseph Budak for "attempting to fleece the government of $61,516 in taxes." The indictment charged that both brothers filed fake returns for the years 1940 and 1941, grossly understating their income. During that two-year period the government claimed the brothers had a combined income of $172,091, for which taxes of $65,924 were due and only $4,409 paid. Frank Budak was unaware of the indictment until contacted by a *Vindicator* reporter seeking a comment.

One of the businesses Joseph Budak was a partner in, and had failed to report income from, was a gambling operation called the All-American Club. (This name surfaced again in Campbell in the 1990s in connection with Lenine Strollo.) Frank was listed as a partner in the Milton Dog Racetrack with late Warren mobster James "Jimmy Munsene" Mancini.

On November 26, the brothers pled not guilty at their arraignment in federal court in Cleveland before Federal Judge Emerick B. Freed. Both men were represented by former Youngstown Mayor Joseph E. Heffernan. A trial date of May 22, 1946 was set. "This tax fraud case, the first involving gamblers ever to be tried in Cleveland, may be used as a model in future prosecutions in the Justice Department's present drive against tax evaders," claimed Don C. Miller the U.S. Attorney in Cleveland. Miller, who was set to prosecute the case, was an American sports legend during the 1920s when he was a member of the famed "Four Horsemen" of Notre Dame.

The government was ready to proceed when the trial date arrived. They had lined up twenty-four witnesses, including ten banking officials from Ohio and Pennsylvania, to testify. In a surprise move, the Budaks' Cleveland attorney entered a plea of guilty before even one potential juror could be called. Before sentence was passed both sides were allowed to speak. A member of the prosecution team told the judge that the brothers had received $200,000 from an Ellwood City, Pennsylvania banker. The defense attorney claimed that the $61,500, the entire amount of the tax evasion, resulted "from money paid out on bets" by the banker to a man named "Alabama," who had recently died. The lawyer said the Budaks had not received the money and that "Alabama" was really the guilty person.

Attempting to clarify the statement Judge Freed asked, "Do you mean to tell me that they made all their money off one individual?" The question drew smirks from both Budak brothers. They realized in seconds their bad judgment when Judge Freed barked out, "I am tremendously amazed and shocked that people get rich from the misfortune and weakness of others. Their smiling and smirking here is an indication of their character." Freed called the case the "worst tax violation I have seen since I served in the district attorney's office and on this bench." With that Freed sentenced the pair to two years and six months each in a federal penitentiary. The sentences were reported to be the heaviest ever handed down in the Northern Ohio Tax Court.

In a May 23 editorial, the *Vindicator* compared the Budaks' conviction to that of Chicago mob boss Al Capone in that it was sad that for all of "Scarface's" crimes all they could convict him of was income tax evasion. In the Budaks' case:

> "It was bad enough for these men to evade paying their share of the cost of government, as other people must do. It was worse that they got their money by mulcting others, breaking down the morals of their community, and debauching law enforcement. In their long career of this sort of thing they went virtually unchecked."

After the brothers' sentences they were taken directly to the Cuyahoga County jail where they remained until June 5, when they were transferred to Lewisburg Federal Penitentiary in Pennsylvania.

In late June, Frank Budak's 13 percent ownership of the Lake Milton Dog Track was attached by the government as part of its effort to recoup unpaid taxes. The dog track, located over the Mahoning County line in Portage County, recently had a change in majority ownership and was about to reopen. Pari-mutuel betting at dog tracks was illegal under Ohio law, but the new operators were looking to get support for a change in that law. Part of their effort included offering payments to a Ravenna hospital and local veterans groups.

In February 1947, federal parole board members met in Lewisburg and set a parole date of April 1 for the Budak brothers. The newspaper reported that the $61,500 tax bill had not been satisfied. Despite the fact that the government had filed liens on property owned by Frank and Joseph Budak, and their mother Mary, they had not foreclosed on any of them. Two months after they were paroled the brothers were back in federal court in Cleveland. The government was about to enter a civil suit against them when the two men agreed to pay $133,111 in back taxes and penalties. Their proposal was accepted, making it the largest settlement recorded in the Northern Ohio district.

On January 3, 1948, Joseph Budak's North Phelps Street operation, Club 22, was raided by Youngstown Police Captain William R. Golden. The raiding party included a young black patrolman by the name of Lloyd Haynes. Club 22 was just one of several clubs raided during the new mayoralty of Charles P. Henderson. There were several reports that Club 22 was involved in after-hours liquor sales. The reports proved reliable as Golden and his men arrived at 4:15 a.m. to find 25 or more people patronizing the club. As Golden entered Joe Budak shouted at him, "You're jumping the gun. You're not supposed to start your campaign until January 5; I'll see my boys about this!"

The January 5 deadline referred to the arrival of Henderson's new chief of police Edward J. Allen. Just who "my boys" was a reference to, Budak never explained, but it was rumored that he had campaigned for Henderson and thought he may have been entitled to some "special privilege." Budak later went to the police station to apologize to Golden, but the captain refused to see him.

Frank Budak was reported to have been one of the "backers" of the Green Acres casino in Struthers when it was robbed on September 17, 1948 (See entry on Green Acres in Section 5). Budak denied having any association with the operation. "I'm not that screwy," he claimed, "I'm on federal parole for twenty months yet." John Sanko, a hood with a long record, was arrested by police as being the "keeper" of the Green Acres operation. He had previously worked for Budak at the Poland Country Club. Three days after the robbery, the gambling and bar equipment from the Green Acres casino was packed up, while a Struthers' police cruiser sat nearby, and transported to the Poland Country Club.

In early October 1948, Chief Allen had Ohio Bell Telephone disconnect and remove the phones from the Poland County Club and the Liberty Pool Room because of "illegal use." Budak went to visit the fiery new police chief to get his telephone service back. He told Allen that the telephone was in his wife's name. When the chief asked if anything illegal was taking place inside the club, Budak replied, "Yes and no."

On October 23, the Budak brothers were arrested less than a month before their paroles were due to terminate on November 21. They were taken to Cleveland and returned to the Cuyahoga County jail to await transfer to a federal facility. Joseph Budak's parole violation stemmed from the Club 22 incident where liquor was being served after hours. Joseph had signed a parole agreement stating that he would not "frequent places where liquor was sold, dispensed or used unlawfully." Violations of Frank Budak's parole were "evidence of his operation of the Poland Country Club where there was illegal gambling and liquor sold."

The *Vindicator* article announcing their arrests stated, "It was reported that the Youngstown underworld had made up a pool on the date of the Budaks' return to prison as parole violators. The pool listed the days until Nov. 21, when the parole ends." The newspaper failed to announce who the winner was. By November 1, the two brothers were back in Lewisburg to complete the last 20 months of their original sentence.

Near the end of November, the IRS announced that equipment from Joe Budak's Club 22 would be sold at public auction with the proceeds going to satisfy unpaid federal income taxes. At the same time, it was announced that the Poland Country Club would also be sold at a sheriff's sale after the Dollar Savings & Trust Company foreclosed on the mortgage.

On November 29, approximately 75 bar and restaurant owners lined up to take part in bidding for the Club 22 equipment. The auction was delayed for five hours because a representative of the IRS couldn't find a key to the club. The high-bidder for the equipment - bar, back bar, piano, tables, chairs, leather booths, a steam table and miscellaneous cooking and eating utensils - was Charles R. Vizzini, an alleged member of the Mafia, who paid $3,005. Vizzini owned the De Luxe Café on West Boardman, which, incidentally, had employed Joe Budak as a night manager until his arrest for parole violation.

Just days after the Club 22 auction, Judge David Jenkins ordered the Dollar Savings & Trust Company's judgement be satisfied by selling the Poland Country Club. The sheriff's office was told to have the property appraised and advertised for sale despite the fact that attorneys for both the Budaks and the government sought postponement. On December 28, after Dollar Savings & Trust Company assigned its judgment to the S. J. Gully Bank of Farrell, Pennsylvania, the property auction was cancelled. The government, which held a $59,000 lien against the property for back income taxes, withdrew its "cross-petition" to the foreclosure. The newspaper summarized, "Thus the Farrell bank now owns the judgement and the property will not be sold unless the Farrell bank files an order for sale." The *Vindicator* reported "bidders were prepared to pay as high as $45,000 to $50,000 for the club house and golf course, which had been appraised at $31,000."

After two weeks of rumors in the local newspapers that the Budaks were going to be released, the two brothers returned to Youngstown on January 6, 1950. Their probation officer explained to reporters that "the Budaks were not paroled in the regular sense but rather were given 'conditional releases.'" Their release was scheduled for June 13, but they were given a six-month reduction for good behavior. The probation officer stated that the men were "model" prisoners while at Lewisburg. Both brothers were trusties; Frank served as a chauffeur for prison officials. In a peculiar statement, while explaining that the Budaks could be returned to prison for any "illegitimate" activity, the probation officer said, "They must engage in legitimate work or business *at least* until the terms of their sentence expire." Joe Budak was no sooner out of prison before his wife of nearly 20 years filed for divorce on the grounds of "gross neglect and extreme cruelty."

In March 1951, the Budak brothers were part of a "secret" nationwide list of 126 underworld figures under investigation for tax evasion. The list was compiled during the Kefauver Hearings. Despite the fact that the brothers had pled guilty in May 1946, they had yet to pay a cent towards the tax bill they were assessed.

Beginning in February 1951, a concerted effort began to padlock the Poland Country Club. Prosecutor Ambrose prepared the writ referring to the club as a "common and public nuisance." Judge Ford signed the writ and a series of hearings followed. On April 30 Judge Ford ordered the Poland Country Club[10] padlocked permanently.

On April 7, 1952, Frank Budak was served a summons for reckless driving after nearly hitting an automobile driven by Municipal Judge John W. Powers. In reporting the incident, the *Vindicator* began the article with: "Youngstown is no place to almost crash into the car of a municipal judge and then expect to get away with it."

The newspaper was proven wrong.

Events began when Frank Budak had a near collision with Power's car at Elm and Woods Streets. Budak took off, with the angry judge in pursuit, and ran stop signs along Wood Street at Hazel and at Wick Avenue. Budak turned on Wick and crashed a red light at Commerce Street. Powers caught up with Budak on West Boardman Street, and seeing a patrolman nearby, ordered the officer to issue a summons for reckless driving. Powers claimed he didn't know that it was Budak behind the wheel, "until he got out of the car."

When Budak failed to appear in court the next day, a bench warrant was issued for his arrest. Budak was quickly arrested and pled not guilty. He was released on a $25 bond with a hearing date set for the following week. At the hearing, after Judge Powers' testimony was heard, Judge Robert B. Nevin tossed the case out because the patrolman "failed to swear and sign the affidavit" in the presence of the chief clerk of the court. The patrolman, who was assigned to the juvenile bureau, explained he was not familiar with the summons process. He claimed he didn't sign and swear to the affidavit because he hadn't seen the actual infraction and that he thought the judge would file a separate complaint.

Through the mid-1950s, Frank Budak managed to remain in the newspapers. Whether it was fighting a zoning bill in Campbell or answering allegations of running gambling operations in East Liverpool, Budak was never out of the public's eye. All the while the tax bill against him remained unsettled.

By February 1956, the IRS, fed up that it was nearly ten years and no effort was made to satisfy the tax judgement, seized Frank Budak's home on McCartney Road in Campbell. The house, a large two-story dwelling, was a "notorious" brothel in the early 1920s when it was known as the "White Kitchen." On March 23, the house was sold for $11,000. The high-bidder was Frank Boback, Jr., Budak's brother-in-law. Boback was the owner of Frank's Food Market on South Avenue, the scene of one of the districts many bombings during the 1950s. It took a year before the property transfer was complete. Shortly thereafter, a real estate transfer was filed in the Mahoning County recorder's office indicating the property was resold for $11,000 to Frank Budak's two sons; Frank, Jr. and Anthony. Frank Budak and his wife Irene continued to live there.

Despite being out of the Poland Country Club and Club 22, the Budak brothers continued to be involved in other gambling operations. One was the American Croatian Club on Poland Avenue, where in January 1958 underworld figure "Big John" Schuller and two of his associates were injured in a car bombing in the parking lot.

Frank Budak's name surfaced again in August 1961, during a U.S. Senate gambling probe. The senators were investigating the Bentley-Murray Company of Chicago, controlled by Thomas Kelly, Sr., at one-time the manager of the Continental Press, the infamous race-wire service. The company printed betting slips, wall cards and bookmaking material. The probers found that during a 19-month period, from January 1, 1960 through July 31, 1961, the company produced 27 million betting slips. One of their customers was a "Mr. Stone" of 8 Short Street in Campbell. The city directory showed the address was listed in Budak's name, while the telephone directory listed it as Budak's Dairy.

Two weeks after this revelation, Irene Budak, in whose name the dairy was titled, issued a statement through the *Vindicator* denying the allegations: "Mr. and Mrs. Budak have never received any package or mail from the Bently-Murray Co., and to their knowledge nobody by the name of 'Mr. Stone' has been connected with their Short St. address since Mrs. Budak started the dairy business [over seven years ago]."

In January 1964, Budak was subpoenaed during a Mahoning County grand jury crime probe. The newspaper referred to him as "an old time numbers king here." Later that year, he was cited for violating the local liquor ordinance for Sunday sales. Keeping a tradition he began over 30 years earlier, Budak pleaded not guilty.

Frank Budak's remaining years were spent being active in various Croatian fraternal societies and organizations. On November 15, 1973, he was visiting friends for the evening when he was stricken with a heart attack. He was pronounced dead a half-hour later at St. Elizabeth's Hospital. Budak was a month shy of his 74th birthday.

American House

The two leaders of the American House lottery syndicate were no strangers to law enforcement in Youngstown. Patrick J. "Pack" Scanlon and Peter J. Higgins were partners-in-crime since the 1920s. Higgins and Scanlon were involved in one of the state's biggest liquor scandals. Known as the "Ohio Liquor Permit Scandal," the crimes took place between May 1921 and June 1922. During this time 22,000 gallons of whiskey were removed from the Hayner Distillery in Troy, Ohio, through the use of illegally obtained medical permits. The plot was uncovered in February 1925. Ten people were indicted, including Higgins and Scanlon, as well as the state's top Prohibition official. Higgins and Scanlon received sentences of 16 months each.

In March 1943, with significant raids already executed against the Big House and the Campbell House, state investigators turned their attention to Higgins and Scanlon at their headquarters in the Steel City Club on Central Square. The club was a popular restaurant and catered to many city and county officials for both lunch and dinner. The raid, carried out on the afternoon of March 12, netted 5,000 bug slips, nearly $1,500 in cash and approximately 30 persons, who were held for questioning by Special Prosecutor Leis. As in the other two raids, no arrests were made.

On June 16, when the grand jury indictments were announced, Higgins and Scanlon were each charged with eight counts. They were arraigned, fingerprinted and photographed, before being released on $2,000 bonds. Both men pleaded guilty and on November 9 were fined $4,000 each by Judge Newcomb. Scanlon was sentenced to a 90-day term in the county jail. The judge declined to impose a jail sentence on the 70 year-old Higgins, despite the fact he was only two years older than Scanlon, due to his age and physical condition. Newcomb granted a stay of sentence until Scanlon's attorney, Andrew M. Henderson, could provide medical testimony about his client. The lawyer stated that Scanlon had a serious heart ailment and a diabetic condition, which required constant care.

After four stays of sentencing for Scanlon, he finally appeared in court on January 20, 1944. Newcomb heard testimony from doctors for both the prosecution and the defense. A point of contention was the insulin injections Scanlon needed for his diabetes. His doctor was also concerned about the effect the strenuous jail conditions might have on his patient's heart. Prosecutor Leis pointed out that the injection could be handled by the jail's visiting nurse. As far as Scanlon's heart was concerned, Leis questioned, "Isn't climbing 32 steps leading to the Steel City Club considered strenuous?" Before leaving the stand the doctor remarked, "Sometimes it's hard to distinguish when prosecution ends and persecution begins."

At the end of the hearing Newcomb let the sentence stand. Henderson persisted, however, and Scanlon was nowhere nearer to jail. Upset that the prison sentence was still being fought by defense counsel, the judge told Henderson that a "reasonable request has not yet appeared in this court." After three delays in reporting to the county jail Newcomb agreed to a final conference with a specialist from the Cleveland Clinic to determine if a stay in jail would further impair Scanlon's health. There was no change in the medical opinion that Scanlon's ailments were not serious enough to prevent him from serving time.

On March 15, 1944, Scanlon reported to the Mahoning County jail, where he claimed, "Maybe this would put an end to the trouble and satisfy everyone." By the end of the month Scanlon was transferred to St. Elizabeth's Hospital due to bronchitis. After examination by the hospital's doctors, he was reported in "fairly good" condition. On June 1 Scanlon was released.

The remaining years of Higgins and Scanlon's lives were spent out of public scrutiny. The Irish branch of the Valley's lottery houses were the oldest in age. In early July 1955, Scanlon, who was ill for several years, suffered a stroke. Ten days later, on July 15, he died at the home of his daughter at the age of 81. Five years after the death of Scanlon, his longtime friend and business partner, Peter Higgins, died of a cerebral hemorrhage at his home on July 5, 1960. Higgins was 88.

South Side House

The final lottery operation was the South Side House overseen by Domenico "Big Dom" Mallamo, one of the Valley's most mysterious underworld figures. Mallamo was born on August 19, 1904, in South Nicola Ardore, Reggio Calabria,

Italy. He arrived in Youngstown in 1918. Mallamo's partners in the operation were Joseph "Joe Peppe" Fezzuogho and Frank Lewis "Frankie Joy" Gioia. Fezzuogho was born in Naples, Italy on August 19, 1905. He and his family arrived in America in 1908. His name sometimes appeared in print spelled "Fezzuoglio" and his nicknames as "Peppe," "Pepe" and "West Side Pepper."

Of the four lottery houses only the South Side House escaped being raided during the investigative period of the secret Mahoning County grand jury. Gioia, however, came to the public's attention after an arrest on March 22, 1943, less than three months before the indictments.

Gioia was under surveillance by two vice squad detectives – William Turnbull and William Golden. The two officers were watching Gioia because they suspected him of conducting the pickups for the South Side House. Gioia was in his automobile at the corner of Elm and Spring Streets when the detectives attempted to question him. Gioia took off with the vice men in hot pursuit. The chase reached speeds of 70 miles-per-hour through the city's North Side before Gioia slipped away. Instead of going into hiding, the numbers racketeer parked his vehicle behind a bar on Federal Street and went in for a drink. Golden and Turnbull returned and found the car, then found Gioia minutes later. The lottery man was arrested for reckless driving, suspicion, and possession of a box of blank policy slips. The detectives also found empty moneybags and adding machine paper in the car. Gioia told the vice men that he drove off because he thought someone was trying to rob him.

Gioia was in court on May 18 charged with another crime – using rationed gasoline in conducting his illegal lottery operations. At the hearing, Gioia admitted to having once worked for the South Side House, but claimed, "I've retired now." His rationing rights were revoked until the end of 1944.

On June 16, 1943 Mallamo, Gioia and Fezzuogho were indicted and charged in 12 counts a piece with being "owners, vendors, backers and operators of lottery outfits." The next morning Gioia walked into the court clerk's office and arranged his bail. He then went by himself to the county jail to be booked. Fezzuogho went through the same process a short time later. Both men were represented by Russell Mock, who refused to allow them to be photographed and fingerprinted claiming the law reads that "unless a defendant volunteers, he may not be fingerprinted or photographed for a misdemeanor."

The legal wrangling began the following month during a hearing before Judge Newcomb on July 2. Attorneys Mock and William P. Barnum (representing Frank Budak) filed a writ to void the grand jury indictment against their clients on the following grounds:

1. The special grand jury was not selected according to law.

2. Subpoenas issued for witnesses were not sent through the regular channels, the clerk of courts office.

3. The state either through its Attorney General, Thomas L. Herbert, or its special prosecutor, Simon L. Leis, here, never filed a complaint charging any specific person with any specific crime.

4. No list was prepared in the clerk's office as to what the special jury was to investigate.

5. Leis was never legally appointed prosecutor in Mahoning County by journal entry.

Newcomb overruled the pleas and motions to quash the indictments, but he allowed for the writ to be filed. The *Vindicator* reported the following as Prosecutor Leis took the stand to answer questions being fired at him from attorney Mock:

> "Mock asked Leis if it were true that search warrants could not be issued for misdemeanors, which include 'bug' writing, slot machines, and other types of gambling which have been investigated by the jury.
>
> "To this Leis replied, 'The record speaks for itself.'
>
> "As Mock asked Leis a succession of questions, he would turn sideways, facing the jury box where a number of attorneys, representing others, who might be affected by the decisions, and the reporter were sitting. After he did this several times, Leis said:
>
> "'Could you wait for my answer before sneering?'
>
> "'Didn't you tell the lottery men to go back to their work after you questioned them – that you weren't interested in them?' Mock demanded of Leis.
>
> "At this point, Judge Newcomb broke into the questioning saying, 'Let's stop this situation here.'
>
> "'I'm not interested in any unpleasant conversation between you and Mr. Leis,' the judge told Attorney Mock.
>
> "Mock then changed his method of questioning and asked Leis questions concerning an alleged promise of immunity to [Gioia] when he testified at the special headquarters at Trinity Church.
>
> "Leis denied he had promised that any person questioned at his headquarters would not be prosecuted. He told Mock he has no statements of any of the persons who have been indicted."

At the time the indictments were announced, Mallamo was reported to be out of town. When he failed to appear at two separate arraignments, Newcomb raised his bond from $2,000 to $4,000 along with those of the still fugitive leaders of the Big House. On July 5, Mallamo turned himself in and was released after posting the higher bond. During arguments to have the bond reduced, attorney Mock claimed his client was taking "treatments" in Hot Springs, Arkansas – a known haven for on-the-lam underworld figures.

In late October, the three South Side House operators appeared before Newcomb. They had recently dismissed Russell Mock as counsel and retained James

Modarelli, who entered guilty pleas for the men. Mallamo was the first to be sentenced. On the afternoon of October 25, Newcomb sentenced "Big Dom" to a 90-day term, but told Mallamo if he were to obtain a defense industry job he would consider granting work privileges. The next morning, when Gioia and Fezzuogho were sentenced, Modarelli asked for the same consideration. Newcomb denied the request stating that of the three defendants only Mallamo had a clean record. Gioia and Fezzuogho received 90-day terms. For the trio of South Side House operators the judge suspended 30 days each on the remaining eleven counts against them; each man was fined $4,000.

The 39-year-old Mallamo began his 90-day sentence in the Mahoning County jail on November 4. In less than three weeks his release on probation to find a job created a heated controversy. At his sentencing Newcomb advised Mallamo's counsel, "Get a bona fide 100 percent war plant job and I'll let him out of jail 10 hours a day, eight to work to help the war effort and one to go to work on and the tenth to get back to jail. Remember that it's got to be a real war job and has to stand up under the investigation of the Mahoning County probation office."

When this was announced in court Special Prosecutor Leis was opposed to the motion, but was assured by Newcomb that a "full notice" of hearing would take place prior to any specific action. When the probation release was issued Newcomb admitted that he "had overlooked" his promise to Leis, but claimed his decision would have been the same.

In allowing Mallamo time to look for employment the judge also granted him time off for the Thanksgiving holiday. While Leis was upset at this turn of events, Mahoning County Sheriff Elser was incensed – especially when, on the heels of the Mallamo release, he received a second notice from Newcomb for slot machines racketeer, Dominic "Moosey" Caputo, to be given a holiday furlough. A disgusted Elser stated, "It looks as though the county jail will be turned into a hotel and the prisoners can come and go as they please." Elser said he would place two large signs outside the jail:

WANTED: HOTEL CLERKS
WANTED: BELL HOPS

"If we're running a hotel with in-and-out privileges, we've got to have experienced hotel help," Elser stated with added sarcasm. He continued, "With the annoying racketeering that we've had in this district and with the work we had to get these fellows where they belong, I had a feeling of Thanksgiving that they were where they belonged. I hoped that they would stay there and I'm speaking as one who has two sons and 11 nephews in the service."

Commenting on Mallamo the sheriff added, "It is thoughtful of these boys at this late hour suddenly to become patriotic and take up defense work which they so neglected. No doubt the war will end much sooner when they are all in defense work. Not too many weeks ago, they had never known nor cared to learn what it meant to earn a few dollars by the sweat of their brow."

On November 27, Mahoning County Probation Officer George F. Hadnett notified Sheriff Elser that Mallamo had landed a job. Elser told reporters, "There is nothing else I can do but release the man. I hope the arrangement turns out to be satisfactory." Mallamo was released daily from 7:00 a.m. until 6:00 p.m. to work for the Ohio Valley Roofing & Painting Company. His job called for him to clean furnaces for repainting. Hadnett was asked, "Is that war work?"

"I'm satisfied that it's war work. It's supposed to be," answered the probation officer.

As the Christmas Holiday season neared, Judge Newcomb again drew criticism as he released Mallamo, Caputo and Frank Cassano, a partner of "Moosey's," for another "vacation." This time the judge caught the wrath of the Ohio assistant attorney general. During a heated exchange Newcomb explained his decision, "These men received the stiffest fines and penalties in Ohio for their misdemeanors. In 55 or 60 other counties, slot machines are operating, and in other cities this type of misdemeanor brings a $10 fine and 15 days suspended." Newcomb told the assistant attorney general that the "court of appeals is wide open to you."

On December 23 a *Vindicator* editorial questioned Newcomb's logic:

> "Is the judge saying that he crucified these men in response to the clamor of the crowd? Either these men had jail sentences coming to them, or they did not. If on second thought he feels he did wrong, he should say so frankly and commute the sentences, instead of granting these vacations from jail which have the aspect of special favors."

Sheriff Elser was not only irate at the new holiday release, but also by the work release accommodations extended on Mallamo's behalf. Initially, "Big Dom's" release schedule was ten hours – eight for work and two for travel. By mid-December they were extended to 13 hours. Elser questioned why "it took five hours for him to get back and forth to county jail." When the request came for Mallamo's Christmas release, Elser denied it because it did not come to him in the form of a court order, but rather as an "authorization" from Hadnett the probation officer. Even though Elser denied the "authorization," after his work was completed Christmas Eve, instead of reporting back to the county jail, Mallamo headed home to spend the holiday with family members. Around 1:00 p.m. Christmas Day, Mallamo was arrested at his home and taken back to the jail. An hour later a hastily called hearing was held at the home of Judge J.H.C. Lyon, who was ill since summer. Elser, who was also ill at the time, got up from his sick bed to answer the writ of habeas corpus. Unable to get anyone from the prosecutor's staff to serve as his legal counsel, Elser arrived at Lyon's home, with Mallamo and two deputies, prepared to act as his own counsel.

The four men were met at the judge's house with Hadnett and several court officials. The encounter between Elser and Hadnett was not a pleasant one. Hadnett admitted that he had told Mallamo to disregard the sheriff's orders. "This is Christmas Day – were all Christians," barked Hadnett, "and I'm tired of being tormented and sick and tired of being dragged into court on these petty larceny cases. I'm not taking a judge's job but when I'm given orders by a judge I can carry out those orders."

Hadnett told Lyons that he was constantly harassed by the press and others since Mallamo was assigned to him. "It isn't easy to carry out court orders when there is no cooperation, but I try to do my best for the persons placed in my care regardless of who they are."

When it was Elser's turn to speak he told the judge he had interpreted the "authorization" to mean that it was up to his discretion to release Mallamo. "I'm not riding this man," Elser explained. He was simply refusing to release him because "morale at the county jail is terrible. I did this for the good of all the prisoners and the conduct in the jail," the sheriff stated.

Judge Lyon's decision was to enforce the request in Newcomb's letter and allow Mallamo to report back to the jail at 7:00 p.m. December 27 (Mallamo was granted an additional 24 hours of freedom due to his Christmas "interruption"). After the hearing Elser and his deputies delivered Mallamo to his front door. Elser then checked himself into a hospital.

On December 27, in an editorial titled "Fast Footwork for Mallamo," the *Vindicator* stated, "Yes, the machinery of the law spun so fast it smoked. And like an overheated motor, it smelled bad. It showed again that there is one sort of treatment for one criminal, another sort for a crook who has money, influence, and good friends in office."

On New Year's Eve, Mallamo was granted another three-day "vacation" by Newcomb. On February 1, 1944, Mallamo was released at the end of his 90-day sentence. Incredibly, Mallamo, who was later called the "Valley's one true Godfather," was out of the public eye for nearly two decades. By that time his nephew, Vincenzo "Jimmy" Prato, was making a name for himself in the Mahoning Valley underworld. Mallamo owned and operated the Workingman's Club on East Federal Street, before retiring in 1965. Mallamo died on April 14, 1987, at South Side Hospital after a two-month illness. He was 82 years old.

Days after Mallamo's release, his partners, Fezzuogho and Gioia completed their sentences. Fezzuogho's name would not surface again until February 1954, when he was named as a "principle" in a federal probe investigating gambling in Youngstown. In November 1956, he was one of 14 gamblers questioned about a series of bombings in the area. When Fezzuogho died, on February 14, 1979, at the age of 73, the obituary claimed he was a "retired self-employed salesman."

Except for a traffic violation, for driving without a license, Frank Gioia kept a low profile until February 5, 1948. During one of Chief Edward Allen's early crusades, a police raid headed by Vice Squad Chief Sergeant Dan Maggianetti resulted in the seizure of 125 cases of bug books – containing 1.5 million numbers slips, valued at $1,500 – in a Mahoning Avenue warehouse. The bug book consignment bore the name of Frankie Joy. The confiscation was the largest of its kind in Youngstown history.

Gioia was arrested and locked up in the city jail where Allen questioned him. It was a repeat performance of his arrest in 1943 when Gioia said he was no longer involved in the South Side House lottery operation. He now told Allen he was a bug writer prior to Mayor Henderson taking office on January 1, 1948. Gioia said he had "been doing nothing" since then.

Gioia appeared before Judge Frank P. Anzellotti the next day for arraignment, where he pled not guilty. His attorney John R. Hooker, who arrived late at court and asked the judge if the plea could be withdrawn and the arraignment postponed, claimed his client would "lose certain rights" if he pleaded now. Declaring that he had not had sufficient time to review all the material, Hooker stated he believed the search warrant and subsequent arrest were illegal.

Granted the delay, a few days later Hooker filed motions to dismiss the case stating that the arrest of his client was illegal because 1) the city ordinance "holds that books must be used in gambling before any indictment can be returned," and 2) Gioia was not at the warehouse when the policy books were found. Anzellotti dismissed the motions and Gioia pled not guilty on February 11 and demanded a trial by jury.

At Gioia's trial in April, an employee of the warehouse testified that between November 1946 and January 1948, some 237 boxes of policy books were delivered to the facility of which 112 were removed. Sergeant Maggianetti told the jury that Gioia "freely admitted" to him that he was in the numbers business for more than a decade and that he averaged more than $300 a day in receipts. In his closing arguments, attorney Hooker reiterated that possession of a blank piece of paper or book of blank pages, which were not used "is not considered gambling." During the trial Hooker had helped support his point by calling police officers that testified they used seized blank lottery books for scratch pads at the city jail. Hooker called the pads harmless pieces of paper and said, "It can't be a crime until two people get together, place a wager and then record it."

Once the jury began its deliberations Gioia raised a few eyebrows by speaking with Lou Tiberio and Anthony Gianfrancesco, both known numbers racketeers, outside the courtroom.

After four hours of deliberations on April 22, a jury of eight women and four men were deadlocked at 7 to 5 in favor of guilty. Judge Anzellotti dismissed the jurors and declared a mistrial. A second trial was scheduled to begin on June 3. Just as jury selection got underway, Gioia, against the advice of attorney

Hooker, pled guilty. Anzellotti fined Gioia $100 and ordered him to pay $68 in court costs, which included empanelling the jury. The judge then ordered the 125 blank lottery books to be destroyed in the city's incinerator.

On July 7, 1950, Gioia was arrested for possession of lottery slips and pled not guilty. Three times he requested that a preliminary hearing be postponed to allow him time to retain counsel. On August 17, without an attorney, Gioia pled guilty and was fined the maximum of $500 by Anzellotti. Gioia paid $100 of the fine immediately, but had to be threatened with arrest before the balance was paid in March 1951.

Since his indictment in 1943, Gioia was referred to in the newspapers as a "top racketeer" and "notorious bug man." That persona changed in April 1953 when he was arrested for assaulting a 15 year-old boy. Gioia was now a "former petty racketeer." His latest arrest followed an egg-throwing incident in which a window was broken at his Olteanul Cultural & Athletic Club on Myrtle Avenue. Gioia chased a gang of youths, but apparently grabbed an innocent teenager and roughed him up. He was fined $100 and given a suspended 30-day sentence. It was the last time Gioia was mentioned in the newspapers.

The era of the Lottery Houses exposed "faction siding" in both the police department and the justice system in Youngstown in the late 1930s and early 1940s. Justice prevailed though. But while the era was relatively a non-violent one, the one that eventually replaced it would not be.

Section I Notes

1 James "Jimmy" LaCapra would never testify against Adam Richetti. Released on January 2, 1935, he was told by an FBI agent to get out of the country for his own safety. Instead, LaCapra went to New York. On August 21, 1935, his body, riddled with bullets, was left on a highway near New Paltz, New York, a town just west of Poughkeepsie.

2 In August 1997 Robert Unger, head of the Urban Journalism Program at the University of Missouri-Kansas City and whose credentials could fill a small filing cabinet, published *The Union Station Massacre*. The 13-year project was based on the FBI's own files and attacked the FBI's most sacred department - the crime lab. Unger's conclusions, again based on the FBI's own files, proved that three of the massacre victims - escaped prisoner Frank Nash, Kansas City Police Officer Frank Hermanson and FBI Agent Raymond J. Caffrey - all received fatal wounds from a shotgun fired by FBI Agent Joe Lackey. Seated behind Frank Nash in one of the automobiles, Lackey was not familiar with how the shotgun operated and, more importantly, was not authorized to carry it.

3 Pictures of the building clearly show the establishment's name as "Tesone's Tavern." A check of the 1930 census shows a James and Michelena Tisone listed, while a great many Tesones are also shown as living in the Youngstown. The *Vindicator* always referred to the establishment as "Tisones."

4 The investigation into Mike Russell's death indicated that he was murdered because "he knew too much" about several gang leaders who were charged with evading income taxes and about to go on trial. Mike Russell's cousin, William "Big Bill" Lias, was the "reputed king" of the Wheeling numbers rackets who earned his moniker from the 400-plus pounds he carried. Russell's wife was charged with the murder of Lias' first wife. She was acquitted in a court trial. A Marino family member suggested that because of Roy and Mike Russell's friendship that "Wheeling gangdom may have wished to shut 'Happy' up." Mike Russell was murdered four days prior to his trial on an income tax conspiracy charge in Clarksburg, West Virginia. His cousin, Theodore Russell, pled guilty in federal court and announced he was "ready to tell all." Despite his release on bail Theodore Russell decided to remain at the Harrison County jail in West Virginia fearing gang retaliation.

5 The six accused Youngstown police officers were Charles Grisdale, Edward Hinman, Joseph Ernst, Herman Mathieu, Joseph Lepo and Steve Birnich.

6 On February 13, 1941, three weeks after his testimony, Captain Charles N.

Richmond collapsed in the Youngstown Police Department. He was rushed to St. Elizabeth's Hospital where he died six hours later of a heart attack. Richmond was a police officer for 28 years. He was born in Cleveland on October 8, 1887, and arrived in Youngstown in 1912. The next year he was appointed to the police department. During his career Richmond served as chief of the vice squad three different times. He also served on the detective bureau. Richmond made sergeant in 1925 and was promoted to captain in 1939. Richmond was on duty on June 19, 1937, when two men were fatally wounded during the "Little Steel" strike. He was a key witness during the National Labor Relations Board investigative hearing. Richmond was said to be the best marksman in the Youngstown Police Department. He was 54 years old.

7 Sergeant William Davis later estimated the damage at $300. A fund, initiated by subscribers of the *Vindicator*, raised $5.35 for the repairs. Workers at the Truscon Steel Company contributed $11.40 to the fund and attached the following note:

"Racketeers Pay for Protection –
Can We?"

"Such acts of violence as the recent bombing of Sergeant Davis' home are a challenge to the citizens of Youngstown as well as to our law enforcing officers. We accept the challenge.

"This contribution for repairs to Sergeant Davis's home serves as an indication of our desire to stand behind our honest law officers in their efforts to clean our city of rackets."

– Office Employees of Truscon Steel Co.

8 In November 1947, John Palermo ran for the Second Ward council seat as a Democrat and was elected.

9 Simon Leis was a staff prosecutor on the case of Anna Marie Hahn in 1938. Hahn was the first woman put to death in Ohio's electric chair for murder.

10 On June 5, 1951, it was reported that a deal was struck to turn the Poland Country Club into a private club for men and women golfers. Several physicians and Leonard Darnell of the *Boardman News* were said to be in negotiations. On July 20, the facility reopened as the Boardman Country Club. The following spring the club was "declared dead." Efforts to reopen faltered and in December 1955 Sam Budak filed for permission to sell it. The court approved the request the following month and while a pending deal was announced nothing more was reported until May 1961 when the Boardman Fire Department destroyed the Poland.

Section II

The 1940s

Photo courtesy of Library of Congress

"When these two teamed up in the white slave racket, some of the most brutal treatment of women that hardened Federal agents have ever investigated came to light. The pair appeared to enjoy hearing women, their 'slaves', scream for mercy and had the distorted belief that beating was the only way to keep the girls in line." – *Vindicator* reporter William Griffith describing "Sugar" Harrell and "Little Joe" Blumetti, February 20, 1944.

6

"Sugar" Harrell and the White Slave Trade

As in previous decades, prostitution and white slavery were a staple in the Mahoning Valley underworld. The 1940s, even with World War II raging, would be no different. During this period, Youngstown would serve host to a vicious white slavery ring that was international in nature.

In exposing all the sordid details of the ring, *Vindicator* reporter, Bill Griffith, wrote a six-part expose. His work commenced on February 20, 1944, with the following opening:

> **MOBSTERS SMASHED BY FBI TRAINED VICTIMS IN CITY;**
> **NAZI-LIKE TACTICS LED TO DOWNFALL**
>
> "Federal agents smashed one of the biggest and cruelest gang of white slave rings ever uncovered in Ohio when they rounded up eight procurers who used Youngstown as headquarters and shunted women around the country and to Honolulu. A two-year investigation revealed that the gang trained their 'women' here and held them under continuous threats by beating, clubbing and stabbing them. This is one of a series of stories about activities of the mobsters and their leader, handsome Baxter Lee 'Sugar' Harrell."

Although Griffith used a fictitious name for the tragic young lady in his series, the newspapers had already identified her as Fay Miller. The story begins in the late 1930s with Miller running away from home, a small coal-mining town in Pennsylvania, and heading to New York City with the dream of becoming professional model. Griffith notes she "had flashy blue eyes, shapely legs, and a well-formed body." After several weeks of being turned away at all the top modeling agencies, Miller walked into a bar on 51st Street in Manhattan, perhaps to drown her sorrows. Instead, Miller met a handsome young man with wavy hair and blue/gray eyes. "I've been following you for several blocks," the man said. "You're in trouble, aren't you?"

After explaining her streak of bad luck, the man offered to buy her dinner at a nearby restaurant where she could finish her tale of woe. As they left the bar the young man said, "They call me Sugar."

"Sugar" was Baxter Lee Harrell, Jr. He was born in 1910 in Indiahoma, Oklahoma, where his criminal career began when he was 11 years old. It was said that "his suave manner made him popular with the girls, who nicknamed him Sugar." Harrell started out with a record of forgery, safe-cracking, and counterfeiting, but with the way he attracted women he soon focused on the white slave trade. By the mid-1930s, Harrell had become a major operator and earned a new nickname, the "coat hanger slasher," due to the vicious beatings he gave to keep his women in line.

Harrell took a liking to Miller and slept with her several times. He then rented a room for her and began sending over men to have sex with her. He convinced her there was good money to be made as a prostitute and with her looks Harrell had little trouble getting top dollar for her. Afraid of losing her, however, Harrell took Miller to Elkton, Maryland, in 1938 and married her. During the mid-1930s there was a vice crackdown in New York City, so Harrell removed his young bride to Youngstown where he had friends.

In Youngstown Harrell's friends were George "Taxi" Elkovitz, involved in the procuring of "customers" for prostitutes for more than 20 years; William Clark, alias Bill Murphy, another customer hustler; Philip "Cueball" Poghen, alias Philip Rose, a small-time racketeer in the city for 15 years; and Joseph Thomas "Little Joe" Blumetti, who operated a brothel at 237 East Boardman Street with his wife, Doris.

Harrell and Elkovitz were close friends until an incident one night in March 1940 when the two got into an argument with a bar owner on Wilson Avenue, who threw them out. Later, the two drove past the place and one fired a shotgun blast through the front door. The owner was seriously wounded and spent several weeks in the hospital recovering. Elkovitz was later arrested and charged with shooting with intent to wound. Despite the case being dropped due to lack of evidence, Harrell and Elkovitz paid all of the man's medical expenses. The incident led to a parting of the ways between Harrell and Elkovitz. Sugar, it was reported, "grew to dislike him for his weakness, since it was 'Taxi' who insisted that the hospital bills be paid."

Harrell had a stronger relationship with Blumetti, who could be just as vicious as he was. In the fall of 1938, Blumetti was arrested for possession and passing counterfeit ten-dollar bills. He was turned over the Secret Service, who in turn handed him over to the U.S. Marshal. The case against him apparently wasn't strong enough as charges were dismissed on December 7. Blumetti's rap sheet showed arrests for suspicion in Philadelphia and Youngstown. During the war he was convicted of making a false statement to the Selective Service. Bill Griffith described Blumetti:

> "A swarthy Youngstown-born Italian, 'Little Joe' had a record of passing counterfeit before Sugar met him. He had two years of high school education and was 'smart' as the rackets go.
>
> "When these two teamed up in the white slave racket, some of the most brutal treatment of women that hardened Federal agents have ever investigated came

> to light. The pair appeared to enjoy hearing women, their 'slaves', scream for mercy and had the distorted belief that beating was the only way to keep the girls in line."

In Youngstown, Harrell placed Miller in a brothel run by Doris Blumetti. Doris, who used the name Elizabeth Florence Blumetti, was in her second foray as a Madame. She had once operated a house in Canton under the name Ginger Brooks. Over Easter weekend 1940, a bandleader from Buffalo had his orchestra in town to play an engagement. After the show he paid a visit to Blumetti's place where he bedded down with the house's top earner, Fay Miller. The next night he returned and told her, "You don't belong in this place." Urging Miller to join him, she agreed and began to pack a bag. Her departure was interrupted when Harrell entered the room.

"I'm going away, Sugar," Miller told her husband.

"I never expected you would do anything like that," Harrell calmly replied. "Okay, you could leave, but you're not on your own." He then told her he would take her back if things didn't work out.

Surprised at his reaction, Miller promised to call when she arrived in Buffalo. After completing an engagement in Cleveland, the bandleader returned to Buffalo where Miller remembered her promise to call. Several nights later Miller was relaxing in the Buffalo Club where her new lover was performing. There was a small commotion in the club and Miller was suddenly confronted by Harrell and Joe Blumetti. Sugar ordered Miller out to the car.

All the way back to Youngstown Harrell beat Miller relentlessly as "Little Joe" drove – singing, laughing, and whistling to drown out her screams. At one point Harrell told Blumetti to stop the car. He got out and found a large stick. When he returned he began striking Miller, who raised her arms to ward off the blows. Sugar beat her until she could no longer keep her hands up to protect herself. After arriving in Youngstown, she was taken to a downtown hotel. Miller described what happened next:

> "Sugar, then went to a clothes closet and brought out a wire coat hanger. He pulled the wire out straight and told Miller to take off her two-piece suit.
>
> "'I begged him not to beat me anymore but he pulled off my jacket and began to beat me across the head and back with the wire,' Miller said. 'He blacked both my eyes so I could not see and my body was black and blue all over.'"

Miller lay in bed for weeks, prevented from seeing a doctor, before she could get up. Harrell stopped by once to tell her, "I beat you because I loved you. I didn't mean to hit you so hard." From that day on the beating Miller received served as a warning to the other women about "loyalty" and "holding out" any earnings.

Several of the operators enjoyed giving a beating to the girls just to keep them in line. One of these sadistic individuals was Philip Poghen. Slim and fair-skinned, Poghen was called "Cueball" because of his bald head. Convicted of a robbery in Beaver County, Pennsylvania, in 1933 he served a prison stretch until December 1939. Poghen became a panderer and bookmaker and once served a 90-day term after pleading guilty to a grand jury indictment after a vice investigation. Poghen opened an establishment on East Federal Street, where he sold soft drinks and got involved in petty gambling. His club soon catered to "minors who had strayed." By now Poghen, who like Sugar and Little Joe brought his wife into the trade, had hooked up with Harrell and soon began to employ "Sugar's methods."

One night a "working girl" from one of the other houses dropped by to have a drink with her sister. Poghen asked the young woman if she would consider working for him, but she politely declined. Poghen and one of the bartenders forced the sisters into a car and drove them out to a lonely country road. Poghen inquired again if the woman would work for him. This time when she refused he punched her in the mouth. He then pulled a revolver and began beating her about the head and shoulders. This was followed by slashing the young woman's hand with a knife, cutting her finger to the bone. She was then shoved out of the car, landing and breaking her right elbow. Poghen then drove off with her sister. After a passing motorist found the injured woman she was hospitalized for eight days.

Like Harrell had done with Miller, the ring members lured women by spending money on them and then convincing them that by being "smart" they could earn big money. Edward Dailey, the youngest member of the ring at 32, made his contribution by "furnishing" teenaged girls to the trade. Many of the young girls he persuaded were taught their "craft" at a house run by Helen Marcus on West Wood Street.

The ring prospered through 1940 and into 1941 with casualties happening to both the women and the men. The working girls were not supposed to have a night off. One, however, received permission from one of the Madame's to take in a movie one night. When Harrell arrived and demanded to know where the woman was, the Madame got scared and said she had left without permission. When she returned from the movie, Harrell beat her bloody while she screamed for mercy. With both eyes blackened and blood sopping through her dress, Harrell, "just for a lesson," made her finish the night working.

On July 28, 1941, someone tried to get even with "Little Joe" Blumetti at his East Boardman Street brothel. Police were not sure if it was a customer or a business rival. No consideration was given to the fact that it could have been one of Blumetti's beating victims. Around 4:00 a.m. that morning, "Little Joe" smelled something burning and went to the window to investigate. Someone had placed a bomb on the windowsill. As Blumetti pulled aside the window shade the bomb went off. Debris from the blast blew in, hitting "Little Joe" in the face and eyes. When he was released from the hospital he was forced to wear dark glasses due to permanent damage to his eyes.

In February 1941, Harrell decided to reward Miller, in the wake of the vicious beating he gave her, for her renewed faithfulness. The reward was a vacation to Honolulu, Hawaii. Harrell drove her to Los Angeles, put her on a steamer and then went to San Diego, where he had "girls on call."

Miller avoided the longing glances of men on the boat eyeing a beautiful woman traveling alone. Once in Honolulu, however, Miller saw the enlisted men flocking in from the Pearl Harbor Naval Base with pockets full of money. Miller forgot about the vacation and went to work. By the time she returned to the United States in July she had put away $5,000. Miller was met by Harrell and Blumetti. After purchasing a new automobile for her husband, she told him all about her new found wealth. Harrell then talked Miller into buying him a ranch in Indiahoma, where he grew up. All the time he was thinking about how to empty the pockets of those sailors. Shortly after settling into his new home Harrell told Miller and Blumetti to pack. They were headed back to Youngstown to round up all the money earners for a sabbatical to the Hawaiian Islands.

Doris Blumetti and Fay Miller began telling the women about the wonderful opportunities abroad. Eddy Dailey and another ring member, Sam Conti, got their girls together while Miller drove to Campbell to get William Clark to recruit more women. It was during this recruitment mission that the bomb went off at Blumetti's place. Included in the group of women headed for the future 50th state were the five ringleaders' wives.

Between September and October, thirteen women traveled to Honolulu where Miller booked hotel rooms. She purchased "entertainers licenses," which permitted the women to "loiter about bars, clubs, and other places where soldiers and sailors gather." The normal fee for sex was $3.50. One of the women later told a Federal agent she made $3,000 in 40 days, but it was "hard traffic." Several of the women, exhausted, sailed for home and hospitals. Not all the profits the girls collected were earned on their backs. Many of the girls quickly discovered a drunken sailor and his money were soon parted. The money train came to a crashing halt, however, on December 7, 1941, "a day that will live in infamy."

Before the women left Hawaii, FBI agents working out of the Cleveland office were gathering information about the ring. Special Agent in Charge, Lee V. Boardman, was placed in charge of the Cleveland office around the time Miller returned from Honolulu the first time. Evidence gathered by the veteran agent showed that he was dealing with a vicious gang of white slavers. He wanted an airtight case. It would not be until almost two years after the Japanese bombed Pearl Harbor that the FBI would make their first arrest.

During the early morning hours of September 28, 1943, government agents, backed by detectives from the Youngstown Police Department, surrounded Sam Conti's "bawdy house" on East Boardman Street. When an agent pounded on the door Fay Miller stuck her head out of an upstairs window and hollered down, "We're closed. Come back tomorrow." She then slammed the window. The agent then took the butt of his gun and banged louder. Miller then opened the door dressed in a revealing red negligee. She complained, "Why don't you drunks..." The words stuck in her throat as a badge was thrust in her face and the lawman stated, "We're Federal Agents. We want to talk to you." Arrested along with Miller were Sam Conti and George Elkovitz.

The two-year investigation was exhaustive. In addition to gathering evidence in the small towns of Ohio – Dennison, Sandusky, Canton, Warren, Niles, and Campbell – the investigation took the FBI to Buffalo, Chicago, Miami, New York City, Oklahoma, Philadelphia, Pittsburgh, San Diego, San Francisco, Seattle, and finally Honolulu. Agents found that the women were being trained in "perversion – atrocities that the average American would believe could happen only in Nazi-controlled countries or Jap prison camps." Yet this training was being conducted in Youngstown, Campbell, and Buffalo, and the women were being sent throughout the country to earn money for the ringleaders.

After the exodus from Honolulu, more and more women were "recruited" by Harrell and his men. Federal Agents questioned hundreds of "girl inmates" across the country in building an "airtight" case. Perhaps the most lascivious activity took place in the Ohio cities of Dennison and Sandusky. In those towns agents were told one-third of the "visitors" were high school boys 16 years old.

Agents moved quickly to arrest all of the conspirators. Local police departments arrested 14 women while 7 procurers were swept up. One man that slipped through the dragnet was Sugar Harrell.

Conti and Elkovitz pled not guilty and were held under $15,000 bond each. Miller was held as a material witness under a $10,000 bond. On October 28, the two men were joined by Blumetti, Poghen, Dailey, Clark, and the fugitive Harrell in being indicted on charges of conspiring to transport women from Youngstown to Honolulu "for prostitution, debauchery, and other immoral purposes." William Clark was arrested in the Allegheny County Workhouse, where he was serving a sentence for burglary. The wives of six of the men were named as unindicted co-conspirators. On November 10, all of the jailed procurers pled guilty and were sentenced by a federal judge in Cleveland to terms ranging from two to six years, but not before he gave them all a severe tongue lashing. Blumetti, Poghen, and Elkovitz received the longest sentences. Blumetti was sent to the Federal Penitentiary in Leavenworth to serve a six-year term, which was to run concurrent with his sentence for making false statements to the Selective Service.

Doris Blumetti and Josephine Zanghi were arrested in Rochester, New York and charged with perjury. They pleaded guilty on December 13 and were sentenced to 90 days. Sam Carroll, alias Sam Cariola, was indicted for transporting his wife, Zanghi, for immoral purposes and was sentenced to three years.

After a nationwide manhunt, Sugar Harrell was captured at his home in Indiahoma. From Washington D.C., J. Edgar Hoover announced the arrest, which, ironically, came on the second anniversary of the bombing of Pearl Harbor. Harrell was arraigned in Lawton, Oklahoma where he pled not guilty to violating the Mann Act.[1] He was taken to Cleveland and held on a $20,000 bond. On February 15, 1944, Baxter Lee "Sugar" Harrell pleaded guilty to charges of violating and conspiracy to violate the Mann Act. He was sentenced to seven years in federal prison.

After his release Harrell returned to Oklahoma. In May 1954, he was found guilty in Comanche County of unlawful possession of two cases of whiskey and sentenced to 30 days in jail and a fine of $100. In February 1961, he was found guilty in Kiowa County of the same charges and received the same punishment. That was the last that was heard from him. Joseph Blumetti would surface again in the late 1950s.

"This is a Christian nation and yet we must wait until gangsters shoot down their fellow gangsters in our streets before the mayor of the city does anything about it." – February 22, 1942. Dr. Donald P. Montgomery, pastor of Pleasant Grove United Presbyterian Church, criticizing the belated response of Mayor William A. Spagnola to the killing of William Scodras. Spagnola ordered Turnbull "to rid the city of gangdom."

7

The Short Career of the "Sledgehammer" – Jerry Pascarella

The Mahoning Valley seemed to produce a charismatic gangster in just about every decade. In the 1940s that distinction went to Jerry "the Sledgehammer" Pascarella. Young and handsome, his criminal career, and his life, was over by the time he 23 years old.

Jerry Pascarella was barely out of his teens when he first got involved in the slot machine rackets. During his early venture into the "one-armed bandits," the newspaper reported Pascarella was told by Dominic "Moosey" Caputo that he couldn't continue to operate unless he "kicked in to the slots king." The newspaper didn't identify who the "slots king" was and it didn't matter to Pascarella anyway because he wasn't paying. Instead, after being forced out of business, Pascarella appointed himself head of a one-man vice crusade and over the next few weeks raided local bars and stores destroying every slot machine he found with a sledgehammer.

In his new role as vice crusader, Pascarella told the newspaper, "The sooner the city gets those slots out of this town, the better off we'll all be." Local gamblers saw it differently. They felt the sooner they got rid of Pascarella, the better off they would be. On September 16, 1941, two Caputo associates, Frank Carey and Frank Chako, "invited" Pascarella to join them for a late night ride. They released their passenger on a deserted road in Trumbull County and, being sporting men, gave him a chance to run while they took turns shooting at him. Pascarella filed a police report and Captain Eugene McEvoy and members of the vice squad arrested the two Franks the next day. Carey and Chako said they heard they were wanted and were on their way to give themselves up when they were apprehended. At the Mahoning County prosecutor's office, Pascarella, represented by Dominic Rendinell and former Youngstown police chief Kedgwin Powell, had an affidavit prepared charging the two men with kidnapping. The two attorneys argued over the document – Rendinell urging his client to sign it and Powell opposing it. Pascarella left without signing the affidavit. The police continued to hold both men on a suspicion charge. In the end, the threat by Caputo's men proved to be in vain as Pascarella not only survived the target practice, but also kept up his "raids" until Christmas 1941.

In early February 1942, Carey tracked down Pascarella in a restaurant at the Pick-Ohio Hotel. With Carey fingering what appeared to be a gun in his pocket, Pascarella leaped behind a counter and ordered the cashier to call the police. When she refused, Pascarella came out from behind the counter and was confronted by Carey again. Both men were armed and faced each other with one hand in their pocket. Carey, after assessing the situation – and the number of witnesses – walked out.

On the night of February 18, Pascarella had plans to go downtown to see a movie. He stopped at a dairy store he frequented at the corner of Madison and Fifth Avenues for a cup of coffee. While Pascarella drank his coffee William "Billy the Greek" Scodras entered the store and began pacing nervously about, walking to the front door several times to look out. After purchasing a candy bar he stepped outside. A witness recalled Scodras then opened the door and called to Pascarella, "Come on out, Jerry, we got it all planned and we want to talk it over."

Pascarella stepped out onto the sidewalk. He later told detectives, "'Billy the Greek' jumped aside and two guys started to fire." Apparently Scodras didn't jump fast enough. A bullet ripped through his neck severing the jugular vein. Scodras managed to make it across the street to a filling station where he told the proprietor, "I've been shot." He was barely alive when he arrived at St. Elizabeth's Hospital. Scodras died a short time later.

Pascarella claimed, "I saw one, a guy with a large nose, and I lunged at him. I think I hit his gun. Then I slipped on the ice and fell. While I was on my stomach I looked up just in time to see him level his gun at me and fire." Pascarella was wounded in the left shoulder, the bullet exiting through his left arm. Women and children in the dairy store barely escaped injury as two bullets shattered a plate glass window and hit a cigarette machine inside. Meanwhile, Pascarella scurried to his feet as the killers were also making a mad dash. Pascarella went back into the store. Heading to the back door he fell again before he found refuge outside behind some oilcans. From this vantage point he watched his would-be assassins escape. Pascarella ran to his car, which was parked on Fifth Avenue, but was unable to start it. He then entered McCready's Drug Store where he cried out for someone to take him to the hospital.

At St. Elizabeth's, Pascarella sat on an emergency room table smoking a cigarette while telling police that Frank Carey was one of the gunmen who fired at him. He even provided the officers with the license plate number of the getaway car. Pascarella said he had seen the vehicle on previous occasions and had warned John "Pinky" Walsh, an associate, to be aware of it.

Where Pascarella had once refused to sign an affidavit charging Carey with kidnapping, after the murder of Billy Scodras and his own wounding, he apparently forgot his underworld code of ethics against "ratting out" an assailant and now signed two different affidavits. Against the advice of his lawyer, Pascarella claimed Carey was the shooter and accused him of killing Scodras. Carey was arrested the next morning and told police he was at a movie during the time of the shooting. He was arraigned before Judge Peter B. Mulholland on February 24, and pleaded not guilty to both charges.

Pascarella soon had second thoughts. On February 28, Carey, represented by attorneys David Shermer and John R. Hooker, appeared in court. Defense counsel claimed they had 15 witnesses, "all good clean citizens," ready to testify on their client's behalf. When the once talkative Pascarella, and attorney Rendinell, failed to appear in court, City Prosecutor Forrest Cavalier dropped the charges due to insufficient evidence and Carey was released from jail.

After Pascarella's no-show performance in the courthouse his next act was to join the Army. Jerry failed in this patriotic endeavor as he received a medical discharge from the service. On November 2, 1943, he was arrested on the degrading charge of violating the city sidewalk ordinance. He was fined $10 and court costs.

On January 31, 1944, Pascarella made the front page again when he, "Pinky" Walsh and seven others were arrested in a gambling raid conducted by Mahoning County Sheriff Ralph E. Elser. As the sheriff's deputies rounded up the men and the evidence, one of the players commented, "I thought the green light was on?" To which a deputy replied, "The sheriff does not recognize green." Walsh, the alleged operator of the game, was fined $200 and Pascarella and the others were hit with $25 fines from Justice B. J. Rosensteel. Walsh did not have the money to pay the fine so Pascarella pulled out a roll of bills and peeled off the $200, after which he stated, "It would have been cheaper to have paid a lookout $10 a day." The *Vindicator*, in editorializing on Walsh's arrest, pointed out, "It should be noted, incidentally, that Pinky Walsh, proprietor of the gambling game, recently was paroled from the penitentiary on a robbery charge – another evidence of the too-familiar result of a loose parole system."

It didn't take long for Pascarella to make news again. Three days after the raid, Jerry was arrested for assault and battery after a 24 year-old woman told police he attacked her. Less than three hours later, the woman was arrested by vice officers after she was found soliciting soldiers in a bar on South Champion. Pascarella pled not guilty and was released on a $100 bail.

On February 24, 1945, shock waves from Cleveland reached the Valley as Nathan "Nate" Weisenberg was murdered on a Cleveland Heights street. Around 11:45 p.m., Weisenberg was in his automobile apparently talking to someone in a vehicle that had pulled alongside his on a suburban street. Two shotgun blasts rang out and the "slots baron," with his face partially blown away, died instantly.

The local newspapers reported that renewed warfare in the slot machine rackets had heated up due to a ban on local horse racing. The 60 year-old Weisenberg was considered the "king pin" of the slot machine rackets in Northeastern Ohio, or at least a figurehead representing Cleveland's notorious Mayfield Road Mob, for the past two decades. In recent months it was rumored that he was expanding his operations, allegedly moving into Mahoning, Summit and Trumbull Counties. Gamblers in the Valley reported that slot machines, belonging to a Youngstown operator with Cleveland connections, were disappearing from saloons, stores and other places in recent months.

On March 30, Pascarella was playing barbut in "Black Sam's," a gambling joint on East Federal Street. Jerry was down several hundred dollars early, but his luck changed as the night wore on and he won $500. During the course of his winning streak two other players became aggravated. One responded by spitting in Pascarella's face. During the commotion to settle the incident the other man threw a punch over one of the peacemakers and caught Jerry flush in the eye, causing it to blacken and swell. The men, who were both armed, threatened Pascarella and any of his "friends" who might choose to retaliate.

The next day, fearing for her son's safety, Pascarella's mother, Mrs. Edward Kurz, went to the gambling house and urged the operators to keep Jerry out of the place that night. Before entering the building, Kurz noticed a large automobile parked out front and got a close look at the man behind the wheel. When she returned home she described the man to her son. Pascarella told her, "You want to watch out for him. He's a bad guy." Later Kurz would identify the man through police photographs.

The same day Pascarella's mother visited the gambling house, Sheriff Elser received a tip that a killing would take place there. The sheriff was told that "a gang of outsiders were scheduled to move in on 'Black Sam's' place Saturday night, not particularly to take over the place...but, to 'settle some issues.'" At 5:00 p.m. on the evening of March 31, Elser's deputies raided "Black Sam's" and chased out 30 gamblers before ordering the place closed. Deputies found two large barbut tables, one they had busted apart just one week earlier, which was repaired by a pretty "good craftsman." The raiders must have been feeling their oats as they moved on to hit six more locations that night. The newspaper reported that the deputies:

1. Raided the Army & Navy Union Club on North Chestnut Street, confiscating liquor and beer.
2. Raided the Short Street Pool Room, on Short Street in Campbell where they smashed three of Frank Budak's slot machines.
3. Broke up a poker game at 208 Liberty Street in Lowellville.
4. Broke up a poker game at a soft drink parlor on Wilson Avenue in Struthers.
5. Broke up a third poker game at 216 Water Street in Lowellville, where they confiscated money and arrested the proprietor.

6. Raided the A. A. Social Club, for the second time in 8 days, where they seized a slot machine as well as beer and whiskey.

It was later rumored that the "tip" Sheriff Elser received came from Pascarella. Apparently this was not the end of the affair. Over the next few weeks, threats continued to emanate from the men who attacked Pascarella. Once, one of the men walked into a shop where Jerry was having his shoes polished. Fingering a weapon he stated, "I can use this if I want to." In another confrontation Pascarella was told, "They missed you last time, but I won't miss you. I'll be standing right in front of you." The continued threats prompted Pascarella to purchase a .38 police Colt revolver for protection.

In mid-April Pascarella divorced Ruth Snyder. He was already planning a May wedding with his new sweetheart, Sylvia Demming. This would be the fourth marriage for Demming, who met Pascarella when she was a manicurist in a downtown hotel. On Monday, April 23, Pascarella went to the bank and withdrew $1,500 with the intention of purchasing both an engagement and wedding ring. That afternoon Jerry placed Demming aboard a bus headed for Canton where she worked for relatives who owned a dress shop. Later that night he telephoned her. Demming would later recall, "He was cheerful...and promised to find an apartment for us." Before hanging up he promised to call the next night. He then headed off to the East Federal Street gambling den.

On Wednesday morning, April 25, a squad car in Cuyahoga Falls, a city located between Akron and Cleveland, found an abandoned Buick sedan along a side road six blocks from the business district. Police discovered fresh bloodstains in the trunk along with clumps of grass, weeds and soil. A check of the license plate showed it was issued to 23 year-old Jerry Pascarella of Youngstown.

The automobile was towed to the Cuyahoga Falls police station. Jerry's brother Ludwig "Wally" Pascarella arrived soon after being notified by the police. During a quick inspection he found his brother's black pocket comb, which Jerry always carried in his breast pocket, lying in the blood-soaked trunk. "That convinced me," Wally told newspaper reporters. "There is no chance Jerry is alive."

There were clods of mud inside on the car's floorboards and a cigarette butt was crushed out on the floor of the back seat. Pascarella had always taken meticulous care of his car leading his brother to theorize that it was not Jerry that drove the vehicle to its side street destination.

Investigators launched two theories about the disappearance. One, that it was brought about as a result of Pascarella's recent fight with the two men in the East Federal Street gambling den; second, that he was a casualty of the same warfare that had taken the life of Nate Weisenberg. While there was a flurry of newspaper reporting on both theories, the first one seemed to be laid to rest when the *Vindicator* reported on May 1 that, although the last two men seen in

Pascarella's company were the two he fought with, "Acquaintances said Jerry had 'patched up' his trouble with the men." This may have accounted for the fact that when Pascarella's apartment was searched police found the .38 Colt he had recently purchased. The newspaper also printed that neither of the men were questioned by the police even though it was reported one had told his lawyer, "I'm in plenty of trouble."

Cuyahoga Falls detective John Stewart was assigned to the case. A search behind the East Federal Street gambling house uncovered the remnants of numbers slips, which had recently been burned, and gravel similar to the type that was found in the trunk of Pascarella's Buick. Stewart's investigation revealed Pascarella was last seen at 10:30 Monday night in front of the gambling house. Pascarella had told his ex-wife, Ruth Snyder, and his cousin that he would call them between 11:00 and 11:30 that night and to make sure their line was clear.

Police focused their search for the body around a swampland area close to where the car was found. On Saturday, Wally Pascarella returned to Cuyahoga Falls to lead a Boy Scout Troop in a search of the swamp area. Both efforts proved to be fruitless. Detective Stewart advanced the theory that Pascarella was killed in Youngstown, the body transported elsewhere and the vehicle driven to Cuyahoga Falls to throw off investigators. He backed up his claim by pointing out that the automobile was out of gas when it was found. Another theory appeared in the *Vindicator* on April 28:

> "...assailants killed Pascarella in Youngstown, then drove the body to Akron to make it appear that he was mixed up in the slots row which resulted in the murder...of Nate Weisenberg, Cleveland slots baron.
>
> "A year ago the body of 'Whitey' Gladish, Cleveland slots operator was found 'dumped' in Cuyahoga Falls."

Why Cuyahoga Falls would be selected as a dumping ground for mob victims was never explained. In 1981, however, the burned out automobile that mob hitman Joe DeRose, Jr. was last seen in was also abandoned in this community.

Police received an anonymous tip claiming Pascarella's body could be found between the towns of Hubbard and Coalburg in a swamp area beyond Swallow Tavern. It was here that police discovered a water filled mineshaft that they believed Jimmy Muche[2] and his automobile were left in after he disappeared in April 1937. A search there for Pascarella's body was unsuccessful. Searchers checked the Brimfield Kennel Club in Portage County where several Youngstown men owned an interest. All culverts located between Cuyahoga Falls and the Milton Dam were searched. Tourist cabins in the vicinity of Lake Milton, where Pascarella had spent a few nights before his disappearance, were also checked.

In early May, Sheriff Elser joined the investigation. He told reporters, "It appears that a murder has been committed in Mahoning County. My office is ready to give any assistance it can." He then indicated that the next 24 hours may bring "sensational developments." After interrogating a witness for four hours Elser announced he would be conducting a search at the Berlin Dam. The search was futile.

Suffering through this ordeal was Pascarella's mother and relatives who received endless telephone calls from anonymous sources. Some turned out to be cruel jokes and at one time Mrs. Kurz had to be placed under a doctor's care. As the investigation heated up strange things began to occur at the Wick Avenue home of Kurz. Around the end of April a person in an automobile began to keep surveillance on the home. One night someone moved close to the house and shined a flashlight through the window before being chased away by Wally Pascarella. On Tuesday, May 1, a mysterious woman knocked on the front door of the Kurz home. When Mrs. Kurz opened the door the lady told her, "I have come to let you know that Jerry is still living. He is being held, so don't worry." The lady left quickly and climbed into an automobile. Police theorized it might have been a woman who had called days earlier claiming to be an astrologer. Shortly after she left, Kurz received two phone calls from a young lady who claimed, "Jerry is all right. His sweetheart knows all."

Detective John Stewart was told that there was a celebration in a Youngstown bar after Pascarella's car was found abandoned. One of the men that Pascarella had words with reportedly left town after the disappearance and returned a week later. The night he came back, two anonymous phone calls were placed to the Kurz household by a woman who claimed he was in a Market Street nightclub spending lots of money and "bragging about getting paid for something."

Without offering details the *Vindicator* reported that, "One of the principals involved in the Pascarella case was a former sweetheart of 'Happy' Marino..." The newspaper wrote the next day that two female witnesses were threatened. One had received several "mysterious telephone calls," the other was warned that it wouldn't be "healthy" to continue to talk. Neither woman was identified as having been the "sweetheart" of Marino.

On August 30, two safety deposit boxes Pascarella kept at a downtown bank were opened. Although the family refused to disclose the contents, Wally had told investigators that his brother had intended to leave a letter behind "in case anything happens" to him.

Throughout the days after Pascarella's disappearance the hot rumor was that it was tied to the Nathan Weisenberg murder in Cleveland and the alleged renewal of slot machine activity in Youngstown. Pascarella's status in the slot machine rackets varied depending on which newspaper article you chose to believe. Here is a sampling of the reporting by the *Vindicator*:

> ***April 25*** – (the day he was reported missing) "In recent months Jerry is said to have placed some slot machines in outlying locations."

> ***April 26*** – "Papers which Jerry left behind indicated that his slot machine operations were on a grander scale than even his intimates suspected. He had telephone numbers and cards of numerous coin and amusement device dealers in Canton, New Kensington, Pennsylvania, Cleveland and other cities. Mrs. Kurz said several Cleveland men were bothering Jerry recently trying to get him to furnish them vest-pocket slot machines. There is every indication that Jerry had plenty of slots, probably 50 or more. Since the slaying of Nate Weisenberg...and the tightening of restrictions Jerry has had trouble placing the machines..."
>
> ***April 27*** – "The theory that Jerry was slain in slot machine warfare was discarded Thursday after it was learned from the mechanic who repaired Jerry's slots that he had sold all but two of his machines. These two were seized in a raid recently by the sheriff. 'Jerry hasn't been operating slots since the heat was turned on,' the repairman said."
>
> ***April 28*** – "Jerry had word that he could 'go' with two slot machines, informants say, and planned to drive to Cleveland Tuesday to purchase them from the man who sent him a telegram February 8. Jerry sold this man vest-pocket machines shortly before Weisenberg was slain."

As the investigation ground to a halt, information from investigators in both Cleveland and Youngstown was revealed. Papers left by Pascarella were said to link him to slain Cleveland businessman Nathan Weisenberg. It was alleged that at the time of Weisenberg's death that his henchmen were "moving in" on slot machine operations in both Lowellville and Struthers. Weeks prior to the February 23 murder of Weisenberg, a meeting was held at Anthony Milano's Italian Villa in what is now Richmond Heights, a small suburb on the eastern edge of Cuyahoga County. A deputy sheriff wrote down the license plate numbers of the automobiles which revealed the names of several underworld figures in and around Northeast Ohio. From the Youngstown area the names Charles Cavallaro and Howard C. Aley were reported; from Akron Michael Adella and Carl LaFatch; and from Lima George, Joseph and Louis Guagenti.

At this meeting it was alleged that plans to take over the slot machines in Northeast Ohio were discussed. Prompting this decision were several factors including the closing of houses of prostitution in Youngstown and the War Manpower Commission's decision to close the racetracks. All of this hampered the mob's ability to make money. Several recent gambling raids by Mahoning County Sheriff Elser didn't help matters either.

To recoup their losses the mobsters decided to go into slot machines "in a big way." In Youngstown, it was reported that the gambling "fraternity" was planning to operate "as openly as near-by Trumbull County," this obviously was referring to the success of the Jungle Inn. Without providing the name a *Vindicator* article claimed, "A big-time racketeer, who lives outside Cleveland and has close connections in Youngstown," sent word that there's plenty of money to be made in the slots business. He warned he could "come in and open them himself," if his directions were not followed locally. As for Pascarella's connection to these operators it was claimed that he was "counted out" of this new deal because he was "stepping on the toes" of the gamblers by demanding "cuts" from their profits. It was reported that local gamblers "feared he would hijack any new slot machines put out."

In Cuyahoga Falls, Detective John Stewart's investigation revealed in early May that Pascarella had disappeared two days after a gambler's "conference" was held in the restaurant of a downtown Youngstown hotel. The conference was held to discuss the return of slot machines to the Youngstown area with machines being placed at Craig Beach and Lake Milton. On May 3 the *Vindicator* reported:

> "There were five men in the conference, including the top slots machine operator in the county. It was learned that Jerry approached the group and asked, 'How about my deal?' One of the gamblers, it is said, got up and walked away saying: 'Oh to hell with you.'
>
> "From other sources it was learned that Jerry had been given an opportunity to 'go legitimate.' It is said he was offered proprietorship or a 'piece' of one of three taverns which the 'syndicate' was considering purchasing as spots for machines.
>
> "Jerry is reported to have refused this offer saying: 'I can do better with my method. Nobody's going to stand in my way.'"

Nine days after the shotgun murder of Nate Weisenberg a coroner's inquiry was held, and Dr. Samuel R. Gerber of Cleveland ordered the arrest of James Licavoli the prime suspect. Licavoli made himself scarce for the next three and a half months. While on the lam Licavoli lived for a short while at a downtown Youngstown hotel. It may have been this hotel where Pascarella walked in on the meeting. Coincidentally, it was while Licavoli was hiding in the Youngstown area that Pascarella disappeared.

On June 15, 1945, Licavoli was arrested by Cuyahoga County deputies as he chatted with a group of men at the North Randall racetrack outside of Cleveland. During questioning, Licavoli claimed he had spent a "lot of time around Cleveland, Youngstown and Warren" since the murder of Weisenberg. He denied being involved in the slot machine and pinball rackets. He claimed that at the time of the Weisenberg murder he was chatting with an attractive cashier in a Cleveland bowling alley.

With Licavoli's capture the coroner's inquest was reconvened. Questioned by Gerber, Licavoli stated most of his time since May 1 was spent at the Cleveland home of Vincent J. "Doc" Mangine, a partner in the Buckeye Catering Company, a joint operation of the Cleveland Mafia and the Jewish Cleveland Syndicate. Licavoli was not charged with the murder of Weisenberg, but as he left the inquiry detectives from Toledo arrested him on an outstanding warrant for a 1931 murder. Licavoli was later convicted for extortion and sentenced to one to five years in prison.

Before disappearing, Pascarella reportedly told a friend that he feared one man at the hotel conference he walked in on, guessing he could be trouble. "That is one man who would hire someone to have a person put out of the way," he said. It's a good bet that the man was James Licavoli and that Jerry "the Sledgehammer" Pascarella may have guessed correctly. The body of Pascarella was never found and nobody ever stood trial for his murder.

"The episode should at least bring the breakup of the gang of hoodlums and racketeers who have been making the hotel their hangout. People who have business there or must pass by are sick of seeing them. Let them loaf and fight in some less public place where their faces will not be a constant affront to decent people." - A *Vindicator* editorial regarding the hoodlum element at the Hotel Pick-Ohio after a New Year's Eve 1946 shooting at the Purple Cow restaurant, the hangout of "Fats" Aiello, located a block away from Youngstown police headquarters.

8

Rise of the Valley's "Big 3" – Fats, Moosey and the Wolf

It's lost to history just how the three mobsters came together, as well as exactly when. It's not even certain what their roles were. But the trio of Joseph Jasper "Fats" Aiello, Dominic "Moosey" Caputo and Joseph "The Wolf" DiCarlo was clearly the first Mafia backed organized crime combine in the Valley. While no one can be sure if Aiello or Caputo were initiated members of the "secret society," it is for certain that DiCarlo, with his bloodlines to a one-time Mafia family leader, was an inducted member of high standing.

With DiCarlo's role in the group defined as "first among equals," it appears the trio began to "muscle in" on gambling activities during the period from 1939 to 1946, although DiCarlo's entry has been more closely tied to the latter date. Their target was the Valley's bookies and their muscle came from control of the area's wire service, which provided horse race results from tracks all around the country.

The activity of the three was brought to the attention of the Kefauver Committee in the spring of 1950, when the Senate investigating body was just beginning its whirlwind tour of American cities affected by underworld gambling with interstate ties. The man responsible for exposing the group was Police Chief Edward Allen who traveled to Washington, D.C. to testify on April 27. Allen produced a statement that was taken from one of the bookies that explained the "muscling in" process:

> "In March 1945, while I was in Florida, I received a call from Youngstown, from my partner, that I had better come home because there was a new setup. I came home and discovered some out-of-town men were 'muscling in' on the book places. I was told if I wanted to stay in business I would have to pay 50 per cent of my business. It was a definite threat that if I did not give them 50 per cent I could not operate.
>
> "I was told, 'You will not get wire service unless you agree, because we control it.'"

The bookie bowed to the pressure and soon was forwarding $3,000 a month to the combine. The pressure had to have been coming from Aiello and Caputo, for DiCarlo was doing a stretch in the Erie County Jail in New York for a gambling conviction from March 1945 until early January 1946.

Allen's testimony at the time of his April 1950 appearance in Washington focused on DiCarlo. In describing the Buffalo hood to the committee, Allen refrained from using DiCarlo's name claiming it might give him "a national reputation." The *Buffalo Courier-Express*, however, reported, "...the Youngstown police boss insisted that the nation's major 'law-breakers are known to each other,' and that the Buffalo man has far-flung connections."

It's reasonable to believe that DiCarlo's muscle and his connections were coming from Cleveland and from transplanted members of Detroit's infamous Licavoli Gang. James "Jack White" Licavoli, the key suspect in the murder of Cleveland slot machine baron Nate Weisenberg and believed to be behind the disappearance of Jerry Pascarella, was certainly a major provider of the "muscle."

While the triumvirate of Aiello, Caputo and DiCarlo created a lasting reputation in the Valley, their actual period of power and profit making was a short-lived period - 1946 through 1947. The beginning of the end came with the advent of the Henderson administration and Chief Allen's harassment campaign. The gamblers were forced to relocate their operations in the "honky-tonk suburbs" of Mahoning County until the "mortal blow" came when Western Union and Ohio Bell Telephone Company pulled their equipment, thus ending the race wire service that the trio's bookmaking operations depended on. Not long after this DiCarlo and Caputo moved to South Florida where they both hoped to find greener pastures.

Joseph Jasper "Fats" Aiello

If the requirements to be a successful gangster are decades of newspaper headlines, little jail time and dying of natural causes, then Joseph Jasper "Fats" Aiello had few equals in the Mahoning Valley. Aiellos' rap sheet included arrests for bootlegging, reckless driving, shooting with intent to kill, carrying a concealed weapon, suspicious person, receiving and possession of stolen property, passing a bad check, breaking and entering, larceny, armed robbery, gambling, speeding, disturbing the peace, flight to avoid prosecution and aiding and abetting abortion. Everything Aiello did seem to make the newspaper whether it was being hauled in for questioning or having a tooth removed. Aiello once made front-page news for failing to show up for questioning before a county grand jury even though the article acknowledged he had never been served with a subpoena requesting his appearance. No mobster generated more newspaper editorials in Youngstown than Aiello. (See appendix A for the names and titles used by the newspapers in reporting his activities.)

Born in St. Louis, Missouri, on August 6, 1913, Aiello once told a probation officer that he quit school in the fourth grade at the age of 12 and for a short time helped his father in the produce business. His family later relocated to Springfield, Illinois. It's believed that "Fats" was related to the infamous Aiello clan of Chicago, whose war with the forces of Al Capone, during the mid-to-late 1920s over control of Unione Siciliana, culminated with the St. Valentine's Day Massacre in 1929. Joe Aiello, the leader of the clan, was cut down in spectacular fashion on October 23, 1930; the coroner dug 59 bullets out of his body. In addition, Aiello was believed to be related to the infamous Licavoli clan, who were also from St. Louis.

Some believe "Fats" tried to distance himself from his notorious relatives, not by changing his name or the spelling of it, but by distorting its pronunciation. The Mid West Aiellos pronounced the name I-Yel-Lo, while "Fats" called himself A-Leo. Others believe the media created the name "distortion." In addition to the distortion of the last name, Aiello's nickname was also a misnomer. "Fats" tipped the scales at 137 pounds. During a trial in the 1960s Aiello would be asked about his famous nickname. "I never walked until I was four years old because I was so fat, and after that everyone just called me 'Fats,'" Aiello explained.

On August 11, 1932, Aiello was arrested for the first time at the age of 19 in Springfield for violating the National Prohibition Act. This was followed by an arrest for burglary on May 11, 1933. Aiello pled guilty in January 1934 and was placed on a year's probation. Making his way to the Valley in the mid-to-late 1930s, Aiello married Rose Sudetic in 1943. Their union lasted over 30 years, but produced no children. Other than an arrest for reckless driving in April 1940, little is known of his activities in the area prior to 1946, but there was some evidence that he was involved in the Jungle Inn operation in Trumbull County in the late-1930s.[3]

Aiello made his debut on the front page of the *Vindicator* on New Year's Eve 1946. The headlines read: "Gamblers Attack Youth At Restaurant." Aiello, despite the fact that the only mark on his record locally was the reckless driving conviction, was labeled in the article, "long a trouble maker in Youngstown and the district." In addition to Aiello, the fracas involved Joe DiCarlo, Sandy Naples and Joe Russo.

The trouble began at Aiello's gambling joint on East Federal Street called the 115 Club. Anthony J. Bova, who used the alias Lou Bogash, was an 18 year-old with more bravado than brains. After stealing a dollar bill from behind the bar he lied to "Fats" about it and was ushered out of the club "unceremoniously" by several of Aiello's toughs. Around 4:00 a.m. the crowd from the 115 Club filed out and headed over to the Purple Cow, an all-night restaurant located inside the Hotel Pick-Ohio at Boardman and Hazel Streets. Bova soon showed up with a friend, John Paul "Jack the Ripper" Zentko, and re-ignited the argument over the stolen dollar bill. "If you'll get rid of the gun you carry, I'll show you that you're not too tough around here," Bova threatened.

With that, one of Aiello's associates threw a cup of hot coffee in the teenager's face. Bova countered by tossing a glass of water in Aiello's direction, and then quickly turned to flee. Both Naples and Aiello drew weapons, but only "Fats" fired. The newspaper reported, "The bullet fired by Aiello narrowly missed the youth's head, it sped past a waitress, who screamed and fainted; it just missed an orchestra member drinking coffee, and glanced off the metal binding of a venetian blind, as at least two score patrons of the restaurant dived under tables and sought other refuge."

Bova made it out the door and into the street where he escaped to safety on foot. His companion was not as fortunate. Zentko jumped into a taxicab only to be dragged out of the vehicle and pistol-whipped. After being kicked and beaten into unconsciousness he was tossed back into the cab and sent home. The Aiello crowd celebrated their victory by kicking up their heels and causing such a ruckus that one member soon warned them that if they attracted the attention of the police "this damn town'll be shut tighter than hell."

The newspaper reported that after the shooting, "police were told...to 'soft pedal' it. Especially they were told not to tell anything to the Vindicator, because 'there'd be too much heat put on.'" It was alleged that Joe Russo went across the street to police headquarters and told a "deskman" to "forget" about the disturbance. It was then reported that the night operator at the hotel was ordered "not to put through any calls to the police station reporting trouble." The hotel's manager later "suspended indefinitely" the night telephone operator, clerk and bellhop for "gross neglect of duty."

The city was abuzz about the shooting that morning. Mayor Ralph W. O'Neill promised to get a weapon's ordinance with "teeth" in it, something the mayor's approach to the city's underworld problem lacked. O'Neill was viewed as a weak mayor when it came to facing the city's gamblers. It was a weakness that attorney Charles Henderson would attack in the upcoming November election.

The Purple Cow was drawing gamblers and the nightclub crowd to its dining room for sometime. Those personalities – mixed with alcohol – created an atmosphere conducive to trouble. The Hotel Pick-Ohio's manager had requested of Mayor O'Neill three months prior that an extra police presence be granted the hotel. O'Neill denied ever receiving any request.

The town's bookies were prepared to close "on a moment's notice" if police were ordered to respond to Aiello's gunplay. The newspaper checked several downtown hotspots and found all were in full operation. The only thing missing since the incident were Aiello, Naples and DiCarlo, who were said to be lying low.

The New Year's Day edition of the *Vindicator* carried the following comments in an editorial titled "Everyone Knew But the Police":

> "When a city government tolerates rackets it can expect just such occurrences as Tuesday morning's brawl in the Hotel Pick-Ohio's restaurant and on the sidewalk outside.
>
> "But it seems strange that none of the two-score witnesses thought of calling the police, or that a disturbance so noisy as to alarm even the gangsters who were making it attracted no attention in the police station, virtually across the street from the scene.
>
> "The episode should at least bring the breakup of the gang of hoodlums and racketeers who have been making the hotel their hangout. People who have business there or must pass by are sick of seeing them. Let them loaf and fight in some less public place where their faces will not be a constant affront to decent people."

The *Vindicator* was intent on getting answers to the Purple Cow shooting and their target was Youngstown Police Chief John B. Thomas. On January 3, a reporter conducted a telephone interview with the chief. Thomas said he would not provide any information until the investigation was complete and scoffed at the idea that the "investigation might be whitewashed and forgotten as soon as the *Vindicator* forgot the incident." When asked why he hadn't questioned the victims or Aiello, Naples, DiCarlo and Russo, Thomas became defensive and replied, "That's not my business. Why do you think I have investigators?" The chief went onto claim that the city was as "clean as it has ever been in reference to vice and crime." The reporter took this moment to point out that the 115 Club was operating wide-open as a gambling joint for several months. "Ah, now listen," Thomas replied. "Places like those were here before my time and they'll be here after I'm gone." The chief avoided some questions and was short or curt on others. When he tired of the reporter's inquiry he simply stated, "Ah, I gotta get my morning coffee." With that he said goodbye and hung up.

Due to the police department's lack of attention to the matter, the Mahoning County grand jury began questioning witnesses about the shooting. County Prosecutor William Ambrose revealed he began investigating the incident when it was first reported in the newspaper, not because of any request from the city. Not wanting the county to react first, the police department arrested Aiello and brought him in for questioning just two hours before the grand jury issued a two-count indictment against him.

Aiello's story to the police was that his gun "went off accidentally" when it fell out of his pocket while he was eating. O'Neill announced the city planned to probe the "dropping" angle claiming that it "could happen to anyone." When informed that the county had indicted Aiello, O'Neill feigned surprise and told reporters, "I didn't even know the grand jury was in session." He then ordered Aiello held in jail overnight.

The grand jury indicted Aiello for carrying a concealed weapon and shooting with intent to wound or kill. After spending the night in the city jail he was transferred to the Mahoning County jail the next morning. He was released on a $5,000 bond and Judge Erskine Maiden, Jr. set arraignment for the following week. Aiello's bond was provided by Mrs. Angeline Constantino, a mysterious woman who thirteen years later would figure in the investigation into the death of William "Billy" Naples.

Aiello was the only person indicted; none of his cohorts were named. The newspaper questioned why police did nothing about Sandy Naples having a gun since he was still on probation from a 1934 conviction. Certainly possession of a firearm was a violation of his parole. The charges against Aiello indicated that neither of the victims had testified before the grand jury:

> "Unless 'Jack the Ripper' was one of the secret witnesses to appear before the grand jury, or was questioned by police, he is said to have dropped out of sight since the Purple Cow brawl. It is unlikely that he appeared before the grand jury, it is believed, since both the counts against Aiello concern his gun action and not anything to do with a beating. Similarly, [Bova] has not been traced."

A *Vindicator* editorial on January 4, 1947, expressed its displeasure with the way the indictment came about:

> "The shooting and beating at the Hotel Pick-Ohio ...was a direct outcome of the city administration's tolerance of rackets. The county action thus leaves the city's law enforcement agencies convicted of failure. Mayor O'Neill and Police Chief John Thomas can now take refuge in seeing that the case is in the county's hands. The edge will be taken off embarrassing questions about the alliance between politics and rackets."

In response to the editorial, O'Neill said his investigators would continue on the case, but "they would concentrate on proving to the public that police were not warned by Aiello's mob to forget" the Purple Cow shooting.

During the second week of January Bova and Zentko were brought in for questioning by police. Zentko denied that Aiello or anyone else had beaten him and fabricated a fascinating tale to account for the stories the newspapers had printed about the incident. The *Vindicator* stood by their eyewitness accounts claiming, "It was reliably stated that the underworld has brought pressure to bear on witnesses." A reporter who checked the apartment building where Zentko said he resided was informed by the owner that he was not one of her tenants. She did not want people "to get the idea 'The Ripper' lived there because someone 'might toss a pineapple at the place.'" Meanwhile, Bova was held for further questioning because police felt he was "evasive" with his answers. When investigators discovered he was an admitted panderer, who kept a young woman in another county, his credibility was shot.

On February 14, Aiello pled guilty to one count of carrying a concealed weapon and threw himself on the mercy of the court. Judge Maiden dismissed the second count of shooting to wound or kill because "sufficient proof cannot be obtained to convict on it." This of course came after "consideration" of Bova's "character and business." Zentko's beating and wild story never played a part in the trial. Zentko's career on the fringe of the underworld would continue and over his lifetime he would be arrested 23 times as a suspicious person.

In handing down Aiello's punishment Maiden stated, "This sentence will run the full 60 days and I don't want any calls about it." Aiello reported to the Mahoning County jail on February 17. Three weeks later Aiello was being hailed as a "model" prisoner by his jailers.

Meanwhile, Bova was taking it on the chin from another Youngstown judge. On March 12, the young woman that Bova had admitted to pandering for was arrested. She told a sordid tale of her relationship with Bova, which included beatings and his stealing her clothes. The young lady, a teenager from Harrisburg, Pennsylvania, met Bova the previous November and he talked her into becoming a prostitute. She worked in Alliance until he moved her to Masury, where she worked for a while at the "Green House," a brothel located on Route 62. She claimed she gave Bova on average $400 a week. When this story unraveled in court, Municipal Judge Robert B. Nevin "threw the book" at Bova. The incensed judge told the 18 year-old, "If I had my way, I'd take a pup like you and drown you in the middle of the Pacific Ocean. You'll serve every day of your sentence. Now get out of here."

Bova was sentenced to six months in jail and fined $300. But first Nevin ordered that Bova be held in the city jail and be given only bread and water until he revealed where he had hidden the girl's clothes. Nevin sentenced the young lady to a 30-day jail term, but suspended the time if she promised to return to her father's home in Harrisburg. When she claimed that Bova had stolen all her money, the sympathetic judge and several police officers in the courtroom donated the money to pay her bus fare home. Because of Bova's "terrible crimes" even Judge Maiden felt compelled to act. He released Aiello ten days early from his sentence, lopping off five days for good behavior for each month he served.

On September 17, 1947, the *Vindicator* published an article which discussed the migration of a "horde of racketeers" throughout the country to the sunny South. While the article focused on Joe DiCarlo making an "exodus," it had the following to say on Aiello:

> "Rumors have had it that Joseph "Fats" Aiello, another Youngstown gambler and underworld character, is to take part in the mob migration from north to south. Speculation on Fat's moving has been based on the fact that he recently sold his home in Euclid Blvd. for 'a fancy price.'
>
> "However, if "Fats" should move, it will only be a temporary departure. "Fats" is said to have only recently bought into The Center,[4] a restaurant and pool room operated by other notorious characters such as Sandy Naples and Pinky Walsh. The Center is located at Center St. and Wilson Ave.

> "Fats" is said to have bought a third of the place, getting his share from Joe Alexander who has taken over operation of another restaurant on the lower South Side.
>
> "If the local boys should join the gangsters on their southern flight, Miami police say they are ready to welcome all of them with 'open arms – with a club in each hand.'"

Mayor O'Neill continued to receive pressure over the Purple Cow incident. Attorney Charles Henderson, during his reform campaign for mayor in 1947, would use O'Neill's oft-repeated remark, "it could happen to anyone," as part of his crusade against the current administration. Henderson was elected in November and took office in January.

Despite being one of the prime targets of Henderson's "Smash Racket's Rule" campaign, Aiello remained free on the streets avoiding the grasp of the mayor's new police chief, Edward Allen. That ended on August 3, 1948, when Allen had Aiello brought in "for investigation as to his means of support." The gambler, picked up outside the Purple Cow, was unable to provide "a reasonable and satisfactory account of his means of livelihood." During their conversation Aiello told Allen, "I can't remember having a legitimate job." It was a statement Aiello would soon regret. The gambler then boasted, "I'll be around here longer than you will." To which Allen responded, "In that case, I'll just keep you a couple of days so we'll be together." Allen ordered Aiello held without charging him so that he could not be released on bond.

Aiello's lawyer, David Shermer, was preparing to file a writ of habeas corpus to get his client released when Allen placed Aiello under arrest using the city's catchall crime of being a "suspicious person," a law on the books since the late 1920s. If convicted he could face a jail term of 30 days and a fine of $25 to $50. Aiello's $500 property bond was again provided for by Angeline Constantino.

Aiello was the first target of Allen to be arrested "in connection with explaining the manner of their livelihood at the present time." The chief explained, "It's time for the racketeers to get legitimate jobs. They have had six months in which to do it. If they can't find legitimate jobs, the racketeers will be picked up and asked why they are not working."

In responding to Aiello's boast to Allen, a *Vindicator* editorial stated: "For the final answer as to whether Aiello or Chief Allen is to 'be around longer' rests, not with the chief, but with the public. In the past, rackets have been stopped temporarily (as in the state cleanup of 1943) but have come back stronger than before. The cause was apathy by voters who would not take the trouble to see that good candidates for public office were nominated and elected."

At a preliminary hearing before Judge Frank P. Anzellotti, attorney Shermer filed a motion asking for a bill of particulars[5] from the police prosecutor's office. The judge asked Assistant Police Prosecutor Frank Franko to respond. Declaring that the case against his client was "vague, indefinite, uncertain, and insufficient in general term and conclusion," Shermer announced he was prepared to take the case all the way to the United States Supreme Court because the charge was "in conflict with constitutional rights."

On August 14, Anzellotti denied Shermer's motion for the bill of particulars stating that the affidavit filed on Aiello clearly outlined the nature of the charge. In brief, the affidavit read, "that during the years 1947 and 1948, Aiello unlawfully obtained his living by criminal means and practices." The basis for this allegation was Aiello acknowledging to Allen that he couldn't "remember having a legitimate job."

In defending the charge, Franko stated that "a municipal operation may define a suspicious person and provide for his punishment." He added that "a general course of conduct or mode of life which is prejudicial to the public welfare may likewise be prohibited and punished as an offense." Franko supported himself by reciting a city code reference, "Any person who obtained his living by criminal means and practice shall be deemed and held to be a suspicious person."

At a hearing on September 10, Police Prosecutor Henry J. Fugett found himself face-to-face with three of the Valley's most talented defense attorneys – Shermer, William P. Barnum and Clyde Osborne. The attorneys attacked on several fronts. First, Shermer renewed his motion for a bill of particulars, claiming that a clause in the city's suspicious person's ordinance was unconstitutional. Barnum stated that Anzellotti's earlier decision denying the motion "constitutes prejudicial error" while declaring that it is "mandatory" for the prosecution to provide a bill of particulars "when reasonably requested."

Clyde Osborne presented a strong argument against the validity of the city ordinance. The city's suspicious person's law was passed as an emergency council measure back in March 1928. While the council minutes, however, showed the passing of the ordinance, "no definition was given to the emergency. It was reported that the ordinance had been passed to curb petty racketeers and gamblers by providing for a jail sentence instead of small fines." Osborne contended that the measure was never passed in council on a "separate roll call."

Anzellotti approved the request of Fugett for a one-week postponement to "study the validity of the ordinance." When court reconvened, Fugett filed a brief supporting the law's validity. Citing case law, the police prosecutor wrote, "The ordinance in question was passed as an emergency ordinance in the manner required by the charter of the city. [Therefore the] ordinance cannot be attacked for irregularities or defects if an emergency clause after the period for referendum has elapsed...the court has no right to inquire into the sufficiency of reasons declaring an ordinance to be an emergency measure."

Defense attorneys were allotted a week to reply and submitted a 19-page response to Anzellotti. On December 3, after spending more than two months reviewing the matter, the judge upheld the validity of the "suspicious person" ordinance, but ordered Fugett to file a detailed bill of particulars. The request was fulfilled a week later and the battle was on to see how long the trial could be delayed. The fact that Aiello had three attorneys made it easy for one or more to be tied up with other cases delaying a court date from being set until June 15, 1949. Fugett was then notified that the municipal judges begin their summer vacations in June and a hearing would not be held until all three were present. That pushed the date back to September 19. A week before the hearing Aiello filed a demand for a jury trial and a date of October 4 was established. The final delay came because the municipal court bailiff had scheduled his vacation.

On Monday, October 17, fourteen months after Aiello was arrested, the trial was ready to begin. At 9:30 a.m. the judge, prosecutors, defense attorneys and potential jurors were seated in Anzellotti's courtroom awaiting one man – "Fats" Aiello. The attorneys told the judge that Aiello must have "misunderstood" the time and thought the trial was to begin at 1:30 after the jury was seated. Anzellotti asked the jury pool to return that afternoon. When Aiello failed to appear at that time, the judge ordered his $500 bond forfeited and issued a warrant for his arrest.

Angry over Aiello's failure to show was his legal counsel, each of whom quickly announced their withdrawal from the case. Aiello had conferred with his lawyers on Saturday and was seen at his normal haunts on Sunday. Osborne told reporters, "When a man of his kind walks out and leaves us holding the bag I don't like it. Let someone else play nursemaid to him." As soon as the arrest warrant was issued Sergeant Daniel Maggianetti and his vice squad began their search.

The *Vindicator* claimed that since the incident at the Purple Cow in December 1946, Aiello's career was on the decline; referring to the gun-play as the "climax to his notorious career." They reported:

> "[The shooting] apparently marked the descent of Aiello's star. Long regarded as one of the leaders in the 'fix,' Aiello is believed to have lost his influence to outsiders.
>
> "In recent months, reports have come out of the underworld that 'Fats' was 'busted." He also is believed to owe several other gamblers large sums of money advanced in the belief he would again have 'something going.'"

The next day a *Vindicator* editorial explained Aiello's disappearance – as the newspaper saw it – and gave credit where credit was due:

> "Fats not only was unable to do business with the Henderson administration at any time, but of late he couldn't do business with the few petty racketeers who are left around here since Chief Allen's cleanup.
>
> "In any case Aiello's absence is much preferred to his company. If it weren't for the principle of upholding due legal process, one would be tempted to suggest that the policemen assigned to finding him shouldn't look too hard. Certainly it is

> in order to recommend that the administration which has made Youngstown too tough for the Aiellos should be kept in office, come November 8 [Election Day]."

On October 19, Chief Allen told reporters, "If Aiello doesn't show up within a day or two, I will order the vice squad to round up Aiello's friends to bring them in for questioning and determine where Aiello has gone." When a reporter responded that this declaration might cause the racketeer friends of Aiello to flee the area, Allen replied, "This will be one way of getting them out of town."

What was unknown to the public at the time was that several racketeers, including Joe DiCarlo and Sandy Naples, were subpoenaed to appear at Aiello's trial. DiCarlo had already left town for a West Coast vacation because of this. Naples was picked up for questioning by the end of the week, but was released after convincing Allen he didn't know Aiello's whereabouts.

On November 10, Aiello appeared in court with his new attorney, Russell Mock, and pleaded not guilty to the charge of being a suspicious person for which he was arrested 15 months earlier. Despite the plea for a $5,000 bond by prosecutors, Judge Anzellotti released Aiello after a $1,500 bond was posted. He set a trial date of November 21. Outside the courtroom, Aiello told reporters that he "had been in the city the whole time," although he ducked questions of where he was hiding and how he avoided capture by the police. The gambler claimed he informed his previous counsel that he would not appear in court when trial opened. His reason for staying away was "to avoid becoming involved in the city's political campaign." Refusing to elaborate further he offered, "I'm just a good guy and don't want to get others involved."

On Monday, November 21, the long awaited trial opened with the selection of six men and six women as jurors. Opening statements followed with Assistant Law Director P. Richard Schumann telling the jury that Aiello had conspired with DiCarlo and Dominic "Moosey" Caputo to extort local bookmakers into paying them 50 percent of their profits in order to operate. This was how Aiello was able to finance his lavish lifestyle while never holding a legitimate job. Mock countered by claiming Aiello's income came from the $27,000 sale of a home he owned and other transactions.

Testimony Monday included a review of the Purple Cow incident. This was followed by an auditor from the Dollar Savings & Trust Company discussing the gambler's bank deposits. Aiello opened an account in October 1939 and listed his business address as the Jungle Inn in Trumbull County. Beginning in January 1947, Aiello's deposits averaged more than $1,000 a month; the largest being $5,800. Totals for the first seven months of 1947 exceeded $16,000. Because of these revelations IRS agents went after DiCarlo and in September 1950 billed him for $3,127 for the years 1946 and 1947.

The next witness was a bookkeeper from the U-Drive It Company, who testified that Aiello had rented an automobile on 31 occasions over a 10-month period. Laughter filled the courtroom when she stated that Aiello's first application was denied because he was deemed a "poor financial risk." On his application Aiello listed his occupation as proprietor of the Center Sandwich Shop on Wilson Avenue and his former occupation as "Jungle Inn."

Clyde W. Osborne was the next prosecution witness. This was not the same Clyde W. Osborne who had once represented Aiello, but rather his nephew, who was named in his honor. Sometimes the nephew would use "Jr." after his name to differentiate himself from his more prominent uncle. The younger Osborne was personal secretary to Mayor Henderson and would later become a prosecutor and a judge. On the stand Osborne testified that a check of city permits and licenses issued to the Center Sandwich Shop over the prior three years did not reflect Aiello's name. Instead, ownership was listed in the names of John "Pinky" Walsh and Joseph Alexander. Sandy Naples, at onetime an owner, had to back out due to being on probation.

The highlight of day two of the trial was the testimony of Chief Allen, who revealed for the first time publicly the full content of Aiello's unsigned statement taken after his August 1948 arrest. According to Allen, Aiello was in a partnership with DiCarlo and Caputo when they muscled in on the bookies handling the area's horse-betting business, collecting 50 percent of the profits. "Fats" claimed that the bookies didn't know about DiCarlo's involvement until they asked Aiello "how they should list their 'partnership' on their income tax returns."

Allen read a list of the group's bookmaking "partnership," which included Charles Cavallaro and Frank Carey, the former adversary of Jerry Pascarella. Later, six of the "partners" were called to testify. Each, including Cavallaro, refused to answer the prosecutor's questions on the grounds that it might be self-incriminating. The chief stated that Aiello told him, "Cadillac Charlie" [Cavallaro] was not a partner of ours after the first year. Whether he got tired of paying us 50 percent I do not know. He would pay us by check occasionally."

The bookies were told to deliver the payoff to Caputo at the Paddock Grill on West Federal Street. "Moosey" would then split the take with Aiello and DiCarlo. Aiello claimed, "The partnership lasted from then [the beginning of 1947] until the present administration took office."

Mock's cross-examination of Allen generated heated exchanges between defense counsel and the prosecution table and drew several admonishments from Anzellotti. Allen admitted that Aiello's statement was voluntarily given and that charges were drawn after "we had digested the statement." Allen testified he "had no personal knowledge of Aiello's activities until the defendant made his statement." Mock asked the chief why the men named in Aiello's statement were not arrested. Allen cheerfully replied, "I can't arrest all of your clients at once. Be patient, their day will come."

The prosecution called Caputo as one of its last witnesses. Questioned by Fugett, "Moosey" said he had known Aiello for several years, but denied being involved in any business with him, least of all extorting local bookmakers.

Fugett and Caputo went nose to nose when the prosecutor demanded to know if "Moosey" ever knew Aiello to be "employed in a lawful capacity." Caputo finally answered that he didn't know.

Mock's strategy was to prove to the jury that Aiello's income came from legitimate sources. He had a realtor testify that he sold a house for Aiello for $27,000. Another man testified that he purchased the 115 Club and its contents for $3,000. Joseph Alexander testified he sold his half interest in the Center Sandwich Shop to Aiello during the summer of 1947 for $5,000. Then Aiello's brother-in-law, Louis R. Sudetic said he ran the combination restaurant/poolroom with "Pinky" Walsh until March 1948 when Aiello sold his interest.

During the trial, the *Vindicator* reported that, "the courtroom on the third floor of the police station building was jammed with spectators, most of them apparently sympathetic to the defense. Whenever attorney Mock succeeded in scoring a point, there were loud outbursts from the crowd which filled the seats and lined two deep against the rear wall."

On Wednesday morning, as the trial was coming to a conclusion, Mock had two surprises. First, he refused to allow his client to take the witness stand. He then declined to present a closing argument. The jury was given the case at 11:30 a.m. and after lunch deliberated for an hour and nineteen minutes before returning to the courtroom shortly after 3:00 p.m. after finding Aiello guilty. Mock said he would file a motion for a new trial and Anzellotti delayed sentencing.

The following editorial appeared in the *Vindicator* the day after the verdict:

Aiello's Conviction

> "It is unfortunate that evidence is not available to bring more serious charges against Fats Aiello than the suspicious-person rap on which he was convicted yesterday. However, this one will do for the present.
>
> "The conviction itself serves justice: the racketeer who so long was able to order police around is brought to book on a charge usually employed in rounding up bums.
>
> "The case served a wider purpose than cutting Aiello down to proper size. It enabled Police Chief Allen to take the public behind the scenes of the underworld, showing the rackets' extent and their ruthlessness, their complete disregard of law or ordinary decency.
>
> "If this record of past evils and of the improvement since Charles P. Henderson became mayor had been published before the recent election, the mayor's majority would have been still larger. Perhaps this is why Aiello hid out when his case was called several weeks ago."

Mock wasted no time in filing his motion for a new trial. On November 25, the attorney filed his paperwork charging Assistant Law Director Schumann with misconduct and Judge Anzellotti with erring in letting Chief Allen read from Aiello's statement and for upholding the validity of the suspicious person's ordinance.

On November 30, Anzellotti denied Mock's motion for a new trial and sentenced Aiello to serve 30 days in the city jail and to pay a $100 fine. He gave Aiello 30 days to file his appeal. Mock took nearly the full month before filing his motion for the appeal, listing more than a dozen errors. In addition to the ones he used in his new trail motion, Mock now claimed his client was, "Deprived of his constitutional right of a speedy trial."

On March 15, 1950, attorneys for both sides made their arguments before the Seventh District Court of Appeals. When the court came back with its ruling on April 5, it was a blow to both the prosecutors and the city. Agreeing with the argument first put forth by attorney Clyde Osborne in September 1948, the appellate court concluded "an ordinance passed by a municipal council as an emergency measure [must comply and state] the reasons for the immediate measure, and if such reasons are not stated by the ordinance it is invalid and its enforcement [not permitted]."

The newspaper pointed out that, "Many of the city's most important pieces of legislation had been passed in the same manner as the suspicious persons ordinance." The wording of such measures in municipal legislation amounted to: "This ordinance is hereby declared to be an emergency measure - necessary for the preservation of the public peace, health and safety and shall take effect upon its passage and approval by the mayor." Over the years the city passed literally hundreds of emergency measure ordinances, which were now in jeopardy of being invalidated by the appellate court's ruling.

Immediately after the decision, Judge Robert Nevin announced he would refuse to rule on "any suspicious person charges brought before him until the court of appeals issues its complete ruling on the ordinance." Nevin then advised city detectives not to charge anyone with the crime until the matter was resolved. Meanwhile, city leaders huddled to discuss filing an appeal to the Ohio Supreme Court. Before the month was over, Ohio Chief Justice Carl Weygandt ordered that Aiello not be freed of the charge until the higher court heard the issue, and that his bond be continued. The legal battle would drag on for another year and a half before resolution, but in the meantime Aiello continued to be front-page fodder.

Temporarily free of legal worries, Aiello's first move was to get a legitimate job - or at least the appearance of one. He accomplished this with a little help from his friends. In late May 1950, he went to the auditor's department at the Mahoning County courthouse and purchased licenses for four cigarette vending machines. Using the name of Anthony Delsanter's National Cigarette Service Company at 15 Oak Hill Avenue, he paid $99 a piece for the machines to be placed around town. The locations were Charlie Cavallaro's South Champion Street bar, the Center Sandwich Shop, the South Bend Tavern and the Wagon Wheel restaurant in Struthers. The latter location was a popular eatery known as "Jimmy's Wagon Wheel." The "Jimmy" was James Constantino the husband of Aiello's bond benefactress – Angeline Constantino. The cigarette machine at the Wagon Wheel was quickly removed when new owners decided to return to the previous vendor.

Many began to believe that Aiello was the real owner of National Cigarette Service. In March 1951, Russell Mock, who represented both Aiello and Delsanter, explained to Chief Allen that "it is Delsanter's money that is in the business, the vending machines are in his name, Aiello is just working for him. Delsanter employed Aiello because the latter knew many people and places in Mahoning County where machines could be set up."

An indication that Aiello's every move was being scrutinized by the press came on June 8 when he was arrested for crashing a traffic light in the city. Aiello was on his way home at 4:30 a.m. when he ran a light on Mahoning Avenue and then attempted to outrun a squad car. Police forced his vehicle to the curb, where Aiello refused to get out until he was told he was under arrest. Described in a front-page story as "petty racketeer turned businessman," Aiello was released on a $50 bond and appeared before Judge Nevin later that morning. He was fined $5 plus $8 court costs.

On August 18, Aiello made national news when he and DiCarlo were named in an interim report submitted by the Kefauver Committee (See Chapter 10 on the Kefauver Hearings). Aiello's name appeared in the report, after hearings held in Miami, with nationally recognized organized crime figures Joe Adonis, "Little Augie" Pisano, Frank Erickson and Meyer Lansky from New York; Charles Fischetti from Chicago; and former Mayfield Road Mob members – Al Polizzi and the Angersola brothers.

With the Kefauver Committee making a scheduled stop in Cleveland in January 1951, Aiello was one of several Mahoning and Trumbull County underworld figures to be served subpoenas by Chief Allen. On January 9, members of the vice squad picked up Aiello and brought him to the police station. After "cooling his heels" for nearly an hour, Aiello told a reporter, "I don't know what's wanted of me this time, but if the chief wants me for dinner, he can always get me at the Purple Cow." Allen soon appeared and served Aiello with the Senate summons.

Aiello was scheduled to appear on January 18. Of the seven area mob figures to be called, only DiCarlo took the witness stand to be questioned. In the committee's third interim report, Aiello and Caputo were named partners of "racket lord" Joe DiCarlo in muscling in on area bookies.

On June 27, the Ohio Supreme Court finalized its decision on the prosecution's "suspicious person's" appeal. The court ruled, "The offense of being a suspicious person does not consist of particular acts, but of the mode of life, habits, and practices of the accused in respect to the character of traits, which it is the object of the ordinance to suppress." With that, Youngstown's suspicious person's ordinance was declared legal. Attorney Mock announced he would appeal to the United States Supreme Court.

Hours later, at the Purple Cow, Aiello was discussing the ruling with some companions. After noticing two vice squad detectives outside, he commented, "I think they are looking for me." Aiello stepped outside and was placed under arrest near the same spot where he was apprehended over two and a half years earlier. Allen had ordered his arrest fearing Aiello might leave town. When it was pointed out to the chief that "Fats" was still under bond, Allen replied that did "not mean anything" to a man like Aiello. After Mock's appearance at the jail, and a subsequent telephone call to Judge Anzellotti, Aiello was released.

A week after the decision, Mock filed for a new hearing with the Ohio Supreme Court. In his application, he stated that the court had ruled "only on the validity of the ordinance, but did not give any ruling on whether or not Aiello had a fair trial." The tenacious lawyer said if he failed again in Columbus he would petition the U.S. Supreme Court. Hours after receiving Mock's notice of appeal, court attaches in the state capital announced that court was in recess for the summer. The appeal would not be heard until September and Aiello continued to remain free on bond.

On October 3, 1951, the Ohio Supreme Court refused to rehear Aiello's case. Mock announced plans immediately to ask the U.S. Supreme Court to reverse the state court's decision. Allen issued orders to have Aiello arrested on sight to begin his sentence. Aiello left home and remained in hiding until a week later when he appeared in court with Mock. The attorney requested that his client remain free on bond stating that "it takes time to get a writ printed, which is required in appealing cases to the U.S. Supreme Court and Aiello's 30-day jail sentence would be served by the time the case came up." Anzellotti said it would take him a few days to rule on the matter and allowed Aiello to remain free. The judge then ordered that vice squad members were to refrain from arresting Aiello or bringing him in for further questioning until the issue was decided. On Monday, October 15, Anzellotti denied Aiello a stay of sentence stating that the defendant has "had a fair and impartial trial by his peers." The judge told Mock and his client that in his five years on the bench he had never studied a case more thoroughly than Aiello's and that he had "bent over backwards" to be fair. At Mock's request Anzellotti allowed Aiello until Wednesday to "arrange his personal affairs." Mock then appealed again to the Seventh District Court of Appeals for a stay of sentence. Schumann advised the attorney that the court of appeals had no jurisdiction in this area. Mock realized the situation was futile and in a last ditch effort went to the newspapers and on local radio pleading on his client's behalf, but to no avail.

The appeals court, just as Schumann had said, ruled it had no jurisdiction in staying the sentence. On Wednesday morning, Aiello paced the corridor outside Judge Anzellotti's courtroom, nervously chain-smoking cigarettes. He told reporters, "I haven't been prosecuted. I've been persecuted. I'm getting railroaded by that publicity hound, Chief Allen." At 11:45 Anzellotti came out of the courtroom and told Mock that his client was to accompany a member of the city vice squad down to the city jail. Aiello turned to a reporter and said, "Well, I'll see you in 30 days. And I'll eat the baloney they serve."

The long ordeal was over. Three years and two months had passed since Aiello's arrest outside the Purple Cow that warm August day. Aiello had already served a 50-day sentence on the concealed weapon's conviction. His jailers had called him a "model" prisoner. Why the long legal battle over a 30-day sentence? Could Aiello have detested jail time so much that he would pay for years of legal assistance for such a short sentence? Did his dislike of Chief Allen fuel the costly contest? Or did Mock's large ego pave the way for the marathon procedure? The Valley would never know for sure.

What was sure was that Aiello's incarceration was not about to keep him out of the newspapers. Three days after entering the city jail Aiello made the front page just for having a tooth extracted. During the procedure he complained to the dentist about his "accommodations" at the jail.

Aiello was released from his sentence shortly before noon on November 15. The smiling gambler told reporters he had lost three pounds while doing time. Mock paid his client's $100 fine and $125 in court costs. Aiello went immediately to the Hotel Pick-Ohio for a haircut, but would not tell the press what his future plans were. Three days later Aiello offered to cater Thanksgiving dinner to some 60 city jail inmates. "These men need a lift in their morale, especially on a holiday, and I think a good substantial dinner would help them in many ways," he stated. Chief Allen's reply was brief, "No, thanks." He stated the prisoners get a "good Thanksgiving dinner."

"Fats" was headline news again on March 27, 1952, when the IRS announced it was going after Aiello, DiCarlo and Vince DeNiro for $12,000 in back taxes. The government had arrived at Aiello's share based on numbers being bandied around by Mock and Allen during the 1949 suspicious person's trial. The tax agents charged that Aiello owed $4,024 for 1947.

On October 26, 1952, rising mob figure Vince DeNiro was brought in for questioning during the bombing investigation of two local union truck drivers. During the interrogation, DeNiro revealed that he had purchased Anthony Delsanter's interest in the National Cigarette Service vending company. Since Aiello was an "employee" of Delsanter, police determined he must now be out of a job. Allen responded by hauling in Aiello an hour after DeNiro's release. The out-of-work gambler remained in jail overnight as Allen and Maggianetti, now a lieutenant, quizzed Aiello about "his plans for earning a living." He was released the next morning and told he would be given "reasonable time to get a job."

In early November, Allen ordered Maggianetti to have his men "pick up all petty racketeers and hoodlums for routine checks until the men either get legitimate jobs or leave town." The order followed Aiello being picked up again for questioning regarding his livelihood. Chief Allen told reporters that Aiello "and others like him can expect to be picked up and questioned on their activities and means of earning a living, from now on. There will be no let up in our campaign until we either get these hoodlums off the street or out of town altogether."

In the fall of 1952, Ed Reid, an award-winning journalist from the *Brooklyn Eagle*, who became the first prolific organized crime author, published the book *Mafia*. The recent Kefauver hearings and Reid's own investigative work into a New York Police Department corruption scandal involving bookmakers, for which the journalist won the 1950 Pulitzer Prize, fueled the book. Reid presented a list of the top 83 Mafiosi in the country "in order of their importance" for one of the book's chapters. The following men, in order of "importance," represented the Mahoning Valley:

8. Anthony De Janero, Warren (Barney Jennings)
16. James De Janero, Mahoning County (James Jennings)
27. John Vitullo, Mahoning County
44. Ray Scalise, Youngstown and Florida
67. Joseph DiCarlo, Youngstown (The Wolf)
68. Victor Aiello, Youngstown (Fats)
69. Frank Cammaratta (sic), Detroit and Youngstown
70. Ralph Palente, Mahoning County

The popular release, in its third printing that year, foot noted that, "Since the 1st edition printing of this list, about all the Mafiosi listed have come under denaturalization proceedings by the U. S. Attorney General's office." The only Mahoning Valley entry this would have affected was Cammarata.

A *Vindicator* article about the book was titled "Book Lists District Men As Black Hand Members." The newspaper still believed the Black Hand and the Mafia were one and the same. The article pointed out that John Vitullo had died four years previously in 1948, and that the names Ray Scalise and Ralph Palente were "not immediately familiar" as "locals." Reid listed Aiello's first name incorrectly as "Victor," but got his nickname "Fats" correct. Reid can hardly be blamed considering all the names the *Vindicator* had assigned the mobster (See Appendix A). Aiello, having been born in St. Louis, obviously could not have been on the government's list of hoods to be deported – much to the chagrin of Chief Allen. The article stated, "Underworld sources have speculated for years that Aiello is under orders from the Mafia grand council to remain in Youngstown and thus has had to 'put up' with the constant harassment by police...and has remained long after most men would have left." Commenting on the book, Chief Allen stated, "Actually, of the district men named, the only one on the list presently residing in Youngstown is 'Fats' Aiello and he's peanuts."

To keep from being harassed by police, Aiello knew he had to establish a legitimate job for himself. His efforts met a solid roadblock – Chief Allen. In late

November 1952, Aiello applied to the city for a soft drink license. He was planning to open a store on West Boardman Street "to sell magazines and soft drinks and operate a shoe shine stand."

"I can see Aiello shining shoes and selling pop," Allen stated sarcastically. "I want to eliminate hoodlum hangouts, not create them." Referring to a South Champion Street "hangout" owned by Charles Cavallaro, the chief recalled, "We had to tear it down to get the hoodlums out."

Reporters questioned whether Aiello had any legal recourse if he were denied the permit. Allen responded, "We deny licenses to cab drivers with bad records so why should we give one to Aiello. Any license is a privilege and its issuance should be contingent upon the type of character of the applicant." The chief advised that if "Aiello is so anxious to earn an honest living he should go to work in industry like thousands of other Youngstowners."

Mayor Henderson supported the denial of Aiello's application for the soft drink permit stating, "I am following the recommendation of my police chief." Aiello then had to apply to the city to get his $5 deposit refunded. His attorney said Aiello might follow through with his plans for the shop and forget about the soft drinks.

Aiello soon abandoned his plans for the shop, however, he told several people that he was going to be involved in the Windsor Tailor Company, a new men's clothing store, which was to open at the West Boardman Street address where he applied for the soft drink permit. On January 9, 1953, the city building inspector halted the remodeling effort because the B & B Construction Company had not obtained a permit. The day after the *Vindicator* reported "Work Halted On Aiello Shop," Fred Beshara, owner of the construction company and a 90 percent owner of the tailor shop, who had testified on Aiello's behalf during his November 1949 trial, announced that Aiello had no connection whatsoever with the Windsor Tailor Company.

Some investigative reporting by the newspaper showed that the owner of the West Boardman building was Charles Vizzini,[6] proprietor of the De Luxe Café. Vizzini was alleged to have links to the "notorious Licavoli gang." An associate of Fred Beshara in the tailor shop venture was Jack Zizzo, a known bookie, who in 1949 threw 300 football pool tickets out the window of his automobile when he was about to be arrested. Finally, Joseph Beshara, a cousin of Fred, was the holder of a federal gambling stamp.

On April 4, 1953, Aiello was one of a dozen men arrested by the FBI for their alleged role in the theft of stolen paintings valued at more than $500,000. Area men arrested were John "Tar Baby" Millovich,[7] John Ralph Lupu of Warren and Charles R. LaCamera of Farrell, Pennsylvania, located just across the Ohio state line. The local arrests were carried out by a group of agents led by Stanley Peterson. FBI agents also made arrests in Cleveland and Chicago. The Windy City arrests included a former assistant U.S. attorney and a deputy bailiff of the Cook County Court.

The theft of the nine paintings took place on November 12, 1952, from St. Joseph's Cathedral in Bardstown, Kentucky. Three of the art pieces were said to have been works of the "old masters," and were a gift from King Louis Philippe of France. The paintings were believed to have been transported through Youngstown to Chicago where they were to be smuggled to Europe and sold.

On April 6, Aiello, Lupu and Millovich were arraigned and charged with conspiracy in interstate transportation of stolen property. As Aiello was being led in handcuffs from the city jail to the Post Office Building for the federal arraignment, the "usually congenial" mobster became angry and held his coat up to his face to avoid photographers. The men pled guilty and were each released on a $2,500 bond. Aiello hired attorney John Hooker to represent him at the trial set for May 22. After his release, Aiello went to a downtown restaurant where he told reporters he knew the FBI was following him for several weeks.

On April 24, Aiello staged what had the appearance of an impromptu press conference. He talked about his unemployment woes and announced that for the past few months he was receiving aid, to the tune of $28 a week, from the Ohio State Employment Service Office. Aiello told reporters that Chief Allen, "can't accuse me now of not trying to make an honest living." He explained, "I report to the employment office once a week and contact three businesses a week and try to get a job. None of them will hire me because of my reputation so I keep drawing compensation. At least Allen can't throw me in jail every time I turn around because I'm trying to find work." Aiello admitted that friends were willing to lend him money but won't give him a job because of police harassment. To add insult to injury, his recent arrest by the FBI for art theft resulted in a stoppage of his state compensation payments.

As the trial date for Aiello neared, the U.S. District Attorney in Cleveland announced that charges would be dropped against the area men if sufficient evidence wasn't produced or if witnesses from Chicago failed to appear. The FBI had to admit that obtaining evidence in the theft case was more difficult than at first believed. On June 2, 1953, the federal government formally dropped the charges against Aiello, Lupu and Millovich, as well as four Chicago men and one in Cleveland.

With the election of Frank X. Kryzan in November 1953, the six-year reign of Mayor Henderson and Chief Allen came to an end. Aiello had made good on his boast to the chief that, "I'll be around here longer than you will." Kryzan selected Paul H. Cress, a sergeant on the Youngstown police force, to be the next chief.

Cress had taken an unusual route to becoming Youngstown's police chief. Born on April 26, 1908, in Butler, Pennsylvania, Cress graduated from the local high school there. Cress decided to go into the ministry. He attended Missionary College in New York State for four years and Pittsburgh Theological Seminary. After receiving a Masters degree in Theology he was ordained in the clergy and assigned to a small church in Johnstown, Pennsylvania. Cress quickly became disenchanted with the lifestyle and on one of his return trips to Butler ran into a former seminary friend who had joined the Pennsylvania State Police. After a brief conversation Cress decided to make a rapid career change. Cress had a furnished house in Johnstown with a lot of personal belongings. He called a church official and told him he would not be returning. When asked what he wanted done with his belongings, Cress answered, "Use it, sell it, give it away, burn it, whatever you want to do with it." He never went back.

Cress was with the state police from 1930 to 1937. During that time he had occasion to be assigned to Sheriff Ralph Elser during several coal strikes in the Valley. Cress liked the people in the area, but decided that he needed a change of climate. He planned to move to the country's SouthWest and told his wife, "I'm going to have to go where the sun always shines." During an interview in 1981 Cress revealed what happened next:

> "I started for Arizona, got as far as Youngstown again, and stopped off overnight to see a policeman friend of mine. I got drunk and stayed drunk for a week. When I got sober, I discovered that I had met a hell of a lot of people. I had met, at the time, about 175,000 hunkies of one kind or another, but the best hunkies on the face of the earth. I liked those people. We had ideas in common. I never left. I made an application to the police department in 1930."

Cress didn't paint a very flattering picture of the Youngstown Police department that operated during the late 1930s and early 1940s:

> "You were sworn in, given a club, a badge, and a gun, and said, 'Now you're a policeman.' There wasn't very much training, but they put you in a cruiser with an old-timer. The old-timer could be one of the these and those guys; he didn't know a felony from a bag of cement, but he didn't need to. He had a strong back and a weak mind and that was all he needed. But, the young policeman learned from him. Unfortunately, he learned not only the little good that he needed to know to be a policeman, but he learned all the tricks of the trade, the negative features. If he was working with a crooked cop, you could depend on it that he was going to be a crooked cop.
>
> "In those days it was hard to tell the difference between a crooked cop and an honest cop. In 1940, the bug business, as we know it around here, was wide open. Business was good, the steel mills were working, everybody had money, the bus situation was good. We had trolley buses and cheap fares. Bug riders would make tours around the neighborhoods and pick up the money everyday and take your bet. Beer joints would have card tables set up just outside the door where you would bet your money on a number or a horse or a football game or basketball game. It wasn't the police department's fault, it wasn't enforced. It was the policy. It was a wide open town and you don't enforce moral laws when the town is wide open."

On January 6, 1954, vice squad members "began rounding up the city's most notorious racketeers for 'talks' with the chief." Aiello was the first to be brought in and warned about the new administration's "get tough" policy toward any renewal of bug activity.

The city was in the middle of an ongoing bombing campaign when Aiello was arrested for suspicion on June 14 along with six other racket figures. Aiello was identified in the newspaper on this occasion as one of the reputed "kings" of the local number's operations. New Vice Squad Chief George Krispli, whose family had recently received death threats, said the men would be "brought in continually for questioning until they convince police they are working at legitimate jobs."

Aiello was arrested again for suspicion on August 8 and questioned about gambling activities and the July bombing of Mahoning County Democratic Party Chairman Jack Sulligan's home. During the interrogation Aiello informed Chief Cress that he was employed for the past two weeks at an industrial company in Farrell, Pennsylvania. Aiello was detained in jail for 25 hours during this most recent arrest and responded by filing a $2,500 lawsuit against Cress and one of his patrolmen. The suit claimed that Aiello's "arrest without charge had deprived him of his right to make a legal living as an assistant labor foreman." Cress laughed and said, "I wish him luck, if he thinks he can get any money out of me. I don't think the American public will give comfort and reward to punks and racketeers that can't justify their existence." In October 1955, a common pleas judge dismissed the suit.

When Jack Sulligan's house was bombed for the second time in a little over two years in November 1956, police, as they had after the first bombing, brought Aiello in on a suspicion charge. Aiello, for some reason in an affable mood, claimed he didn't mind being picked up or questioned by the vice squad men. When he professed to be willing to talk to "anyone about anything," the detectives used the opportunity to see if he would take a lie detector test. Aiello flat out refused. A request to be examined under "truth serum" was also denied by him.

On January 15, 1957, Aiello was arrested downtown on an "open charge" by detectives from Youngstown and Warren. He spent the night in the Warren city jail. Aiello was questioned by Warren Police Chief, Manley English, who later told reporters, "We only wanted to ask him a few questions...and he had nothing to say." A detective captain related, "The only positive bit of information we were able to get out of him is that he doesn't like our jail." The newspapers speculated the questioning had to do with a couple of robberies in the area during late 1956.

The harassment of Aiello reached a peak on April 9, 1957, when he was picked up three times for questioning during a 12-hour period. With no break in the on-going bombing campaign, Kryzan issued an order to "bring in known underworld characters on any excuse and to harass them and also quiz them for any information they may have on the blasts." Chief Cress told reporters, "If necessary we will pull these gamblers' and racketeers' cars off the streets and we don't care if they are Cadillacs. We're going to follow the mayor's orders to the letter."

As usual, Aiello was the first to be picked up – due mainly to the fact he was always easy to find hanging out at the Purple Cow. Police found him there at 3:00 p.m. and brought him in for questioning. Eight hours later, another team of vice detectives found him in the restaurant and again hauled him down the street to the police station. When he returned to the Purple Cow at 1:30 a.m., he was grabbed for the third time.

Captain William R. Golden explained, "On the three arrests the various vice squad men did not know Aiello had been arrested and questioned earlier." Aiello complained he would be better off working in a steel mill. He told Golden he would never be given a legitimate job "because his picture is hanging on the walls of police headquarters with many other wanted men and known racketeers, gamblers and bombing suspects."

Golden was unimpressed with the gambler's plight, "I don't think Aiello would last long anyway if he got a job in a steel mill. He would probably work three or four days and then file for unemployment compensation."

Anything that happened to Aiello seemed to be news in Youngstown. Whether it was an arrest for gambling, robbery or just suspicion, the underworld figure made good copy. In July 1955, an automobile accident he was involved in was reported, as well as an injury he suffered to his knee while getting out of his car in May 1957. Aiello was clearly Youngstown's version of the "walking media event," the label that was bestowed upon New York City mob boss John Gotti in the late 1980s. In August 1957, Aiello was front-page news again as the IRS seized his new 1957 Ford convertible for non-payment of income taxes from 1947. This was the culmination of the tax agents' work that began back in 1952. The Ford convertible was scheduled for auction on September 10 at the U-Drive-It Company garage. When potential buyers found out a finance company held a $2,300 mortgage on the automobile, no one bid on it. IRS agents gave up trying to sell the car and abandoned it so it could be repossessed by the finance company.

Aiello was next brought in for questioning on July 15, 1958. Again picked up outside the Purple Cow, Aiello told police that while he didn't have a job he was living off the money he received from the settlement of an auto accident in which he was involved.

The year 1959 proved to be a watershed year for Aiello. In January, a Trumbull County grand jury secretly indicted him on three counts of robbery. In the first count he was charged with robbing the Greenwold Company on November 30, 1956. Aiello was alleged to be one of four gunmen who entered and then hid until the store closed. The robbers made off with $20,000. He was charged in the

October 1956 burglary at the Rappold Company where $10,000 in cash and furs were taken. The last charge involved a burglary at the Strouss-Hirshberg Company in 1958. The thieves in that robbery blew a safe and made off with $8,000.

On May 26, 1959, in an article that could not have made his wife of sixteen years happy, the *Vindicator* reported that Aiello was arrested by FBI agents and a Mahoning County chief deputy sheriff at "the home of a Wickliffe girlfriend." Although the charge was later dropped, Aiello was initially arrested at the home for "flight to avoid prosecution." The article stated Aiello was arrested without incident. "He had just begun eating a steak dinner, but lost his appetite when the officers arrived. Aiello has been a frequent visitor to the Wickliffe home." The next day Aiello was released from the Trumbull County jail after a bond of $37,000 was posted.

On October 14, Aiello was indicted by a Mahoning County grand jury and charged with violating the state banking laws by writing a check for $28,500 that bounced. This latest incident began back on March 27. In what was alleged to be his "habit," Aiello would go to an area bank just before Friday closing and cash a check for a large amount. He used the money, according to a newspaper report, "to finance floating gambling games for high-stakes in the district that night and then deposit the money [in his own bank] to cover the check as soon as the bank" opened for business Monday morning.

The rumor was that Aiello had lost big on this occasion and was unable to cover the check. At Union National Bank, where he had cashed the check, the bank's policy was to verify a check of that size could be covered by the bank it was drawn on – in this case the Dollar Savings Bank of Niles – or at least have the approval of a bank official. Because the procedure was not adhered to, the teller, a ten-year employee, was dismissed.

Why the bank failed to take immediate legal action was not explained. Instead, they approached Aiello, who agreed to pay back the money in increments of no less than $250 per week. Aiello's payments, which totaled $3,500, stopped soon after he was indicted for the Warren robberies. In July, an attorney for the Union National Bank filed a complaint and an arrest warrant was issued for Aiello. Arrested on July 9, Aiello was free on a $25,000 bond the same day after his latest attorney, Donald Hanni entered a not guilty plea for him in Judge Cavalier's courtroom. In August, Aiello was held over to the grand jury in the matter and two months later was indicted.

As the decade of the 1950s was coming to an end Aiello was facing another highly publicized trial.

Dominic "Moosey" Caputo

Of the "Big Three," Moosey Caputo was the only one who had his roots in the in the Valley. Dominic A. Caputo, Jr. was born on November 1, 1902, the sixth of nine children of Dominic and Porsia Caputo, who raised their large family in the Brier Hill section of Youngstown. During the Prohibition years his father ran a local saloon and the family lived on West Federal Street.

Four of Moosey's older siblings died before they reached their 30th birthday. Peter, the oldest brother, was the first to pass away. During the mid-1910s, Peter was attending a circus at Wright Field on the city's East Side. Like many of the circuses that traveled around the Midwest at that time, one of the attractions was a boxer who offered to "take on" anyone in the crowd. If the challenger could go three rounds with the pugilist there was usually a monetary reward. Peter Caputo came out of the crowd to challenge the boxer. After three rounds Peter was declared the winner of the bout. The embarrassed loser responded by stabbing Caputo when his back was turned, partially severing his lung. Peter never fully recovered from the devastation caused by the wound and a few years later, after contracting pneumonia, died at the age of 20 on April 18, 1918.

On July 18, 1922, Michael Caputo, described as a prominent businessman, died at his home in Girard at the age of 29. The second oldest brother, after graduating from Brier Hill School, worked for several years in the local steel mills. Michael, whose birth name was spelled Michele, saved enough money to purchase a grocery store in Girard, where he was successful and became a highly respected member of the community. While he was reported in poor health for the past few years, his death came as a shock to both family and friends. Michael left behind a wife and young son.

The Caputo's second daughter, Margaret, passed away at the age of 22 on May 8, 1927. The beautiful young lady died after complications from a two-month illness.

The Caputo's third son, Anthony, was murdered during what was described as "bootleg warfare," in August 1928.

Tall and handsome with black wavy hair, Moosey Caputo was always particular about his dress. Caputo got his nickname at a young age. When he didn't get his way he displayed a long face and sulked, which in Italian was referred to as *muso lungo*, and his family and friends called him "Moosey" for short. Caputo didn't particularly like the nickname and tolerated being called that only by a select group of people. According to city directories, Caputo worked at Youngstown Sheet & Tube Company in the early 1930s. In the 1920s, Caputo married Margaret Reider and the couple had a son they named John. In August 1930, Caputo and Margaret were granted a divorce. The couple made amends and remarried, later having two more sons.

Moosey made the newspapers for the first time on March 29, 1923 when, at the age of 20, he was arrested by federal agents for violating the Volstead Act. The Valley's Chief Federal Prohibition Enforcement Officer, William L. Bence and his men "invaded the premises of Dominic Caputo" at his Brier Hill home on Dearborn Street. It was no small cache the agents uncovered. Confiscated were four 50-gallon stills and 30 gallons of newly distilled raisin jack. More than 1,100 gallons of mash were seized.

Less than a year later, on March 7, 1924, Caputo was arrested for suspicion after a raid at 2448 West Federal Street. The building housed a restaurant, poolroom and confectionery. The newspaper reported that "Caputo was the only person in the place and is believed to be the owner of the building although he has not been alleged to have taken any part in liquor sales." When booked, Moosey told officers he was a farmer. In January 1926, an overheated hot water heater caused a fire which gutted the poolroom and confectionery and damaged the restaurant. At that time the building's owner was reported to be Frank Caputo.

On July 2, 1934, Caputo was arrested for operating a gambling house on North Chestnut Street. A squad of deputies, led by Mahoning County Sheriff William J. Engelhardt, broke through a barred door and raided the place at 1:10 a.m. The owner of the place, Emanuel H. Dupuy, was arrested during a raid five weeks earlier at the location. Caputo, whom the newspaper claimed used the alias "Joe White," was fined $100.

The North Chestnut Street location was gaining a notorious reputation. In August 1934, an arrest warrant was sworn out for Caputo and Dupuy after attorney Kedgwin H. Powell claimed his client, a downtown businessman, lost some $400 to $500 of his store's money in a crooked dice game there. Powell also pointed out that another individual, who won $800 in the gambling joint, was slugged and relieved of his winnings as he left building. On August 29, Caputo and Dupuy turned themselves in at police headquarters. After pleading not guilty at arraignment, both were released on a $100 bond. On September 27, the two were found guilty before Municipal Court Judge Henry P. Beckenbach. The judge reduced the $100 fines he handed the pair to $50 each. The businessman testified in court that Caputo and Dupuy tried to have the case fixed through the police chief's secretary, a charge that he denied. When questioned the next day the secretary claimed attorney Powell had approached him and said, "If something isn't done to get this fellow's money back, I'll blow the roof off things."

The reporting of Caputo's first name caused confusion for years. During his arrests in the 1920s he was referred to as Dominic. Arrests in the 1930s had his name as Moosey. For years after that the newspapers listed his name as Donald B. Caputo. In fact, Caputo once used that name in the city directory. He was referred to as Donald in the newspapers well into the 1960s. During the late 1930s and early 1940s, when Caputo operated the Paddock Bar at 258 West Federal Street, he was listed on the ownership papers as Dominic.

Moosey ran the Paddock Bar with his older brother Frank. Born on June 20, 1900, in Youngstown, Frank attended Brier Hill School. On April 18, 1920, police broke up a fistfight Frank was involved in and discovered he was in possession of a handgun. He was charged with carrying a concealed weapon. Indicted, Frank pled guilty and was fined $100. In April 1925, Frank was accused by a Spring Lane resident of hitting him over the head "with a blunt instrument without warning or provocation." In March 1927, the city filed a suit against Frank and his bondsman to recover a $100 bond after Frank failed to appear in court on a charge of reckless driving. On April 10, 1930, after being involved in another fight, he was arrested for assault and battery; he paid a $25 fine. On October 31, 1934, tragedy struck when Frank's 24 year-old wife, Catherine Schonhut died after a brief illness. The couple was married for seven years and had a young daughter. Frank later married Evelyn Coxey in the late 1930s.

Moosey Caputo became associated with the Jungle Inn during the latter half of the 1930s. In November 1940, the operators of record, in addition to Caputo, were Mike Farah, Edward Flannigan and Moosey's old North Chestnut Street gambling partner Emanuel Dupuy. Shuttling patrons from the Paddock Bar to the Jungle Inn became a family effort as Moosey's brothers Frank and John, and brother-in-law Phillip Micklas, helped with the transportation. In addition to working as a bartender at the Paddock, Micklas served as a "coopman" at the Jungle Inn. He entered the gun turret and from this vantage point had a complete view of the gambling den, where he watched for anyone with intentions of robbing the place. Dominic Caputo left the Jungle Inn after Edward F. Tobin became involved.

During the trial of Jerry Pascarella in December 1941, in which he was charged with carrying a concealed weapon, he explained that he needed it for protection from Frank "Cowboy" Chako and Frank Carey. The two were gunmen employed by Moosey Caputo, who had ordered Pascarella to "kick in" profits from his small allotment of slot machines or "get out of the business." During his testimony Pascarella let the judge know that Caputo was "said to run all the rackets here."

Caputo and Frank Cassano were targets of Simon Leis and his special grand jury that was investigating gambling and criminal activity in the Valley during the first half of 1943. On February 17, Mahoning County deputies seized 71 slot machines owned by Caputo from the home of Anthony Napolita. The same day the home of Jack Zizzo was raided and 14 machines belonging to Cassano were confiscated. Napolita and Zizzo were described as "second in command" to the slot machine owners.

Just days after the lottery house operators were indicted in June 1943, another 16 men were named in a separate indictment. On June 29, all of the men were charged with making book on horse races except Caputo and Cassano, who were charged as being slot machine operators. The two went into hiding for a short period before surrendering at the Mahoning County jail on July 6. Both men were released after posting a $4,000 bond.

Trial was scheduled for October 5, but the day before the two men pled guilty before Judge Newcomb. Caputo, who had never spent a day in jail, was convicted of "exhibiting gambling devices." The "devices" were slot machines, which were placed in drug stores and candy shops all around the city. Caputo was charged with ten counts, Cassano with six. The charges carried a penalty of 90 days in jail and a $500 fine. Newcomb ordered that the sentences run concurrently for both men and he fined Caputo $2,500 and Cassano $1,000. Both were allowed eight days to "wind up their affairs" before reporting to the county jail.

After the sentencing, Special Prosecutor Leis wanted the slot machines destroyed and the scrap metal donated to the defense industry. Attorney David C. Haynes convinced the judge that since a third man, Joseph Rango, who was serving in the Army, had a financial interest in the machines, that their "destruction be held up as a matter of courtesy" until Rango returned from the service. Promising that the machines "will be destroyed eventually," Newcomb agreed to the "stay" of destruction.

On October 13, Caputo began his 90-day term in the Mahoning County jail. It was a memorable one. Two days after he entered, attorney Haynes went to court with a doctor and another medical professional to claim Caputo was physically unable to serve a 90-day sentence. The doctor told Judge Newcomb that his client suffered from "a painful illness which had its origin in the nerve center and affected the legs and back." In the doctor's professional opinion, 90 days in stir "would aggravate Caputo's condition." Reports of Caputo's health in the newspaper caused an embarrassing moment for the gambler when he received a "beautifully wrapped box of flowers" in his jail cell. An attached note read: "With sympathy during your illness while in county jail." It was signed, "A Friend." Caputo received "quite a ribbing" from his fellow jail mates, which included Cassano, Frank Budak, and South Side lottery house leaders "Big Dom" Mallamo, Frank Gioia and Joseph Fezzuogho. The incident caused Caputo to abandon his efforts for a medical release.

Years later Caputo's nephew Thomas Micklas chuckled about Moosey's health problems. "He was as healthy as a bear. It was just his lawyer's effort to get him released." Micklas, the son of Moosey's oldest sister Fannie, remembers his aunt, Caputo's wife Margaret, preparing huge feasts for Moosey. Micklas helped deliver the pasta meals – complete with meatballs, sausage, braziole and even bottles of wine – to the county jail.

Sundays had always been a festive time in the Caputo household. After the death of Moosey's father in 1938, his mother would cook large meals for her children, grandchildren and their friends. Before a falling out between them, Frank Carey was one of the Sunday regulars. Micklas recalls that Carey always began the meal by spilling wine on the tablecloth to anoint it. Micklas said, "Big, tough guys would come to the home for dinner and always pay respect to Caputo's mother Porsia. My uncle brought only a few, select people around and they were always closed-mouth about their activities. Moosey was very secretive about his business and questions were never asked. After the meals Porsia would gather the clan together and say, "*Vi racconto una cosa.*" Let me tell you a story. Moosey would thank his mother by massaging her feet for hours while she told stories in Italian."

The 90-day term didn't prevent Caputo from enjoying the Thanksgiving holiday with his family. Citing that Caputo's son, John was being inducted into the Army, Judge Newcomb allowed the mobster a furlough to mark the occasion. (John was later wounded during the Battle of the Bulge.) This was followed by five days of hospitalization in mid-December when Caputo was ill with the flu. Less than a week after he returned to jail, Judge Newcomb granted Caputo, Mallamo and Cassano a Christmas leave from December 24 until January 3. On January 12, 1944, Caputo and Cassano were released from the county jail. Between hospital time and approved releases Caputo had spent a total of 72 days in jail; Cassano served 80 days.[8]

Two and a half years later Caputo was back in the news. In June 1946, the Caputo brothers paid a fine of $2,800 for overcharging on drinks at the Paddock Bar. The fines came after customers complained to the Office of Price Administration in Cleveland. In the wake of the OPA incident, the Caputo brothers were told to vacate the West Federal Street building that housed their bar. In the early months of 1947, Frank was searching for a new business location when family and friends noticed that he was growing despondent. He began to suffer severe headaches. Family members believed this was caused by the drinking binges Frank sometimes went on. While a patrolman in the early 1940s, future Police Chief John Terlesky remembered several occasions when he was called out to a bar where Frank had gotten drunk at. "I would get Frank into the squad car and take him home to his mother. She would then proceed to chew him out in Italian," Terlesky recalled with a smile.

Frank's drinking may have been behind a cover-up shooting at the Canteen Club on North Chestnut Street during the early hours of March 12, 1941. Witnesses reported seeing an "intoxicated man" shooting a gun in front of the establishment and that police disarmed him and took him home. Despite the fact that police officers were seen collecting spent shells from the sidewalk in front of the club and that there was a fresh bullet hole in the front door, Police Captain Eugene McElvoy denied there was shooting and claimed the noises witnesses heard was an automobile backfiring. Some witnesses claimed that the Caputo brothers were outside the club and that Frank was the one doing the shooting. When asked for a comment about the incident by a reporter, Moosey stated, "You can bet all the tea in China" that no shooting took place. "This town's too small to keep a thing like that quiet." Canteen Club operator, Carl Rango, who was seen holding the "intoxicated man" in the club doorway until police arrived, denied statements made by witnesses and blamed the noise on somebody "shooting fire crackers out of season." Rango also denied that either Caputo brother was present. Despite Frank Caputo's drinking, which had brought on his problems in the past, he was well liked in the community and was known to be quite generous.

On March 31, 1947, Frank was working at the Paddock Bar. Around 6:15 that evening he received a telephone call. After hanging up, Frank went to a small office, which was used to cash checks, where he said goodbye to an employee on her way out. Frank quietly closed the door, pulled out a .38 caliber revolver and placed the gun to his head. Employees heard a muffled shot and when they unlocked the office door found Frank on the floor with the revolver gripped so tightly in his hand they had to pry it loose. Rushed by ambulance to South Side Hospital, doctors pronounced the 46 year-old dead on arrival. When the *Vindicator* reported his death the next day they printed a picture of Frank from one of his arrests with the jail numbers appearing. Veteran *Vindicator* columnist Esther Hamilton, at one time a recipient of Frank's generosity, was provoked at the newspaper's insensitivity and commented as such in one of her columns. A nicer picture of Frank was then printed in an obituary that appeared the next day.

Another Paddock Bar was opened in Brier Hill and owned by John Caputo, Phillip Micklas and another relative. While the operation was short-lived, one of the personalities that appeared there was singer Vic Damone.

For the remainder of the 1940s Moosey Caputo avoided the limelight that engulfed Aiello and DiCarlo. Many believed that of the three men Caputo was just a muscleman. His name seemed to appear in print only when he was being referred to in connection with the other two. After the exposure received by the trio during the Kefauver Hearings in the early 1950s, Caputo and Joe DiCarlo, according to an October 30, 1951 *Vindicator* article, "pulled up stakes and pitched their tents in a new climate - Florida - after selling their expensive homes at less than cost just to get away from Police Chief Edward J. Allen, Jr." Caputo had actually begun traveling to Florida in 1938 and was associated with the Valhalla Club there.

In October 1952, Caputo ended his Florida hiatus and returned to Youngstown and was immediately questioned by the vice squad. Caputo claimed the reason for his return was his 80 year-old mother's recent illness, and a bout of rheumatism he was suffering. He planned to bring his family up from Hollywood, Florida, after the end of the 1953 school term. Caputo informed the detectives, concerned about his employment, that he had a position as a used car salesman at a North Side dealership.

Caputo boasted that while in Florida he had helped organize the Italian-American Civic League in Hollywood. He stated that Florida Governor Fuller Warren was a guest speaker. Chief Allen was quick to counter that the Kefauver Committee had criticized Governor Warren for failing to cooperate with its investigation two years earlier.

In October 1953, Chief Allen announced he had reports that Caputo "and a group of hoodlums" had muscled in on The Ranch, a gambling house on Route 422. Allen revealed that, "A co-owner of The Ranch property told me last week that he became 'scared' when he saw Caputo and his band of assorted hoodlums taking over the nightspot. This man said he has been trying to sell his interest in the gambling joint."

In May 1954, Caputo had a different story to tell police about his local presence. His relocation from Florida to Youngstown was only temporary. He was now operating a construction company in Hollywood, but planned to spend the summers up north visiting his elderly mother and a sister. After his latest return he dropped into the police station voluntarily to let vice squad chief George Krispli know that he did not "plan to enter or help set up any rackets during his stay."

Caputo's real reason for returning was revealed a week later when private detectives working for the Waterford Park Race Track in Chester, West Virginia, threw Moosey off the grounds for running a bookie service there. During the 1953 racing season Caputo began booking bets at the track and returned the next season to pick up where he left off. The detectives put him under surveillance after seeing him huddled with a number of track patrons. He tried to mask his activities by jumping in and out of the track's legal betting-window lines. Once caught, Caputo was escorted to a private office and questioned before being ushered off the premises with the promise that if he ever returned he would be arrested for trespassing.

Nearly three years passed before Caputo was back in the news. It was again in Chester, West Virginia, this time at a gambling casino called Club 30. Chester is one of West Virginia's northern-most cities, making it a convenient locale for gamblers from the Mahoning Valley, Pittsburgh and Wheeling. The club was a popular hangout, operating as a restaurant, bar and casino for several years. The newspaper claimed the casino's "drawing power" from the Valley was Caputo, who reportedly worked there since he was tossed from the Waterford Park Race Track.

Gambling at the casino was believed to have come to an end in January 1957 with the election of a new sheriff. A *Pittsburgh Post Gazette* story stated that the new sheriff was under the impression that gambling had shut down there once he took office. A March 13 *Vindicator* article reported the alleged closing of the club "came as a surprise to many Youngstowners who spent the evening drinking, dining and gambling at the Route 30 casino Saturday night." The story continued:

> "Youngstowners who like to eat and drink where they can gamble reported the club 'in full swing' Saturday night. They said parking lot attendants take your car when you reach the main entrance and you may enter the club without questioning. This is always an indication that the operators are not worried about the law.
>
> "There were three roulette tables, three crap tables several poker games and a big bingo game, with the bingo followers getting into the other forms of gambling during the frequent intermissions."

The publicity generated by the two newspaper articles forced the club to shut down within days. By mid-May the casino was operating again under a new name – the Tri-State Social Club.

Caputo continued to make trips to Youngstown, "at least once a year," to visit his sister. One of these trips, in July 1958, caused speculation that he and DiCarlo were returning to "take over the rackets." Caputo was in and out of town before police could pick him up. The newspaper reported that, "Detective George Krispli, morals squad chief...learned of the rumor the two 'bigwigs' were planning to move in to Youngstown and take a 50 per cent cut of any and all rackets." Police responded by dragging in Vince DeNiro at 1:00 o'clock in the morning to question him about the rumors. DeNiro claimed he had not seen either man in the past ten years and that the rumor couldn't be true "because there aren't any rackets here to take over."

Joseph "Joe the Wolf" DiCarlo

Joseph J. "Joe the Wolf" DiCarlo was one of the few Mahoning Valley mobsters of whom it could be said that he was born of gangland stock. DiCarlo's father was the first recognized Mafia boss of Buffalo, New York. DiCarlo was born in Vallelunga, Sicily in 1899. He came to the United States with his family in 1907 and settled in New York City. After a couple of years the family relocated to Buffalo. DiCarlo's father Giuseppe was affectionately known as "Don Pietro" and became known as the first Mafia boss of Buffalo sometime during the 1910s. Joe DiCarlo's uncle (a cousin by marriage), Angelo "Buffalo Bill" Palmeri was reputed to serve as the second-in-command or "underboss" of the family.

Before Joe DiCarlo reached the age of 23 his family suffered a series of tragedies. In 1918, his brother Frank died of tuberculosis while still in his teens. A year later his mother died of cancer at the age of 45. His father, only 49 years old, suffered a heart attack and died in 1922. According to an FBI file, an informant claimed that Joe DiCarlo "was suggested to succeed his father as czar, but was considered too young and irresponsible for the position." Instead, Stefano Magaddino is alleged to have taken over the family and ruled it for 52 years until his death in 1974, making him one of the longest serving Mafia family leaders in the nation's history. Still, young DiCarlo left his mark on the city. The titles of "Public Enemy #1," "Racketeer #1" and "the Al Capone of Buffalo" were bestowed upon him by law enforcement and the media.

During the early 1920s, Buffalo gained a reputation as a hub of illegal narcotics activity. On January 6, 1923, the "most sensational dope seizure ever made" in New York State took place as 20 state and federal narcotics agents swept through the city and made over 40 arrests and confiscated more than $100,000 worth of heroin, morphine, opium and cocaine. One of the first locations raided was a drug store in the city where agents arrested six people including DiCarlo. He told agents he was there to purchase a cigar. DiCarlo was released on bail and the charges against him were soon dropped due to lack of evidence. He returned to operating his Auto Rest Inn, a roadhouse located in Williamsville, New York. Oft raided for prohibition violations, DiCarlo operated the inn with his partner Minnie Clark, a woman known as "Jew Minnie."

One of the men arrested during the raids was Joseph "Busy Joe" Pattituccio. A former infantryman during World War I, Pattituccio developed a drug addiction after he was wounded during fighting in France. He had recently completed a six-month term in the county jail for a narcotics violation. On July 23 he was sentenced to two years in prison by Federal Judge John C. Knox.[9] A few days before Pattituccio was to be transported to the Atlanta Penitentiary, he testified in secret before the mayor about police corruption in the city. On July 29, Judge Knox released Pattituccio on a $17,000 bond after a "writ of error," a prelude to a new trial, was granted.

On the afternoon of August 21, with information supplied by Pattituccio, two undercover narcotics agents met with DiCarlo associate Peter "Pete the Slash" Giallelli in front of the Ford Hotel to purchase $35 worth of morphine. DiCarlo, who was alleged to be part of the transaction, was seated in a car across from the hotel. DiCarlo recognized the men and shouted to Giallelli, "Look out for the two agents." With that DiCarlo gunned the engine and made a "sensational getaway," but not before one of the agents got his license plate number. Agents had a search warrant for Giallelli's home and found four ounces of cocaine there. Both Giallelli and his wife were taken into custody.

Federal officials claimed Joe DiCarlo was the "brains" of the dope ring and that it was operating for the past four years. With the arrests in January, members of the ring were starting to "rat out" DiCarlo. Pattituccio helped set up the buy; Giallelli had implicated DiCarlo as a participant in the drug transaction; and two inmates in Atlanta were claiming to have purchased their drugs from him. DiCarlo was arrested twelve hours later in front of the same hotel. U.S. Attorney William J. Donovan[10] rushed in from New York City in time to make sure DiCarlo's bail was set high. "I want to make sure that DiCarlo does not get out easily. We have him now and I don't want to take the chances of his running away. Bail of $25,000 would be mighty cheap. He could produce it in no time," claimed Donovan. The $50,000 bond Donovan demanded, however, was furnished just as fast and DiCarlo was a free man. Meanwhile, Giallelli was left in a cell to fend for himself.

At the upcoming trial, Pattituccio was scheduled to be one of the government's key witnesses. Around 11:30 p.m. on New Year's Day 1924, Pattituccio and his common-law wife, May Gilmore, had just finished dinner at a restaurant and were returning to their automobile. A car containing four men pulled alongside the curb behind them and DiCarlo and Giallelli jumped out and began shooting. The first bullet, fired by Giallelli, slammed into Pattituccio's chin. He spun around and ran as seven more bullets whizzed by him, two of which struck his clothing, one imbedding itself in his coat. At the end of the street he was stopped by a Buffalo police officer who escorted him to a nearby hospital. Pattituccio's wound was not serious. After it was attended to he went to the police station to make a statement.

DiCarlo was arrested at the Auto Rest Inn, while Giallelli and two other men, Gaetano Capodicaco and Joseph Ruffino, were quickly rounded up. Held on $100,000 bonds each, within hours money for all, except Giallelli, was raised by family and friends. Police also arrested Philip Mangano, who they believed to be a fifth member of the gang, as a material witness. Mangano[11] had arrived in town a week earlier from New York City. He had little trouble in making his $15,000 bond. As in his earlier arrest, Giallelli was left behind to languish in jail. Numerous witnesses were secured to testify before a federal grand jury just thirty-six hours after the shooting. Pattituccio appeared before the panel still wearing the same bloodstained clothes he wore the night of the shooting.

On February 6, testimony began in what was described by the *Buffalo Morning Express* as a trial based on "charges of conspiracy to obstruct the administration of justice by interfering with a government witness." The courtroom was crowded with relatives and friends of the defendants who, on more than one occasion, were admonished by the judge for their outbursts. Pattituccio was the third witness called and described for the jury the events of the evening he was wounded. He pointed out DiCarlo and Giallelli as his assailants. Under cross-examination Pattituccio admitted his past as a dope peddler in the city and discussed his previous arrests. He admitted that he had enjoyed several glasses of wine that night with dinner.

Later that afternoon the prosecution put a convicted narcotics dealer on the stand. The government called him to tell the jury that DiCarlo and the others had threatened to murder Pattituccio. The witness backfired though and testified that Pattituccio had told him that he would "hang DiCarlo if it was the last thing he ever did."

The next morning things didn't get any better for the prosecution as May Gilmore took the stand. The 25 year-old testified that she was Pattituccio's common-law wife for two years and that she was a drug addict, who only recently had "taken the cure." After reviewing events leading up to the time of the shooting, Prosecutor Donovan asked Gilmore if she saw the men who fired at her husband.

"I did not," May replied.

"Did you not tell before the federal grand jury that you did see the men and gave their names?" the astonished Donovan exclaimed.

"I did, because my husband told me to do it," she responded. "He told me before I went before the grand jury that he was not positive it was DiCarlo and Giallelli, but was suspicious of them. We were both intoxicated on the night of the shooting."

At this point Federal Judge George S. Morris cut it. "You were under oath before the grand jury...and you were under oath here?" he asked.

"I guess so," May Gilmore answered.

"Well, I order you in the custody of the court and the United States marshal on a charge of perjury," the judge stated. Gilmore was whisked out of the courtroom.

Donovan was able to counter the damage by calling several police officers to testify that neither Pattituccio nor Gilmore were drunk the night of the shooting and that Gilmore named DiCarlo and Giallelli as the assailants.

When the defense began their case they presented nine witnesses who placed DiCarlo at the New York Central Railroad Depot at the time of the shooting. He had taken his uncle Angelo Palmeri, who was leaving on a trip to New York City, to the station. The witnesses included a city detective and an employee of the railroad. DiCarlo was the only one of the four defendants who did not take the stand.

One witness, employed by the Yellow Taxicab Company, testified that he spoke to DiCarlo at the station. Prosecutor Donovan questioned, "Let's see, John Montana[12] owns the Yellow Taxicab Company, doesn't he?"

"He does," the witness replied.

"And how long have you known DiCarlo?" Donovan asked.

"I was brought up in the same neighborhood with him, I knew him well," came the answer.

As a rebuttal witness, the government put on a New York Central Railroad detective who testified that a lawyer, whom he wouldn't identify on advice of the prosecutor, had offered him a bribe. The man was accompanied by Giallelli's attorney, who walked away before the bribe offer was made. "If you will be right in this thing, I have $1,500 in my pocket for you, all you have to do is go easy on this case," the detective stated he was told. He admitted to seeing DiCarlo at the station that night, but claimed he left shortly after 11:00.

On February 11, after closing statements, the jury received their instructions from the judge and began deliberations around 6:00 p.m. After deliberating for over six hours they returned to the courtroom with their verdict at 1:15 a.m. All but Gaetano Capodicaco were found guilty and Judge Morris sentenced the men immediately. DiCarlo and Giallelli[13] were each handed a six-year sentence and fined $5,000. Ruffino was sentenced to two years and fined $1,000. Ironically, although DiCarlo was convicted of obstruction of justice in the narcotics case, he never stood trial for the actual August 1923 narcotics arrest.

After appeals failed, DiCarlo reported to the Atlanta Federal Penitentiary on April 16, 1925, to begin his sentence. DiCarlo remained there for a little over a year before being transferred to the U.S. Industrial Reformatory in Chillicothe, Ohio, on July 23, 1926. He was incarcerated there until he was paroled on October 19, 1928. DiCarlo remained on parole until September of the following year. When he was released in 1928, DiCarlo signed what was called a "pauper's oath," which rendered the $5,000 fine "temporarily uncollectable." DiCarlo's non-payment of this debt would come back to haunt him decades later.

After his release DiCarlo returned to Buffalo and waited out his parole. In June 1931 he was one of 33 people arrested during a grand jury investigation probing a protection racket involving bootleggers in what was known as the Niagara Frontier section. Even though police believed that DiCarlo was the ringleader, when the grand jury issued their indictments his name was not on the list. This did not stop Police Commissioner Austin J. Roche from bestowing the title of Public Enemy No. 1 on DiCarlo.

Police kept the heat on DiCarlo throughout 1931, but couldn't charge him with anything substantial. The charges ended up being dismissed (vagrancy), or he was acquitted (election fraud), and once he was forced to pay a $5.00 fine (traffic violation). In March 1934, new Police Commissioner James W. Higgins removed the public enemy label stating, "Joe rode the wave of publicity and built himself up until he believed he was a big shot. I believe he was overrated as a so-called public enemy by my predecessor in office [Roche] for they never fastened anything on Joe."

Despite the apparent public demotion, DiCarlo was listed as "No. 1" in the "packet galleries" carried by all detectives. Meanwhile, DiCarlo was responsible for the new wave of slot machines that began arriving in the Buffalo area by June 1932. When the competition reached the point of violence during the summer of 1934, DiCarlo was arrested and questioned about it. During the booking process DiCarlo gave his occupation as florist.

On June 3, 1935, DiCarlo was arrested under the state's newly enacted Brownell Law, consorting with known criminals. Nabbed while conversing with Anthony Battaglia in front of a theatre, DiCarlo howled, "You ain't got nothing on me. I ain't bothering nobody." Battaglia, hardly a master criminal, had a rap sheet that showed arrests for disorderly conduct, playing cards on Sunday, vagrancy and corner lounging. The two were soon bailed out.

On July 30, 1936, DiCarlo was arrested after a bookie accused him and John "Peanuts" Tronolone of assault in Cheektowaga, New York, a suburb east of Buffalo. It was believed that DiCarlo was involved in another protection racket, this time it was the local bookmakers. In explaining his stand to the police, the assault victim stated, "I'm going through with this. I won't kick in to the racket men, and I won't let DiCarlo or any of his mob get away with this." When the case came to trial on March 1, 1937, the victim suddenly got cold feet and claimed he was unable to identify his assailants. Defense counsel asked for the charges to be dismissed, but a determined judge denied the motion. The next day, a juror reported that he was threatened by telephone the night before. The judge then declared a mistrial, released the jury and ordered a new trial to begin immediately. On March 3, the new jury found DiCarlo and Tronolone not guilty.

A year later, on St. Valentine's Day 1938, DiCarlo was arrested after being accused of trying to "muscle in" on the cigarette vending machine business. The following month, during the trial the victim testified DiCarlo threatened to "smash my head in," and then promised "after this thing is all through, you'll find Joe DiCarlo is still running this city and there won't be any room for you fellows." On March 10, after deliberating just 44 minutes, the jury returned a verdict of guilty of coercion. On April 1, DiCarlo was sentenced to one-year in the Erie County Penitentiary and fined $500.

DiCarlo was not back in Buffalo for long before he was in trouble again. On September 7, DiCarlo, Tronolone and several others, including two police officers, were named in a secret indictment by the grand jury. DiCarlo fled to Ohio when charged with conspiracy and extortion. A fugitive for two months, DiCarlo was indicted by a Federal grand jury for flight to avoid prosecution. He remained a fugitive for six months before negotiating a deal to surrender. On May 31, 1940, he was arrested and pled guilty to the conspiracy charge. He was sentenced to the maximum – a year in the penitentiary and a $500 fine. The *Buffalo Evening News* reported:

> "Within an hour after his arrest, he admitted his guilt in a conspiracy with three other defendants to extort money and property from persons and groups by influencing police in their duties. They also were charged with seeking control of bookmakers and dealers in slot machines and mechanical musical instruments."

DiCarlo, who had not paid the fine from his 1925 conviction, signing the "pauper's oath," was told if this fine wasn't paid he would serve an additional day for each dollar owed.

In January 1945, DiCarlo and Tronolone were named in yet another indictment, this time for gambling-conspiracy. Indicted with them was Buffalo Police Captain Thomas F. O'Neill, charged with failure to perform his official duty. During a trial in late April all three were found guilty. DiCarlo and Tronolone received 12 months in the penitentiary, entering on April 27, and were fined $500 apiece. Captain O'Neill was later exonerated.

DiCarlo was released from the Erie County Penitentiary on January 10, 1946. With all his legal problems over the past 25 years, Buffalo's Public Enemy No. 1 was thinking of leaving the city on Lake Erie for good. DiCarlo had left Buffalo in the past – during times the authorities were looking for him or when he was considered "hot" – but this time it was said he was looking for a more permanent move. A close associate of DiCarlo was quoted in the *Buffalo Courier-Express* as saying, "I told Joe he has worn out his welcome in Buffalo and that he better take his operations elsewhere. I suggested he might transfer his amusement interests to Ohio or Pennsylvania, where he is well known." If DiCarlo was moving he wasn't packing alone. "Peanuts" Tronolone, his long time friend, announced that after his latest sentence he, too, was leaving Buffalo. "There seems to be no future for me here," he bemoaned.

No one is sure when DiCarlo actually began his association with "Fats" Aiello and "Moosey" Caputo, but by the spring of 1946 he drew the attention of the local police. In an April 29 letter from William W. Reed, the chief of detectives for the Youngstown Police Department, to his counterpart in the Buffalo Police Department, the official asked for a photograph of DiCarlo and a copy of his police record.

On February 1, 1947, just a year and a few weeks after DiCarlo left town, the *Buffalo Evening News* ran an article entitled, "Pastor Says Buffalo Gangsters Run Things in Youngstown, O." Reverend Eugene C. Beach, pastor of the First Christian Church in Youngstown, stated, "The situation in Youngstown is the worst it has been..." He accused the "Buffalo gangsters" of running policy and other gambling rackets. The *Buffalo Evening News* was quick to point out that the "Buffalo gangsters" Beach was referring to were DiCarlo and his sidekick Tronolone.

On May 27, 1947, DiCarlo received a telephone call from Salvatore Messazalma, with whom he was incarcerated in Chillicothe. Messazalma arranged a meeting between DiCarlo and Al Silvani, the manager of middleweight boxer Jake "the Raging Bull" LaMotta. At the meeting DiCarlo offered $100,000 to LaMotta if he would take a dive in his upcoming bout with Tony Janiro, which was to take place on June 6. Janiro was a Youngstown boxer whom DiCarlo had befriended. LaMotta rejected the offer and went on to beat Janiro in the tenth round of the match. Word of the meeting reached the New York County district attorney's office and DiCarlo, Messazalma and another man were brought in for questioning. The incident would not come to the public's attention until 1960.

In September 1947, Brooklyn, New York Detective Chief William Whalen, an expert on underworld activities, wrote that DiCarlo was "one of the many big time mobsters in the country who are taking part in the great gangster exodus from northern cities to a safer haven in Florida." In his investigation, Whalen listed DiCarlo as a brother-in-law of Anthony "Tony the Chief" Bonasera of Brooklyn, "an ex-lieutenant of Al Capone." It's highly unlikely that Bonasera had any connection with Capone; however, he had a long criminal record in New York City dating back to 1916.[14] In August 1932, he was one of eight men arrested in a "murder ring" suspected of killing Pittsburgh Mafia boss John Bazzano and dumping his body on a Brooklyn Street. Whalen claimed that DiCarlo, Bonasera and Johnny "Bath Beach" Oddo of Brooklyn "were planning to muscle in on Miami, (Fla.) concessions reportedly controlled by Chicago hoodlums and "Little Augie" Pisano." Police sources in Youngstown were quick to confirm that DiCarlo was still residing at his Volney Road home, near the Mill Creek Park district, with his wife, the former Elsie Rose Pieri, whom he married on November 29, 1924. Elsie was the sister of Joseph, John and Sam Pieri – future bigwigs of the Buffalo Mafia family. An article commenting on Whalen's report stated, "DiCarlo's position in Youngstown in the last couple of years or so has been a rather nebulous one. Some sources even report him to be one of the master minds behind all of Youngstown's rackets and gambling joints."

During a campaign speech on November 1, 1947, mayoral hopeful Charles P. Henderson named DiCarlo and Caputo as the leaders of the city's numbers rackets. After Henderson was elected on his campaign pledge to "Smash Rackets Rule," he hired Edward Allen as his chief of police and DiCarlo immediately became one of his prime targets. Chief Allen's efforts to shadow DiCarlo led to a sitdown between the two men. In late August 1948, DiCarlo and attorney Russell Mock met with Allen and vice squad chief Dan Maggianetti at police headquarters. During the meeting DiCarlo complained that he was being watched by police "from morning to night." Police cruisers tailed him even when he was walking down the street and were passing his house "more often than they pass police headquarters."

Allen suggested that DiCarlo must have a guilty conscience. "Otherwise you would welcome a police cruiser on your street," the chief offered. "Most residents complain because they don't see one often enough." Allen assured DiCarlo that he was paying no more attention to him than to "other punks" in Youngstown. DiCarlo, who explained that he had legitimate business operations in Buffalo and was a part owner of the Italian Village restaurant in Miami Beach,[15] inquired of Allen if there was any law prohibiting a person from having a home in one city and his place of business in another? Allen responded, "In your case there could be."

Allen later described the mobster's demeanor as friendly, but whenever he asked DiCarlo a question pertaining to his livelihood Mock advised him, "You don't have to answer that." DiCarlo informed the chief that he had turned over a new leaf, but wouldn't admit that it was due to the racket-busting efforts of Allen and the Henderson administration.

Allen had intended to keep the meeting private, claiming DiCarlo had expressed a desire to keep his name out of the newspapers. The *Vindicator*, however, was made aware of the interview through Mock, who told a reporter, "They had gone to answer any questions the chief cared to ask." The next day the *Vindicator* ran an editorial discussing the meeting and a statement Allen made at a Rotary Club gathering earlier in the week. The editorial closed with:

> "Chief Allen made one comment in his speech to the Rotarians which everyone who wants Youngstown to be a safe and clean city should note and remember. That is, that you can't have a law-abiding city unless people back up the police. Youngstown, under Mayor Henderson, is fortunate in having a police chief who deserves public confidence and support. It has not always been so. Most of our police chiefs have been very lenient in their attitude toward rackets, usually under orders of their superiors. Mayor Henderson and Chief Allen both stand for what is right and honorable. Youngstown is a different and a brighter place since they took office. Good citizens will unite to keep it so."

Early in the Henderson administration, Allen harassed DiCarlo's operations to the point where he was operating only in the rural areas of Mahoning and Trumbull Counties. A newspaper article confirmed, however, that DiCarlo "has been having difficulty in Mahoning County because of the enmity of Prosecutor William A. Ambrose, whose agents are constantly following DiCarlo and his henchmen and ordering them out as fast as they set up operations."

On September 17, 1948, five masked bandits entered the Green Acres casino in Struthers, and robbed about 250 guests of an estimated $25,000 to $30,000 in cash and valuables (See entry on Green Acres in Section 5). The most discussed aspect of the daring heist was the allegation that the bandits relieved DiCarlo of a diamond ring valued at $2,000. That rumor became suspect the next day when DiCarlo was stopped in his Cadillac for a lane change violation on Market Street. The patrolman noted that DiCarlo was wearing "a big diamond ring." The report of DiCarlo having been robbed was even bigger news in Buffalo than Youngstown. A Buffalo reporter interviewed Chief Allen about their former Public Enemy No. 1:

> "Police Chief Edward J. Allen told The Courier-Express last night by telephone that the former Buffalo gangster has been 'pretty quiet and appears to be laying low.'
>
> "Chief Allen said DiCarlo is living in one of Youngstown's best residential sections but claims to have no business connections there. He has told police that he is associated in 'legitimate businesses in Buffalo and Miami Beach, Fla.,' the chief added.
>
> "Indications are that DiCarlo and his henchmen are not operating in Youngstown at present, Chief Allen declared. He said several gambling places are being run in nearby villages, but city police do not have jurisdiction there."

On October 6, DiCarlo was arrested at the Hollenden Hotel in Cleveland, a hotspot for many underworld figures in that city. DiCarlo claimed he was there to try to purchase tickets for the World Series, which the Cleveland Indians were appearing in for just the second time in their history. Police questioned DiCarlo about the recent murder of Sam Jerry Monachino, a Cleveland hood. Monachino was a suspect in the Green Acres robbery along with Julius Petro. Both men were also believed to have been involved in the famous Mounds Club robbery in September 1947.

Nearly a year passed after the Green Acres robbery before DiCarlo was linked to a new gambling operation. On August 8, 1949, the *Vindicator* printed a front-page article about the new club:

> "The revival of gambling in Mahoning County moved ahead unmolested Saturday night with the opening of a new dive called the Green Village near Lake Milton. Bingo and slots continued their rapid pace in other parts of the county, and Jungle Inn had its usual quota of about 3,000 patrons.

> "The newest gambling emporium in Mahoning is reportedly owned by Joe DiCarlo, former Buffalo racketeer. Disguised as a gasoline station, the remodeled residence housing slots and table games is located on Route 18 about a mile and a half east of Lake Milton.
>
> "Reports circulating among the gambling fraternity here said that DiCarlo has become active again as the head of gambling activities in Mahoning, and linked him with Joseph "Red" Giordano.
>
> "The Green Village opened its peep-hole door to the public for the first time Saturday night, offering free beer and sandwiches and selling whisky without the benefit of a state liquor license."

The article claimed that dice, slot machines and chuck-a-luck were the offered entertainment, and that the "grand opening" was widely advertised. Then the writer took a swipe at the operation's clientele stating, "Few of the customers looked as if they were the type who had money to throw away on dice games. Most of the gullible were young couples, inexpensively dressed housewives, and stags not too well dressed." No more than 50 people were reported to have visited during opening night.

In October 1949, after "Fats" Aiello failed to show for his "suspicious person" trial, Chief Allen revealed that a number of the gambler's associates were subpoenaed to appear – but had disappeared, instead. DiCarlo was reported to have fled to the West Coast, but Allen said he had reliable information that he would be back in time to vote in the November election. Allen referred to DiCarlo as Aiello's "mentor" and told reporters: "We are not reliably informed which candidate DiCarlo is supporting for mayor. But we are reliably informed that he had advised intimates that anyone who bets against Henderson is a sucker. And we are reliably informed that Mr. DiCarlo is an expert on suckers."

On November 29, 1949, the *Vindicator* printed a front page story titled, "Link DiCarlo With Missing Buffalo Man." The article discussed the disappearance of a Niagara Falls gambler and convicted drug dealer who was missing since April. Patsy Quigliano, a well-known underworld figure in the Buffalo area, was the owner of a dry-cleaning concern that was a front for a gambling joint. The article reported, "Mrs. Caterina [Quigliano's sister] told police that on the evening of April 2 she drove her brother to Buffalo where he was to meet DiCarlo and accompany him to Cleveland." In Buffalo the local newspapers reported that Quigliano met up with Sam Pieri, DiCarlo's brother-in-law, that night. The only mention of DiCarlo's name in the many articles that came out about the disappearance was a quote in the *Buffalo Evening News*: "Mrs. Caterina emphatically denied that she had ever told police 'or anyone else' that her brother was to meet Joe DiCarlo." How the *Vindicator* made the mix-up was never explained.

In April 1950, Chief Allen's testimony about DiCarlo to a Senate investigative committee sparked a renewed interest in the fact that the former Buffalo mobster still had an outstanding fine from his 1924 conviction. The U.S. attorney in

Buffalo, George L. Grobe, began action to collect the outstanding $5,000 fine DiCarlo had failed to pay 26 years earlier using new laws that were passed allowing the government "to collect fines from persons living in other federal districts." A subpoena was issued for DiCarlo to appear before a U.S. commissioner to be interviewed about his income and property in Youngstown. At question was his home on Volney Road, which was listed in the name of Elsie DiCarlo, as was his 1948 Cadillac. Grobe stated, "We intend to do everything we can to collect this fine as we understand that DiCarlo has made plenty of money in Youngstown."

On May 29, 1950, DiCarlo appeared in federal court in Buffalo, where he declared that he owned no real property, stocks, bonds or life insurance. He also claimed his bank account consisted of $100, "more or less." DiCarlo promised to submit a payment plan within 30 days to payoff the $5,000 fine. Exactly one month later, the Buffalo district attorney's office received DiCarlo's proposal – $500 down and $50 per month. A check for $500 was enclosed. At this rate it would take the mobster seven and a half years to pay the debt. An investigation of his assets by deputy marshals confirmed that the home was in his wife's name, while the gangster's Cadillac suddenly could not be located.

DiCarlo made front-page headlines in January 1951 as he was subpoenaed to appear before the Kefauver Committee in Cleveland (see Chapter 10 on Kefauver Hearings). After his testimony before the committee – or rather, lack there of – DiCarlo fought a yearlong battle over a contempt of Congress charge. By now, the newspapers were already referring to him as the "deposed Youngstown racket king." Chief Allen was given credit for "deposing" the gangster. Just weeks after being subpoenaed to Cleveland to be grilled by the Kefauver committee, it was reported that DiCarlo was selling his Volney Road home at "a big sacrifice." The newspaper reported that, "There is speculation that DiCarlo is broke or nearly so and needs the money from the sale of his house." DiCarlo let it be known that his plans were to remain in Youngstown, but "I just want a smaller home." In June, the sale of the house was completed to a local doctor for $30,000. It was rumored that "real estate men" had placed the value of the home and its furnishings at $80,000.

DiCarlo was facing a backlash from his exposure at the Kefauver hearings. In addition to the contempt citation, Chief Allen kept up the pressure within Youngstown on the mobster. On April 22, DiCarlo was picked up at 11:30 p.m. and held for questioning for more than three hours. Capitalizing on the awareness gained from the hearings, Chief Allen launched his latest wave of "hoodlum harassment," which targeted "all persons connected or formerly connected with various rackets in the city." Allen stated, "My men are continually checking all hoodlums and known racketeers and DiCarlo can expect to be picked up for questioning at any time until he gets a legitimate line of work or leaves the city."

Chief Allen and the Kefauver committee were not the only ones seeking a pound of DiCarlo's flesh. In early May, the mobster returned to Buffalo to attend the funeral of a cousin. At 5:00 o'clock on the morning of May 4 he was awakened in his hotel room and subpoenaed to appear at the district attorney's office at 10:00 that morning. DiCarlo was clearly irritated with the summons because it coincided with the funeral mass. Missing the funeral, DiCarlo went directly to the prosecutor's office where he was subpoenaed again – this time he was ordered to appear later that week before the grand jury, which was investigating the city's gambling operations.

DiCarlo accused the district attorney of using him to gain publicity. "This is the biggest joke there ever was. I don't have any interest in Buffalo, as I don't live here anymore. The only time I come is to visit relatives or attend a funeral, as was the case this time. There is nothing I know and I cannot give the grand jury any information." On May 10, DiCarlo appeared and refused to sign a waiver of immunity on the advice of counsel, resulting in the grand jury refusing to ask him any questions. He quickly left the grand jury room and, though still under subpoena and subject to recall, headed home to Youngstown.

In mid-September, Chief Allen informed the media that DiCarlo had vacated the city and was listing Miami Beach as his new address. Allen hinted that DiCarlo might "team up" with "Moosey" Caputo, who had also relocated to the sunny climate of South Florida. While dismissing Allen's claims as being inaccurate, the *Vindicator* did confirm that Elsie DiCarlo was living in Miami, "where she has been ordered for her health." DiCarlo, they claimed, was looking for a "small apartment" and still intended to call Youngstown "home."

Except for his legal battles on the contempt of Congress charge, DiCarlo remained out of the public eye until late 1953 when he was arrested in Miami Beach on an old charge of failing to appear in court on charges of "conspiring to violate Florida gambling laws." On December 16, 1953, DiCarlo attended the second-degree murder trial of New York City hoodlum Eddie Coco, a former fight-manager he knew. In attendance at the trial was Daniel P. Sullivan, director of the Greater Miami Crime Commission, who recognized DiCarlo and informed sheriff's deputies who then tailed the gangster and arrested him outside his motel room. DiCarlo was released on a $500 bond. Authorities claimed DiCarlo was arrested back in December 1949 for running a gambling game out of a hotel room. While this was reported in the *Vindicator* on December 30, 1953, the *Miami Daily News* reported on January 4, 1954, that DiCarlo was arrested that day on a gambling warrant issued four years prior for operating a gambling house. That arrest of DiCarlo came just two days after a Miami area task force made several raids resulting in the arrests of Sam DiCarlo (Joe's brother), John Tronolone and his cousin Carmen all on gambling charges.

Joe DiCarlo was indignant over the arrest and told reporters that police had the wrong man. Indeed, a check of police records indicated that it was Sam DiCarlo who was arrested during a raid four years earlier along with 14 other men. Only one of the gamblers appeared at the arraignment and bench warrants were issued for the others. Authorities told Joe DiCarlo, who was released on a $2,500 bond, that if there was a case of mistaken identity it would have to be resolved in court.

In February 1955, despite the fact that the $50 monthly payments on his federal fine had stopped, DiCarlo threw a wedding celebration for his daughter Vincinetta that cost him an estimated $35,000.[16] Held at Ciro's Restaurant in Miami Beach, the rental of the facility alone was $3,000. Providing entertainment for the reputed 900 guests were Jimmy Durante, Milton Berle and Sammy Davis, Jr. DiCarlo's new son-in-law, John W. Johnson, was no stranger to crime, he had served time in the Indiana State Farm in 1952.

Word of DiCarlo's extravagant spending on the wedding generated a public outcry in Buffalo. The U.S. attorney sent word about the unpaid fine to Miami and DiCarlo was called in by the district attorney. DiCarlo promised to return April 1 and pay "something" on the fine. A *Buffalo Evening News* editorial claimed, "The attorney forgot that was April Fool's Day. Joe did not show up." The following comments appeared in an *Evening News* editorial on April 14, 1955:

> "What mystifies the average law abiding citizen who never misses being called up over a $10 discrepancy in his income tax is how DiCarlo can travel in the company he does, drive a big car – registered in his wife's name – and toss an expensive wedding party, meanwhile pleading poverty.
>
> "DiCarlo may be a hero to his underworld satellites who rate him as a big shot because he has been able successfully to defy the government, but it's about time that the Justice Department cut him down to ordinary size. They did it with Al Capone – and he was big.
>
> "Joe is getting 'hot' and the syndicate doesn't like 'hot' characters around. It may decide he ought to pay up."

The response from the U.S. attorney's office in Miami was an effort to embarrass DiCarlo into paying by harassing his friends. In mid-April, Michael "Trigger Mike" Coppola, a former New York City enforcer known for his violent and sometimes sadistic temper, was called in to be questioned about DiCarlo's finances. Coppola was reported to have picked up part of the expenses for the wedding bash. Whether this is true or just a story circulated at DiCarlo's request was never confirmed. DiCarlo resolved the situation by coughing up another $1,000 along with a promise to "pay the remainder of the five within a reasonable length of time."

A month and a half later DiCarlo was crying poverty again. This time the U.S. attorney's office dragged him in along with John Angersola. Known as Johnny King, Angersola was a former member of Cleveland's Mayfield Road Mob and a close associate of Al Polizzi, the former Cleveland boss, in some South Florida business ventures. During questioning about his finances DiCarlo invoked his Fifth Amendment rights. He was given until July 1 to answer questions or be cited for contempt. Angersola, on the other hand, refused to even be sworn in. In mid-July, DiCarlo handed over an additional $1,000 and was given until January 2, 1956, to make good on the balance. It would not be until May 1957 that DiCarlo paid the final $100 installment to complete the fine levied some 33 years earlier.

The heat generated by the Kefauver hearings had hardly subsided when a new Senate investigation was underway. The Senate Select Committee on Improper Activities in the Labor Management Field, also called the McClellan Committee, was known to mobsters nationwide as the "Rackets Committee." The committee was established in January 1957, with Arkansas Democratic Senator John L. McClellan as chairman and Robert F. Kennedy as chief counsel. One of the Senators on the committee was John F. Kennedy.

On July 1, 1958, a year and a half into the committee's investigative work, the *Vindicator* announced in front-page headlines: "Cammarata, DiCarlo Named in Mafia Quiz." In addition to these two, James Licavoli was also mentioned as being a "figure" in the probe. Sparked by the revelation of the now infamous Apalachin Summit on November 14, 1957, the newspaper reported that the list on which the local hood's names appeared was titled, "Individuals at Apalachin and names of some of their contacts and associates."

On July 5, a *Vindicator* editorial, responding to the negative publicity the city was receiving due to the McClellan probe, was entitled: "Echoes from a Crime Era," and read in part:

> "Once again Youngstown has received unwelcome notoriety on a national scale, as the result of one of the city's worst crime-ridden, racket-dominated eras in many years – a period in the 1940s when gambling dives, unlicensed saloons and houses of prostitution flourished within blocks of City Hall, were draining off a half-million dollars or more a year.
>
> "Youngstown unfortunately still suffers from its big splurge into crime, a lapse which should never have been permitted."

Sadly, the gist of the editorial was that through the efforts of former law enforcement officials Chief Allen and Sheriff Elser the crime problem here was brought under control, but there was still an embarrassing stigma left to deal with. This embarrassing stigma would only multiply during the early 1960s leaving the city of Youngstown with a reputation it has never lived down.

"Youngstown has had bad government for so long that people here do not know good government. We are so tolerant of evil that we accept it as the natural course of events."– Attorney Benjamin F. Roth, Republican candidate for President of Youngstown City Council, April 26, 1947.

9

"Smash Racket Rule" Allen and Henderson

The reader should keep in mind that Chief Edward Allen's interplay with the various underworld figures in the Valley are contained in the chapters devoted to them and not repeated here. The same goes with his participation in the Kefauver Committee hearings.

The Mahoning Valley in the 1940s was a conglomeration of organized crime, vice and political corruption. Beginning with "Sugar" Harrell's white slave trade the decade got worse as the triumvirate of Aiello, Caputo and DiCarlo began their activities. Slot machines, punch boards, and the lottery houses provided much of the cash that lined the pockets of the Valley's gangsters and crooked politicians.

The problems continued through the war years, but 1947 proved to be a watershed year. It began with Mahoning County Democratic Chairman John C. Vitullo[17] directing a Youngstown City Council move. Democrat Councilman Nicholas P. Bernard left to begin a term in the Ohio State Senate. Vitullo sent fellow Democratic council members Stephen P. Olenick, Edgar G. Morley and William D. Holt to sunny Florida so council could not reach a quorum on Bernard's replacement. A law on the books gave power to Mayor Ralph O'Neill, a Democrat to name a successor, thus avoiding the chance a Republican winning the seat.

Even more bothersome was that the AWOL councilmen left in the company of Jack Lombard, alias Napolitana, the former proprietor of the Savoy Club, on South Hazel Street. State liquor agents raided Napolitana's club on March 15, 1941 with city police – liquor and gambling equipment were confiscated. On May 7, Napolitana was fined $300 for selling liquor without a license. The Savoy later became the 330 Club. Repeated raids by Sheriff Elser in early 1945 caused the owners to relocate. Before the month of January was out, Vitullo was back on the front pages after admitting to writing a letter to State Liquor Department officials to help push through a liquor permit for the McGuffey Athletic Club during the last days of Governor Lausche's first administration. Vitullo's letter stated, "I would appreciate it greatly if you will rush this through, as the boys were a great help in the last campaign and we would like to keep them that way for future elections."

The fallout from the letter led to a probe by the State Liquor Director into a rash of liquor permits being granted to other private clubs around the state during the same period. By February, the probe had expanded and on March 6 it was announced that 33 private clubs in the Mahoning Valley were found not to be legitimate clubs under the terms of law. Before the end of March a number of the permits were revoked. On March 25, during a hearing on the clubs, Assistant Ohio Attorney General Charles Schnur revealed that the club owners were paying $50 to $100 a month to local officials in order to operate.

In addition to the continuing political corruption, there was turmoil in the Youngstown Police Department. On April 29, John B. Thomas, in his third year as Youngstown police chief, resigned and returned to the detective bureau after another embarrassing incident under his command – this latest one involved the damaging of a squad car by the chief's 16 year-old son. During his regime Thomas had come under fire a number of times for allowing gambling to flourish in the city. His one claim to fame seems to have been a "one man campaign" against Zoot-suiters in 1944. Zoot suits became a popular fashion craze in the mid-1940s, originating in Los Angeles. The suits, popular with blacks and Mexicans, featured wide-legged, tight cuffed pants and a long jacket with wide lapels and broad padded shoulders. On one occasion, he personally arrested 21 of the snazzy clad group and ordered a crackdown on them throughout the city. The low point for Thomas came in 1945 after a black man he allegedly beat while disbursing a crowd of loiterers, swore out an arrest warrant against him. The case never came to trial. Thomas was replaced by Captain William J. Cleary, a 46 year-old with just 12 years in the department.

Amid the corruption and turmoil a 36 year-old attorney by the name of Charles Packard Henderson promised to "clean out the powers behind the scenes and to make certain that no others enter to take their places." Henderson, whose family once owned a section of the city where many of the town's brothels were located, was a Republican and a "political greenhorn," whom many thought would get chewed to pieces by Vitullo's Democratic political machine. So sure of his defeat were the members of his own party, that Henderson was forced to run his campaign like an independent.

Charles Henderson was born in Youngstown on March 3, 1911. His father, Andrew M. Henderson was a prominent attorney in the city. In 1921, he served on the defense team representing Safety Director David J. Scott, who was convicted of bribery charges. Charles Henderson attended McKinley and Rayen schools locally, before enrolling at Princeton University. He received his law degree from the University of Michigan Law School. After passing the bar exam in 1935, he joined his father's law firm. In 1941 he was elected municipal judge, serving in that capacity for 18 months before joining the Army. During World War II, Henderson was a military intelligence officer working for the OSS, the forerunner of the Central Intelligence Agency.

Henderson began a vigorous campaign. While delivering a speech at the VFW Auditorium, sponsored by the Mahoning County Women's Republican Club, Henderson recalled hearing several returning servicemen comment that in Youngstown "things have gone from bad to worse." He told his audience, "To have good government there must be fair and firm law enforcement. When there is government by racketeers and special interests, you do not have good government." In the same speech, Henderson took a shot at the current problems in the Youngstown Police Department stating, "My son is six years old, but I assure you he will not be driving a police cruiser."

In the May 1947 primary, Henderson won by a two-to-one margin over opponents in four of the seven wards and was now ready to carry his campaign slogan, "Smash Racket Rule," against Democratic incumbent O'Neill in November.

Throughout the spring, summer and fall Henderson carried on his "Smash Racket Rule" campaign, bashing the O'Neill administration at every turn. Henderson spoke out about two areas in the police department. The first was the growing traffic problem in the city and the department's laxity in enforcement and planning. The second was a promise to keep politics out of the department. "It is not right for police to have their morale so destroyed they feel it is useless to carry out their duties because the offender will be released anyway because of his politics or political connections," he declared. "Officers should have a free hand to enforce laws and make arrests."

In late October, just a week before the election, Henderson used O'Neill's oft-recalled remark, "it-could-happen-to-anyone," regarding the shooting by Fats Aiello at the Purple Cow, to again embarrass the mayor. The comment was delivered at a political rally, again sponsored by the Mahoning County Women's Republican Club at the VFW Auditorium. Henderson addressed the audience:

> "The administration is using the campaign slogan that its 'record of achievement is a pledge for the future.'"
>
> "Take heed, therefore, that you have been pledged for the next two years to an administration of bombings and fires [and] illegal establishments which the vice squad has not seen fit to close.
>
> "To further becloud the questions at hand, [O'Neill] has asked you, the citizens of Youngstown, to re-elect him on his record. Never has an issue been clearer cut. His record is one of absolute indifference to the welfare of the citizens.
>
> "[The mayor] absolutely failed to provide citizens of Youngstown with even the necessary services such as adequate garbage collection, adequate police protection and adequate fire protection."

Throughout the campaign Henderson attacked the "corrupt Vitullo machine," charging it with dictating policy and decisions at City Hall. "My opponent is not O'Neill," Henderson declared, "I am running against Vitullo and his henchmen." Calling the mayor a figurehead, Henderson stated, "O'Neill reports he runs a business-like administration and frequently confers with his cabinet and councilmen. He, however, forgot to mention one person with whom he confers constantly. That man is Vitullo, boss of the Democratic Party. After all, Vitullo really is mayor of Youngstown." During a huge rally before the Young Republican's Club at the VFW Auditorium, Henderson openly named bug men, gambling house operators and identified bookie joints, declaring they were all protected by the O'Neill administration.

On Election Day 1947 all the bookie joints and lottery houses in the city were closed as the men were called to duty to help in the O'Neill campaign. Despite this strong effort to keep O'Neill in office, Henderson won by 3,000 votes. He then set about forming his cabinet, most important of which would be a new police chief to implement his "Smash Racket Rule" promise to the citizens of Youngstown.

On December 22, Mayor-elect Henderson issued the following statement to the Republican Executive Committee in announcing his selection of Youngstown's new chief of police:

> "I have chosen Edward J. Allen of the Erie police department as my chief of police because I believe him best fitted of the available men I have considered to carry out my campaign platform of firm law enforcement.
>
> "As an outsider, he is free from the many political influences which have hampered the efficiency of the department for many years. He will be able to perform his duties as chief without fear of reprisals during future administrations, since he will not return to the ranks at the end of his term as chief.
>
> "Finally, he is a professional policeman, and as a recent graduate of a National Police Academy of the Federal Bureau of Investigation, he will be able to give the Youngstown police department the benefit of modern ideas and techniques in police administration and law enforcement.
>
> "Most of the members of the Youngstown police department are honest and capable. Those whom I know personally I like and admire very much. Given good leadership and freedom from political interference, they will be able to give Youngstown the kind of law enforcement the people have a right to expect.
>
> "I am satisfied that Edward J. Allen will furnish that type of leadership. He has been recommended to me by J. Edgar Hoover, director of the Federal Bureau of Investigation, as qualified for the position as chief of the Youngstown police department. I have complete confidence in his ability, integrity and sincerity of purpose."

Meet Eddie Allen

Edward J. Allen, Jr. was born into a family of police officers on November 13, 1907. His father served as Grand President of the Fraternal Order of Police, where he focused his attention on the working conditions of police officers. He was known as the "father of the eight-hour law for policemen in Pennsylvania." Another relative, John T. "Jack" Grant, an uncle, served as a sergeant in the Erie Detective Bureau until his death in the line of duty during a shootout in 1912.

Allen attended local schools in Erie, graduating from Central High School in the class of 1925. Allen didn't attend college; instead he enrolled in the General Electric Company's technical school. He was later hired by a local bank, where he worked his way up from messenger boy to teller.

In 1935, Allen became a member of the Erie Police Department. During his early years in the department he walked a beat, and served as a radioman, traffic officer and desk sergeant. During the early 1940s, Allen was a key figure in two police investigations. In one, five Erie officials were indicted on a number of charges, including perjury and bribery. Due to a technicality the case was dismissed. The second case took place in 1943 when Joseph Calafato, "a leading policy operator," attempted to bribe Allen with $1,000 up front and $50 a week if he would lay off the policy writers in town. Allen set up a second meeting where the offer was repeated in front of two witnesses. Calafato was arrested and pled guilty in court. The judge fined him $750, but suspended a six-month jail sentence. Allen was livid and expressed his views in a public statement. The local Fraternal Order of Police approved a resolution to censure Allen. The official who signed the order later became the police commissioner; he was convicted in 1955 of accepting bribes and sent to prison.

With America's involvement in the war in 1941, Allen was assigned to work as a liaison officer with the FBI office in Erie. In this capacity, Allen worked exclusively with special agents of the bureau "against subversive elements." During this time he performed internal security work and undercover activities, which resulted in the indictments of members of two Nazi organizations in the Erie area – the Kyffhauser Bund and the Erie chapter of the German-American Bund. Both cases resulted in the conviction of members for subversive actions.

At one point during the early years of the war Allen considered enlisting in the Navy. When rumor of this got around one Erie underworld figure quipped, "If that man goes into the Navy, we ought to take up a collection and buy him a battleship to get him out of here quicker."

After the war Allen returned to his regular duties with the Erie Police Department and was soon promoted to detective sergeant. Years later, an article in *Look* magazine stated, "in Erie he had won the reputation, even as a mere sergeant, of being a one-man police force. Almost single-handed he had brought gambling and prostitution there to a standstill." He still kept close ties with the FBI, graduating from the FBI National Police Academy in March 1947, after a three-month course in firearms, fingerprinting, investigative procedures, instruction and administration. Allen's expertise as a marksman led him to organize the first firearms training class and every member of the Erie Police Department attended. He inherited from his father a concern for the working police officer and served as treasurer and vice president of the Fraternal Order of Police. In 1945, Allen was named "Policeman of the Year" by the Kiwanis Club of Erie.

Allen found time to get married to the former Dorothy Davenport in 1937; the union lasted 52 years and the couple had a son and a daughter. Outside of police work, Allen had varied interests – sports, philosophy, poetry and religion. As a young man Allen was a semi-professional basketball player and an amateur boxer. He loved reading about the great philosophers of history and could quote the likes of Plato and Thomas Aquinas. Allen was a devout Catholic and wrote religious poems and sonnets. In April 1953, a book of sonnet meditations called *Way of the Cross* was published by Youngstown Catholic Bishop Emmet M. Walsh. Years later he became a staunch supporter of the anti-abortion movement in California.

The New Chief

Henderson interviewed Allen in mid-December, after receiving the recommendation of FBI Director Hoover. Allen's concern was the personnel and the need for cooperation within the department. In accepting the position he stated, "I will endeavor to do an efficient job for Youngstown. My success or failure will depend upon the cooperation of the citizenry and especially that of the officers with whom I will be working." Some who knew Henderson wondered if he would get along with Allen. It was rumored that the new chief was a reformed alcoholic and very opinionated, while Henderson was known to be a "nice quiet, guy."

Charles Henderson took the oath of mayor on New Year's Eve 1947. That day the *Vindicator* reported the Youngstown Police Department's four captains – former, now acting chief, William J. Cleary, Harry Fickes, William R. Golden and Eugene McEvoy – were already in agreement to give the city's racketeers the heave-ho. In a kind of "state of the underworld message," the newspaper reported that due to the new regime at city hall, and the resolve of police to rid the city of gamblers, "that the bookies, the back room gambling spots, the all night gambling joints and others of the same ilk might beat the police to the punch by moving out" on their own.

There seemed to be a renewed spirit in the department. Suddenly the officers found themselves unshackled from political hands and free to do their jobs. As one officer looked forward to lowering the boom on gamblers, he explained, "We don't need orders to do this. It is our duty to do it. I don't know how the people of Youngstown are going to like this sort of thing, but it's going to be done. We're going to act like policemen now that we have the backing to do so."

The article stated, "The general consensus has been that the gamblers and racketeers were going to close, lay low and await developments to see if there won't be a possible change to come back into business under the Henderson administration." New reports indicated the exodus of "horse players, crap shooters, poker players and gamblers" had already begun, in addition to "stickmen, dealers and other men employed to run the game." Lottery houses and gambling joints were closing or closed and slot machines in public places had dwindled to just a few. Speculation was that Trumbull County's infamous Jungle Inn would have to expand to handle the famished Youngstown gambling crowd.

The article, in conclusion, stated the city's underworld figures "have decided to give once-lucrative Youngstown the go-by and head for Florida, the West Coast and other places where the weather is hot, but the law isn't."

Just four and a half-hours after Henderson took office, two patrolmen answered a call about a disturbance at the South Side Vets' Club on Oak Hill Avenue. They found nothing unusual going on when they arrived, but when they noticed a broken window at the club they attempted to enter the premises. When the proprietor, Alfred Ross angrily ordered them out, they called for assistance and it arrived in the form of Sergeant William Davis. Ross suddenly backed down in the presence of the no-nonsense Davis. Without confrontation the officers searched the club and seized three slot machines. Ross was brought before newly elected Municipal Judge Frank P. Anzellotti, serving his first day on the bench, who released him on a $100 bond. The judge later fined Ross and ordered the slot machines destroyed.

The January 3, *Vindicator* reported, "Police today said the town is 'down' – meaning gambling and the rackets are not operating. The bookies aren't booking – the gamblers aren't gambling – the bug isn't selling (well) – and the whole after-legitimate-hours aspect of the city Friday looked almost as dark as a black pig in a poke."

At 4:15 that morning, Captain Golden and a raiding crew hit Joe Budak's Club 22 on Phelps Street, causing the former Campbell House lottery figure to issue his famous outburst, "You're jumping the gun. You're not supposed to start your campaign until January 5, I'll see my boys about this."

All the other bookie joints in the city appeared to be closed tighter than a drum. "Cadillac Charlie" Cavallaro's place on South Champion Street was dark and the rumor was he had packed up and moved "lock, stock and barrel."

The cops were still at it on January 4, the eve of Eddie Allen's arrival in the city. Back in December two patrolmen – Joseph Battaglia and Mitchell Simmerlink – raided a gambling game at the Vets Sandwich Shop on Albert Street. There they ran into a snarling Frank L. Glio who informed them, "This is your last day on this beat. You flunkies are not going to tell me what to do." Now, on the last night before the big department change, they raided the Bridge Club on Oak Street and arrested Vince DeNiro, who was later fined $500 with $400 suspended. Both officers stated that after arriving at the club they got the same greeting every other officer seemed to be getting, "What's the matter with you fellows? You weren't supposed to arrest anyone until January 5."

Allen arrived in the city on the night of January 5, after finalizing plans for a leave of absence from the Erie Police Department. The next morning he was sworn in by Judge John Ford in Mayor Henderson's office. The "soft-spoken, mild mannered, 40-year-old" announced three goals. First, he hoped to make a personal friend of every man in the department; second, to see Youngstown possess the finest police department in the United States; and third "cleaning up the city."

Allen's message to the city's underworld was short, but sweet, "Get going, keep going." Some of the racketeers were already lying low or had vacated the city waiting for the dust to settle. Allen demanded, "Continued exodus of all racketeers and would-be gangsters," declaring "they are nothing more than parasites living off the fruits of other men's labors."

Over the next two days Allen devoted his time to addressing the troops. He demanded a strict observance to departmental rules, with emphasis on two areas. "I will not tolerate any intimacy between members of the Youngstown police force and underworld characters except in the necessary performance of duty," he declared.

The second area was a zero tolerance approach to drinking while on duty. "My chief aim is to raise the standard of the entire department," Allen proclaimed. "No member of the force will be allowed to hold back the department through the infraction of rules or regulations. Those whose duties it is to demand a strict observance of laws from citizens must first begin by obeying their own regulations. Police officers should be men who are willing to exercise self discipline."

Allen next addressed his plan to implement "a permanent and continuous school of instruction for Youngstown policemen." Officers would study all phases of police work and the FBI would be invited to send representatives, schooled in specialized areas, to give instruction to the men. In addition, judges and prosecutors would be called to review legal procedures to be followed during arrests and searches.

One of the controversial decisions the new chief made was to initiate rotating turns of duty. Many of the newer officers complained about always having to work second or third turn (shift). Allen let the entire force vote by secret ballot about changing this system. The majority wanted a change and the rotating turn system was set up giving each officer and patrolman "an equal share of daylight work." The department's veterans were livid about the change. (Days after Allen left the department the old system, giving officers with the most seniority the daytime 7:00 a.m. to 3:00 p.m. shift, was restored.)

While Allen was busy addressing his force, the *Vindicator* reported that 15 to 20 Youngstown racketeers "invaded" Erie, Pennsylvania, to seek new fields of operations. Allen responded that the underworld figures were "probing" his record from the detective bureau to "get something" on him. The next day, a report claimed the mayor of Erie ordered police officials to drive "all visiting mobsters" out of the city. The directive came after a "diamond-studded Youngstown man" was discovered with two Erie men involved in the policy rackets. The bejeweled man, identified as Robert Howell manager of the 40 Club on East Federal Street, told police he had come to Erie because Eddie Allen was making it "too hot" to remain in Youngstown.

It took Allen just one week before his first clash with city council. Allen's position on politicians was clear. He stated there's "nothing a policeman dislikes more than a ward-healing politician to put pressure on him. I do not interfere with the affairs of politicians, nor do I appreciate their attempts to interfere with operations of the police department." For decades political appointments filled the Youngstown Police Department's ranks. Depending on who was in the mayor's office, many potential policemen needed a letter from their councilman to apply for a position. This left him indebted to the councilman for the job. For years councilmen selected the vice squad members to assure themselves of knowing what places were going to get raided in their wards.

Allen and Henderson went to council with a proposal to elevate three of the fourteen sergeants to the position of lieutenant in order to create a level of command above sergeant in case one of the shift captains was unavailable, sick or on vacation. At the time the Youngstown Police Department was operating without the position of lieutenant in its ranks. While the proposal would create a budget increase of $900, it would not increase personnel; there simply would be three less sergeants. The lieutenant posts would be filled though civil service examination.

Opposing the action was Democratic Fourth Ward Councilman Edgar T. Morley, who became a nemesis to Allen. Morley wanted to speak privately to "captains, sergeants and other members of the force to determine how they feel" about the proposal. When Allen objected to the councilman's request, Morley tried to draw him into an argument.

"I'm not going to lower myself to the level of political bickering," Allen stated.

"What do you mean by that, chief?" Morley demanded.

"I mean your proposed action in talking to every man on the force," Allen answered.

Morley contended that the establishment of the lieutenancies would create confusion within the civil service examination process. Kathryn Klee, secretary of the Civil Service Commission, declared Morley's argument had no basis.

The next day Allen issued the first of many pleas to the populace of the Valley encouraging citizens not to "feed" the hoodlum element by participating in illegal gambling activities. Mayor Henderson introduced Allen to a packed audience of the Junior Chamber of Commerce. In his opening remarks Allen, a gifted speaker, expressed his appreciation for the warm welcome he received in Youngstown, confessing he had some "misgivings about the reception" he might encounter – that as an outsider he might be resented. Allen explained that the drive to eliminate lawlessness was a "community call to duty like God's call to man. It is on a personal basis." The key points of his speech were:

◊ The citizen is the front line of defense in a program of stopping racketeers.

◊ We are freedom loving, and don't want to be stopped. If a law doesn't suit us, we feel we can violate it. But we are bound as citizens to live within the law the same as the racketeer.

◊ Where does the racketeer get the money to buy elections? He gets it from the people.

◊ Don't be so quick to throw money into the racketeer's coffers. He'll use it against your best interests.

◊ The policemen are your servants. They administer the law as people demand it...When police feel the public is behind them they will do a good job. The only thing discouraging to them is political interference or outside interference with their duty. Even law enforcement officers who are politically corrupt want to free themselves of their shackles. It is up to the people to let them be the free men they want to be.

◊ The same mentality as breeds a Hitler, Stalin, or Mussolini breeds gangsters, hoodlums and violent delinquency here at home. The Joe DiCarlos and would-be gangsters are nothing but small imitations of Hitler. We must get rid of them.

◊ [In ridding the city of the underworld element] It is nothing that cannot be done by a return to good, old fashioned discipline. That you will get from this administration. Get behind it. Don't let knockers put you aside.

Allen demanded that his men continue with the arrests, revealing he was informed the racketeers were "whispering, the heat is off." He ordered the captains during role call to tell the men "to keep on cracking down on the rackets." Particularly irritating to Allen were the bondsmen who came to bail out the hoodlums, reaching into their pockets and peeling off $500 in ten $50 denominations. The bug was still being played, but reports were that the headquarters was re-established in Campbell and Struthers and in Trumbull County. Players, however, were complaining because they had to wait up to 48 hours to be paid on a winning ticket.

Closing the Race Wire Service

One of Chief Allen's first targets was the race wire service. The service provided daily horse race results from tracks around the country. Subscribers received the service, which was relayed over Western Union wires and Ohio Bell Telephone Company lines. The Continental Press was the national supplier of the wire service; it was provided locally by the General News Agency. When it first began operating in Youngstown, in the late 1920s, the office was located in Suite 409 of the Keith-Albee Building downtown. Managing the new service was William Hamilton.

The General News Agency soon became the Empire News Service and was owned by Morris "Mushy" Wexler of Cleveland. Wexler, as a young man, worked for Arthur "Mickey" McBride and James Ragen, owners of the Continental Press. Both men played an important role as circulation managers during Cleveland's newspaper circulation wars during the early 1910s. Wexler worked as one of their newspaper truck drivers.

In 1931, members of the Youngstown vice squad raided the race wire headquarters. The officers treated the place like it was a speakeasy, destroying furniture and ripping the phone wires out of the walls. The raid, as it turned out, actually resulted in providing Empire News Service with "legal" protection for nearly two decades. After the raid, attorneys were able to obtain a court injunction prohibiting police from destroying furniture and equipment again. The court order was only to protect the property, but Hamilton and later Sammy Alpern convinced police that the injunction meant Empire News Service was a legitimate operation and precluded them from ever coming on the property.

In late March 1940, Cleveland Safety Director Eliot Ness, the famed leader of "The Untouchables" conducted an investigation of Empire News Service. His probe led him to Youngstown. Working with Youngstown Chief of Detectives William Reed, Ness and two detectives visited a number of local bookmaking joints including:

Hazel Smoke Shop, 28 South Hazel Street
Stambaugh Athletic Club, Room 2 over 10 North Hazel Street
Hartman's Place, 26 North Phelps Street
Wick Club, 19 Wick Avenue, above the Palace Grill
Hagerman's, 16 East Commerce Street (official Daily Racing Bulletin Company)
Joe Budak's Place, 26 East Federal Street (rear) over Regent Billiard Parlor
Steel City Club, over 43 Central Square
Roy's Smoke Shop, 116 South Champion Street
Empire News Service Company, 409 Keith-Albee Building

At the Empire News Service, Ness and the detectives entered and went upstairs. In his official report, the surprised safety director recorded what happened next:

> "[The detectives] waited at the end of the hall near the elevator, as they could not accompany me into the place, due to the fact that the Youngstown police were enjoined some time ago from interfering with the operation of this establishment by court order."

With the local police hoodwinked into believing the race wire service was legally off limits, it continued to thrive...until Eddie Allen arrived.

During the 1940s, the management of the local Empire News Service was taken over by Sammy Alpern. The "suave little gent" once worked as a telegrapher for Western Union in Pittsburgh, before moving to Youngstown where he was employed for Postal Telegraph. He soon discovered more money – much more money – could be made in the race wire field. Alpern was hired by "Mushy" Wexler and was in charge of the new office when it moved to 31 North Walnut Street. Allen described this new location in his book:

> "From his headquarters – a dingy, second story office in a dilapidated neighborhood – this national race track service was piped direct to the various local "bookie" joints via loud speaker systems. Other county and state drops were serviced by telephone and telegraph from the same headquarters."

Allen soon paid a personal visit to Alpern. The bookie was open and at ease with the new chief, no doubt feeling that the copy of the court injunction he held was a force field for protection. He spoke freely about his operation and those whom he serviced. Allen's ears perked up when Alpern admitted he was servicing "three local men." The chief was quite aware of the muscling-in on the bookies in the Valley by Aiello, Caputo and DiCarlo. Allen vividly recalled that Alpern "kept waving a copy of a court injunction which, he triumphantly announced, forbade the police from interfering with the race-wire operation."

Alpern then made a fatal mistake and the protection that Empire News Service enjoyed for 17 years flew out the window. He let Chief Allen read the injunction. Allen revealed in *Merchants of Menace: The Mafia*:

> "The court rightly held that this type of 'raid' was not to be repeated. That is all. The court, of course, did not prohibit the police from gathering sufficient evidence to prove a connection between the illegitimate bookmakers and the renting of the race wire service, nor did it preclude the presentation of proof of a conspiracy to violate the gambling laws. Yet this decrepit document was the 'gimmick' that had stymied police action against the Empire News Service and its predecessor in Youngstown for almost a score of years."

Allen and his new Vice Squad Chief Dan Maggianetti began a careful preparation of their assault on Empire News Service. Both realized that under city statutes a conviction resulted in a mere fine, and the wire service would continue business as usual. Allen consulted with Cleveland Safety Director Alvin J. Sutton and Police Chief Frank Story. He then met with Lieutenant Martin J. Cooney, who had fought a similar battle in Cleveland. Cooney related how he had received the cooperation of the telephone company and Western Union. When Allen's investigation was complete he sent his reports and evidence to officials at both companies. After serious perusal by their legal staffs, both companies agreed that their regulations forbade the usage of their electronic lines for gambling purposes.

On May 14, 1948, the first step in "Smash Racket Rule" was achieved. With the flick of a switch, power to Youngstown's race wire service ceased to exist.

Attacked by the F.O.P.

On the day the plug was pulled on the race wire service, an obscure service station proprietor named Joseph J. Shepard wrote a letter to Law Director H. Herschel Hunt demanding that the city stop paying Chief Allen's salary. The letter was conveyed through the law firm of Powers, Church & Church, of which two principals were former members of previous mayor Ralph O'Neill's administration – John W. Powers (city law director) and Henry Church (assistant law director).

According to the *Vindicator*, "Shepard says Allen is not qualified under the state constitution, that he was appointed without compliance with requirements of city and state civil service laws [meaning he didn't take a competitive examination for the chief's position], and that he was not a member of the Youngstown police department when appointed."

Mayor Henderson, impressed with the knowledge of civil service and state laws the filling station operator possessed, explained that Allen's appointment was made under the "provisions of Youngstown's home rule charter." Chief Allen initially believed two recent incidents led to this attack. First was the race wire service cut-off, and the second was an incident outside the Purple Cow when he cleared the sidewalk of a group of rowdy Democratic committeemen. It soon came to light that members of the Fraternal Order of Police were backing the ouster, this coming after Allen's re-organization of the department.

The chief told reporters, "If this is an effort to bring about relaxation of the campaign against racketeers, gamblers and other law violators it will fail because as long as I am chief I intend to pursue the same vigorous course of law enforcement."

The *Vindicator* attacked the effort to remove the chief in their editorials claiming the election of Henderson and the appointment of Allen to be "one of the best things that has happened to Youngstown in many years." After Shepard's name was used in the editorial he quickly dropped his request, offering as his reason for the removal demand, "Sometimes we're forced to do things." The *Vindicator* advised the FOP to do the same – which they did...for a while.

One month later, Peter R. LaPolla, an assembler at the General Fireproofing Company, filed a new demand asking Law Director Hunt to seek an injunction preventing the city from paying Allen. LaPolla, not surprisingly, was represented by Henry Church in the suit in which the previous grounds were cited.

When approached by reporters, LaPolla stated he would "rather not discuss" his reasons for demanding Allen's removal, but admitted he didn't even know the chief.

This time when the *Vindicator* editorialized it wanted the action to be heard in court so it would be cleared once and for all. They wrote, "It is hoped that the present action will be sued out, to get a clear and final settlement of Chief Allen's status." Then, commenting on the achievements of the "Smash Racket Rule" leaders, the newspaper stated, "They have put honesty and efficiency into the police department. An officer no longer has to get off the sidewalk for a racketeer's punk, or find out whose second cousin an offender may be before arresting him. Most of the policemen like their new dignity and independence – and most of the people who pay their salaries like it, too."

Allen was furious when he found out that officials of the FOP were behind the effort. Their stand was that Allen shouldn't be chief because he was an "importee." Allen wrote years later:

> "None of Mayor Henderson's opponents seemed perturbed about the fact that the boss racketeer in their community was, like their new police chief, also an out-of-state "importee." Indeed, the astute leadership of the local Fraternal Order of Police hailed the police chief into court charging that his appointment was "illegal." The same police leadership had never even brought Joe DiCarlo in for questioning, much less arrest and court action, although his "position" in the community had been patently "illegal" for years."

The FOP was again accused of being behind the lawsuit. They tried to preempt the criticism by claiming an auxiliary unit known as the FOP Associates sponsored the suit. A spokesman for this unit issued a statement vehemently denying the allegation and declaring the FOP was clearly engineering the move.

If the pending court case affected Chief Allen he didn't let it show. On August 26, he appeared before the Youngstown Rotary Club in 97-degree weather. With sweat pouring down his brow, he addressed an audience of more than 200 local businessmen and told them that crime detection had increased 43 percent during the first six months of 1948 over the same period the prior year. He reported that the department's pistol team, which he initiated, had met the Erie department's team twice and beat them on both occasions. "We expect to challenge Cleveland and Pittsburgh," he advised.

Allen told the crowd, "Law enforcement is a mutual problem. Indifference to law enforcement on the part of the public is Public Enemy No. 1. We are attempting here to establish law enforcement in the hope that it will be permanent." The chief updated the audience on the educational program he had instituted and promised he could develop a department on the same level as the FBI. "Police work is a profession," Allen declared, "and should be accorded its place with other professions and paid for the job. The day of 'the dumb cop' is over. We are trying to better our conditions to attract better men into police work." He then announced that he was going before city council to ask for "15 more policemen, substantial pay raises and additional equipment." The chief's speech ended to a thunderous applause.

Allen's court case on the injunction suit to stop his salary began on September 9. A panel of three common pleas judges – David Jenkins, John Ford and Harold Doyle – heard arguments against Allen and City Finance Director J. Emerson Davis. No witnesses were called and all the facts were presented by mutual agreement of the two sides. The case boiled down to whether or not the state and civil service rules outweighed those of home rule. Lawyers for Allen pointed out that since the home-rule charter was passed in 1924, no promotional examination for chief had ever been held and that this was the first time its provision for chief was challenged.

The hearing was completed the next day and the judges promised an early ruling. On September 15, the panel agreed unanimously to throw the injunction suit out ruling:

1. That Allen's position is a "public employment, not a public office" as the injunction alleged.
2. That because Allen does not hold a public office, his former out-of-state residence does not affect his appointment.
3. That the city charter, not the state civil service laws, governs appointment of a Youngstown police chief.

In arriving at the ruling the panel concluded that "the mayor, himself, by state law and city charter, is the sole conservator of the peace, and Allen, serving as police chief, is the mayor's deputy, and thus keeps his job at the will of the mayor."

Before the dust had cleared from this latest incident, it was rumored that Allen was leaving Youngstown to become the police chief of Albuquerque, New Mexico. Allen denied the rumors, which originated in Erie, claiming that the southwest city had simply put out feelers looking to see who might be interested. When questioned, Allen told reporters, "I would never leave Mayor Henderson in the lurch. He brought me here to do a job and I am doing it to the best of my ability."

At the end of the first year of the Henderson administration the *Vindicator* discussed Allen's achievements. The newspaper pointed out that "major rackets have been driven, for the most part, from the city and that some notorious racket bosses (mainly the Budak brothers, Joe and Frank) have been returned to jail." Nothing was more telling though than the success against the policy writers. The new vice squad, of which Allen placed Sergeant Dan Maggianetti in charge, made 90 arrests in 1948 compared to zero the year before. During the first quarter the police made 39 arrests. At this point the bug men began operating out of different homes and using the telephone to take the bets. The vice squad officers quickly caught on to the new tactics and telephones were removed or service shut off and bug writers were nabbed after leaving the homes. Fines issued by the court totaled $21,000, with $14,000 suspended, which added $7,000 to the city coffers. In addition, before the end of 1948, Allen had cleared out all the bookie joints that offered the race wire service. Allen and Henderson were praised for their accomplishments in editorials and the chief was honored with a "Man of the Year" award issued by American Legion Post 472. Despite these achievements a thorn remained in Allen's side just over the border in Trumbull County.

The Jungle Inn

According to Eddie Allen, "The Village of Halls Corners, Ohio was conceived in infamy as a 'front' for a brothel operated by a Trumbull County criminal syndicate. The brothel later became the Jungle Inn, and eventually one of Ohio's most notorious gambling dens."

In August 1938, William M. McLain, assistant Trumbull County prosecutor, gave the following characteristics of Halls Corners.

> "The incorporation was made solely for the purpose of securing a liquor license and to defeat the purpose of the Liberty Township electors who in November, 1936, voted against permitting the sale of liquor by the glass.
>
> "The fact that the incorporation is a fraud is further indicated by the failure of the electors in Halls Corners to hold a municipal election last year though the ballots for this purpose were sent to the community by the Board of Elections."

When Halls Corners, located in the southeast corner of Trumbull County, just north of the Mahoning County line, was incorporated, the village consisted of nine voters, "all of whom became city officials and were connected with the Jungle Inn either personally or through some relative," Allen claimed. The gambling den was actually closer to Youngstown than to Warren and most of the patrons seeking taxi service to and from the Jungle Inn hailed from Youngstown. The Jungle Inn itself consisted of two frame buildings, one 57' x 125', the other 53' x 88'. The larger building was used as a bingo hall, horse race book and game room; the smaller one contained a restaurant, bar and living quarters.

In November 1940, the alleged operators of the Jungle Inn were named publicly for the first time when a woman filed suit against the gambling den to recover nearly $1,200 she claimed to have lost while playing bingo. According to the suit the operators were Mike Farah, Dominic "Moosey" Caputo, Emanuel Dupuy, and Edward Flannigan. The woman, a Youngstown resident represented by attorney Clyde W. Osborne, eventually settled out of court.

After the war there was evidence the Jungle Inn served as a sort of headquarters for Valley mobsters and that members of Detroit's infamous Licavoli Gang had moved in to organize and take charge of local gambling operations. The early months of 1945 had seen the murder of Cleveland's slot machine czar, Nate Weisenberg, followed by the disappearance of Jerry Pascarella. James Licavoli was a prime suspect in both incidents. A *Vindicator* article claimed, "Those in the know in the underworld say that many of the petty racketeers and mobsters who infest Trumbull County are imported from Detroit through the Mounds Club [Cleveland]."

Trumbull County Sheriff Ralph R. Millikin, who had once pledged "full enforcement of the law" after ordering the closing of the Jungle Inn, now claimed he had no authority to enter private clubs. Millikin later claimed that "enforcement of the law in Halls Corners was the responsibility of the local officers and he would not step in unless called upon to do so." Millikin, who by most accounts was being paid to look the other way, failed to acknowledge that Halls Corners had no law officers.

During the heyday of the Jungle Inn, crowds of up to 2,000 patrons appeared nightly to play poker, roulette and other games and to feed the slot machines on the premises; while a majority of the people still played bingo. An insight into the activities is provided by a *Vindicator* report:

> "Chief attractions at Jungle Inn still are bingo and the 80 odd slot machines which line the walls. Horse racing is the main afternoon feature at the spot, with the big 'run-down boards' indicating that bets are accepted for all the leading tracks.
>
> "Two poker tables continue to keep 22 card 'sharps' interested, and the chuck-a-luck, crap and dice games retain their specialized patrons. The roulette wheel is drawing more fans than in the past, however, as district gamblers get used to such fancy devices.
>
> "As usual, the crowd ranged from the very young to the very old, but the chief 'customer' of the Jungle still seems to be the motherly appearing middle-aged woman. The young gamblers were there in spite of signs warning: 'No minors allowed.'
>
> "The bingo crowds come in the free taxis provided by the gambling spot's management, or in thousands of automobiles parked in the spacious lots around the place. Many of the cars bear Pennsylvania licenses."

During the late 1940s, a partnership was formed known as the Jungle Novelty Company. The purpose was to operate a gambling casino called the Jungle Inn. The new partners of record were John and Shamis Farah, Ralph and Tessie Coletto, Edward F. and Catherine Tobin, and Anthony Delsanter.

In October 1948, Chief Allen requested a sit-down with Sheriff Millikin. Allen traveled to Warren with his Vice Squad Chief, Dan Maggianetti. When they arrived Sheriff Millikin and Deputy Earl Bash met them, but refused to allow

Maggianetti into the meeting. Allen pointed out that a gun used in a recent murder in Cleveland (the killing of Sam Jerry Monachino on September 29) was traced to a card dealer who worked at the Jungle Inn. The chief recounted, "I asked Sheriff Millikin to close down the Jungle Inn as a crime prevention measure because my investigations have led me to believe that the establishment is now having dangerous individuals." The sheriff refused Allen's request without elaboration.

At the next Youngstown City Council meeting, Allen promised to take action against the Jungle Inn. "The hoodlums who frequent the gambling dives are a menace to Youngstown," Allen stated. "People over in Warren are too far away to be affected by [the Inn's] activities, but many of the men who work out there live here in Youngstown."

Allen told council about a recent incident where a Jungle Inn employee asked a Youngstown police officer to saw-down several shotguns. The chief claimed that "too many guns were being funneled through Youngstown via the Jungle Inn to suit local authorities." Allen advised council members that he was checking with his law department to determine what state statutes, if any, would allow him to seek recourse against the Jungle Inn.

Not everyone in council was impressed with the chief's concerns. Allen's meeting with Sheriff Millikin met with criticism from council members Edgar Morley and Third Ward Councilman Anthony B. Flask, Jr., a future mayor. Both claimed the visit was politically motivated. Just how, they didn't explain. "Stay on your own dunghill, chief," advised Morley, "and give Youngstown the benefit of your great talents."

The night after Allen addressed city council, reporters paid a visit to the Jungle Inn only to find the 80-plus slot machines were removed. (When law enforcement officials raid gambling joints and seize the equipment with plans to destroy it, the slot machines are the most expensive to replace.) Nearly 2,000 people, however, were on hand to play bingo, poker and patronize the chuck-a-luck wheels and dice and roulette tables. That night there was a different atmosphere in the club with the door drawing more security, and armed guards watched the patrons carefully.

On October 21, Chief Allen exercised one of his "recourses" and had the Ohio Bell Telephone Company cut off service to the Jungle Inn. The telephone, in the name of Halls Corners' Councilman Charles Sedore, Sr. – whose son was the village mayor – was being used in connection with gathering horse race results. "You call the Sedore number and get the odds and instructions on how to place a bet," Allen told company officials. Despite Allen's further scrutiny of state laws, hunting for a legal means of raiding the Jungle Inn and his latest attempt to get Western Union to cut the wire service supplying track results, within a month the slot machines were back and gambling was going full blast.

In November 1948, Allen called Halls Corners' Mayor Charles Sedore, Jr. and asked him to come to his office. Sedore obliged the chief, but when Allen began talking about "violations within the mayor's jurisdiction," Sedore stood up and walked out. In talking to reporters afterward Allen "hinted" that a raid was being planned. "It'll come when the gamblers least expect it," he promised.

Allen's last recourse was to take the matter up with Governor Lausche. Sometime in 1949 the chief and Mayor Henderson paid the state's chief executive a visit. The raid Chief Allen hinted about came, but it took nine months to materialize and it was not Allen leading it. On Friday night, August 12, 1949, Ohio's Chief Liquor Enforcement Officer, Anthony A. Rutkowski and Ohio Department of Liquor Control Director, Oscar L. Fleckner closed the Jungle Inn forever during a raid that would live in infamy in Trumbull County.

The unarmed raiders were bullied and threatened by Jungle Inn thugs under the control of John Farah. At one point Farah ordered a guard in a gun turret to open fire on Rutkowski and Fleckner. As state liquor control agents the men had no power of arrest. They radioed Sheriff Millikin for assistance. The sheriff, who was at the Trumbull County Fair, didn't show up for three hours. Meanwhile, the thugs terrorized the agents, roughed up a newspaper photographer, and built a barricade to keep the agents from removing the gambling equipment. Despite this, the days of the Jungle Inn were over.

Less than three months after the Jungle Inn was closed Henderson was reelected with a margin of victory of nearly 12,000 votes, beating out Democratic challenger William D. Holt.

Frank Cammarata

Frank Cammarata was a Detroit Mafia figure with a long rap sheet. More annoying to Eddie Allen was the fact that Cammarata was deported to Italy in 1937, but sneaked back into the country two years later. Arrested in Solon, Ohio, just outside of Cleveland, in July 1946 the government began a 13-year battle to deport him again. It wasn't until Cammarata fell into Allen's cross hairs that the effort gained national attention.

After jumping bond in Cleveland, Cammarata looked for a place to live in Warren, but was unsuccessful. By his own admission, he went to Youngstown and lived at the home of Sam Belinky on Rush Blvd. After eight months in the Belinky household, he relocated to Warren.

Cammarata's presence in the Steel Valley is linked to the juke box dispute. What can be pieced together is that Cammarata was asked to intercede in a juke box dispute in Detroit during the mid-1940s. The dispute involved the placing of a new style of juke box, distributed by the Seeburg Company, into bars and restaurants in a city that was monopolized with machines provided by Wurlitzer Company and overseen by Vincent Meli. Due to Cammarata's association with Detroit Mafia figure Angelo Meli during the Prohibition years, he was able to convince the respected Mafioso's nephew, Vincent, not to take such a hard-line stand with the Seeburg distributor. Many believed it was Cammarata's success in this endeavor that resulted in his relocating to the Mahoning Valley to serve as an intermediary in the same type of dispute that was occurring in Youngstown, but of a more destructive nature. Whatever the case, Cammarata moved into a modest home at 161 Avondale Avenue, on the city's south side with his wife and three children.

In March 1948, Cammarata was arrested in Grosse Pointe, Michigan with five other men, all members of the Licavoli clan. Cammarata was a member of the clan not by association, but by marriage. He was married to the sister of Peter and Thomas (Yonnie) Licavoli. A couple days later, Cammarata was loaded on a train headed for Ellis Island for "re-deportation."

Once in New York, an attorney hired by Cammarata filed a petition in federal court asking for a stay of the deportation order. While a judge reviewed the request, Cammarata was released on bond while friends and relatives sought the help of the Mahoning Valley's powerful Congressman – Michael J. Kirwan. On April 20, 1948, Kirwan placed a bill in Congress to hold back the deportation until the Department of Justice could do a "thorough investigation." House Bill H.R. 6286, "A Bill For the relief of Francesca Cammarata," stated:

> *Be it enacted by the Senate and House of Representatives of the United States of America in Congress assembled,* That the Attorney General is authorized and directed to cancel the deportation proceedings presently pending against Francesca Cammarata, and that the facts upon which such proceedings are based shall not hereafter be made the basis for deportation proceedings.

During Chief Allen's investigation of violence in the local jukebox industry during June 1950, the deportation delay resulting from Congressman Kirwan's bills came to his attention. It's not for certain if Kirwan's efforts were made public before this, but at this juncture they exploded in the headlines right as the Kefauver Crime Hearings were beginning their 14-city tour of America.

Allen admits it was Youngstown's "juke box war" that initially brought Cammarata to his attention. He wrote: "The monopolistic practices of owners and union leaders in and around the juke box business were the cause of this war, which had begun to erupt in the hurling of stink bombs, acid bombs and dynamite bombs by those who wished to retain control and those who were trying to muscle in."

Cammarata was allegedly overseeing this muscling in and in June 1950, Allen had Cammarata brought in for questioning. The mobster informed the chief that he was president of the American Records Company, which had a branch office in Cleveland. He claimed at the moment the company was "not very active" locally, but if it did get active he was entitled to receive 45 percent of the profits. Despite repeated questioning from the chief, Cammarata never explained his duties or responsibilities with the record company. Cammarata did reveal he was compensated to the tune of $100 each week from the Berger Music Machine Company of Lorain, Ohio (located west of Cleveland), but again refused to explain his function.

During their conversation, Allen said he was told by Cammarata the first congressional bill was introduced by Kirwan at the insistence of his wife, Grace. On the second one, he "personally went to see Congressman Kirwan in Washington D.C. and requested Mr. Kirwan to introduce another such bill." He said the Congressman assured him that he would continue to do whatever he could for him. (Kirwan claimed that the introduction for the second bill came at the request of others.)

After questioning Cammarata, Allen called in James Licavoli, Cammarata's cousin by marriage. The suspected killer of Jerry Pascarella and Cleveland's Nate Weisenberg had recently been named by Virgil Peterson, director of the Chicago Crime Commission, as one of the "most powerful racketeers in Youngstown and Trumbull County," during his July 7 testimony before the Kefauver Committee.

On Sunday, July 9, the *Vindicator* reported that Allen had sent a registered letter to Kefauver in Washington D.C. accusing a politician, "with good White House connections," of blocking federal prosecution of a local racketeer. Allen wrote, "The official's intercession is so powerful that he has been able up to now, to stop the wheels of justice of the investigating agencies which are pushing the case against this criminal."

When asked why the letter was sent to the crime-crusading Senator, Allen replied that it was "prompted by a request from Kefauver for information on enforcement officers or politicians," who were protecting criminals. Allen then revealed details of his meeting with James Licavoli. According to Allen, "This criminal only last week told me that he had enough influence in Washington to force his racketeering operations into Youngstown. So far, we've heard endless testimony in Washington charging that powerful connections were safeguarding criminals. As yet, I haven't heard anyone mention the name of a powerful politician. Now one name is in the hands of the Senate committee. I named this politician in my letter, together with a request that the Senate committee aid me in keeping this racketeer [Licavoli] out of Youngstown."

Allen claimed Licavoli would extend his gambling operations into Youngstown, "as long as this national political figure stands in front of him and protects him." The chief promised that if the Senate committee didn't release the name of the politician, he would...and soon. "If the Senate doesn't help us in exposing this Washington politician, than [Licavoli] is right," Allen declared. "Neither federal agencies nor local police can curb the criminals if this type of high influence continues in the nation's capital."

The next day a front-page *Vindicator* story revealed the politician to be Congressman Michael Kirwan. After receipt of the letter Senator Kefauver spoke directly with Kirwan about the accusations. Kefauver told reporters that Kirwan had relayed to him that he had received "an adverse report" from immigration officials on Cammarata and was dropping the case. Kefauver sought to appease both parties. He stated, "Chief Allen is a good man trying to do a diligent job, and his assistance has been invaluable." The Senator in support of Kirwan, a fellow Congressman, said he believed the representative "acted out of good motives."

Allen's comments proved to be the first time Kirwan was attacked publicly for introducing the bills. He responded with a formal statement in which he declared, "I have no apology for introducing a bill in behalf of the Cammarata family." Then, in a stinging rebuke to Chief Allen, he ended the statement with "the faster the citizens of Youngstown deport you back to Erie, it will be a much better city." Incensed by Kirwan's comments, Chief Allen challenged the Congressman to appear before the Kefauver Committee and "tell his story" publicly. It was a challenge the representative declined.

In November 1950, the Michigan parole board, which had allowed the deportation of Cammarata, finally charged Cammarata with parole violation and sought his arrest. Michigan authorities were giving consideration to a full pardon for Cammarata until Chief Allen's investigation resulted in a label of "influential racketeer" being place on him. The *Vindicator* explained, "The parole violation thus is actually a violation of commutation of sentence and Cammarata would be liable to serve out the remainder of his sentence."

On December 14, Cammarata was arrested by Warren Police Chief Manley English and three officials from the Ohio Parole Board. Cammarata was booked in Warren, but transferred to the Youngstown jail where he was held without charge while extradition details were worked out. The prisoner would be handed over to Michigan authorities unless he decided to fight extradition. On December 16, Cammarata's attorneys, Russell Mock and Patrick J. Melillo, filed a writ of habeas corpus demanding the release of their still uncharged client. Judge Erskine Maiden, Jr. set a hearing date for Monday, but refused to free the prisoner. Mock met with Chief Allen and offered to provide a bond of $15,000 to insure Cammarata's appearance in court. Allen refused, after conferring with Michigan officials, citing Cammarata's "record as a bail jumper."

On Tuesday afternoon, Chief Allen was called to testify as to why Cammarata was a bad risk for being granted bond. Questioned by Assistant Law Director P. Richard Schurmann, Allen stated that Cammarata "probably will not be here when extradition papers arrive from the governor of Michigan to return him as a parole violator." Allen backed up his statements with newspaper clippings from the *Detroit Free Press*, which reported how Cammarata had jumped bond after his 1925 arrest in Detroit for the bank robbery. A *Vindicator* article reported:

> "Allen said that the Black Hand Society known as the Mafia, is greatly interested in Cammarata's hearing and that the chief indicated that Cammarata's son-in-law

> Emmanuel Amato of Cleveland, a front man for juke boxes in Youngstown, appeared in court Tuesday along with a local cafe owner. The latter, Allen said, had attempted to take over the entire vending machine business in the Youngstown district.
>
> "The Chief said he began his investigation when he learned that Cammarata was 'trying to muscle in on the juke box business here." He named the café owner as Charles Vizzini[18] of 848 Fifth Ave., and said he was the head of the Mafia in the Youngstown area. Vizzini has denied any connections with the Mafia."

Mock responded that Cammarata had "lived an exemplary life," claiming that his arrest record held only two convictions – a concealed weapons charge in 1927 and one for armed robbery, for which he had served his jail sentence. As for "bail jumping," Mock pointed out that Cammarata was still under bond to immigration officials for $10,000 since 1948. On Wednesday afternoon, Judge Nevin denied Cammarata's petition for bond and committed him to the county jail, setting a 30-day limit for the extradition process to take place.

Thus began a long and arduous legal battle to return Cammarata to Michigan to serve out his sentence, or at least have him re-deported. In the end both happened.

In the meantime, during the mayoral race in the fall of 1951, Mayor Charles Henderson and Michael J. Kirwan traded heated barbs, triggered by the congressman's bill to keep Cammarata from being deported. Kirwan came out in support of John A. Bannon, the Democratic candidate for mayor. Henderson claimed Kirwan "injected" himself into the campaign because of his personal resentment over Police Chief Edward J. Allen's exposure of Kirwan's sordid role in keeping the convict Frank Cammarata from being deported." In the fall election, Henderson beat the Kirwan-supported Bannon by 7,500 votes.

Cammarata finally lost all his appeals and was returned to Michigan in July 1953. He served additional time for his 1931 bank robbery conviction until May 1958, when he was released with orders to be deported. Cammarata remained until December when he was called before the McClellan Committee and questioned about his previous jukebox activities by lead counsel Robert F. Kennedy. Days after the hearing he left for Cuba never to return. In early May 1965, while in a Cuban "concentration camp" prison on drug charges, he died of acute edema of the lungs and hypertension of the heart.

Chief Allen was successful in removing a number of outsiders from Youngstown – Buffalo's Joe DiCarlo had packed for the sunny south with "Moosey" Caputo at his heels, Detroit's Frank Cammarata was returned to a Michigan prison cell, and St. Louis's "Fats" Aiello was reduced to "peanuts," according to the chief. This left Youngstown with a power struggle, however, with many local underworld figures trying to seize the brass ring. The main contestants were Sandy Naples and Vince DeNiro, but others would vie for the right to the Valley's gambling profits. In doing so, the balance of the 1950s would turn into a prolonged bombing war until the key participants eliminated each other in a bloody battle of attrition during the first three years of the 1960s.

The citizens of Youngstown showed their appreciation of Henderson's and Allen's accomplishments by re-electing the incumbent mayor in November 1949 and again in November 1951.

As was the case with most good police chiefs, Allen could be sensitive when it came to territorial issues. In the spring of 1950, when a Western Union executive testified before a Senate subcommittee that three race wire services were operating in Youngstown, Allen took the man to task. The official went back before the committee and admitted he "erred," that the three in question were in Wickliffe, a neighborhood west of Youngstown on Mahoning Avenue in Austintown Township.

Allen told reporters that, "There hasn't been any wire service operating in Youngstown since they were cleaned out in 1948, and there won't be any." When informed of these latest operations Allen immediately sent a letter to Mahoning County Sheriff Paul Langley and informed him. The previous year, Langley had boasted of closing several gambling joints in Youngstown, insinuating that Allen's men had missed them. Allen was quick to retaliate. The chief stated, "Since Langley has boasted he is sheriff of the entire Mahoning County, I now challenge him to clean up the entire county if he can or if he dares – or else deputize some of our men and we will show him how it is done."

Allen then revealed that he had informed the sheriff of a bookie headquarters behind the Saunders Restaurant on Mahoning Avenue at which automobiles belonging to Joe DiCarlo and "Cadillac Charlie" Cavallaro were spotted. Langley never acted on it. The chief dashed off a note to the sheriff, "As you know, your jurisdiction in the county has always been respected by this office, and we have not made arrests in the county, as yet. I call your attention, however, to the clause in the law that grants us extra-jurisdictional authority. It is my considered duty to protect the good names as well as the lives and properties of the citizens of Youngstown. I shall use every legitimate means to prevent causes leading to disparagement."

Allen then informed Langley that he couldn't plead ignorant to not knowing the location of the race wire tickers in the county. "Western Union will not lease race wires in the Youngstown district without first consulting the police chief. This courtesy is likewise extended to you as chief law enforcement officer in the county," he advised.

In March 1950, Allen was invited to speak at the FBI National Academy in Washington D.C. by Director J. Edgar Hoover. The audience was made up of police representatives from large and small cities across the nation. Because of his recent success in cleaning up gambling in Youngstown, Allen discussed the model he used in his effort. The chief claimed that gambling could not be eradicated without a "four-fold" program, which included the input and participation of the mayor, the police department, the prosecutors and the judges. "Meet with these officials," he urged and then release a joint public statement to get the citizens on board.

Allen openly blamed police and elected officials for allowing the problem to get out of hand. "It would have been easy to stop it if they didn't go along with the appeasement or open connivance with racketeers who since prohibition days, seems to have been accepted into every branch of society," he stated.

The chief pointed out that, "Since we cannot guarantee that there will be no more larcenies, burglaries and murders, we cannot guarantee that there will be no more gambling. But we can and do guarantee that no one will operate openly and that no hoodlums or racketeers will exact tribute from anyone with any sort of police or political protection."

Allen then expressed his own point of view on the recent influx of slot machines. "There are no slot machines, either openly or in private clubs in Youngstown. There are no punchboards, [or] pinball games and gambling is at an almost irreducible minimum. There is one point on which we as local law enforcement officers might justly differ with some federal authorities, and that is the practice of licensing or exacting a tax on slot machines. This practice, it seems, gives at least tacit approval to their operation and transportation and a certain cloak of legality. It is my opinion that the government sets a wrong example by this policy."

By the end of 1950, Henderson and Allen's efforts were now drawing nationwide attention. In September, Henderson accepted "The American All-City Award" for 1950 for "progressive work in better government." The accomplishments were chronicled in the October issue of *National Municipal Review* [19] and the December 19 edition of *Look* magazine, which stated, "Honest government plus a relentless police force has made "Little Chicago" the most law-abiding city its size."

Battle with City Council Over "Bug" Laws

Allen and Henderson waged their biggest battle with city council over a proposed amendment to the bug ordinance, which called for a jail sentence for offenders. Previous attempts on getting ordinances introduced came in May 1949 and April 1950. Both times council tabled the discussions and refused to act. In the next attempt, the battle turned ugly during a council meeting on April 30, 1951.

The current law called for fines of up to $500, of which the municipal judge normally suspended all but $100. This was not a hardship to bug operators who were raking in amounts much larger than that on a daily basis. Henderson's proposal called for a six-month jail sentence for possession of "apparatus, devices, sheets, slips, tickets, books and other devices used in gambling." The mayor pointed out that during the prior week a New Castle, Pennsylvania judge sentenced a Youngstown policy racketeer, who was caught peddling his trade there, to a year in prison. These types of penalties, the administration declared, were needed to make a dent in the policy rackets here.

Members of council opposing the ordinance – Council President Frank X. Kryzan; First Ward Councilmen John W. Barber; Second Ward Councilman John "Jack" Palermo; and Third Ward Councilman Anthony B. Flask – claimed the police should have the case prosecuted under the state law, which contained provisions for a prison term. Police Prosecutor Henry Fugett explained that under the state statute the arresting officers had to catch the suspect actually purchasing or selling the number's slip, pointing out that arrest on possession alone was not enough.

Kryzan questioned, and correctly so, that since judges normally levied fines well below the maximum, what reason was there to believe that they wouldn't impose brief sentences instead of giving those convicted the maximum?

To this Allen responded, "Your duty will cease when you give us a good law."

It was then that the fireworks began.

Anthony Flask questioned Fugett, "Do you make the arrested man sign an affidavit admitting his guilt or else book him on suspicion so that he will be held in jail for 72 hours without legal aid?"

"Tony," Allen cut in, "that's what the racketeers say."

"I resent that," Flask shouted.

"Well who told you?" Allen demanded.

"It wasn't a racketeer and I still resent the remark," Flask countered.

"You can resent that until hell freezes over," Allen responded.

Flask told the chief that he represented his ward "to its best interests" and "you never will tell me what to do."

Allen seized the moment and answered, "The best interests would be the passage of that law. Rackets exist because we have inadequate laws. You are failing in your duty if you do not pass it."

At this point John Palermo interrupted. The former bodyguard of Mayor Spagnola, who once did time for sucker-punching attorney Dominic Rendinell, struck again, this time with a verbal barrage at the chief. "You talk like a child," Palermo said. "You are a disgrace to the FBI if you can't get a conviction on a nickel bug writer." It was apparent the councilman was not up to speed with what the argument was about. The police had no problem getting convictions against "nickel bug writers," they just felt that the fine alone was not sufficient punishment.

Kryzan took this moment to get in his own shot. Accusing the chief of timing the introduction of the ordinance with approaching elections, he demanded, "Are you interested in electing the mayor or in getting your name in the headlines?"

As the meeting progressed Allen was writing his thoughts, preparing to deliver them at the appropriate time. The *Vindicator* reported his message to council:

> "When Allen took the floor in council chambers nearly an hour later he told councilmen that they can best identify their stand on gambling by 'giving us stringent laws to cope with the ever-changing tactics of the criminal element.'
>
> "'The police department cannot do the whole job. We are willing and anxious to do our part, and feel we have the right to expect council to do its part by passing adequate laws.'
>
> "Allen pointed out that the Senate [in the midst of the Kefauver hearings] has recognized its responsibilities in the crime investigations, spending millions of dollars, whereas the passage of the law here would cost nothing.
>
> "Allen continued that 'for over three years the department has been tireless and unrelenting in its efforts to rid the community of organized racketeering and gangsterism.'
>
> "'Are we not justified in expecting whatever help council has the power to render? But instead the power of council has favored the racketeer as against the police department and the general public as is undeniably apparent by their consistent refusal to attach a jail sentence to the numbers ordinance.'
>
> "'There is no valid reason for their failure to support their police department in its determined efforts to cleanse the city of undesirable elements and characters who, incidentally, in large measure, came here from other states to bring shame and disgrace on the fair name of Youngstown.'
>
> "'But the assistance of council has been conspicuous by its absence in all of our efforts to rid the community of their presence as well as their influence. To which influence, a vast number of Youngstown citizens may attribute council's action tonight. Failure to discharge these duties in the public interest seems to me tantamount to failure of public duty,' Allen stated.
>
> "Allen stated that the previous ordinances were tabled June 20, 1949, and Nov. 13, 1950, 'neither of which date had any significance so far as local elections are concerned. Further, a little political acumen or reflection would discover that there could be no political significance to the present amendment or its timing.'
>
> "'If there was a political motive involved, I assure you that a date nearer the fall election when there will be a contest would have been more propitious.'
>
> "'But apparently the jaundiced hue of politics has so discolored your outlook that it is difficult for you to see through its fog, even in the serious matter of legislating for the safety and welfare of its citizens.'
>
> "'The opponents of the law in council can prate loud and long of how much they are opposed to racketeering but their action in council proves otherwise. Actions speak more eloquently than words,' Allen concluded."

Kryzan responded to Allen's statement by accusing him of using his office for persecution instead of prosecution. "It is time to give great consideration to anything you ask for," Kryzan declared.

Allen stated that Kryzan's remarks were "a bald and malicious lie" and said he expected a public apology "to discover whether or not you possess character and decency."

Jumping into the attack against Allen was Barber and Palermo. Stating that he resented the chief's remarks, Barber criticized the new ordinance reiterating, "The judge can send a man to jail under the state statute."

Palermo's response was a little more condescending. Claiming that the department didn't give the state law a fair test, Palermo said, "Allen made no effort to use this law and, until he shows me he is honest and sincere, I will oppose the amendment. Other administrations have convictions under the state law. But our chief can go to Detroit and tell them how to run the country but he can't get evidence on a five-cent bug writer."

The day after the council meeting Kryzan came out publicly and suggested that a public hearing be held on the jail-sentence proposal. Henderson welcomed the suggestion and discussed this, as well as council's accusation that politics were behind the ordinance, telling reporters:

> "The only political aspect is that which members and the president of council have seen fit to inject into it. Any such charge of politics can be completely removed by council's passage of the needed legislation.
>
> "I believe that the people of this community will leave no doubt in the minds of members of council how they feel about the issue. I welcome a public hearing.
>
> "The members of council know fully as well as the administration does, how helpful in a law enforcement program our requested legislation would be.
>
> "I am completely amazed and entirely at a loss to conceive how council can logically deny our request especially now in the face of so much evidence in the current news that the public is overwhelmingly in support of that which we are endeavoring to do."

The mayor pointed out that local ordinances are full of provisions contained in state laws, sometimes being stated almost verbatim. "Why," he questioned, "This special consideration for the racketeers." As for his chief's clash with members of council, Henderson was diplomatic. He applauded Allen for "his great courage and ability to stand up and fight for the things he believes to be right." He agreed, however, that some of his chief's statements were made "in a much stronger and personal manner than was called for, especially in the light of opportunity for sober reflection."

In the end, throughout the entire Henderson Administration, city council refused to pass an amendment to provide jail time to its bug ordinance.[20]

Ordinance or no ordinance, Allen's vice squad kept up their pursuit of the bug writers. Nothing showed the desperation of these men more than an incident on July 17, 1950. Patrolmen and Vice Squad Officer William Campanizzi stopped an automobile containing Sam J. Thomas, his two young children, and the nine-year-old son of Louis Pannunzio. The elder Pannunzio had just moved his bug headquarters to a new location after the cutting off of telephone service to his home. Police were following Thomas' movements for two weeks before they stopped him. The officers were at first disappointed when a search of the automobile failed to uncover any policy slips. Officers then went through the pockets of the three children where they found 30 slips in the pocket of the Pannunzio youth. Thomas and Pannunzio pleaded guilty the next morning before Municipal Judge Nevin, who berated the men for "hiding behind juveniles to escape the law."

Another example of Allen's success in Youngstown and Mahoning County was the ever-increasing gambling activity that was beginning to occur in Trumbull County to the north.

The Buddy Fares Incident

Nothing brought out the junkyard dog in Eddie Allen faster than being accused, or having his men accused, of being in cahoots with the underworld. In 1953, Bud J. "Buddy" Fares crossed this line bringing the chief's wrath raining down on him.

Buddy Fares seemed like a jack-of-all-trades in Youngstown. In the early 1950s, this former internationally known bodybuilder was the publisher of a weekly entertainment guide called *The Youngstowner*. The pamphlet, distributed for free in nightclubs and hotels, highlighting upcoming performances and events, also served as a sounding board for Fares' public views.

Sounding off was just what Fares did in the publication's release for the week of February 9, 1953. In his weekly column Fares wrote:

> "For the past year, we have heard and in some instances seen certain instances involving members of Police Chief Edward Allen's vice squad that left no doubt in our mind that there is an alliance between certain members of the vice squad and certain members of the local gambling syndicate. Rumors persist, and many of our informers have taken oath in our presence, that the numbers racket in Youngstown is directly controlled by about six members of the vice squad. We find it difficult to deny that statement as sensational as it may seem... because our observations seem to bear out this co-operation."

In his story Fares asked, "Why does the vice squad and Allen pickup just certain operators, while the other three or four bug banks continue their ...operations unmolested?" Also included, was a claim that a member of the vice squad visited Sandy Naples in late December looking for a "Christmas present." Naples allegedly "booted the officer out, kicked him, spit on him and reviled him."

An incensed Chief Allen conducted an immediate investigation of his department and declared it completely vindicated. He then made several requests for Fares to voluntarily come to police headquarters to substantiate his allegations. When he refused, Allen had the small-time publisher arrested by vice squad members on the night of February 17.

At the police station, Allen questioned Fares and recorded the interrogation without the prisoner's knowledge. Fares gave him three names as the sources of his information. He named Sandy Naples first, who was then brought in and questioned before Fares. Naples denied supplying any information about a "fix" with the vice squad. The next two, Harry and Joseph Beshara, were also questioned in the presence of Fares, who claimed he was present when a vice officer shook down the two at their Poland Dry Cleaning Shop several months earlier. The brothers denied Fares' allegations and claimed, "We've been out of the rackets for sometime because of activities of the vice squad."

Allen disgustedly told reporters, "Even the gambling figures named by Fares as his sources of information have no use for him."

The chief kept Fares in jail overnight. The next morning his attorney filed a writ of habeas corpus and Common Pleas Judge Harold B. Doyle ordered police to file charges by 2:15 that afternoon or release him. Allen then called in the 12 members of the vice squad and told Fares to pick out any of the six men that he had accused. When Fares was unable to identify any of the officers, Allen charged him with criminal libel just minutes before the afternoon deadline. Fares was arraigned before Municipal Judge Robert B. Nevin, who set bond at $1,000. After the hearing Fares boasted to reporters and courtroom observers, "I'll blow the lid off this town before it's over. You can say we're not worried. We'll substantiate in court all the things I've printed."

On the eve of Fares' case being bound over to the grand jury, Allen told reporters that his vice squad chief – now Lieutenant, Dan Maggianetti – and the City Law Director, P. Richard Schumann, were handling the case. The chief stated, "As far as I'm concerned, it in now a matter for the courts to decide. We gave Fares every opportunity to give us information and to help clear up the matter. If he is right in his charges we have a job to do, but if he is wrong the court will have a job to do."

The next morning, February 27, Fares' attorney Patrick J. Melillo, waived a preliminary hearing, pleaded his client innocent of the charge of criminal libel, and asked for the case to be referred to the grand jury.

On September 5, after being "batted around by two or three grand juries," the charges against Fares were finally decided. The panel indicted him on two counts of criminal libel. The first was against Chief Allen, the second against six unnamed members of the vice squad. In the weeks after the charges, Melillo filed motions to have the indictments quashed. The *Vindicator* reported the attorney argued before Common Pleas Judge Erskine Maiden, Jr., that the indictments should be dismissed on the grounds they did not support a charge of criminal libel under Ohio law. The article stated, "Attorney Melillo said that in order to be criminally libelous, Fares statements would have to be directed at the character of an individual with direct intent and not merely innuendo. He said the article was a criticism of alleged official acts of the chief and vice squad and was not aimed at their character."

After hearing arguments from Melillo and First Assistant County Prosecutor Harold Hull, Judge Maiden ruled on October 22 that the second count of the indictment be quashed. The judge ruled that Fares' comments about "six members" were not specific without naming individuals or designating the entire group.

On December 10, 1953, Fares home, at 633 Almyra Avenue, was bombed at 3:00 a.m. when a dynamite explosion destroyed a porch railing, broke two large windows, damaged the porch floor and destroyed the front door and a storm door. Damage was estimated at $500. Fares told police he had received seven telephone threats during the latter half of October. He claimed he was warned to "lay off Chief Allen and the vice squad," and if he didn't stop his writing campaign that his home would be "blown sky high." Fares stated, "I don't know who actually did this, but I have some pretty good ideas as to who may be responsible." Fares was out delivering his publication at the time of the blast. His wife and two daughters were home, but not harmed.

During the initial questioning of Fares, he said he didn't know who planted the bomb at his house, but he had a couple of motives. Fares said he recently had trouble trying to collect monies due him for advertisements in *The Youngstowner* by restaurant owners and used car dealers. A second motive mentioned by Fares was his recent attacks on Chief Allen and the Henderson Administration.

The restaurant owners Fares referred to were Vince DeNiro, part owner of the Colonial House on Market Street; and Sandy Naples, owner of the Center Sandwich Shop. The used car dealer was Vince's brother, Frank DeNiro, owner of the Century Auto Mart on Market Street.

Police questioned Vince DeNiro first. The dapper gangster claimed he didn't owe Fares anything and that if there was anything about the Colonial House in *The Youngstowner*, it was placed there without his permission. DeNiro said he was at George Economus' Skyway Tavern on the Belmont Avenue Extension at the time of the explosion.

Frank DeNiro was questioned next. He too, claimed he didn't owe Fares any money, even though advertisements for his used car business appeared in the publication. He claimed Fares kept calling the Century Auto Mart looking for Vince, but was told to contact him at the Colonial House.

Up next was Sandy Naples. He also denied owing money to Fares, and said he was at the Purple Cow with two friends when the bomb went off.

Police went back to Fares after questioning the three men. Fares now claimed he was being blamed for the recent arrest of Hartley Moore, a local bug dealer. Moore was arrested on December 9 by Detective Lloyd Haynes for possession of lottery slips. Why Fares would be blamed for having a role in the arrest was not revealed.

In February 1955, more than a year after Chief Allen left office, the case finally came to trial. County Prosecutor William A. Ambrose explained that the delay in pursuing the case was due to the illness of attorney Patrick Melillo, who suffered from heart trouble.

As the trial date neared, Fares announced that Vincent DeNiro would be subpoenaed for the defense. All of a sudden Fares was now claiming, "DeNiro supplied much of the information." This revelation, of course, came after his previous stated "sources," Sandy Naples and the Beshara brothers, crapped out.

County Prosecutor Ambrose encountered a number of surprises on the first day of trial. First, he was under the impression the case would be tried without a jury. Next, he didn't realize how well known both Allen and Fares were in Mahoning County. The potential jury panel of 24 was exhausted before the first day was over and an additional allotment was needed the next day. One of those questioned said he didn't know either Allen or Fares, but knew the prosecutor. When asked by Judge Maiden how close their association was, the man answered, "Why, your honor, I've campaigned for him many times."

In his opening statement a confidant Melillo said, "The informers produced evidence [for the article] that Mr. Fares personally investigated. We will prove everything in the article was true to our best information and belief." The attorney claimed the story, to him, was "classified under qualified privilege." The jury might have bought the attorney's story, had he produced any evidence to back it up.

The courtroom was filled to capacity as former Youngstown Police Chief Eddie Allen took the stand. It became public for the first time that Allen's interrogation of Fares was taped after his February 1953 arrest. Allen admitted on the stand that the questioning ran beyond the length of the tape, and that Fares was unaware he was being recorded. Ambrose did not offer the tape as testimony saying he didn't need it to make his case. He offered it to the defense, to which Melillo declared that since it was incomplete it would be tantamount to "confronting a half truth."

The former chief testified that Fares "couldn't or wouldn't" backup his charges against the vice squad members. During the interrogation, Fares at first said he couldn't give Allen the names of his "informers" because the time wasn't "ripe for blowing the lid off." Fares followed this claim with the statement that on two occasions he was present and witnessed payoffs between racketeers and vice squad members. When he was asked to identify the officers, he balked, again claiming "the time isn't right."

Allen told the court that he ordered the underworld members Fares claimed had informed him of the fix brought in. The first was Sandy Naples, who denied Fares' claims and instead told Allen that Fares ran a "shakedown" publication. Naples told the chief that if he thought he could have bought members of the department, he would have done so. The hard-nosed Allen advised the court he was just repeating his conversation with Naples and that he would no more trust the word of the mobster than he would anything the defendant had to say.

Allen said Naples was followed by the Beshara brothers. Allen stated Fares had told him he overheard a telephone conversation where a vice squad member apologized to one of the brothers for arresting one of their "bug" runners. The Besharas were brought in, but Fares denied making any such allegations to Allen and Maggianetti in the brother's presence.

When the state completed its case, the defense offered no witnesses or evidence. The talk of subpoenaing Vince DeNiro apparently was just rumor. In the state's closing, Prosecutor Hull attacked Fares for not testifying, "For not having the courage like this very capable Chief Allen to get on the stand and name names."

Melillo told jurors that Fares didn't take the stand because he was protecting his sources, his "informers." He declared that his client's publication was "just criticism" of a public official, claiming it was Fares' "duty as a newspaperman" to do so.

William Ambrose's closing rebuttal was the highlight of the trial. Called "dramatic and thundering," he attacked both the defendant and his counsel. Ambrose ripped into *The Youngstowner*, asking the panel, "Who ever heard of it accorded the dignity of being a newspaper? Why, it's no more a newspaper than a seed catalogue. Fares never believed himself that he was a newspaperman until Melillo told him."

The prosecutor then ripped into Melillo charging, "He made more out of nothing in this case than any other lawyer that I have contacted in a long time."

Although the prosecutor and the former chief didn't see eye-to-eye when they worked together, Ambrose had kind words for Allen. "Chief Allen," he began, "while here tried very hard to combat all crime. Allen was conscientious. He made enemies; he couldn't help it.

"He believes that the petty thief of today is the master thief of tomorrow. Therefore he went all out to get the petty thief.

"You'll have to admit the man was honest, conscientious and dedicated to his duties. He had courage and cared not whose toes he stepped on in performing these duties. I know what I'm talking about."

Ambrose finished by telling the jurors Fares "defied you by not taking the stand; he simply ignored you."

The case was quite intricate. The *Vindicator* tried to explain the complexities as the jurist charged the jury:

> "Judge Maiden told the jury before it retired that he was ruling that the article Fares wrote Feb. 9, 1953, linking former Police Chief Edward J. Allen with the rackets here, was libelous.
>
> "Therefore the question for the jury to decide concerning Fares' guilt or innocence was whether the libelous accusation made by Fares was the truth or was false.
>
> "The jurors also were told to determine in their judgment whether it was published for a good reason.
>
> "At one point Melillo argued that the indictment terms The Youngstowner "a newspaper" and that it had been stipulated when the trial began that it was a newspaper and that Fares was its publisher.
>
> "Therefore, Melillo argued, the jury should be charged on the law contained in

> the immunity act whereby a reporter, editor, etc., of a newspaper in Ohio cannot be forced to reveal the source of his news.
>
> "This has been a bone of contention in the trial, since Fares refused to take the stand to name racket men and gamblers who he has charged told him of tie-ups with the vice squad and thence with Allen.
>
> "Judge Maiden refused to charge the jury thus because Fares had not been required to testify, which is a stipulation of the immunity law."

The jury began deliberations at 2:40 on the afternoon of March 1 and by 4:55 had reached a verdict – guilty. Maiden withheld sentencing pending defense counsel's motion for a new trial. More than four months passed before Maiden overruled Fares' motion for a new trial and imposed sentence. The statute called for a fine of $500 or a year in the penitentiary. Maiden declared, "The court did not feel the offense warranted the jail sentence," then meted out a fine of $300.

Melillo appealed the case and on December 8 the Seventh District Court of Appeals confirmed the conviction. Five months later, on May 2, 1956, the Ohio Supreme Court refused to overturn the decision.

In the end, the reason for Fares' attack on Chief Allen and his vice squad was never revealed. Did Fares have a beef with the police official or was he just writing pulp fiction for his readers? Had underworld figures really supplied him with the information and then retreated after Allen's ire when the incident became public? We'll never know.

End in Sight

By June 1953, there was speculation that Charles Henderson would be defeated in the fall election by Council President Frank Kryzan. If that were the case Allen would surely be out as chief of police. Still, with the storm clouds gathering, Allen never wavered in his loyalty to Henderson and the city.

That spring, Allen was offered the position of chief of police of Palm Springs, California. Since the city had a manager form of government, Allen would be free of the political nonsense he detested in Youngstown. The city, which offered beautiful surroundings, a mild climate and higher pay, was concerned primarily with the protection of its wealthy homes from burglaries. In declining the tempting offer Allen stated, "Mayor Henderson and the good people of Youngstown have given me their loyal support and friendship to an exceptional degree. These are treasures I am reluctant to voluntarily surrender. I am pleased and happy to continue in service here."

At the time, Allen was embroiled in a bitter battle against pornography and obscene publications. His efforts to eradicate the material were challenged by a lawsuit in federal court. The chief's religious beliefs fueled this latest crusade. In September 1953, he traveled to Detroit where he delivered a talk on "Lascivious Literature and the Times." The address was delivered during the annual police chiefs' convention being held in the Motor City. After reviewing a copy of the speech, FBI Director J. Edgar Hoover commented, "The magnitude of this threat to our nation's morals definitely calls for prompt and decisive action. Frankly, it is time that more people were awakened to the extent our nation's youth have been affected by this tide of pornography."

On the eve of the November 1953, election Allen received the "Badge of Honor" award from *Police Detective* magazine as the nation's law officer of the month. The story that accompanied the award described Allen as "a fearless policeman who transformed one of the country's worst sin cities into a law abiding community."

Unfortunately for the city of Youngstown, Mayor Henderson was defeated the next day by less than 1,500 votes. Frank Kryzan, the incoming Democratic mayor, announced just one day later that Allen would not be re-appointed chief of police. Kryzan's selection was Paul H. Cress a registered Republican, which surprised some. The *Vindicator* reported Cress got the nod, "partly because of the urging of an influential wing of the Democratic Party here."

When interviewed by reporters, Allen stated he had no immediate future plans, but that whatever they were, they would involve law enforcement. Commenting on his accomplishments as police chief, Allen praised his boss. "The real police chief in Youngstown," he stated emphatically, "has always been Mayor Henderson. If any effective law enforcement has been accomplished it is due to his unswerving support and permitting the police department to be completely free of petty, partisan politics.

"His strength enabled me not only to achieve results in traffic and unseating formerly entrenched underworld characters, but in all other phases of law enforcement.

"He has been the kind of mayor every police chief dreams about but very seldom encounters."

On December 29, the eve of his departure, Chief Allen presented to City Council a 13-page report summarizing his achievements in the Youngstown Police Department. The report discussed a 35 percent decrease in felonious crimes and nearly a 50 percent cut in the traffic fatality rate through the first five years of the Henderson administration. Among his accomplishments Allen listed the fact that patrolman's salary increased 60 percent, from $230 a month to $362. This combined with 40-hour workweek and overtime considerations made the department one of the best-paid police forces in the nation.

Allen was most proud of his success against the Empire News Service, claiming that cutting off the race wire was a "knockout blow to the racket czars who ruled the underworld here and who yielded such great influence politically." He also listed his battle to keep Detroit mobsters from muscling in on the local jukebox rackets here one of his top accomplishments. This effort resulted in the jailing of Frank Cammarata and his later deportation.

Allen was especially proud of his men in the traffic division and thanked them personally before he left. He called on each member to "give your loyalty to both your new police chief and the administration in the same full measure as you have in the past." Sergeant Paul Cress, who was slated to be the new police chief, was a member of that department, who Allen had sent to Northwestern University for traffic courses.

On January 7, 1954, Eddie Allen was feted at a dinner at the Youngstown Country Club by 100 invited guests. Organized by Dr. John J. McDonough, the special guests were former Mayor Henderson, Reverend Emmet M. Walsh, bishop of Youngstown and Reverend Dr. Roland A. Luhman, pastor of Pilgrim Collegiate Church. When Bishop Walsh spoke he told the audience that Allen "is a genuinely Christian man. I hate to see him go. May God speed him on his way and give him years of service."

The most touching words of the night came from Henderson. He told the group that "it was comforting to have a department head you never had to worry about. You knew he was always doing a good job and fighting for things we stood for and that in Eddie Allen Youngstown had the best chief in the country."

McDonough, head of the committee for the Chief Allen Recognition Fund, presented Allen with the keys to a brand new 1954 Chevrolet in appreciation of his six years of dedicated service to the city. Allen was told there was one string attached to the gift – "please don't drive it too far away from Youngstown."

Days after leaving the department Allen received a personal letter from J. Edgar Hoover. The FBI Director wrote:

> "I want to take this means to let you know what a great pleasure it was for my associates and me to work with you during your tenure as chief of police at Youngstown.
>
> "You must indeed find a great deal of personal satisfaction in the knowledge that you were able to serve your community in a manner in keeping with the highest traditions of the law enforcement profession.
>
> "It was a real privilege for all of us in the FBI to cooperate with you and we wish you every success in your new endeavor."

The new endeavor was enforcement chief of the Ohio Liquor Control Department. There he reported to Director Anthony Rutkowski, the man who closed the Jungle Inn. Even before he left as police chief, Allen turned down the opportunity to return to the Erie Police Department, from which he was still listed as being on a leave of absence. Allen stated he was resigning from the Erie police force, "because I have no intention of returning to Erie. I have several offers which are so much better than what I would return to." What Allen dreaded was returning to a department controlled by politics.

Life After Youngstown

If Allen thought the Ohio Department of Liquor Control was free of politics he was sorely mistaken. His appointment by Governor Frank Lausche drew immediate criticism from Mahoning County Democrats, including the new Youngstown mayor. It was at this point that Kryzan proclaimed publicly his reason for not retaining Allen as chief. The *Vindicator* reported:

> "Kryzan said he lost interest in the possibility of retaining Allen as police chief when Allen began campaigning actively and publicly for the re-election of Mayor Charles P. Henderson last October. The mayor said this act meant that Allen stepped out of his role as public servant into the realm of politics so that when Allen's team met defeat, he was deserving of a politician's fate in loss of his public office."

Many supporters of Allen were quick to point out that the chief should have been retained on his ability to do the job, not his political position, a fate too many law enforcement officials have faced. But Kryzan's feelings must have run deeper than just the political aspect. After the Allen appointment to the liquor department by the governor Kryzan was quoted in the newspapers as stating he was "not too happy" with the decision and that he hoped "the entire state will not be subject to such national notoriety as the city of Youngstown experienced in the last six years because of Allen." The lawlessness during Kryzan's administration, and the early years of the approaching decade, would make this statement ludicrous. But proved no more ludicrous than Cress' statements a month later when he spoke before the Lions' Club. The new chief stated Allen had some noteworthy accomplishments, "but in the last year and a half of the Henderson administration Allen had outlived his usefulness" and during his last six months as chief "survived on hot air."[21]

Two days later Allen gave a speech in Canton before the Daughters of the American Revolution. Declaring he was "far too busy to enter into political tirades that may emanate from disgruntled politicians," Allen simply stated that his record while chief "stands open for all to examine."

Allen was content to focus on his campaign on morality. During his program called "Moral Principals," the former chief stated, "If we do not recognize the evils of immorality we are far less wise than out forefathers." He stated that standards of morality are forever fixed and true and do not shift and change, despite some false notions of pseudo-liberals."

Allen was quite successful as an enforcement officer in the liquor control department, winning the praises of his superiors and from Governor Lausche. His tenure there, however, was short-lived. He announced his resignation on May 6, 1955, after accepting the position of chief of police in Santa Ana, California, then a community of 52,000 residents. Allen stated that one of his reasons for accepting the offer was the fact that if new leadership was elected, as in the case of Mayor Henderson, he could very well be out of work with the liquor department. Lausche applauded Allen's efforts and had highly recommended him when questioned by Santa Ana officials.

In discussing Allen's departure from the Buckeye State, the *Vindicator* wrote:

> "The name Edward J. Allen has been a symbol of honest and courageous law enforcement in Ohio since the 'stranger from Pennsylvania' took over as police chief of racket-ridden Youngstown in January 1948.
>
> "His departure to California...saddens foes of rackets, racketeers and corrupt politicians. Law abiding citizens had the assurance that an honest job was being done when Allen was in command."

Allen was in his new position for nearly three years when a Long Beach State College professor of police science did an appraisal of the Santa Ana Police Department. In his report to the assistant city manager, the professor wrote, "In examining reports of the very large departments with very great reputations, I have rarely witnessed a more commendable sign of integrity and public confidence." In the analysis of the department's accomplishments it was found that 70 percent of all stolen property in the city was recovered.

By 1960, the Santa Ana Police Department had doubled in personnel and increased the pay of its officers. As he had done in Youngstown, Allen made traffic safety one of his top priorities. That year the California Traffic Safety Foundation awarded Santa Ana officers for being leaders in the country's traffic safety programs, making it the fourth year in a row the city had received such high awards.

Allen was still involved with the International Association of Chiefs of Police and served as chairman of the organized crime committee of the association. In September 1960, he traveled to the association's national convention in Washington D.C. and was a member of a panel presenting information on the notorious Apalachin Summit, the nefarious meeting of Mafia bosses from across the nation held on November 14, 1957, in upstate New York.

During the summer of 1962, Allen wrote, *Merchants of Menace - The Mafia*. The book not only covered the underworld activity that took place in the Mahoning Valley, but was an in depth study of the Mafia and its far reaches. He focused on the connection between organized crime and politicians. Allen was involved in fighting the secretive underworld society for years. At a conference of the International Association of Police Chiefs, held in Colorado Springs during October 1950, Allen compared the Mafia to the growing concern of Communism in America. He told his audience that the Mafia is "just as un-American, just as destructive to our government, and just as determined and powerful in infiltrating into high political and social and commercial power." In summing up the current state of Youngstown he wrote, "It is glaringly apparent that neither the Youngstown politicians nor the majority of the voting public have been militant enough to free themselves from the 'chains' their own votes have forged."

Eddie Allen served as police chief until August 1972, when, at the age of 65, he was forced into mandatory retirement. Allen remained a religious man and served as a lector for St. Joseph's Catholic Church of Santa Ana. He helped establish a "jail ministry" and twice a week visited local jails to share the word of God. In addition, Allen was a member or served on the boards of numerous community groups, many of which served young people.

After his retirement Allen became involved in the anti-abortion movement in Southern California. During the summer of 1986, while demonstrating in front of an abortion clinic, Allen was arrested for trespassing after entering the building and trying to speak with the clinic manager. Allen refused an offer to plea bargain and was sentenced to four months in jail, of which he served 15 days.

In late December 1989, Allen became ill. He contracted pneumonia and was hospitalized in St. Joseph Hospital. On January 6, 1990, he died there at the age of 82.

As for Charles Henderson, the former mayor remained out of public office until October 1965, when Governor James A. Rhodes, appointed him Mahoning County Probate Judge, filling an un-expired term. In 1970, he turned down an opportunity to run for the 19th District Congressional seat. In February 1985, after 20 years on the probate bench, Henderson retired.

Henderson moved to Marion, Massachusetts. On September 15, 1990, Henderson and his wife of 51 years, were at LaGuardia Airport in New York City getting ready to board a flight for the Bahamas for a summer vacation cruise. Henderson was stricken with a heart attack and died. He was 79 years old.

At the farewell dinner for Allen when he left the Youngstown Police Department, the former chief said of Charles Henderson, he "was not so much a boss as he was a wise and judicious counselor, a patient and understanding friend. His high endeavor was like a beacon light that kept the path before us always bright. He never flinched or gave way where matters of principal were involved."

Section II Notes

1 The Mann Act was also known as the White-Slave Act of 1910. Proposed by James Robert Mann, Republican Congressman from Illinois, the law was intended to address prostitution and immorality. The law banned the interstate transportation of women for immoral purposes. The first person prosecuted under the act was Jack Johnson, the heavyweight boxing champion of the world. Johnson encouraged a woman to leave her work at a brothel and travel with him. Although he later married the woman, he was prosecuted, convicted and sentenced to a year in prison.

2 James "Jimmy" Muche, a popular ex-boxer and gambler, disappeared on April 23, 1937. That night Muche had been fired from his job at the Jungle Inn by management after he "failed to report receipt of certain money at the inn." It was reported that Muche argued with mobsters from Cleveland outside the club that night. Muche was never found. For years whenever a body was discovered anywhere near the Mahoning Valley, speculation was always ripe that it was Jimmy Muche.

3 An August 14, 1949, *Vindicator* article states, "The Jungle Inn has other names, too, which are familiar to Youngstowners including J. J. "Fats" Aiello, Youngstown racketeer who is a cousin of Mike Farah. "Fats" stepfather is one of the leaders of the notorious Mounds Club near Cleveland which was closed recently by the state fire marshal." While doubtful, Farah could have been a cousin through marriage, but there is no information to backup that Aiello had a stepfather or that the stepfather was involved in the Mounds Club.

4 The "Center" would become infamous as the headquarters of Sandy Naples. The building still exists today as a restaurant and bar and the headquarters of a vending machine concern. The location was called many names over the years including the Center, the Center Restaurant, the Center Street Lunch Room and the Center Sandwich Shoppe. As not to confuse the readers with the various names the newspapers and others used, we will simply call it the Center Sandwich Shop except when referring to it in a direct quote.

5 A "bill of particulars" is defined as a form of discovery in which the prosecution sets forth the time, place, manner and means of the commission of the crime as alleged in complaint or incident. The purpose is to give notice to the accused of the offenses charged in the bill of indictment so that he may prepare a defense and avoid surprise – *Black's Law Dictionary*, fifth edition, 1979. In Aiello's case, the prosecution contended a bill of particulars was not necessary because the indictment sufficiently informed the defendant of the crime to enable him to prepare for his defense.

6 In a memorandum dated June 6, 1950, from Harry J. Anslinger, the Commissioner of Narcotics, to the Kefauver Committee, Charles Vizzini was described: "This man is the leader of the Italian Mafia in Youngstown, Ohio, and one of the most important members of the organization in the state. In late years, Vizzini has appeared to be conducting himself as a legitimate businessman; however, he is known to be very influential in gambling and other rackets in Youngstown and vicinity. Other activities in which Vizzini has been engaged are liquor violation, counterfeiting, extortion and murder. He is closely associated with members of the Mafia throughout the State of Ohio and in Illinois, Pennsylvania, New York, Florida and California. The subject is the owner of the DeLuxe Café at 201 W. Beardioux (sic) and resides at 848 5th Avenue, Youngstown."

7 John "Tar Baby" Millovich was the brother of George Millovich, a member of the Youngstown Police Department and head of the vice squad during the early 1960s. John Millovich was an armed robber and burglar. Most of his crimes were committed outside of Youngstown. He was arrested for crimes in Farrell, Pittsburgh and Mercer County, Pennsylvania; Bardstown, Kentucky; and Warren and Trumbull County. At one time in 1953 Millovich was under indictment for five separate crimes.

8 On January 24, 1946, Frank Cassano was killed in Leonardsburg, Ohio, a small town northeast of Columbus, Ohio. Cassano was riding in an automobile returning from the London Prison Farm, where he and a companion picked up Frank LaRocco, who had just been released from a sentence for a hold-up he committed in December 1938. The car crashed into a loaded freight truck and Cassano was killed instantly. The other two men received serious injuries. Cassano was 34 years old and was reported to be an employee of the Jennings Night Club in Niles.

9 In 1941, Judge John C. Knox would preside over the extortion trial of Willie Bioff and George E. Browne. Convicted, the two men would become government witnesses in the infamous "Hollywood Extortion" case, which sent the top leadership of the Chicago Outfit to prison including Paul "The Waiter" Ricca and Louis "Little New York" Campagna, and led to the suicide of Frank Nitti. Knox chronicled his 25 years on the bench in a 1943 autobiography titled *Order In The Court*.

10 During World War II, Colonel William J. "Wild Bill" Donovan would be promoted to the rank of general and become Director of the OSS, the forerunner of the CIA.

11 Philip Mangano was the brother of Vincent Mangano, one of the original bosses of New York City's five Mafia families. Many believed the two brothers

jointly ran the family. The family's underboss was the notorious Albert Anastasia. When Anastasia decided to take over the family in April 1951, Vincent Mangano disappeared forever. Philip Mangano was murdered on April 19, 1951. Shot three times in the head, his body was found near Jamaica Bay in the Bergen Beach section of Brooklyn.

12 John Charles Montana was a businessman, politician and civic leader in Buffalo with close ties to both the Magaddino family and Joe DiCarlo. In 1927, he was elected to Buffalo City Council and served four years in that capacity. As of 1957 he had no criminal record. Buffalo Mafia boss Stefano Magaddino's son Peter was married to Montana's niece. Montana's nephew, Charles, was married to Magaddino's daughter.

13 "Pete the Slash" Giallelli had an extensive criminal career after serving his sentence. In the mid-1930s after being arrested in Buffalo on a vagrancy charge it was found that he was wanted in three states – Pennsylvania, Missouri and New Jersey. In the latter he was indicted for participation in a $130,000 bank robbery in Penns Grove on February 2, 1934. As for Joseph "Busy Joe" Pattituccio, it was later reported that he committed suicide.

14 Anthony Bonasera, a brother-in-law of Joe DiCarlo, was born on June 1, 1897, in Sicily. His police record reflected 29 arrests between July 1916 and June 1958 – three for murder – but there were only two convictions for which he spent less than six months in prison. During one of Lucky Luciano's arrests in Italy, police found Bonasera's name and residence in his address book. During testimony in 1960, Bonasera was said to have been "quite prominent among the guests" at the wedding of Anthony Tocco, son of Detroit mob leader William "Black Jack" Tocco, and Carmela Profaci, the daughter of New York mob boss Joseph Profaci. In addition, Bonasera was the uncle of the wife of light heavy/heavyweight boxer Tami Mauriello.

15 Allen later put the information he collected from DiCarlo into a memorandum. Regarding the Italian Villa restaurant, the memorandum stated: "Subsequent investigation however revealed there was no such partnership recorded on any legal papers with his name, but that he did frequent the place along with other hoodlums. We were informed many such partnerships existed in a financial way without any legal papers drawn up."

16 Prior to the DiCarlo family's exodus to Florida, Vincinetta was believed to have been dating, and may possibly even had been engaged to, singer Vic Damone. Thomas Micklas recalls that Damone came to the Paddock Bar, after it was relocated to Brier Hill, and was accompanied by Vincinetta. Nobody remembers what happened to the relationship, but on November 24, 1954, Da-

mone married Italian movie actress Pier Angeli in Hollywood. Among Damone's ushers were singers Dean Martin and Tony Martin. Although the newspapers called it the "wedding of the year," only 700 guests attended compared the estimated 900 who were invited to Vincenetta's wedding reception a year later.

17 John C. Vitullo was a powerful leader in Mahoning County Democratic politics in the mid-1940s. During the administration of Mayor Ralph W. O'Neill many considered Vitullo not only the "real" mayor of Youngstown, but also the head of the local rackets. Vitullo was born on December 22, 1902, on Wood Street to Italian immigrant parents. Vitullo's entry into politics came through the board of elections, to which he was appointed clerk in 1936. He was elected a member of the board in 1940 and in 1944 he became chairman.

By the end of World War II Vitullo had built himself a solid power base. Some said he had complete control of the police and other city departments. His strength could be seen countywide as he helped get Democratic mayors elected in Campbell, Struthers and Sebring. The *Vindicator* wrote of him:

"Few political figures have arisen in the Youngstown district who have excited as much interest or aroused as much controversy. His political enemies denounced him; and his political friends swore by him. All attested his ability as a political organizer.

"As an organizer, Vitullo depended heavily on getting out the vote on Election Day, and probably no Mahoning County political leader ever developed the art to such a high point."

As Mahoning County Democratic Chairman, the apex of Vitullo's career came in July 1947 when he was among a number of Democratic chairmen nationwide called to a conference in Washington D.C. by President Harry Truman.

In November of that year, Vitullo suffered a debilitating heart attack. He never fully recovered and Jack Sulligan eventually assumed his position. One of Vitullo's dreams was to serve as a delegate to the Democratic National Convention. Named to attend during the summer of 1948 his medical condition prevented his attending. On October 19, 1948, at the age of 45, Vitullo suffered another heart attack and died at North Side Hospital. He left behind a wife and five children.

18 See Chapter End Note 6. Since the memorandum dated June 6, 1950, from Harry J. Anslinger, the Commissioner of Narcotics, to the Kefauver Committee labeled Charles Vizzini as "the leader of the Italian Mafia in Youngstown," it is possible that Allen was just relating this information to the press. Vizzini's name appeared infrequently in the *Vindicator.* On November 30, 1948, he purchased equipment from Joe Budak's Club 22 at a public auction; on July 16, 1954, it was reported he filed a suit against the Rank Manufacturing Company on Oak

Hill Avenue for allegedly violating a sales contract involving aluminum decorative grills; on December 3, 1955, the IRS dismissed liens on property owned by him after tax judgments had been paid for the years 1947, 1948, 1950 and 1954; and on December 7, 1956, a lawsuit was filed against Vizzini for not keeping to the terms of his lease involving the DeLuxe Café. In addition, he was questioned in June 1954, following a threat to Vice Squad Chief George Krispli. There was never anything revealed about Vizzini to support his alleged status as a Mafia chieftain in Youngstown by either Anslinger or Allen.

19 The *National Municipal Review* article was written by Frederic Sondern, Jr. the author of *Brotherhood of Evil: The Mafia*, which was published in 1959 about the Apalachin Meeting held on November 14, 1957 and its aftermath. The magazine article appeared in condensed form in the November 1950 issue of *Reader's Digest.*

20 On June 8, 1954 First Ward Councilman Michael J. McCullion proposed emergency legislation that would put gamblers behind bars from 30 days up to six months. The legislation needed six votes to pass. With one of the councilmen conveniently absent, several of the dissenters knew the proposal couldn't pass so they voted for it. The vote turned out 5 to 1 for approval and didn't pass. The nay vote came from Second Ward Councilman John Palermo, who again said the city should adopt the state law, in which the police had to catch the gamblers "in the act."

Whereas Eddie Allen had been an ardent supporter of the bill, Chief Cress, when asked for his opinion of the ordinance gave a milk-toast reply, "It is a good tool toward accomplishment of a good end. I don't think it is a perfect answer. It would be a step in the right direction."

On June 15, with council at full strength, the ordinance was put to the vote again. Prior to the vote, Mayor Frank Kryzan, who had butted heads with Allen in vehement opposition to it before, was concerned about criticism due to the current lawlessness and asked council to approve it. "Let's remove the black eye. I'll appreciate your doing it," he stated.

This time, three of the Democratic Councilmen who had voted for it when they knew there was no way it could pass, now voted against it. Changing their votes were Third Ward Councilman Anthony B. Flask, Fourth Ward Councilman Paul E. Dolak and Seventh Ward Councilman Michael J, Dudash. Two of whom claimed to have changed their vote because there was "a hidden motive" behind the ordinance, but would not elaborate on what it was.

A *Vindicator* editorial the following day suggested the four dissenting councilmen of being "in partnership with the racketeers."

21 In February 1981, former chief Paul Cress was interviewed by John M. Bukovinsky of Youngstown State University as part of that school's Oral History

Program. Cress gave Edward Allen solid credit for educating the police department. Cress stated, "He set aside certain hours for certain groups of men to study traffic, study search and seizure, study arrest and criminal procedure. After a while the whole police department got to know the difference between a felony and a misdemeanor and that helped them of course. They have been fairly progressive ever since down there." In reorganizing the department Allen had upset a number of the veteran officers, many of whom had achieved rank. Allen wasn't as popular in the department as he was to the citizen on the street. Cress more than likely summed up Allen's ability in the eyes of these veteran officers when he candidly stated, "Eddy Allen wasn't as good as Eddy Allen said he was, but he wasn't as bad as we said he was either."

Infamous Mid-West Crime Wave bank robber killed in the Valley. Cleveland Press Collection

Roy "Happy" Marino, Valley gambler and murder victim on September 11, 1937. Cleveland Press Collection

John Anthoulis, Steubenville gambling boss convicted and sentenced to life for the murder of Roy Marino. Cleveland Press Collection

Solly Hart, Cleveland gangster sentenced to life in prison for the murder of Roy Marino. Cleveland Press Collection

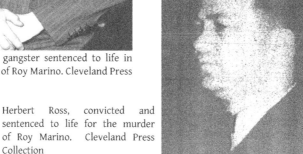

Herbert Ross, convicted and sentenced to life for the murder of Roy Marino. Cleveland Press Collection

Youngstown police mugshot of Baxter Lee "Sugar" Harrell. Youngstown Police Department

Joseph Blumetti, white slaver and labor racketeer. Youngstown Police Department

Vice Squad. Front Row: J. Dalley, Captain Eugene McElvoy, Chief John Turnbull, C. Young Back Row: T. Mitlow, George Krispli, Joseph Lepo, W. Collins (circa: early 1940s). Courtesy of William E. Gruver

Youngstown police mugshot of Jerry "The Sledgehammer" Pascarella. Youngstown Police Department

Youngstown police mugshot of William "Billy the Greek" Scodras. Youngstown Police Department

Pin ball machines or "Marble Boards" which brought much gambling attention in the late 1930s. Cleveland Public Library

Dominick "Big Dom" Mallamo. "The one true Godfather of the Valley." Courtesy of Donald Hanni

Adrian G. Newcomb, Cuyahoga County Common Pleas Judge selected to oversee grand jury investigating Lottery Houses. Cleveland Press Collecton.

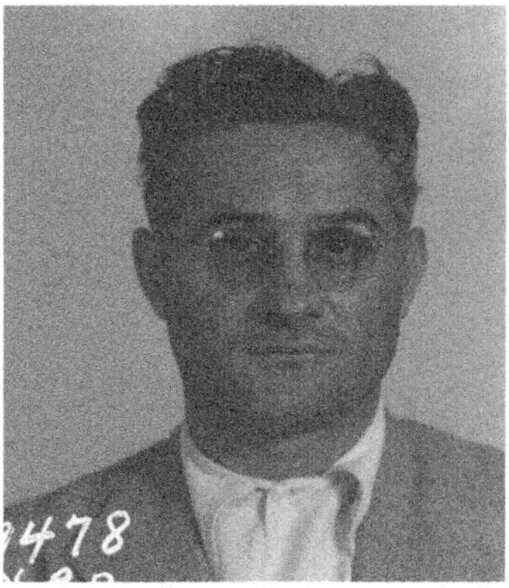

Frank "Frankie Joy" Gioia, Southside Lottery House member. Youngstown Police Department

Captain William J. Davis. Courtesy of William E. Gruver

The infamous Jungle Inn gambling den on Applegate Road in Halls Corners. Courtesy of Bruce Birrell

John Farah, who ran the Jungle Inn for the Cleveland Mafia Family. Cleveland Public Library

Mike Farah, Jungle Inn operator and Valley murder vicitm on June 10, 1961. Cleveland Public Library

Family grave marker for Mike and John Farah in Lake View Cemetery, Cleveland. Author's Collection

Frank Cammarata, Detroit Mafia transplant. Courtesy of Paul Kavieff

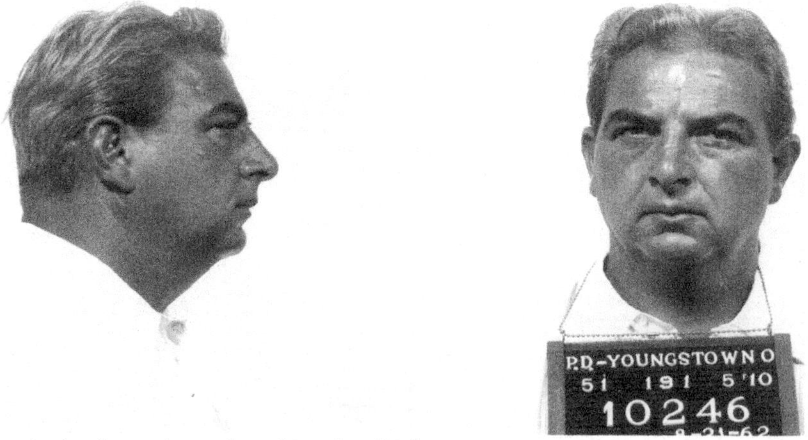

Cleveland Mafia member Anthony "Tony Dope" Delsanter. Youngstown Police Department

Dominic "Moosey" Caputo. Courtesy of Thomas Micklas

Joe "The Wolf" DiCarlo at Kefauver Hearings in Cleveland during January 1951. Author's Collection

Joseph Jasper "Fats" Aiello. Youngstown Police Department

Youngstown most famous Police Chief - Edward J. "Eddie" Allen. Cleveland Press Collection

Democratic Senator from Tennessee - Estes Kefauver. Cleveland Press Collection.

Charles Henderson, Mayor of Youngstown and brought on "Smash Racket Rule" campaign. Courtesy of William E. Gruver

James "Jack White" Licavoli and attorney Dominick J. "Duke" LaPolla (left) before the Kefauver Committee in January 1951. Cleveland Public Library

The Hotel Pick-Ohio, home of the infamous Purple Cow restaurant. Courtesy of William E. Gruver

Home of Joseph DiCarlo on Volney Road. Author's Collection

Bomb damage at the home of Bud J. Fares 633 Almyra Avenue on December 10, 1953. Youngstown Police Department

Bomb damage at Johnnie's Grocery, 1157 West Rayen Avenue, May 28, 1954. Youngstown Police Department

The twice-bombed home of Mahoning County Democratic Party Chairman Jack Sulligan at 1966 Smithfield Street. Youngstown Police Department

Bomb damage at the home of Jack Sulligan 1966 Smithfield Street, July 17, 1954.. Youngstown Police Department

Bomb damage at the Circello Grocery on Jacobs Road, August 28, 1954. Youngstown Police Department

Entrance to Circello's Grocery where bomb went off on August 28, 1954. Youngstown Police Department

Bomb damge at the Steel City Club, 2123 Belmont Avenue on November 6, 1955. Youngstown Police Department

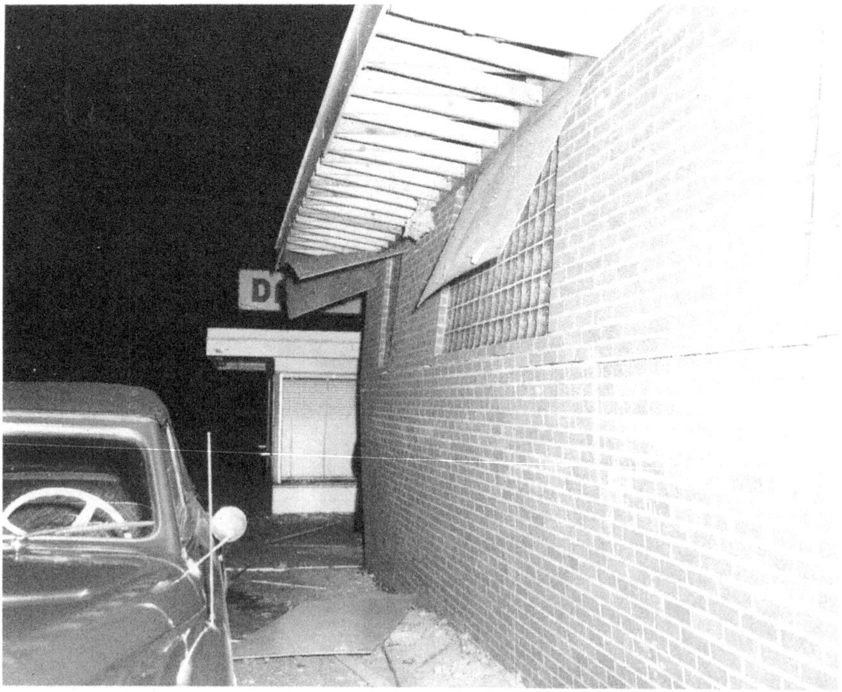

The buckled wall of the Steel City Club on Belmont Avenue after November 6, 1955 bombing. Youngstown Police Department

Bomb damage at Frank's Food Market, 3305 South Avenue on August 1, 1956. Courtesy Youngstown Police Department

Bomb damage at the home of Charles Bower 3522 Dover Road on April 6, 1957. Courtesy Youngstown Police Department

Bomb damage to the home of Youngstown Police Detective Lloyd Haynes, 3049 McGuffey Road, August 13,1957. Youngstown Police Department

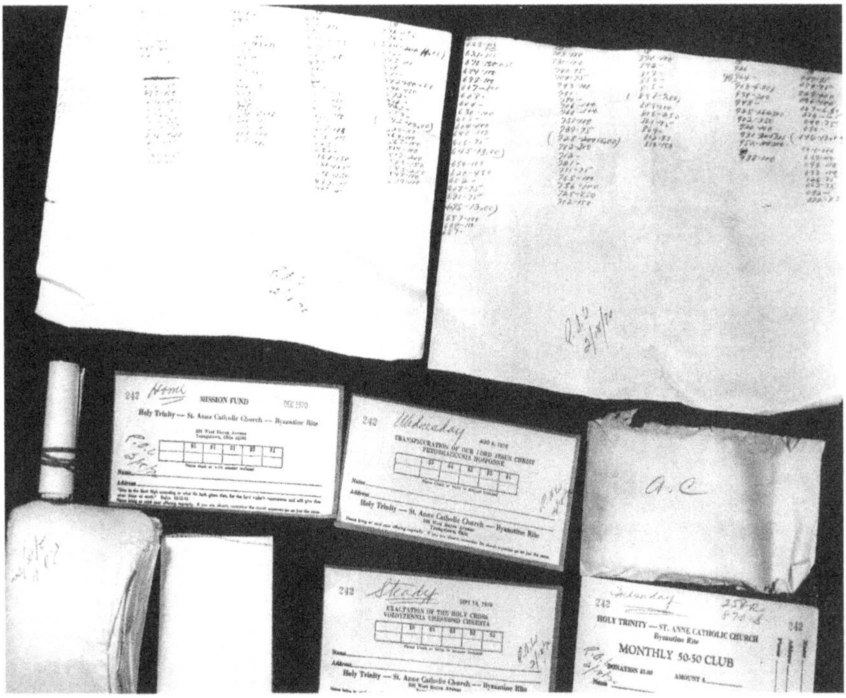

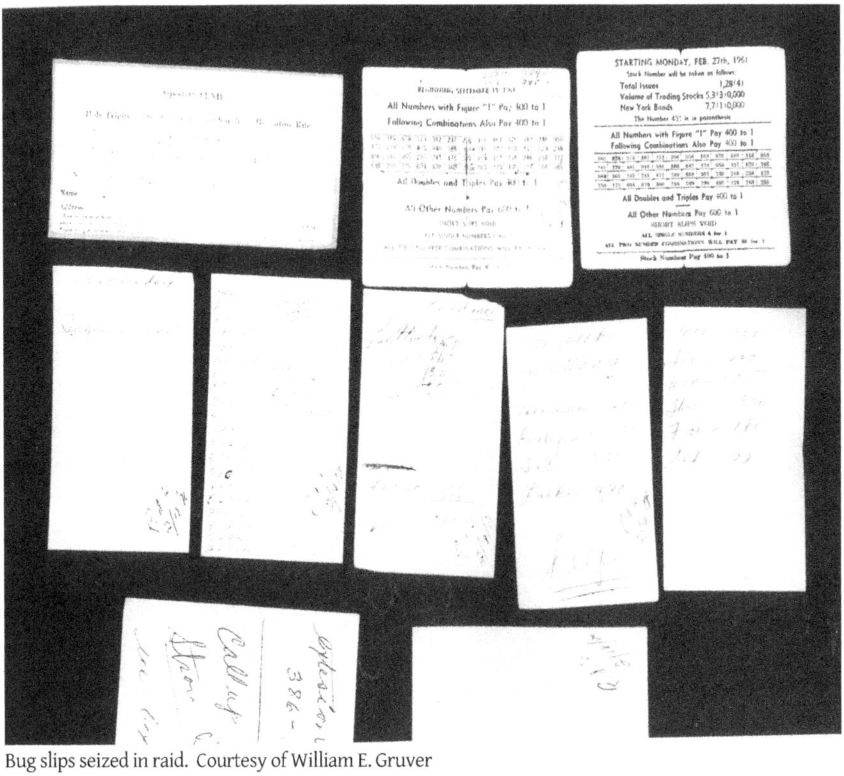

Bug slips seized in raid. Courtesy of William E. Gruver

Bug slips seized in raid. Courtesy of William E. Gruver

Frequently arrested bug seller Anthony "Booze" Gianfrancesco. Youngstown Police Department

Surveillance photo from roof of Northside Hospital showing Gianfrancesco selling the bug Courtesy of William E. Gruver

Naples Brothers' bug headquarters the Center Sandwich Shop. Courtesy of William E. Gruver

Building that housed Center Sandwich Shop in the year 2000. Author's Collection

Closed hidden bug drawer where bug slips were kept at the Center Sandwich Shop. Courtesy of William E. Gruver

Open hidden bug slip drawer at the Center Sandwich Shop. Courtesy of William E. Gruver

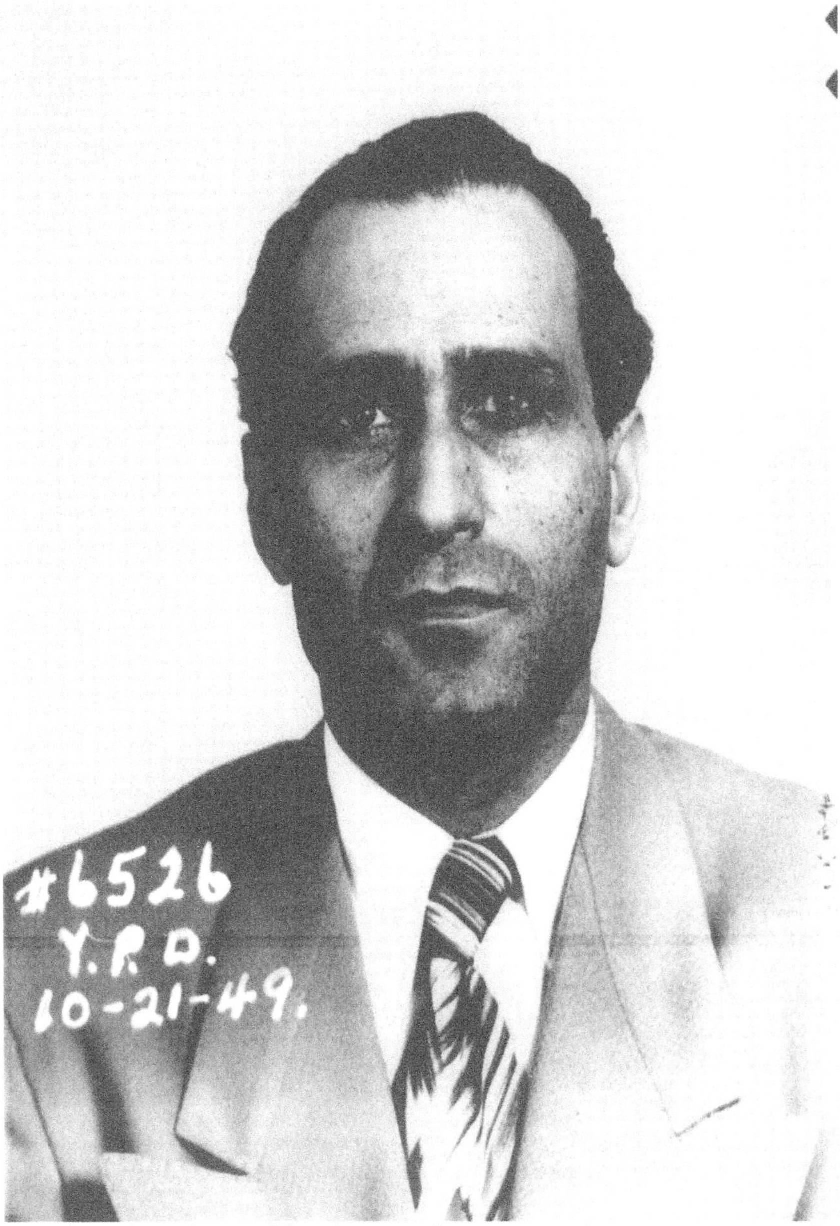

S. Joseph "Sandy" Naples one of the Policy Kings of Youngstown in the 1950s. Youngstown Police Department

Vrancich home, 623 Caledonia Street where Sandy Naples was murdered on March 11, 1960. Youngstown Police Department

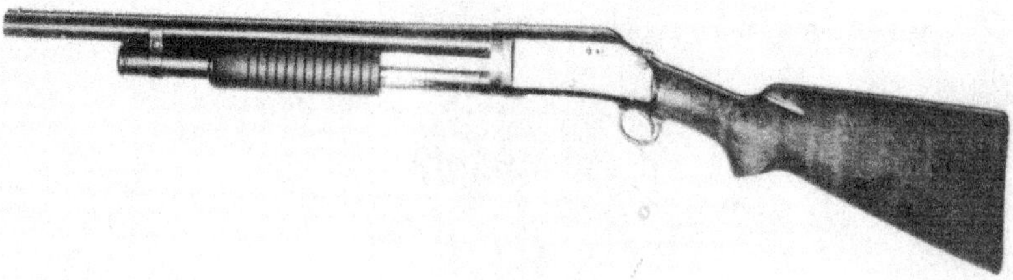

A shotgun found at the murder scene of Sandy Naples and Mary Ann Vrancich. It was stolen from the Canton Police Department.. Youngstown Police Department

The sprawling home of Sandy Naples at 605 Carlotta Drive. Author's Collection

Headstone of Sandy Naples in Calvary Cemetery. Author's Collection

The headstone of Mary Ann Vrancich in Calvary Cemetery. Author's Collection

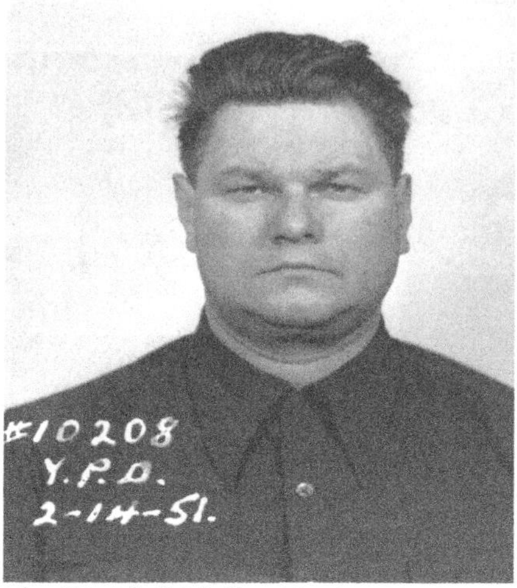

John "Big John" Schuller. Courtesy Youngstown Police Department

Vincent Innocenzi, a safe-cracker and murder victim whose body was found in Virginia-Kendall Park. Cleveland Press Collection

Headstone of Vincent Innocenzi at Lake View Cemetery in Cleveland
Author's Collection

Anthony Libertore, Cleveland cop-killer and Mafia member, suspect in Innocenzi murder. Warren Police Department

James Vincent "Vince" DeNiro one of the Policy Kings in Youngstown during the 1950s Courtesy Youngstown Police Department

Location where DeNiro's restaurant Cicero's one stood on Market Street in the Uptown District. Author's Collection

Aftermath of car bombing that took the life of Vince DeNiro on Market Street July 17, 1961. Youngstown Police Department

Remains of 1961 Oldsmobile convertible DeNiro was killed in. Youngstown Police Department

Bomb damage caused by explosion of DeNiro automobile. Cicero's restaurant can be seen in the background. Cleveland Press Collection.

This strip of 13 stores, just down the street from the bomb blast which killed Vince DeNiro, had their windows blown out. Cleveland Press Collection.

A shoe left in the rubble of Vince DeNiro's automobile bombing on July 17, 1961. Youngstown Police Department

The headstone of James Vincent "Vince" DeNiro in Calvary. Cemetery. Author's Collection

Family marker for the DeNiro Family in Calvary Cemetery. Author's Collection

William "Billy" Naples his death on July 1, 1962 may have come at his own hands. Youngstown Police Department

Front end bomb damage of autombile Billy Naples died in July 1, 1962. Youngstown Police Department

Bombing scene where William "Billy" Naples was killed. Youngstown Police Department

Home of William "Billy" Naples at 505 Carlotta Drive. Author's Collection

Family marker for the Naples Family in Calvary Cemetery Author's Collection

Headstone of William "Billy" Naples in Calvary Cemetery. Author's Collection

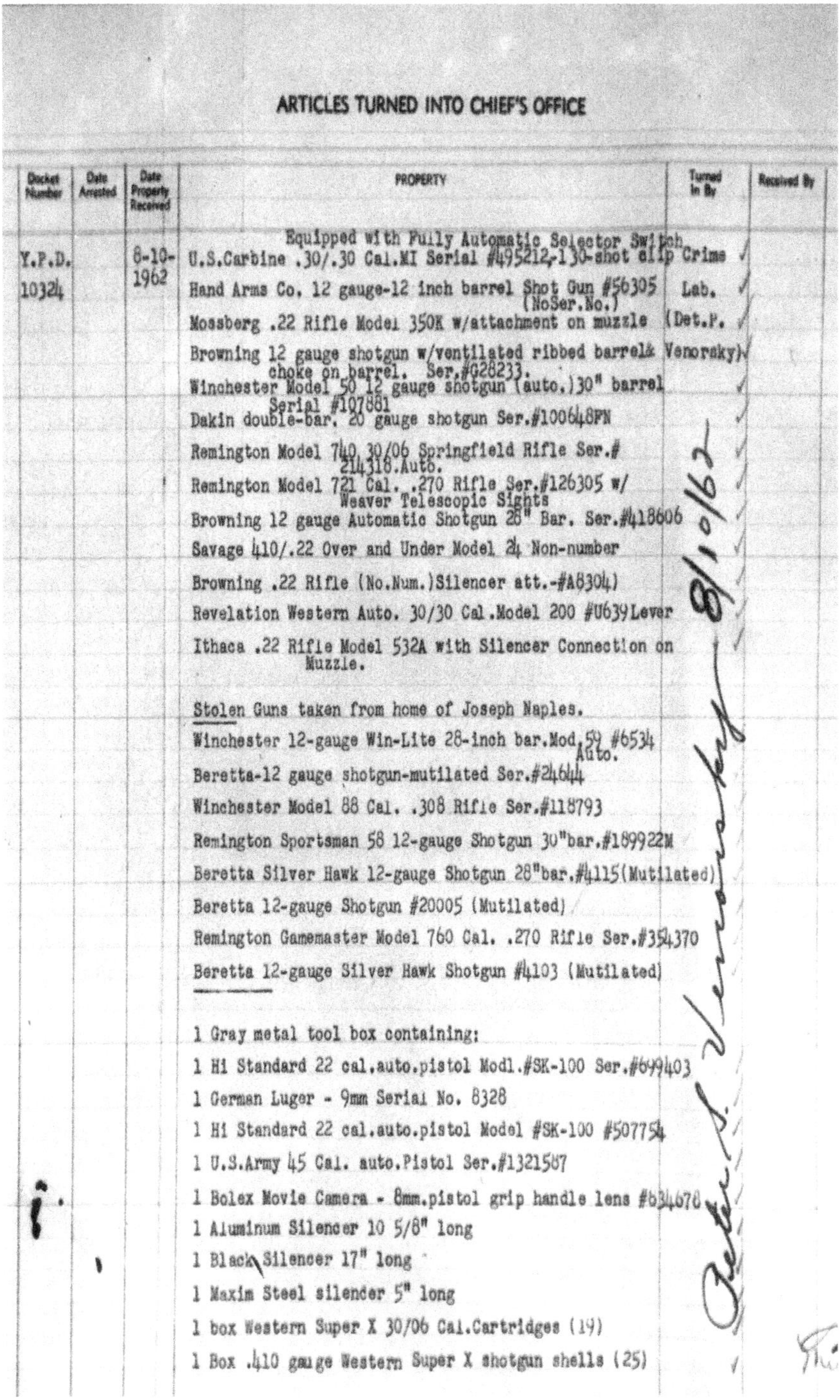

ARTICLES TURNED INTO CHIEF'S OFFICE

Docket Number	Date Arrested	Date Property Received	PROPERTY	Turned In By	Received By
Y.P.D. 10324		8-10-1962	U.S.Carbine .30/.30 Cal.MI Serial #495212-130-shot clip Equipped with Fully Automatic Selector Switch	Crime Lab. (Det.P. Venorsky)	
			Hand Arms Co. 12 gauge-12 inch barrel Shot Gun #56305 (NoSer.No.)		
			Mossberg .22 Rifle Model 350K w/attachment on muzzle		
			Browning 12 gauge shotgun w/ventilated ribbed barrel& choke on barrel. Ser.#G28233.		
			Winchester Model 50 12 gauge shotgun (auto.)30" barrel Serial #107881		
			Dakin double-bar. 20 gauge shotgun Ser.#100648PN		
			Remington Model 740 30/06 Springfield Rifle Ser.# 214318.Auto.		
			Remington Model 721 Cal. .270 Rifle Ser.#126305 w/ Weaver Telescopic Sights		
			Browning 12 gauge Automatic Shotgun 28" Bar. Ser.#418606		
			Savage 410/.22 Over and Under Model 24 Non-number		
			Browning .22 Rifle (No.Num.)Silencer att.-#A8304)		
			Revelation Western Auto. 30/30 Cal.Model 200 #U639Lever		
			Ithaca .22 Rifle Model 532A with Silencer Connection on Muzzle.		
			Stolen Guns taken from home of Joseph Naples.		
			Winchester 12-gauge Win-Lite 28-inch bar.Mod.59 #6534 Auto.		
			Beretta-12 gauge shotgun-mutilated Ser.#24644		
			Winchester Model 88 Cal. .308 Rifle Ser.#118793		
			Remington Sportsman 58 12-gauge Shotgun 30"bar.#189922M		
			Beretta Silver Hawk 12-gauge Shotgun 28"bar.#4115(Mutilated)		
			Beretta 12-gauge Shotgun #20005 (Mutilated)		
			Remington Gamemaster Model 760 Cal. .270 Rifle Ser.#354370		
			Beretta 12-gauge Silver Hawk Shotgun #4103 (Mutilated)		
			1 Gray metal tool box containing:		
			1 Hi Standard 22 cal.auto.pistol Modl.#SK-100 Ser.#699403		
			1 German Luger - 9mm Serial No. 8328		
			1 Hi Standard 22 cal.auto.pistol Model #SK-100 #507754		
			1 U.S.Army 45 Cal. auto.Pistol Ser.#1321587		
			1 Bolex Movie Camera - 8mm.pistol grip handle lens #634678		
			1 Aluminum Silencer 10 5/8" long		
			1 Black Silencer 17" long		
			1 Maxim Steel silencer 5" long		
			1 box Western Super X 30/06 Cal.Cartridges (19)		
			1 Box .410 gauge Western Super X shotgun shells (25)		

Peter S. Venorsky 8/10/62

Youngstown Police list of weapons taken from a hiding spot in the basement of Sandy Naples Carlotta Drive home. Joey Naples was arrested for having possession of them, some of which were stolen. Courtesy of William E. Gruver

Charles "Cadillac Charlie" Cavallaro. Youngstown Police Department

Home of Charles Cavallaro at 164 Roslyn Drive. Author's Collection

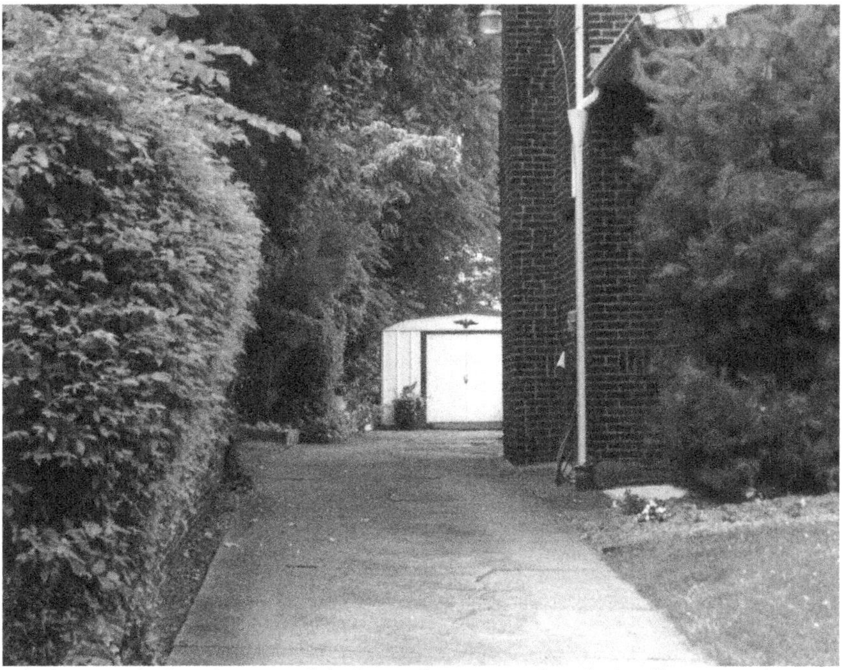
A shed now stands where the garage of Charles Cavallaro once stood. Author's Collection

Headstone of eleven year-old Thomas "Tommy" Cavallaro in Calvary Cemetery. Author's Collection

Dominic Moio. Warren Police Department

Headstone of Charles Cavallaro and his wife Helen in Calvary Cemetery. Author's Collection

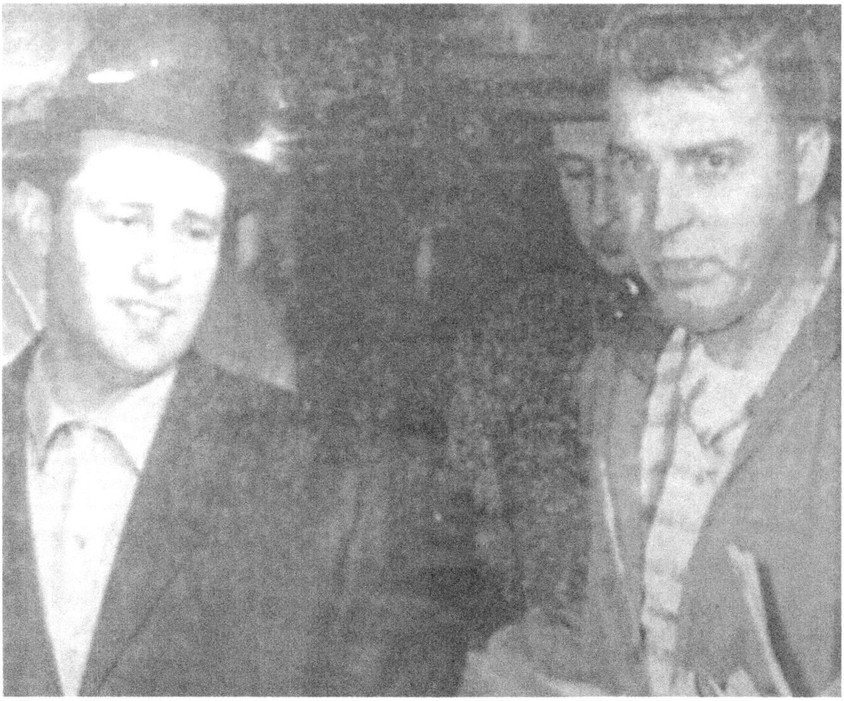

Officer William E. Gruver arresting Joey Naples. Courtesy of William E. Gruver

Joseph "Little Joey" Naples, youngest of the four Naples brothers. Youngstown Police Department

Donald Hanni - assistant city prosecutor, municipal, judge, defense attorney, Mahoning County Democratic chairman. Cleveland Press Collection.

Officer William E. Gruver. Courtesy of William E. Gruver

Officer Randall A. "Duke" Wellington. Courtesy of William E. Gruver

Randall A. "Duke" Wellington, the only man to serve as Chief of the Youngstown Police Department and Sheriff of Mahoning County. Courtesy of William E. Gruver

Chief of Police John Terlesky. Courtesy of William E. Gruver

Youngstown Police Captain Donald Komara. Courtesy of Donald Komara

Dan Maggianetti. Courtesy of William E. Gruver

Lieutenant Frank W. Watters. Courtesy of William E. Gruver

Sergeant Charles Bush

Lieutenant Harold Faust

Officer Andrew Kovac

Captain Joseph Lepo

Officer John Lynch

Lieutenant George Maxim

Captain Eugene McEvoy

Chief of Detectives William W. Reed

Chief of Police Cyril Smolko

Photos this page courtesy of William E. Gruver

Back Row from left: Clyde Osborne, John Leskovansky, Martin P. Joyce and Charles Henderson Front Row: Forrest Cavalier, Sidney Ridelhaupt and Elwyn Jenkins. Courtesy of William E. Gruver

Calagero Malfitano, Mafia mentor of Vince DeNiro. Youngstown Police Department

Joseph "Stoneface" Romano, gambler who was critically wounded after the murder of Sany Naples. Courtesy Youngstown Police Department

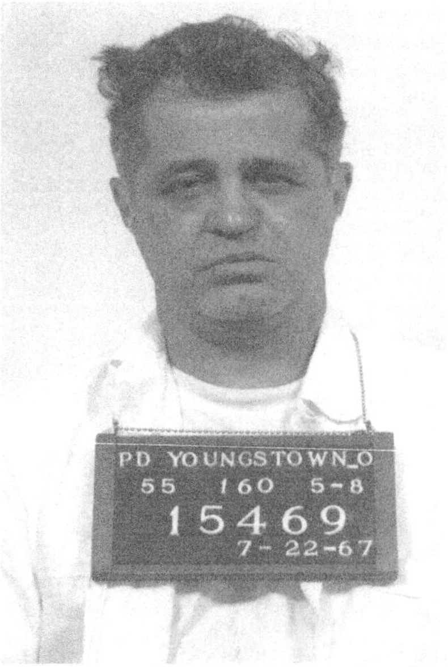

Michael Romeo alleged Mafia leader in the Valley. Youngstown Police Department

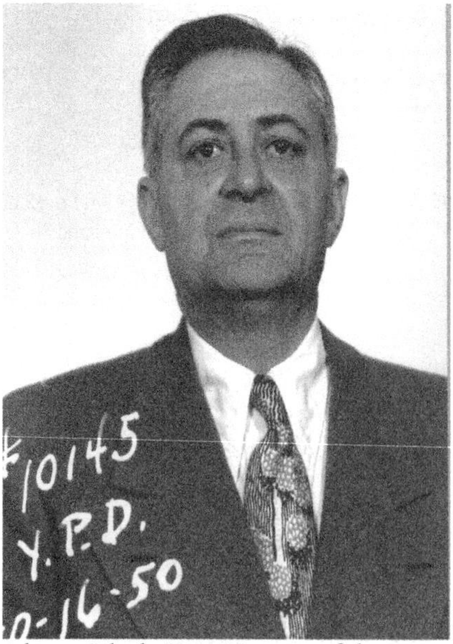

Calogero "Charles" Vizzini, owner of the DeLuxe Café, who was reputed to be Mafia leader in the Valley. Youngstown Police Department

Joseph Alexander. Youngstown Police Department

Charles Carabbia. Mahoning County Sherriff's Office

Ronald Carabbia, one of three brothers. Ronnie was a suspect in the bombing murder of Chris Sofocleous. Youngstown Police Department

Peter Fetchet, along with his brother Frank, were the main bug competitors to Sandy Naples and Vince DeNiro. Youngstown Police Department

James "Jimmy" Naples, one of Sandy's three younger brothers. Youngstown Police Department

Nello Ronci, gambler and floating dice game operator. Youngstown Police Department

Louis Tiberio owner of the Tropics Night Club and Lottery House operator. Youngstown Police Department

Carmen Tisone. Youngstown Police Department

John "Jack the Ripper" Zentko. Youngstown Police Department

Victor Acierno, bug seller and operator of Vic's Confectionary. Youngstown Police Department

John Burnich - bug operator. Youngstown Police Department

Zollie Engel, bookmaker who was pushed out of business by the "Big Three". Youngstown Police Department

Philip Kimla, the last man to see "Big John" Schuller alive. Youngstown Police Department

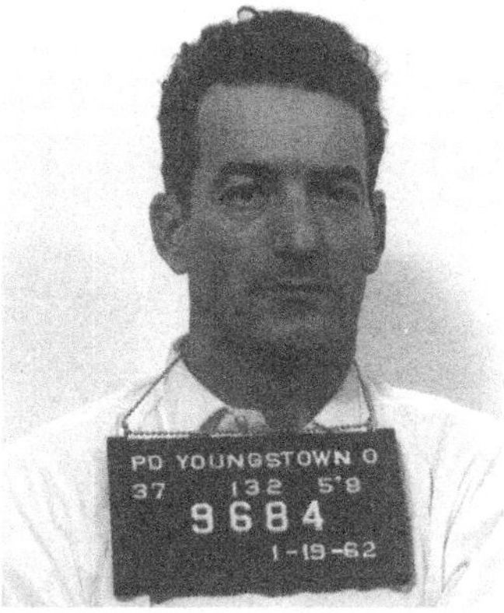

John "Johnny the Greek" Magourias, admitted bomber, but not convicted. Youngstown Police Department

Phillip "Fleagle" Mainer, key bombing suspect in the late 1950s. Youngstown Police Department

"Little Pete" Skevos, bug operator and owner of the Parthenon Bar on South Avenue. Youngstown Police Department

Sam Vona. Youngstown Police Department

Section III

The 1950s

Photo courtesy of Mahoning Valley Historical Society.

"This is a complete surprise to me. I don't know what they want me to talk about. I'm willing to tell them anything I know, but I don't know anything they would want. I have all my records and my accountant has all my income tax material. Anything the committee wants to know about me, I'll tell them. But I can't imagine what information I can give them." – Joseph DiCarlo talking to William A. Mullen of the Courier-Express in late December 1950 after being served a summons to appear before the Kefauver Committee.

10

Cleveland's Kefauver Hearings

The Special Senate Committee to Investigate Organized Crime in Interstate Commerce began as a Senate Resolution bill submitted by Democratic Senator Estes Kefauver of Tennessee on January 5, 1950. The Senate passed the resolution on May 5, 1950, a week later Kefauver was appointed chairman and the Kefauver Committee[1] was born.

According to the Senate investigating body's interim report:

> "The function of the committee was to make a full and complete study and investigation to determine whether organized crime utilizes the facilities of interstate commerce or whether it operates otherwise through the avenues of interstate commerce to promote any transactions which violate Federal law or the law of the State in which such transactions might occur.
>
> "The committee was also charged with an investigation of the manner and extent of such criminal operations if it found them actually to be taking place and with the identification of the persons, firms, or corporations involved.
>
> "A third responsibility which was charged to the committee was the determination as to whether such interstate criminal operations were developing corrupting influences in violation of the Federal law or the laws of any state."

On April 27, 1950, Youngstown Police Chief Edward Allen was in Washington, D.C. to testify before a Senate subcommittee prior to Kefauver getting his appointment. During questioning by Republican Senator Homer Capehart of Indiana, who grew up in Buffalo, Allen painted a sordid tale of Joe DiCarlo and his activities in both Buffalo and Youngstown without mentioning the mobster's name. This testimony paved the way for the Kefauver committee to include the Mahoning Valley among the areas they wanted to hear testimony about.

The next day the *Buffalo Courier-Express* reported on Allen's testimony:

> "So diligently did the Buffalo man ply his trade...that he was able to move into a 'palatial home in one of the most exclusive residential sections in Youngstown.'
>
> "'This big shot still has his palatial home' there, said Allen, but as a result of strict law enforcement since 1948, 'he does not operate in Youngstown' any longer.

> "Chief Allen did not, at the hearing, disclose the identity of the Buffalonian who prospered in the Ohio city. He told the subcommittee he did not wish to mention the name because it might give him 'a national reputation.' However, he later told The Courier-Express:
>
> "'The Buffalo man to whom I was referring at the hearing is Joe DiCarlo.'"

Allen also told the subcommittee members that, "byand large professional politicians and racketeers have much in common. They need money to operate. Both major parties do the same thing. They accept contributions and in this way racket men buy immunity. Behind the career of every racket man is a political protector or protectors."

On June 5, Allen was back in the nation's capital where he was scheduled to address the FBI National Academy on gambling law enforcement. While there Allen met with Rudolph Halley, chief counsel for the Kefauver Committee. Halley was an outstanding contributor to the Truman Committee, a legal council investigating World War II contract scandals, where he advanced to the position of chief counsel. Allen provided Halley with general background information on DiCarlo and some of his associates in the Valley; promising more detailed data at a later date.

Allen was impressed with the committee's progress to date and was delighted that they showed interest in DiCarlo's activities. After his return to Youngstown, Allen told the local media, "DiCarlo is the type of criminal with interstate connections that the Kefauver Committee is going to look into. Believe me, they can do a good job if they go at it the way they are starting." Allen advised that DiCarlo, Aiello and Caputo could all receive subpoenas to testify before the committee. "It looks like the committee is going into every phase of gambling - including racketeer's incomes, consorts and political protectors," he reported. Benefiting the committee, according to the chief, was their ability through federal powers to subpoena income tax records and call the racketeers to appear in person and testify.

While Allen was clearly impressed with the committee, the committee was also impressed with him. Kefauver stated, "Chief Allen's contribution has been particularly helpful. He seems to be doing a fine job in Youngstown, and it is a pleasure to work with conscientious law enforcement officers like him."

The first stop on Kefauver's 14-city tour was Miami. During the hearings in that city DiCarlo's name was mentioned prominently as well as "Fats" Aiello. Both men were reputed to have made the Wofford Hotel in Miami Beach, in which gambler Frank Erickson had ownership, their "winter headquarters."

Miami was a key city in the committee's investigation. It was known in mobterms as an "open" city, meaning no single Mafia family could claim it. The same would later be said of Las Vegas. After the hearings there a spokesman for the committee stated, "findings in Miami have been very profitable for the lines to go out from there to all points in the nation, due to the fact that [Miami] is an assembly ground for racketeers from many areas. It is here that many interstate conspiracies are hatched for division and control of the underworld and its lush profits. You can definitely say that we intend to track down the activities of every racketeer we found mingling in the company of the Erickson mob."

One of the key witnesses to testify in Miami was former FBI Agent Daniel P. Sullivan, now head of the Greater Miami Crime Commission. In discussing DiCarlo he told committee members, "In Youngstown he associated himself with Joseph "Fats" Aiello, Charles "Cadillac Charlie" Cavallaro and Nicolone Tamburello. In Youngstown they organized the numbers and the horse bookmaking racket in conjunction with a man by the name of Ray Linese.[2]

"Ray Linese, according to the chief of police of Youngstown, is a nephew of Joe Massei,[3] and has been operating the Italian Village Restaurant on 23rd Street, Miami Beach, which has been a place which a great many of these characters frequented."

In late December, the first subpoenas involving Youngstown underworld figures were issued. DiCarlo was served his summons at 7:30 in the morning at Buffalo's Hotel Statler (not to be confused with Cleveland's Hotel Statler) after being surprised in bed by Youngstown detectives and local police.[4] The subpoena, one of several sent to Chief Allen to serve, took a week to be delivered, as detectives could not locate the mobster.

DiCarlo held court later that morning at a restaurant where he told reporter William A. Mullen of the *Courier-Express*, "This is a complete surprise to me. I don't know what they want me to talk about. I'm willing to tell them anything I know, but I don't know anything they would want. I have all my records and my accountant has all my income tax material. Anything the committee wants to know about me, I'll tell them. But I can't imagine what information I can give them."

Mullen suggested that they might ask about his relationship with Joe Adonis, Frank Costello and Lucky Luciano. DiCarlo replied, "I don't know any of those fellows. That is I don't know anything more than I have read in the papers. I'm just a hometown boy."

DiCarlo said that he was "wounded" by reports that he was hiding out at the Hotel Statler. "I was registered in my own name," he claimed. "I was around the lobby quite a bit and even talked to some policemen I know. Why should they say I was hiding?"

After the Kefauver committee set a hearing date of January 17 in Cleveland, additional subpoenas were issued. Chief Allen received additional summonses for Aiello, Charles "Cadillac Charlie" Cavallaro, Leo "Dutch" Manley, Sam Alpern and Joseph Melek. Alpern was the former supplier of the Empire News Service, the Valley's race wire service; Melek was a Mahoning County bookie who handled bets on horse races. Melek proved to be an elusive target. He reportedly left Youngstown by bus and police were never able to serve him with the subpoena.

On January 10, Chief Allen and Vice Squad Captain Harold E. Faust,[5] once a key member of Sergeant William J. Davis' "special vice squad," traveled to

Cleveland to spend the day with associate counsel Joseph L. Nellis and Cleveland Safety Director Alvin J. Sutton.[6] When the committee was preparing for the important New York City hearings, the work of Nellis so impressed the committee members that they promoted him from assistant to associate counsel.[7] Allen and Faust provided background information on the Valley mobsters who were subpoenaed. It was standard procedure for investigators to gather evidence and sometimes question subpoenaed witnesses in advance of the committee members arriving in town in an attempt to streamline the hearings.

The Kefauver Committee hearings began in Cleveland on the morning of Wednesday, January 17, 1951. At 10:15 a.m., in room 318, on the third floor of the Federal Building, Senator Estes Kefauver calmly announced, "The Committee will come to order." Kefauver was the only member of the five-Senator committee to appear in Cleveland. In a "blinding flash" of photographer's flashbulbs, the crime hearings got underway. The media frenzy had begun too. The limited courtroom space was shared among reporters, government and police officials, and spectators. Almost knocking each other over, radio and newspaper reporters jockeyed for position around two large tables in the courtroom. In addition, they filled up the two rows of seats in the jury box. Four of the six courtroom benches were set aside for spectators and could accommodate 28 people. The other two benches were occupied by Internal Revenue investigators, FBI agents, Cleveland police detectives, and other interested "government hawks."

Chairman Kefauver introduced the committee's first witness Frank J. Lausche. The Ohio Governor discussed the raid on the Jungle Inn in Trumbull County, recounting all the problems the state liquor agents incurred. He then reviewed where the trouble spots were in the state, and what was currently being done about them. These locations included Mahoning and Trumbull Counties, as well as Lucas County, where Toledo is located.

On Thursday afternoon, Anthony A. Rutkowski, chief of the enforcement division of the Ohio Department of Liquor Control appeared. Rutkowski began with a statement outlining his responsibilities and stating that in his position he has no legal authority to investigate gambling or conduct gambling raids. The enforcement work he completed was done at the personal request of Governor Lausche. Rutkowski then told the story of the raid at the Jungle Inn in Warren.

Kefauver asked Rutkowski if he had any suggestions for the committee. Rutkowski replied, "Yes, Senator. I would like to suggest, in order to break up this powerful syndicate of gamblers operating gambling places in one state and living in another, that it may be possible to destroy them by the passage of legislation . . . which would make it a federal offense punishable by penitentiary sentence for any person to keep, operate, conduct, or own stock in a corporation which is conducting gambling in one state (while) he resides in another state."

Chief Allen was the last witness called during the afternoon session on Thursday. Allen told the committee he was engaged in a constant battle with organized crime since the day he became police chief. He reported the criminal power in Youngstown came from the Licavoli gang and Aiello, Caputo, and DiCarlo, all associates in the bookie business. Aiello and Caputo had muscled in on the local bookmakers, demanding 50 percent of their profits. The bookies caved in to the mobsters, figuring "half a loaf was better than none."

The chief declared that DiCarlo and his associates in the Valley "are without question members of the Mafia, better known as Black Hand Government." Allen described the Mafia as an "association of persons with the purpose of gaining illicit control of both legal and illegal enterprises." It is interesting to note that Allen had such a strong opinion of the Mafia and its activities in light of the fact that he was so highly recommended by Hoover. The FBI director was a firm believer that the Mafia didn't exist.

Allen said that DiCarlo left Buffalo and went to Cleveland. From there he was "told to move on to greener fields in Youngstown. [DiCarlo, Aiello and Caputo] managed to corner about 50% of the bookmaking business in Youngstown until they were driven out by a reform organization in 1948. Apparently all Joe had to do was to put up his share of the bankroll and he was in. When the Youngstown bookies learned that DiCarlo had a political in, they permitted him to organize them."

"Why did DiCarlo leave Buffalo; was the heat on him?" Nellis asked.

"That's correct, they didn't want him in Buffalo," Allen answered. "But he had built up a reputation in Buffalo. When he came to Cleveland and Youngstown he had to 'see the boys' before he could operate. You just don't come into a city and take over without the approval or acquiescence of those in control."

Claiming that DiCarlo's associates in the Valley "beyond question are members of the Mafia," Chief Allen explained his version of the organization to the committee. "The Mafia is an association of persons whose purpose is to gain illicit control of both legal and illegal enterprises," he stated. The DiCarlo gang operated very successfully by inducing fear in and around Youngstown."

With the use of a chart, carefully put together by Allen, a complete picture of organized crime in the Youngstown area, showing ties to Detroit, Toledo, Cleveland, Erie and Buffalo unfolded before the committee. Allen, without a doubt, had the most thorough understanding of the organized crime structure throughout the region and impressed the committee with his knowledge. In discussing the men on the chart, Allen told the committee, "The amazing thing is that their records show lots of arrests but few convictions. Perhaps a reason is that the police were unable to find prosecution witnesses when they were needed."

During Kefauver's questioning of Allen, the matter of Frank Cammarata's stay of deportation came up. Kefauver said that he had asked Congressman Michael Kirwan about it and was told that at the time he introduced the bills he wasn't aware of the mobster's record. Not wanting to use Kirwan's name for some unexplained reason, Allen answered, "It is wrong for a Congressman or Senator to obstruct law enforcement. It wasn't necessary to file a bill for Cammarata as the congressman in question could have picked up his phone and found out easily this man's record dating back to 1922."

When Friday morning's session began, DiCarlo and James Licavoli were the main witnesses. DiCarlo appeared first, accompanied by attorney Russell Mock. Nellis began the session by going over DiCarlo's criminal record. The 52 year-old DiCarlo was arrested 28 times between 1920 and 1945, all but twice in Buffalo. The charges, in addition to his conviction in 1924, included assault, reckless driving (3 times), improper lights on his automobile, vagrancy, illegal registering for an election, disorderly conduct, speeding, coercion, extortion, conspiracy, accepting bets on horse races, public intoxication, use of profanity, and resisting arrest.

Nellis questioned DiCarlo about his take over of the rackets in the Valley, with Aiello and Caputo between 1946 and 1948, by muscling in on the bookies. The questioning reflected Allen's testimony from the previous day. DiCarlo denied the accusations. When asked what his business was in Youngstown, he refused to answer on the grounds that he might incriminate himself. DiCarlo's attorney, Mock, tried to convince the committee that his client's refusal to answer questions was based on litigation that was currently going on involving a gambling investigation. After arguing points of law, Kefauver directed DiCarlo to answer the question, but he still refused. When Nellis continued to question DiCarlo, Mock jumped in and stated, "Oh, you are just trying to find the old cat that's in the closet for Chief Allen."

Nellis led DiCarlo through a slate of names, inquiring as to his knowledge of and / or relationship with them. DiCarlo admitted knowing James Licavoli, but claimed that he did not know what business he was in and that he had no business dealings with him. He admitted knowing Pete Licavoli and his brother John for almost 25 years. Cleveland mobsters he claimed to know were Al Polizzi and the Angersola brothers; he left out Frank Brancato, a mobster he had dealings with, which later came to light. Several of the persons Nellis mentioned were arrested during the raid at the Cleveland Statler Hotel in 1928.[8] Included in that group of mobsters was DiCarlo's brother Salvatore, known as Sam. When queried about his knowledge of this raid, DiCarlo stated that he was in prison in Atlanta at the time. Actually the meeting, if there was one before police raided the hotel, took place on December 5, 1928; DiCarlo was paroled from the reformatory at Chillicothe, Ohio a month and a half earlier on October 19.

Defiant and short with his answers, DiCarlo claimed he couldn't remember when he came to America from Italy. Having admitted that he arrived in New York City, Halley tried to find out which borough DiCarlo lived in. The following exchange took place:

Mr. DiCarlo: I know I lived in New York, but I wouldn't know just where.
Mr. Halley: I mean, you do know whether you lived in Manhattan, Brooklyn, the Bronx, Queens, Staten Island?
Mr. DiCarlo: I will tell, at this time I didn't know that there was so many boroughs there.
Mr. Halley: How long did you live in New York?
Mr. DiCarlo: Off hand, I would say – well, I don't know – maybe a year, 2 years.
Mr. Halley: A year or 2 years?
Mr. DiCarlo: Yes, but I wouldn't know the exact time.
Mr. Halley: And then in a year or 2 years you never found out what borough you lived in, Mr. DiCarlo?
Mr. DiCarlo: I wasn't acquainted to the boroughs in them days. I mean, now I would know if I lived in New York or Brooklyn.
Mr. Halley: You were about 10 years old?
Mr. DiCarlo: Yes. Well, I don't remember.
Mr. Halley: You don't really expect me to believe that, do you?
Mr. DiCarlo: Do you want me to say New York if I don't remember?
Mr. Halley: Is that it, you don't remember, or you didn't ever know where you lived?
Mr. DiCarlo: I know we lived in New York. I really don't know where.

This strained line of questioning went on with Halley trying to put together an early background on DiCarlo. When asked about his jail sentence in 1924, the following dialogue took place:

Mr. Halley: What did you go to jail for?
Mr. DiCarlo: All I know is conspiracy.
Mr. Halley: Conspiracy to do what?
Mr. DiCarlo: ...intimidating, if I'm not mistaken.
Mr. Halley: In connection with what?
Mr. DiCarlo: Why, I just wouldn't know.

As the committee went through his arrest record, DiCarlo professed he had pled innocent on several of the charges, but was found guilty by the court. He couldn't comment on the crimes because he was an innocent man, falsely charged and convicted. After getting out of Chillicothe, DiCarlo claimed he went into the amusement business –vending machines, cigarette machines, and jukeboxes – but not slot machines. His business was called the Chippewa Amusement Company, which he operated with Joseph Anzalone. When asked where Anzalone was, DiCarlo answered he hadn't "seen him in 10 or 11 years." DiCarlo said he gave up the amusement business and left Buffalo for Youngstown in 1945. He then "denied emphatically" Chief Allen's testimony from the previous day that he had left Buffalo "because the heat was on." After that he refused to answer any questions about his business in Youngstown or his involvement in gambling operations.

Halley asked DiCarlo if he knew Frank Costello, Joe Adonis, Joseph Aiello or Willie Moore (Moretti), to which the witness replied, "No." Halley pressed him, trying to get him to admit to a relationship with "Fats" Aiello in the bookmaking operations in the Valley. After DiCarlo again refused to respond, Kefauver directed him to answer. DiCarlo shook his head, no.

Mr. Halley: Well, do you have any legitimate business now?
Mr. DiCarlo: No.
Mr. Halley: When did you last have a legitimate business?
Mr. DiCarlo: I sold my vending machine business in 1938.
Mr. Halley: Where were you from 1938 to 1945?
Mr. DiCarlo: I guess I was in jail at that time.
Mr. Halley: That's a nice legitimate business.

Actually DiCarlo only spent two years between 1937 and 1945 serving prison time; nonetheless he still had no legitimate job. Halley questioned him about a month long vacation he took in Florida during this time:

Mr. Halley: So that except for the period during which you were in jail, you had no legitimate occupation?

Mr. DiCarlo: I was out of work, counselor.

Mr. Halley: Well, out of work. You couldn't afford to spend a month at the Wofford Hotel (Miami) in the season with your family, could you?

Mr. DiCarlo: Well, I – there is a lot of retired people go to Miami if I am not mistaken.

Mr. Halley: Are you a retired gentleman, Mr. DiCarlo?

Mr. DiCarlo: Well, not exactly. Right at the present time I am.

As with most of the underworld witnesses the committee had their tax returns along with both personal and business records. Nellis asked DiCarlo about his connections with the Woodworth Novelty Company, described as "a slot machine outfit located near Woodworth south of Youngstown." DiCarlo claimed he knew nothing about the company. After Nellis pointed out that his tax returns showed receipts from the company for the years 1946 through 1948, DiCarlo replied, "I don't remember."

At the completion of the examination, Kefauver informed DiCarlo that because of his refusal to answer certain questions of the committee, "I will have to make a recommendation that some appropriate action be made."

DiCarlo responded, "Thank you, Senator."

In addition to the threat of an impending contempt of Congress citation, DiCarlo was also informed that he was still under subpoena and could be brought back before the committee for another appearance.

On May 1, when the committee filed its interim report, they portrayed the case of Joseph DiCarlo as a "typical enforcement operation." The report stated, "DiCarlo was a criminal with a long and unsavory record in Buffalo, N.Y. For reasons unknown, he decided to transfer his operations to Ohio, coming first to Cleveland and finally settling in Youngstown. Shortly after his arrival in Youngstown, DiCarlo and his partners, Aiello and Caputo, made their rounds of the local bookies and advised them that as of a certain time, the partnership was going to take 50 percent of the gross receipts of the local bookies. Two basic means of intimidation [were] used by the DiCarlo partnership to effectuate its orders to the bookies. First, the partnership threatened to use political influence to drive the bookies out if they did not succumb to the enforced arrangement and, second, they threatened physical violence. These familiar muscling-in tactics resulted in a complete surrender on the part of the bookies."

If the committee was frustrated with the lack of cooperation they received from DiCarlo, the next witness did little to improve their disposition. James Licavoli, of the infamous Licavoli clan, and his attorney, Dominick J. "Duke" LaPolla, now settled in before the committee. Licavoli answered questions about his criminal record, conceding that he was arrested "many times." In 1945, he was convicted in Toledo of extortion and sentenced to one to five years in prison. He couldn't recall any of the facts of the case, having "copped a plea" in the matter. After probing his family relations, Nellis questioned Licavoli on his current business affairs. Here the fireworks went off:

> Mr. Licavoli: Well, Senator, excuse me. I refuse to answer all questions.
> The Chairman: You refuse to answer all questions?
> Mr. Licavoli: Yes
> The Chairman: Any and all questions?
> Mr. Licavoli: Any questions, all questions.
> Mr. LaPolla: Anything pertaining to his business.
> Mr. Licavoli: Business or not, I refuse to answer all questions.
> The Chairman: Anyway, answer the question, what business you were in. The Chairman directs you to answer. (Do) You refuse to answer?
> Mr. Licavoli: I refuse to answer.

During nine months of hearing testimony and dealing with many recalcitrant attitudes, Kefauver had developed a style of handling even the most belligerent of witnesses. His technique was to keep asking the questions, calmly but firmly, until the witness gave in to his mesmerizing style. He never browbeat a witness, but instead treated them all with respect.

After some legal formalities on Licavoli's refusal to discuss his business, the inquiry moved forward. Nellis, as he had done with DiCarlo, went through the usual procedure of asking whom Licavoli knew, how he knew them, and what business dealings he had with them. Licavoli admitted that he knew DiCarlo, but couldn't remember where he met him or who introduced them. He denied having any business involvement with him. He knew Sam DiCarlo, whom he called "Toto," and acknowledged having met him during his days in Toledo. He also admitted that he knew Frank Brancato and that Frank Cammarata was married to his cousin, Grace.

Licavoli was questioned about his past in St. Louis and Detroit. He denied ever hearing of the Purple Gang. Halley asked him about the time he was shot by a police officer in St. Louis. Licavoli admitted to having been wounded, but could not offer an explanation as to why the officer shot him. He divulged that he was arrested "maybe two dozen" times in St. Louis, 22 times in Detroit, 2 or 3 times in Toledo, and a "couple" of times in Cleveland. The arrests included murder charges on more than one occasion. Licavoli denied currently being involved in any gambling operations.

Kefauver took a moment to inquire how Licavoli's life of crime had gotten started. This line of questioning resulted in the Senator concluding with, "I really think it is a sort of sad situation."

After one more, "I don't know," and another, "I refuse to answer that question," the Licavoli testimony came to an end.

Since the thrust of Licavoli's questioning pertained to his pre-Mahoning Valley activity, DiCarlo officially was the only Valley underworld figure who testified. The committee adjourned late Friday afternoon ending speculation that it might hold another evening session or one on Saturday morning. The feeling was that any discussion to question the "lesser lights" would result in "a repetition of the big wheel's revelations under oath."

The "lesser lights" from the Valley still waiting in the witness room were Aiello, Cammarata and Cavallaro. They were brought into the courtroom at the end of the day, along with six others including Joseph Aiuppa[9] from Chicago, who the committee thought had failed to answer their subpoena. Kefauver asked the group en masse if they had any information they wanted to volunteer. The newspaper reported Kefauver and counsel, "received nothing but a deep silence from all nine men." As Kefauver and members of his committee were preparing to leave it was suddenly brought to their attention that Aiuppa, who had ducked their subpoena in Chicago, was among the men in the courtroom. Kefauver re-opened the hearings.

Aiuppa was subpoenaed by the committee to answer questions about a racing handbook in Chicago that took in $1.9 million in bets during 1947. Aiuppa ran Taylor and Company for the Chicago Outfit, which manufactured roulette wheels, dice and crap tables and other gambling paraphernalia. Taking the stand Aiuppa gave his name and address. He then told the committee, "Gentlemen, I am going to stand on my constitutional rights and refuse to answer all questions on the ground that they may tend to incriminate me." He then refused to answer questions as to how old he was, where he was born and whether he was married. "My answers are all the same," he stated.

The witness sat mute, chewing gum and staring blankly at the committee. At one point he thrust an unlit cigar in his mouth and began chewing it along with the gum. Kefauver asked one final time if he was going to answer the questions and Aiuppa stared at him in silence. Kefauver ordered him off the witness stand, telling him, "I hope each question you refused to answer will be adjudged a separate offense. We will take whatever action we can to see that you don't get by with this contemptuous treatment of the Senate."

There were four witnesses whom Kefauver announced were slated for contempt of the U.S Senate citations – Al Polizzi, James Licavoli, Joseph Aiuppa and DiCarlo. Polizzi, in order to avoid the contempt charge, traveled to Washington, D.C. at his own expense and testified in February. The basis for the contempt of the U.S. Senate charge occurs when a witness refuses to answer a question and is then "directed" by the chairman to respond. If convicted, the sentences of jail terms of 30 days to a year and/or fines of $100 to $1,000 on each count could be imposed. A contempt charge could be brought on each question the witness refused to answer at the discretion of the chairman. In DiCarlo's case, the committee counsel estimated that he "refused to answer 20 to 30 pertinent questions about his bookie operations, connections with national vice and crime lords and past record in dealing with slot machine operations in and around Youngstown." Russell Mock, after reviewing the hearing transcripts, claimed the number of "citable refusals" were only eight to ten.

On January 20 the *Vindicator* acknowledged:

> "Three days of probing into northern Ohio's crime picture by a U.S. Senate investigating committee here brought out the national alliance of criminals and corrupt practices of gamblers, but failed to throw any new light on the Youngstown district's underworld and the city's past record of crime."

When the committee met in Detroit in February, Pete Licavoli was one of the key witnesses. The alleged leader of the Licavoli clan was the brother of Thomas "Yonnie" Licavoli, who was doing a life sentence in the Ohio Penitentiary; the cousin of James Licavoli; and the brother-in-law of Frank Cammarata. The connection between Detroit, Cleveland and Youngstown was further investigated and was confirmed by Pete Licavoli's comment that he "stays in touch" with DiCarlo and former Cleveland Mayfield Road Mob boss Al Polizzi.

On February 21, DiCarlo was one of 13 witnesses nationwide to testify who were cited for contempt of Congress by an approval of the committee. In addition, the Senate ordered 17 arrests warrants for people who had ducked subpoenas. In the Valley, Joe Melek was the only one to avoid the summons. The newspaper reported "the Senate apparently considered him too 'small time' to bother about issuing a warrant. Had Melek obeyed his subpoena he probably would not have been called to the witness stand in Cleveland anyway."

DiCarlo, Licavoli and Aiuppa were tried in Cleveland. To date, contempt charges had only been prosecuted against Harry Russell, a gambler from Chicago and Miami. In that case, Russell was acquitted by a federal judge who ruled the gambler was within his constitutional rights in refusing to answer questions from the committee. Despite that decision, Kefauver was of the opinion that no precedent was set and that each contempt case would be decided on its own merit. Each of the Senate citation requests had to go before the appropriate federal grand jury. On March 27, the grand jury in Cleveland issued indictments against the three men. DiCarlo was charged with eight counts of contempt of the U.S. Senate. The next morning, a deputy U.S. marshal went to DiCarlo's Volney Road home with the indictment, but DiCarlo wasn't there. Before noon, DiCarlo, accompanied by his wife, turned himself in at the Post Office Building in Youngstown. DiCarlo claimed he had gone to Russell Mock's office, but when he found his attorney was away he decided to "surrender voluntarily." A U.S. commissioner set bond at $15,000.

While this was being handled, DiCarlo, "affable and at ease," spoke with reporters. DiCarlo used the opportunity to criticize his adversary Chief Allen. "Why does he always want to inform people I am always moving out of town? I intend to stay. You can tell that publicity crazy Allen he can stop worrying. I am here to stay and I intend to stay and not sell my home."

Meanwhile, federal men were looking for James Licavoli. Living under his nickname "Jack White," Licavoli was reported to have been residing in Trumbull County since January. Assistant U.S. Attorney John J. Kane, a former assistant prosecuting attorney in Youngstown who was handling the case, stated arraignment would be delayed until all three men were served with the indictment. Licavoli's attorney, LaPolla claimed his client had left for vacation at an undisclosed location. The lawyer assured authorities that, "Licavoli has no intention of evading arrest. As soon as he knows he has been indicted, he will come back."

On April 13, all three men appeared before Federal Judge Charles J. McNamee in Cleveland and pled not guilty. Attorneys for the three men huddled with the judge and prosecutor Kane and asked that charges be dismissed. Attorney Mock brought up the argument that because Kefauver was the only Senator present at the Cleveland hearings there was no quorum. Mock claimed he had evidence to support that a subcommittee of Congress, with just one member acting for the committee, "is not a competent tribunal to call for citations for contempt." The judge gave defense counsel 15 days to file briefs arguing for dismissal. The prosecution then had an additional 15 days to respond.

Two days after filing their briefs, defense counsel's motions were denied on May 16. Months dragged by, but still no trial date was set. As time passed government prosecutors began to realize there was little chance of gaining a conviction against the mobsters. On December 5, 1951, the *Vindicator* explained:

> "The main reason for the belief that a conviction cannot be obtained is based on a U. S. Supreme Court decision. The court said, 'A seemingly innocent question might lead to the disclosure of some illegal activities indirectly.'
>
> "The men are thus expected to explain they did not answer the series of questions put to them on business ventures and associates on the ground they might lead to self-incrimination."

The case finally came to trial on December 17. Despite having lost all other contempt cases generated by the Kefauver Hearings, due to Fifth Amendment rights, prosecutor Kane fought on. His case was based on the fact that, "The amendment protects persons only against self-incrimination regarding federal crimes. It does not cover state and municipal crimes, which he felt applied to Licavoli, DiCarlo and Aiuppa." In addition, Kane said the government's stand was "that each question about gambling and racketeering activities that the witness refused to answer before Senator Estes Kefauver is basis for a citation for contempt." Speaking for all three defendants, attorney Mock insisted that the men could only be tried on one count each. The trial lasted one day and both sides were given until early January to present final arguments to Judge McNamee.

On February 7, 1952, over a year after their appearance before the Kefauver Committee, DiCarlo and Licavoli were found not guilty. The judge ruled "the issue of state's rights was involved and that Congress could not take away the immunities of self-incrimination guaranteed by the U.S. Constitution." Judge McNamee claimed the two men were not just ordinary gamblers, and were alleged to be involved in "more serious violations of state laws" connected to gambling. Those more serious violations were reputed to be "intimidation, violence and even murder." Therefore, the judge decided, the two had justification for refusing to answer the committee's questions. The men had "reasonable fear" in responding to the queries.

Ironically, the judge found Joseph Aiuppa guilty on three counts of contempt and sentenced him to six months in jail and a $1,000 fine – he was freed on a $10,000 bond pending appeal. Aiuppa had refused to answer any questions outside of his name and address. The judge ruled that questions he refused to answer could not have incriminated him. In passing sentence, McNamee said Aiuppa was "probably the most contemptuous witness to appear before the committee."

From the first session held on May 26, 1950, in Miami, Florida, Kefauver had traveled over 52,000 miles, holding meetings in 14 different cites. Questioning witnesses from almost every state in the union, Kefauver heard shocking and incredible testimony that he listened to with "mounting indignation and revulsion" about this national disgrace, organized crime. In hearing testimony from an estimated 800 witnesses and reading "hundreds of thousands of words" of additional corroborating memos, the committee arrived at the following conclusions:

◊ A nationwide crime syndicate does exist in the United States, despite the protests of criminals, self-serving politicians, blind fools, and others who may be honestly misguided, that there is no such combine.

◊ Behind the local mobs, which make up the national crime syndicate, is a shadowy, international criminal organization known as the Mafia, so fantastic that most Americans find it hard to believe it really exists.

◊ Although dishonest politicians and officeholders are a small minority compared with the hundreds of thousands of devoted, honest public servants, political corruption in the United States seems to have sunk to a new low.

◊ While law enforcement is primarily a local responsibility, and everywhere we uncovered a monotonous picture of corrupt or passive local officials, much of the responsibility for what is going on rests squarely on federal enforcement agencies.

◊ Infiltration of legitimate business by known hoodlums has progressed to an alarming extent in the United States.

The exposure Estes Kefauver received from the hearings catapulted him to national political popularity. This springboard to political fame propelled him to be nominated as Adlai Stevenson's vice presidential running mate in the 1956 Presidential Election. They were defeated by incumbents Eisenhower and Nixon.

Kefauver's committee did not put an end to organized crime by any means. The committee issued 45 citations for contempt of Congress, of which three ended up in convictions. Of the 19 new crime-fighting laws they recommended, only one passed and it proved to be unenforceable by the courts. An investigation of the citizenship status of over 500 mobsters was begun, but resulted in the deportation of only 24. The Internal Revenue Service, however, was able to indict 874 racketeers on income tax violations.

What the Kefauver Committee did accomplish was to put a face on organized crime in this country. This, combined with the investigation of the Senate Select Committee on Improper Activities in the Labor or Management Field, formed in January 1957, raised the public awareness of the presence of a nefarious underworld society. If the hearings helped to arouse J. Edgar Hoover from his slumber in acknowledging the existence of organized crime, then the Apalachin summit in November 1957 would be his final wake up call. By the end of the 1950s, he was ready to pit his FBI organization in a head-to-head battle with organized crime.

Federal Gambling Stamp

In the wake of the Kefauver hearings a new Federal law was enacted by Congress which required bookies, numbers men and sports pool operators to purchase a federal wagering tax stamp (also known as the federal gambling tax stamp). At certain intervals the gambler had to report his earnings to the Internal Revenue Service and pay a ten percent tax on it. The tax was to be paid on the gross receipts, meaning the gambler could not deduct payouts that he made. In obtaining the stamp, the purchaser could declare himself, or herself as a "principal" or an "agent." As a principal, the purchaser indicates that they actually operate a policy business or another form of gambling activity.

The gambler was instructed to purchase the $50 stamp, identify his business address and list the names of his partners and every employee and agent. In purchasing the stamp, and providing the information, the gambler was admitting his illegal activities and where they were being carried on. Still, gamblers purchased the stamps nationwide and it's fairly certain that any declarations of income were grossly understated. Attorneys for the gamblers weren't too concerned. Most felt that if the law were ever tested in court the government would find it ruled unconstitutional because, in effect, the very purchase of the stamp was tantamount to having to testify against one's self. Hank Messick and Burt Goldblatt in *The Only Game in Town: An Illustrated History of Gambling* state, "Government attorneys said privately that the legal eagles were probably right, and for that reason they advised the IRS and the Justice Department not to demand vigorous enforcement of the law."

The new law was set to go into effect November 1, 1951. The *Vindicator* reported the day before that, "Bookies and lottery operators in the Youngstown area say they will go out of business tonight rather than be subjected to a new federal gambling tax." A little over a month later Chief Allen reported, "I think things are tighter now than they've ever been." Policy operators all over the county had shut down. It wasn't just the bug men who went underground, locations that catered to poker players and craps games had virtually closed and horse bets were being taken only on a "friend-to-friend" basis.

On December 5, the Internal Revenue Service in Cleveland released the names of 13 area gamblers who had purchased the new tax stamp. Not a single purchaser lived in Youngstown. The most prominent name in the group was Vince DeNiro, who used his Lowellville address. The IRS reported an additional 41 applicants had their applications returned due to insufficient information, eleven from the city of Youngstown. Chief Allen announced that as soon as the information is passed along to him he will raid every address. With that, the harassment campaign was on.

The bookie business seemed to be the hardest hit. By February 14, 1952, sales of race information sheets was reported off in the city by 75 percent. When applications for the stamp were due again by the end of July, the Cleveland IRS office reported that of the 22 northeastern Ohio counties under their jurisdiction, only 55 bookmakers had applied, compared to 566 the prior year. The Cleveland collector reported, "Those who bought last year, but haven't bought this year must either be going underground or out of business. If they are going out of business, fine. If they are going underground, who do they think they can fool? We have a list of them, and the police have a list of them. If the local police pick them up, we'll move in. Then they'll be liable to fines of from $1,000 to $5,000 and possible prison terms."

Over the next few years the names of Sandy Naples, Vince DeNiro and Peter Fetchet were repeatedly on the list of purchasers released by the IRS and printed in the *Vindicator* (See Appendix B). While the agency could announce who purchased the stamps, they couldn't say what each person was declaring in taxes, therefore proving that they were actively in business. Paul H. Cress, who replaced Eddie Allen as police chief in January 1954 complained, "The Internal Revenue Department apparently isn't interested in whether or not a man is gambling, because they issue him a stamp and collect the taxes on that stamp. To me, possession of a gambling tax stamp is no proof that a man is gambling. However, the Internal Revenue Department knows who is gambling and how much money he is making by gambling because they collect taxes on it every year. The bureau is not permitted to tell local enforcement agencies who is gambling and who isn't. The public knows this, but we, as policemen, must prove the fact a man is gambling before we can take him into court."

During a harassment campaign in November 1955, all the holders of the stamp were ordered to come to the police station for interviews by Vice Squad Chief George Krispli. On the first day, John Burnich, Peter Fetchet, Nick Lavaglio and Sam Zappi announced they had quit the gambling business and "suspended operations." Burnish went a step further and relinquished his stamp to the police. The other three vowed to follow suit. The next day, Sandy Naples and his brother "Little Joey" surrendered their stamps. A spokesperson for the IRS in Cleveland called the surrender a "hollow gesture," claiming that the men "can tear up the stamps as for as we're concerned," explaining that the stamps were simply receipts for taxes paid to the government on winnings, not a license to gamble. A year later, when the new holders were again announced, Sandy and Joey Naples were back on the list.

In March 1957, it was reported that Youngstown area gamblers who possessed the gambling stamp paid $294,000 in wagering excise tax during the prior year. Since the tax rate is a flat ten-percent, gamblers earned $2,940,000 – assuming they reported all their gambling income, which is unlikely.

By August 1958, the number of gambling stamp purchasers for the 22 counties in Northeastern Ohio had dwindled over a six-year period from 598 to 88. Throughout the decade, gamblers tried to avoid getting their names in the newspaper when it was periodically announced who the purchasers were. One of these methods was to have the stamp taken out in the name of only one partner. Sometimes the stamp was purchased by a principal, at other times the agent. Many times the purchaser waited until after the deadline to make his purchase. By 1963 the district was down to only 10 purchasers of the gambling tax stamp. A year earlier the government came up with a new gambling tax stamp, this one for gambling devices. The new stamps cost $250 and were sold annually to individuals and businesses operating gaming devices.

In the end, the government had not found a way to stop gambling, only to profit from it.

"That jerk don't know what he is talking about. If I had to carry on business the way he described it, I would never make a nickel in the business." – Sandy Naples responding to the testimony of Youngstown Police Sergeant Clayton Geise, a former vice squad member, who took the stand to explain how the numbers rackets operated.

11

The Policy Kings

Sandy Naples

There is as much mystery surrounding Sandy Naples' birth, as there is his death. In *Brier Hill, USA*, local Italian historian Tony Trolio states that when Giuseppe DiNapoli and his wife Lucia Alteri were on their way to America by boat she was pregnant with Sandy. The book lists his date of birth as January 7, 1907. Sandy's death certificate lists the date as December 7, 1907. Sandy's grave stone in Calvary Cemetery, however, lists the year of birth as 1906. Attempts to locate the birth certificate at South Side Hospital proved fruitless, which also would have provided his actual first name. The newspapers referred to him for the most part as S. Joseph "Sandy" Naples, while the death certificate listed him as Sandy Joseph Naples. There is some belief though that the "S" actually stood for "Santino," and just as the DiNapoli name became Naples, Santino became Sandy.

Giuseppe, who used the Americanized name of Joseph, eventually settled into the Brier Hill area in a house at the corner of Poplar and Calvin Streets. His three brothers came to live in the same area. In addition to Sandy, Lucia and Giuseppe's other children were sons James, William, Joseph and daughters Madeline, Annette, Rose and Dorothy. Giuseppe worked as a plumber for the city until he was struck by a hit-and-run driver in the 1940s.

Between 1931 and May 1934, the 5 foot, 4 and a half-inch tall, 145 pound Sandy Naples was arrested ten times. His rap sheet revealed the following entries early in his criminal career. All arrests took place in Youngstown unless otherwise indicated:

August 11, 1931 – arrested as a suspect in the robbery of the Grennan Baking Company three days earlier. He was released on August 20, no charges were filed.

October 10, 1931 – arrested on suspicion of robbing Frank Laney of Samuels Street. He was released the same day.

January 23, 1932 – arrested on suspicion. No crime is indicated and he was released four days later.

February 2, 1932 – arrested on suspicion. Released the next day after the plaintiff refused to press charges.

December 5, 1932 – arrested for assault and battery. Naples and two other men assaulted a Wilson Avenue man. They were released three days later after the victim refused to press charges.

January 27, 1933 – arrested for violation of the liquor law – possession. Three days later he pled guilty in Municipal Court and was fined $200 and costs.

October 7, 1933 – arrested for assault and battery. Naples was accused by Edna Mitchell of beating and kicking her. On October 24, he was released after Mitchell refused to press charges.

November 6, 1933 – arrested in Warren, but no crime or disposition is listed.

November 22, 1933 – arrested for contributing to the delinquency of a minor. On December 4 he pled guilty in juvenile court and was fined $100 and costs and sentenced to 30 days in the county jail.

May 13, 1934 – arrested as a fugitive from justice. The next day he was turned over to Warren authorities and arrested for breaking and entering. There was no disposition given.

May 18, 1934 – arrested in Butler, Pennsylvania for robbery. A May 18 newspaper article said attorneys for Naples had filed a writ of habeas corpus in Warren to obtain his release (this obviously refers to his May 13 arrest). The article claimed he was indicted for attempted burglary in Trumbull County, but was to be extradited to Beaver, Pennsylvania where police wanted him "on a charge of assault with intent to commit a felony in connection with robbing and beating an aged farmer."

This latest arrest involved the home invasion of Theodore Bedonner of Economy Township near Butler, Pennsylvania. Bedonner was held by Naples and two other Youngstown hoods who were seeking the hiding place of his savings. To force their captive to talk one of the men burned his feet. Naples was convicted on June 16 of robbery and receiving stolen goods. He was sentenced to 10 to 20 years in the Western State Penitentiary in Bellfonte, Pennsylvania. On June 16, 1944, Naples was paroled and released to Youngstown.

In January 1946, Naples formed the Center Amusement Company with John "Pinky" Walsh and Joseph Alexander. The "company" purchased property at the corner of Center Street and Wilson Avenue. The building housed Haselton Gardens, also known as Tesone's Tavern where James Tisone was murdered in

September 1937. The men paid $15,500 for the property and signed a mortgage for $11,500.

The *Vindicator* printed the following description:

> "The property, located near a number of large plants, includes the old Wilson Theater (now a garage), three store rooms on the first floor, four apartments on the second floor, and four apartments on the third floor. The downstairs rooms have been occupied by the Haselton Confectionery, a barber shop, and Haselton Gardens, a tavern."

The article also pointed out that Naples was "reported to have joined Walsh as a partner following the disappearance of Jerry 'Sledgehammer' Pascarella last summer." Walsh and Naples were allegedly "connected with local slot machine groups and reports indicate Walsh 'took over' a number of machines formerly owned by Pascarella on the grounds that the latter owed him some $1,200 at the time of his disappearance."

The announcement of the property purchase drew immediate attention to the fact that Naples was still on parole from his 1934 conviction in Beaver, Pennsylvania. Parolees were not permitted by law to purchase property without the permission of the parole board. Just days after the article appeared, Naples filed a quitclaim deed and his share of the property fell, legally, into the hands of Alexander and Walsh.

Alexander, Naples and Walsh approached Buddy Fares, the publisher of *The Youngstowner*, a pamphlet advertising local nightclubs and restaurants, in 1949 to borrow money to complete the remodeling of the Center Sandwich Shop. The total amount borrowed was $1,400, and only Alexander's name appeared on the note for the loan. Before any of the money was repaid, "Fats" Aiello purchased Alexander's share of the restaurant. Sometime later, when Fares approached Aiello about the loan, "Fats" claimed he was no longer involved, that he had "walked out" of the deal because he wasn't making any money. Meanwhile, Sandy Naples was sent back to prison for a parole violation and when he returned, Fares confronted him about the money that was due. Naples said he couldn't pay him and to go see Alexander, because his name was on the note. Fares, tired of all the "buck pushing," threatened Naples with a lien on the building. Sandy responded by threatening Fares with, "bodily injury" if he carried out the placing of the lien.

Naples next encounter with negative publicity came after the infamous shooting at the Purple Cow, where "Fats" Aiello unleashed a round at Anthony Bova on New Years' Eve 1946. The incident clearly showed that Naples was tied to Aiello after his return from prison. Naples was said to have drawn a weapon at the same time, but didn't fire. Immediately after the shooting, Naples and others gave a savage beating to John "Jack the Ripper" Zentko, who made the mistake of accompanying Bova into the Purple Cow. Two days later the newspaper again disclosed Naples actions took place while still on parole.

An official from the Ohio State Bureau of Probation began an investigation of Naples, but it wouldn't be until mid-June 1947 that action was taken. Naples was "quietly" placed in the Mahoning County jail, but quickly had his lawyer file a writ of habeas corpus. When the case came before Judge John Ford on June 30, the evidence against Naples was overwhelming and the writ was withdrawn.

Officially Naples was charged with "failure to adjust himself to the parole system, associating with the wrong people and not going into a legitimate business." In addition to the Purple Cow incident, parole officers cited the fact that Naples was connected with "Pinky" Walsh in a gambling operation going on in the backroom of the Center Sandwich Shop and that Sandy was "running one of the city's more prosperous bug outfits from his home." The *Vindicator* claimed he was operating the policy business for "another local racketeer," but failed to name him. Naples was returned to the Western State Penitentiary.

In announcing Naples' incarceration the newspaper reported, "Mahoning County, officials said, 'has proved a pitfall for parolees, mostly because of the wide open opportunities for criminals to fall back into the ways of vice, crime and corruption.'

"Investigators commented that nowhere else in the state had they seen or heard of as many parolees mixed up in the gambling racket as in Youngstown."

Despite the reported problems, when Naples was re-released in August 1948, he was allowed to return to Youngstown. Six months later, after Naples' legal team applied for the commutation of the maximum limit of his sentence, the request was granted by Pennsylvania Governor James H. Duff. The commutation meant that state parole officers could no longer look into Naples' affairs.

Naples returned to a Youngstown that was cracking down on the underworld element in an effort led by Mayor Charles Henderson and Chief Edward Allen. Naples' first session with the hard-nosed chief took place on October 21, 1949, when he was hauled in for questioning regarding the whereabouts of "Fats" Aiello, who had gone into hiding the day his suspicious person's trial began. Later, during Aiello's trial, it was revealed that Naples was again co-owner of the Center Sandwich Shop with "Pinky" Walsh.

Around 11:30 on the night of December 6, 1949, Naples and Vince DeNiro were allegedly discussing "business" at the Center Sandwich Shop when Sandy rose to make a phone call. Naples had received a necktie as a birthday gift and was calling to thank the sender. Just then two men entered the restaurant and one, armed with a .45 automatic, fired a single shot at Naples as he stood at the wall phone talking.[10] The slug tore through Naples' right thigh and embedded itself in his left leg causing a compound fracture of the bone. Naples later said he didn't see or hear a thing. He asked DeNiro to call an ambulance when he felt the lower part of his body go numb. Naples was rushed to St. Elizabeth's Hospital, where he told attending physicians, "It was just an accident."

At the restaurant police questioned DeNiro and a waitress. DeNiro, while admitting to seeing the two gunmen enter, said he didn't recognize either one. The waitress said she fled to the basement at the sound of gunfire. A witness outside the restaurant claimed six people fled after the shooting. One, a local steelworker, was taken in the next day questioned and released.

With Naples and DeNiro unable, or unwilling, to shed any light on the assailants, the investigation came to an abrupt end. Police concluded the bullet that struck Sandy was intended for someone else inside the restaurant after an argument there and that Naples was hit by accident. For Naples it was a long recovery period. He was not released from St. Elizabeth's until March 20, 1950, some three and a half months after the shooting.

Through the remainder of 1950 and the early months of 1951, the Valley's attention was focused on the Kefauver Hearings. Despite the attention given to the hearings both Naples and DeNiro escaped the media blitz.

Around 9:45 on the night of March 11, 1951, Youngstown police were called to investigate a disturbance outside the Center Sandwich Shop. After arriving officers found John R. Price, an inhabitant of the Central YMCA, lying on the sidewalk outside the restaurant bleeding from a vicious beating that was administered to him. When police questioned Sandy he told them that Price spat on the front window and then tried to kick it in. Price returned ten minutes later and kicked out the glass from a door on the side of the building.

Mrs. Ruth Parks, described as Price's companion, told a different tale. She said the two were at the Worker's Tavern, directly across Wilson Avenue. After they crossed over to the bus stop in front of the Center Sandwich Shop, Price was attacked by William "Billy" Naples and Stephen J. "Skin" Bajnok, the latter was at times listed as the manager of the eatery. Parks claimed she was bruised on the legs while trying to break up the melee. Price was taken to South Side Hospital. According to medical testimony, later introduced at trial, Price suffered a brain concussion, a broken nose, broken cheek, multiple bruises of the head and paralysis of the pupil in one of his eyes.

Billy Naples and Bajnok were arrested the next day and pleaded not guilty to disturbance charges before being released on their own recognizance by Judge Frank Anzellotti. An investigation determined Sandy was also involved. One week later, police filed charges of assault with intent to kill against him. Sandy quickly hired Russell Mock as his counsel. On April 11, one month after the attack, all three men were bound over to the grand jury on charges of assault with intent to kill. Bond was set at $1,000 apiece. On May 28, the grand jury indicted the trio.

Before the case came to trial, Sandy and Billy were arrested again on robbery charges. Shortly before 3:00 a.m. on June 19, an anonymous woman caller phoned the Niles Police Department to inform them, "There is a lot of noise and commotion over at the Jennings." The "Jennings" of course was the notorious

Jennings Club in Niles, which at the time was "only" being used for bingo. As a police cruiser sped to the scene it narrowly missed hitting a man running from the club on Mason Street. Police took off after the man and the chase ended when the suspect hit a fence and fell to the ground. He was soon identified as "Pinky" Walsh.

Less than two hours later, based on a description given of another man seen fleeing the club along Mason Street, Niles police arrested Sandy Naples near a Crandon Avenue Street corner. At the crime scene, the second floor apartment of Joseph "Pobo" Jennings, Jr., who was vacationing in Canada, police found four smashed doors and the combinations knocked off two strong boxes. Police could not tell how much money, if any, was stolen. When the two men were searched at the station they had $28 between them.

Both men were indignant while police questioned them. Walsh stated, "I've been coming to Niles for 30 years and nothing like this ever happened before. I was just up here doing a little drinking. Asked why he ran from police Walsh replied, "There was lights and yelling and who wouldn't run!" Naples insisted that, "I came up to shoot some craps, that's all. I got in a fight, that's all." Sandy stated that he had come to the city alone. When told that Walsh had already admitted that the two came together Naples became abusive and began swearing at his interrogators.

During the course of the night, Billy Naples went to the Youngstown Police Department to inquire if Sandy had been arrested. Curious as to why they were being asked, police arrested Billy. They then drove out to the Center Sandwich Shop where they arrested John "Jack the Ripper" Zentko, who apparently made amends with Sandy, James Corsell and Joseph "Little Joey" Naples, the youngest of the four brothers. All were held on open charges. The newspaper reported, "These four were arrested in connection with the mysterious movements of a 1949 gray Cadillac club coupe believed to have been used in the burglary. The car was left at the Skylight Restaurant in Girard and later picked up after a telephone call was made" to the Center Sandwich Shop.

The next day Naples and Walsh pleaded guilty to suspicious person's charges, were fined $50 and costs, and were released from the Niles jail. Police lacked evidence and witnesses to tie them to the break-in at the Jennings Club. In Youngstown, Sandy's brothers and the other two men were also released. In a move reminiscent of the proverbial adage, "Closing the barn door after the cows have left," Niles City Council, buoyed by ridicule from local communities, moved to amend its suspicious person's ordinance to include jail time.

On June 25, the trial of Stephen Bajnok got underway. In his opening statement Assistant County Prosecutor Michael Kosach stated Bajnok beat Price with the butt end of a cue stick. Due to the viciousness of the beating and the use of a "deadly weapon," the assault was meant to kill Price, who was hospitalized for 18 days. Attorney Mock, in his opening remarks, denied that Bajnok had any "weapon" and that Price was injured as the result of a street fight.

During the course of the trial it was revealed that two fights actually took place that night. Ruth Parks, who married John Price shortly after he was released from the hospital, testified they had planned to go to a restaurant for dinner that night and crossed the street to the bus stop in front of the Center Sandwich Shop. Outside the restaurant it was alleged that Bajnok and Billy Naples witnessed Price spit on the recently washed front window. Bajnok rushed out and fought with Price landing punches "about two times."

Price and Parks retreated back across the street to the Worker's Tavern where Price "cleaned up" in the men's room. Returning to the bus stop, Price went to the side door of the restaurant and began shaking it. He testified that he did this to attract the attention of whomever it was who beat him and to demand an explanation. (It's interesting to note that the *Vindicator* reported, "Neither Mrs. Price nor her husband...identified Bajnok as one of the men involved in the fight.") At this point Bajnok, who claimed Price "kicked in the door, breaking the glass," went back outside and engaged Price, whom he claimed threw the first punch, and pummeled him "eight or ten times." Bajnok also testified that Billy Naples, not he, used a blackjack, not a cue stick. In Ruth Price's account of the second fight she claimed three men beat John on the head and shoulders "with what I called a stick" until he was left bloody and his eyes swollen.

After two days of testimony, closing arguments were heard on June 26. Mock claimed that Bajnok acted in self-defense, stating that a man "has a right to protect himself and his property." What property Bajnok owned that he was protecting wasn't specified by the attorney. In his instructions to the jury Judge Ford let them know that they could return with a lesser verdict of guilty of assault and battery. It was this charge that the jury found Bajnok guilty of. On July 5, Judge Ford sentenced Bajnok to six months in the county jail. Despite the fact that he had no previous record, the judge imposed a longer sentence due to the brutality of the beating.

After the conviction of Bajnok on the lesser charge of assault and battery, some court watchers believed the Naples brothers might plead guilty to the same charge to avoid trial and the possibility of being convicted of the intent to kill charge, which carried a sentence of from one to twenty years in prison.

The trial of Billy Naples got underway on the morning of August 8, with the seating of a jury of six men and six women. When the handsome, younger brother of Sandy Naples took the stand the next day it seemed as if he was more intent on defending his older brother than himself. He testified that once Price returned and engaged Bajnok in the second fight, he grabbed a blackjack from behind the counter and rushed outside. Naples claimed Price kicked him in the groin. Billy responded by whacking Price several times with the blackjack before Sandy came out and ordered a halt to the fight. During the trial Billy claimed that his brother James owned the restaurant. As in Bajnok's case, the jury returned with a guilty verdict to a lesser charge of assault and battery. On August 10, Judge Ford sentenced Billy to six months in the county jail, but allowed him to remain free on bond while Mock appealed the case to the 7th District Court of Appeals.

By the time Sandy's trial began on September 17, Bajnok was already serving his sentence and Billy was out on bond pending appeal. Despite the fact that both Bajnok and Billy were convicted of the lesser charge, and had testified that Sandy had no role in the fracas, and that he had even tried to break it up, the elder Naples was still tried on a charge of assault with intent to kill. The trial lasted less than two days. A jury of five men and seven women found Sandy not guilty after less than an hour of deliberations.

Billy Naples' appeals process was a long drawn out affair. On April 3, 1952, the 7th District Court of Appeals confirmed the conviction and Judge Ford's sentence. During June 1952, Billy and Stephen Bajnok were arrested during Chief Allen's harassment campaign. After nearly 24 hours they were released. On October 9, the Ohio Supreme Court dismissed Naples appeal, finding that "no debatable constitutional question was involved. Billy didn't turn himself in after this final appeal failed and delayed the start of his jail sentence until sheriff's deputies arrested him and delivered him to the county lock-up on January 30, 1953. After being informed by Sheriff Langley that Billy Naples was a model prisoner, Judge Ford gave him an early release on May 14 after he had served three and a half months of his six-month sentence.

On January 2, 1952, FBI agents entered the Center Sandwich Shop to arrest Armando DiMartino on a Mann Act violation. In February 1949, DiMartino allegedly transported a 20 year-old woman from Youngstown to Farrell, Pennsylvania, just across the state line. Agents reported that "Sandy's henchmen became frightened" when they realized the men who entered the restaurant were federal men. According to the G-men, John Zentko, who was seated in a booth with DiMartino, was "visibly disturbed as the FBI men approached the table but gave an audible sigh of relief" when he realized he was not the man the agents had come for. Patrons in the establishment were seen attempting to hide their faces while others "quickly eased" out of the eatery.

Despite speculation that Sandy Naples was involved in the Valley's policy rackets since the late 1940s, the first real accusation came on February 2, 1952, during a vice crack down by Campbell Police Chief John Putko. The police chief was arresting Campbell gamblers, who had purchased a federal gambling stamp, and ordering them to return the stamps to the government or face being charged with being a known gambler. By early February, Putko's crusade had resulted in the arrest of seven gamblers, all released on $200 bonds to await "known gambler" charges, and caused four tax stamp holders to turn them back over to the government. One of the tax stamp holders arrested was Joseph Frano.[11]

Frano used his allotted telephone call to reach Sandy Naples to ask him to post his bond. When Naples told Frano he didn't generate enough business for him to go through the trouble of bailing him out, the bug pickup man was incensed. Frano told Putko that he averaged $1.75 to $2.00 a day in number slip pickups (Therefore confirming Naples' charge that he wasn't worth the trouble). Frano went on to say that he was making pickups for the past four years, but just recently began dropping them off with Naples at the Center Sandwich Shop and receiving a ten percent commission. After three days in jail, Frano was fined $200 by Campbell Mayor Michael J. Kovach and released.

Frano's revelation caused shock waves in Chief Allen's police department. Lieutenant Dan Maggianetti, who recently succeeded Captain Harold "Dutch" Faust as vice squad chief, was called on the carpet by the chief and told in no uncertain terms that, "if the men we have now can't make arrests, we'll get some more." The irate Allen, upset that his men had failed to make an arrest after Frano's confession, had Naples picked up immediately for questioning and then locked up for further interrogation. Allen told reporters that "Putko's efforts will help breakup this operation that affects both communities. This is the kind of co-operation that is needed to benefit both cities, especially when such statements are testified to in a court of law." Allen emphasized that the hoodlums would not be walking about if there were jail sentences instead of fines for policy convictions.

In arresting Naples, vice squad officers went into the Wilson Avenue restaurant and ripped up floorboards, seat cushions and looked under counters and in closets for lottery slips, but found none. Two doors down from the restaurant, officers encountered and arrested Armando DiMartino, out on bond from his Mann Act arrest, and Mario Centofanti, a 1947 candidate for the Democratic nomination as 2nd Ward councilman. Police found five bug slips on Centofanti.

The next day, Allen had a different story for reporters. "There is no criticism of Lieutenant Dan Maggianetti, chief of the vice squad, and never has been. And from what I know of him there never will be. It was he who commanded the squad when it accomplished the difficult original cleanup job effectively and efficiently. He is one of the best and most industrious officers," the chief proclaimed. Allen pointed out that Maggianetti, who served as vice squad chief from 1948 to 1950, was reassigned to the squad in November 1951. Two-thirds of the 12-man squad were chosen just recently and were still "learning the ropes." As far as Frano's accusation about the Center Sandwich Shop, Allen dispelled reports of the raided restaurant being a bug bank, but instead described it as a pickup station. The chief continued to claim there were currently no policy banks in the city.

With the notoriety Sandy Naples and his Center Sandwich Shop were generating, Chief Allen soon added him to his "hoodlum harassment" campaign as he had done with Aiello and DiCarlo. Sandy was picked up frequently, arrested for "suspicion," and questioned about his bug activity. On June 23, 1952, Naples was awakened at his Poplar Street home by Stephen Bajnok, calling from the restaurant, and told vice squad members were "taking over the place."

During an interview, Naples claimed, "I hurried to the restaurant, and the first thing I know [two vice squad officers] jumped on me and said, 'we are staying here'"

An angry Naples responded, "No, you're not. I'll close the place first."

With that, Naples claimed the officers "called the wagon" and he was taken to jail for refusing to answer questions and was booked on suspicion. At the station, Naples complained about police tactics, declaring that he would rather burn down his shop and go to jail than have the "police department come to my restaurant and bother my good steady customers. They can do anything to me they want, but when they come in and stand behind my counter and push my customers around, they got another thing coming."

The next day, while Sandy was waiting to be arraigned, the two vice officers returned to the Center Sandwich Shop to monitor phone calls and check for "suspected lottery men." Reached at the courthouse, Sandy became enraged after being told by his brother James that the men were answering telephones inside the restaurant. Naples, represented by attorney Samuel S. Fekett, was released after pleading innocent to disturbing the peace and resisting arrest in Judge Cavalier's courtroom (the following week Naples pleaded guilty to the charges and was fined $25). Fekett immediately announced he would seek a court order to prevent members of the vice squad from interfering with Naples' restaurant.

The activities of Allen's vice squad provided "reasonable grounds" for Ohio Bell Telephone officials to remove the pay phone from the Center Sandwich Shop, believing it was being used for gambling purposes. The telephone was listed in "Pinky" Walsh's name. Commenting to reporters on the removal, Chief Allen stated, "The Center Sandwich Shop had become a major sore spot in gambling operations here. It's an information center for gamblers at the very least." Allen used the opportunity to push his agenda for a new city ordinance that would provide jail sentences in addition to fines for those who sold lottery tickets. "I think the operation of this place shows that numbers operators aren't too disturbed about going into court and paying fines – particularly when sometimes not even the maximum fine is imposed," Allen stated. "If city council would pass the gambling ordinance we've requested so often, bug operations would be held to a minimum if not eliminated altogether."

Sandy Naples was brought in for questioning in early August 1952, after the release of the latest list of federal gambling tax stamp purchasers was released. Questioned by Allen, Naples said the purchase of the stamp was "to settle up with the government on past gambling activities." Allen reported that Naples "claims to have told the internal revenue bureau he earned money on betting with various restaurant customers on baseball, basketball and football games," but has now ceased all gambling activity.

Three other men hauled in for questioning with Naples – Peter Fetchet, Joseph J. Beshara and Roosevelt Rivers – all declared that they had left the gambling business. Beshara was arrested as recently as June 5 for possession of policy slips.

Four days later, both Naples and Peter Fetchet were arrested on the charge of "being a known gambler." Naples was nabbed at the Center Sandwich Shop and released on a $100 bond just 20 minutes after he was charged before Judge Cavalier. The newspaper reported, "Under the city ordinance, a person found guilty is subject to a fine of $50 and costs and a 30-day jail sentence. A person arrested on the same charge more than once can be sentenced to a year in jail and fined $50 and costs.

While awaiting trial on the "known gambler" charge, Naples was arrested with James Corsell on September 4. Corsell, just 19 years old, was described as a henchman of Naples. He was picked up for suspicion over a year earlier when Naples and Walsh were arrested in Niles. During the summer of 1952, Corsell pled guilty to possession of lottery slips and was fined $100; was fined $200 on a similar offense; and was arrested for reckless driving as he tried to escape from two vice squad officers who wanted to question him. The latest incident got underway when vice squad officers received a report of a man handling lottery pickups on Arlington Street. Staking out the area, they spotted Corsell entering a home. Apparently Corsell had spotted the officers at the same time and called Sandy. When Naples arrived Corsell ran from the home and jumped in Naples' automobile as it pulled to the curb. At arraignment Corsell was charged with being a "known gambler" before Judge John Powers.

Despite the fact that no policy slips were found in either Naples or Corsell's automobiles, the newspaper reported for the third time that Sandy "is definitely connected with 'bug' operations in the city." Chief Allen was quoted; "Naples can no longer continue the fiction that he is not mixed up in the numbers racket. Any attempt to do so brands him as a public liar, among other things, after he personally tried to assist one of his pick-up stooges to get away from the vice squad."

When Naples' December 16 date for the "known gambler" trial was "indefinitely delayed" by Judge Cavalier, Allen became irate and lashed out calling it the "same old familiar pattern of postponement and delay." The chief's comments were taken as a personal affront by Cavalier, who was quick to respond in a written statement. Cavalier wrote that if Chief Allen had:

> "Accorded this court the courtesy of a call before criticizing me for the continuance of the Joseph 'Sandy' Naples case, I would have been glad to give him the reason for the continuance.
>
> "On December 8 the prosecutor brought into my office a copy of a demurrer and brief filed by Clyde W. Osborne Sr.,[12] counsel for the defendant, attacking the

legality of the ordinance under which the defendant was charged.

"Since the demurrer raised important legal and constitutional questions, the prosecutor's office desired an opportunity of preparing and filing an answer brief and it was at their suggestion that the case was continued.

"This court is interested in the speedy disposal of all cases and of course is opposed to dragging out litigation."

The principals in the case held a hearing on December 30. Judges John Powers and Cavalier listened to arguments from a defense team comprised of Clyde Osborne, Martin P. Joyce and John Hooker and the prosecution team consisting of Henry Fugett and Assistant City Law Director Richard Schumann. Attorney Osborne argued that Youngstown's gambling ordinance was invalid because the section charging a defendant with being a known gambler does "not specify the elements describing the crime committed. Under this law a once-a-week poker player might possibly be described as a known gambler."

Fugett and Schumann responded by pointing out that a similar case, tried in Cincinnati, was held valid by the Ohio Supreme Court, which ruled it was not necessary to prove any specific acts of gambling.

On January 6, 1953, both judges upheld the constitutionality of the city's known gambler ordinance. They cited the previous conviction of "Fats" Aiello on the city's "suspicious person" ordinance, which had gone to the Ohio Supreme Court, as their case law.

In an expose article, the *Vindicator* reported on January 18, 1953:

"Bug Racket Seen Making Return Try"

The article pointed out that Naples and a store employee were seen taking numbers over the telephone and from two runners in "plain view" of patrons inside the restaurant. This was in contrast to the action at Kissos Confectionery where the numbers player "would be taken behind a partition next to the lunch counter to transact his business." In addition to Naples, only two other men were mentioned – Charles Cavallaro and Robert Owens. The article didn't mention the reason for the comeback of the "bug."

Two weeks after the expose appeared, and a week before Sandy Naples' trial was scheduled to begin, the vice squad raided the Center Sandwich Shop. At noon on February 2, Sergeant Clayton Geise and the vice entire squad, several dressed in street clothes, surrounded the Wilson Avenue eatery and moved in. They seized "200 bug slips, 75 Treasury pool tickets, a dozen turn-in bags with coded names, two large rolls of Treasury pool result sheets and $10 in cash." Two officers found the bug slips and paraphernalia in a false panel in a cellar stairwell. Arrested at the scene were Sandy and Joey Naples, Stephen Bajnok, John and Ben Salvatore, Donald Davidson and James Cataland. Commenting on the raid, Lieutenant Maggianetti stated, "This raid is a culmination of more than two months of serious planning, based on the theory 'give the punks enough rope and they'll hang themselves.'"

The next day, in Judge Robert Nevin's courtroom, Sandy Naples was charged with possession of lottery slips, keeping a building and room used for gambling, and renting a place to be used for gambling. Ben Salvatore of Campbell was charged with possession of lottery slips and keeping a room where gambling is permitted. Both men pleaded not guilty and were released on a $1,000 bond. The other men were released.

On February 19, Naples went into court asking for a delay in his known gambler trial due to recent articles about the raid and his latest arrest. In his motion, Naples claimed stories that appeared in the *Vindicator* "may have such an effect as to prejudice some or all of the jurors selected to hear the case." Naples also declared he "has no connection" with the Center Sandwich Shop, which he said was owned by his brother James. Five days later, Naples entered the municipal court and pled guilty to being a known gambler before Judge Cavalier. The judge suspended a 30-day sentence and fined him $50 and costs. Cavalier told Naples, "Since it is the first offense on this particular kind of charge, the law is interested in correcting any future conduct of the defendant, and I therefore place you on probation for six months and warn you that any violation during this period will bring you before me and the 30 days will be placed in effect."

According to the newspaper, Chief Allen "voiced vigorous objection to the leniency shown Naples:

> "'When this type of verdict is given to an arrogant, long-time racketeer, it makes it undeniably clear why certain racketeers still continue to operate in Youngstown,' Allen declared.
>
> "'The police department,' the chief added, 'spent a lot of time and expense in getting Naples to court, and the net result to the citizens of Youngstown is nil. The fact that Naples entered a plea of guilty shows the vice squad did an efficient job. If the police department is to get the blame for everything that happens in Youngstown along the line of crime, let's put the blame in the Naples' verdict where it belongs.'"

Again, Judge Cavalier responded to Chief Allen's accusations in a written statement to the *Vindicator* on February 25, 1953:

> "I am loathe to engage in a newspaper controversy concerning the disposition of cases which appear before me. I am sure the dignity of the court is not enhanced by such practice. However, in view of the extremely grave charges of Chief Allen impugning the motives of the court in the disposition of the 'Sandy' Naples case, I have no choice other than to issue this clarifying statement.
>
> "I, of course, assume full responsibility for the sentence given to the defendant, Naples. The defendant had been charged with being a 'known gambler.' The

> maximum sentence allowed under this charge in our city ordinance is $50 and costs and 30 days in the city jail. The court sentenced the defendant to the maximum. The days were suspended and the defendant placed on probation upon the request of the attorney for the prosecution, who was the representative of the city and the chief in the case. Since this was the defendant's first offense on this charge the recommendation of the prosecution was adopted.
>
> "However, the probation given the defendant is, in some respects more severe than the actual days would have been, since any subsequent offense by the defendant during the period of probation will result in immediate imposition of the 30-day sentence, plus the severer sentence which would be allowable under a second offense.
>
> "I trust the press will accord prominence to this clarifying statement equal to that accorded the charges of the chief of police."

Judge Cavalier's revelations touched off a controversy at City Hall. The *Vindicator* reported, "Witnesses at the pre-hearing conference in the judge's chambers differed on what Schumann might have said in regard to probation. All agreed there was some discussion of leniency, between counsel for Naples and Schumann. The discussion was brief and reports vary on exactly what was said."

Schumann said there was talk of probation for Naples at the pre-hearing conference, but denied making any recommendation. He claimed that Naples' guilty plea "came as a complete surprise to him because he understood the racketeer was going to fight the 'known gambler' charge and the possible jail sentence it carried." The newspaper also reported, "One observer who attended the conference in the judge's chambers said he believed the judge may have *interpreted* Schumann's remarks with Naples' attorneys as a recommendation for a suspended jail sentence."

When questioned by reporters about the pre-trial hearing, attorney Osborne quoted Schumann as saying, "Well, supposing we suspend the jail sentence," Osborne claimed this came after his announcement to the group that Naples would plead guilty. Osborne said he then asked that "consideration be shown," because the plea was saving the city the expense of having to prosecute the case.

When called before Mayor Henderson and asked if he had given his passive consent to leniency, Schumann replied, "I did." Henderson later told reporters he did not want to comment on the controversy.

While certainly disappointed that Naples was not going to jail, Chief Allen had a card up his sleeve. Back on February 6, an undercover rookie patrolman, Angelo Peruzzi, entered the Center Sandwich Shop and was sold two lottery slips by Naples. Allen would later say that Naples was not charged immediately "because police were busy with other phases" of the Naples case. On February 26, just two days after being handed probation and a $50 fine, Naples was arrested on a warrant sworn out by Lieutenant Maggianetti. The head of the vice squad announced that Naples was being charged with a violation of the state law, which carried a $500 fine and a six-month jail sentence for first offense and a $1,000 fine and a jail term of one-to-three years for a second offense. The newspaper disclosed the state law was "seldom used...because most 'bug' counts are based on possession rather than selling of slips."

After his arrest Naples was allowed to post a $1,000 bond. He was in jail for less than half an hour. The next day he was arraigned and pleaded not guilty before Judge Nevin. On March 5, Naples' defense attorney made the usual delaying tactic of asking for a trial by jury. Sandy was now facing two trials – the one for his February 2 arrest during a Center Sandwich Shop raid was still pending. On March 30, on the advice of attorney John Hooker, Naples pled guilty to the state charge of selling a lottery ticket to Officer Peruzzi. Naples was handed a 90-day jail term and fined $500 by Judge Nevin. In the plea bargain, the charges from the February 2 raid were dropped at the request of Maggianetti, who asked for the dismissal due to "lack of evidence." At the same time, Ben Salvatore was fined $500 after he pled guilty to possession of policy slips. Additional charges against him were also dismissed at the request of the vice squad. After the fine was levied, Salvatore "strolled" over to the clerk of courts, pulled a roll of bills from his pocket, and peeled off 50 ten dollar bills. Nevin allowed Naples 24 hours "to complete his personal business."

On April 1, 1953, Sandy began his 90-day sentence in the county jail. For the first 45 days, his brother Billy was a fellow inmate. On April 25, after complaining of stomach pain, Naples was ordered taken to the hospital by Mahoning County Physician Dr. William Welch. At North Side Hospital, Naples was diagnosed with kidney stones and treated. Five days later, after being returned to the county jail, Sheriff Paul Langley announced x-rays showed Naples was suffering from a stomach ulcer.

In mid-May, Dr. Welch wrote to Judge Nevin and advised him of Naples' condition, claiming the prisoner needed "special diet, medication and rest." He suggested to Nevin that Naples be sent "home for the duration of his sentence and if he is found in the streets or in his place of business have police pick him up and return him to jail to suffer his ulcer pains and discomfort." Nevin denied the suggestion and advised Sheriff Langley, "because of Naples' ulcer, you have my permission to permit Mr. Naples, at his own expense, to have proper dietary food sent in to him at county jail."

On June 15, with fourteen days left on his sentence, Judge Nevin released Naples "because he is in ill health and because it is customary to shorten sentences for good behavior." Nevin placed Naples on parole for one year and declared that if he were found in violation he would be returned to jail to serve out the remainder of his sentence.

Just days after the administration of Mayor Henderson and Chief Allen ended, newly appointed police chief Paul Cress rounded up several of the Valley's top mobsters for questioning. On January 7, 1954, "Fats" Aiello, Sandy Naples, Charles Cavallaro and Vince DeNiro had individual meetings with Cress in which they were told that Youngstown would not be "opening up."

It was around this time that Paul R. Van Such, the Campbell solicitor and an ardent vice crusader, helped close down the "wide open" city of Campbell after conducting a thorough investigation of that town's gambling activity. His probe brought out that Naples and DeNiro were "in control" of the Valley's bug rackets and that Naples was considered the "head man."

Van Such's allegations were seconded on February 13, when it was announced that, "The federal government today named S. Joseph (Sandy) Naples and Vincent J. DeNiro reputed bosses of the numbers racket in Youngstown, as 'principal' operators of gambling businesses." The *Vindicator* revealed that, "Their federal rating as 'principals' was disclosed in a list of current holders of federal gambling stamps."

On March 11, 1954, vice squad chief George Krispli had a meeting with Mayor Kryzan "to discuss rumors that the city's vice squad is not doing a thorough job in cleaning up bug activity." After the meeting, it was reported by the *Vindicator* that, "Rumors that Krispli may have been asked to explain to the mayor are that vice squad men have been taking direct orders from several big racketeers who control certain sections of the city; that several vice squad men have been 'looking the other way' at times and that only small time operators have been arrested." Krispli denied the rumors and told reporters that he and his men have done everything possible to "kill bug operators."

By the end of March, rumors were leaked to the media that members of the vice squad were on the payrolls of DeNiro and Naples. Chief Cress commented, "You can count on the fingers of one hand the policemen who would be taking a buck and God help them if I find out about it." The chief believed the rumors were actually started by the gamblers themselves in an effort to get Cress to shake up the vice squad because the members couldn't be bribed. Cress stated, "The game was pretty well broken up when we took office and we will keep it that way." It should be noted that five months later, during a speech by Kryzan, the mayor cited a different state of affairs. He told reporters "we have made progress but everybody must remember that the major problem in law enforcement when we took over was the flourishing numbers rackets here." The mayor was responding to comments about the police department and his chief. Kryzan denied that Cress was on his way out and blamed those rumors, as the chief did about the vice squad, as being spread by the gamblers. The mayor claimed that DeNiro was the biggest bug operator, but "we'll get him." Kryzan closed with, "It is unfortunate that we have to devote so much time in the [police] department to eliminating this phase of vice. There are other phases we want to attack, including dope peddling. But we have to spend so much time fighting the bug that we are weakened on other fronts."

Just hours after the March 11 meeting between Krispli and the mayor, a formal request was made to have the telephone service at the Center Sandwich Shop disconnected. A notice was sent to Sandy Naples from Ohio Bell Telephone stating the telephone would be cut off on the third business day after the mailing of the notification unless court action was initiated restraining the phone company from doing so.

Judge Harold Doyle granted a temporary restraining order on March 15 after a lawsuit was filed by "Pinky" Walsh and James Naples, who claimed they were the actual operators of the restaurant. In the petition the men declared the telephone had not "been used by the plaintiffs or any other persons in connection with and in the furtherance of gambling operations nor – for any unlawful or illegal purpose." Removal of the telephone would "deprive them of the lawful use of a public utility," and since the removal of the pay phone by Chief Allen in 1952, leave them with no telephone in which to conduct normal business matters.

Two days after the restraining order was issued, James Naples was back in the news. On St. Patrick's Day a police officer stopped Naples' automobile on a South Side street. During a cursory search of the car the officer found policy slips in the glove compartment. James responded by speeding off. Three hours later, after having had time to discuss the situation with Sandy, James surrendered to police at the city jail. He was booked on charges of unlawful possession of lottery slips and reckless driving. Held overnight, he pled innocent to both counts at arraignment the next day and was released on a $1,000 bond by Judge Franko.

An hour after James' release, Sandy appeared at police headquarters after being asked to come down to speak to George Krispli. James claimed the slips belonged to Sandy and he was taking them home for his brother when he was stopped. Krispli wanted to get Sandy's side of the story. "Sure, the slips belong to me," Sandy confessed. "The kid was doing me a favor and for that he winds up in jail. He has never been in trouble with the police before. This is the first time." On March 30, James was fined $500 after pleading guilty to possessing lottery slips. Three days later, he was fined $50 for reckless driving for fleeing a police officer and had his license suspended for 90 days.

About 12 hours after James pled guilty to reckless driving, vice squad detectives arrested Sandy. Based on James' guilty plea to possessing lottery tickets owned by his brother they charged Sandy with, "being the unlawful depositary of slips used in the process of gambling." James would be the prosecution's key witness against his brother. The prosecution simply believed that James would repeat his story on the witness stand. Sandy was bonded out later that night and the next morning was arraigned and pled innocent before Judge Franko. Krispli eagerly told reporters that the citation charging Sandy as the "depositary" identified him as "the man the slips actually belong to – the ring leader of the bug outfit."

At a hearing on April 15, Naples' counsel, attorney S. S. Fekett, told Judge Franko he needed additional time to prepare his case. Franko granted him until April 20. On the day the trial was to begin Sandy revealed that James Naples had left for Florida and would be away for six months. With the key witness gone Prosecutor Irwin I. Kretzer asked Franko to issue a bench warrant for James' arrest, even though the city had no jurisdiction outside of Ohio. Kretzer also asked for a delay until April 29 to begin the trial.

Naples and Fekett both balked at the request for a delay. Sandy, who in the past was always looking to have his court cases delayed, cried, "I want to go to trial today and not on April 29." Fekett informed the court that he was "sailing for Europe May 1 and wants the case disposed of by then." Kretzer was clearly annoyed at the turn of events. He claimed if Sandy were convicted there would be more in store for him than just the $500 fine. The prosecutor pointed out that Naples was still on probation from his 1953 gambling conviction and still had 14 days to serve on that sentence.

On April 29, Franko granted the prosecution an additional two-week postponement to find James Naples. At this time Kretzer said he would jail James to assure his presence at the trial and if the case were dismissed, he would jail him for contempt when he did reappear. During the hearing, Assistant Prosecutor Donald Hanni contended that a "conspiracy" might exist between James and defense attorneys. This allegation brought Fekett and co-counsel Mock to their feet in protest. Hanni claimed that Fekett was heard to say he could get in touch with James "with one call at any time." Fekett reminded Hanni that anything defense counsel said outside of the courtroom was "inadmissible as evidence." Sandy Naples called the accusation a "lot of bull" and threatened to punch Hanni, if he could "catch him before he left the courtroom."

The day after the raucous hearing, Judge Harold Doyle granted a motion to dissolve the temporary injunction against the removal of the telephone from the Center Sandwich Shop by Ohio Bell. One week later, on May 6, Sandy Naples and Vince DeNiro sat in a booth at the restaurant and sipped coffee as Ohio Bell Telephone workers removed a telephone from behind the counter at the front of the restaurant and an extension from an office in the back. Naples, who claimed, "I'd be crazy to use it for gambling after all this publicity," decided not to fight the matter in court because he believed it would turn into a lengthy battle. In September, Ohio Bell officials would return to disconnect a "bootleg" phone hookup.

On May 13, Judge Franko ordered prosecutors Kretzer and Hanni to proceed with their case declaring the city had sufficient time to produce their key witness – James Naples. When the two prosecutors informed the judge they could not proceed, Franko dismissed the case. Kretzer promised he would reopen it when James was apprehended. As soon as Naples "shows his face in the city, we will have him picked up on a warrant and hold him on bond as a material witness."

Two weeks later, after police were alerted that James had returned, they summoned him to appear at police headquarters. On May 28, James Naples walked into vice squad chief Krispli's office and announced he was back from vacation, and claimed his absence from the city was not an effort to prevent him from testifying against his brother. Within the hour Sandy was arrested at the family home on Poplar Street. Pleading not guilty before Judge Cavalier he was released on a $1,000 bond. Once outside the courtroom, Sandy confidently stated, "I don't have a lawyer yet, but even I can see that this is a plain case of double jeopardy."

Youngstown Law Director Felix Mika reported, "We knew that Sandy's younger brother, James Naples, was back in town for several days, but we didn't call him in until we had carefully checked the law on double jeopardy." Obviously "double jeopardy" was on everyone's mind – Sandy Naples', the prosecutors and the *Vindicator*, which reminded its readers that, "Federal and state constitutions guarantee that a person may not be tried more than once for any alleged offense." Felix Mika, in a *Vindicator* interview, pointed out the city's position:

> "'The rule doesn't apply in this case because of two reasons,' Mika said. 'First, the original prosecution was under the city ordinance, while this one is under the state law. The courts have held that a person may be tried more than once for a crime if the same act violated laws of different sovereignties. Prosecution under the laws of the city thus would not bar prosecution under the state laws.'
>
> "'Secondly, there was no jeopardy at all under the first case, because the city never got to present its case against Sandy,' Mika said.'"

Mika also pointed out that the case would be tried before Judge Cavalier instead of Nevin after the latter disqualified himself because he was one of those who heard Sandy Naples admit that the lottery slips found in the possession of his brother belonged to him. Therefore, he could be called as a witness in the case.

Before the trial got underway it was brother Billy who popped into the headlines in an embarrassing moment involving the police department. Back in January, Billy and Joey were in Billy's Cadillac taking care of lottery business when police spotted them and gave chase. During a wild chase on the city's North Side, Joey pitched a handful of bug tickets out the window before Billy, thinking they were in the clear, ended the episode. The two were arrested and while Joey was convicted and fined $613 for possession of lottery tickets, which the police recovered, Billy was fined $25 for reckless driving and had his license suspended for six months. In handing down the sentence Judge Nevin warned Billy that if he were caught driving during this period he would face a maximum of $500 and be sent to jail for six months.

Billy apparently heeded the judge's warning even to the extent of requesting police assistance in his travels. On May 28, 1954, Billy was looking at new 1954 Cadillacs at Barrett Cadillac Company perhaps in anticipation of celebrating the end of his driving suspension. His automobile shopping completed, Billy spotted Youngstown Police Sergeant Alonzo Wilson. Billy asked the sergeant for a ride from the car dealership on Wick Avenue to the Hotel Pick-Ohio. Wilson obliged and the misguided "servant of the people" delivered Billy downtown. Much to the chagrin of the accommodating sergeant, Chief Cress witnessed the deed and suspended Wilson for a week for "permitting a non-member of the police department to ride in a police cruiser."

Sandy's trial got underway on Thursday, July 1, 1954. A jury trial was waived and Judge Cavalier heard the case. Twenty minutes into the trial, defense counsel asked for a dismissal on the grounds of double jeopardy. Kretzer argued that double jeopardy didn't apply due to the fact that this case was now being tried under state code. He then stated "the law provides that no claim of double jeopardy can be made on a plea of not guilty and that when Naples was arraigned May 27 on the second charge he entered a plea of not guilty, thereby waiving all rights to double jeopardy." Cavalier adjourned the court to study law covering the double jeopardy clause. When he returned Cavalier ruled against the defense.

The prosecution's case centered on Sandy's statement that the policy slips found in the possession of his brother belonged to him. Vice squad chief Krispli and John R. "Jack" Gates, the police reporter for the *Vindicator*, testified that Sandy stated in the vice squad office, "The slips belong to me." When James Naples was called to the stand he denied his previous statement and now claimed that the slips belonged to him. Hanni told the court that James' testimony came as a complete surprise to the prosecution. He asked that a statement by James be read to "refresh" his memory, but Cavalier denied the request ruling that it had not been made in Sandy's presence.

Sandy was in a feisty mood on the first afternoon of the trial. His attitude in court was similar to the style that John Gotti employed in New York City courts some thirty-plus years later. The newspaper reported, "Hanni complained to the court that Sandy has threatened retaliation. He said Sandy leaned across the table in the courtroom 'and said he was going to take care of me after the trial.'" Sandy could also be heard complaining to his attorney, Clyde Osborne, or anyone else within hearing distance for that matter, he was being tried in a "kangaroo court." The *Vindicator* provided the following description of the "Dapper Don" – the Youngstown version:

> "From the top of his curly head to the tips of his pointed shoes, the debonair Sandy presented a picture of snappy sartorial splendor as witnesses answered (or ducked) questions in the court of Municipal Judge Forrest J. Cavalier.
>
> "Naples demonstrated to the satisfaction of all that he is no man to take a rap

> – bum or not – sitting down. On frequent occasions he was on his feet, breathing down the neck of his defense counsel or engaging in undertone soliloquies on the nature of the testimony.
>
> "His fascinated audience – swelled by many hangers-on – was nearly blinded by sunlit reflections from a diamond-encrusted wrist watch worn by the defendant. It appeared to contain enough separate stones to provide respectable engagement rings for all the eligible females of a medium-sized community. Sandy said it cost $5,000.
>
> "Sandy may, in his lifetime, be accused of many things. He can never be charged with being inconspicuous."

Before the start of the Friday morning session, Judge Cavalier warned Sandy that any additional comments would result in a contempt of court charge. James Naples was then recalled to the stand. Hoping that the threat of a perjury charge would jar his memory, he was questioned again about his statement that the slips belonged to his brother. James replied, "I don't remember. Sorry."

When Sergeant Clayton Geise, a former vice squad member, took the stand he described how the numbers rackets operated. This caused Sandy to respond, "That jerk don't know what he is talking about. If I had to carry on business the way he described it, I would never make a nickel in the business." That remark, and others made by the arrogant Naples, returned to haunt him as both Assistant Prosecutors Hanni and John Leskovyansky took the witness stand and testified about statements made by Sandy at the defense table.

One part of the prosecution's case was to prove that Sandy was a "numbers ring leader." The prosecutors subpoenaed 14 convicted "bug men" in hopes of showing that they were working for Naples. The men weren't much help. George Battle, who had received $1,260 in wages in 1953, told the court, "I got paid but I don't know where it came from." When a withholding tax statement was introduced, Battle claimed a "mysterious stranger" filed his income tax. He then denied he had ever conducted business with Sandy and that the money he received from being a pickup man was paid to him by someone he didn't know." As the bug men were being sworn in, Sandy would turn to the prosecution table and say, "I don't know why you called him. He's not one of my boys." Every witness called denied being in business or working for Sandy. When the witness was asked if they knew the defendant, Sandy would stand up and listen intently while they each repeated, "I never saw Sandy before."

Before court ended on Friday, the prosecution "hinted" that they had a surprise they would spring when the trial convened on Tuesday after the Independence Day holiday. The surprise was a plan to recall James Naples. A subpoena was issued on Monday to insure his appearance. On Tuesday, however, the surprise was on the prosecutors – James had pulled another disappearing act.

Tuesday morning's session was dominated by bug men and one bug woman, whom the newspaper reported, hinted at mysterious 'higher-ups' behind the district's numbers operation but refused to tie Sandy with the racket." The three men who testified were well-known and "oft-arrested" policy people – Sam Zappi, Anthony "Booze" Gianfrancesco, and Alfred Catoline, the latter a DeNiro relative. While all admitted that their "racket bosses paid their court costs and fines" they had no idea who these individuals were.

Described as the "most defiant" of the witnesses, Gianfrancesco chewed gum while answering prosecutor's questions. He admitted to being arrested "five, six or seven times," but when asked who paid the fines, he responded, "I don't know. Someone handed me an envelope with the right amount to pay the fines and costs and I went over and paid." Gianfrancesco said he didn't know who handed him the envelope, "A couple of times it was a woman, a couple of times it was a fellow."

On July 7, Judge Cavalier continued the trial for a day to allow law enforcement to track down James Naples. Police received a tip that he and his family had gone to Geneva-on-the-Lake, located along the shore of Lake Erie between Cleveland and the Pennsylvania border. Two vice-squad officers with a subpoena were sent to find him. The officers were unable to locate Naples and on Thursday morning the trial resumed and the final prosecution witness took the stand.

Mrs. Millicent Brooks seemed to hurt the city's case more than help it. She testified that when she was arrested three years earlier, Vince DeNiro paid her $500 fine. When asked if she was working for DeNiro, she replied, "No," that a man named "Jimmy" was the pickup man who stopped at the poolroom / confectionery she and her husband ran on West Federal Street. Brooks stated that numbers were written at their place "until three months ago and that Jimmy picked up the numbers daily in his big white-looking Cadillac." She concluded her testimony by claiming she never saw the defendant, Sandy.

Closing arguments were delivered on Thursday afternoon. Hanni began first and told Cavalier that he must decide, "Was James Naples promoting the game? If the court answers in the affirmative it should find Sandy guilty as charged." State law "provides that any person who aids, abets or procures another to commit an offense must be prosecuted and punished as if he were the offender."

Hanni stated that Sandy had failed to testify on his own behalf to deny the accusations against him, and that "he has admitted he does employ pickup men." Hanni was referring to the comments Naples whispered to the prosecutors' table during the trial. Hanni concluded, "We are not dealing with any ordinary pickup man but with one who had the audacity to tell police he had procured another man to commit a crime and practically defied police to do anything about it."

During Osborne's closing statement he asked, "What has Sandy failed to testify about? He hasn't denied he said those slips were his or that 'only two of those boys [the bug men who testified] are mine.'" Osborne explained away Sandy's statement to prosecutors by claiming the defendant was referring to the fact that they were restaurant employees who worked at the Center Sandwich Shop as "dishwashers, waiters or cleanup men – not numbers men."

Asking the judge to set aside inferences, Osborne stated, "What do you have left? Nothing but statements by Sandy Naples in front of Jack Gates...that 'those are my slips.'" The attorney argued that James Naples, based on prosecution witness testimony, could have been taking the slips to the DeNiro bank. Osborne emphatically stated that the prosecutors had failed to prove Sandy was operating a numbers game.

Osborne, nodding toward his client, concluded, "We know he is one of those fellows who doesn't work in the mill, paint houses, practice law or preach in a pulpit. Still, he shouldn't be convicted unless evidence points directly as guilty under the charges as made here. I don't expect you to convict upon implication and inference. There is no evidence of any connection between Jim and Sandy in a business transaction. And the fact that somebody had slips in his possession does not constitute running a bank."

Prosecutor Kretzer's closing rebuttal was an impassioned one. In urging Cavalier to convict Naples for "procuring another to commit a crime," Kretzer declared, "The eyes of all the good citizens are on you, hoping and praying you have the courage to stop this racket which is the forerunner of all crimes. You will be telling hoodlums to stay away from Youngstown."

When Judge Cavalier reached his decision on July 15, it was Sandy Naples' own remarks that had done him in. In announcing his guilty ruling, Cavalier cited Naples remark made during Sergeant Giese' testimony as one of the factors. The judge wrote that Sandy's comment "proved inescapably that the defendant was referring to his numbers business." This along with Naples' admitted ownership of the policy slips found in his brother's possession; the fact that he did not take the stand to contradict prosecutor's accusations; and because he was the purchaser of a federal gambling tax stamp made it "apparent that the defendant was unlawfully promoting and carrying on" a numbers operation.

Osborne immediately requested a new trial and Cavalier held off sentencing Naples until he ruled on the attorney's motion. On July 21, Cavalier denied defense counsel's request for a new trial. The next day the judge sentenced Naples to six months in the county jail and fined him $500. He delayed the execution of the sentence pending appeals by Sandy's defense counsel.

In a strange editorial, which appeared in the *Vindicator* on July 24, the newspaper complimented the "good work" and "ingenuity" of prosecutors in the Naples' case, but did not mention one person on the three-man prosecution team.

As the appeals process dragged into the next year, Naples made news again on March 14, 1955, when he interfered with another raid on the Center Sandwich Shop. Police received a tip that the restaurant was again being used as a bug bank. Officers "took over" the restaurant around 2:30 in the afternoon and were refused access to a drawer behind the counter by Naples. Sandy was adamant, declaring that he'd rather be "taken down to headquarters than open that drawer for you guys." Police accommodated his request and he was jailed for two hours and grilled by Chief Cress.

While in the neighborhood, the police also stopped and searched a club down the street from the Center Sandwich Shop. At the Copa Club, at 1214 Wilson Avenue, Naples was reported to be in a partnership with Nick Constantino. Described as a "one-time Campbell racket figure," Constantino once ran the Club Merry-Go-Round on Salt Spring Road, which had federal tax liens of over $30,000 filed against it when it was forced to close in February 1953. The Copa Club had had gained a notorious reputation since it opened in September 1954. Previously known as the Colony Club, the nightclub was watched by vice squad members for gambling operations and by federal narcotics agents for drug activity. The *Vindicator* wrote, "This atmosphere of police suspicion clashed with the plush cabaret atmosphere the operators tried to create, including hiring of 'big-time' entertainers." The only "big-time" attraction the newspaper listed was Denise Darcel,[13] a "Hollywood actress" who appeared at the club for a week during its second month in business. In early June 1955, vice squad chief Krispli reported the Copa Club had closed and that the owners reportedly lost $38,000.

Meanwhile, the Center Sandwich Shop was having ownership problems too. In the midst of Sandy's July 1954 gambling trial, Mary Walsh, the wife of "Pinky" Walsh filed a civil law suit to partition the jointly owned property on which the restaurant stood. Representing Mary Walsh was former Municipal Judge John W. Powers. The Center Amusement Company was split into thirds with Mary Walsh owning one-third; James Naples and his wife Irene another; and the last third owned by Sandy Naples, "Pinky" Walsh and Joseph Alexander. The *Vindicator* tried to determine the cause of the suit. They reported:

> "There are rumors of discontent in Sandy's camp, based on Sandy's too-frequent bouts with the law in recent months and Vince DeNiro's ascension to the No. 1 spot in the racket underworld. But Mrs. Walsh reports everyone is 'buddy-buddy.'
>
> "'The partnership is still in effect so far as I know and Pinky and Sandy are not on the outs – not that I know of,' Mrs. Walsh explained.
>
> "Pinky said he isn't happy with the current arrangement.
>
> "'I am tired of being an inactive partner,' he said. 'I haven't received anything from the shop since it opened.'
>
> "And Sandy's trouble with the police is reported to be bothering Pinky, who has had a few scrapes with the law himself.
>
> "'Every time Sandy opened his mouth he got in trouble,' Pinky declared."

While it appeared to some that there might have been a parting of the ways between Naples and Walsh, others didn't see it that way. Many believed that the Center Sandwich Shop had become "too hot" for the gang to continue to run their numbers operation due to the scrutiny of the vice squad. One unnamed observer stated, "It just isn't good business to have so many cops coming in and out of the place." The newspaper said bluntly and rightfully so, "Sandy's operations have kept the Wilson Avenue property in the headlines for many years, and at times his dealings have been so open that even a policeman could play the bug there."

Two months after the closing of the Copa Club it was reported that the Center Sandwich Shop would be sold at a sheriff's auction. In an August 11 article the newspaper wrote," The lawsuit was filed by Walsh's wife, Mary, more than a year ago, and during the entire time it has been pending, the defendants, including Sandy Naples, have failed to file briefs. So far as it is known, they have no attorney in the case. The failure to file briefs outlining their stand is seen as an aversion to airing the restaurant's business in the courts."

A week after the announcement of the sheriff's auction, Mary Walsh dropped the suit only to re-instate the action in September. Her reversals must have prompted Sandy to action because by October it was announced that a settlement was reached and the case was dismissed in Common Pleas Court.

On October 14, 1955, more than 15 months after Naples was found guilty of gambling charges, Common Pleas Judge Harry Doyle upheld Judge Cavalier's Municipal Court conviction. Attorneys quickly prepared a motion for the Seventh District Court of Appeals – and the process dragged on.

A political bombshell went off in the Valley on February 11, 1956, when Assistant City Prosecutor Donald Hanni claimed he was fired for his refusal to shield Sandy Naples and other racketeers from certain jail time and for not backing certain political candidates supported by Democratic leaders. In a prepared statement released to the media, Hanni claimed:

> "My first break with the Kryzan administration and Jack Sulligan occurred when I prosecuted Sandy Naples. Both Sulligan and Felix Mika approached me and Irwin I. Kretzer and asked that I take it easy on Naples.
>
> "I informed them both that when I tried a lawsuit I was out to win.
>
> "My second run-in came when Mika and Sulligan again approached me and asked me to reduce the charges against [Peter] Fetchet and [Steve] Kilame[14] from a state numbers charge to a city charge, the reason being that the state charge carries a jail sentence and the city charge does not. Kretzer was approached on that also.
>
> "When both Kretzer and I refused to make such a recommendation, Mika went personally to Judge Nevin and asked him to reduce the charge or suspend the jail sentences. Of course Nevin refused.
>
> "More recently Felix Mika called me in and told me that if I insisted on supporting Franko for county prosecutor that he was going to request that the mayor fire me.
>
> "The grand climax came in filling the 4th Ward vacancy in Council. When I refused to pressure [Thomas W.] Caldron, the councilman in my ward, into vot-

ing for Sulligan's choice the mayor said that 'this was the last straw' and said he would have to ask me to resign, emphasizing that he was strictly a party man and down the line with Jack Sulligan. Of course I refused to resign.

"Mayor Kryzan called me at 9:30am Friday and I again repeated my decision ... that I would not resign. In a few minutes his secretary appeared in my office and handed me a letter from the mayor which, in effect, was my discharge. Within minutes after that the mayor phoned Kretzer and told him that I was to be given half an hour to clean out my desk and vacate the premises."

The following responses came from people who were asked to comment about Hanni's statement:

Mayor Kryzan: I wouldn't dignify them [Hanni's comments] with an answer. The sour grapes reveal Hanni's true character.

Law Director Mika: I do not care to answer the wild rantings of a disgruntled employee who didn't know how to behave decently.

Democratic County Chairman Sulligan: I don't even know what he's talking about.

City Prosecutor Kretzer: As long as I've been in office nobody ever told me to take it easy on anyone and I wouldn't if anyone did.

While downplaying Hanni's accusations, Judge Nevin did admit that he was approached by Mika to "discuss the possibility" of reducing the charges against Fetchet and Kilame, but he refused.

On March 27, attorney Martin P. Joyce was appointed by Mayor Kryzan to replace Hanni. It was an ironic choice because Joyce had recently been hired by Sandy Naples to file the motion with the 7th District Court of Appeals on his gambling conviction. In accepting the position, Joyce had to withdraw from the Naples case as well as from all other criminal cases he was handling. This only helped to drag the appeals process further along.

During the fall of 1956, Sandy Naples was identified as one of two football pool sellers who were having success in the Valley. Naples' "Sport" pool sheets were in competition with a group called the "Brier Hill mob" who produced the "Kick Off" pool sheet. The sheets, which had all the teams listed, had printed at the bottom, "News information Only. Not to be used in violation of any law." Early in the season some sellers found themselves faced with padlock action by the city. These bookmakers quickly restricted their business to known customers.

With the success of Naples' gambling operations, he decided in October 1956 to move his family from the Poplar Street dwelling into what the newspaper described as a "beautiful ranch house in one of the North Side's most fashionable residential sections." The new home at 605 Carlotta Drive was being built at the cost of $30,000 (others believed the cost of the home, to which the building permit was issued to Joey Naples, was much more) and was a block away from where Billy Naples had built a home the previous year. The 3-bedroom, 2-bathroom home also had a two-car garage to house Sandy's Cadillacs.

On November 2, the 7th District Court of Appeals arrived at a unanimous decision in denying Naples' appeal. The Appellate Court's opinion stated, "In a word of summary, defendant Naples convicted himself by the statements made at the police station at the time his brother was under arrest, which statements remain undenied, he not having taken the witness stand." Three days later, Naples attorney, Edward L. Williams, filed an application for a rehearing based on the grounds that the "case contains no record that a jury trial was waived and that instead 'the affidavit indicates a jury trial was demanded June 10, 1954." The motion for a rehearing was denied by the Appellate Court on December 27.

In a front-page *Vindicator* story on January 24, 1957, the newspaper reported Sandy spent $14,680 in purchasing two 1957 Cadillacs. One, an Eldorado Biarritz convertible, cost nearly $7,900 and was listed in the name of his sister Lucy. The second Cadillac was listed in his name. The publicity surrounding the cash purchases may have been the cause for Billy to seek financing when he purchased his 1957 Cadillac from Barrett Cadillac two months later. The newspaper quoted an "interested individual" as stating, "Those boys in the rackets usually have the cash; they don't need big mortgage arrangements for cars. Maybe he arranged to pay for it that way to make it look good; like he didn't have that kind of cash on hand."

The seemingly endless bombing epidemic in the Valley during the 1950s reached the doorstep of Sandy Naples on March 16, 1957. At 2:00 a.m. a massive explosion ripped through the nearly completed home on Carlotta Drive causing an estimated $20,000 damage. So far, it was the costliest of all the bombings in the Valley. A description of the damage appeared in the newspaper as follows:

> "A good number of dynamite sticks [were used]. The explosion occurred in a shower stall in the bathroom near the front master bedroom. It damaged virtually every room and left a heavy odor resembling 'rancid sauerkraut.'
>
> "It blew a large hole in the hardwood floor, tore a hole eight feet in diameter in the ceiling, ripped a large section of the roof off the corner of the house and blew out three large plate glass windows in the front. A cedar-lined closet was ripped and splintered like matchwood.
>
> "The blast was so powerful that a heavy I-beam in the basement directly under the bathroom, was bent enough to weaken the entire front section of the house."

Former vice squad member, now captain, Stephen N. Birich arrived at the scene shortly after the blast. While surveying the damage he reported that Sandy Naples "pulled up with his fancy car and fine clothing." The police were not sympathetic towards Naples' loss. He was arrested and held for nearly nine hours for questioning. The newspaper reported, "Several policemen said

'Shaky' (a nickname allegedly given to Naples by "underworld characters" because of his violent temper) will never get over this one. It just might kill him because his ulcers will be activated now!" Sandy had his own comment for the press, "I don't have any idea why this should happen to me. If I did know, it's for sure I won't tell a newspaper." Later that morning Stephen Stanec, the Trumbull County contractor who was building the home, viewed the damage. He told investigators he was heartsick, and that he wasn't sure what part of the home, if any, was salvageable.

Reporters from the *Vindicator* immediately speculated that a disgruntled lottery player planted the explosive. The newspaper recently disclosed in an expose that, "the number 607 received extremely heavy play and was the winner in other cities having the numbers racket. Youngstown players that day got paid on 606 instead." Naples responded to their inquiry with, "You guys don't know what you are talking about."

In editorializing on "the district' 44th bombing since 1951" the *Vindicator* stated:

> "The obvious inference is that Sandy was expanding his operations and some other racketeer who was adversely affected gave him a violent warning against poaching.
>
> "It may be said that if racketeers fight among themselves, specifically if Sandy Naples loses $20,000, it's no skin off the public's nose. Yet you can't enforce the law for one person and not the other without breaking down law enforcement generally, and the public will wish the police success in finding out all they can about either Sandy's enemies or his own operations."

Chief Cress revealed the next day that Naples informed him that he had "no idea why the bombing occurred but he promised to do his own checking to find out why." Cress told reporters, "If he does find out, I don't know if he will tell us." The chief then put a new spin on the bombing stating; "I'm wondering where this bombing was directed. Was it actually at Naples or was it aimed at the contractor? Once we decide who was hurt, we will know how to conduct our investigation." Part of the chief's speculation was due to a rumor that Stanec had used some non-union workers on the job, an accusation that the contractor vehemently denied.

On the morning of March 18, an anonymous caller told the *Vindicator* that Sandy Naples "was warned last week" to pay off on the disputed 607 number or his Poplar Street home would be bombed. Instead they targeted his new home. That same morning the city building inspector met with Naples and Stanec and determined, "Not less than $35,000 will be needed to fix up the damage." While the three men surveyed the scene a steady flow of automobiles, loaded with gawkers, drove slowly by doing their own surveying.

Chief Cress was still working the angle that Stanec was somehow the target. A week after the bombing he was given a lie detector test and passed. Cress announced the results in a prepared statement declaring, "He has been cleared completely as to any participation in the bombing or having any knowledge as to the perpetrator." Cress must have been surprised when a warrant was issued the following month in Trumbull County for Stanec and Naples' arrest for contempt for failing to appear for a hearing on a cognovit note[15] action on March 22. The action was filed by a Masury man seeking $3,500 on a promissory note Stanec had failed to pay for construction work. Naples was pulled into the case to disclose his indebtedness to Stanec and to see if he owed any money to the contractor that the court might attach.

On April 11, Naples was arrested at his home and brought before Trumbull County Common Pleas Judge G. H. Birrell. Naples told the judge that he had failed to appear at the hearing because Stanec had assured him that "everything was taken care of." Birrell released the gambler from the contempt charge, but ordered him to appear before a court referee to explain his financial dealings with Stanec.

Naples was in a rare talkative mood before the referee. The newspaper reported he was, "Talking so fast that he sometimes had to stop and wait for the court stenographer [to catch up]." The candid Naples revealed that he had paid a total of $46,700 in cash for the Carlotta Drive home. He said $16,000 was handed over before construction began; $4,500 was paid for the lot; and, in addition to subsequent payments, Sandy's 1955 Cadillac valued at $3,500 was given to the contractor. Naples claimed all payments were in cash and that he was never handed a receipt. "I never write checks. I'm goofy for doing business like that," Sandy confessed.

Naples told the court he was to receive a $17,000 payment from an insurance company settlement on the bombing. Although Stanec had taken out the policy, Naples was the beneficiary. Without going into detail, Sandy claimed he was served "with 15 subpoenas" as a result of doing business with Stanec. The next day Stanec was arrested and immediately given a three-day jail sentence by Judge Birrell on the contempt charge. Stanec continued to be plagued with legal problems. In November 1957, he was indicted by a Mahoning County grand jury for accepting $5,000 to build a new home and never completing the work. In May 1958, he was indicted for passing four bad checks totaling $370. Unable to raise a $4,000 bond he was placed in jail.

The media coverage of the bombing and Sandy's extravagant spending overshadowed his continuing court fight to avoid prison. It was now going on three years since his sentence. The latest legal wrangling came after his newest attorney Edward Williams filed a motion called a "diminution of record." The newspaper explained, "This type of action usually is filed when a correction is sought in the record. While uncommon, a motion for diminution of record is a routine maneuver regarded as a delaying tactic."

The point of contention was whether the waiving of a jury trial by Naples and his attorneys was properly handled. As of April 13, the Appellate Court had sent the case back to Judge Cavalier to make any corrections he might deem proper. On June 12, Cavalier reopened the case and heard testimony from court employees who oversaw the paperwork regarding the defendant's waiving of a jury trial. It was noted that the "Municipal Court code says a defendant must sign his own demand for a jury trial," which Naples had not done.

On June 13, Cavalier corrected the transcript of the original case regarding the demand for a jury trial and sent the matter back to the 7th District Court of Appeals. In his ruling the judge noted:

> "Based on evidence in this hearing on the part of the deputy clerks, notes appearing on the affidavit, plus testimony of the court, this court finds the Atty. Martin P. Joyce, acting as attorney for the defendant, filed a jury demand June 10, 1954.
>
> "The court orders the clerk to correct the record of this case to indicate the filing of a jury demand by the defendant."

Judge Cavalier pointed out in his ruling that "no objection was made to trial by the court."

The *Vindicator*, which said its files showed that late attorney Clyde Osborne had waived the jury trial, commented that "bets are now that the higher court is going to send the case back again for an entirely new trial, this time by a jury." In their article they called the matter the, "Delaying tactics of [a] strutting little racketeer..."

In October 1957, defense lawyers produced, for the first time, the written demand for a jury trial, which apparently was misplaced for some three years. Defense counsel was asking for Naples' six-month jail sentence to be voided. Law Director Felix Mika claimed the mysterious jury demand was not properly signed and was not permissible because the agreement to waive the jury trial was arrived at in open court. On October 29, the 7th District Court of Appeals reaffirmed its November 1956 decision to uphold Naples' conviction.

In April 1958, the Ohio Supreme Court refused to hear the case after all seven justices agreed that there was no debatable question involved. A week later the "official papers" arrived from Columbus and Naples was notified that he had until Monday to handle any pending personal matters.

On Monday, April 28, a smiling Sandy Naples arrived at Municipal Court shortly after 9:00 a.m. He arrived alone explaining, "My attorney [Edward Williams] ain't feelin' so good, so I came over here to get it over with."

The *Vindicator*, which had taken to calling Sandy, "Shaky, the Dandy," provided the following description of Naples:

> "The little man, in usual tonsorial splendor, wore a dark blue Italian silk suit with dark maroon necktie and diamond stickpin and a midnight blue Ivy League hat to match his black pointed shoes. He smoked one cigarette after another and he perspired during his long wait in the hall outside the courtroom where he talked with newsmen."

Naples was forced to wait for over an hour for Judge Cavalier to arrive and get the process going. At one point he joked, "They better hurry up or my ulcers are sure going to kick up." During that time he spoke candidly to newsmen. Sandy admitted he "would have been better off to have served my time way back there instead of spending all this time and good money." This statement left many wondering if "Fats" Aiello, Vince DeNiro and Peter Fetchet had all arrived at similar conclusions. It also brought up the question of whether it was the attorneys for the men who were responsible for the expensive, long drawn out – and ultimately unsuccessful – legal proceedings.

When asked about the bombing of his home, Naples responded, "I sure would like to find the answer to that one." Sandy claimed he would do another six months in jail if he could find who was behind the destruction of his Carlotta Drive home. Naples admitted he was still under a doctor's care for his ulcers, but claimed, "I ain't gonna worry about how they feel while I sit over there and serve my time." He said he would spend his time, "reading and swallowing my pills when I need them."

Less than two weeks into his sentence the ulcers were beginning to bother Naples. Sheriff Langley reported that by May 11 Sandy had suffered two attacks. "There is no doubt in my mind the man is sick and has a bad stomach. I don't care if he is Sandy Naples. We are dealing with a human being who is sick and needs medical care. Therefore, I recommend his personal physician see him, "Langley advised.

Naples was eating jail food for the most part, but was permitted to "send out for orders of roast beef sandwiches" when the food was something he couldn't eat. Speaking to *Vindicator* reporter Jack Gates, Langley revealed, "I'm a little concerned about the man's health. He is getting pretty gray and thinner than the last time I saw him. He looks like he may have something besides ulcers and I want to find out for sure."

Naples, who had struck up a friendship with Gates, confessed to the reporter, "But am I glad I ain't got my brother Jimmy's ulcers because I didn't think I could last in here." Pulling out a bottle of pills, he quipped, "just got a new supply of the latest ulcer pills to ease the pain, try some Jack, or did your ulcers stop bothering you?"

Gates reported that Naples had adjusted to the life of a county prisoner and had even volunteered to "do a little work" to keep himself busy. Sandy and Sheriff Langley denied reports that the prisoner had a television set in his cell. Langley said, "He isn't getting any special treatment and he hasn't asked for any." Naples asked, "Who needs a television set? Why, Jack, as long as you can write them nice stories about me and I read the newspaper I don't need a set. I sure did appreciate that nice send off you gave me, but those radio and television stories didn't do me justice."

The "Sandy Watch" was on in the newspaper as daily reports appeared on the front page of the *Vindicator*. On May 12, Langley reported, "Our jail doctor talked with him this morning and told him to have X-rays of his lungs and stomach. The rest is up to him because we aren't going to pay any medical bills or cook him special meals. If he has to go to the hospital, then he'll have to see the judge who sent him here."

Naples, who was drinking as much milk as he could each morning claimed, "I don't want any of the prisoners feeling I'm getting special treatment. Look at me. I've lost ten pounds since I've been here." Naples, after being checked out by his own physician, was asked if he would pay for a hospital stay if it were recommended. Sandy replied, "They put me here; let them worry about it."

The next day the town was again abuzz over Naples' ailment. In what was becoming his daily routine, Sheriff Langley issued the latest statement on Sandy's condition. After having talked with jail physician Dr. William Welsh, the sheriff reported that Naples would be advised to get a 48-hour check up to determine his exact illness. "He will not order him to do it because we aren't going to pay the bill," claimed Langley in what was becoming his main concern with the matter – the expense. "But when he learns the exact illness, he will present it to the court. There is no doubt the man is sick...I won't upset a 10-year routine by setting up special diets or catering service for one man." Meanwhile, after Naples had suffered his third ulcer attack since entering the county jail two weeks earlier, his attorney, S. S. Fekett, petitioned Judge Cavalier for a hearing about Sandy's condition.

The situation was quickly turning into a soap opera. On May 14, Judge Cavalier called for a hearing and asked the following to attend: Sheriff Langley, Dr. Welsh, S. S. Fekett, and Dr. David A. Belinky (Sandy's personal physician since 1953, who became the Mahoning County Coroner.) Welsh immediately informed Fekett that he would not attend because he was "too busy" and that all he could testify to was that Naples' examination shows he has "gastric symptoms."

Dr. Belinky agreed to appear and testify that he treated Naples for a duodenal ulcer, but "I can't testify to anything else." Belinky had already advised Dr. Welsh that Naples be placed on a "full and strict program," which Langley had already stated he would not provide.

During the hearing Judge Cavalier stated that he felt responsible for Naples' condition while he was in jail. "I simply want to know whether or not he is getting proper medical care," Cavalier said.

When it came Langley's turn to address the court he declared, "Unless ordered by a court there will be no special diets. We have numerous complaints of stomachaches and colds and there are no special diets for the other prisoners. The sheriff's job is not to baby the prisoners. We have 101 prisoners over there and we have a job to do. If we allow one prisoner to have special food, then all will want it."

Dr. Belinky then testified that Naples ulcer could lead to complications if not properly treated. He recommended that Sandy be on a strict diet. Belinky also stated that "aggravation and smoking" would bring on additional attacks. This coming after Naples was seen extinguishing a cigarette just prior to entering the courthouse. Sandy admitted, after being questioned by the judge, that he had a pack-a-day habit. Naples told Cavalier that it was "almost impossible" for him to receive a special diet at the jail. "They can't give me two poached eggs and not give them to the other prisoners," Sandy offered.

Outside the courtroom Langley stated to newsmen, "Cavalier cannot give me orders about how to run this county jail." This added fuel to the soap opera as it was reported that Judges Erskine Maiden, Jr. and Harold B. Doyle, in "off-the-cuff" opinions, claimed the whole matter should be under the jurisdiction of the Common Pleas Court instead of the Municipal Court, which Cavalier represented. While soft-peddling these views to a *Vindicator* reporter both judges claimed they weren't interfering with the case, but Judge Cavalier's jurisdiction "could be officially questioned" if the sheriff decided to take action.

A May 15 *Vindicator* article reported:

> "It was also the opinion of the judges that Judge Cavalier can in no way shorten Sandy's six-month sentence in county jail or release him. After execution of the sentence, the matter left Judge Cavalier's hands, they say.
>
> "Under the law the sheriff and the county jail are both under the jurisdiction of the Common Pleas Court. The lawyers and judges felt that since the question of Sandy's ulcer diet is a matter concerning the running and management of the jail, the present legal question technically should be under the Common Pleas Court and not the Muny Court.
>
> "Judges Doyle and Maiden also said that they believed Sheriff Langley could rightfully refuse to carry out any order by Judge Cavalier regarding Sandy's diet or his release before the sentence legally expires."

Not surprisingly, when Judge Cavalier issued his ruling on May 16, he stated Naples should apply to the Mahoning County Common Pleas Court "for relief of his ulcers."

Attorney Fekett, after speaking with his client, decided to back down from any further action. Although he had suffered another attack, Fekett reported that Sandy didn't want to "put anyone on the spot" by being singled out as a special prisoner. Sandy would just try to persevere. People were quick to take notice of the sudden change in Sheriff Langley's attitude toward his ailing prisoner. When asked for an update on Naples' condition the sheriff replied, "How should I know I don't talk to him and I don't particularly care, either."

On June 18, Naples suffered his eighth ulcer attack. Jail personnel reported that Sandy "turned several shades of blue...and we really got worried about him." Naples refused Langley's request to go to the hospital to be X-rayed. The sheriff said he believed Sandy refused "because he is afraid they might find something else."

When asked if he might try to assist Naples, Judge Cavalier replied, "I have nothing to say at this time. I want to check into the matter." A few days later, after Cavalier had time to "check into the matter," he was all for allowing Naples an early release. The judge informed reporters that he "never intended that Naples serve the full six-months in jail when I sentenced him but after checking the law I feel my hands are tied." Cavalier was told – in no uncertain terms – by Prosecutor Kretzer and Law Director Mika that they would fight any effort to give Naples an early release.

With the judge's revelation in late June came rumors that Sandy was about to be released. The newspaper reported, "One rumor circulating in city hall today indicated that Naples was so sure of his release that his brother came to county jail...with a complete change of clothing." Sandy would have to wait – but not too long. On July 26, ninety days after he entered the Mahoning County jail, Judge Cavalier made the following entry in the case file:

> "It appearing to the court that the defendant has served 90 days of his sentence, during which time his conduct has been good; that he is and has been in ill health requiring medical attention and special diets which the county jail cannot adequately furnish resulting in a number of ulcer attacks; therefore, in the interest of justice, the court deems the defendant has been sufficiently punished and merits probation."

At 11:40 a.m. Naples walked out of the Mahoning County jail, just ten minutes after his brother Billy paid the Municipal Court Clerk the $500 fine and associate costs. Sandy was released to Dr. Belinky and placed on probation for one year. He left the jail "grinning broadly" and after a few hours with family he was undergoing treatment at North Side Hospital.

Mayor Frank Kryzan quickly registered his disgust at Naples' early release. "We are tired of getting these guys convicted and then having them released on the pretext of a bellyache," Kryzan declared. He then announced that Law Director Mika was checking Ohio laws in an effort to appeal the release. These efforts centered on what jurisdiction a municipal judge had over a prisoner of the county.

On July 31, Mika filed a petition in Common Pleas Court in an effort to get Naples back to jail to complete his sentence. Angered by the actions of the Kryzan administration, Judge Cavalier responded that he did the "right and just thing." Naples was my prisoner and comes under my jurisdiction. If I can't release him, no one can. With the filing of the court action a writ was issued by

Judge Maiden, which Cavalier would have to respond to. While Cavalier pondered his decision, Naples was released from North Side Hospital five days after entering for treatment of his ulcer.

On August 4, a hearing was held before Judge Maiden in Common Pleas Court. Representing Judge Cavalier was a battery of attorneys, Edward L. Williams, one of Naples' lawyers; William A. Ambrose the former, long-time county prosecutor; W. Glenn Osborne, the nephew of the late Clyde W. Osborne and brother of future prosecutor and judge Clyde W. Osborne; and Philip A. Morgante. Forest Cavalier found himself in an unusual seat – the witness stand – as he was called to testify and answer Mika's questions.

During the two day hearing the highlight was a clash between Mika and attorney Williams. The co-defense counsel accused assistants in Mika's law department of making requests and recommendations in the past, with the law director's knowledge, to municipal court judges to release prisoners before their jail terms were up. Mika vehemently denied the charges.

At the completion of the hearing Judge Maiden's ruling was that Ohio law forbids a judge to change his sentence once it is imposed. Maiden also pointed out that Cavalier had received a mandate from the Ohio Supreme Court to carry out the sentence. In what must have been a painful moment for the proud judge, Cavalier admitted he made a mistake and ordered Sandy Naples to return to jail to complete his sentence. With Maiden's permission, Cavalier gave Naples 24 hours to report back. Maiden then ordered Sheriff Langley into the courtroom and told him that the county jail physician could examine Naples on request and, if the doctor recommended it, Sandy was to receive a special diet. And, if necessary, be hospitalized. Many wondered if this decree were issued earlier by one of the "off-the-cuff" opinion-offering Common Pleas judges that matters would not have reached this point. Judge Maiden commented, "There is no doubt in anyone's mind of Judge Cavalier's sincerity, integrity and honesty. It takes a big man to admit when he has made a mistake."

While the events of the first half of Naples's sentence certainly proved bizarre; no one could have predicted the absurdity that the second 90 days would bring.

On August 6, after enjoying eleven days of freedom, Sandy Naples returned to the Mahoning County jail. Smiling and wearing a pair of dark sunglasses to protect a swollen eye caused by a mosquito bite, Naples arrived with attorney Glenn Osborne. Spotting his favorite reporter, Jack Gates, the gambler quipped, "For you, Jack, I spent most of yesterday with my girlfriend but I don't think you'd better print it because her mother might get mad."

When questioned about his health, Sandy replied, "I don't know about my ulcers, because my doctor hasn't given me a full report." Sheriff Langley, after booking Naples, said he would have Dr. Welsh conduct an examination before deciding on a course of action.

Sandy remained out of the public eye until the last day of August. Then his "friend" Jack Gates wrote about Naples suffering from a bout with sciatica, a chronic nerve problem in lower back and hip area. The article was entitled "How Did Sandy Get 'Labor' Pains in Jail?" The reporter poked fun at Naples for wearing silk underwear and for being treated as "the king" of the county jail.

Gates' next article seemed like a plea from the gambler for the reporter to back off. "I got more pills to try to kill this new pain and I'll probably need more for my ulcer if you write this thing up again," Naples complained. "Don't say another word in print about my sickness, because if you do I'll stay upstairs in my cell. Please, Jack, don't write no more stories about me. Too many people are complaining that you know too much about me and what I'm doing in this place."

While Naples was in jail the police continued to watch the Center Sandwich Shop for numbers activity. Police suspected that an unauthorized telephone was in operation at the restaurant. At 9:00 on the morning of September 10, two patrolmen, recently assigned to plain-clothes duty, entered the restaurant, getting there before the "lookout," who normally arrived at 10:00 a.m. As the officers entered they saw Stephen Bajnok hurriedly placing a telephone under the counter. After crawling around on his hands and knees, one of the men finally found the hookup hidden deep under the counter top, but the phone had no dial tone. The officers noticed that while they were searching for the connection, Bajnok had walked away from the area and turned on the jukebox. When one of the patrolmen turned off the jukebox from a wall switch, the music stopped and the dial tone returned. At that point the telephone rang and the officer answered. "Skin, this is Moon. What's my ribbon?" the caller asked. The ribbon was the total from the adding machine tape of the day's numbers receipts. The quick thinking officer replied that he didn't have it totaled and to call back in ten minutes. "Moon" did not phone back.

The efforts of the officers to search the place were hindered by Bajnok, a waitress and the just-arrived lookout. The patrolmen went immediately to Chief Cress' office to show off their find. Cress ordered the men back to the restaurant to arrest anyone there telling them, "We may be able to close the place on a complaint it is a hangout for hoodlums." When the officers returned they arrested Bajnok, Billy Naples, David Coman, and Pat Carlini, who was reportedly operating the Center Sandwich Shop in Sandy's absence. The waitress was sent home and the restaurant closed. All four men were later released.

On Monday, September 29, Sandy Naples reached legendary status in the Valley. He was caught by *Vindicator* newsmen running back to the Mahoning County jail at 8:35 in the morning after having a sexual tryst at the home of his girlfriend Mary Ann Vrancich. The newspaper reported that, "The dapper little racketeer, clean shaven and clutching a half carton of his favorite cigarettes, jumped from a private car at the entrance of the jail drive way and dashed down the drive into the arms of a waiting reporter."

The newspaper claimed it was following up rumors for three weeks that Naples was leaving the jail on weekends. Naples' position as a trusty of the jail placed him in his "usual spot" in the jail's garage during the weekday. After the supper hour Sandy was confined to an area on the fifth floor of the jail with other trusties. When Naples couldn't be found in the garage area and a deputy was asked of his whereabouts the reply was always, "He is lying down resting."

After his embarrassing encounter with the *Vindicator* reporter, Naples claimed he had been to see his doctor about his sciatica. Sandy denied he was away from the jail cell all weekend and told the reporter, "You can check with my doctor. He will tell you I have been seeing him for treatment." Sandy wouldn't name the doctor he went to see, and refused to explain how, with his sciatic problem – not to mention his ulcer – he was able to run full-speed down the driveway from the car to the jail.

"If you write this story about me being away from jail over the weekend, you're going to look silly," Sandy warned.

Sheriff Langley said he wasn't aware of the incident until informed by the *Vindicator* around 10:00 o'clock that morning. He spoke to both Sandy and then Frank Naples, a deputy at the jail that happened to be a cousin of the prisoner. Both related the same story – but one different from the first one Sandy told reporters – that Frank had driven Sandy to his Carlotta Drive home so the gambler could retrieve clean underwear and socks. Langley then "indicated" to reporters that he accepted their explanation, but was still investigating the rumor that Sandy was gone the entire weekend. Langley was asked why Sandy was allowed to be taken home instead of having the items of clothing delivered. "I'm not going to comment on that," the sheriff replied.

This was a story that would not soon be relegated to the back pages of the newspaper. The indignation was targeted at Sheriff Langley. County Prosecutor Beil was called on by Governor C. William O'Neill to take "appropriate action" against Langley "if any of these allegations" about weekend passes for Sandy Naples were true. While the legal battle was on as to how to address the matter with Langley, the newspaper reported that, "Sandy's leaves have not been confined to the weekends; that he has often staggered his times of departure and return, just in case anyone was watching."

Beil's response to the problem was to throw it back into the lap of the governor. In a letter to O'Neill, Beil, quoting from the Revised Code wrote, "it is our opinion that...neither the common pleas judges nor the prosecuting attorney can take any type of action against a sheriff for misconduct. The only person who has this statutory right and duty to commence proceedings against a sheriff is the governor of the state."

Meanwhile, Langley announced he had completed his investigation of the incident. Still believing Sandy and his own deputy, Frank Naples, the sheriff accepted that the two left the jail between 7:30 and 8:00 a.m. to retrieve underwear and socks from the gambler's home. Langley did take action against Frank Naples. "I have suspended my deputy indefinitely, he stated. "For how long I don't know. I have made my report to the Common Pleas Court and that's all I have to say on the matter," although he said he would "welcome" a grand jury investigation to clear his name. Langley's suspension of deputy Naples for "giving preferential treatment" to a prisoner officially ended the sheriff's investigation. (On October 31 the sheriff announced that his "indefinite suspension" of Frank Naples would be 30 days. On November 1, Naples reported for duty at 8:00 a.m.) Langley later claimed that "Frank Naples is as good a man as I have to help run the jail." This revelation raised a few eyebrows in the county.

While the newspaper claimed there were no reports from Langley they could find filed with any of the judges, they did report, "Deeply disturbed and near tears the sheriff said he spent a sleepless night over the news story about the goings-on of his notorious prisoner. Langley said it was a shame his family has to suffer for 'something like this.'"

Governor O'Neill appeared irritated with Beil's letter pointing out "that the prosecutor himself made no charges, but that throughout the letter repeated charges or allegations [were]made by representatives of the *Vindicator.*" Beil then went to Ohio Attorney General William Saxbe and asked him to rule on whether the prosecutor and Governor O'Neill should act to oust the sheriff. While Saxbe reviewed the matter, Beil announced on October 7 that he would make a "limited investigation" into Naples special privileges. This followed receipt of a letter from Governor O'Neill in which he stated, "I would suggest that, as chief law enforcement officer of Mahoning County, you make an investigation to determine whether or not these newspaper allegations are true, with a view to taking appropriate action." In response to the governor Beil said, "Of course this office will cooperate with the governor at all times. I will initiate and carry out any reasonable request made by him if within my authority under law." The newspaper followed up with "if Saxbe rules the governor should act he [Beil] will give the results of his limited investigation to O'Neill as this would come under 'appropriate action.'"

The newspaper announced the "latest theory" regarding Naples' field trips from the jail. "He supervised weekend work on his lucrative football pools which flood the county and city every week," they reported

On October 15 Attorney General Saxbe backed Prosecutor Beil in his stand that O'Neill should initiate ouster proceedings against Sheriff Langley. The *Vindicator* reported:

> "Beil and Common Pleas Judges David G. Jenkins and John W. Ford originally agreed there were only two ways an ouster against Langley could be initiated.
>
> "One was the complicated method of Beil getting 15 percent of the electorate in the total vote for the governor in the county in the last elections to sign petitions

> authorizing Beil to file the charge in Common Pleas Court.
> "The other method is for the governor to initiate the proceedings in Common Pleas Court. His signature alone would take the place of the signature of 15 percent of the voters.
> "In either case, the ouster move would be for misconduct in office on the part of the sheriff."

Beil quickly forwarded all of the information he had gathered to-date in his investigation to the governor, and said he would cooperate fully with any investigator O'Neill may send. The governor responded that as soon as he received the information he would then take "appropriate action." A week later the governor appointed Fred Moritz, Superintendent of the Ohio Highway Patrol to conduct the investigation.

In the midst of the investigation, on November 3 Sandy Naples walked out of jail a free man. Even this was done in unusual fashion. The suddenly media-shy Sandy had the sheriff awakened at 5:00 a.m. for permission to leave. The deputy making the phone call told Langley that Naples wanted to leave immediately to avoid the "newspaper group." The sheriff later told reporters, "I told the deputy to go ahead and release him and good riddance." Sandy was whisked away from the county jail by his brother Joey. The man responsible for one of the most publicized corruption scandals in the county's history was not forced to spend an extra minute in jail over the matter.

The probe by Moritz went no where due to that agency's inability to conduct a proper investigation. On November 19, Moritz reported to the governor that, "The patrol was handicapped in its investigation by the fact that it has no lawful power in these matters to issue subpoenas, to compel attendance of witnesses or put witnesses under oath."

On January 2, 1959, in a letter to Prosecutor Beil, O'Neill stated, "I recommend for your consideration taking the matter before the grand jury, where you have at your command the power to subpoena witnesses and records and to take the testimony under oath." When Beil finally responded to O'Neill's letter, he took a swipe at the outgoing governor.[16]

> "Although the attorney general and local common pleas judges have stated it was clearly the duty of the governor, he has refused to act. I will do the job.
> "I found Governor O'Neill always adept at dodging a real decision.
> "Sheriff Langley has previously stated he would welcome an investigation by the grand jury as it would afford him an opportunity to answer the charge. We will grant him this privilege. If he is innocent his name should be cleared. If he is guilty of misconduct it should not be ignored."

Langley was contacted by reporters at his home. The sheriff had just been released from the hospital where he was being treated for an intestinal ailment. He informed reporters, "No comment. I have nothing to say."

On January 27, the Mahoning County grand jury began hearing testimony in the misconduct investigation of Sheriff Langley. Witnesses included *Vindicator* employees Jack Gates and photographer Lloyd Jones; the Mahoning County chief jailer, the chief deputy sheriff, another deputy and, of course, Sandy Naples. While waiting to be called, Naples told reporters, "This stuff is taking me away from my work." Sandy wouldn't comment on what that work was.

The grand jury spent a total of two days questioning eight witnesses. On February 3, they decided not to indict Langley for misconduct and instead issued a "mild" reprimand. The grand jury recommended that the sheriff keep "a closer surveillance of his deputies and prisoners" and that the jail's garage door, which Naples had re-entered that morning, be kept locked at all times. The panel stated that the 30-day suspension of Deputy Frank Naples was a fitting reprimand. When informed of the body's findings, Sheriff Langley stated, "I feel very pleased; I also feel I have been completely vindicated by the grand jury." Sandy Naples was not available for comment.

In April 1959, police received a tip that a numbers pickup man was collecting bets at the Mahoning County Tuberculosis Sanatorium and the Woodside Receiving Hospital. Officers staked out the area and on April 21, stopped Felix Black. When police searched his car they found bug slips totaling 324 lottery bets in a hollowed out armrest. Black was fined $200 by Judge Martin Joyce the former assistant police prosecutor, who once represented Sandy Naples. During the questioning of Black, he admitted that he worked for "Shaky."

It was the last time Sandy Naples made the newspapers as the turbulent decade of the 1950s came to an end in Youngstown. The highly publicized activities of the lottery kingpin were not over. Sandy would make one more media splash just three months into the new decade.

Vince DeNiro

James Vincent "Vince" DeNiro was born in Youngstown on November 19, 1921, the son of Frank, Sr. and Helen Catoline DeNiro. A brother of Helen, Dr. Raymond Catoline was named Youngstown police physician by Mayor Frank R. Franko in 1960. Vince DeNiro was one of five brothers; the other boys were Michael, Frank Jr., Louis and William.

Vince grew up on the city's East Side, where his early education came from Immaculate Conception School. He later attended East High School but quit before graduating. Looking for work as a teenage dropout, DeNiro found a job in the produce department at a Kroger supermarket. He quickly tired of this and joined the army, serving two years during World War II.

While in uniform, DeNiro married Mary Sekula, an attractive 21 year-old, in November 1943. A New Castle, Pennsylvania, justice of the peace performed the simple ceremony. After his discharge from the Army, DeNiro returned to a

Youngstown flowing with money from the war year's boom. With workers looking for a way to spend their pay checks, DeNiro became part of the local underworld and helped exploit the gambling that was available to the Valley's residents.

As his career in the underworld moved forward his married life took a backseat. In May 1947, Mary DeNiro filed for divorce, claiming gross neglect. The couple reconciled and the case was dismissed a year later. In September 1950, she filed again and the divorce was granted two months later. Mary was given custody of the couple's two daughters – Joanne and Helen Marie.

DeNiro's first brush with the law came on January 3, 1948, when he was charged by the Youngstown police with operating a gambling house. DeNiro pleaded not guilty, but on January 14 was found guilty in municipal court. Judge Anzellotti fined him $500, but suspended $400 of it and gave DeNiro two years probation. His second arrest was for suspicion after the wounding of Sandy Naples in the Center Sandwich Shop on December 7, 1949. DeNiro, who was with Naples when he was shot in the legs, told police he could not identify either gunman and was released the next day. Police records showed at that time that his height was 5'4 7/8" and his weight was 141 pounds. DeNiro gave his occupation as "Proprietor of Pool Room, 628 Oak St. Youngstown." He was of medium build and light complected with dark chestnut hair, while the color of his eyes were "D. Mar." The report stated DeNiro was married, but listed separate addresses for both him and his wife, Mary. DeNiro's next twelve arrests, through May 1959, except for two traffic violations, were all for suspicion.

On December 5, 1951, it was reported that DeNiro was the first of 25 district gamblers who purchased the new federal gambling stamp through the Cleveland office of the IRS. DeNiro gave his address as Lowellville on the mail-in application. By purchasing the stamp DeNiro drew the attention of both Chief Allen and the IRS. Allen questioned him at length at police headquarters. The IRS quickly delved into DeNiro's tax returns and an investigation resulted in a tax lien being filed against him on March 18, 1952 for the years 1948 through 1950 totaling $4,920 in unpaid back taxes. In May, the government filed an additional lien totaling $7,184 against him. In May 1955, it was reported that three federal tax liens were filed against DeNiro totaling $9,664 for the years 1949 through 1953. The liens were filed for three different addresses that DeNiro used.

Police kept a close eye on his activities. On April 1, 1952, vice officers arrested him at a "suspected 'bug' headquarters" on Lincoln Park Drive, the address of the DeNiro Produce Company. Officers banged on the front and back doors of the home until being allowed to enter by DeNiro after several minutes. Inside they found burnt papers, believed to be bug slips, and DeNiro was arrested and held overnight. During questioning by vice squad lieutenant Maggianetti, DeNiro related that he still had his federal gambling stamp, but was earning his money legally through his produce company.

During the early hours of September 2, 1952, two creosote acid[17] bombs were thrown at the homes of Dominic R. Delbone and Paul Duritza. Around 2:30 a.m. the first bomb was thrown through the window of Delbone's North Watt Street home. Forty-five minutes later the exercise was repeated at Duritza's South Bruce Street residence. Both men were truck drivers and members of Local 377 of the Chauffeurs and Teamsters Union. In August, local "stewards" of the Teamster's Union arbitrarily raised the monthly dues of the members by one dollar. Delbone and Duritza sent a letter to Teamster's Union President Daniel J. Tobin requesting that he investigate the situation in Local 377. When the national headquarters, then in Indianapolis, responded that dues increase was unconstitutional the two proclaimed they would not pay. Local leaders warned them, "You'll pay or you won't work!" The duo then set about collecting signatures in protest of the raise. The acid bombings came in response.

When Chief Allen questioned the drivers, both told him they believed union "goon squads" were responsible for the bombing. By now the two were scared and reluctant to discuss the reasons for the bombing. Subsequently the story began to come out that the extra dues were being used to finance automobiles for the personal use of union officials, including Joseph Blumetti, the former convicted white slaver.

During the ensuing investigation sources told police that DeNiro "was stopping at the homes" of the two men. Allen brought Delbone in for questioning again in October and was told that DeNiro stopped "once or twice during the past month" and asked him to "keep quiet" about the bombings and affairs of the union. In return DeNiro promised to pay for damages caused by the bomb.

Chief Allen sent detectives to the home of Local 377 Secretary-Treasurer John J. Angelo. A request was made that all officers of the local come to the chief's office and submit to a lie-detector test "in an effort to solve the bombing situation." Allen was soon contacted by a union attorney who informed him, "The men are not coming in."

The frustrated chief told reporters, "The union officials told me last week they would be willing to cooperate in any way necessary to clear up the bombings here. I regard their refusal as a definite indication they will not aid my office in trying to get at the bottom of this mess in the union here."

Teamster President Dan Tobin sent Thomas J. Flynn, an international union representative, to investigate the local. Flynn immediately took over as trustee of Local 377 and promised "a complete report on charges of illegal elections of officers and expenditures of funds." In late March 1953, Flynn reported that his "investigation failed to uncover any connection between union officials or members and the creosote-bombings of the homes of the two truck drivers." After the report, union members voted immediately to ask the international president to give control of Local 377 back to its elected officials.

Meanwhile, Allen stated, "We are not interested in intra-union controversies, but we are interested in the bombings of homes of innocent people. DeNiro's contacting the two drivers shows there are hoodlum connections in the driver's union. That fact, together with the peculiar silence of union leaders, is beginning to give this case a peculiar smell." DeNiro was brought in the next day and questioned. One of the first things police found out was that DeNiro had purchased Anthony Delsanter's interest in National Cigarette Service, Inc., a vending machine concern. The immediate effect of this information was the realization that "Fats" Aiello no longer had a legitimate job.

Chief Allen was quick to come to the conclusion that there was a movement underway "by ex-convicts and racketeers to gain control of local unions affiliated with the vending machine industry." The following people were linked by the chief to this movement:

◊ Carl Rango, a partner in National Cigarette Service. Rango managed the Colonial House located in the Uptown District and was reported to be a partner of Frank Fetchet in a Brier Hill bug operation.

◊ Joseph Blumetti, the convicted white slaver who served his sentence and returned to Youngstown and became the business agent and vice president of the Vending Machine Employee Council, as well as a member of the Teamsters and Electrical Workers Union.

◊ William "Billy" Naples, an officer in the Vending Machine Employees Council and the younger brother of Sandy Naples.

Allen claimed that the recent action was similar to the tactics used two years earlier during the juke box bombings in the area. In an October 27 *Vindicator* article, Allen told a reporter:

> "This type of union leadership not only attempts to intimidate its members, but tries to control the operators.
>
> "The point is that unless underworld characters are permitted to use tactics like bombing and intimidation they can't operate a legitimate business successfully."

The chief claimed that because of "close police surveillance," Delsanter and Aiello were unable to "make out" in the National Cigarette Service and now their successor has "resorted to tactics of intimidation." Delbone told Allen that he was informed by DeNiro that "the investigation was hurting his business, but he wouldn't explain what he meant." When DeNiro was questioned by the chief he "confessed" that he had warned the two men not to talk to police and that he offered to pay for the damages to their homes. Allen stated, "DeNiro said he was not going to pay for the damages from his own pocket, but he refused to say where he would get the money." A disgusted Chief Allen had no choice but to release DeNiro. "This is obviously interference with police investigation, but apparently under Ohio law is not a specific violation." Allen finished his interview with the newspaper by stating:

> "In view of the apparent security the operators feel in taking the law into their own hands, who can tell whose home or whose wife will be attacked next unless the rotten mess is cleaned up. The police gather evidence, but in the absence of specific laws and in the face of powerful political favoritism that task of law enforcement is most difficult."

One hour after the release of DeNiro, Allen armed with the information about the new ownership of National Cigarette Service had Aiello thrown in jail and then questioned about "his plans for earning a living."

During the early months of 1953, two DeNiro relatives were arrested for gambling violations. In February, Joseph F. DeNiro was arrested after throwing lottery slips out of his car window during a police chase. He was fined one dollar by Judge Nevin. On March 6, Alfred J. Catoline was apprehended for possession of policy tickets. The same judge fined him $500. By May 1954, when Catoline was arrested for the sixth time, his fines had reached $1,550.

At 5:00 o'clock on the morning of March 30, 1953, someone placed or tossed a bomb at the corner of the back porch of the home of Frank DeNiro on Lincoln Park Drive. The ensuing explosion knocked several bricks out of the side of the house, damaged part of the porch and broke two windowpanes. In addition, there was damage reported to the homes of two neighbors.

Although Vince DeNiro listed his home address as Lowellville, he was asleep on the third floor of the house, which was the home of his parents. It was reported he spent most of his time there. Asked about the explosion he replied, "I don't even know if it was a bomb that went off. It couldn't have been much of a bomb because it only did about $25 to $50 damage."

Taken in for questioning by police, DeNiro was anything but cooperative. Chief Allen stated, "He said he doesn't know anything – who, why or anything else. From the way he answered questions, I doubt if he'd tell us if he does know anything. It looks like his refusal to talk has us pretty much stymied. We have to make two investigations – one of the victim himself, and the other of any enemies he might have." There was no evidence left of the bomb for police to investigate other than a few burned pieces of cardboard. Asked by a reporter about hiring a "bomb expert" to assist, Allen replied that it was useless, "There was nothing left of the bomb except the smell."

If an anonymous telephone call to the *Vindicator* can be believed, DeNiro would have had reason for not knowing anything. Just after noon on the day of the bombing an unidentified man told an operator, "I am calling about the bombing this morning. We got the wrong house; it should have been Second Ward Councilman John Palermo's house." Palermo, who lived a few doors away from the DeNiro's, told the newspaper he "knew of no reason why anybody should attempt to bomb his home."

Whoever the bombers were they made it clear that they had not mistaken the DeNiro home for that of Councilman Palermo. On April 16, just seventeen days later, and again at 5:00 o'clock in the morning, a second bomb went off, this time causing $200 damage at the Frank DeNiro home. This time the bomb was placed on the front porch near the door. The explosion ripped a small hole in the floor of the porch, damaged a storm door and broke two large windows in the home. Vince DeNiro left quickly to avoid being hauled in again and questioned by police. Detectives believed that the explosive this time was several sticks of dynamite, which were reported stolen from a Boardman construction warehouse earlier in the week. Nothing came of the investigation.

On October 21, DeNiro was ordered arrested and held by Chief Allen to be questioned about his connection to The Ranch, a gambling den on Route 422. DeNiro's car was seen in the parking lot on several occasions. Twelve hours of interrogation failed to provide the police with any useful information and DeNiro was released. The Ranch was raided days earlier by Ohio liquor enforcement agents who rounded up 20 dice players at 3:00 a.m. Leo Ferranti, one of the operators, was fined $150 after pleading guilty to gambling charges. Sheriff Paul Langley said he had granted permission to Ferranti to "run a series of stag parties" at The Ranch.

The Ranch was closed by an order of Judge John Ford in 1953. Ferranti remained loyal to DeNiro and soon joined him in another venture in Coitsville Township on Route 422. In October 1956, Ferranti was arrested at the Petrie Club on McGuffey Road and held on an open charge before being released. During the raid a chuck-a-luck game, two decks of cards and some dice were confiscated, however, no gambling activity was detected.

During the summer of 1955, DeNiro was operating what the newspaper labeled a "raid proof," gambling casino on Route 422 (McCartney Road) in Coitsville Township. DeNiro's partner in the operation was reported to be Sandy Naples. The building was fronted by a drive-in restaurant / coffee shop. The casino was actually chartered by the state as the Dry Men's Social Club on May 7. In the charter, the official purpose of the club was to provide an "atmosphere of complete sobriety where members may promote social affairs devoid of any alcoholic drinks whatsoever." One of the three trustees of the club worked for DeNiro at one of his legitimate operations.

Patrons attending the club had to pass muster with a lookout man stationed in the coffee shop. It was reported, "If the lookout man in the coffee shop doesn't know you, that is as far as you can go." Describing the operation in a front-page article the *Vindicator* wrote:

> "The elaborate casino, which opened earlier this year, has an estimated net take of $100,000 monthly. There are several gambling compartments, with lookouts

> guarding each one and long corridors separate them, thus permitting delaying tactics in the event of a raid. The spot has a beautifully decorated lounge, while inside are collapsible dice tables which can be changed into innocent-looking pool tables in short order."

It didn't take long for the casino to gain a reputation in the small township and for people to react. A July 3 article in the *Vindicator* reported:

> "A mother of four children has written to the sheriff, telling him that her husband gambles from 10 p.m. to 5 a.m. at the coffee shop. He is losing the money he earns in the mill and some days is unable to go to work after gambling all night.
>
> "She reports that her husband has borrowed money from some of the men at the joint. They come to the home demanding payment, making threats. The family doesn't even have enough money for food."

Additional efforts to get the help of the sheriff were made by Reverend Delbert Poling, the pastor of Coitsville Presbyterian Church. In early summer, Poling reported the gambling operation to a deputy who promised to have Sheriff Langley contact him. Several weeks passed without the pastor hearing anything from the sheriff, so Poling and the local constable paid a visit to the restaurant. In a room adjoining the coffee shop the men found a pool table, a baseball ticker and a scoreboard. While they were there they met DeNiro. Referring to himself as a member of the "private club," DeNiro was cordial with his guests and invited Poling to join him in a game of pool. The pastor declined the invitation.

Perhaps embarrassed by the newspaper article, Sheriff Langley responded to the *Vindicator*, "I have been out there at least six times since it opened up several months ago and I found nothing. If there is gambling out there and I find it I'll take action." When pressed about ignoring Poling's complaint, Langley stated," We talk with so many people and investigate so many things I don't remember anything about a preacher complaining."

Comparisons were quickly drawn to the Jungle Inn in that both locations seemed to enjoy immunity from the county sheriffs. By mid-August, Governor Lausche was being called on to intervene just as he had done with the Jungle Inn and the Mounds Club. His first step was to have the State Highway Patrol announce that they would begin to check the license numbers of the automobiles parked at the club hoping that the threat of publicity would drive the patrons away.

As this effort was getting underway, the police received another report of a bombing at the home of Frank DeNiro. At 12:47 a.m. on August 16, an anonymous caller reported, "DeNiro's house is bombed!" A police squad rushed to the Lincoln Park Drive home but could not find any damage. They set up surveillance for a short while before leaving. Later that day family members claimed they were unaware of the call to the police and said no one was at the home that night. They refused to discuss the incident further with reporters.

On Thursday, August 25, a series of unrelated events began to occur at the club. Late that night a burglar reportedly kicked in a side door and smashed open two pinball machines, stealing an undetermined amount of change. During the evening, prior to the break-in, the owner of the property, Victor Kosa, an interior decorator, left a quart of cobalt and some other chemicals outside the building. Kosa, who used the chemicals for making stained glass, later told authorities that he was unloading the chemicals from his automobile and accidentally slammed his finger in the car door. "I wanted to get home and fix my finger," Kosa explained. "The pain was bad, and I guess I forgot to pick up the chemicals."

Sometime after midnight "the fluids, which were in glass bottles wrapped in chemical-saturated rags, apparently exploded through spontaneous combustion," according to a newspaper account. "The blast rocked nearby houses and smashed a small window in the west side of the drive-in coffee shop which masks DeNiro's gambling casino." The explosion caused immediate speculation that DeNiro's club had become the target of his gambling rivals.

When questioned by the authorities, Kosa scoffed at the suggestion that DeNiro was running a high-class casino in the building. "Why, DeNiro is losing his pants. He can hardly get together enough money to pay me the rent," Kosa confided.

On Saturday night, August 27, two local constables and four deputized men, accompanied by *Vindicator* reporters and a photographer, lurked behind the darkened Coitsville Township Hall ready to spring a raid on DeNiro's Dry Men's Social Club. They had a search warrant signed by Justice of the Peace John P. Almasy. At approximately 12:30, after a number of cars appeared in the parking lot of the club, the raiders moved toward the entrance to the coffee shop. The first person the raiding party encountered was Leo Ferranti, the former front-man at The Ranch. Ferranti was seated at the end of a short hallway near the rear of the coffee shop. As soon as he saw the men approaching he pushed a button signaling to the men inside that law enforcement officials were present. Ferranti tried to stall for time by demanding to read the entire three-page search warrant. Instead, all the constable let him see was the page with Almasy's signature.

Ferranti then demanded to know who were the men accompanying the constables. When informed that they were from the *Vindicator*, Ferranti shouted, "You guys can go in, providing you don't have any cameras. See all you want, but positively no pictures." The raiders accepted Ferranti's terms and moved into the club. The first room they entered was a small lounge, which extended out to a patio. There they found two men huddled over a chessboard. A trip to another room revealed two men engaged in a game of pool. A search of the kitchen area, including stove, refrigerator and cabinets, failed to uncover alcohol or anything else illegal. In the last room searched they found six men in a large area intently watching a television program; none of whom bothered to look up. While DeNiro was not on the premises, the raiders did come across Victor Kosa busy painting signs in one of the other rooms. The only incriminating material the raiders found was the baseball ticker and the scoreboard.

While some observers blamed the failure of the raid on a "leak," others claimed Ferranti's quick actions gave the men inside enough notice to switch to legal activities. Still, another suggested that the raiders struck too early and they should have waited until 3:00 a.m. because business doesn't begin to "boom" until then. The newspaper tried to put a positive spin on the effort claiming the "curtailment of activities is largely a result of the governor's orders to highway patrol investigators to keep a watch on the place and take license numbers of patron's cars."

The day after the raid Sheriff Langley sent a letter to the *Vindicator* seeking vindication for his past inability to find evidence of gambling at the club. He suggested that the newspaper take its battle to the Secretary of State's office because they were responsible for issuing the club's charter. In defense of his department, Ohio Secretary of State Ted W. Brown explained that charters were issued for $25 to anyone who applies for them, that no investigation is conducted. Brown stated that, "From the name and stated purpose clause in the application I would say that it sounded like a group connected with Alcoholics Anonymous."

In March 1956, Victor Kosa and his wife sold the property to "satisfy thousands of dollars of judgments and liens" pending against him totaling more than $22,000. The sale price was reported to be $16,800. The buyer was Frank Dota, whose family claimed he was making the purchase as an investment.

With the next round of gambling stamp purchases, police brought in DeNiro and Sandy and Joey Naples for questioning. Vice squad chief Lieutenant Krispli announced, "We are bringing all those in for questioning about their business and the reason for the purchase of the stamp." Sandy Naples, who was held for nearly 12 hours, had a novel explanation for Krispli. Naples explained he "had to take the stamp because the federal government sent it to me." Naples, instead of arguing with the government said he would "rather pay the $50." It should be noted that in the *Vindicator* article discussing the incident the newspaper wrote that DeNiro was "a competitor with Naples in the race to control Youngstown's rackets." It was the first time the newspaper had indicated that the two mob heavy weights were on opposite sides.

A further split was recognized in late September. John "Jack the Ripper" Zentko, who was once beaten outside the Purple Cow by "Fats" Aiello's men, was seen walking into a suspected bug operation on East Boardman Street. When Zentko departed, he was stopped by two officers who searched him. While they failed to find any policy slips on his person, a search of his automobile uncovered four bundles of slips inside a brief case.

On September 27, Zentko appeared in court before Municipal Judge Franko. Zentko pled guilty, but before Franko passed sentence he ordered a vice squad member to bring Lieutenant Krispli to the courtroom. Officers located the vice squad chief in a barbershop and Krispli came on the run, curious as to what the summons was about.

The *Vindicator* reported what happened next:

> "The judge declared that not one of DeNiro's men has been brought before him and then asked Krispli, 'Do you know why? Can you tell me if Zentko is a DeNiro man?'
>
> "Krispli, white-faced with shock and anger, said, 'My men have orders to pick up anyone violating the vice laws. I set no policy and I am doing a job as I deem it. I know nothing of any policies set.'
>
> "Without waiting for further comment, Judge Franko shouted, 'I don't see why DeNiro should be free from arrest. He has the biggest bug bank in town,' and then jumped up and said $500 and costs and stomped off the bench."

The newspaper stated Franko's accusation left the inference that vice squad men had orders to concentrate their efforts on lottery operators they might believe were friendly to Franko. Many courtroom observers regarded Judge Franko's blast as political.

Less than two weeks later, Franko's indignation reached a new high. In announcing that he was leaving the bench to campaign for Mahoning county prosecutor, Franko stated, "The courthouse gang and the Colonial House clique permeates the vice squad. The vice squad is being used as a political wedge against my candidacy. It is no longer a vice deterrent squad but a Vince DeNiro squad which fronts for the Colonial House clique."

Triggering this latest outburst was the case of Nicholas Kritas, co-owner of the Kisso Confectionery. Despite the store being raided many times for policy activity, Franko claimed that Kritas, who was 70 years-old, was the first DeNiro man "ever to appear before me." When Kritas entered a plea of guilty for playing the bug, Franko refused to accept the plea and ordered Assistant City Prosecutor Martin P. Joyce "to draw up a new affidavit charging him with possessing lottery slips."

The newspaper reported, "Judge Franko declared the police records in the vice squad office and press reports by the *Vindicator* are true proofs that Kisso's joint is a DeNiro joint engaged in the numbers."

"Judge Franko charged that 'this case demonstrates conspiracy between the Ambrose gang and courthouse and Colonial clique and vice squad against my candidacy.'"

"I am going to sacrifice my vacation time," he said, "since I have been receiving unfavorable comments from the political editor of the Vindicator, to crusade so that the power that is invested in the few be relegated back to the people. I shall commence today to campaign and not cease until election day."

In response to Franko's outburst, DeNiro was arrested on the night of October 23 by vice squad men Lloyd Haynes and William Kenny at "Fats" Aiello's hangout, the Purple Cow. This was the third bug arrest in eight hours. Previous to this, Joey Naples and John Zentko were arrested on East Boardman Street while they were "making the rounds" collecting bug slips. The newspaper pointed out that it was the ninth time in four years DeNiro was arrested for suspicion and each time he was released without being charged. This time proved no different. DeNiro was released after denying "any connection with local gambling activities, asserting his only source of income is his salesman's job with a cigarette service."

The newspaper proclaimed that DeNiro was being used as a "political football" in the three-man race for county prosecutor. It called the contest "one of the hottest election campaigns on record for the office." The election turned into a bitter mudslinging, three-man race between longtime incumbent William Ambrose, Judge Franko and Republican candidate Thomas A. Beil. With a campaign slogan claiming he's the "only candidate with no strings attached," Beil went about bashing Ambrose and Franko for their ties to the Valley's "kingpins of crime."

On October 17, 1956, Beil, during a speech in Canfield, attacked Ambrose's record stating, "It is apparent that as long as he is prosecutor, not only will gambling and racketeers be with us, but they will have nothing to fear." Beil told the voters, "If you want DeNiro, vote for Ambrose; if you want Naples, vote for Franko." Beil promised to rid the county of "DeNiro domination." A week later, at a meeting of the Youngstown Business & Professional Women's Club, Judge Franko again accused Ambrose of "protecting" Sandy Naples and challenged him to padlock Naples' Wilson Avenue restaurant.

The campaign for county prosecutor was an unusually bitter one and led to the following front page editorial by the *Vindicator* on November 5, 1956:

> "Never in all of Youngstown's history has a candidate for public office made such a bold attempt to deceive the voters as Frank R. Franko has made in this campaign.
>
> "Mr. Franko was elected municipal judge as a Republican. He then changed his party and registered as a Democrat. But in this campaign he sent letters to Democrats asking them to support him as a Democrat; to Republicans asking them to support him as a Republican; and others he addressed as 'Dear Fellow Independent.'
>
> "As a judge of municipal court Mr. Franko misused his office to build himself up by letting traffic violators off easily, and in this campaign he asked them to repay him by voting for him as judge.
>
> "It was improper for Mr. Franko to run for another office while serving as judge of municipal court. (He still has three years to serve). Besides he does no have the experience or legal ability to fill the higher office of prosecuting attorney."

In the election the next day, Thomas Beil won by 14,000 votes over Franko and Ambrose who virtually ran a dead heat. Despite the huge margin of victory, Franko requested a recount. The judge had finished third behind Ambrose by a scant 44 votes. The newspaper reported the "Reason for the recount, it was said, is because of the large number of bets placed on the relative positions of Franko and Ambrose."

In July 1957, one of DeNiro's most profitable "pick up" stations was raided by the newly formed police bomb squad,[18] The operation, on Market Street and Philadelphia Avenue, was the Betras Confectionery where police arrested Mary Rose Betras, the sister of attorneys Anthony and Peter Betras. Ironically, Peter shared a law office with Anthony Kryzan. The one-time councilman was the brother of current Mayor Frank X. Kryzan, who had given the bomb squad a free hand to conduct raids and make arrests. The newspaper stated, "To date the arrests made by the bomb squad have exceeded those by the vice squad which devotes full time to this type of activity." Despite admitting that the lottery slips in the store were hers, Mary Rose pled not guilty at arraignment.

By July 1957, the Dry Men's Social Club in Coitsville Township was operating for more than two years. Despite a *Vindicator* editorial rating it as the number one "betting parlor in the Ohio-Pennsylvania area," with gambling going on until 5:00 in the morning, both County Prosecutor Beil and Sheriff Langley claimed they were planning no action. That was until the following editorial appeared in the newspaper on July 15:

Miniature Jungle Inn

"One thing seems certain about Vince DeNiro's flourishing gambling joint on Route 422 – it is operating with the consent of one or more highly placed county officials.

"Sheriff Langley asserts today that he has 'found nothing to support suspicion of gambling' in the Coitsville Township building, despite repeated checks in the last several months.

"However, the sheriff never has conducted a raid on the casino in the two-and-a-half years it has been in operation and can learn little about the true situation by stopping for neighborly chats at the coffee shop which serves as a front for the gambling den.

"The fact is that informers (who must remain anonymous) have supplied details of the casino's setup and the gambling games that go on every night of the week. There can be no doubt that the joint is one of the largest gambling headquarters in this section of the state.

"It is bad enough for Mahoning County to harbor what amounts to a miniature Jungle Inn. What is even worse is the possibility that this 'raid-proof' den serves as a headquarters for DeNiro's 'bug operations in Youngstown and surrounding communities. If this is the case, effective action by the sheriff's department would be a serious blow to the rackets.

"The next move is up to Mr. Langley and Prosecutor Beil, the county's top enforcement officials. The sheriff wants 'bona fide' evidence against the joint and

> has the means to collect it. Mr. Beil also has broad authority, including the power to request that the courts padlock the casino. County residents will not be satisfied until these weapons are brought to bear against DeNiro and his henchmen."

The newspaper interviewed both county officials. Langley was in a belligerent mood as he told a reporter, "My men have checked that place time and again. They have a charter on the wall out there and it is legal as far as I'm concerned. I checked it with the secretary of state and it's okay.

"If anybody can present either to me or the prosecutor bona fide evidence to prosecute, then I will. Our boys haven't been able to find any gambling out there. I'm not going to make a chump out of myself without evidence.

"Tell your boss that if he can give me specific evidence of gambling out there I'll prosecute. If it is a gambling joint I haven't found out yet."

When asked about bringing in DeNiro to be questioned, Langley responded, "I'm not going to call anyone in. I don't have reason to. I don't even know he operates the place, let alone know if he owns the building."

Prosecutor Beil's comment was much shorter. "I'll have to talk it over with my staff," said Beil. "After all, I'm not a policeman."

The newspaper's own investigation revealed, "DeNiro visits the coffee shop at 3:30pm daily, leading observers to speculate that one of the building's secret compartments is DeNiro's bug bank, biggest in Youngstown and Mahoning County. DeNiro also drops in between midnight and 1 am to check on operations." The *Vindicator* pointed out that Sandy Naples, "Youngstown's No. 2 racket king pin," frequents the casino often. Claiming that, "His Cadillac is parked outside the joint nearly every afternoon," Langley said that might be true, but he is also "downtown a great deal."

After the *Vindicator's* editorial and follow-up articles, some members of Beil's Republican Party were expressing dismay over his comments, remembering his promise to end "DeNiro domination" in the county during his election campaign. The newspaper, in a July 16 article, stated, "These Republicans say they expected Sheriff Paul J. Langley to continue to turn his back on the plush gambling casino, but they expected Beil to follow through and fight DeNiro, not only at the coffee shop but at his flourishing bug operation in Youngstown and Campbell and throughout the county."

Under pressure from members of his own political party, Beil back-peddled, claiming the *Vindicator* misquoted him and issued the following statement: "I will prosecute anyone in Mahoning County when I, through investigation or from other sources, obtain evidence of gambling or anything illegal in Mahoning County."

On July 22, Judge David Jenkins issued a temporary padlock order on the coffee shop and the Dry Men's Social Club. The order stated that the real estate and the building on it "shall not be used for any purpose whatsoever until further order of this court."

As was the case in the closing of the Jungle Inn, it took agents from the state liquor department to come in and perform the work local law enforcement couldn't – or wouldn't. The gambling evidence local officials were crying for was obtained by a state liquor agent, who entered the premises, gathered information and filed an affidavit. Named as defendants in the suit were Frank Dota, who had purchased the property from Victor Kosa and his wife, and the Dry Men's Social Club. DeNiro was not named in the suit.

The agent had entered the casino on July 13 and visited different gambling rooms within the building where he observed black jack, craps and high stakes poker. He also drew a sketch showing the layout of the operation. During the time he was in the casino he counted approximately 15 employees and several dozen patrons. At a converted billiards table the agent lost $65 shooting craps with 18 players.

After the issuance of the padlock order, Prosecutor Beil said he would have the sheriff close the club immediately and post notices. Judge Jenkins ordered Langley to seize all the gambling equipment and take inventory. Robert B. Krupansky,[19] the director of the Ohio Department of Liquor Control, stated during the announcement of the action that he and Beil had "been observing the coffee shop for some time and the padlock action would not have been possible without the cooperation of the prosecutor's office."

On Monday afternoon, July 22, Beil, two deputies, a state liquor agent and a county maintenance man arrived at the Route 422 gambling den to padlock the facility. Sheriff Langley was conspicuous by his absence. Additional state men had staked out the building earlier in the day, keeping it under surveillance to make sure nothing was removed. There were approximately a dozen people there – mostly in the coffee shop – many reputed to be horse bettors and bug pickup men. The officials entered and immediately went to the rear of the building, which housed the Dry Men's Social Club, accompanied by reporters and cameramen. Finding the door locked and after having no response to their knocking, one of the deputies kicked it open. Once inside the officers made a casual search before approaching another locked door. This time when they knocked the door was opened by DeNiro.

The gambler was handed the court's padlock order and he asked for time to read it, closing the door in the officer's faces. After a few minutes deputies rapped again. DeNiro took his time responding and when he did stated, "This is a house here. You've got the club. When you get another warrant you can come back here." When a deputy pointed out that the order gave them authority to search the entire building, DeNiro allowed them entrance but refused to let any photographers in.

Inside the "comfortable living quarters," DeNiro explained they were in the residence of Dominic Frank, the owner of the property – at least on paper. Despite the presence of a number of filing cabinets with boxes of envelopes piled on them, not to mention a telephone that rang constantly, the deputies and Beil looked around and quickly walked out.

The state liquor agent – who was said to be only on the scene as an observer – told Beil that the court order allowed the deputies to execute a complete search and remove any gambling evidence on the premises. Reporters overhearing this asked Beil why he hadn't looked in any of the envelopes. The prosecutor pointed to the deputies and stated, "It's up to them." Newsmen then posed the question to one of the deputies. "We'll look anywhere you want us to," he replied. A return trip to the office for a look inside the envelopes revealed them to be receipts from the restaurant.

The *Vindicator* reported, "Neither Beil nor the deputies made any attempt to find any evidence of DeNiro's bug or horse-betting operation. Nor did they 'turn the place upside down' to make sure they got into every room. They concentrated on the gambling room where the state man lost money."

After a meaningless cursory search, DeNiro was told he and the other patrons would have to leave the building immediately. The maintenance man then began the padlocking exercise. What should not have come as a surprise to anyone, the worker had only been supplied with three padlocks to accommodate seven doors.

As the people filed out, James V. "Dankers" Petrella, manager of the Sportsman's Tavern on Belmont Avenue, apparently secreted away in one of the hidden rooms, ran out with a waitress and a cook and quickly drove away. Petrella had made headlines back in May after he was hit in the legs with a shotgun blast outside the tavern. His rap sheet showed arrests for selling policy slips, football pools and possession of lottery tickets, as well as for questioning about several bombings. Booked four times for suspicion, Petrella refused to cooperate with police when questioned about the shooting.

When informed that the gambling joint had finally been closed, Sheriff Langley told reporters, "I'm very happy they found some medium for closing the place, and I hope it remains closed. I want the public to know that I wanted the place closed up."

On July 24, Chief Deputy Frank Reese received a call from an anonymous source stating that the telephones at the Dry Men's Social Club were still in service. A check with Ohio Bell Telephone confirmed the fact that the phones at the gambling casino were not disconnected. Reese, Sheriff Langley and four deputies headed out to Coitsville. Along the way Reese stopped and made a phone call to the casino. When a man answered, Reese hung up and continued on his way. When the officers arrived they found all the doors either padlocked or locked. Langley ordered one of his men to kick open one of the doors. When they entered waiting for them was DeNiro.

The officers arrested DeNiro and he was charged with contempt of court for violating the padlock order. He admitted that he went to the club to retrieve a lawn mower and found a door open – apparently something the officers were unable to find. DeNiro readily confessed that he was clearly in violation of the order. Judge Jenkins sentenced DeNiro to spend 30 days in jail. Jenkins maintained the purpose of the contempt proceedings was "to show all men, no matter how big they think they are, that they are nothing compared to the law." It was the first jail sentence DeNiro had ever received. Jenkins, however, refused to fine the gambler, stating that money meant nothing to DeNiro.

The prosecutor recommended a delay before DeNiro began his sentence for "good cause shown the court," even though no explanation as to what that "good cause" consisted of. The judge gave DeNiro until August 8 to report to the county jail. The time allowed DeNiro was to let him handle "immediate and pressing business."

After DeNiro's arrest at the club, the sheriff and his men again came under criticism for not searching the club thoroughly. Rumors were reported that others were on the premises booking bug action and hid when the officers came crashing in. A July 31 *Vindicator* article reported:

> "Those supposedly in the know say there were two henchmen of DeNiro in the place at the time, but that they escaped detection. The joint is a sprawling place with several different rooms, some of them which are said to have remained untouched and unexplored despite the recent raid..."

In addition, weeks after the padlocking of the social club, two alleged DeNiro bug locations in the downtown area were facing padlock petitions. The Variety News Stand, located on East Boardman Street and operated by Anthony Greco and James Ricciuti, and the Family Wine Shop on West Federal Street, which was operated by the wife of DeNiro henchman "Dankers" Petrella, had padlock petitions filed against them by First Assistant City law Director Frank J. Battisti.

As many expected, DeNiro used his "pressing business" jail delay to file an appeal. Six days before he was to begin his sentence, his attorney, Paul W. Brown, filed the paperwork. The appeal, "based on points of law," along with a $5,000 appeal bond was provided by the defendant and a stay of execution pending the outcome was granted.

While the appeal process was carried on, two events raised eyebrows about what appeared to be a let up in the crackdown on DeNiro. First, after running a red light at Belmont Avenue and West Federal Street on August 7, DeNiro pleaded guilty before his old nemesis Judge Franko. The judge, who once cursed DeNiro's name, "took it easy," fining him $5 while suspending the $8 court costs. Then on September 5, Judge Jenkins "relaxed" the padlock order. The judge said his original ruling was too sweeping after attorney Paul Brown contended that a padlock injunction could only be enforced on a place used for gambling and that it should not offset other legitimate operations in the building. The newspaper reported that, "Under the modified order, the coffee shop or any part of the building may be used for any lawful purpose until the first hearing is held on a permanent injunction." After a year under the padlock order the Dry Men's Social Club was reopened as a restaurant under new management.

Judge Jenkins quickly attempted to head off speculation about DeNiro's sentence by stating, "The modified order will in no way affect his finding DeNiro guilty of contempt of court for violating the order several days after the place was closed."

In late September, the 7th District Court of Appeals heard DeNiro's case. Attorney Brown represented the defendant, while venerable Assistant County Prosecutor Harold H. Hull[20] argued for the state. On October 9, the court unanimously upheld Judge Jenkins' sentencing. Brown immediately announced he would appeal the sentence to the Ohio Supreme Court. On January 30, 1958, the high court agreed to review DeNiro's contempt sentence.

In May 1958, the *Vindicator* exposed DeNiro's investment in the Sans Souci Hotel in Las Vegas. The article claimed that DeNiro's "earnings," to the tune of $250,000, were sunk in the casino and he was losing money and looking for additional Youngstown investors. Local people already involved included Edward F. Tobin, who once held an interest in the Jungle Inn; Michael Velardo, who worked for DeNiro at the Dry Men's Social Club; and Sam "Ricky" Filigenzi, originally from New Castle, had worked the dice table at The Ranch in 1953.

Filigenzi was out in Las Vegas for three or four years and had just recently been hired by the Sans Souci. He had a bad habit of getting vocal about losses the casino was incurring. One night DeNiro got tired of hearing the complaints and told him to shut up. Filigenzi responded by punching DeNiro and knocking him down. The hot-tempered employee was immediately fired.

Tobin was the only area man whose name appeared on the gambling license. The newspaper stated that, "Tobin's record of gambling arrests would not block him from getting a license in Las Vegas because it is the official policy of the Nevada Tax Commission to license men for gambling casino ownership 'without care' if their background indicates only gambling offenses. The reasoning is that gambling is recognized as legal. In fact, the commission prefers that those going into the gambling business have some gambling background."

The article didn't point out any official capacity DeNiro might have in the financial structure. The 1,000 plus stockholders, which made up the landlord corporation, were not allowed to "exercise control" of the casinos under penalty of losing their gambling license. According to the newspaper, DeNiro made "weekend trips there almost every Friday to look out for his interests." This couldn't have lasted long. According to Chief Allen's information, "The Sans Souci opened as a gambling casino in Las Vegas in October 1957 and closed at the end of August 1958, a period of nine months."

During July 1958, police arrested DeNiro and kept him overnight to question him about rumors that Joe DiCarlo and Moosey Caputo were returning to the Valley to "take over the rackets." DeNiro claimed he hadn't seen either man in the past ten years.

Nine and a half months after agreeing to review DeNiro's sentencing case, the Ohio Supreme Court heard arguments on October 13. Again Paul Brown represented DeNiro, while Harold Hull argued for the state. During the hearing, Hull pointed out how reporters from the *Vindicator* entered the club to gamble and to expose the operation. Chief Justice Carl V. Weygandt asked the prosecutor if the reporters won or lost money during their investigation. Hull replied that when he questioned the reporters about it they "took the Fifth." On December 3, by the slimmest of margins – a four to three ruling – the Ohio Supreme Court upheld the Appeals Court decision. The prosecutor's office announced a bench warrant would be issued for DeNiro's arrest.

Like "Fats" Aiello, DeNiro was not going to jail until all legal efforts were exhausted. Attorney Brown filed a motion for a rehearing, which, even if it failed, would give DeNiro another ten days of freedom. After the high court refused to reconsider its ruling, Paul Brown announced he would take the case to the United States Supreme Court. Unlike "Fats" Aiello, who was denied a stay of sentence, DeNiro's attorney Brown got permission from Weygandt for a stay of sentence until the nation's highest court could consider the case. The stay was granted on December 22, and the newspaper announced, "Vince DeNiro will be home for Christmas ...and probably Easter." The newspaper was being facetious, but as it turned out they could have added Memorial Day, Flag Day and the Fourth of July to the list of holidays DeNiro would be celebrating at home.

In February 1959, the *Vindicator* announced that DeNiro was bankrolling a plush new cocktail lounge and restaurant to be called Cicero's. Located in a section of Youngstown called the "Uptown District," Cicero's was taking the place of the former Burton's Grill at 2609 Market Street. Involved in the new venture was Victor Kosa, who applied for the building permit to make $15,000 worth of alterations to the building. Kosa had owned the building in Coitsville Township in which the Dry Men's Social Club once operated.

The article reported, "There are underworld rumblings that DeNiro's entrance into the Uptown district as a Colonial House competitor[21] indicates a feud between himself and Frank Fetchet, tops in North Side booking operations. The Fetchet family has a piece of the Colonial House and one of its members, Peter Fetchet, is currently 'on vacation' in the Mahoning County jail serving a four year old sentence."

The Colonial House and DeNiro's connection with it is somewhat an enigma. During a grand jury investigation in April 1964, the *Vindicator* reported, "DeNiro was a partner of [Carl] Rango's when the restaurant opened about 16 years ago." If DeNiro did own a piece of it this could explain his presence in the parking lot when he was arrested during a bombing investigation in 1954. DeNiro was said to have been in competition with the Fetchet's who, as far back as May 1948, owned a piece of the Colonial House with Carl Rango. Oddly enough, Rango was a partner of DeNiro in the National Cigarette Service.

As spring turned into summer in this final year of the 1950s, DeNiro's focus was on his appeal to the U.S. Supreme Court. On May 8, attorney Brown was given a week to file briefs. On May 17, the *Vindicator* covered the key points of the Ohio Supreme Court's decision and DeNiro's U.S. Supreme Court appeal:

> "The Ohio Supreme Court upheld the conviction for contempt of the padlock order but noted 'we agree with the defendant that the evidence will not support a finding that his presence on the premises was connected with gambling.'
>
> "The majority of the state court held that granting of the temporary injunction closing the coffee shop premises for any purpose extended the court's power beyond that authorized by Ohio law but that the resulting order was 'voidable rather than void.'
>
> "In DeNiro's appeal, he denies that this interpretation in effect 'decided that the innocent entering of the padlocked premises by the defendant justified the imprisonment of the defendant for the violation of an order that has no historical precedent or statutory authority.'
>
> "The appeal contends that such an order 'never before in the history of American jurisprudence has been found to be valid or necessary' and that the order was not asked for by the county prosecutor, intended by the court or required by the circumstances."

Attorney Brown filed his argument on May 18, and County Prosecutor Beil was given 30 days to respond. Beil and Hull hammered out their response just days later. On June 15, the U.S. Supreme Court refused to hear the appeal.

It took until July 21, until the clerk of courts received the U.S. Supreme Court mandate upholding DeNiro's conviction. The next day – the second anniversary of Judge Jenkins padlock order – DeNiro appeared at the Mahoning County jail just after 11:00 a.m. to begin his sentence. There to greet him was *Vindicator* photographer Lloyd Jones – who in the 1940s had taken two different beatings for his photography work – and a reporter, who followed DeNiro in.

Escorting DeNiro to his cell was Frank Naples. The deputy sheriff, who served a month's suspension because of the *Vindicator*'s exposure of Sandy Naples' excursion from the jail, was not happy to see the reporter and told him so. "You know everything and make it tough by scooping everybody else," he said. "A bomb ought to be thrown in Vindicator Square."

Sheriff Langley was home that morning dealing with an upset stomach when contacted by the newspaper. Langley was asked in a sarcastic tone if DeNiro would receive the same freedoms Sandy Naples enjoyed. Langley replied indignantly, "You guys are always looking for something." The sheriff claimed he didn't know DeNiro and more importantly, "I don't care to know him."

Two days after DeNiro was tucked away in jail, a local sporting goods owner sought to collect a judgement from the gambler. In 1958, the store won a court judgement of $170 for equipment used to sponsor a team supported by National Cigarette Service, because DeNiro never paid them. When the creditor approached the jail in an effort to collect he was given $16 of the $19 DeNiro walked in with. The $3 was left so DeNiro could purchase cigarettes.

On August 21, sometime before 6:00 a.m., DeNiro was released from the county jail before reporters and photographers could arrive to record the event. DeNiro was described as a "model prisoner," but sheriff's department personnel were reluctant to say much more.

Fetchet Brothers

During the bug wars of the 1950s, the Fetchet brothers, Frank and Peter, survived and by the end of the decade were called the "Number 3" operators behind Vince DeNiro and Sandy Naples.

Frank was born on St. Patrick's Day, 1918. He had his first bug arrest before the age of 20. Between December 1937 and March 1939, as a numbers writer for the Big House, Frank was arrested six times for possession of lottery slips. None of these arrests resulted in any fines or convictions. In June 1939, he testified at the trial of Herbert Bodine, who tried unsuccessfully to sue the Big House operators for $400,000.

During the vice crusade in 1942, after the bombing of Sergeant William Davis' home, Frank Fetchet was arrested twice – May and August – for possession of bug slips. Each time he pled guilty and received fines of $25. On July 31, 1943, Frank was arrested by Sergeant William Golden at a dry cleaners on Mahoning Avenue for possession of lottery slips and books. This time he decided to plead not guilty and was released on $100 bond. When his court date came, on August 13, he pled guilty and was again fined $25 and court costs.

Over the next seven and a half years, Frank Fetchet kept a low profile, but was believed to be continually building his operation. Two of his alleged bug stations were the Tasty Sandwich Shop at 1505 West Federal Street and a house on Dearborn Street in the city of Girard. After Allen was named police chief, there were several raids at the Tasty Sandwich Shop located in Brier Hill. In September 1948, Frank Del Guidice was arrested for possession of football pool tickets. In July 1948, Alfred Delmont was convicted for possession of policy slips. On March 7, 1949, after a fire at the shop, investigators found basketball pool sheets, scoreboards, adding machines and other gambling paraphernalia at the location. The fire coming a day after a vice squad search came up empty.

A March 29, 1951, *Vindicator* article spotlighted the "Girard Bug Bank" on the front page, as well as printing a picture of the small home on Dearborn Street. The article said the house in Girard, "now ranks as the biggest bug center in the Ohio-Pennsylvania area...The spot takes lay off bets from New Castle, Sharon and Pittsburgh and serves as bank for Youngstown operations." As for the

Tasty Sandwich Shop, the article identified Joseph Margiotta as the proprietor. Margiotta's "sporty" convertible was seen parked near the Girard bug bank on occasion. While the article never mentioned Frank Fetchet, it did say, "A North Side man whom downtown gamblers call the 'boss' of the lottery syndicate in this area, also is closely associated with the Tasty Sandwich Shop."

Chief Allen was determined to close Fetchet down, but was not having much luck. By March 1951, Allen had Frank picked up on suspicion twice, holding him once overnight. Except for a gambling arrest in September 1950, in which Fetchet forfeited a $15 deposit, he stayed clear of Allen's clutches. That is not to say Allen didn't try. The chief was frustrated because a large portion of Fetchet's lottery operation was handled by telephone through the house in Girard. Allen wanted the Girard police to cut the telephone lines. Describing the operation as the "lifeline of the lucrative racket," Allen made the following statement: "If law enforcement agencies don't work together these racketeering hoodlums will continue to wield whatever power lax law enforcement or political policy affords them." Irritated by Allen's remarks, the response from Girard Police Chief W. R. Flory was that his city was "lily white" and free of vice. It's just a private house," argued the chief. "If anyone was operating at 246 Dearborn St. I am sure they went away. Youngstown has more than we have in the way of gambling. If bug men were here when we called, they probably are back in Youngstown now. There is none here that I know of." Vice squad members also came up empty at the Tasty Sandwich Shop. Officers were reported to have "camped" there, but "nothing has ever happened when they are there."

In March 1951, Allen sent an officer with a search warrant to Frank Fetchet's Felicia Avenue home. The newspaper reported that once on the premises, "The vice squad member answered the phones trying to get evidence of bug operations but apparently the word was out. Shortly after the officer arrived the calls ceased."

Fetchet, annoyed with Allen's efforts, "admitted that in the past he had been involved in policy operations, but claimed he "quit four years ago." He told reporters, "I don't see how he can say anything about me. He's been giving me a hard time by using Gestapo methods. Why, he even searched my home a few times, had me stopped on the street, but found nothing. The chief even had a fellow sitting in my home for over two days. So if I had some connection with the bug they'd have found something." When told of Fetchet's comments about his retirement from the numbers business and the chief's "Gestapo methods," Allen replied, "Fetchet is a liar on both counts."

Confirmation of Chief Allen's beliefs came on April 12 when Joseph D'Agostino was arrested near New Castle, Pennsylvania. Charged with operating a lottery, police found a book in D'Agostino's possession which contained the telephone numbers of Fetchet, the Tasty Sandwich Shop and one for "Mose," who was identified as the man who ran the Girard bug bank for Fetchet. A firm Pennsylvania judge sentenced D'Agostino to a year in the Allegheny County workhouse and fined him $500. During the sentencing the judge told the numbers man that Youngstown's racketeers "should stay in their home territory." Allen hailed the sentence stating, "We could do something here if we had a legislation and court policy to back us up." Mayor Henderson had already submitted to council an ordinance requiring a six-month maximum sentence for policy convictions. The current law handed down only a maximum fine of $500 for convictions and no jail time.

Encouraged by the information revealed in D'Agostino's book, Chief Allen sought an order to have the telephone and a ticker-tape machine, used in bookie operations, removed from the Tasty Sandwich Shop. Judge John Ford granted two lawsuits seeking restraining orders on Allen's request.

Meanwhile, Frank's younger brother was beginning to gain some notoriety. Born on June 25, 1920, Peter James Fetchet's rap sheet began with a reckless driving conviction when he was 18 and an arrest for suspicion in May 1949. On June 27, 1951, Peter Fetchet was driving on West Federal Street near the Tasty Sandwich Shop when he was stopped by a pair of vice squad members, one of which was William Campanizzi, who were "making a routine check" of the street. The officers found 30 policy slips hidden in his jacket and arrested him. At his arraignment Fetchet demanded a jury trial and was released on a $500 bond. Peter later changed his plea to guilty and on July 5 was fined the maximum $500.

On June 19, 1952, Peter was arrested at a home in Boardman that was purchased the prior month by his brother Frank. The home was previously owned by J. Earl Schoaff, who was indicted by a Lawrence County, Pennsylvania grand jury on December 4, 1951, for running a prosperous policy ring that operated between Boardman and New Castle, with the bug bank located at the Boardman home on Leighton Avenue. Schoaff didn't fight the charges, but did not appear for sentencing, and although he purchased another home nearby, there were rumors that he had fled to Canada perhaps to avoid a year's term in prison like Joseph D'Agostino received.

When officers, from the Mahoning County Sheriff's Department, entered the back door of the Boardman home they found Peter Fetchet and Steve Kilame. The deputies reported, "Two large desks with extension phones were found in the basement. Hundreds of lottery slips, race horse and baseball tickets were piled high on the desks. Otherwise the large frame house was completely empty, but had Venetian blinds and curtains on the windows." The officers told the pair they were watching the place for three weeks. Peter, speaking openly, claimed they had only moved in a few days earlier. He told the deputies his workday consisted of taking phone bets from 11:30 a.m. until 4:00 p.m. Both men were taken before Justice of the Peace Bert Rosensteel, where they pled guilty to possessing gambling equipment. They were each fined $300.

After the raiding of the Boardman location, Chief Allen announced, "There are no bug banks operating in Youngstown to our knowledge. (This soon changed as Sandy Naples and his Center Sandwich Shop began to gain notoriety.) We don't know of any bug banks in Youngstown, either large or small, but we are happy to hear Sheriff Paul J. Langley finally closed the one in Boardman. That one has been operating at least three years that I know of. I hope Langley makes it permanent."

Six weeks after the raid, Peter Fetchet made the front-page again as one of three Youngstown gamblers who purchased the federal gambling tax stamp. The announcement of the purchases of the stamps by the Cleveland IRS office brought about the arrest of Fetchet by Chief Allen's men on charges of being a "common gambler." The newspaper reported, "Possession of the stamp along with two previous convictions for gambling and Fetchet's own statement he had purchased the stamp to avoid federal prosecution ...is grounds enough to file the charge."

With conviction carrying a 30-day jail term, Fetchet pleaded not guilty and asked for a jury trial. It was a long wait. A year passed and Fetchet purchased another gambling tax stamp – for which he was brought in and questioned again – and still no trial. Part of the problem was the lengthy illness of City Prosecutor Henry Fugett, who was unable to handle any cases between January 1 and July 7, 1953. Another reason was assistant prosecutor Frank Franko was not allowed to try cases in Judge John Powers' courtroom since he was campaigning for Power's municipal judgeship seat.

On July 16, over 11 months after his arrest, Peter Fetchet was back in court where he had to plead not guilty again because the original charge of being a "common gambler" was revised to read "known gambler." The case never came to trial.

After being out of the public eye since May 1951, Frank Fetchet was back in the news on April 3, 1954, after a bomb went off outside his home on Felicia Avenue. Fetchet, whose wife and daughter were in Florida, said he fell asleep after watching the Friday Night Fights on television. He awoke around 2:00 a.m. and got into his car and drove downtown to purchase a newspaper and a sandwich. Police suspected that around 2:30 a small bomb was placed about a foot away from the cellar wall near the side of the house. The explosion broke four windows, damaged wood paneling on the side of the house, destroyed some shrubbery and cracked several cement blocks.

When Frank Fetchet returned home around 3:00 a.m., he was followed into his driveway by a police cruiser. He went to police headquarters later that morning to answer questions. According to officers who interrogated him, Fetchet "stated that he knew of no reason why anyone wanted to bomb his house. He further stated that at the present time he is not engaged in anything illegal and has had no trouble with anyone trying to shake him down or anything of that sort." The police questioned Sandy Naples, who provided an "account of his time" and said he hadn't had anything "to do with Fetchet for a couple of years." Fetchet left for Florida to be with his family within days of the bombing.

On July 3, 1954, after purchasing a new gambling tax stamp for fiscal 1954-55, the "known gambler" case pending against Peter Fetchet was rehashed again in the newspaper. The *Vindicator* reported that it was one of 200 cases that were carried over from the Henderson administration that came to an end in January 1954. The newspaper, which was still referring to Peter's brother Frank as a "numbers kingpin," said that the case against Fetchet was "thin" and after nearly two years "would require considerable work."

Less than a week later, vice squad detective Lloyd Haynes and his partner arrested Peter after they observed him visiting homes on the city's North Side and believed him to be "drumming up business for the bug racket." When questioned Fetchet admitted to police that he had purchased the gambling stamp in order to "get into the numbers business," but his explanation for going door to door on the North Side was that he was attempting "to sell a house and was contacting prospects."

Fetchet was released, but just four days later his Grant Street home was raided by seven vice squad members including vice squad chief George Krispli, William Campanizzi, and led by Police Chief Paul Cress. Officers were let in by Mrs. Fetchet and they arrested Peter and Steve Kilame, who was also living at the address. Police found a large quantity of bug slips on the kitchen table and in a second floor office found a desk, phone and a large quantity of blank lottery pads. Although the slips recovered represented between $2,000 and $2,500 in bets for the day, no money was found in the house. Cress reported that they also found items "resembling credit bills, indicating Fetchet may be in the business of lending money."

At the arraignment, City Prosecutor Irwin Kretzer filed both state and city charges against Peter Fetchet, who was released on a $2,000 bond. During a hearing on July 29, Fetchet requested a jury trial in municipal court. Perhaps the fact he was never brought to trial on the last charge, the "known gambler" arrest, led him to make this request again.

There were a large number of policy arrests during the summer of 1954 where the defendants demanded jury trials. This created a backlog in the court system and Judge Robert Nevin realized something needed to be done. He explained, "All summer long these cases have been battered from pillar to post because the men have asked for jury trials. These demands are delayed because many court officials are vacationing and it is difficult to empanel juries for the same reason." The judge declared, "The day of reckoning is at hand." On September 10, six defendants dropped their demands for jury trials and accepted fines of $500 each. The judge showed his fairness when Joseph J. Beshara, one of the men picked up after purchasing a gambling tax stamp, asked Nevin if he could have a couple of months to pay the fine down after he informed the court he could only afford $200. The judge gave him until November to satisfy the balance.

Judge Nevin and City Prosecutor Kretzer had reason to want to work out deals. By mid-November they had 15 jury trials to conduct. Kretzer told a reporter, "We are hoping to clear up all these cases, which include lottery, suspicious persons, indecent exposure, liquor cases and such, before the first of the year."

Regarding Peter Fetchet's case the *Vindicator* reported:

> "[Nevin] said he will give Fetchet and Kilame ...a 'break' if they drop their demands for juries. He said he would give them fines of $500 and costs, jail sentences of six months, but suspended 90 days of the sentence if they will plead guilty to the charges. However, he said, if they insist on going through with the jury trials and are found guilty, they will get the maximum fine and jail sentences."

Both men refused and their attorney used the offer against Nevin. On December 2, Russell Mock, new counsel for Fetchet and Kilame, filed affidavits of prejudice against the judge and asked to have him removed from the case. Mock claimed Nevin had "given communications to newspapers relative to the cases and has expressed an opinion relative to the defendants and the punishment that will be given." It was asked that Judge Forrest Cavalier be given the prejudice issue to decide. City Prosecutor Kretzer said he would "contest any action" to have Judge Nevin removed.

On February 5, 1955, after deciding that "the weight of the evidence against Judge Nevin does not substantiate any charges of bias or prejudice against the defendants," Common Pleas Judge Harold B. Doyle ruled the judge could preside over the numbers trial of Fetchet and Kilame. Attorney Mock's response to the ruling surprised no one as he immediately appealed Doyle's decision to the 7th Court of Appeals.

On March 11, vice squad members spotted Peter Fetchet in a truck and took him in for questioning. After searching him, police found nearly $1,000 on him. Fetchet claimed he was just a truck driver and the money was his savings, which he was on his way to deposit in the bank. Police released him claiming "he must be one of the highest paid drivers in this area."

That same day, Frank Fetchet accidentally walked into a front-page story by being in the wrong place at the wrong time. The scene was the office of Judge Franko, who was embroiled in a heated argument with Chief Cress over the issuance of traffic tickets during the new rush hour parking ban downtown. Members of the press, who were hovering nearby, reported, "Frank Fetchet, one of the city's kingpin bug operators, sauntered into the judge's quarters unannounced at the height of the argument. Franko turned on the cigar-smoking racketeer [who] beat a hasty retreat after Judge Franko ordered him out." Fetchet's reason for visiting the judge was never revealed.

The following month, vice squad members watched as Peter Fetchet left a different Grant Street address. When Fetchet spotted the officers he attempted to get away, but was apprehended near Belmont Avenue. Police held him for six hours during which time Fetchet told them that the $283 found on him was "part of his personal savings and the savings of his little daughter." He still claimed he was employed as a truck driver for a Mahoning County painting contractor.

On May 2, 1956, Steve Kilame was acquitted of promoting a gambling game stemming from the July 1954 raid. Although Kilame didn't testify at his trial, he was the key defense witness at Peter Fetchet's trial and was called to appear on May 4. Under questioning from attorney Mock, Kilame claimed that all of the "bug paraphernalia" seized in the Grant Street home of Fetchet belonged to him. The witness said he rented a room in the home from Fetchet, but did not conduct any policy business on the premises. Kilame explained that he was a pickup man for a numbers bank in Niles and that after he made his various stops throughout the area he returned to the Grant Street address.

The newspaper reported that, "under cross-examination by City Prosecutor Irwin Kretzer, Kilame said he had only been in the numbers racket two weeks before the raid. He was about to destroy the huge pile of numbers slips, pads and books when the police moved in. He said radio and television news stories about police bug raids in the area prompted him to attempt to burn the bug material. Kilame, who refused to take the stand during his own jury trial, said he did not know who operated the bug 'bank' in Niles, and that he turned his slips and money over to a man there he knew only as 'Harry.' Kilame insisted he was no longer in the bug racket. Asked by Kretzer if he admitted the bug items were his because he wanted to take the 'rap' for Fetchet, Kilame said 'no.' He also denied that he picked up bug bets and slips and turned them over to Fetchet. He said he 'couldn't remember' the bug pickup stations where he made daily stops. 'It was a long time ago,' Kilame testified."

Attorneys Russell Mock and Joseph Vouros filed a motion for a new trial claiming "prosecutor misconduct" by Kretzer for comments made during his closing statement. Judge Nevin granted a stay of sentence during the appeal. In late July, Nevin denied the new trial motion. Mock then filed a motion to appeal the municipal court decision with the court of common pleas. On May 29, 1958, Common Pleas Judge Harold Doyle reviewed Fetchet's May 1956 conviction and held that the "evidence was sufficient to warrant the conviction."

Sometime during 1955, Fetchet moved from the Grant Street address to a home in Liberty Township. It was rumored that Fetchet was operating his bug business out of his new home. On August 18, 1956, an explosion occurred near the home. Despite the fact that the Trumbull County Sheriff's office claimed no reports of a bombing were called in, there was apparent damage done to the Fetchet home. The newspaper reported, "That in addition to a shattered picture window in the ranch-style home, there appeared to be trifling damage to some exterior bricks and there was a possibility that some of the interior foundation was broken loose." There were numerous reports from people in the neighborhood who heard an explosion around midnight. Why none of these were called into the sheriff's department was a mystery in itself.

During a new harassment campaign in July 1958, Fetchet was hauled in for questioning. Found with $470 on him, Fetchet told George Krispli that he was now a half-owner of Ohio Auto Sales, a concern located on Market Street. He was taking the money to deposit it in the bank. Three months later Fetchet was brought in again and held five hours for questioning.

In October, attorney Mock and, now Youngstown Law Director, Irwin Kretzer argued before the 7th District Court of Appeals over Fetchet's conviction. On October 22, in a two-to-one decision, the appellate court upheld the conviction. Still believing that there was no evidence to prove gambling on the part of his client, Mock appealed the case to the Ohio Supreme Court. On February 4, 1959, the higher court refused to review the case. Mock said he planned no further appeal. A week later when Fetchet appeared at Judge Nevin's courtroom eager to get "it over with," he was informed that the paperwork had not been received from Columbus. Nevin reminded Fetchet and his attorney Vouros, that the court was forced to wait over four years while his conviction was being fought. "Certainly a few more days won't hurt," the judge advised.

After a four-year legal battle Peter Fetchet was finally jailed on February 17. Discussing his dress and demeanor after arriving at the courthouse the *Vindicator* wrote:

> "Just opposite the flashing dresser Naples, Fetchet wore a bedraggled pair of slacks, sweater, sports shirt, tan topcoat and brown hat. He kept his hands to his face or turned away each time the photographer snapped a picture."

Fetchet completed his 30-day sentence and was released at 6:00 a.m. on March 18.

"I don't have any idea why I got it. I don't know what it might have been I uncovered to make somebody uncomfortable, but all I know is that working on these bombings is like hunting an invisible man in the desert." – Vice Squad Detective Lloyd Haynes, after the bombing of his home on April 13, 1957.

12

A Decade of Bombings

In the 1950s, the Mahoning Valley and surrounding area witnessed 69 bombings. During most of the decade the bombings served as a terror tactic to get someone to either do something or to stop doing something. Most of the explosions caused relatively little damage; the monetary loss sometimes amounting to only $25 to $50. Many times the bombers blew apart porches, garages, empty automobiles; in some cases stench bombs made of pungent liquids and acids were used. By the end of the decade the bombs used became more powerful and the bombings became more vicious. Instead of being utilized to scare or threaten a victim, they were now being used to eliminate them. In 1958, two men were severely injured, leaving one nearly crippled, and the next year the bombings claimed their first life. The bombing practice only intensified as it carried over into the 1960s producing horrific results. While only 31 bombing incidents took place in Youngstown during the 1950s,[22] the city could not escape the blame or the media attention, which resulted in Youngstown receiving the first of its three infamous nicknames – "Bomb Town U.S.A."

By mid-1954 the consensus was that a full-scale underworld struggle among Youngstown racketeers for the gambling profits and political favors was underway. Law enforcement in Mahoning County felt they had achieved a major victory back in June 1943 with the closing of the lottery houses. Years later, reflecting back, retired Police Chief John Terlesky recalled, "We went from three lottery houses inside the city of Youngstown, where there was little if any fighting, to some eighteen independent operators involved in a city-wide bombing campaign." Terlesky believed that Vince DeNiro might have been behind many of the numbers related bombings in the area. If not to take over their operations, then at least to collect a percentage of the profits – creating, in effect a protection racket.

Around this time, a mysterious figure was becoming known in the Valley. Calogero Malfitano, according to the vice squad, was a member of the sinister Mafia, and was said to have become DeNiro's mentor or counselor. Malfitano, born in Sicily on December 17, 1889, entered the United States illegally in 1923. In 1941, in federal court in Cleveland he was sentenced to two years in the Federal Penitentiary in Milan, Michigan for a violation of the internal revenue act. Later the sentence was suspended and Malfitano paid only a small fine.

Police reported that Malfitano came to Youngstown around 1946. His only arrest in the city came that same year when he was picked up for possession of lottery slips. Malfitano held a ten-percent interest in DeNiro's National Cigarette Service. It was said he was taken in as a partner shortly after DeNiro's father's home on Lincoln Park Drive was the target of two bomb attacks in early 1953. During the prolific bombing year of 1954, Malfitano was picked up for questioning concerning several of the attacks in the area. He was held for two days and refused to take a lie detector test. On August 27, 1954, the 64 year-old Malfitano was arrested by U.S. Immigration officials for his illegal entry back in 1923. He was released on a $2,500 bond.

The bombing epidemic that made the Valley famous seems to have gotten started in the late 1940s. There were three incidents that took place during the fall of 1947 that captured front-page news. The first involved the Ohio Tavern on Route 62 where a bomb was exploded in the doorway. About 40 hours later there was a similar explosion at the Acme Club located on Market Street. The handmade bomb was comprised of black powder, packed in newspaper, and went off around 9:30 on a Sunday night under the steps leading to the side door of the club. The blast ripped the steps apart and shattered a basement window of a nearby home. Police questioned Abe Schwartz, one of the proprietors, but he could offer no explanation for the bombing.

The Acme Club had a notorious reputation as an after-hours joint and gambling club. Between October 1944 and August 1946 the club was raided six times. Neighbors claimed the place was a nuisance, with cars coming and going between midnight and 4:00 a.m. making it difficult to sleep. During one of the raids, Sheriff Elser arrested Leo Ferranti on a gambling charge. The next day, after carpenters repaired the stairway, the club was open and doing business. Sixth Ward Councilman, George L. Stowe asked Chief William J. Cleary to "investigate and close – and keep closed – the Acme Club."

Earlier in the day that Sunday, Joe Melek's Club 43 was set ablaze in Central Square. The "gambling dive" was reported on fire shortly before 8:00 a.m. The fire was started on the second floor of the building that also housed four apartments and the Center Square Grill, which was located on the first floor.

The *Vindicator* reported, "There were more than 50 chairs in the bookie joint with the usual boards and signs. Deep water in the gambling room washed horse racing betting stubs and football pool tickets out into the corridor and down the stairway. Valuable communications equipment, through which the bookie shop received race results from a central point at 31 N. Walnut St. [Sam Alpern's Empire News Service], was destroyed and adding machines were ruined." Melek, who soon arrived to watch the firemen put out the blaze, commented that he "knew of no reason why anyone would set fire to his place." Like the Acme Club, Melek's Club 43 was open for "limited" business on Monday. Some of the rooms were completely unusable, but the race wire service, emanating from 31 North Walnut Street, was quickly restored and the horse betting windows were open.

Several times during the 1950s the *Vindicator* printed summaries of the bombings, arriving at a "to-date" total. The starting point was normally October 3, 1951, the first bombing of the Croatian Fraternal Union Club. Over the years, however, some area bombings were left out and dates were listed incorrectly. Toward the end of the decade the newspaper, as well as radio and television, began referring to each new bombing in number sequence. The following list of bombings is not an attempt to tie-in to the *Vindicator* total, but rather to list, examine and summarize each incident (See Appendix C).

October 3, 1951 – the Croatian Fraternal Union Club on Route 422 in Trumbull County. A dynamite explosion caused $10,000 damage to the recently constructed nightclub. The front door was "jimmied" open and dynamite placed inside. The owner, Joseph Sarkies, said the blast leveled a bar, walls and a ceiling in the club. Sarkies was also the superintendent of Pineview Memorial Park, a cemetery, located across the highway from the club. Prior to relocating, the club had operated for many years on West Market Street in Youngstown. With a response that was to be repeated time and again throughout the decade, Sarkies told investigators that he had "no enemies."

December 15, 1951 – the Croatian Fraternal Union Club was bombed for the second time in a month and a half when a dynamite explosion rocked the empty club. The blast, which took place around 4:00 a.m., blew apart a glass block wall in the front of the club. A portion of the ceiling was knocked down, two booths were destroyed, as well as a quantity of liquor. Damage was estimated at $3,000.

February 14, 1952 – the former Croatian Fraternal Union Club. For the third time in just over four months the building was bombed. The fraternal society that rented the building had vacated the premises ten days earlier. The 1:30 a.m. blast knocked a two-foot hole in the back of the concrete block structure, knocked a door from its hinges and scattered debris throughout the inside. A woman living next door to the club called Sarkies at his home in Youngstown to inform him of the latest explosion. She later told police, "I didn't have to look to know what happened."

March 6, 1952 – the garage at the home of attorney Frank Mastriana, 4030 Hudson Drive, Boardman. At 1:20 a.m. an explosion ripped an 18-inch hole in the corner of the garage, shattering windows in the garage and home. Damage was estimated at $200. Mastriana told Mahoning County deputies that he believed the blast was caused by heating fluid stored inside the garage. An investigation by deputies, however, revealed the bomb exploded outside the structure. Mastriana told investigators, "I have no enemies I know of." The attorney lived next door to Edward J. DeBartolo and served as counsel to the M. DeBartolo Construction Company. The men's wives were sisters.

March 11, 1952 – the M. DeBartolo Construction Company, 216 Alexander Street, Youngstown. At 12:02 a.m. dynamite, placed in the doorway, shattered 16 windows in the building, destroyed two frame doors and caused extensive damage to the walls and ceilings. In addition, several nearby homes suffered damages. The blast injured a 43 year-old woman who was walking nearby on her way home. She was showered with bricks and debris and taken to South Side Hospital with a possible fracture to her arm and injuries to both legs.

The construction company was run by Michael DeBartolo, who told police that the bombing must have some connection with the one at the Mastriano garage. "My relations with my employees have been very good. I have been in business for 40 years and never had any trouble with employees." His son, Edward, president of the company, explained that they were not involved in any competitive bidding contracts and in recent years focused their construction efforts on developing shopping centers.

Despite each man believing the explosion was the work of "pranksters," the next day both asked for police protection and offered a $1,000 reward for information leading to an arrest. Chief Allen, who was contacted by Mastriano, said the police would keep a close eye on DeBartolo property within the city, which included the West Side Shopping Center, the Uptown Shopping Center and the company offices on Alexander Street. Sheriff Langley was to protect the suburban homes of the two men as well as shopping centers in Boardman and Poland. Chief Allen later commented, "We have accumulated a wealth of information on all phases of the explosions, but haven't found anything conclusive so far." That included a motive.

April 29, 1952 – the automobile of Hubbard Mayor Joseph J. Baldine in Newton Falls. At the time Baldine was running for the Democratic nomination for Trumbull County sheriff. The explosion took place in the parking lot of the Newton Falls Community Center where the mayor was speaking. Baldine, whom the newspapers described as "a leading contender in the eight-way" race for sheriff, claimed the bomb was set off by his political enemies in an attempt to intimidate him. Governor Lausche ordered an investigation by the state highway patrol.

In 1949 the community of West Hubbard was the scene of two bombings believed to be related to a heated debate over the annexation of "considerable property to Hubbard Village," a proposal that had the backing of Mayor Baldine. At 2:45 a.m. on August 13, a bomb damaged portions of the living room and basement of the C.W. Kirkwood home on Washington Street. Again at 2:45 a.m. on September 8, a bomb collapsed the front porch of W.S. Wissinger, located just 100 feet from the Kirkwood home. In both incidents, the explosives were thrown at the homes.

August 16, 1952 – the home of Valentine Milton, 407 West Marion Avenue, Youngstown. At 1:30 a.m. a dynamite explosive, placed on the porch railing, tore a hole in the porch roof, ripped off the front door and destroyed part of a wall. The blast caused an estimated $800 in damage as it shattered more than 15 windows in the neighborhood. The 45 year-old Milton, worked as a recruiter for the A.E. Anderson Construction Corporation of Buffalo, New York. He advised investigators that due to his work with explosives he was able to detect the odor of dynamite immediately after the blast. Milton told police he had no enemies.

September 2, 1952 – the home of Dominic R. Delbone, 264 North Watt Street, Youngstown. At 2:30 a.m. a container with creosote acid was thrown through the bedroom window of the Delbone home. Helen Delbone, who was nursing her year-old baby, was splashed on the back and neck resulting in first-degree burns. She was treated and released at St. Elizabeth's Hospital.

September 2, 1952 – the home where Paul Duritza resided at 145 South Bruce Street, Youngstown. At 3:15, just 45 minutes after the attack on the Delbone home, John S. Schmidt was wakened when a jar containing creosote acid was tossed through his living room window. The acid damaged a rug and a lamp. Duritza, Schmidt's son-in-law, had left for work moments before the incident.

Both Delbone and Duritza were employed by the Commercial Motor Freight Company as truck drivers and dock men. They were also members of the Chauffeur, Teamsters and Warehousemen's Union Local 377 and were vocal about a recent increase in dues (See chapter 11).

February 5, 1953 – the home of John O. Robinson, Trumbull Avenue, Hubbard Township. The home, unoccupied and under construction, was the scene of an explosion around 3:50 a.m. causing an estimated $500 damage. The bomb was placed in an oil drum and set in the middle of the living room. The blast blew out 23 panes of glass and sent the oil drum through a large picture window and onto the front lawn. Robinson, who was doing most of the construction himself, had no insurance on the home.

Robinson, a black man, was at onetime a Trumbull County sheriff's deputy until he was dismissed by Sheriff Ralph Millikin. Robinson then served as Mayor Joseph Baldine's bodyguard and was later appointed a special constable for Hubbard Township by the mayor. Baldine, who lost in his bid for Trumbull County sheriff in November 1952, believed the bombing was linked to Robinson's raids on several gambling houses in Hubbard Township. Robinson believed that too, telling reporters, "I have been strictly enforcing stop sign regulations throughout the township, but the raids on the gambling joints are the only explanation I can think of for the bombing."

The next day Baldine came up with another motive for the bombing. He now claimed it could have been the result of a bitter election campaign for director of the United Steelworkers of America District 26. Robinson, in addition to his constable duties, was an employee of the Brier Hill plant of Youngstown Sheet & Tube, and a shop steward. Robinson campaigned hard for Danny Thomas who was up against James P. Griffin in the upcoming February 10 election.

Countering Baldine's accusations, Griffin stated, "It seems to me that Baldine and his associates have a penchant for being involved in bombings during campaigns. This bombing is further proof to us that racket elements backing Thomas are attempting to get control of the union and District 26."

March 14, 1953 – the cab of a truck in the garage of the Central Trucking Company, Niles-Cortland Road, Niles. Around 3:00 a.m. dynamite exploded inside the cab of a dump truck parked inside the company garage. Nelson Brutz, secretary-treasurer of the firm, claimed the bombing was carried out by business rivals. He reported that several months earlier sand was poured into the gas tank of one of the trucks.

March 19, 1953 – the garage of the Central Trucking Company, Niles-Cortland Road, Niles. For the second time in six days bombers struck at the trucking concern. At 1:30 a.m. an explosion tore a two-foot hole in the roof of the concrete block garage and destroyed several windows. After being reported to the Howland Fire Department it took them an hour to find the source of the explosion.

March 20, 1953 – State Road Shopping Center, Cuyahoga Falls. Being built by M. DeBartolo Construction Company.

March 30, 1953 – home of Frank P. DeNiro, 116 Lincoln Park Drive, Youngstown. *This was covered in the chapter on DeNiro* (See chapter 11).

April 16, 1953 – home of Frank P. DeNiro, 116 Lincoln Park Drive, Youngstown. *This was covered in the chapter on DeNiro* (See chapter 11).

June 19, 1953 – the Golden Gate Night Club, Route 422, north of Warren. At 3:15 a.m. an explosion, caused by either dynamite or nitroglycerine, tossed onto the roof, blew a two-foot hole in the roof and tore out a five-foot section of the barroom ceiling. A glass bar-back was also shattered. Carmen Cesta and Adrian Belmaggio, co-owners of the restaurant, could offer no excuse for the bombing. They claimed they had no union problems and no enemies. Both the new sheriff and the county prosecutor were in Columbus at the time of the bombing – attending a crime conference. Investigators believed a "personal grudge" was behind the bombing.

July 7, 1953 – a dump truck parked in the rear of Nelson Brutz' home, 404 Lincoln Avenue, Niles. In what was being called "inter-union strife," the Central Trucking Company suffered a third attack in just over four months. Around 4:00 a.m. dynamite placed beneath the cab of a company owned dump truck sent pieces of the vehicle flying, which shattered windows in houses along Lincoln and Washington Avenues. The newspaper reported, "Pieces of fenders, transmissions, panels and other metal were found in lawns a block away. Leaves were ripped from trees and awnings were ruined in many Washington Ave. residences by heavy pieces of metal and other debris." Mrs. Brutz' automobile had its roof gashed open by a section of the truck's tailgate.

Gasoline from the gas tank ignited and showered down on a concrete block garage. Brutz, the secretary-treasurer of the company, rushed to the garage and with the help of several neighbors was able to remove another truck from the burning structure.

Brutz said that the company was no longer engaged "principally" in trucking, but turned its focus to installing driveways. A couple of truckers who worked for the company recently dropped their affiliation with the AFL truck drivers' local.

December 10, 1953 – home of Bud J. Fares, 633 Almyra Avenue, Youngstown. *This was covered in the chapter on Allen and Henderson* (see chapter 9).

February 13, 1954 – the home of Paul P. Marr, 130 Ridgeway, Struthers. A bomb placed on a brick and cement railing at the corner of the Marr home exploded around 2:10 a.m., just ten minutes after Marr's wife and 11 year-old son went upstairs to bed. The blast ripped a hole in the living room wall, breaking several windows and spreading debris throughout the room. Struthers police said the bombing was the work of an amateur. Marr stated, "I don't have an enemy in town as far as I know."

Marr had formerly run the P & M Billiards Hall on South Bridge Street. Although Marr claimed he no longer owned it, Struthers Police Chief G. Woodrow Sicafuse said Marr was frequently at the pool hall, and "as far as I am concerned the place is in his name." Marr's police record showed an arrest in January 1950, for keeping gambling equipment at the pool hall and a June 1950 arrest for keeping a gambling room. He pled guilty both times and was fined. Marr owned the Summit Motel on Route 422 with his brother Anthony and brother-in-law Rocco Constantino.

March 28, 1954 – Tauro Dump Truck Service & Marino Coal Company, 226 Pratt Street, Niles. A window was broken and a stench bomb was tossed in causing damage to walls and furniture. Louis Tauro, the operator-manager of the firm said the concern operated five company-owned dump trucks and had 30 to 40 driver-owners operating trucks under its P.U.C.O. permit. He knew of no motive for the attack.

April 3, 1954 – the home of Frank Fetchet, 2044 Felicia Avenue, Youngstown. *This was covered in the chapter on the Fetchet brothers* (see chapter 11).

April 24, 1954 – the Towne Plaza Shopping Center, Massillon. The 22-unit, $1.5 million complex suffered $20,000 in damage when a dynamite bomb, hidden in a pile of lumber exploded. Towne Plaza, Inc. was owned and operated by William S. Cafaro of Warren. The shopping center was being built by the B & B Construction Company of Youngstown, which was owned by Fred Beshara. The blast ripped a hole in the floor of the W. T. Grant Company store, shattered several plate glass windows in that section and embedded fragments of wood and bomb particles into the walls and ceiling. The explosion, which occurred around 11:00 on a Saturday night, drew hundreds of onlookers to the scene. John Cafaro told police he knew of no labor difficulties which could have led to the incident. "The people of Massillon have been wonderful to us," he stated.

May 12, 1954 – the home of Roland Leibert, 156 Wilson Avenue, Niles. The 11:00 p.m. dynamite blast tore a hole in the breezeway and garage and shattered eight windows in the home. The damage was estimated at $1,000. Mrs. Leibert narrowly missed being showered with glass in the kitchen; two young children sleeping upstairs were unharmed. The blast was similar to the one in Massillon on April 24, in that it occurred at a reasonably early hour, 11:00 p.m., and attracted crowds of onlookers.

Leibert, an oiler on a power shovel, was described as an influential member of the AFL Operating Engineers' Union. It was reported that, "A pending strike of truck drivers on the turnpike may have been responsible for the incident." Members of the Teamsters' union felt they could strengthen their bargaining position for higher wages if members of Leibert's union supported them. Leibert was approached by the Teamster members and "urged" to stay away from work on the day of the bombing. Leibert refused. One police report identified Leibert as "a known bug operator," and concluded that the bombing had something to do with his activities.

May 13, 1954 – the home of Raymond White, 245 Gypsy Lane, Youngstown. A stench bomb inside a glass jar was tossed through the front window of the home around 4:00 a.m. causing an estimated $200 damage to the carpeting, a couch and a chair. White was a partner in Cleveland Auto Wrecking Company, Inc. He told investigators he had "some ideas as to who might have done this, but I certainly will not make any charges until I am sure." Inside the house at the time were White, his brother Morton, Raymond's 4 year-old son and a housekeeper. The housekeeper told police that when she heard glass breaking she thought it was just "Raymond and his brother coming home."

May 14, 1954 – the Towne Plaza Shopping Center, Massillon. For the second time in three weeks, the W. T. Grant Company was the target of bombers. This time, however, the blast caused a mere $100 damage. Police surmised a "homemade" explosive was placed atop a concrete slab at the rear doorway of the store, which had scheduled its grand opening for June 15. The bomb went off at 9:20 p.m., just 20 minutes after the closing of adjoining stores. The complex owner, William Cafaro, could offer no explanation and stated that B & B Construction Company, which was building the shopping center, wasn't having any labor problems "whatsoever."

May 23, 1954 – Tauro Dump Truck Service & Marino Coal Company, 226 Pratt Street, Niles. After a stench bomb incident in March, the company suffered more serious damage when a dynamite explosion ripped through the office at 1:55 a.m. causing $2,000 in damage. The *Vindicator* reported, "A dynamite bomb slipped beneath the structure, which is supported by concrete block, ripped a hole nine by 12 feet in the flooring, tore open a ceiling, smashed glass in six windows, crushed a calculating machine and reduced a typewriter to a mass of twisted metal." In addition, records were strewn about the room, furniture was knocked around and a fuel pump near the building was damaged. The blast was said to have "rattled windows in the police station."

Louis Tauro told police he was at a loss as to who might be responsible for either incident. "We have been checking around trying to find out if anybody wants anything from us or is harboring a grudge. We haven't been able to find out a thing and nobody has approached us for anything. That's why it's all so mysterious," Tauro said. Drivers employed by the company were members of Local 377 Chauffeurs & Teamsters Union. Louis' brother, Joseph A. Tauro, was an agent in the Warren office of the IRS.

May 25, 1954 – the Union Distributing Company, 1141 South State Street, Girard. A dynamite bomb was thrown on the roof of the building causing about $55 in damage. Described as a "beer distributing agency," one of the owners was Youngstown Third Ward Councilman Anthony B. Flask, Jr., who claimed the explosion was the result of a refrigeration compressor blowing up. Flask refused to allow photographers to take pictures of the damage. The newspaper claimed, "All the [recent] blasts were at places whose owners had some connection with trucking in Trumbull County." Union Distributing Company used a fleet of twelve trucks to deliver its beer to locations in Columbia, Mahoning and Trumbull Counties. A police report claimed, Leo "Shine" Jennings of Niles was connected with Union Distributing Company of Girard and his wife, Alice, was a director and stockholder.

May 28, 1954 – Johnnie's Grocery, 1157 West Rayen Avenue, Youngstown. Around 11:50 p.m. a dynamite explosion broke nine plate glass windows in the store, destroyed the front door, a screen door and damaged a section of brickwork in the doorway. The damage caused to the small grocery store, operated by John Burnich, Jr. and his brother Steve, totaled only $61. Police had two theories on the bombing. First, it was connected with the attack at Flask's Union Distributing Company earlier in the week because the distributor supplied Johnnie's Grocery with beer and wine. The second theory was that it was related to the numbers competition. Burnich, who had recently purchased a federal gambling tax stamp, had turned it over to the vice squad after it was reported in February that he was a "principal" in the gambling racket. Although the police department had a number of complaints about bug activity there, there hadn't been an arrest in the past four years. Other than an arrest for suspicion in August 1945, John Burnich had no police record. A *Vindicator* headline screamed, "Report War Among Lottery Men." The article said the bombing was a "reflection of an undercover war among city bug operators," this war was fought over "the scraps and tatters of the once flourishing city numbers racket."

During the police investigation over the ensuing weeks several men were taken in for questioning and given polygraph tests including John Burnich. Two brothers emerged as prime suspects – Stephen Nicholas Kisan and Anthony John Kisan – although they were never charged. Officer Robert Balog, who conducted the polygraph tests, summarized as follows:

> "John Burnich Jr.: The subject showed a very pronounced reaction to the following two questions. 1. 'Do you know who bombed your store?' 2. 'After the bombing, did anyone contact you in regards to a shake-down?' It is the opinion of the examiner that the subject lied when he denies having any knowledge of who was responsible for the above mentioned bombing.
>
> "Stephen Kisan: It is the opinion of the examiner that the subject lied when he denies having anything to do with the above mentioned bombing. It is also the opinion of the examiner that the subject is directly involved."
>
> "Anthony Kisan: It is the opinion of the examiner that the subject has some knowledge of the above mentioned bombing but doesn't seem to be directly involved."

The day after this latest bombing, Governor Lausche called for a "concentrated effort" to end the wave of terror sweeping the Valley. The governor stated, "Bombings such as these constitute one of the major assaults against society and law and order." Then, perhaps taking a shot at the Valley's law enforcement, said, "Regrettably, most local officials do not look upon them in that light."

The *Vindicator* reported that in 28 incidents over a 30 month period there had not been a single arrest, let alone a trial or conviction. "Police in most cases," the newspaper stated, "have not even been able to find anyone to arrest for questioning." They also reported that in addition to the 28 bombings, "There seems good reason to believe that some incidents have been 'covered up' either by law enforcement officials or the persons directly involved." Theories as to motives in these attacks fell into four categories – labor difficulties, inter-union strife, competition for gambling interests and revenge.

Heading a state probe into the recent bombings of the Union Distributing Company and Johnnie's Grocery was newly appointed State Liquor Enforcement Chief Edward J. Allen. The former Youngstown police chief had replaced Anthony Rutkowski, who had recently been appointed to the common pleas bench in Cleveland by Governor Lausche. Allen promised a thorough investigation of the incidents a day after Lausche's plea for a "concentrated effort." Many surmised Allen would not get much cooperation from Flask. The councilman, who was a political enemy of Allen during his days as chief, had failed to cooperate with Girard city officials after the blast in which the cause took two days to be reported correctly in the newspapers.

Meanwhile, the *Vindicator* reported that a local "free nightclub publication," not identified as Bud Fares' *The Youngstowner*, had printed a story that Flask and Leo "Shine" Jennings had joined together and had taken over the "wholesaling of one of the district's most popular beers." Jennings had previously operated a gambling den in Niles.

By mid-June some elements of the Valley's underworld believed new Vice Squad Chief George Krispli had "gone far enough" with his investigation into the recent bombings. An anonymous caller threatened to "harm his wife." On June 15, the newspaper reported, "Seven Youngstown men, many of them notorious racket figures allegedly connected with the dreaded Mafia or Black Hand Society, were given an ultimatum after their arrest Monday: 'Get legitimate jobs or face constant police harassment.'"

Krispli said the seven men "will be brought in continually for questioning until they convince police they are working at legitimate jobs." The vice squad leader had hoped to identify the voice of the man who had phoned in the threat about his wife. During questioning the suspects denied any connection to the bombings or anything else illegal. All refused to take a lie detector test. The seven arrested were "Fats" Aiello, Vince DeNiro, Sandy Naples, Charles Cavallaro, John "Tar Baby" Millovich, Charles Vizzini and Joseph Romano. Chief Cress told reporters afterwards that "This is just the beginning of a continued program to encourage this criminal element to leave our city."

The *Vindicator* reported, "All of those questioned were vehement in their denial of any knowledge of the bombings. It was reported they may have been the result of underworld warfare to gain control of the city's rackets after a reported split between DeNiro and Naples. The two were said to have been operating the lottery independently after DeNiro became angered at Naples' numerous arrests by city police."

The bombing of Johnnie's Grocery Store followed the attack on the home of Frank Fetchet by less than two months. These two events signaled the beginning of the bombing war as it pertained to the policy kings.

It was only a matter of time after the "Smash Racket Rule" regime of Allen and Henderson came to an end in January 1954, that the policy brokers were back in full force in the Youngstown. The *Vindicator* reported in November 1955, that the number of policy outlets had doubled over the previous year, while the arrest of "bug runners" had dwindled to an average of less than three per month.

The newspaper documented its claims by conducting what they termed periodic "surveys," in which lottery bets were placed at various locations, and through their scrutiny of the police arrest blotters. The surveys were conducted during the summer of 1954, December 1954, September 1955 and November 1955. They divided the lottery operations into three categories:

1. The downtown or near-downtown restaurant, tavern, grocery or poolroom where large groups of people ordinarily go.
2. The neighborhood center which sends runners to homes throughout a given area.
3. The "home" at which neighbors drop in to leave bets under the promise that the place is "protected" by one of the several big bug operators.

The *Vindicator* revealed that, "Home bug spots have expanded the most among those covered by the surveys. Where one house took bets a year ago in the North Ave. area, now there are three. A talkative party connected with one of these said a month's gross totaled $1,400. All of it went to Vince DeNiro, another stamp holder, who paid the operator a salary and "guaranteed" no interference from police."

The newspaper shared the results of their investigation with the police department, but claimed little was done. The list of bug operations was handed to both Vice Squad Chief George Krispli and Police Chief Paul Cress in early November 1955. By the end of the month the newspaper reported that so far no raids were conducted, "police have done nothing against habitual offenders except to threaten padlock action."

What follows is a rundown of the most active policy locations based on the *Vindicator*'s November 1955 survey:

American Poolroom, E. Federal St., also under DeNiro supervision and recently moved from a South Ave. location.

Archies, Jacobs Road, a fairly recent DeNiro joint.

Carlyle Grocery, 656 High St., sells whiskey, beer and bug regardless of age or sex; frequented by women and children.

Center Sandwich Shop, Wilson Ave., catches the mill workers as they come off the end of the Center St. Bridge; one headquarters of Sandy Naples; sells generally to persons known as customers. Sandy has been a prime target of police. His shop has hardly been touched.

Family Wine Shop, 901 W. Federal St., took the attention of vice squad members in October and November 1954; arrests were made. One player claimed, "This place catches all the business along W. Federal St."

Federal Billiards, W. Federal St., does business mainly with runners; also some crap games in rear; raided once in two years by police.

Greek-Syrian Coffee House, South Ave., is the place where you can get the bug number by dialing RI 6-9355 after 6 p.m. It's like getting the time. You just dial it and a voice gives you the winning number for the day. Operated by Gus Leamis.

Himrod Cigar Store, 626 Himrod Ave., also caters to women and children. Milkmen and soda pop truck drivers also drop in.

J and G Grocery Store, Himrod and Penn Ave., takes some play away from Himrod Cigar.

Johnnie's Grocery Store, 1157 W. Rayen Ave. Johnnie's writes bets only for those who are well known to the operator and clerks. Owned by John Burnich.

Kissos Confectionery, on E. Boardman St., four blocks east of City Hall. Bug players often stood in line to lay their money on a number.

State Bar / Restaurant, three blocks east of City Hall on Boardman St., sells numbers daily. Policemen in uniform occasionally sit at lunch counter while numbers are written in rear.

United Lunch, 16-18 South Ave., caters to runners who drop in about noon.

Under media pressure, Chief Cress finally launched a series of raids on February 2, 1956. Included with the raiding parties, which were divided into three units, were nine photographers and news reporters from the *Vindicator* and local radio stations. Except for the arrest of a man and woman at Carlyle Grocery, the raids were a complete bust most likely due to the fact that the targets were notified ahead of time.

At Jimmy Naples home a photographer watched as a young child was hustled out of the house just minutes before police arrived. Steve Burnich, brother of John and co-owner of Johnnie's Grocery Store, sat calmly reading the newspaper as raiders searched the home. Another raiding party came up empty at the home of Frank Fetchet on Felicia Avenue.

When police arrived at the Poplar Street home of Sandy Naples they encountered his parents before finding Joseph, the youngest brother, still asleep in his bed. Sandy remained calm as the raiders searched the house, but used the moment to talk to reporters.

"You think I'm crazy?" he questioned. "They ain't going to find anything here. You think I'm stupid? What the hell does that Cress have for brains?"

When the *Vindicator* conducted its fifth "survey," during the summer of 1956, it reported, "While the volume of sales in the illegal, million-dollar racket shifted somewhat from place to place in the downtown area, all previously publicized joints continued to book bets and a number of new spots got into the act."

The newspaper pointed out that the most active of the "new spots" was the Variety News Stand, on East Boardman Street.

June 11, 1954 – the Canada Dry Bottling Company, 2680 Youngstown Road, Warren. A two-by-two foot hole was blown in the roof of the plant by a bomb, which went off at 2:20 a.m. Although the explosion was heard for several blocks and Warren police cruised the area, it wasn't until 7:00 a.m. when the plant was opened that the damage was discovered. Windows were smashed and there was some equipment damaged. Total damages were estimated at $200. The plant was run by Martin and James Jennings, Jr. Both were sons of James "Sunny Jim" Jennings, who was listed as the president of the bottling concern. As far as a reason for the bombing, "There must be some crackpot, similar to a pyromaniac, running loose," claimed Martin Jennings. "Sunny Jim's" brother Leo was connected with the Union Distributing Company, which was bombed on May 25.

July 17, 1954 – the home of Mahoning County Democratic Chairman Jack Sulligan, 1966 Smithfield Street, Youngstown. Around 2:30 a.m. a dynamite bomb exploded on the steps leading to the front porch of the Sulligan home. The wooden steps were splintered, windows were shattered and the siding was badly damaged. Lead fragments sprayed the front of the home as well as a house next door. Sulligan was alone in the house asleep; his wife and a daughter were at their Lake Milton cottage, while another daughter was out of town and had taken Sulligan's car – possibly leading the bombers to think the house was empty. Police discovered a pickup truck containing an open case of dynamite on the Oak Street Extension approximately 45 minutes before the explosion. The truck was stolen at 11:30 the previous night from a quarry in Pennsylvania owned by the New Castle Limestone Company. Chief Paul Cress boasted, "The police department has a pretty fair idea who is doing the bombings."

Sulligan was the Democratic County Chairman since the death of John C. Vitullo in 1948. Sulligan told police, "I think perhaps there are still some persons who are unhappy because of the heat downtown which is keeping them from opening up rackets. I am in hearty agreement with the mayor to keep the town closed." Sulligan claimed that when Frank Kryzan was campaigning for mayor they were offered money from several racketeers, but refused it.

Both Kryzan and Cress felt a lot of pressure to solve this latest bombing. Kryzan, the first Democrat to hold the mayor's office in six years, was indebted to Sulligan for helping him get there. The newspaper reported that the bombing was being "interpreted" as a "slap in the face" to the Kryzan administration after they promised a continuance of the Henderson administration's "Smash Racket Rule."

Kryzan, on the offensive, declared he would order "more action against rackets and racketeers," but offered no details. Cress offered up an even more bizarre statement, "We have enough to work on, with the exception of eventually accomplishing something."

Both the mayor and police chief offered some insight as to what they believed was going on. Sandy Naples, convicted of promoting the bug racket, was sentenced to six months in the county jail three days before the latest bombing. Kryzan reflected, "If this [the bombing] is an indication of the way some bums and hoodlums react against law enforcement, I am more determined than ever that I will not let down until the day we can get all of these undesirables either behind bars or out of the community."

Chief Cress saw a pattern developing during shifts of power in the numbers rackets. "Taking, for example, the bombing of the home of Frank Fetchet," Cress stated. "Just before that Sandy Naples got in trouble with the law and for some time was kept busy in court. Consequently, he didn't have much time to attend to whatever affairs he may have had on the outside. Perhaps someone else during that time invaded Naples' field and took some of his business. At any rate, somebody dropped a bomb at the Fetchet home."

Cress called the bombings "a special language" of the numbers men, a warning to "get in line and do, or quit doing, whatever has irked the bombers." He reiterated that the bombings were a warning and that, "Nobody gets hurt!"

During Cress' investigation Vince DeNiro, "Fats" Aiello and Nick J. Jardine were arrested and held for questioning. Aiello was found outside his favorite restaurant – the Purple Cow – while DeNiro was picked up in the parking lot of the Colonial House Restaurant on Market Street. Jardine had two convictions on his record, a liquor violation in 1929, when he was fined $100, and for possession of counterfeit gasoline ration stamps in March 1944, for which he spent ten months in a federal prison. What his connection might have been to the Sulligan bombing was not revealed. All three men were questioned and released. In addition, Cress had Sandy Naples, Charlie Cavallaro and Calogero Malfitano hauled in for questioning.

By early August, the police were still investigating with no results. On August 10, the *Vindicator* printed the names of eleven underworld figures the police wanted to question, most were those listed as recent purchasers of the federal gambling tax stamp. The next morning Peter Fetchet, John Burnich and Joseph Romanchuk arrived at police headquarters with their lawyers ready to be questioned. One of the first questions asked of Burnich was why he had legal representation with him. Burnich replied that he was trying to stave off bad publicity because of working at his in-laws store, Terlecky's Appliance, and his partnership with his brother Steve at Johnnie's Grocery Store. While being interrogated, he claimed he was in the process of selling his share of the grocery store to his younger brother.

Burnich admitted to being a childhood friend of Frank Fetchet, but claimed he never did any business with him and knew nothing about the bombing of his house back on April 3. He did admit to owing money to Peter Fetchet, which he said he borrowed to pay off creditors in the appliance business.

The interrogation of Burnich, while raising some interesting points, did not bring the investigators any closer to those responsible. Here are a few of the more interesting exchanges. On the subject of the bombings at Johnnie's Grocery Store:

> Question: After the bombing of your store you once stated that you went looking for Sandy Naples and found him at a girl friends on Caledonia Street and you asked him about the bombing of your store?
>
> Answer: If I did go there I don't recall, it's been some time ago if I did, I don't remember asking him anything about the bombing.
>
> On the subject of the bombing at Jack Sulligan's home:
>
> Question: Do you attribute the bombing of Jack Sulligan's home due to the fact that since the first of the year there has been a crack down on numbers business in this city?
>
> Answer: That I couldn't answer. Many a man gets chased for taking out another man's wife.
>
> On the Mafia in the Mahoning Valley:
>
> Question: Do you know if there are any remnants of the Mafia Gang in this district?

Answer: I don't know what the Mafia Gang means and never heard about it until it came out in the paper just recently, and it must have been before my time.

Finally, on the lie detector analyst's conclusion that he had lied during the polygraph test after the bombing of Johnnie's Grocery Store:

Question: How do you account for the difference in your answers and your reactions on the lie detector?

Answer: Being a high strung person with a critical ulcer, which made me very nervous, which may have been responsible for my reaction on the machine.

Joseph John Romanchuk was born in Youngstown in September 1927. A 1945 graduate of Rayen High School, he then joined the Marines and was honorably discharged in 1947. Romanchuk had several notches on his rap sheet, including possession of lottery slips and suspicion. During his interrogation he stated he was a salesman at Terlecky Appliance, where his boss was Burnich. The two men were friends since childhood.

Romanchuk was asked why he was the holder of a federal gambling tax stamp. He replied, "John Burnich and myself would put our money together, and shoot crap and play cards, and we wanted to be honest with the government so we got a wagering stamp."

Romanchuk was involved with local politics at one time and was elected precinct committeeman, serving one term from 1951 to 1952. He was succeeded by Anthony Kisan, who was questioned, along with his brother, in the Johnnie's Grocery Store bombing agreeing to take a lie detector test. Romanchuk was asked, "What sort of feeling is there between you and Jack Sulligan?" He answered, the "same feeling as there always was, I didn't know him and he didn't know me." He claimed he was no longer involved in politics because, "This last time I didn't run as a precinct committeeman, because the last time that I was arrested, Chief Allen tried to make an issue of it." In October 1953, when Allen arrested him on bug charges. In court Municipal Judge John W. Powers, who once worked at having Allen removed from office, freed Romanchuk of the charges.

Both Burnich and Romanchuk declined the offer to take a lie detector test claiming they didn't believe it was "accurate." During the interrogation the two were questioned only about three bombings – Johnnie's Grocery Store, Jack Sulligan's house and the home of Raymond White back on May 13. If there was some connection between the White bombing and the other two it was not made apparent.

Cress was angry with the *Vindicator* for this turn of events. He snarled at a reporter saying, "This certainly wouldn't have happened if your paper had not printed the list of names the police department is interested in." He promised that in the future he would see to it that the newspaper "did not learn the names of any new suspects so that the men wanted cannot learn of police plans in advance and consult attorneys."

Cress was not deterred in his master plan. "We'll keep picking up local racket figures until we find enough evidence for a conviction," he promised. The plan was to continually pick up every racketeer off the street and re-question him, by "the second, third or fourth time around, somebody will get his story scrambled and provide a working basis toward prosecution."

July 31, 1954 – the uncompleted home of Paul Calderone (identified as Paul Brown in the newspapers), Belle Terre Avenue, Niles. Police found two sticks of unexploded dynamite at the under-construction ranch home around 8:00 a.m. after being called to the scene by Calderone. The bomb was found near a heating duct between the living room and kitchen; a long fuse was "carelessly connected" preventing it from detonating. A neighbor recalled hearing dogs barking around 1:00 a.m. Calderone, the vice president of the Central Trucking Company, was perplexed by the attempt claiming he had no problems with unions or anybody. "I just work my 12 hours a day hauling slag or anything else I get a contract for and causing nobody any trouble," he declared. This despite the fact that this was the fourth incident involving the trucking concern.

During the summer of 1954, the Ohio State Highway Patrol conducted an investigation of the bombings in Mahoning and Trumbull Counties. After reviewing 29 incidents, they concluded that the motives for the bombings were, 1) to intimidate others for the purpose of accomplishing their (hoodlums and racketeers) personal desires; 2) revenge – grudge fights; or 3) personal or political gain.

In arriving at the *modus operandi* of the bombers, the investigation claimed:

> "Hired hoods are presumed to drive their motor vehicles to the vicinity of the proposed location to be bombed, parking their automobiles and walking to the building placing their bombs equipped with delayed fuses, dynamite, stench and duds, scare bombs, returning to their vehicles and driving away unnoticed."

The investigators determined the suspects to be, "Hired hoodlums from the Cleveland area." The report ended with information regarding two men whose involvement they suspected:

> "Louis Marchionte, 941 Lincoln Ave., Niles, Ohio. (Believed to be responsible for the bombings involving the Central Trucking Company).
>
> "'Shine' Jennings, believed to be the go-between between the Cleveland hoodlums and local individuals.

> "Information obtained from an informant indicates a strong possibility of Louis Marchionte being involved in the bombings, stating that the bombings of the Central Trucking Company started to occur shortly after Mr. Marchionte contacted the officials of the Company and requested readmission to the Company. However, he was refused and sometime later the bombings started to commence.
>
> "Mr. Marchionte was then accepted by the Company as a part-time official. The bombings immediately subsided and remained that way until just recently when Mr. Marchionte started to exert some pressure upon the Company officials demanding interest in the Company.
>
> "It was reported that Shine Jennings approached Mr. Marchionte and ordered him to refrain from future bombings, as the publicity has created adverse sentiment among influential citizens in this area and if the bombings continued an extensive investigation no doubt would be made and consequently the possibility of their racket being exposed.
>
> "The following day after the scare bomb was found at the residence of Paul Calderone, Mr. Marchionte was observed by our informant as appearing to have been beaten up, stating he had a black eye and other facial bruises. It is assumed by him that he was beaten up for placing the bomb at the Calderone residence."

August 2, 1954 – the automobile of Elman Burnett, 338 Park Avenue, New Castle, Pennsylvania. Around 3:00 a.m. an unidentified explosive was tossed under Burnett's 1953 automobile, which was parked on Logan Street around the corner from the Burnett home. Burnett and his wife claimed they heard a muffled sound, but when they looked out the window they saw nothing suspicious and went back to bed. Burnett discovered the bombed car when he was leaving for work at 6:00 a.m. He was employed by the Morain Coating & Construction Company on Market Street in Youngstown. Burnett could offer no reason for the bombing

August 3, 1954 – on Denver Drive near Route 90 in Poland. Sheriff's deputies believe a test bomb was exploded on the street. The blast, which tore a large hole in the berm of Denver Drive, occurred around 9:30 p.m., but wasn't reported by residents until 4:00 the next afternoon. Deputies found roofing material and parts of a rain sprout that they believed were used as the outside casing for the bomb.

August 28, 1954 – the Circella Grocery Store, 2047 Jacobs Road, Youngstown. The 3:45 a.m. explosion caused about $200 damage to the small grocery operated by Anthony Circella. The blast shattered two large windowpanes and several smaller ones, and damaged the front door and two brick walls leading into the store. The dynamite bomb was placed at the corner of the recessed doorway. Six members of Circella's family, including his parents, were asleep in an apartment above the store; all were frightened although no one was harmed. Neighbors reported that two cars were seen in the vicinity just prior to the explosion.

During a canvassing of the neighborhood the police got practically the same answer from everyone they questioned, "There was no reason for it, the Circellas were liked by all and never engaged on anything illegal." While the police were questioning Anthony Circella and his mother at the station they left the room at one point, leaving a tape recorder secretly running in hopes of picking up some information during an exchange between the two. The results were negative. Police hauled in Sandy Naples, Vince DeNiro, "Fats" Aiello and Benjamin T. Guerrieri for questioning.

The newspaper reported, "Circella said that he had not been in the numbers racket, has never written or played the bug, and said he could give no reason for the bombing." The blast came less than 24 hours after Mayor Kryzan launched a verbal attack against the numbers racketeers operating in the city.

When a city councilman said that he would ask the FBI to get involved, the bureau was quick to acknowledge that since no federal laws were broken the agency would take no active role in the investigation.

September 24, 1954 – the garage at the home of Joseph "Jugg" and Sam "Hobo" Sanfrey, 270 Maryland Avenue, Warren. The dynamite blast, around 2:20 a.m., caused $1,500 damage to two cars, the garage and windows in a neighbor's home. Sam Sanfrey was convicted and served a six-month sentence for running a "disorderly house" in Deforest, a neighborhood on the city's north side, in November 1953. A week earlier a fire in Deforest destroyed the Ivy Inn, a one time notorious house of prostitution on South Main Avenue. Sanfrey told detectives he had "no idea who might have done such a thing, it might have been the work of some punks."

October 22, 1954 – the home of Julius Benson, 26 Sycamore Street, Youngstown. The explosion took place at 1:30 a.m. and broke two windows in the house. Benson said he told Chief Cress about the blast, but the newspaper, which didn't report the incident until five days later, said it was "suppressed by the police." The *Vindicator* reported that it was not known whether a firecracker or dynamite caused the blast. The incident could have been a "prank of all-night Halloweeners." Benson was a former manager of the 40 Club.

October 26, 1954 – the Sunrise Confectionery, 1601 McGuffey Road, Youngstown. The explosion went off at 1:45 a.m. after dynamite was placed against the front door at the store owned by Emideo DiFrangia. The front door and two large windows in the entrance were destroyed. There was damage to the front exterior of the building and broken windows on the second floor. DiFrangia and his wife were asleep in an apartment on the second floor. The damage was estimated at $600.

The newspaper reported that, "The friendly operator said he never has written a 'bug' number in the 25 years he has operated his store and never has had trouble with fellow workers in the transportation department of Republic Steel Corp., where he is a foreman." As with the blasts at Johnnie's Grocery Store and Circella's, DiFrangia claimed he had "a C-2 beer and wine carryout permit," but this portion of their business was small. The storeowner claimed he did business with many distributors, but only purchased "a couple of cases of beer from anyone who comes to the store when I need it."

October 26, 1954 – a strip-shopping plaza owned by State Road Plaza, Inc., State Road (Route 8) Cuyahoga Falls. A triple blast destroyed the fronts of three stores in this shopping plaza, which was preparing to open in February 1955. Edward J. DeBartolo was the president of the corporation and the stores were being built by the M. DeBartolo Construction Company. Damage was estimated at $7,000 to $9,000. The damaged stores were J. C. Penney, People's Drug Store and the Thom McAnn shoe store. Company officials could offer no explanation stating there was no labor difficulty.

October 29, 1954 – the Warren Richey Elementary School, East High Avenue and Early Road, Youngstown. An early morning blast caused $700 in damage to this school on the city's East Side. The dynamite explosive was believed to have been hung on the school's front door. The blast destroyed the front door and 42 windows. School officials claimed there was no trouble at the school and that it must have been the work of "vandals or some mentally unbalanced person." The newspaper reported that former principal Warren L. Richey, for whom the school was named, was a vice chairman of the Youngstown Metropolitan Housing Authority, which was involved recently in a bitter dispute regarding a nearby public housing project. On the day of the blast, a Friday, the school was closed for NEOTA day, a district teachers' meeting day.

A front-page article in the *Vindicator* on October 30 cited the frustration everyone seemed to be feeling about the rash of bombings. The newspaper claimed the bombings had now fallen into the following categories, "rackets, beer distribution, politics and labor union disagreements," but declared the school bombing didn't fit into any of these. Despite the range of categories, the article suggested the bombings might be the work of one individual:

> "Who does he work for, this criminal who seems to have an unlimited supply of dynamite? Can anyone in the underworld hire him for a 'job' against an enemy or a potential threat? Or is the syndicate for which he works as vast that its interests cross the lines of all four bombing categories and into an elementary school as well?"

For the first time since the bombings began three years earlier there was a touch of indignation finally in the newspaper, apparently triggered by the attack on a schoolhouse. Chief Cress announced that two detectives were assigned to investigate the bombing on a full-time basis. "We are going to concentrate on this case until we get something to work with," Cress stated. The newspaper reported, "In the past, investigators have been sidetracked with other duties and investigations and have not been able to work full-time on any one of the city's last five mysterious bombings."

Cress told reporters, "We are not going to let up on this investigation. I have had a feeling all along that some of the victims surely know why they were bombed, but with some of these I'm not too concerned. However, when the school board is involved, we enter something far more serious than the bombing of a bookie joint or labor troubles." The chief considered that the bomber could even be a psychopath, but in the school's case stated, "Certainly you don't have a disgruntled third grader who is responsible."

December 27, 1954 – the State Street Tavern, 186 State Street, Struthers. A bomb planted in a flowerpot outside the front entrance exploded around 4:30 a.m. smashing windows on the first and second floor of the building and damaging a neon sign. Police arrested two men, one a 16 year-old, and stated that the bombing may have resulted from a fight involving four women, which began in the tavern on Christmas Eve.

January 28, 1955 – the home of Paul Kurosky, 831 Garland Avenue, Youngstown. Around 2:00 a.m. an explosion left a four-inch hole in the flooring of the front porch, causing an estimated $25 damage. Kurosky's two married daughters lived at the house. Although the sisters were awaken by the blast, they concluded that a gas hot water tank had exploded somewhere in the neighborhood. The damage wasn't discovered until the next morning by Kurosky. One sister was married to Joseph J. Costello a contract painter. Costello, who recently formed his own painting company, was in Ashtabula working for the B & B Construction Company doing a job for William Cafaro. Costello said his desire to begin his own company had the blessing of the Painter's Union and could offer no reason for the attack.

August 9, 1955 – the front porch of Joseph "Shorty" Bardinello, 491 Catalina Avenue, Youngstown. A stick of dynamite was found on the porch by Bardinello's young daughter around 10:00 a.m. Police weren't notified until late afternoon when the girl pointed it out to her father. The fuse had gone out before reaching the blasting cap.

It was seven months since the last incident and police had a variety of motives to pursue. Bardinello, like Costello, was a painter in the employ of the Ohio Valley Sheeting & Painting Company. The owner of the company, George Glaros, was active in Democratic politics. Finally, Bardinello was described as a "small-time bug operator and petty racketeer who formerly owned the Spot Club in Market St.," an alleged gambling joint. When asked for a comment by a reporter Bardinello replied, "I don't want to discuss anything about this thing with you or anyone else."

August 14, 1955 – the automobile of Thomas Ciarnello, owner of the Ohio Tavern, 1525 Hubbard Road, Hubbard. The Valley surely escaped its first fatality when three sticks of dynamite, wired to the engine of Ciarnello's car, failed to detonate. Ciarnello operated the Ohio Tavern, an alleged gambling joint in Trumbull County. The *Vindicator* reported:

> "Ciarnello told police he left his tavern about 4:15pm and drove to a nearby restaurant for a milkshake. He said he noticed the hood of his auto unlocked when he came out and slammed it shut before he drove off.
>
> "The tavern operator said he drove to Logan Ave. and Hubbard Road and stopped at a service station because the motor was not functioning properly. He said he opened the hood and found a paper potato bag and wires attached to the third cylinder. He removed them and threw them to the ground.
>
> "Police said they opened the bag and found three quarter-pound sticks of dynamite with cap and wires wrapped in a pink towel. The bag containing the device was placed between the battery and wiring of the motor block."

The article revealed, "Crime lab technicians said the three sticks of dynamite would have completely destroyed the automobile and caused damage to nearby objects if it had exploded." Then, in a questionable piece of reporting, the newspaper stated, "They said the bomb did not explode because of failure to remove a small metal ring on the two wires, which prevented electric current from passing through when the car started." If the bomber was in doubt as to what went wrong the newspaper certainly cleared up the mystery for him.

Although it was outside his jurisdiction, and even though he admitted not knowing Ciarnello personally, Chief Cress was quick to comment, "I know one thing! He's connected with hoodlums and punks who hang around his tavern and adjoining joints." In a candid interview, Cress said the people behind these incidents were "connected with rackets some way or other." The chief was not shy in announcing who he believed was behind the attempt. He called the incident, "part of a program, possibly by number one racketeer, Vincent DeNiro, to channel all gambling into one central location." The location was identified as DeNiro's new club on Route 422 – the Dry Men's Social Club.

The next day Cress backpedaled on his comment about Ciarnello, stating that he did not say that Ciarnello was associated with hoodlums and punks, but rather that the Ohio Tavern was a hangout for hoodlums and punks.

At 12:47 a.m. on August 16, an anonymous caller told police headquarters that DeNiro's home on Lincoln Park Drive was bombed again. Police rushed to the house only to find it was a false alarm and that no one was home. Two hours later police were called to the Alcatraz Bar on Wilson Avenue. Detective Lloyd Haynes discovered three bullet holes were fired through one of the windows. It was reported that a "preliminary investigation shows the shooting may have been done by one of DeNiro's lieutenants."

November 6, 1955 – the Steel City Club, 2123 Belmont Avenue, Youngstown. (This should not be confused with the club of the same name which was operated during the 1920s and 1930s by Patrick Scanlon and Peter J. Higgins located at 37 Central Square.) Several sticks of dynamite were placed inside a front passageway leading into the bar around 4:00 a.m. Sunday morning. The blast tore a hole in the concrete two-feet wide and eight-inches deep, shattered the front door, blew a hole in the upstairs floor and buckled a brick wall that sheltered the entrance and a concrete front wall. Numerous windows in the club, as well as several in a nearby Dairy Queen were shattered. The damage was estimated at $5,000.

The recently remodeled Steel City Club had in years past been the scene of numbers activity, but recently was declared "pretty clean" by Chief Cress. The owner of the club, Donald "Slick" Gaetano, was in Florida recovering from a heart condition. Police were called by Edward Markusic, who managed the club and lived in an apartment above it. When police arrived they found Hartley Moore cleaning up. Moore, once employed at The Ranch as a dice game operator, was associated with Vince DeNiro, as was Leo Ferranti, another ex-employee of The Ranch. Moore was questioned during the bombing investigation of Jack Sulligan's home in July 1954.

On November 9, when detectives returned to the club, they again found Moore there and this time arrested him. Moore was alleged to have been a partner of Gaetano in operating a football pool racket in Trumbull County. Moore denied any knowledge of the bombing, or being involved in any illegal betting, and claimed that Gaetano had called him and asked him for his help in cleaning up the place. Moore refused to take a lie detector test.

Claiming the blast was the result of political unrest, Chief Cress stated that "a 'Dynamite Incorporated' is at work, offering intimidation by bombing at a price." The chief again changed his tune and said, "There is a good possibility that other factors may be involved with this case and I intend to find out by questioning Gaetano. We will also check on his financial status to learn how his business has been and if he has any outstanding debts."

Markusic was ordered to come to the station for questioning. He agreed to take a lie detector test, and when the results proved inconclusive he was booked on suspicion, but later released. After Gaetano returned from Florida he went to the police station to answer questions. During the interrogation he admitted that DeNiro and Charles "Red" La Camera visited his place. Gaetano could offer no explanation as to why the club was targeted. One rumor making the rounds was that Gaetano and his wife were having marital problems. Gaetano admitted that a divorce action was pending, but they were trying to reconcile. Police later questioned Gaetano's wife, Katherine.

The Ohio State Liquor Control Board began an investigation of the blast and quickly confiscated the Steel City Club's records.[23] A review of the books showed that Gaetano was elected secretary-treasurer of the club back in January. When questioned by a state liquor official he denied being an officer. A $3,000 building permit, to begin repair work on the club, listed the owner as Katherine Gaetano, Donald's estranged wife.

On November 16, Chief Cress announced that Gaetano, his wife, and Markusic were cleared of any involvement in the bombing. Cress told reporters, "We will now review all bombing cases in an effort to find some common denominator that can trace this bombing to one specific cause to learn if it be strictly a beer war, gambling or bug activity." The chief then indicated again that it may be the work of a psychopath because, "there seems to be no rhyme or reason" to the pattern of bombings.

April 2, 1956 – the Oak Street School, New Castle, Pennsylvania. A bomb, believed thrown, exploded at 10:42 p.m. at this East Side New Castle school breaking windows and knocking a door off it hinges. The New Castle School District had recently given approval for the building to be used as a technical training center. A witness told police he saw a late-model, light colored Ford sedan speeding from the scene after the blast.

April 2, 1956 – the apartment of George Sledge, 142 North Fruit Street, Youngstown. At 1:25 a.m. a stench bomb was tossed through the front window of Sledge's house breaking the window, damaging the carpeting and some clothing. The bomb contained mercaptan and motor oil. Mercaptan, a foul-smelling, sulfur-containing substance, was mixed with the oil to give "persistency" to the concoction. Sledge, who described himself as a "good church member," may have been the target of some ill-informed hoodlums. He had moved into the first floor apartment two weeks earlier from a suite on the second floor. The previous occupant, Edmond "Billy" Brown, operated the Sportsman's Grill on Foster Street on the North Side. The restaurant had a raucous reputation. Brown admitted that he may have been the actual target of the bomb because, "I don't want to do no peddling for nobody." An hour after the police crime laboratory technicians completed their investigation five shots were fired into the front of the house from a gunman in a passing car.

During the investigation, Brown stated that he had turned down an offer of $3,000 from Billy Naples for a half interest in the Sportsman's Grill. Three weeks earlier, Billy had approached him about "picking up numbers for their outfit." Brown was turning his numbers over to "Dog" Benson, but Billy Naples wanted Brown to meet with his brother Sandy to listen to an offer to loan him money to open a grocery store and dry cleaning business at 138 North Fruit Street. Brown was told "they would take care of him if he did business with their outfit." Brown claimed he refused their offer after speaking with Sandy. He then warned Naples' pickup man George Beverly, "not to come into the Sportsman's Grill and conduct business."

After the acid throwing incident and shooting, Brown received a telephone call at 4:30 a.m. He was told that he had better straighten up or something would happen. The automobile from which the shots were fired, was described as a 1955 Buick with a light green top, dark green bottom and having a spare tire on the back. Three men were seated in the front seat and the driver fired the shots. After the shooting Brown drove to the Purple Cow looking for Sandy. Brown spotted Naples' Cadillac but could not locate Sandy. Outside the restaurant Brown spotted the two-tone green Buick.

April 16, 1956 – the Hillcrest Sportsman's Club, 138 Walton Street, Struthers. Around 1:30 a.m. a "homemade" dynamite bomb exploded in the doorway of this poolroom / sandwich shop. The blast ripped off the front door, depositing it on a neighbor's lawn, and broke windows in two nearby houses and a welding shop. The owner of the building, who lived above the club, knew nothing of the explosion until awoken by police. Thomas Colaluca, a local steelworker who managed the club in his off-hours, could offer no explanation. The poolroom had previously been used for gambling, but nothing unlawful was reported in recent years. Police offered that the bomber wanted "only to throw a scare into the poolroom owner for some unknown reason."

August 1, 1956 – Frank's Food Market, 3305 South Avenue, Youngstown. A dynamite bomb, tossed onto the roof of the store around 4:00 a.m., blew a hole fifteen inches in diameter in the ceiling. Police received several reports of an explosion, but could find no sign of damage in the early morning darkness. Frank Boback, the brother-in-law of former Campbell House lottery kingpin Frank Budak, discovered the damage when he arrived at the store around 8:00 a.m.

The only motive police could ascertain for the bombing was that Boback was scheduled to testify later that day in the trial of Ray York, who was charged in the robbery of Boback and two other men during a dice game held at the Structural Ironworkers Hall on July 13. York was free on bond, but was arrested and questioned about the bombing and even passed a lie detector test.

August 18, 1956 – home of Peter Fetchet, 3496 Fifth Avenue, Liberty Township. *This was covered in the chapter on the Fetchet brothers* (see chapter 11).

November 5, 1956 – the Martin Brothers Trucking Company, East Poland Avenue, Bessemer, Pennsylvania. A dynamite bomb, planted under the hood of a cement truck, damaged five cement-hauling vehicles and tore a hole in the sheet metal roof of the garage. The blast occurred at 8:30 p.m. on a Sunday night. Thomas W. Martin, a partner in the cement-hauling concern, had no explanation for the incident. He claimed his firm and Teamsters' Local 261 were on excellent terms.

November 9, 1956 – the home of John S. Basista, 843 East Boston Avenue, Youngstown. Two stench bombs, contained inside of fruit jars, were tossed through the front window just after 11:00 p.m. causing damage to a carpet and several pieces of furniture. Around 11:00 p.m., Mrs. Basista watched as a red and white automobile pulled in front of the house and parked. One man exited the car, poured something into a bottle and then got back in. Moments later two men got out of the car approached the front of the home and each tossed a glass fruit jar through the front window. At 12:15 a.m. Basista, an employee at Republic Steel Corporation received a telephone call stating that next time the home would be bombed. Basista and his wife believed the attack was carried out by someone they "had differences with" over a year ago.

November 19, 1956 – the home of Jack Sulligan, 1966 Smithfield Street, Youngstown. A stick of dynamite, wrapped in paper and placed in a tin can, was set under the front porch between two trees. The blast at 7:45 p.m. caused $200 in damages. A front window was shattered, portions of siding on the front porch were ripped loose and a wooden lattice piece at the side of the porch was damaged.

The timing of the explosion made this the boldest attempt to date and could have resulted in serious injuries. A women passed in front of the home just seconds before the blast occurred; Sulligan's daughter narrowly missed being hit by flying glass inside the house; and across the street a 69 year-old neighbor, who witnesses two windows shattering in her home, collapsed and was taken to St. Elizabeth's Hospital.

For the first time, perhaps due to the early hour, the bomber was actually seen by a witness. Sulligan's neighbor, who had installed spotlights outside his home after the first blast at the Democratic official's home in 1954, was drawn outside due to the barking of his dog. After opening his door and calling to his dog, he noticed a "prowler" who then raced from the rear of the Sulligan home to a vacant field which fronted Burbank Avenue. He described the man as "hatless, coatless, tall and slender." Just before going outside, the neighbor said goodbye to a friend whom, ironically, had stopped to borrow money to play bingo. It was this woman who narrowly escaped injury as she walked past the Sulligan home.

Sulligan, who was at the county Democratic Headquarters, was incensed by this second attack. "They are the lowest people in the world," the Mahoning County Democratic Chairman stated. "If they want to get at me, why don't they pick on me instead of the kids in my house?" Sulligan's two infant grandchildren were asleep in the home. "They know I am at the Democratic Headquarters," Sulligan said. "They can put a bomb in my car."

The newspaper reported that the investigation revealed, "On Nov. 15 two threatening phone calls were made to Bryon Wade, clerk of the Mahoning County Board of Elections, warning him the election 'better go the right way.' Neither call mentioned what race the caller was interested in, but apparently it was the sheriff's race."

On November 20, the *Vindicator*, in an editorial entitled "Is Youngstown Civilized?" made the following comments:

> "An attack upon [Sulligan] is an attack upon everyone in public office. It is an attack upon everyone who refuses to take orders from the rackets. It is warning to all decent citizens to do what the rackets tell them or suffer the consequences – which may be much worse than having their homes bombed.
>
> "Three considerations are pertinent. First, the city can't accept the bomb victims' protestations that they have no idea what it is all about. Clearly the bombs are intended as warnings. They are so placed as probably to avoid injury, loss of life or heavy property damage...A warning would be pointless unless the recipient knew it as such. Mr. Sulligan and the other victims should tell law-enforcement agencies what they know.
>
> "Second, so long a list of bombings should not be beyond the power of human ingenuity to solve. Perhaps undercover work on the FBI model is needed. If the police officers are too well known to provide it, the department could bring in outside help.
>
> "Third, there is more than a suspicion that quarrels among racketeers, probably over territory, are responsible for most of the bombings. Taking the profit out of the rackets would remove the motive. This consideration calls for renewed action to cut rackets to their lowest possible minimum. [In short, a call for the residents of the Valley to quit gambling and to stop playing the bug.]

In an ironic turn of events Kryzan, who had praised Sulligan for helping him to achieve the mayor's office, now allowed him to agree to take a polygraph test to clear his name. Chief Cress reported the results of the questioning session:

1. Sulligan does not know who bombed his house
2. He does not know why it was bombed
3. He was not threatened by anyone
4. He made no commitments that he failed to keep
5. He has no personal differences of any serious nature
6. He has no belief or theory as to who bombed his home or why

Cress then claimed he would ask other bombing victims to submit to the same questioning. The chief declared, "If we can elicit the same cooperation from other persons involved in local bombings, we shall soon have the answers we seek so earnestly. We are going to put more pressure on this town than it has ever seen."

A November 23, *Vindicator* editorial agreed with the polygraphing and stated, "When so prominent a public figure as the Democratic county chairman submits to a test, others will have little excuse for refusing to do as much.

"As to Mr. Sulligan, perhaps some group wants to get him out of the county chairmanship, or the deputy chairmanship of the Board of Elections which he also holds, by terrorizing him. These foes might be either a political or a racketeering faction in whose way he has stood in one or the other of his political positions. Probably both rackets and politics are concerned, since usually they are mixed."

Of course many in the Valley were anxiously waiting to see if Cress was going to "slap the wires" on Third Ward Councilman Anthony B. Flask in connection with the Union Distributing Company bombing, an incident which he had already publicly denied.

In the meantime, Chief Cress began a round of the "usual suspects" hauling in 12 suspects including Sandy Naples, John Zentko, James Petrella, Joseph Fezzuogho and Gus Leamis. In hoping to solve the rash of bombings Cress declared, "We intend to pick up every racketeer, gambler and hoodlum in town and everyone who associates with them." Of the 12 rounded up, 11 were released before habeas corpus hearings could be held. Leamis was found holding lottery slips and charged.

Meanwhile, a movement was begun in city council to offer a $5,000 reward for the arrest and conviction of anyone responsible for any of the district's bombings since 1951. A great idea, but no one could foresee the impending bureaucratic nightmare it became. In making the proposal to council, Michael J. Dudash of the Seventh Ward contended that it was about time "someone finds a solution. There is a great deal of excitement when the news of a bombing is fresh, but we don't seem to be too concerned in between the blasts."

Deflating the hype of offering a substantial reward for the bombers was City Law Director Felix S. Mika, who informed city council that they were not authorized to offer or pay a reward, "either by general law or under the home-rule provisions of the charter." Mika indicated that the board of county commissioners was empowered to do so, but pointed out that many of the bombings took place outside the city's corporate limits. Councilman Dudash immediately requested that the law department draft a resolution urging Mahoning County commissioners to consider the $5,000 reward that he had proposed to city council. Two of the three county commissioners were quick to respond. Edward J.

Gilronan stated, "If the police can't find out who is responsible for 24 bombings in the city, $5,000 won't apprehend the criminals. It's up to the police." Commissioner Fred A. Wagner was a little less opinionated in his response. The offer of a reward would "be impossible," he claimed. "The county has no money!" The third commissioner was ill.

It was certain that Mahoning County Sheriff Paul Langley was in favor of the reward. The day after the county commissioners thumbed their noses at the proposal an unidentified woman called the sheriff's office and said, "I overheard two men say the sheriff's office will be bombed tonight." The woman caller hung up before a deputy could get any further information. Langley realized that Bryon Wade of the elections' board had received a similar threat, followed by the bombing at Sulligan's home. Still Langley boasted, "If they think they can scare me they better think again, because I don't scare easily." With his thoughts then turning to his family, the sheriff asked Youngstown police to keep an eye on his home.

Langley felt the threat might be tied to his recent recount petition filed with the board of elections. Langley stated publicly that he wondered if someone at the elections' board was promised something if certain results were achieved. "This sort of thing is not fair to the public," the sheriff said. The results of the November 6 election were that Langley had lost the Mahoning County sheriff's job to Republican candidate G. Stanley Kreiler by 247 votes. After several tabulating errors were detected in various precincts, by November 8 the margin was down to 170 votes out of some 111,000 cast. By the time the "official" count was complete Kreiler won by a mere 23 votes and Langley asked for a recount. At the end of the recount process the incumbent sheriff had a 211-vote lead.

Kreiler and his campaign manager, Lloyd Phipps, filed a bill of particulars with state officials and asked for an investigation. The bill cited 16 instances of alleged irregularities that took place during the recount. On December 10, Ohio Secretary of State Ted W. Brown initiated an official probe. During a three-day hearing nothing but "generalities and hearsay" developed regarding the 16 points made by Phipps and Kreiler. In fact, Phipps failed to appear and testify. All four Republican officials who were said to have signed the bill of particulars requesting the investigation testified they had not signed the document. The *Vindicator* claimed the recount hearing was "much ado about nothing." The Mahoning County Board of Elections certified Langley's election victory.

On February 13, 1957, Councilman Dudash formally sponsored a resolution requesting the Mahoning County Commissioners to offer a reward stating that they had the "statutory authority" to do so.

March 16, 1957 – the under-construction home of Sandy Naples, 605 Carlotta Drive, Youngstown. *This was covered in the chapter on Sandy Naples* (see chapter 11).

April 6, 1957 – the home of Charles Bowers, 3522 Dover Road, Youngstown. The blast at 2:23 a.m. caused $500 damage to the Bower's home and $100 to the house of B. D. Gamble next door. The dynamite, placed alongside Bowers' garage, "ripped siding from the building and weakened the superstructure." Windows in the garage and home were smashed. Bowers' automobile suffered slight damage. At the Gamble home four windows were broken.

Bowers, who worked at General Fireproofing, had suffered a heart attack a year earlier and was not fully recovered. He, his wife and four sons were asleep in the house. The blast attracted about three dozen neighbors to the scene. After an investigation of Bowers, Captain Stephen Birich reported, "I am well satisfied that Bowers is a reputable, hardworking family man. He and his wife and family form the kind of a home we like to call 'typical American.'"

Police believed the intended target was Phil Rose, who lived on the other side of the Bowers' home. Rose, who used the name Ross, had a reputation as a bookmaker handling horse races. Rose told police he had no enemies and knew of no reason why anyone was out to get him. Another theory involving Rose was due to his recent role in Judge Franko's unsuccessful campaign for county prosecutor.

The bombing placed four children in harm's way, touching off a wave of public indignation and a cry for Governor C. William O'Neill to call a special grand jury investigation. Edward Gilronan, chairman of the county commissioners, stated, "I feel our police and law enforcement officials are very negligent in not finding out who is responsible for the bombings. The people of Mahoning County should insist something be done, and if there are no results they should appeal to the governor." Members of the following groups expressed their outrage: Mahoning County Bar Association, Youngstown Council of Churches, Youngstown Federation of Women's Clubs, Organization of Protestant Men and the League of Women Voters.

The bombing of the Bowers' home and the ensuing hysteria drove Mayor Kryzan to issue the following emotional plea:

> "The Saturday morning bombing of the Charles Bowers home at 3522 Dover Road has, needless to say, disturbed me greatly, and as a father of two children has caused me great concern for the safety of our citizens who may be innocently subjected to great dangers while certain elements of our society are venting their private grudges upon each other.
>
> "I want to assure my fellow citizens that none of the bombings committed in the city has gone unheeded, but rather, they have been given the closest police scrutiny of any crimes committed in this community in the past six years, with the least success. A special detail has been assigned to this task. A highly trained and efficient crime laboratory, trained under FBI methods, has joined in the fight and, to date, no solution seems near. So it becomes evident that additional steps must be taken and to this purpose I have devoted the greater part of the past two days.
>
> "The most recent bombing has been labeled the 45th in the district. I wish to

point out this number dates back to December of 1951 and includes a wide area. There have been 22 bombings in the city of Youngstown including those which occurred before I took office. There have been 23 outside of Youngstown, stretching from New Castle, Pa., to Massillon, Ohio. They were perpetrated in at least seven cities and involved the police authorities of those seven cities and the sheriffs of four counties. With all the individual effort of the police authorities of these several communities, the sheriffs, and with the cooperation of the FBI, not one solution has been accomplished.

"A further analysis of these bombings indicates that the victims have included members of the building trades, contractors, publishers, schools, merchants and just plain citizens, as well as people with criminal records. Fortunately, it is pure luck that no injuries have occurred up to now. In view of these circumstances the situation calls for further measures to be taken in order to bring about an end to this reign of terror.

"Since the individual efforts of the various police authorities have failed to cope with the situation, I am calling and inviting the sheriffs and prosecutors of Trumbull County, Stark County, Lawrence County and Mahoning County, and the mayors and chiefs of police of Hubbard, Girard, Warren, Niles, Massillon and New Castle to meet with me and our police officials on Tuesday, April 15, at 10 a.m. to combine and unite our thinking on this perplexing problem. I am also inviting Gov. C. William O'Neil (sic) to be present, or to send his representative to this meeting, and will request that the FBI be represented.

"I do not care to usurp the authority or responsibility of other elected officials, but I shall offer my complete cooperation to the prosecutors of Mahoning and Trumbull counties, should they see fit to bring these matters to the attention of their respective grand juries.

"I feel that some of our citizens may possess some knowledge which might help toward a solution but which they fear to impart to the police. I think a reward might induce them to action. Last year the Mahoning County commissioners were requested to offer such a reward. I am today, officially, forwarding a request to Edward J. Gilronan, chairman of the commission, to offer a reward of $5,000 for information leading to the arrest and conviction of the perpetrators of these nefarious crimes, since the county commissioners are the only political body so authorized to act by law.

"I am personally reviewing this problem with our police with a view of further concentration on this matter, and making this not only the problem of the officers charged with the bombing investigation, but am further ordering every member of our department, from the newest rookie to the top brass, to give the solution of this problem his topmost consideration. I am making it plain that I will leave no stone unturned to assure our citizens that these criminal acts will be stopped.

"I urgently request every member of our community to impart to our police any information, no matter how minute he may think it to be, which may be connected with the recent bombing or with any of the past bombings. We have at our disposal men specially trained with the FBI, such as Lt. Maxim, Detective Edward Przelomski, Lt. Watters and other officers with years of experience, who may be able to connect the information furnished with one of these crimes.

"Nothing short of an all out effort will be accepted by me in this war against the bombing crimes, and this is the least that the people of our city can expect.

"Frank X. Kryzan, Mayor."

On April 9, before going off-duty at the end of his turn, vice squad member Detective Lloyd Haynes filed the following report:

> April 9, 1957
> 1:30 A.M.
> Chief George Krispli:
> Please be advised that I ran into a former employee of the 422 Club on McCartney Road and started to talk to him about the bombings in and around the City. He stated to me that he would tell me something if I promised not to let his name be known. (I made that promise). He stated that if the 422 Club, which has recently remodeled, was closed, the bombings would stop. He further stated that the following men have a piece of the 422 Club:
>
> Vince DeNiro......general manager
> Joe Romeo.....Mafia contact (protection from being bombed)
> Sandy Joe Naples.......on percentage
> Dominac Frank......
> Mike Valando.......
> Joseph Mafitiana aka "Akron Joe"
> Phil Ross......
> George Glaros......(Columbus contact) He has ok from Governor O'Neil.
> ? .....County official
> ? ......County Official
>
> My informer stated further that Joe Romeo was probably the man who bombed Phil Ross and several others, too. He stated that the above co-owners are always fighting amoung (sic) themselves and it is his belief that somebody is going to get hurt.
> When I asked him where the bomb would probably come from. He stated that Joe Romeo probably has out of town contact and can get a bomb placed anywhere he wants it placed. He stated that Joe Romeo can be found at club 422 any night.
> L. Haynes

Hours after the report was filed Kryzan met with the top brass of the police department for over an hour. When they were through each officer had a copy of the mayor's new directive:

> "The police department and the administration must at all times be sure that we are exerting every effort in protecting the life and property of our citizens.
> "As the top officials of this department you and your men as well as this administration are charged with this responsibility.
> "The recent series of bombings has led to some conjecture that these bombings are racket connected and these bombings reflect an influx of rackets and the necessary struggle for the evil spoils associated with them.
> "Therefore, so that there may be no misunderstanding as to our position in this matter and what yours should be, I am issuing the following as a direct order to you.
> "I want every hood, punk, racketeer, gambler, criminal, suspicious person, burglar, thief and every companion and associate of criminals and dissolute persons

> arrested for every unlawful act they commit. They are to be arrested, not warned or given summonses or other consideration of any sort.
>
> "These persons are to be arrested for any and every unlawful act, jaywalking, parking, reckless driving, stop sign or red light violation, loitering, sidewalk ordinance, or any other of the many laws on the books. They are to be arrested, booked, cars towed in. If they fail to carry a driver's license or registration card they will be booked until they prove ownership or produce drivers' licenses.
>
> "Daily written reports will be turned into the chief's office by every member of the Police Department who sees one of these persons. The reports will state where he was seen, the time, the circumstances, the names of persons with whom he was seen, number of the car he was in if in a car, what he was doing in the place he was seen, and this will involve interrogating him for being where he is seen. If he cannot give a reasonable explanation of his being where he is found, he will be arrested and held on suspicion.
>
> "Any member of the Police Department found fraternizing with known criminals and racketeers will be dismissed summarily from the department and prosecuted if a charge can be found. Every car and foot man, traffic as well as blue division, will check every known or suspected 'illegal joint' on his beat with one and only one purpose – to find a violation of law and make an arrest."

On April 11, Governor O'Neill told the *Vindicator* that in response to a request for help from Mayor Kryzan he sent a letter "offering every assistance and cooperation that we can and willingness to exhaust every avenue at my command." O'Neill agreed to send a personal representative to the mayor's special conference to be held April 16 and said that after the meeting he may appoint a special state investigator to aid in the probe. References were being made in the newspapers to the special investigation back in 1943 when the lottery houses were brought down.

Meanwhile, the police crackdown was on and in the first 48 hours the following policy men were hauled in: James Petrella, Louis DeLuca, Michael Karas, Sam Zappi, William Lantini, Frank Thomaselli, William Murphy and Calogero Malfitano. The newspaper was quick to point out that untouched were racket leaders Vince DeNiro and Sandy Naples.

On April 13, Chief Cress announced the formation of a "special seven-man squad" to investigate the unsolved bombings. Selected to lead the new "bomb squad" was Lieutenant Frank Watters.[24]

The crime crusade continued with a raid at the Farris Food Market on Wilson Avenue, where Joseph Farris was arrested after several lottery slips were found in his possession. A request to have the telephone removed was made by Chief Cress to Ohio Bell Telephone. The next day the Variety News Stand was raided by police and state liquor officials. James V. Ricciuti, the owner, was arrested for possession of lottery slips. This was followed by a raid at the Navy Club, Post 541, on Salt Spring Road where Ralph Angle was arrested with bug slips in his possession.

The mayor's efforts should have generated a united front against the bombing terror that had gripped the city, but they failed to do so. One reason was the relentless efforts of City Law Director Mika to stonewall any attempt to offer a reward for the arrest and conviction of the bombers. Instead of working to find a way for the city to make this reward available, Mika spent his time digging up case law showing that in the past the raising of city funds for such an effort was not within the power of city government. Even after County Prosecutor Beil ruled that county commissioners could authorize a $5,000 reward and suggested that the city match it to make it more attractive, Mika refused to allow it to be put before the courts for a ruling.

Two days before Kryzan's "crime conference," a Democratic hopeful for mayor, Vince Farrar, set off his own explosion by blasting the administration's efforts. "Why doesn't Mayor Frank X. Kryzan call in the Army, the Navy and the Marine Corps?" questioned Farrar. "Anyone who is honest and sincere about putting a stop to these bombings can do so in a few weeks time. That's exactly how long it would take a good conscientious public servant to eliminate this shameful and degrading condition that has no place in our community life."

Farrar offered the following three-step program:

1. Close all the active gambling joints
2. Take the handcuffs off policemen and permit them to perform their duty in conformance with their oath of office
3. Stop wasting time trying to fool the public by picking up the same persons all the time

On this last point Farrar stated "These persons have been out of action since Mayor Charles P. Henderson's administration and Mayor Kryzan knows it." Farrar concluded by stating that the public wasn't as "dumb" as Kryzan thinks.

Finally, one of Kryzan's past decisions returned to haunt him. The mayor was firmly behind an effort by Sixth Ward Councilman George L. Stowe to introduce legislation calling for jail terms of up to a year for lottery ordinance violations. Donald J. Lewis, a candidate for mayor in the Republican primary, reminded Kryzan that during the Henderson Administration the mayor and Chief Allen were adamant about the same type of ordinance. Kryzan, then city council president, had opposed their efforts.

In making the proposal Stowe stated, "This seems to be the best way to attack two problems – bombing and gambling – at one time. Apparently gambling is the factor behind most of the bombings, so as long as gambling is tolerated by officials here there is going to be a war."

The mayor was fair game for Republican contenders. No sooner had Lewis leveled his barrage than attorney Alvy T. Witt came with his. "In the brief period of three years, the present administration has put the underworld back in business and completely surrendered to it," Witt declared. He went on to claim that the bombings were the result of a "total breakdown in law enforcement," which had occurred under Kryzan.

On April 16, ten days after the bombing at the Charles Bowers' home, Mayor Kryzan's crime conference was held. The mayor began by stating that 20 of the bombings, which he now concluded totaled 45, occurred inside Youngstown and of these only "eight could be attributed to the rackets." At the conclusion of the two-hour meeting, Kryzan requested that Governor O'Neill send a special investigator to head a probe of conditions in the Valley. "I want a complete investigation of bombings and rackets. And we don't care what area the governor gets into." After the probe the mayor wanted a "grand jury investigation based on facts compiled by the state investigators, the special city bomb squad or any investigative body in the area."

The crime crusade continued with Lieutenant Watters' bomb squad making their first numbers arrest. One week after the unit was formed, members arrested Vic Acierno, owner of Vic's Confectionery on Wilson Avenue, for possession of lottery tickets. Joseph Francis DeNiro, a cousin of Vince, was arrested for possession. Police also made an arrest at Carlyle's Grocery, where they nabbed a woman as she tried to hand ten bug slips to someone in the store. The next day, bomb squad members arrested Dutch Frazier, described as one of the more active bug pickup men in the city, and Louis Melieno, a convicted numbers man. The success of the bomb squad against numbers operators continued. The newspaper reported, "Since the crackdown, it is reported that several of the large 'banks' plan to merge and move outside the city limits to set up one major 'bug bank.' All bets will be taken by telephone and no slips will be used." A persistent rumor claimed that due to the success of the 7-man bomb squad the regular vice squad, consisting of 15 members, might be on its way out.

If the people behind the bombings in the Valley were concerned with the new efforts of area law enforcement they certainly didn't show it. Just hours after Kryzan's plea for help to the governor, 460 sticks of dynamite were stolen from the D. W. Winkelman Construction Company at a Route 82 relocation work site in Trumbull County.

Incredibly, the legal battle over the offering of a reward was still raging. The Ohio attorney general's office responded to Prosecutor Beil's inquiry into an opinion about the city offering a reward by stating it was up to the city law director to seek the opinion. The bureaucratic response was that the attorney general's office declined "to express opinions to a prosecuting attorney in regard to a question relating purely to municipal affairs since the prosecuting attorney himself has no official concern with such matters." The bureaucracy extended to the county as well as Commissioner John Palermo confirmed the $5,000 the county was offering could only be paid in 1957. A separate resolution would have to be approved if the reward were to be offered in 1958.

Vince Farrar took this opportunity to do some more Kryzan-bashing. The mayoral candidate called for a "citizen's fund-raising drive" to collect the reward money. He said the drive would arouse the voters to "ridding City Hall of an administration that tolerates these bombings. We all know that it is impossible for criminal elements to rove our city unless the mayor, the chief law enforcement officer, knows something about it."

May 6, 1957 – a brick building on Liberty Road, Trumbull County. Around 4:00 a.m. dynamite was placed against the wall of a two-story building in a section of Trumbull County referred to as the Liberty Street district. The blast tore out a section of an enclosed stairway and shattered several windows. The building was owned by the Mathie Real Estate Company of Warren and leased to Lawrence Breckenridge, who had a police record for gambling and liquor violations. A search of the building revealed two jukeboxes. After questioning residents, police theorized that the place was used only on weekends, probably as a "cheat spot."

Amid the chaos that was taking place in the Valley the bombers made their most brazen move to date.

August 13, 1957 – the home of Lloyd Haynes, 3049 McGuffey Road, Youngstown. This was the first time since the bombing of Sergeant William Davis' home in April 1942 that a police officer was targeted. The dynamite blast, which occurred at 12:50 a.m. damaged a long flower bed, tore the front door loose, and shattered a front picture window and two bedroom windows. The front wall of the home suffered damage both inside and out and a bookcase on the other side of the front wall had its contents scattered. The damage was estimated at $1,500.

Haynes was a member of the vice squad for the past two years. In addition, he graduated from the Youngstown University Law School and was admitted to the Ohio bar. Haynes[25] lived at the home with his wife, Helena, the couple had three daughters and a son.

Haynes told police he had just retired to his bedroom when he heard the family dog, tied up in the back yard, begin to bark. Haynes recalled, "The dog was on a chain, my daughter, Loretta, age 14, yelled to me in my bedroom and said, 'Daddy, you better go outside because Lobo is barking the same way that he barks at the gas man.' So I got out of bed, went through the living room, through the kitchen, reached over to turn on the lights...and saw a big red flash followed by a loud explosion in the front of my house. I ran out the back door and my dog was trying to go across the back yard. I turned him loose with the intention that he may follow the person who placed the explosive on my door. Instead, the dog turned and ran into the house. I don't have any idea why I got it. I don't know what it might have been I uncovered to make somebody uncomfortable, but all I know is that working on these bombings is like hunting an invisible man in the desert."

One of the first suspects to be interrogated was Olivia Britt, a bus driver, who had recently accused Haynes of blocking his efforts to be appointed to the police department. Britt claimed that he received a phone call from Haynes two weeks earlier where the detective accused him of telling his wife Helena, "that he was running around with a white girl in Campbell." Britt was questioned about his connection with Wilbur "Shorty" Underwood, who ran a house of prostitution out of a home rented from Britt's late mother. Britt said he ordered Underwood out of the house after his mother's death. He denied having done any business with Underwood, but stated, "If anyone was a partner in this enterprise, it would be Lloyd Haynes." Britt went on to claim that he had heard from different people that Haynes had no "use for him" and that the detective would do "anything he could do to mess him up." None of the accusations Britt made were ever substantiated. When detectives tracked down Underwood he denied that he had any connections with Haynes. Britt was released after police verified his movements at the time of the bombing.

On August 16, Haynes was questioned by Lieutenant George Maxim and Detective Edward Przelomski (See Appendix D). While Haynes was being questioned he was asked about a possible suspect. He replied, "As far as I know I have only one enemy, he's Blue Johnson a dope addict, who I have sent to the Ohio Penitentiary. Several people have approached me while on my tour of duty and stated that Blue Johnson told them that the last thing he does he will get Steve Krispli and I if he goes to the penitentiary." Police contacted the warden's office at the penitentiary to obtain a list of all visitors that saw Arthur "Blue" Johnson and a check of censored mail was made to see if Haynes' name appeared.

On August 16, the police bomb squad issued the following statement (typos omitted):

AN APPEAL TO THE PUBLIC

> On Tuesday, Aug. 13, 1957, about 12:50am, Youngstown recorded its 23rd bombing. As members of the newly formed Bomb Investigation Squad, the dubious distinction of solving this, and the other bombings falls to us. As you all know, the last bombing was perpetrated upon the home of a police officer.
>
> For about four months now we have endeavored to put together bits of information we have picked up in an effort to come to some logical conclusion and to try to place the blame where it belongs. That the racket element is to blame for the bombings, we have no doubt. Proving this however, is another matter.
>
> When this squad was first formed, Lt. Watters, who is in command of this unit, made a public appeal to the citizenry through press and radio channels, that we would welcome any information from any citizen who thought the information they had could have any bearing on our problem. A phone call, a post card, or even an anonymous message would be thoroughly investigated by our unit. To date, I am unhappy to report, we have had not one phone call, letter, or communication of any sort, from the people who pay our salaries. We feel certain that somewhere in our city there is some honest person, not connected with rackets, who may know something or even hold the key to successfully terminating this

investigation. This complacency or lack of interest on the part of the people of our city, has been very disheartening to our squad, to say the least. We do intend leave the impression that the public alone is guilty of this lack of interest. We have little or no information from the victims themselves, or other police officers. We do not intend to let up and are not admitting defeat, we are simply registering a bit of disgust.

In the absence of any help from our legitimate citizens, we now turn to the racket element. Everyone who earns a living by illegal methods, know by now that they are naturally suspects in all the bombings. Some of these people know from our actions, better than others. We will continue to harass them from now on. It may take us a little more time to reach some of them than others, but they know eventually that they will talk with us. We are willing to simplify matters for them. Anyone who fits in this category, can clear themselves as suspects, if they are not guilty of any of the bombings, or if they do not know who is responsible, simply by coming to our office and volunteering for a lie-detector examination. The questions asked will refer only to the bombings. NO OTHER QUESTIONS WILL BE ASKED. If they can pass this test, they will be removed from the list of suspects, and allowed to leave. If they are guilty, then perhaps it would be better not to contact us, because we feel we will be able to contact them, by process of elimination.

This is a bona fide offer and we will be guided by the results of the test. If there are no takers for this offer, we can only appeal to our good citizens again and ask indulgence in our efforts to successfully conclude our investigation.

Members of the Bomb Squad

Two days after the bombing of the Haynes' home Toufi Saadi, owner of the Carlyle Grocery, received a bomb threat by telephone. This was the second time in the past month that Saadi was targeted by extortionists. In the first incident he was told to place a certain amount of money on his front porch or his home would be destroyed. Since that threat the Carlyle Grocery was threatened with padlock action by police after gambling was uncovered there. While insisting that he had no enemies, Saadi told reporters he would not discuss the latest threat with them. "It's nobody's business but my own," he declared.

On September 11, 1957, it appeared that there was a response from the appeal of the bomb squad to the public. After receiving an anonymous tip in a letter, police arrested John "Johnny the Greek" Magourias for the attempted bombing of Thomas Ciarnello's automobile back on August 14, 1955. Magourias, who had received a dishonorable discharge from the Navy, had a police record, which included contributing to the delinquency of a minor and aiding and abetting in a burglary and robbery – all in 1949. Between 1953 and 1956 he was arrested several times for disturbing the peace and suspicion.

During questioning at police headquarters Magourias claimed that he was hired by Dominic DeBonis to plant the bomb in Ciarnello's car. DeBonis had owned the Ohio Tavern until he sold it to Ciarnello and police theorized that a "personal feud" had developed in the wake of the transaction.

Two days after Magourias' arrest, police picked up DeBonis, whose record went back to 1931 when he was sentenced to serve six years in the Atlanta Penitentiary for the shooting of a federal probation officer. Since his release he was arrested for cutting with intent to wound or kill and for a liquor violation. Both men were charged with illegal possession of an explosive when they were arraigned on the afternoon of September 13 before Judge Cavalier. As Magourias was being led from the elevator to the courtroom he began a struggle with officers in an attempt to hide his face from newspaper photographers. "I don't have to have my picture taken," he screamed. In the courtroom the two men pleaded innocent. Cavalier set bond at $10,000 apiece, an amount Magourias, who was represented by attorney Donald Hanni, couldn't raise.

On September 17, four days after the arrest of Magourias, Lieutenant Watters addressed the public stating, "In the five months we have functioned as a unit, we have received only one anonymous letter. This letter contained certain information which resulted in the apprehension of the two charged. We feel there are more citizens who know something about the bombings. Please contact us, and do a great service for your community." In a seemingly cryptic closing Watters concluded with, "We also wish to communicate further with the sender of the anonymous letter. Please use the same identification as you used on the first letter." On October 4, DeBonis and Magourias were indicted for illegal possession of explosives by the grand jury; they were both slated for separate trials.

On Tuesday, January 28, the trial of John Magourias began in Common Pleas Court before Judge David Jenkins. Handling the prosecution were Clyde W. Osborne and Elwyn V. Jenkins.[26] Magourias was represented by Don Hanni and John T. Jakubek. The prosecution's key witness was Detective Jerome Bernat, who took two statements from Magourias after his arrest on September 11. Bernat went over the first statement where Magourias confessed to being hired by DeBonis and planting the bomb in the Ciarnello automobile. In the second statement Magourias claimed he was approached by Philip Kimla, an associate of John Schuller, to plant a bomb at the home of Detective Lloyd Haynes. On cross-examination by Hanni, the former police prosecutor tried to bring out that the statements given by the defendant "were not entirely voluntary."

On Wednesday afternoon, Magourias took the stand in his own defense. He admitted to making the detailed statements to police, but claimed that the answers to the questions asked him by Detective Bernat were "suggested" by the officer. Magourias said he agreed to the statement because Bernat said he would release him if he implicated "higher ups" in the investigation and DeBonis was considered one of the "higher ups."

According to the statement, DeBonis offered Magourias $1,500 to plant the bomb. Magourias said he went to the DeBonis home, watched him retrieve the dynamite from the attic and prepare the bomb in his garage workshop. Magourias then said he placed the bomb in the Ciarnello automobile on the night of August 13, 1955.

The defense had earlier tried to call subpoenaed photographers from the *Vindicator* and television stations WFMJ and WKBN, who took pictures of Magourias after he made his statement. The defendant claimed he was slapped by Bernat. Judge Jenkins refused to allow the jury to see the photographs.

Hanni then called Phil Kimla to the stand. Kimla was mentioned in the Magourias statement as having asked the defendant to plant the Haynes' bomb. Kimla denied having ever contacted Magourias. It is interesting to note that Thomas Ciarnello was not called to testify.

On Thursday, both sides gave closing arguments and the jury of five men and seven women received the case at 11:50 a.m. After deliberating for twelve hours the jury came back just after midnight with a verdict of not guilty. The next day, at the recommendation of Prosecutor Beil, Judge Jenkins dropped the charges against Dominic DeBonis. Later in 1958, Magourias pled guilty to a charge of burglary and larceny and was sentenced to one to 15 years in the penitentiary.

The only bombing case that was brought to trial during the decade turned out itself to be a bomb.

January 22, 1958 – the automobile of John K. "Big John" Schuller parked in the back of the American-Croatian Citizens Club, 1639 Poland Avenue, Youngstown. At 1:10 a.m. Schuller and two companions – Mike Fedchina, Schuller's brother-in-law, and Edward Tabus – left the club and climbed into a 1955 Cadillac. Schuller was in the driver's seat, Fedchina was to his right and Tabus was seated in the back. When Schuller turned the ignition dynamite, wired to the distributor, exploded. The newspaper described the damage, "The hood landed in Poland Ave. approximately 300 feet away. Both front fenders were ripped off, one striking a nearby house. The engine and front end were demolished and the dashboard and steering wheel crumbled. The windshield and rear window were broken out completely and other windows were shattered. The rear seat was hurled outside the car." In addition, 12 windows at the club were shattered, as were another ten in a nearby house.

Schuller suffered compound fractures of both legs below the knees and deep cuts in his abdomen, groin, right foot, left leg and hand. His right foot was also fractured. Fedchina had a fracture of the left leg and cuts to his left thigh. Tabus was blown out of the back seat by the blast and, aside from complaining of ringing in his ears, was basically unscathed. Schuller and Fedchina were rushed to South Side Hospital, where Schuller went right into surgery.

Frank Budak was listed as the "steward of the American-Croatian Citizens Club. Budak was the former owner of the oft-raided Poland Country Club and was indicted back in June 1943 as the principal of the Campbell House lottery ring. The newspaper reported that Budak's new "Poland Ave. place has been a hangout for hoodlums and racketeers for six months." An informant claimed that dice and card games were going on there "since last summer." The man indicated that the weekends are the busiest, and the club never closed on weekends until 5:30 a.m. or 6 a.m. Budak, he said finally had most of the cars park behind the building, but everybody in the neighborhood knew there was more going on than met the eye. A dice table was brought in after hours and remained until after play was complete. The newspaper stated, "The place was loaded with cars most every night."

In commenting on the club Cress stated, "We have had complaints the club was open all hours and there was gambling. Checks were made frequently but the vice squad never found evidence to support the complaints." Vice squad members kept track of the goings on at the club and reported to Cress that club members had "voted Budak out." Vice squad chief George Krispli had recently confronted Budak on the street and warned him about staying open after the mandatory 1:00 a.m. closing time. Budak assured Krispli that he was "getting out of the club."

After meeting with Chief Cress later that morning, a frustrated Mayor Kryzan conceded, "I'm at a loss as to what I can do further. I have instructed the 278 policemen on our force to report daily on the whereabouts of known hoodlums. I have detailed and have had working for approximately one year the highest grade members of our investigating department, known as the Bomb Squad. I don't know what else I can do."

Edward Tabus was jailed for questioning. His rap sheet showed seven arrests in Youngstown between September 1951 and February 1955. The charges ranged from being picked up for desertion from the Army to grand larceny and forgery. There were no convictions. Tabus told police that on the night of the bombing they had stopped at the club for a drink and were only there a half-hour before departing. If this were true the bold bombers had only 30 minutes to plant the bomb in the Cadillac, which was parked just six feet outside the back door. During a polygraph session, conducted by Lieutenant George Maxim, the officer began asking about the activities of the trio and possible problems Schuller might have encountered. The polygraph technician noticed that Tabus began "getting weaker and when he felt he might volunteer some information he got up and said he did not want to continue." Tabus was later released from jail even though he refused to complete the lie detector testing.

Police were anxious to question Schuller after surgery. A doctor refused their request claiming Schuller was still on oxygen and not doing well. Physicians were concerned about the possibility of infection, as several pieces of metal had to be "laboriously" removed. Schuller's first exchange with police was to tell them that he was concerned about somebody trying to "finish the job." After it was reported that two suspicious men tried to enter Schuller's room, Lieutenant Watters ordered a 24-hour guard posted outside.

Schuller's record showed one arrest for suspicion back on February 15, 1951. He was questioned and released without being charged. At the time he said he worked as a salesman of novelty items.

Meanwhile, Watters reported that a search of Schuller's Cadillac revealed "burglary tools." Police found "several pinch bars, jimmy bars and bolt cutters, dark glasses worn by welders, a torch lighter, and hammers in the trunk." A check of the automobile's Pennsylvania registration showed that a John Karl of Hillsville was the owner. Police were unable to track him down because his address was a post office box and he was believed to be a "long distance truck driver." The name Karl also happened to be Schuller's middle name.

At noon, on the day of the bombing, a seven-man search party led by Chief Deputy Sheriff Frank Reese headed to the Hill Crest Motel, located on Route 422 between Youngstown and New Castle, Pennsylvania. The motel, which advertised "deluxe cabins and modern rooms," was home to both Schuller and Fedchina. What officer's uncovered in Schuller's quarters amazed them. The *Vindicator* reported, "Found in the various rooms were more than 200 dynamite caps, a large amount of black powder already fused, charge caps, cutting torches, two slot machines, a gallon jug of bootleg whisky, a tear gas gun and two gas shells, a sawed-off shotgun, a U.S. carbine, a Luger, three automatic Colt pistols, including a .25, .32 and .45; a .32 Smith & Wesson pistol and a pair of steel knuckles." All the serial numbers on the weapons were removed.

This discovery made Schuller a leading suspect in the Valley's bombing investigation. Police didn't believe he was connected with local numbers activities but, because of the items recovered from the automobile, felt the men were part of a burglary ring operating in the area.

Police received a tip that the two men responsible for the bombing were preparing to leave town. At 5:30 a.m. on January 27, police went to the Toddle House on Wick Avenue where they arrested Phillip "Fleagle" Mainer and Steve Milanovich. The two men were held for questioning and Mainer's 1957 Cadillac was impounded and searched. An investigation of Mainer and Milanovich showed the two men had alibis for the night of the bombing – both were in various bars on the city's North Side. When the investigation showed the men to be associated with Schuller, they were kept in jail while police then tried to connect them to several local burglaries. Both men were eventually released due to lack of evidence.[27]

Four days had passed since the bombing and police were still unable to question Schuller due to the pain he was suffering. By that time they had determined that Fedchina was an "innocent victim," who apparently was in the wrong place at the wrong time. His record showed only one arrest for a disturbance in September 1954. Fedchina was released from the hospital on February 11. Six days later, due to "a manpower shortage," police removed the 24-hour guard from Schuller's room.

By early April, doctors decided Schuller could be released from the hospital to continue his recovery at home, which was now an address in Lowellville; a deal, however, had to be worked out with his lawyers and Sheriff Langley. The sheriff agreed that Schuller could recuperate at home providing he made bond. To accomplish this, an agreement was reached with attorneys Donald Hanni and John Hooker. On April 7, Schuller was arraigned in his hospital room by a county judge. Schuller pled innocent to a charge of illegal possession of explosives and bond was set at $5,000.

Schuller posted bond and was released later that day. The newspaper never reported what police learned when they finally questioned Schuller, or if they even had fully interviewed him about the bombing. Whatever he had to say is now lost to history. Over the next 12 months, Schuller underwent treatments for muscle injuries at the Mayo Clinic in Minneapolis. During this time he was never indicted by the grand jury. On January 16, 1960, nearly two years after the incident, Schuller and Fedchina filed separate lawsuits against the American-Croatian Citizens Club. Schuller asked for damages totaling $350,000 for his injuries and $3,000 for his Cadillac. Fedchina asked for $150,000. In the lawsuit the club was being blamed for not having adequate lighting or a watchman, and, incredibly enough, "for allowing unknown explosives to be stored in the parking lot." The men's attorneys were claiming the dynamite was in the parking lot and that Schuller had parked his vehicle over it. On February 24, 1960, the Mahoning County grand jury refused to indict Schuller for illegal possession of an explosive. Schuller was murdered later that year (See chapter 13) while his lawsuit for damages was still pending.

After the Schuller car bombing, the mayor and the police department found they were now fighting a war on two fronts – against the bombers and the media. The spark that ignited the new war was an editorial that appeared in the *Vindicator* on January 22. Entitled "Bombers Laugh at Police," the scathing piece, which seemed to single out Krispli, stated:

> "Since 1951 the Youngstown district has been waiting for its authorities to do something about the bombings which have damaged homes, business places, automobiles and now, in the 57th of these outrages, seriously injured two men. They could just as easily been killed.
>
> "All of the bombings naturally have been associated with underworld operations involving liquor sales, the numbers racket and gambling concessions. The club parking lot in which the [latest] bombing occurred has been 'loaded with cars most every night,' one observer said. Weekend operations lasted until 5 or 6 o'clock in the mornings.
>
> "Vice Squad Chief George Krispli comes up with the usual lame, time-worn excuse: 'I didn't know of any gambling going on there.'
>
> "Mr. Krispli should be able to say either that there is or isn't; and if there is, it should have been stopped. Does Mr. Krispli think he's fooling anyone?
>
> "If, however, Mr. Krispli should be right and after his years of police experience

he does not know about crime and vice conditions in Youngstown, then he ought to get out or be put out of the police force.

"If Youngstown's police officials have gall enough to say they don't know who the racketeers are and what they are doing, then there ought to be a wholesale shakeup of the department. They have made themselves and the City of Youngstown, the laughing stock of the country.

"The responsibility rests not alone with Vice Chief Krispli, but with Police Chief Paul Cress and, finally, Mayor Frank Kryzan.

"The people of Youngstown and the people in the district annoyed by Youngstown's racketeers, deserve a better police administration."

The next day Mayor Kryzan announced that a conference of the top police brass would be held and that it was open to the press, radio and television. "The meeting is for the purpose of discussing and further making clear the administration's official position in the matter of law enforcement," Kryzan stated. When asked if the meeting was a forerunner to a departmental shakeup, the mayor replied, "You'll get all the news there is to get tomorrow morning."

Kryzan's meeting with top police brass – five captains, seven lieutenants and three division chiefs – in front of a media audience, brought the following sweeping changes to the department:

1. The current 16-man vice squad, which included a four-man narcotics unit, was to be replaced by a ten-man "Morals Squad," which would continue to include the four narcotics officers, by February 1. The Morals Squad "will perform the duties... in the area of narcotics, prostitution, license investigations, mental cases and other cases involving morals."
2. Claiming that "vice is not a squad problem; vice is a departmental problem," Kryzan declared there would no longer be a separation of duties within the department. The newspaper reported, "Cress emphasized that the new order is an attempt to break down a longstanding practice whereby policemen assigned to certain departments are hesitant to handle any violations which are the specialty of another police division."
3. Kryzan ordered police to bring in all holders of federal gambling tax stamps, as well as the Valley's other known racketeers, and to "continue a program of harassment that will drive these elements from the community."
4. The ordering of daily reports to be made by every member of the force. The newspaper reported, "These reports will include an account of what every officer is doing every minute of the day. [Cress] said that his men will be allowed 10 minutes for such a thing as a coffee break, but if it takes 12 minutes he wants to know why and what the officer was doing. If the reports show that an officer, for instance, makes no arrests it will mean one of two things. Either the beat is clean and the officer can be assigned elsewhere because he's not needed on it, or he's not doing his duty."
5. The mayor asked Mahoning County to offer a reward for information leading to the conviction of the area's bombers. Kryzan stated if the county refused he would "ask state legislators to sponsor legislation enabling cities to offer rewards."

Throughout the meeting Kryzan referred frequently to what he called "unjustified" criticism of the department. He declared, "I am not going to wage a war of words with the local press or permit members of the department to do so, but conditions are better today than ever in the history of this community." The statement raised the eyebrows of many in attendance.

Kryzan told media representatives that, "It appears every event that occurs within 75 miles of the community becomes our responsibility. We will not hesitate to assume this responsibility, but because of jurisdictional limits we must confine our activities to Youngstown." The mayor ended by saying, "Police work is a profession. The majority of policemen are decent, honest workers. Some are lemons. We will weed them out and you'll have to help."

While the mayor was conducting his meeting, WFMJ radio criticized the chief and the administration and read – verbatim – the entire *Vindicator* editorial on the air. An angry Chief Cress denounced the program and accused the *Vindicator* of using "maliciousness" and "journalistic blackmail," claiming that the newspaper had "grossly exaggerated the bombing record."

On the day the editorial appeared, the newspaper also printed a listing of 57 bombings that took place since 1951. Cress felt that since the area was identified as the "Youngstown district," that he and the city were being unduly criticized. He pointed out that only 28 of the bombings occurred within the city limits and that eight of those took place during the Henderson administration. An outraged Mayor Kryzan asked radio station officials for airtime for Cress. Claiming that the radio program and the editorial were a "disgrace," he added that the only difference between former Police Chief Allen and Cress was that the current police chief was getting "bad press."

On Monday, January 27, Cress appeared on the radio show "Coffee An'" for a scheduled 15 minutes. The *Vindicator* reported several of the chief's comments and some of the exchanges:

> "In answer to the question on the difference between the vice squad and the new morals squad, Cress said the name "vice squad" had a bad connotation and "many cities our size are calling it a "morals squad." He added that it is just a change of name. The new squad will have ten men, compared to 16 on the present squad.
>
> "Asked if the bombings represent any pattern which might be indicative of the Mafia or "Black Hand," Cress said some of them fit that pattern but not all. He added that there was no single modus operandi fitting all the bombings.
>
> "Cress said the police department does know in many instances who is doing a particular bombing and why, but does not have a case that will stand up in court, mainly because the victims themselves refuse to testify.
>
> "Cress maintained that Schuller knows who bombed him and why and that he knows, as he lies in South Side Hospital, that they are still trying to kill him. He

said the police have evidence that two men tried to get in to see Schuller several nights ago in such an attempt, and added that a guard had been placed around the victim.

"Cress accused the Vindicator of 'needling' him and said it just occurred to him that maybe the editorial was a way of needling him to get information.

"In defending their criticism of last Friday, the WFMJ staff members explained to Cress that this is not a police state and 'we have the perfect right to be alarmed by the bombings and ask questions about them."

Vice Squad Chief George Krispli was selected to head the new Morals Squad. The squad was increased from 10 to 12 members "so they could work in pairs" and "take care of the shifts and days off."[28]

January 29, 1958 – the Simon Sheet Metal shop, 780 South Avenue, Youngstown. Around 7:15 p.m. an explosion blew a hole, 14 inches in diameter, in the roof of the metal shop owned by John Simon. The blast shook houses and rattled windows in nearby homes. The shattered window and the hole in the roof of the metal shop were at first believed to be an attempted robbery. This caused Chief Cress to comment, "I hope the *Vindicator* does not try to link this to the bombings. It was just an attempted burglary, from what I am told."

January 30, 1958 – the Youngstown Boat & Supply Company, 2209 Mahoning Avenue, Youngstown. This blast, around 7:10 p.m. and caused an estimated $200. It was similar to the Simon Sheet Metal bombing one day earlier in that the explosive was tossed onto the roof. This time, however, police were able to get a break. Mayor Kryzan reported that, "an unexploded TNT cap found on the roof of the bombed building appears to give us the basis for asking FBI assistance, since the cap is government issue and there is reason to believe it was stolen." The mayor immediately sought help from the local FBI office. It was reported that the FBI could only enter the case if a report of the TNT being stolen from a government facility were filed. Lieutenant Maxim, head of the police crime lab, was quoted as describing the "salvaged bomb as TNT, of the type made for Army ordinance."

While Lieutenant Watters declared that there was no connection between the two bombings, Kryzan's analysis was, "If there is a repeat of these two incidents under similar circumstances, it might indicate a mental problem." One police source said the attack could have been labor related since Walter Paulson, the owner of the supply store, had recently put on a new addition without utilizing union workers. The explosion occurred in the newly constructed section.

May 9, 1958 – the C & S Club, Route 90, Youngstown. Sometime before 2:00 a.m. a bomb consisting of five to six sticks of dynamite was placed near the front door of the club. The fuse apparently went out and when an employee discovered the bomb he pulled out the remainder of the fuse and threw the bomb into a field beside the club. The bombing attempt went unreported until an informant brought it to the attention of Lieutenant Watters. The story didn't appear in the newspaper until May 28.

The club was formally known as the Calabrese & Sicilian Social Club and was reputedly operated by a trio, one alleged to be a member of "the old Farah gang of Warren." The operator's name was not mentioned in the newspaper coverage. Rumors were that barbut was being played at the club every Wednesday and Friday nights and that during a game played within a week of the newspaper report, "a well-known Youngstowner won $18,000" in the game.

During the bloody turmoil that dominated the early 1960s, many believed that controlling the barbut game was the root cause of the killing that took place. The incident at the C & S Club brought about the association of barbut, for the first time in nearly a decade, with the bombing activity in the Valley. A September 25, 1954, *Vindicator* article revealed this about the popular Greek dice-game.

> "The barbut game is believed to be a large-scale game, with as much as $5,000 changing hands nightly, which has moved from location to location throughout the area for some time. It reportedly has drawn racket figures and ex-convicts from Youngstown, Struthers and Campbell and from Farrell and Sharon across the state line a few miles away.
>
> "Noteworthy because of its nomadic tendencies, the barbut game allegedly moved to its present spot after a fruitless raid last Feb. 27 by Hubbard Township constables and Trumbull deputies on the Bell-Wick Auto Sales, also on the Youngstown-Hubbard Road about a half mile from the present location.
>
> "Other spots where the game previously was located were on the Hubbard-Church Hill Road and on Route 62, directly across from the Ohio Tavern.
>
> "The game was tied in with Youngstown racketeering earlier this year when Hubbard Township officials complained that Youngstown racket interests were moving into the township."

October 19, 1958 – the Wallace Building, which contained Muller's Bar and the Struthers News Agency, 30 State Street, Struthers. The blast, which occurred at 3:50 a.m., ripped a two-foot hole in the concrete in front of the building and broke the front doors and shattered a plate glass window showering the inside with debris. Shattered windows elsewhere in the building narrowly missed several sleeping children. Police believed the explosive was a homemade black powder bomb. The building's owner, John P. O'Hara, purchased federal gambling tax stamps over the past few years and was a reputed "bookie joint operator" in Struthers. The building on State Street was located just a mile away from the American-Croatian Citizens Club where John Schuller was the victim of a car bomb in January. The two buildings were actually on the same street; Poland Avenue becomes State Street at the Struther's city limits.

October 19, 1958 – Larry's Sideway Inn, 136 Broad Street, Struthers. This blast, at the opposite end of downtown Struthers from the Wallace Building, came just 3 minutes after the first explosion. The blast gouged a hole in the sidewalk in the front of the bar, destroyed the front door and shattered windows in the front of the building. The bar owner, Larry Sheldon, who had operated the bar for seven years, told police, "I can't understand it. I've never had any trouble with anybody." Sheldon claimed he had no connection with O'Hara.

Struther's Mayor, Harold Milligan downplayed the idea that the explosions were underworld related. He "scoffed" at the belief the bombings were part of an ongoing gangland war for gambling supremacy. "The town is clean," he boasted. If O'Hara was doing any gambling he's just "picking up a few horse bets on the street." Milligan went on to say, "The police and I have been talking it over and have come to the conclusions that the bombings could have been done to embarrass the police department because of the good work they are doing." It was pointed out that, "Just one month ago the city administration issued an order removing all marble boards from Struthers. Charles Carabbia, a known police character, admitted owning the boards and complied with the order."

The *Vindicator* didn't see the bombings in the same light as the Struther's mayor. In a front-page article the newspaper stated:

> "Apparently a gambling feud is behind the double bombing which rocked the city where some racketeers have been prospering without interference from city or county officials. As in most Youngstown bombings, the blasts seemed to be warnings to either the victims themselves or to someone else who would understand their significance."

Mayor Milligan and his police chief, G. Woodrow Sicafuse denied that racketeers were "prospering" and said a check of the city's record of gambling convictions would bare that out.

The rash of bombings and the publicity surrounding them were certain to give people the idea of calling in a bomb threat. During the latter half of the 1950s this was a common occurrence and added an additional burden to the already overworked bomb squad. The main target of these "pranksters" was the school system. The schools received many bomb hoax calls where the buildings were evacuated and the police called in to conduct time-consuming searches. Most of these calls were believed to be perpetrated by students who attended the target school. Normal procedure when a bomb threat was called in involving a school was for a fire drill to be conducted while the bomb squad members carried out a systematic search of the building. One of these senseless pranks resulted in tragic consequences. On March 18, 1959, during a hoax bomb scare at Cardinal Mooney High School, more than 1,000 students were forced to wait outside, most without hats and coats, in 20-degree temperatures. Four days later,

17 year-old Barbara Jayne McClay was hospitalized with severe pneumonia and died the following month.

There was an arrest made in November 1958, of a 39 year-old man who had a record as a "mental case and an alcoholic," who over a year's time had telephoned in false bomb reports involving at least four schools that authorities could identify. The man was captured after an alert officer recognized his voice and got the man to admit he had called about an unrelated incident just 20 minutes before making another hoax call. Police had to deal with the epidemic of false bomb threats well into the 1960s.

Another problem that was taking place was pranksters using explosives, some just as simple as firecrackers, to destroy mail boxes and creating other kinds of mayhem that took up additional police time and effort.

On April 10, 1959, the *Vindicator* reported, "Over-zealous radio and television newsmen today created a near riot at Harrison School when they broadcast news of a bomb threat before the bomb was supposed to explode at 10:30 a.m." The threat was called directly to the school. This was a deviation from most phone threats, which were called into the police station. The Youngstown police, however, had recently announced they would begin taping the numerous bomb calls they received at headquarters in hopes of apprehending the culprits.

December 18, 1958 – a brothel located on the Mahoning / Starke County border, Jennings Avenue, Alliance. On December 22, two area residents received telephone calls from a man who claimed to represent a detective agency. They were told if they didn't take action to "get the house of ill-repute closed," their homes would be bombed. A fire prevention inspector went out to the home of Bertha Ciferno, known as "Ginger King," the next day and after looking at the premises discovered that the house was the target of a bombing almost a week earlier. The inspector found that 20 new windows were installed along with two new doors, one with an entire frame. In addition, the inside revealed that there was some recent plasterwork. The house was built with the front door facing one county, while access to the rear faced another. Ciferno was arrested numerous times for prostitution and for keeping a brothel. The home at one time was padlocked.

January 13, 1959 – the University Athletic Club, 801 Mason Street, Niles. A dynamite bomb, placed between the screen door and the front entrance door of the club, exploded at 1:25 a.m. The blast tore a small hole in the concrete stairs and caused extensive damage to the inside of the club. Vending machines were over-turned; tables, pictures and a davenport were wrecked. In addition to four windows in the club being shattered, 20 more were broken in nearby buildings.

The University Athletic Club, which was listed in the city directory as a "billiards" joint, was owned by A. C. "Squint" Fredericka, the brother of Niles 3rd Ward Councilman Rockie Fredericka. Once investigators entered the club they found evidence of "dice, horse race betting slips, basketball pools and playing cards." One man, wishing to remain anonymous, stated, "That Squint must be a mind reader. Normally there's an all night dice game that lasts until about 6:00 a.m. But the other night he cleared everybody out at 8:00 p.m." The club was reputed to be frequented by "Fats" Aiello.

The *Vindicator* reported the following:

> "It is believed that outsiders have been trying to muscle in on Squint's operation or demanded a percentage of the joint's 'take.'
>
> "If the pattern follows that of other Niles bombings, it is possible that the dynamiters are imported from Cleveland or New York.
>
> "Past investigations have disclosed that in two similar bombings here an 'expert' from New York received $1,000 for his work and in another instance a Clevelander received $500.
>
> "It was learned from a reliable source, however, that one series of bombings ended when victims applied to the 'Court of Last Resort' – the Cleveland Mafia – for relief from an individual who had been engaging in a personal vendetta for a fancied wrong."

March 6, 1959 – the home of Niles Police Chief John A. Ross, 1332 Robbins Avenue, Niles. At 12:40 p.m. a mailman found five sticks of dynamite on the front porch of Niles Police Chief John A. Ross. A 14-foot fuse, which authorities said would have taken 28 minutes to reach the charge, had burned out. Chief Ross considered the incident a threat, but stated, "I haven't the slightest idea of who may be responsible. I have received no other warnings and have been involved with no serious arguments with individuals arrested." The chief had asked the local newspapers to withhold the story in hopes of "expediting the investigation."

May 8, 1959 – the automobile of Christ Sofocleous, outside 385 Park Avenue, Youngstown. The bombing epidemic in the Valley finally claimed its first victim. The 30 year-old Sofocleous died on an operating table at St. Elizabeth's Hospital four hours after the blast.

Sofocleous, who did not have a criminal record in the Valley, was the son of Pete Sofocleous, a Campbell coffee shop owner, who was arrested for operating a gambling joint on several occasions but was never charged. Although Sofocleous was married to Pauline Guerrieri, he had recently been dating attractive 23 year-old blonde divorcee, Mary Higgins Vigarino, who lived in an apartment at the Park Avenue address with her four-year-old son. Neighbors said Sofocleous was a frequent visitor to the apartment and often took Vigarino, who went by the name Higgins, and her son on outings in his automobile.

Higgins, however, had another suitor. Ronald Carabbia had dated the young lady and it was reported that he and Sofocleous had recently had a fistfight over her "affection." The six-foot, 250-pound Sofocleous would have made a formidable opponent for the shorter, lighter Carabbia.

Sofocleous arrived at Higgins' apartment between 1:30 and 2:00 a.m. on Friday, May 8 and spent the night. He parked his car on Park Avenue, just East of Belmont, 1,000 feet from St. Elizabeth's. At 11:50 the next morning, as Higgins and her son were eating breakfast, Sofocleous left the apartment and climbed into his 1954 Buick. As he turned the ignition key a dynamite charge detonated. The *Vindicator* described the actions of two local citizens following the explosion:

> "Robert Shirilla, a pharmacist at Lester's Pharmacy in the Bel-Park Medical Building, heard the blast and ran to the car. He opened a door but was unable to see anyone until dense smoke began to clear.
>
> "He said when he found the victim, his chest and abdomen were torn open, his head and legs severely gashed. He was conscious but in severe pain and shock.
>
> "Shirilla ran into the medical building and got Dr. Henry Shorr, who made a quick examination, ordered a narcotic from Shirilla and gave the man a shot to ease the pain until the ambulance arrived. Police had some trouble getting the victim out of the damaged car."

The blast had blown chunks of the automobile's firewall, like shrapnel, into Sofocleous' abdomen and chest. Higgins came running out of her apartment, dressed only in "shortie pajamas," and had to be restrained by neighbors at the sight of the devastation. Police stated it was only "by chance" that Higgins and her son were not in the car with Sofocleous that day. When police and medical attendants finished placing the dying man inside the ambulance, and it was headed for St. Elizabeth's, Higgins chased after it – in front of hundreds of onlookers who had gathered – running barefoot down the street. All of this was captured by a photographer from WFMJ. Still shots from 16mm movie film appeared on the front-page of the *Vindicator* the next day where Mary Higgins was dubbed the "aluminum blonde." The last photo showed the distraught young lady being escorted by officers back to her apartment. She was arrested and held overnight for questioning.

At St. Elizabeth's Hospital Sofocleous was rushed into surgery. Doctors performed extensive repair surgery to the heart, intestines and kidneys. Sofocleous received 11 pints of blood while the surgery was in progress. Despite the valiant effort of the doctors, Sofocleous died at 3:40 p.m. without regaining consciousness. Dr. David Belinky confirmed that the cause of death was shock and hemorrhage due to shrapnel wounds of the heart and abdominal organs.

Police were making arrests before Sofocleous' body arrived at Putko, Rich & Wasko Funeral Home in Campbell. In addition to Higgins, police held Ronnie Carabbia, Dominic Senzarino (Carabbia's cousin) and Donald "Bull" Jones. While Jones agreed to take a lie detector test, and passed, the other three refused. Whatever reason Higgins had for not taking the test was never clear. After spending the night in jail she agreed to take it the next day and was released after "being cleared."

Police had one more suspect they were looking for. Shortly after the blast they put out an alert for a 1957 Cadillac bearing Indiana plates. The automobile belonged to Phil Mainer, who was a suspect in several of the Valley's bombings including the January 1958 blast that injured John Schuller. When Mainer found out through friends that he was a suspect, he called his Youngstown attorney, S. S. Fekett and from his home in Hammond, Indiana agreed to turn himself in at the detective bureau by 9:00 a.m. Monday morning.

Fekett was asked if his client would submit to a lie detector test. The attorney replied, "That's one thing he won't do if he asks my advice. I can't agree with something, the results of which are not admissible in court."

On May 11, Mainer flew in from Hammond and, after meeting with attorney Fekett, went to see Lieutenant Watters. After Hammond, Indiana, police were able to account for Mainer's "every movement from midnight Thursday until Friday," he was cleared of any connection with the murder. Later that day, Mainer and the three remaining suspects were released. Watters claimed that despite the release, it didn't mean the men were dismissed as suspects. "You can hold these people only so long without charging them. As of now, the circumstances do not permit any charges to be filed." Police then issued a public plea for assistance.

On Monday, May 11, while police were questioning Mainer, the funeral for Sofocleous was held. There were 250 mourners in attendance at Archangel Michael Greek Orthodox Church in Campbell, including Pauline Sofocleous and her husband's lover, Mary Higgins. Dressed in black, Higgins arrived with two female companions and waited outside the church until after family members entered. Sitting in one of the last pews, Higgins wept several times during the service, which was delivered in Greek. Sofocleous' mother, overcome with grief, broke down as she left the church.

At the cemetery chapel, Higgins got too close to family members and was warned off by a sister of Mrs. Sofocleous. The newspaper reported, "While the family and friends were in the chapel Miss Higgins[29] stood alone under a tree."

While Carabbia, who was also questioned in the Schuller bombing, was considered the prime suspect in the killing of Sofocleous, police had one other motive for the murder. In September 1958, Sofocleous was granted probation after he testified against his accomplices in two robberies in Virginia. During break-ins at the Little Creek Amphibious Base and the Norfolk Naval Air Station, both naval commissaries, the burglars got $14,700 and $23,000 respectively. With Sofocleous' testimony four people were convicted. Ben Guerrieri,[30] Sofocleous' brother-in-law, was sentenced to six years in prison and sent to Lewisburg, Pennsylvania. Clayton T. Grimmer, also of Youngstown, received five years in the Atlanta Penitentiary. The men were sent to federal prisons since the crimes took place at government facilities.

The other two were Mike Milanovich and his wife Virginia.[31] Both were convicted in the Little Creek burglary and acquitted of the other. Mike Milanovich received five years and his wife concurrent sentences of five and ten years on two counts. They both appealed their sentences and were currently free on bond. Police considered that relatives and friends of the four people Sofocleous helped convict might have motive to get back at him.

October 6, 1959 – the automobile of attorney Joseph Molitoris, 764 Genesse Drive, Warren. Someone placed a homemade time bomb under the attorney's Cadillac, which was parked in the driveway of his home. The newspaper reported, "The bomb included an alarm clock with the face removed, but the hands intact, a battery, the blasting cap and the charge of dynamite." The electric blasting cap exploded, but failed to detonate the charge.

Molitoris told police he was awakened by his barking dog around 3:10 a.m. He heard a noise, which he thought was an automobile backfiring. Around 4:00 a.m. he took his wife to the train station and when he returned home he found officers searching the area. Police had received a telephone call at 4:18 where an anonymous caller stated, "You'd better send a cruiser to Joe Molitoris' house, there's a bomb out there."

Molitoris could offer no reason for the bombing attempt. Police noted that he was associated with attorney George Buchwalter, who was currently representing Mike Farah in an assault with intent to kill case after he had given a beating to Jean P. Blair, chairman of the Trumbull County Republican Party. Molitoris was also active in local politics.

On March 17, 1961, two days after a bomb damaged the home of Warren Municipal Judge James A. Ravella, police brought in Robert Suckow, William "Chico" Graham and William Whitman in for questioning. Chief Manley English had suspected the three of the Molitoris bombing, but had no evidence on which to charge them. During questioning Graham and Whitman denied involvement. Suckow, after "intense questioning" by Captain Harold Rhoda, broke down and admitted he had conspired with Graham in making the bomb and planting it under the attorney's automobile.

Suckow said Graham wanted to scare Molitoris "as retribution" for a court case involving one of Graham's friends. When Graham didn't hear the time bomb go off, he called police and said that a bomb had exploded in Molitoris' vehicle. The three were arraigned on March 21 before Judge Ravella.

November 3, 1959 – the automobile of Laura DeJacimo, East Market Street School, Warren. A Trumbull County voting board aide whose firing triggered the Farah / Blair incident – a highly publicized assault case in which Farah was charged with attempted murder.

Mrs. DeJacimo was at the East Market Street School serving as an election worker. During the day a smoke bomb was wired to the spark plugs under the hood of her car. The bomb was wired incorrectly and, instead of exploding, caused the vehicle not to operate properly. The next morning DeJacimo took the automobile to a service station where attendants discovered the device.

DeJacimo took the bomb to the police department and personally handed it to Chief English. After receiving no response from the department, DeJacimo telephoned the newspapers. Reporters contacted Chief English the next day. He told them he felt the device was harmless and he "didn't want to take detectives off more important work." English stated he had the bomb dusted for fingerprints, but none were found. He said no attempt was made to retrieve prints from DeJacimo's automobile and no written report of the incident was prepared for news people to view.

December 14, 1959 – in the night deposit box of the Dollar Savings & Trust Company, Lincoln Knolls Plaza, Youngstown. At 9:35 a.m., a teller at the bank opened the night deposit box and found a brown cardboard box with enough dynamite inside to "blow the bank sky high." The teller alerted the branch manager who carried the box to a field some 75 yards away, and then notified police and the FBI.

The newspaper reported, "It takes a key to open the night deposit box and the would-be bomber had one. The La France Dry Cleaning store at the Lincoln Knolls Plaza was looted over the weekend and three night depository keys were stolen." The bomb, set to go off with an electronic charge, didn't detonate. Police thought it was mishandled.

Youngstown's bomb squad was not sent to investigate. The squad was disbanded and its members reassigned to the crime lab, detective bureau and other duties.

Section III Notes

1 The other Senators who made up the initial Kefauver Committee were:

Herbert O'Connor - Democrat - Maryland
Lester C. Hunt - Democrat - Wyoming
Alexander Wiley - Republican - Wisconsin
Charles W. Tobey - Republican - New Hampshire

2 Ray Linese is a mysterious figure for which there is little information available. Outside of his ownership of the Italian Village restaurant in Miami Beach the only reference to him is his alleged illegal activity in the Valley. Linese is not mentioned in Allen's *Merchants of Menace - The Mafia*, nor Hank Messick's *The Silent Syndicate.* It's possible that in Ed Reid's *Mafia* he may have been referring to Linese when he made his list of the top 83 Mafia figures in the country. At number 44 he had "Ray Scalise, Youngstown and Florida." A November 1952, *Vindicator* article about the book stated that the name of Ray Scalise, as being one of the "locals," was "not immediately familiar."

3 Joseph Massei was described by author Paul R. Kavieff in *The Violent Years* as "a downriver bootlegger, rumrunner, and gunman. Massei was a highly respected, well-liked leader in the Detroit underworld. ...[he] was eventually to become an important national underworld figure." In 1928, Massei, Joe Galbo and Pete Licavoli were convicted of bribing a customs official to let them bring liquor across the Detroit River. Massei was suspected of several murders in Detroit including that of Jimmy Hayes, said to be the alleged gambling boss of Toledo. In Hank Messick's *The Silent Syndicate* the author writes, "Joe Massei was to become one of the biggest gangsters in the country. The arrangement with him was part of the working alliance Dalitz had formed with his old Detroit connections and with the Mafia. It was called the 'Combination,' consisting, as it did, of both Jewish and Sicilian elements. Long after the Prohibition era ended, the 'Combination' continued to control gambling and related rackets in Toledo, Youngstown, Buffalo, Pittsburgh, Port Clinton, and to a lesser degree, in Detroit." In Florida, Massei's $90,000 home was built by a construction company owned by Al Polizzi.

4 There was some uncertainty as to who actually served the warrant. The Buffalo *Courier-Express* reported it was served by Detective Chief William T. Fitzgibbons and Detective Sergeant William J. Madigan of the Buffalo Police Department and two Cleveland detectives. The *Vindicator* claimed the papers were served by vice squad men Thomas Kelty and William Turnbull and Buffalo policemen.

5 Captain Harold E. Faust, a 13-year veteran of the Youngstown Police Department, collapsed and died at the wheel of his automobile on April 14, 1953. He was 47 years old.

6 Alvin J. Sutton, Jr., a former FBI agent, was Cleveland's point man for the serving of subpoena's in that city. Sutton was Cleveland's youngest safety director. He was appointed to the position by Mayor Thomas Burke at the age of 31, a year younger than Eliot Ness, who was 32 when appointed in December 1935 by Mayor Harold H. Burton.

7 In 1973, Joseph Nellis co-authored the book *The Private Lives of Public Enemies*, with organized crime authority Hank Messick.

8 The infamous Statler Hotel meeting occurred on December 5, 1928, in Cleveland, Ohio. Twenty-three mobsters from cities such as Brooklyn, Chicago, Buffalo, Newark, Tampa and St. Louis attended. All of the men were Sicilian leading some historians to believe the men were meeting to select a new national leader of the Unione Siciliana. There was recent strife in the organization with the murders of Frank Uale, alleged to have been the previous national president, in Brooklyn on July 1, and the sensational killing of Anthony Lombardo and his bodyguard on a crowded Chicago street on September 7. Major figures arrested in Cleveland were Joseph Profaci, Joseph Magliocco (both of whom were arrested at the Appalachin Meeting in November 1957), Vincent Mangano, Pasquale Lolordo and Joseph Giunta. The last two would both become president of the Unione Siciliana in Chicago and be brutally murdered in 1929. Days after the arrests all of the men were released with the exception of one who was wanted for a murder in New Jersey.

9 Joseph John Aiuppa was known as "Joey Doves" or "Joey O'Brien." His obituary claims he began his "criminal career as a muscleman and gunner for the Capone mob in 1935." Depending on which source you read, Aiuppa made it to the top rung of the Chicago Outfit or served as a figure head under Anthony Accardo in the 1970s. Aiuppa was sentenced to prison in March 1986 after being convicted in the FBI's "Operation Strawman" case, the skimming of Las Vegas casino money, and died there in February 1997 at the age of 89.

10 While conducting interviews for the book I was told that it was Vince DeNiro who shot Sandy Naples. The interviewee stated that when Naples was incarcerated in the Western Penitentiary he developed a close friendship with several members of the Pittsburgh Mafia family. When he was released they put him in charge of the numbers activity in New Kensington. With his new found wealth Naples was expanding into Youngstown where DeNiro held sway. I never

found a clear explanation of the relationship between the two men and was unable to confirm that DeNiro had anything to do with the Naples' shooting – especially in lieu of the fact that DeNiro remained at the restaurant.

In August 1954, when the newspaper printed the latest names of the purchasers of the federal gambling stamp, DeNiro and Sandy Naples were referred to as the "reputed leaders" of the local numbers rackets. It was also stated that DeNiro, "maintains much of a behind-the-scenes position in city rackets, but is regarded by many observers as Naples' equal in the gambling hierarchy."

By the mid-1950s no one was sure what the relationship between Vince DeNiro and Sandy Naples was. Did DeNiro work for Sandy? Was Sandy considered a mentor or a competitor? In May 1954, while the telephones were being removed from the Center Sandwich Shop, because of reported bug activity, the two men sat together in a booth casually drinking coffee and watching the workmen. During Naples' trial in July 1954, DeNiro was linked to Sandy's brother James in the collection of the numbers profits. Both Mayor Frank X. Kryzan and Municipal Court Judge Frank Franko claimed DeNiro was the "kingpin" of both the numbers and the gambling operations in the Valley.

11 The other tax stamp holders were J.S. Pakkac, Chris W. Gorgian and brothers Charles and John Eidelman.

12 It is interesting to note that Judge Cavalier attached "Sr." to the end of the Clyde W. Osborne name to differentiate him from his nephew of the same name, who at the time was serving as Mayor Henderson's personal secretary.

13 Denise Darcel was a French-born actress who appeared in ten films including *Thunder in the Pines* (1948), *Tarzan and the Slave Girl* (1950), *Westward the Women* (1951), *Dangerous When Wet* (1953), *Flame of Calcutta* (1953) and *The Seven Women from Hell* (1961). In 1954 she hosted a short-lived television series called *Gamble on Love*, a quiz program involving married couples.

14 Steve Kilame's last name was listed at various times in the newspapers as Kilone, Kilam, Kilane and Kilamee.

15 Cognovit is a legal term, meaning a written admission by a defendant of his liability, made to avoid the expense of a trial – *The American Heritage Dictionary: Second College Edition.*

16 Ohio Governor C. William O'Neill was defeated in the November 1958 election by Michael V. DiSalle

17 Creosote is an oily substance created by the distillation of coal and wood

tar. The liquid has a burning taste and penetrating odor. Its commercial use is as a preservative for wood.

18 Other members of the new "bomb squad" were Lieutenant George Maxim, Detectives Peter Venorsky, Gerald Brace, Edward Przelomski, Joseph Zetts and John Lesko.

19 Robert B. Krupansky went on to a successful legal career, leaving the bench as the federal circuit court senior judge. In 1969, he was named U.S. Attorney for the Northern District of Ohio. He conducted the investigation that led to the indictment and conviction of United Mine Workers Union President Tony Boyle for the murder of his predecessor Jock Jablonski and his family. The next year he led the grand jury investigation into the Kent State University killings. Later that year he was appointed to the U.S. District Judge of the Northern District. As a federal judge he took over the Cleveland school desegregation case in November 1994, replacing US District Court Judge Frank J. Battisti of Youngstown.

20 Harold H. Hull was born on August 23, 1885, near Grove City, Pennsylvania. His family moved to Greenville when he was a young boy. He grew up there and attended local schools. He went to college at Allegheny College, graduating in 1907. He received his law degree in 1910. Hull moved to Youngstown that same year and passed the Mahoning Bar exam.

Hull began his public career in the Mahoning County prosecutor's office in 1916, as an assistant to J.P. Huxley. Three years later, Huxley resigned and Hull was appointed to fill out the un-expired term. As prosecutor in 1921 Hull faced his most notable trial when he prosecuted the David J. Scott case. Scott was the safety director of Youngstown and was indicted for accepting a bribe from prominent bootlegger Moe Baron to allow him to move his liquor shipments through the city. Scott was convicted and sent to the Ohio Penitentiary. Hull's opponent in the trial was defense attorney A.M. Henderson, the father of future Youngstown Mayor Charles P. Henderson.

In 1924 Hull retired as county prosecutor and went into private practice. In 1930 he decided to run for common pleas judge, but lost to Erskine Maiden, Jr. Hull remained in politics, serving as the executive secretary of the Mahoning County Republican Campaign Committee.

William A. Ambrose, a Democrat, was elected county prosecutor in 1936. One of his first appointments was to name Hull an assistant. Except for brief interludes, Hull remained in that capacity until his death.

Hull was often referred to as "Dean" by the young lawyers he encountered. He was recognized statewide as an authority in interpreting Ohio law. It was not unusual for Hull to be approached by judges for legal advice on questions of law.

During the summer of 1960 Hull was in San Marino, California visiting the home of attorney Ray L. Thomas, who had assisted him in the Scott trial. Hull suffered a heart attack and died on July 25. He was 74 years old.

21 The Colonial House at 2619 Market Street was physically located just two doors down from Cicero's, which was at 2597 Market Street.

22 The breakdown of the 69 bombings – Youngstown (31); Niles (9); Warren/Trumbull County (9), Struthers (5); Cuyahoga Falls, Hubbard, Massillon, New Castle PA, (2 each); and Alliance, Bessemer PA, Boardman, Girard, Liberty Township, Newton Falls, and Poland (1 each).

A further breakdown of the 69 bombings during the 1950s reveals for motive or reason (author's best analysis) – related to gambling, numbers, vice, etc. (26); union or labor related (24); political in nature (6); and unknown (13). As far as locations that were bombed – homes (23 – 3 of which were under construction); garages (3); automobiles (7); bars, clubs and restaurants (12); office, factory, warehouse or commercial garages (9); commercial shopping malls (4); commercial vehicles (3); grocery stores (4); schools (2) brothels (1); and (1) bomb seemed to be a test bomb set off on the side of a road. Seven of the bombings were of the "stench bomb" variety, an acid-type substance inside a glass container thrown at the home.

23 When Donald "Slick" Gaetano tried to renew his liquor license he was rejected on February 11, 1957, by the Ohio Department of Liquor Control. The department claimed "he was operating the Steel City Club for his own interest, not that of dues-paying members as required under private club permit regulations." The club appealed to the Board of Liquor Control, which upheld the department's decision in October 1957. Gaetano took the matter to Franklin County Court of Common Pleas, which also upheld the ruling. A last ditch effort before the Franklin County Court of Appeals was also shot down.

The slick Gaetano, however, lived up to his nickname. In November 1958, the proprietor of the Poland Café transferred his nightclub permit to Gaetano, which allowed him to serve liquor at his new Key Club, located at the Belmont address. The liquor department determined there was nothing illegal in the transfer procedure and the Steel City Club lived on under a new name.

24 Other members of the "bomb squad" were Lieutenant George Maxim. Detectives Peter Venorsky, Gerald Brace, Edward Przelomski, Joseph Zetts and John Lesko.

25 Lloyd Renaldo Haynes was born on December 31, 1916 in Dublin, Georgia. He moved to Youngstown as a child and attended local schools here. He gradu-

ated from Rayen High School in 1936, where he was a member of the All-City Basketball Team. In 1944, Haynes was appointed cadet on the Youngstown police force. While working as a police officer he attended law school at Youngstown College (now Youngstown State University), passing the Ohio bar in 1951. While with the police department, Haynes worked on the vice squad and later with the detective bureau. In 1969, Haynes left the police department when he was appointed Assistant Mahoning County Prosecutor. Haynes became Youngstown's first Black Municipal Court Judge in 1972 when Ohio Governor John J. Gilligan appointed him to the bench. Elected in succeeding years, Haynes served as judge until his retirement in 1989. Haynes was married to Helena Harvey Haynes. The couple had four children. Their daughter Loretta died in a tragic boating accident off Los Angeles in 1976. His son, Lloyd R. Haynes, Jr. became a lawyer also. In retirement Haynes moved to Houston, Texas, where he died on June 10, 2006 at the age of 89.

26 Elwyn Jenkins was the son of Judge David G. Jenkins, who was presiding over the trial. More than 45 years later I asked former prosecutor and judge Clyde Osborne if this was a conflict of interest. He told me that none of the defense attorneys challenged it because, "David Jenkins was a straight shooter who would put his own grandmother in jail if she was found guilty. There was no question that it would be a fair trial"

27 In April 1958, Millanovich was arrested by the FBI on Youngstown's North Side as a prime suspect in an armed robbery involving the Beneficial Finance Company in Columbus, Ohio, on April 2. Millanovich was also wanted for questioning about robberies in Chicago Heights, Illinois, Lansing, Michigan, and Gary and Fort Wayne, Indiana.

28 The new "morals squad" was comprised of George Krispli, the chief; former vice squad members Sergeant Clarence Brown, Patrolmen Andrew Kovac and Peter Polando; narcotics squad members Detectives Sam Schiavi and Steve Krispli and Patrolmen William Campanizzi and Walter Cegan; and new squad members Patrolman Joseph Olexa, Ray Polombi, Ben Smith and Michael Terlesky.

29 Less than a month after Christ Sofocleous died in the fatal bombing, Nick Vigarino, the ex-husband of Mary Higgins Vigarino, filed a lawsuit to gain custody of his 4 year-old son Nick. The Vigarino family claimed Mary was an unfit mother due to her relationship with the dead man. In a hearing on June 6, 1959, Mary told the court Sofocleous had only been at her home for an hour that morning before he was killed.

Domestic Relations Judge Henry P. Beckenbach postponed his decision for a month and ordered investigations into the home lives and backgrounds of Mary, her parents and Nick Vigarino's parents, as both of the child's grandparents were seeking custody. At the time, Nick Vigarino was enlisted in the U.S. Army and stationed at Fort Knox, Kentucky.

On July 21, Judge Beckenbach granted custody to Mr. and Mrs. Nick Vigarino, Sr., the paternal grandparents of the child. The judge's investigation, which did not look into Mary's home life, concluded that both sets of grandparents "have excellent reputations," however, the Vigarino's were raising a four-year-old son of their own. The judge felt this would provide a better home life for the child. In making his ruling the judge told Mary, "Because of your past reputation I must give the child to someone else, at least for now." In his comments Beckenbach admitted, "I know the boy will be losing some of the close attachment he has had for his mother, but that's her fault because of her own conduct, not his." It was pointed out by juvenile authorities that while Mary drove a Cadillac and wore nice clothes she hadn't been employed since November 1958. Mary and her parents were granted visitation rights.

During the hearing Beckenbach refused to allow Mary's attorney Phil Morgante to present witnesses on behalf of his client. Two days later, Morgante filed an affidavit of prejudice against the judge for this refusal. Beckenbach, sparing himself having to go through a hearing of prejudice before the Ohio Supreme Court, transferred the case to Common Pleas Judge John W. Ford.

On December 21, the custody fight got underway. A probation officer for the court testified that the homes of both grandparents would be an excellent environment in which the child could be raised. The officer also admitted that Mary's home and life had not been officially investigated.

On New Year's Eve 1959 Judge Ford ruled that Mary could keep her four-year-old son, providing she moved into her parent's home.

30 After his arrest by the FBI, for the Norfolk Naval Air Station theft, Benjamin T. Guerrieri was facing life imprisonment as a habitual criminal. At the time he was out on bond for the March 1958 attempted burglary at the Consolidated Tire & Paint Company on West Commerce Street and was convicted and awaiting sentencing for the attempted burglary of the Isaly Dairy Store on Hillman Street in October 1956. Another burglary charge was pending against him in Ambridge, Pennsylvania, after an attempted break-in there. In addition, Guerrieri was considered a prime suspect in the holdup of the Girard Amerital Club in August 1956, where $7,000 was taken, and the $5,000 burglary of the Schweibel Baking Company on Midlothian Blvd. that same year. Police believed he was responsible for a number of unsolved burglaries in Youngstown and Guerrieri was frequently picked up for questioning during the wave of bombings going on in the area.

Guerrieri, whose criminal record began in 1949, spent time in the Mansfield Reformatory for assault with attempt to rob. In 1954, Guerrieri was arrested twice for bug offenses. The next year he received a severe beating and was hospitalized. Police believed it was due to his activities in the numbers' business.

31 If there was any relationship between Mike Milanovich and the Steve Milanovich who was arrested as a suspect in the Schuller bombing it was not indicated by the newspaper.

Section IV

The 1960s

Photo courtesy of the Cleveland Press Collection.

"It's like a toothache. After awhile everyone gets used to the pain. But we want to know what we can do to prevent this again." – Mitchell Stanley, station manager of WFMJ-TV conducting an interview in the wake of Vince DeNiro's car bombing murder.

13

Murder Town

The 1960s began with the carryover of the "bug" war that marked the end of the 1950s. The Youngstown Police Department was operating at furious pace, but the gang killings continued. No one, however, could predict that what was on the horizon would turn the city of Youngstown into "Murder Town" and "Crimetown USA." This reputation, earned during the first few years of the 1960s, would never be lived down by the maligned city or its residents.

January 16, 1960, was a big day in the life and career of Lieutenant Frank W. Watters. He became the chief of the Morals Squad, the latest rendition of the vice squad. In his new position Watters immediately began putting pressure on the bug writers. The two largest factions vying for the Valley workers' wages were led by S. Joseph "Sandy" Naples, and the handsome James Vincent "Vince" DeNiro. Profits were down for the gang leaders as Watters' units toiled away arresting the numbers runners regardless of who they worked for.

Less than sixty days had passed since Watters took command and the squad had made 18 bug arrests, compared to 26 for all of 1959. In January alone his men stopped and searched 125 suspects and raided and searched 73 business establishments. The totals were up again in February. There were 216 suspects searched, 53 vehicles stopped and searched, and 93 businesses raided and searched.

Despite Watters' impartial efforts, members of the DeNiro faction complained the police raids favored the Naples' side. As the pressure grew, both sides took drastic measures to ensure their profits. DeNiro, Naples and the few independent operators who dared challenge them, began changing cars and drivers repeatedly during their pickup rounds to throw off Morals Squad members who trailed them.

Three rumors were prevalent during the early months of 1960. The first was that Naples was given the "green light" to begin full numbers operations throughout the city. Second, was that he and three other underworld figures had formed a new syndicate. Although Watters' men investigated both these rumors, neither was substantiated. The third rumor was that Naples, DeNiro and members from a Brier Hill group were to divide the city when the new administration took charge. There was no doubt that Watters' activities hurt both sides, but they all seemed under the impression the lid would come off in the city with the new administration of Frank R. Franko.

Despite the rumors, Watters raids brought the numbers operations in the city to the point of crisis. An underworld informant told police that, "The boys are mad about the way things are going in the numbers game and Naples is pretty mad. There's going to be shooting soon, maybe by early March." The talk on the street was "one bug bank was getting hit too hard and Sandy's was left untouched." The prediction of an early March shooting proved to be right on the mark.

Watters vehemently denied the accusations that one side was being favored over the other. "Everybody is crying because of the pressure we have been putting on them," the lieutenant claimed. He reported that men from his squad were at the Center Sandwich Shop, "practically every day" in efforts to uncover evidence of numbers operations. Watters told the *Vindicator* that, "they had been unsuccessful because the money and slips were sent to different spots outside the city."

Murder of Sandy Naples

Sandy Naples was in love with a pretty blonde named Mary Ann Vrancich. Naples began dating her while she was still a student at Woodrow Wilson High School. Sources claimed the two had dated for fourteen years, which would have made Vrancich only fourteen when they first starting seeing each other. In March 1960, Naples was 52 years old and Vrancich 28.

Vrancich lived near the top of steep Caledonia Street in a white two-story home at the corner of Maple Street. She shared the home with her invalid 68 year-old mother and a sister. Mrs. Vrancich had a serious heart condition and seldom left home since the death of her husband the previous summer. Mary Ann, described by neighbors as the perfect daughter, spent the day taking care of her mother, seeing to her needs and making few trips outside the home. She had accepted an engagement ring from Naples four years earlier, but no wedding date was set. Sandy's official home was still the house on Carlotta Drive, which he shared with his mother, father and younger brother Joseph. The relationship and living arrangement seemed strange to many.

Despite her loving attitude towards her mother, Mary Ann had a dark side too. Five years earlier she was arrested during a roundup of drug users after police found her in an automobile in the company of another suspect. She was released without being charged. While the newspaper reports didn't report it, there was speculation that Naples was supplying her with heroin.

The highlight of Sandy Naples' day was his nightly trips to the house on Caledonia Street. Neighbors said he arrived like clockwork at the house each night around 11:00. His brother James confirmed, "He was the most punctual in the family. He always kept to the same time schedule."

On Friday evening March 11, 1960, Naples left the family home on Carlotta Drive just before 9:30 and drove to the Center Sandwich Shop. As was his custom, he got a couple of sandwiches and the newspaper and headed off to see Mary Ann around eleven o'clock. Naples drove down Maple Street and parked his cream-colored 1960 Chevrolet Impala beside the house. In addition to the sandwiches and newspaper, Naples also had $4,000 in cash, a snub-nose .38 revolver, which he carried in a specially made gun pocket inside his waist band, and eleven capsules of heroin hidden inside a pack of cigarettes.

Naples got out of the car and walked down Maple Street to the sidewalk in front of the corner home. It was still late winter and while there were only a few inches of snow left on the lawns of the houses, the snowplows had pushed the snow into piles two feet high along the street. Naples climbed the few steps leading up to the porch and was about to knock on the door.

Suddenly two gunmen, who were hiding behind the house, emerged and took up positions on the sidewalk on either side of the walk leading to the porch. One man was armed with a 12-gauge pump shotgun, the other a .45 automatic. The killers had the drop on Naples. A bullet from the .45 struck Naples in the upper back near the neck, while a shotgun blast grazed his head. Despite his wounds and the suddenness of the attack, Naples spun around, drew his revolver and took advantage of the scant protection offered by the wooden porch siding. He then emptied his revolver.

Two doors away from the Vrancich home lived Stanley Novak, who was on his way out to pick up family members from a skating rink. Novak told police, "I had just stepped outside the door on the way to my car when I saw this man run out from between the Dressels and Vrancichs [houses].

"He had a repeating gun and it sounded like a machinegun. It went off so fast I couldn't count. Sandy sort of crouched, like he'd been hit, then fell behind the porch railing and began firing.

"The man with the shotgun was running up the street toward Maple Street firing as he went. He fell at the corner of the two streets. I thought he was hit, but they couldn't find any blood. He might have slipped on the sidewalk, which was pretty icy. Then he disappeared west on Maple. I didn't hear any car."

At the sound of gunfire Mary Ann Vrancich rushed to the front door, dressed in pajamas and a robe. She was silhouetted in the doorway from the lights in her living room. A slug shattered the glass door and hit her in the left breast, puncturing her lung. She tumbled forward out onto the porch and fell next to Naples.

On patrol nearby that night were officers Donald Komara and John Koneval. Even the police were aware of Sandy Naples' penchant for punctuality. Over 40 years later the events of that evening were still fresh in Komara's mind:

> "I recall very vividly driving on Midlothian Boulevard going east. I was working with another officer named John Koneval and a call went out. We were in the Schweibel Bakery area near Lake Park. The call was that there was a shooting on Caledonia. John and I immediately looked at each other and I commented, 'Well, they got Sandy.' We proceeded to the scene and sure enough there was his girlfriend on

> the porch, frantic and screaming, and I ran to the porch and there was nobody else in sight. There was Sandy lying on the floor of the porch of the house, a .38 snub-nose revolver in his hand. He obviously emptied it blindly into the banister of the porch. He was conscious. I attempted to get some information from him, however, he didn't respond at all – with any words. He was in agonizing pain. I was rather shocked when I found out later from the hospital that she [Vrancich] had expired. I wasn't surprised to find that he had expired."

During a search of the area Officer Komara found the shotgun, which was abandoned in front of Naples automobile.

Before police arrived, Charlotte Carr, a neighbor, heard Mary Ann cry out, "Help me! Please, won't somebody help me." She placed her robe over Mary Ann and tried to comfort her. Carr later told police that Mary Ann told her she didn't know who did the shooting, but that she knew she was dying. Mary Ann was crying out over and over, "Be careful of my mother. Don't tell her."

The ride to South Side Hospital was a desperate and futile trip. Naples struggled to breathe, grasping his tongue with his hand he gasped for air. His expensive suit and overcoat were drenched in blood. Mary Ann lay on a cot beside him. With an oxygen mask attached to her face she rolled from side to side saying to herself, "Oh my God, Oh my God." Vrancich died in the ambulance and was pronounced dead when it arrived at the hospital at 11:45. Ten minutes later Naples followed her in death.

Back at the Caledonia Street home, Mrs. Vrancich was taken to the Dressel's home next door and kept in the dark about the condition of her daughter until the next day. Told that she had gone to the hospital to be with Naples, the mother kept asking about him. Calling him a "beautiful, wonderful man," she stated, "He always bring sandwiches, [make] coffee, eat and drink and talk, every night."

Shortly after midnight James, Billy and Joey Naples arrived at the hospital. They refused to answer most of the reporter's questions. Jimmy, however, made the comment, "Everything was going smoothly. There was no trouble anywhere." The newspaper was quick to point out that, "Some predicted the death ended the Naples' setup because 'there is nobody to fill his [Sandy's] shoes now.' His brothers aren't expected to continue on a big scale."

Immediately after the double-homicide police began looking for all known hoodlums. Within the hour John "Pinky" Walsh and Joseph Alexander were in police custody. Alexander was working at the Sands Restaurant & Cocktail Lounge, which he owned, when a customer told him about the Naples murder. Alexander was asked to go to the Youngstown Police Department in a patrol car. He was interviewed for an hour before another patrol car returned him to the restaurant. During the interrogation Alexander admitted that he was once a partner with Naples in the Center Sandwich Shop. After nine months the partnership ended because Alexander "saw no future in it." He was also quizzed about being in business with two other suspects the police brought in for questioning – Joseph Romano and Carmen Tisone.

Romano was with Alexander at the Sands and had nothing to offer the police during questioning. Tisone, questioned days later, said he was at home on the night of the killing. He found out about it the next day at his "beer garden," Tesone's Tavern, on Wilson Avenue. During the interrogation he was grilled about his business with Alexander and Romano in a new bug operation. Tisone denied the allegation.

Another who was questioned was Peter "Little Pete" Skevos. Born in Sparta, Greece, the 67 year-old Skevos told police he was at the Marwood Club on South Avenue when he heard about the killing on television. He said police soon entered the club and told them to close down. Skevos said Fred Stevens owned the Marwood Club, but he had previously owned the building in which the club was located. Skevos ran a coffee shop there before closing in July 1959. Two months later, he rented the building to Stevens so he could open the Marwood Club.

Police Chief Peter Venorsky reported on Saturday that racketeers had fled their known haunts. That morning Mayor Franko made the following statement:

> "I have ordered the police department to stay on an around-the-clock alert until an arrest leading to successful prosecution has been made. I am determined that Youngstown will tolerate terrorism no longer, no matter in what form or what source it manifests itself. Chief Venorsky and his capable assistants have a free hand and complete authority to round up, detain and question anyone they suspect of having information of this vicious, violent crime."

The numbers business suffered that Saturday as local police forced operators big and small into hiding to avoid arrest. The *Vindicator* was quick to pickup on the narcotics end and comment about its relevance. The day after the shooting the newspaper reported:

> "The finding of narcotics in Sandy's possession lent some credence to the theory of a Mafia slaying. Victor Riesel,[1] noted columnist, has written several articles reporting that the elders in the Mafia hierarchy have ordered all members out of the narcotics rackets and have threatened violence against some who won't comply. This was reported to be one reason for the Apalachin conference of the Mafia which police broke up in New York two years ago."

Although not publicized, the Youngstown Police Department gave a polygraph to a former boy friend of Mary Ann Vrancich on March 14. During the questioning James Walsh revealed that he was "going" with Mary Ann during the summer of 1953. At the time, both of them were using heroin. They began by snorting the drug before turning to mainlining (needle injection). Naples wanted to see Walsh and sent one of his "boys" to tell him to come to the Center Sandwich Shop. When Walsh arrived he was told by Naples to "lay off Mary Ann." Walsh claims he continued to see her because he was in love with her. Naples again threatened Walsh by having a "few boys" warn him to stay away from Mary Ann. Walsh stated he "eventually" stopped seeing her, at which time he began to "kick" his habit.

Walsh told investigators that it was common knowledge around the "narcotics circle" that Sandy Naples was a user and had been for the past six years. Naples was a source of supply for the addicts. Mary Ann, according to Walsh, was also selling heroin. The last purchase Walsh made was during the early summer of 1959. He made the deal with her over the telephone and then she met him later in an automobile. He purchased "four caps" of heroin from her. Walsh claimed that after consuming the "caps" he became violently ill.

Sandy Naples obituary indicated that in addition to his parents, he was survived by three brothers and four sisters and a married daughter named Loretta, who was living in San Diego. On Saturday evening, Naples' body was available for viewing at the Schiavone Funeral Home on Belmont Avenue. During the night, 300 people filed past the mahogany casket to see Sandy, laid out in a conservative dark blue suit and neck tie. One of his trademark pearl-gray felt hats was placed at the foot of the coffin. One of the largest floral pieces on display was made up of 200 red roses from a Pittsburgh florist. The wake continued on Sunday with an estimated 4,000 people paying respects. All of the funeral home's parking spaces were filled and hundreds of automobiles used the parking lots of supermarkets along Belmont Avenue.

On Monday morning, March 14, the funeral for Naples was held. An estimated 1,500 people crowded into the Schiavone Funeral Home for the service. While the Catholic Church refused to allow a mass, an assistant pastor from St. Anthony's Church in Brier Hill led a prayer service. Naples' mother leaned over the coffin, hugged her son and kissed him on the cheek. In Italian she spoke these last words to him, "Mothers' love, mothers' darling. Why did a death like this have to be?" Naples' father, ill and bed-ridden from a recent stroke, could not attend. After the prayer service, Sandy Naples' body was taken to Calvary Cemetery for burial. His hearse led a 92-car procession down Belmont Avenue.

The next morning the funeral for Mary Ann Vrancich was held. Over 1,000 people, many the morbid curious, filed past her coffin. The attractive blonde, "lay in state" at the Vaschak Funeral Home. Adorned in a white lace gown, she wore the glittering 5-carat diamond engagement ring Sandy had given her. Services were held at both the funeral home and at Saints Peter and Paul Church. Jimmy Naples and two of his sisters attended the Requiem Mass. Mrs. Vrancich tearfully repeated her daughter's name over and over again.

In the days after the double murder there was speculation that Mary Ann, who was a suspected narcotics user, may not have been killed as an innocent bystander. An unidentified source stated, "Sandy really loved that girl and visited her home just about every night. There's no telling what he told her about the rackets. If Sandy's killers had killed him and not her, she might have spilled the beans." The source also pointed out the killers could have shot Sandy at any point from the time he left his car until he reached the top step of the front porch.

There were few clues to help investigators. Police ballistics personnel were checking the seven .45 shells they found at the scene to determine if they might have been fired from a Thompson submachine gun as opposed to a handgun. The 12 gauge shotgun left at the scene was found to have "disappeared" from the Canton, Ohio police department. The Chicago Police Department asked for several shots to be fired and the shells sent to them to determine if the shotgun might have been used in the December 16, 1959, murder of Roger Touhy in that city.

On March 15, Vince DeNiro, who the police were looking for since the night of the murder, turned himself in at the Youngstown police station to answer questions. There was some confusion as to DeNiro's actual position in the city's policy rackets, at least by the newspaper. One article called him, "the acknowledged head of the numbers lottery operations in Youngstown." In an article two days later, DeNiro was referred to as the racketeer "who long had sought to unseat Naples in the numbers rackets."

DeNiro said that he was at his Market Street restaurant, Ciceros, and decided to have a steak. He was enjoying his meal in the kitchen, located downstairs, when William Coleman, the restaurant manager received a call from DeNiro's brother Louis. Coleman told Louis to call back on the downstairs' line and he proceeded to the kitchen to tell Vince the call was coming. Louis told Vince that he had received a phone call from the Purple Cow informing him that Sandy and his girlfriend were murdered. Coleman later recalled that Vince DeNiro seemed to be in a state of shock when he received the news. DeNiro told police he had last seen Naples two days before the killing when he stopped by the Center Sandwich Shop to have a cup of hot chocolate.

While DeNiro shed no light on what happened, the *Vindicator* reported on March 15 that, "A vicious western Pennsylvania gang known as the 'Mannarinos'" might have been responsible for the killings. Operating out of New Kensington, Pennsylvania, the Mannarino brothers' gang was reputedly trying to muscle in on the lucrative numbers rackets in the Valley, but was rebuffed by Naples.

Allegedly acting as front man in the Mannarino brothers' efforts was Joseph "Red" Giordano, the former Youngstown hood who was involved in the December 1947 fur robbery at the home of Rocco Marino. Giordano had ties with Joe DiCarlo in some Mahoning Valley gambling operations. More recently he was convicted of attempting to transport guns stolen from a National Guard armory in Canton, Ohio to Fidel Castro in Cuba.

Youngstown Detective Chief William W. Reed[2] called the speculation about the Mannarino brothers, "so much poppycock." He told the press, "We'll continue to pick up men associated with Naples until we learn enough to lead us to an arrest." In addition to DeNiro, whose questioning lasted an hour, the police questioned Gus Leamis, a coffee house operator and convicted numbers operator from South Avenue; and Nick Andrew, co-owner of the American Pool Room, the scene of several raids, on East Federal Street.

On March 15, members of the Morals Squad raided a home on North Center Street near Naples' sandwich shop. They arrested four men and seized 50 capsules of heroin. Lieutenant Watters sought unsuccessfully to find a link between the drugs seized and what Naples was carrying the night he was killed.

As the investigation into the Naples' murder moved into April, the list of people questioned grew to include "Fats" Aiello, Charles "Cadillac Charlie" Cavallaro, Philip J. "Fleegle" Mainer and Frank Fetchet. The police rounded up only local mobsters who refused to respond to "invitations" to come in for questioning.

The newspaper used the opportunity to attack the police handling of Frank Fetchet over the years due to the fact that he was arrested eleven times for gambling, convicted on three occasions, but was never fingerprinted or photographed. The *Vindicator* reported, "The police record room also has no 'package' on Fetchet, although it is routine for 'packages' to be prepared, with 'mug' shots and fingerprint cards, for others convicted of gambling."

Frank Watters could offer no explanation as to why the department was lacking this information on Fetchet. He told reporters that he was the first police officer to arrest Fetchet. The bust, in 1937, came after a foot chase down West Wood Street on the city's North Side. Fetchet was nabbed for being in the "bug business." Police Captain Joseph Lepo, recently appointed to head up the identification and records department, assigned members to "dig out" the records from all arrest and complaint reports and complete a "package" on Fetchet.

Despite the intense police investigation clues soon dried up. On June 9, 1962, more than two years after the murders, two school mates, aged nine and eleven, were playing on Shady Run Road just two blocks from the Caledonia Street home where the murders occurred. When one child knelt to tie his shoelaces he looked into a sewer grate and saw what appeared to him to be a toy gun. After the two youngsters fished the weapon out they discovered it was real and ran to one of the boys' homes where police where called. Officers arrived and found the badly rusted weapon was a .45 caliber Army issue M-3 sub-machinegun, commonly called a "grease gun." The cocked weapon had a clip containing 24 live rounds of ammunition in place. The clip for this weapon normally holds 30 rounds. Assuming that one round was already in the chamber this would account for the seven empty shells that were recovered at the murder scene.

Police theorized the killers tossed the gun into the sewer during their escape after the shooting. After the discovery, police "technicians" spent hours cleaning the gun, which was pitted and rusted from the sewer mud, waste, and natural elements over the two years it was hidden there. It was deemed unlikely that they would be able to fire it in order to do a ballistics' test on the bullets.

Under pressure to explain why city workers had never discovered the weapon, Streets Superintendent Joseph Booth responded that the grating was used as an overflow chamber and had no manhole or access from the street surface. Booth pointed out that several months earlier workers had found a machinegun clip containing .45 caliber bullets, as well as several revolvers. Lieutenant Watters said the weapons were "checked out" but nothing was found to allow further investigation.

The M-3 sub-machinegun was sent to the FBI laboratory in Washington D.C. to see if a serial number could be lifted, and if the gun could be restored so it could be test-fired.

The Sands Restaurant Bombing

The first man questioned in the slaying of Naples and Vrancich was also the first person to be retaliated against – Joe Alexander. The one-time partner of Naples in the Center Sandwich Shop had his own restaurant targeted with a bomb just six days after the double murder. The Sands Restaurant & Cocktail Lounge, a plush $100,000 Austintown "night spot" at the corner of Mahoning Avenue and Meridian Road, was slightly damaged around 10:30 p.m. on St. Patrick's Day 1960.

The explosive device, believed to be a small stick of dynamite or a blasting cap, was placed next to the wall on the east side of the building. The blast left two holes, one two feet deep in the ground and the other in the ceiling of the restaurant's kitchen, located in the basement, which caused plaster to fall. Three employees working in the kitchen at the time were unharmed. In the days after the blast the few pieces of bomb residue recovered were sent to the FBI lab in Washington D.C. for analysis.

It was apparent that there was a concerted effort by the Alexander brothers to keep the blast from becoming a community spectacle. Despite the fact that local television and radio stations and the *Vindicator* were swamped with inquiries, there were no calls placed to either the Austintown or Youngstown Fire Departments from anyone at the restaurant. The Youngstown Police Department dispatched several cruisers to investigate an area of the West Side bordered by Mahoning, Manhattan and Winchester Avenues and Four Mile Run Road. The first official at the scene was an Austintown constable. After seeing the hole and a black circle of powder stain on the wall, he got back into his radio-less police car and drove to the Wickliffe Fire Station to call for assistance. After his return he discovered the hole was filled in and the wall washed down with water. When police and fire officials arrived, the Alexanders tried to convince them that it was only a small gas line explosion, but after a quick inspection by East Ohio Gas Company employees they found all gas lines intact and no evidence of leaks.

The fact that Joe Alexander was the first suspect questioned and the first retaliated against caused some in local law enforcement to believe he was behind the Naples / Vrancich murders. He was immediately put on the hot seat and the ownership of the restaurant came under intense scrutiny. In August 1958, a $25,000 permit was taken out in the name of Nicholas Alexander for the construction of the restaurant. Once completed, The Sands Restaurant & Cocktail Lounge became a popular spot and one of the "most luxurious" in the area. Just across the Youngstown municipal limits, the restaurant raised suspicions of Austintown authorities and the Mahoning County Sheriff's Department, but neither agency ever raided it.

On March 19, Joe Alexander, while being questioned by Mahoning County Sheriff Paul Langley, claimed he knew of no reason why anyone would want to harm him or his restaurant. While Alexander freely admitted his previous gambling arrests and connections to racket figures in the Valley, he affirmed, "Positively, I have no racket connections now. I have no desire to be the Number One man in Youngstown rackets or to have any part in them." One of the rumors that were circulating had Alexander taking over the local rackets due to his long friendship with Mayor Franko. The newspaper made much of the fact that Franko and the Alexander brothers were friends and pointed out that the mayor had dined at the restaurant just days prior to the bombing. It was also revealed that Joe Alexander accompanied Franko on a recent trip to Miami and Cuba.

Franko went on the defensive regarding these statements, claiming that Alexander was in Florida at the same time other local businessmen were. The *Vindicator* reported Franko's remarks and wrote, "The mayor added that he has been a friend of the Alexander family for 30 years and was a classmate of Nick Alexander at East High School. He said he eats there [Sands Restaurant] no more frequently than at other restaurants in the area."

Alexander denied being connected to the Woodworth Novelty Company, claiming instead that he only repaired jukeboxes and marble boards for the firm. He told the sheriff he had not been associated with Sandy Naples since 1946, when he sold his share of the Center Sandwich Shop. Alexander denied that there was anyone else involved in the ownership or management of the Sands Restaurant other than himself and his brothers Nicholas and Elias, "no one outside the family has any financial or other interest in the restaurant."

Based on what was reported in the newspaper, Alexander did contradict himself as to the cause of the explosion. In a March 20 article the *Vindicator* wrote, "Alexander said he really thought the blast was caused by a gas line because there was gas line trouble in the basement just before the place opened..." In the same article, however, it was reported he claimed, "He has half expected a phone call or some kind of word referring to the blast and making some kind of demand, but none has come." By his own estimate the explosion caused only $50 worth of damage.

Shooting of Joseph Romano

The underworld guns of Youngstown roared again less than four months after the Naples/Vrancich murders. This time they nearly took the life of Joseph Romano outside his Tod Lane home on the city's North Side. Romano, who was born in Altavella, Italy on May 5, 1900, had ties to Sandy Naples and was questioned by police after his murder.

Romano was a bit of a mystery. The police files noted he used the alias Joseph Dolci – his underworld nickname was "Stoneface." Morals' Squad leader Watters claimed he knew very little about the gambler. "The first time his name came to my attention was after a raid on the [Route] 422 Club. Romano supposedly was one of the backers, but it was never proved he had an official connection."

Romano's rap sheet showed no arrests for gambling, just three for suspicion, the earliest in December 1937, and one for speeding. He operated quietly and in the background – often seen, but seldom heard. Also a mystery, was what Romano did for a living? Officially he was said to be a cigarette salesman servicing machines and jukeboxes for Joseph Alexander. During the interrogation after the Naples murder, Romano claimed he "was self-employed, but was associated with the Alexander Music Company where he serviced cigarette vending machines." Alexander told police he paid Romano $200 to $300 a month for cigarette vending machines that he placed. Recently it was rumored that "Stoneface" had attempted to open a barbut game at the Marwood Club on South Avenue above the coffee shop, but when that venue was denied he planned to run the game from a second floor room at 5th Avenue and West Federal Street.

Shortly after 1:00 a.m. on June 4, Romano returned home to his apartment. It was reported that Romano was called out earlier that evening for a "downtown meeting." He parked his car in the garage and was heading toward the front entrance. Two gunmen, armed with shotguns, one sawed-off, were sitting in a car in front of the two-family dwelling. As Romano drew near the guns went off. The first blasts stunned and staggered Romano. He turned and ran back toward the garage area. The driver of the gunmen's car steered the vehicle toward Romano and as they drew close another volley was fired, this time dropping the victim.

After the gunmen screeched the automobile off to a safe getaway, the next sound heard was that of Romano calling out, "Help, I'm dying." By coincidence the fire department ambulance that arrived was manned by the same two attendants that had rushed to the Vrancich home in March. John Punceker described the trip to St. Elizabeth's Hospital with Romano, "He said nothing, just lay there. We picked him up in a stretcher, carried him to the ambulance, and drove to the hospital. He neither complained about his wounds nor said a word. He kept silent as we took him into emergency at the hospital."

Romano was in bad shape when he arrived at St. Elizabeth's. The 12 gauge shotgun pellets had ripped into his chest, abdomen and right arm. Several rounds hit his liver and 16 pellets peppered his bowels. He was in grave condition after three hours of emergency surgery. Two days later, Romano was still only given a 50/50 chance to live.

Youngstown police responded quickly. The automobile the would-be assassins used was found in Liberty Township on Colonial Drive. The car was purchased recently in Canton at a used car lot by a man who gave a false address. The weapons were found abandoned in a culvert nearby. One of the guns was stolen from a store in Mill Creek Township, a suburb of Erie, Pennsylvania. Police in Mill Creek were baffled by the break-in due to the fact that with a large variety of expensive merchandise only a few handguns and shotguns, as well as several ladies blouses, were stolen.

It was the second time that week activities in Youngstown were tied to Mill Creek Township. The previous Saturday night, Youngstowners Nello Ronci and Joseph Margiotta and two others were arrested in a Mill Creek motel. Police confiscated $5,000 worth of crooked dice.

Without providing an explanation, the Youngstown police asked that two Warren men be picked up. One, with a colorful past, Leo "Lips" Moceri, was taken into custody by the Warren police at 4:20 the Saturday morning of the attack. Later that morning, a half-block from Moceri's apartment, Ernest Fusco was arrested. Both were released without being charged.

Rumors were growing that there was more trouble coming in the wake of the Naples murder. It was reported that Romano was one of the names on the short list, along with "a certain politician who was reported to be marked for some form of violence." One of the rumors was that pressure was being put on policy and horse betting operators to pay a street tax of $500 and then 30 percent of their profits to Vince DeNiro. Lieutenant Watters questioned several of the operators who were allegedly shaken down, but none were willing to cooperate.

Murder of Vincent Innocenzi

Two months after the wounding of Joseph Romano a man's body was found near Akron, Ohio. The murder would forever be associated with the unrest that was taking place in the Mahoning Valley, even though there was little evidence tying it to these events.

Vincent Innocenzi was described as one of Northeast Ohio's top safe crackers and burglars. He came to the attention of the Cleveland police in the late 1940s and early 1950s as a member of the infamous Julius Petro gang. Innocenzi was nicknamed "the Horn," and "the Beak" due to his large nose. Although he was arrested on numerous occasions, he served prison time only once, for a burglary in California. In 1951, he pled guilty to stealing a safe from the Singer Sewing Center in Cambridge, Ohio, and was given an intermediate prison sentence. After this incident he told his wife, "Never, again" would he do anything that would put him back in prison. He was "scared" to go back.

In 1951, he was arrested in Fairmont, West Virginia for a supermarket burglary. At trial his lawyer claimed Innocenzi had met the other men in the store "because they wanted a place to hold a reunion." The jury didn't buy it and Innocenzi and two Cleveland men were convicted in June 1960. While still out on appeal "the Beak" was killed.

Innocenzi's increased criminal activity and time away from home on "jobs" put pressure on his family life. The fact that he had taken up with a young lady of "questionable character" didn't help matters. Audrey "Audie" Shaw, at 23 year-olds, had a hard look to her. So hard that she usually gave her age as 31 or 32 when she used the name Carla DeMarco, or another alias. While she was not referred to as a prostitute or a call girl by the newspapers, they reported that she was "known" in Akron, Youngstown and Warren, Ohio and Erie, Pennsylvania – the latter being listed as her hometown. On November 28, 1959, Shaw was arrested in Cleveland with Innocenzi and charged with "false hotel registration" after she checked in using the name Mrs. Ann Paulette. Word must have gotten back to Innocenzi's wife, Juanita, as she filed for divorce, charging cruelty and gross neglect, the following month – but she failed to pursue further court action.

In January 1960, Innocenzi and Shaw were living together in a Liberty Township home on Roosevelt Drive. Innocenzi, described as a "dapper" dresser, was also particular about the furnishings in the places he lived. The apartment the couple shared had wall-to-wall carpeting and many modern features. The apartment was so nicely done that when Innocenzi was forced to leave, Philip "Fleegle" Mainer, another local hoodlum, moved in with his wife, a former nightclub dancer from Chicago. When Mainer was sent to prison Joe DiCarlo took up residence there.

The cozy living conditions between Innocenzi and Shaw didn't last long. Shortly after they moved in Shaw was taken to North Side Hospital, so severely beaten that she was in a coma for two days. Shaw told police she was injured in a fall from a moving vehicle. Despite the unmistakable signs of an assault she refused to press charges against Innocenzi. Local deputies warned the safecracker "to stay out of Trumbull County." Officials believe the couple then rented an apartment above the Alibi Lounge at Boardman and South Phelps Streets in Youngstown, although Innocenzi was still residing at times with his wife in a Cleveland area apartment. On February 1, Shaw, Innocenzi and two other men were arrested at a lakefront restaurant in Cleveland and taken in "for investigation."

On June 11, $20,000 was stolen during a burglary at Idora Park. Six days later Innocenzi was questioned by new Youngstown Police Chief Frank Watters, the former "Morals Squad" leader. In early August, three associates of Innocenzi were captured in the middle of cracking open a safe in Napoleon, Ohio. The gang's lookout escaped causing some to believe it was because he had tipped police to the crime. The lookout was alleged to be Innocenzi.

On Wednesday, August 3, Audrey Shaw checked out of a Cleveland hotel and went with Innocenzi to Akron where the two registered in a room together. The next day Innocenzi, who was driving his wife's 1960 Chevrolet Impala, illegally parked the vehicle on State Street during rush hour and the Akron police had it towed. Innocenzi called a local bail bondsman who he knew and told him he had used his last dime to make the call. The bail bondsman loaned him $16.50 to cover the cost of retrieving the automobile.

That Saturday, August 6, Innocenzi was back with his wife and two young sons. In the early evening he told Juanita he was leaving to meet someone at a drive-in restaurant. When he walked out of the home at 7:30 p.m. it was the last time he was seen alive. Police believe Innocenzi drove his wife's Impala to the parking lot of Chanel High School in Bedford, Ohio, and left it there, getting into another vehicle. The school was near the restaurant where Innocenzi said he was going.

Shortly after 12:30 on the afternoon of August 10, John M. Hall was on his way to mow the grass along a lonely lane called Pump House Road in Virginia-Kendall Park, located in northern Summit County. Hall, who was part Delaware Indian, thought he saw a "bundle of clothes" off to the side of the road. He soon realized he was looking at a corpse rotting away in the hot August sun He immediately notified police.

When and where Innocenzi was killed was the subject of conjecture. While authorities agreed he was murdered – three .38 slugs in the back of the head – late Saturday night or early Sunday morning, there was a question of where the killing took place. Investigators believed Innocenzi must have been at ease with the men he was with as he was found with his hands in his pockets. Police said this was a frequent habit of the dead man.

George Vaughn, Summit County Chief Deputy, told the *Vindicator* that he believed the murder took place where the body was found. He claimed the amount of blood on the ground confirmed this. Meanwhile, the Cleveland *Plain Dealer* reported, "Summit County authorities said there was no doubt Innocenzi had been dumped there after being shot elsewhere." Sheriff Russell M. Bird thought the killing probably took place in Cuyahoga County.

Juanita Innocenzi was taken to the Central Police Station in Cleveland for questioning. Mercifully, police did not take her to the morgue to identify the body, which was decomposing, and the head largely destroyed from the impact of the bullets. Identification was made through fingerprints. Not surprisingly, one of the first questions from investigators was why Juanita hadn't reported her husband missing. Hunched over and weeping, she replied that it was not unusual for her husband to leave and not be heard from for several days. Also questioned was Armand Innocenzi, the victim's brother. He claimed he knew nothing about his brother's activities, calling him the "black sheep" of the family.

Mrs. Innocenzi had some harsh words for her husband's murderer. "A snake is low," she stated. "But any man who would shoot another in the back is lower. He didn't have the nerve to look Vince in the face when he killed him." Juanita told police Innocenzi was a "good husband who loved his children." Despite her claim that when he left home he "didn't have a dime," police found five $20 dollar bills in his pocket, even though his wallet was never recovered.

Police hoped that by finding the Impala it might reveal some clues to the killing. A description of the automobile was given in the newspapers and on the evening news. When it was found, police technicians came up empty in the search for clues. The keys were never found. A search revealed a pair of black leather gloves and a box of metal washers. Police claimed the washers were a "typical hoodlum trick" for cheating on long distance telephone calls. It should be noted that two other prominent mobsters with Mahoning Valley connections were also arrested for using washers and slugs. Leo Moceri, while a fugitive, was arrested in Hollywood, California in 1952 for using washers in a Vine Avenue telephone booth. James Licavoli was once arrested while placing slugs in a vending machine in Florida.

In an ironic piece of reporting the *Vindicator* wrote, "Local law enforcement officials here learned today [August 11] that a special underworld meeting was called for last Friday in Cleveland. Innocenzi was reported to have attended the meeting with several local hoods." Neither the Cleveland *Press* nor the *Plain Dealer* reported this meeting. No other details of the alleged meeting were offered.

On the evening of Sunday, August 7, the Warren police chased and stopped a speeding automobile, containing Anthony Libertore and Cecil Angelberger. While the men were being held and questioned, detectives searched the area along the chase route and found a .32 caliber revolver and six sticks of dynamite in a waterproof bag that were tossed into a ditch. The two men were questioned about the discovery 18 hours after they were arrested. After Angelberger passed a lie detector test he was released. Libertore also passed the test, but was immediately sentenced to a ten-day jail term for reckless driving.

Libertore had a notorious reputation in Cleveland having been involved in the murder of two Cleveland police officers while robbing a filling station in December 1937. Libertore received a life sentence, but was paroled in 1958. Chief Deputy George Vaughn traveled to Warren to question Libertore. The cop-killer told the Summit County investigator, "I'm just the original hard luck kid. First I'm stopped and arrested for nothing. Then they find dynamite in a ditch near where I was arrested. Now they think I'm connected with the murder of a guy I don't even know. The first time I ever left Cuyahoga County and broke parole, what happens?"

The investigation into the murder of Vincent Innocenzi soon fizzled out. No one was ever brought to trial for his killing. Despite the fact that there was no information to connect him to the Naples murder or the Romano shooting, his death was still tied to the ongoing unrest in the gambling activity in the Valley.

Sadly, his death was not the only tragedy for the Innocenzi family. On August 19, less than a week after Vincent's funeral, Sylvio Innocenzi committed suicide. The older brother, in poor health and distraught over Vincent's death, wrote a note and then tied an electric cord to a rafter in his garage before stepping off the trunk of his automobile and hanging himself. Although ruled a suicide, some family members felt there was foul play.

Murder of John Schuller

The bloodshed for 1960 in the Mahoning Valley was not over. Ten days before Christmas the guns of the underworld took another life. John "Big John" Schuller had barely survived the car bombing that nearly left him a cripple in January 1958. He wouldn't be as fortunate the next time.

Schuller, whose nickname came from a hulking 230 pounds on a six-foot, one-inch frame, wasn't having much luck on December 15, the last day of his life. Around 1:00 in the afternoon he arrived at the home of Philip Kimla near Vienna, Ohio. The two men climbed into Kimla's son's black 1960 Cadillac and headed for Cleveland with a woman friend. According to Kimla, the trio went to a store where Schuller wanted to purchase a mirror. Finding the store closed the three drove to Norwalk, Ohio, a small town south of Sandusky, to visit a mutual friend. The friend was not home so they headed back to Kimla's house.

Shortly before 9:00 p.m. Schuller, who was driving the automobile, was stopped for speeding on Route 5, just west of Warren. He was asked to drive to the Warren Police Department where he was arrested and booked. Schuller paid a $25 bond and was released at 9:20. Ten minutes later Schuller was back at Kimla's home. It was a frustrating, not to mention costly day, but things were about to get worse.

After turning down an invitation for a cup of coffee Schuller got into his car, a 1954 pale-blue Chevrolet. Due to the late hour Schuller was unable to see that his right-rear tire was nearly flat. He pulled away from the Kimla residence and headed down Route 82 toward a Coitsville motel that he and his wife, Rosa, called home. It didn't take Schuller long to realize he was driving on a flat tire. A quarter of a mile from the Kimla home Schuller pulled his car off the road, parking it in the wide accommodating driveway apron of Mr. and Mrs. Paul Landes. Irritated that his streak of bad luck was continuing, Schuller examined the flat tire before opening the trunk to retrieve the spare. He jacked up the rear-end of the car and removed the deflated tire. Placing the spare on, Schuller was about to replace the lug nuts when he turned his attention to a car that pulled up behind him. Whether it was the automobile itself or one of the occupants calling out to him will never be known, but Schuller stood up to address the situation.

Inside the Landes home the couple's television viewing was interrupted just before 10:00 p.m. by what sounded like two quick backfires. While Mr. Landes paid little attention, his wife looked out the window to see a car parked at the end of the driveway. She immediately sent her husband to investigate. Landes found the 42 year-old Schuller crumpled and bleeding on the ground still clutching the bumper jack.

"I'm shot, call an ambulance, please help," Schuller begged.

Landes ran back to the house and called the State Highway Patrol in Warren for an ambulance. He then went back outside where he placed a blanket under Schuller's head and did his best to comfort the mortally wounded man. When the first law enforcement officer, Clarence Draghi, arrived at the scene, just minutes after the call, he reported that blood was still spurting from the right femoral artery in Schuller's wounded groin, as well as from wounds in the right side of his chest.

Draghi said Schuller "refused to identify his murderers." As his life was draining away on the Landes's driveway, Schuller whispered to Draghi, "Hold my hand, I'm dying." Big John, who had cheated death less than two years earlier, died in the ambulance on his way to Trumbull Memorial Hospital, where he was pronounced dead at 10:24. The official cause of death was hemorrhaging from ten pellets from a double-barreled sawed-off shotgun.

Schuller's death was reported during an 11:00 p.m. radio newscast, which Phil Kimla and his son were listening to. The father and son hurried to the motel to inform and comfort Rosa Schuller. State police arrived soon after and arrested all three, taking them in for questioning.

There was no physical evidence left at the scene. Investigators could not tell if the assassin had gotten out of the automobile; a gathering crowd had obliterated any chance of finding footprints left behind by the killer. The next morning, a snowplow pushed slush and snow over the remainder of the crime scene. A cane still used by Schuller was in the car and in his wallet was found a listing of the weapons he owned that were confiscated shortly after the car bombing. Testing done on the flat tire found no puncture or leak, confirming in the minds of the authorities that the air was purposely let out.

The first suspect the police quizzed was Philip Kimla, who refused to take a lie detector test. The 46 year-old was no stranger to law enforcement. In 1935 he was charged with "obtaining charitable relief by false pretenses." The next year he was indicted for an arson fire set at an East High Avenue house in Youngstown – at trial he was acquitted. Since then, except for a fine for a driver's license violation, his only arrests were for suspicion in Youngstown, the last one coming in 1957.

While Kimla was being held as a material witness and questioned by the police, "Dankers" Petrella and Joseph Joyce paid a visit to his wife. Detectives, investigating the case, spotted the two men leaving the Kimla home and picked up the pair. Petrella told police he had no knowledge of the murder and had simply stopped to "see if they could help Mrs. Kimla while police were quizzing her husband." When police questioned Mrs. Kimla she claimed she only knew the pair slightly. Asked if she would receive money from the two if her husband stayed in jail, she replied, "no." Her husband, however, when told about the visit, said he had known both men for a long time and that they would have aided his wife if the need arose.

When questioned by the police Rosa Fedchina Schuller stated that her husband "had not been involved in any questionable activities since he was injured" in the bomb blast. She claimed he "only tried to help people" during his lifetime and had not – to her knowledge – been mixed up in any "gangland escapades."

Sheriff's deputies claimed their investigation was hindered because people were frightened to talk. "Most residents of the area and Schuller's friends did not want to implicate themselves in the slaying. Apparently they are afraid of gang vengeance if they give information to the police," the *Vindicator* reported.

As soon as the investigators ran out of people to question, theories and comments from alleged informants began springing up in the newspapers. The *Vindicator* reported, "Underworld informants predicted early this fall that several hoodlums, gamblers and riff-raff were marked for murder to begin shortly after the November election." On December 18 the newspaper stated, "Several theories have been offered to explain the circumstances leading to the slaying. Some contend it was the aftermath of a rift between Schuller and the late S. Joseph "Sandy" Naples, who reportedly had borrowed a large sum of money from Schuller and then refused to repay." The same informant added that Schuller may have fired the bullets that killed Naples and his girlfriend March 11, and was avenged by Naples' associates. This seems unlikely due to the fact that seven months later Schuller still needed the use of a cane due to the car bombing. It should be remembered that witness Stanley Novak told police the man shooting at Naples was running as he fired. No car was reported in the immediate area so both killers had to hoof it to where one was parked.

The newspaper reported, "Both Schuller and Naples had been suspects in the unsolved vendetta slaying of Andrew Gerlach in 1957. Each blamed the murder on the other when questioned by police. Gerlach's body was found near the now defunct Jungle Inn gambling resort. Other sources maintain Schuller was slain because he was trying to muscle in on a large-scale bootlegging operation in southern Ohio."

A *Vindicator* story pointed out that, "Three gangland killings and a near murder – all unsolved – make 1960 the bloodiest year in the history of Youngstown's underworld." The newspaper was still trying to connect all the murders – to what, they didn't say. They put a new spin on the Vincent Innocenzi killing by claiming he was a "close associate" of "Fats" Aiello. They also reported that Aiello was shot in early December while "making a move" at an all-night barbut game. Police, however, had no information about the shooting, only that Aiello claimed he accidentally shot himself.

Murder of Mike Farah

The calm in the Mahoning Valley after the murder of John Schuller lasted less than six months. On June 10, 1961, Mike Farah, the former part-owner of the infamous Jungle Inn, where he was known as "the man in the black suit," was gunned down on the lawn of his home.

As with the murders of Sandy Naples and John Schuller, rumors surfaced that an attempt would be made on Farah's life in early 1961. One *Vindicator* article reported, "The same rumors said Cleveland gambling interests were unhappy with Farah and insisted the Cleveland group hoped to control gambling in the area with Farah out of the picture."

On the warm, sunny Saturday morning of June 10, Farah was out in his yard hitting golf balls and waiting for a golfing partner to arrive. Shortly after 9:15, a 1959 Chevrolet sedan arrived at the home on Kenilworth and South Avenues. Farah had no time to notice the strange set-up of one man driving and a second man in the backseat before the first shot was fired. The blast, from a .12 gauge shotgun loaded with nine pellets of "double-O-buck" shot, tore into the ground near Farah's feet. A second shot ripped into the basement window casing on Farah's home behind him. Perhaps frozen in terror, Farah didn't move and the last blast caught him in the abdomen, hip and thigh.

Mortally wounded, Farah was helped from the yard into the kitchen by his wife, Grace, and his 16 year-old daughter, also named Grace. Both women witnessed the shooting from the kitchen window, which looked out onto the lawn where Farah was standing when shot. Police arrived quickly after being summoned by the daughter. Warren Police Sergeant Herbert Rising was the first to speak to Farah. The dying man gave Rising a description of the automobile, but said he didn't recognize the occupants.

Farah, in a semi-conscious state, was rushed to Trumbull Memorial Hospital bleeding profusely from the damage caused by the nine shotgun pellets. Gathered at the hospital were mother and daughter, son Albert and Farah's twin brother John. They were waiting near the entrance of the emergency room when the bad news came. Another son John, who arrived late, was informed by his brother that their father had passed away.

An emergency room physician informed the press that Farah had died at 10:25, but was revived and lived for another 40 minutes. At 11:15 a.m. he succumbed to internal bleeding and shock on an emergency room table.

Farah's oldest son, John, barked out, "They ought to pick up Tony and the whole fucking bunch." Although he later refused to elaborate, the "Tony" he was referring to was Anthony "Tony Dope" Delsanter, the onetime partner of the Farah brothers in the Jungle Inn. Another family member denied John ever made the outburst.

Albert Farah told police he couldn't understand "why anyone would want to harm his father since he retired from active business about ten years ago." Trumbull County Sheriff Robert Barnett was also perplexed. "We have some hit and run numbers business and some sporadic floating gambling, but I have been making my own checks for some time and I know the county is quiet," he claimed.

Just hours after the shooting, Warren detectives found the automobile, a half mile from the murder scene, abandoned in the parking lot of the Heltzel Steel Form Company on Niles Road. The vehicle was stolen on March 15 in Canton. This was the third shooting in just over a year with a Canton connection. The shotgun found at the Sandy Naples murder scene was stolen from a Canton police cruiser and the automobile that was used in the Romano shooting was stolen in Canton. Searching the area around the car detectives discovered the murder weapon – a .12 gauge Remington shotgun – in some bushes behind the automobile. The weapon was equipped with a "choke," a device that helps to keep the shotgun pellets from spreading as they leave the barrel.

Funeral services were held in Cleveland on June 13 for the 56 year-old. Warren detectives were dispatched to look for "anyone of importance from the rackets world." Among the 70 mourners, mostly family and friends from Cleveland's Syrian community, were two "minor" police characters. After the church service Farah was buried in Cleveland's historic Lake View Cemetery, the final resting-place of President James A. Garfield, multi-millionaire industrialist John D. Rockefeller, and fabled crime-fighter Eliot Ness. Less than a year earlier it was the final stop for Vincent Innocenzi.

After the murder, Warren Police Chief Manley English denied published reports that Tony Delsanter was the "prime suspect" in the investigation. English said police were looking to question an ex-partner of Farah, along with "many other characters." Still, Warren police issued a "pick up" order for Delsanter. The day after the funeral Delsanter was picked up in a Mahoning Avenue restaurant, where he "nonchalantly munched" a sandwich. The 50 year-old Delsanter was questioned and released after his alibi of playing golf in Akron was confirmed by detectives from that city. A second suspect, Nicholas "Nick Brown" Papalas, a holder of the federal gambling tax stamp throughout most of the 1950s, was also picked up. Papalas, a former employee of Farah, had recently been found working with Delsanter. He claimed he was home asleep at the time of the murder.

In 1981, a book about the life of Mafia turncoat Aladena "Jimmy the Weasel" Fratianno titled *The Last Mafiosi* was published. Author Ovid Demaris, in discussing Fratianno's lifelong friendship with Delsanter writes, "[Delsanter] had recently done some work [Mafia terminology for taking a life], clipping Mike Farah, who had fronted the Jungle Inn for Blackie Licavoli." There seems little doubt that Delsanter was behind the murder of Mike Farah, if not indeed the triggerman himself.

Murder of Vince DeNiro

The decade of the 1960s was less than two years old and already it was one of the bloodiest on record in the Mahoning Valley. Naples, Vrancich, Innocenzi, Schuller and Farah were all in their graves, and Joseph Romano was filled full of buckshot. If, and how, they were all related was an unanswered question. But in July 1961 the murders got scarier and more sensational.

The underworld scuttlebutt in the summer of 1961 was that Joseph "Stoneface" Romano had become "titular" head of the rackets as of July 1, "dethroning DeNiro and a Wilson Avenue tavern operator." The provider of this information claimed that Romano was operating as a front man for Joe DiCarlo, who reportedly "has everything in his control now – both the city and county."

Another rumor held that DeNiro was still in power, but Romano was running the day-to-day operations. In this scenario, the unnamed Wilson Avenue tavern operator was only a bookie. Romano's position in the underworld since his near fatal shooting was tenuous. Reports said he stayed close to home after his release from the hospital in early 1961. There were also plans on his part to return to Italy for a while. As he grew healthier, it was reported that he was again the "top man" in the local barbut game, running it unmolested from the police at a South Avenue location. Romano, during the spring and early summer, was a regular on West Commerce Street and could be seen almost every afternoon at the Strouss-Hirshberg restaurant. By July 1, however, he had dropped out of sight, the prominent rumor being that he had gone to the Mayo Clinic in Rochester, Minnesota for tests.

The latest adversaries in this life and death battle for dominance of gambling operations in the Valley were alleged to be Vince DeNiro and Joe DiCarlo. Recent reports had DeNiro struggling with his interests in the Sans Souci Hotel in Las Vegas and trying to make inroads into gambling operations in White Sulphur Springs, a town in the southeastern section of West Virginia. DeNiro had reportedly partnered with Al Gearhart in a gambling casino in this resort town at the foothills of the Appalachin Mountains.

As for DiCarlo, the rumor was that he was back – or trying to get back – in business in the Valley. In addition, he was already said to be operating in White Sulphur Springs, thus creating conflict with DeNiro on two fronts. There was also a rumor that DeNiro was trying to muscle in on the Struthers rackets, a dangerous plan of action as this was the home turf of the Carabbia brothers.

Youngstown's new police chief, Cyril Smolko – the third of the young decade – dispelled the DiCarlo rumors, claiming no one had seen the old gangster in the city. More than one source, however, claimed that "the Wolf" had visited to the Valley several times in recent weeks, making the journey from White Sulphur Springs.

The tinderbox was stoked and was waiting to be ignited. A few minutes after midnight on July 17, 1961, it went off.

On Sunday, July 16, survival was paramount in the mind of Vince DeNiro. He had taken to driving five different automobiles, never letting anyone know which car he had plans to take. Despite the constant threat of peril, DeNiro made time for a few friends he had known since childhood on this warm summer evening.

James E. Modarelli had grown up with Vince DeNiro and Robert Parella on Youngstown's East Side. Stricken with polio since the age of two, Modarelli never had the opportunity to be like others his age and participate in sports as a youngster. DeNiro took a special liking to Modarelli and the two, along with Parella, remained lifelong friends. Modarelli got into the jewelry business and developed a decent operation. From his store he also sold paintings. When DeNiro opened Cicero's he suggested to Modarelli that he exhibit some of these paintings at the restaurant with his business card attached. In mid-July, DeNiro called his friend and told him that someone had offered to purchase a couple of the pieces. The two men made plans to get together to discuss a price.

That Sunday night, around 8:00, DeNiro arrived at Parella's Pizza Oven Restaurant at 2833 Southern Blvd. Fifteen minutes later Modarelli entered. The two left and Modarelli drove DeNiro to the Lincoln Park Drive home of his parents and from there to a location on Himrod Avenue, where DeNiro had parked a gray 1961 Oldsmobile convertible. They both drove separately to Market Street and DeNiro parked the Oldsmobile directly across the street from Cicero's and climbed into Modarelli's car. DeNiro had a taste for steak that night. Since Cicero's was closed and the Pizza Oven didn't serve steak, they picked up Parella around 10:00 and the three friends headed for the 422 Club near Warren for dinner.

Modarelli said that after dinner the trio drove around to check the activities of various restaurants before dropping Parella back at his place of business around 11:45 p.m. DeNiro asked his old friend if he minded making a stop so he could visit his children. After a five-minute stop at DeNiro's ex-wife's house on

West Glen, the two men headed back to Market Street. Modarelli pulled his car behind DeNiro's and let him out. It was a few minutes past midnight. The two friends said goodnight and as Modarelli backed up his car and prepared to pull out, DeNiro got in his Oldsmobile and turned the ignition.

At 12:10 a.m. a deafening explosion rocked Youngstown's Uptown District. Pieces of twisted metal and flesh rained down on the street and rooftops in a 200-foot radius. It was by the grace of God that the night's only victim was Vince DeNiro. The blast mangled the lower part of DeNiro's body – he was actually blown out of his shoes. One shoe was found on the floor of the driver's seat, the second on a rooftop. The lower portion of one leg was never recovered.

The steering column was forced into DeNiro's chest and stomach by the blast and knocked him into the backseat of the automobile. The handsome gangster's nose was broken and his lips cut. Incredibly, DeNiro lived for some fifteen to twenty minutes after the explosion. Police and firemen, who arrived quickly at the scene, said DeNiro was gasping for air as they placed him on an ambulance stretcher. He was unable to answer any questions and died soon afterward. His death was caused officially by hemorrhaging from severed arteries in his legs and shock. DeNiro was pronounced dead at South Side Hospital at 12:35 am.

The *Vindicator* described the carnage at the scene:

> "The tremendous blast which ripped the automobile reduced the entire front end to rubble. A bumper part was found 40 feet south in Market Street, and a fender was blown into Fron's Candy Store where the car was parked. The left front tire was blown across the thoroughfare and south through the display window at George Yates & Son store. Other parts of the vehicle were found on nearby roofs and in the parking area west and behind the stores.
>
> "Large plate glass windows on virtually every store in the Uptown between Indianola and Princeton and in the office suites and apartments on the floors above were shattered by the concussion. The blast was felt for miles and rocked homes for blocks...signs and other portions of the facades and interiors were damaged by the concussion or flying debris. Articles on display in the shop windows also were destroyed or damaged.
>
> "The blast lifted parts of the car on to remaining utility lines, many of which were snapped."

Police claimed it was a miracle that no one else was injured at what was considered one of the city's busiest sections. Within minutes, a crowd of curious onlookers, who came to view the macabre scene, reached several thousand. Firemen roped off the area as workman from Ohio Edison, Bell Telephone Company and East Ohio Gas Company arrived to begin repair work.

By 2:00 a.m. a massive cleanup effort had begun by the business owners and managers of the affected stores in the area. Extra officers were placed on duty and special police were called to guard the damaged shops from being entered. Ironically, Cicero's was one of the few places not damaged by the blast.

The police investigation began immediately with the roundup of the usual suspects. The first to be arrested was an East End operator of a billiards parlor. Chief Smolko notified the Struther's Police Department that they wanted to question Charlie Carabbia. The oldest of the three Carabbia brothers arrived at the police station at 10:30 on the morning of the bombing ready to be questioned. In addition, police sought John Burnich, Dominic Mallamo, James Prato, and Carmen Tisone. "Fats" Aiello called the Youngstown police from Springfield, Illinois, where he was visiting his gravely ill father, and informed them that he would appear for questioning when he returned later that week. Also picked up and brought in during the course of the investigation were Ronald Carabbia, Joseph Sarich, Billy Naples and Louis J. DeLuca. All were questioned and released. DeNiro's friend, Robert Parella, was held as a material witness for 12 hours before he was released. None of the men questioned shed any light on the investigation.

During the hours after the blast, police tracked the ownership of the death car to Edith Magnolia, a 39 year-old former waitress and girlfriend of DeNiro. Friends stated that the automobile was made available to DeNiro's daughters, Joanne and Helen Marie, to use on weekends. Magnolia's son, Daniel, was brought to the scene by police to identify the automobile. A *Vindicator* photographer captured the horrified look on the young man's face as he viewed the bombed car.

In addition to the police investigation, Mayor Franko requested assistance from Ohio Governor Michael V. DiSalle. Franko placed a phone call to DiSalle before 4:00 a.m. that morning, but an aide refused to wake the governor thinking it was a prank call. After the governor and mayor spoke later that morning, Franko sent the following telegram:

> "Request you send state bomb squad here immediately to assist Youngstown police to investigate situation which obviously transcends city and county boundaries. Latest bombing here jeopardized lives in one of the city's busiest business sections."

The state bomb squad Franko requested did not exist. Instead, DiSalle asked the state fire marshal to take action and an investigator was dispatched that morning to assist the police department. The Monday of the murder, Governor DiSalle signed two "bomb bills" into legislation that were introduced by a pair of Youngstown area state senators. In describing the two pieces of legislation the *Vindicator* wrote, "One bill prohibits the malicious placing and exploding of bombs or other explosives with intent to damage property or [cause] injury to a person. The other requires the state fire marshal, at the request of a sheriff or mayor, to investigate a bombing. It does not create a 'bomb squad'"

In the governor's comments regarding the legislation, he pulled no punches in describing the situation in Youngstown and what needed to be done. As the newspaper put it, "DiSalle teed off in no half-hearted" manner:

> "It is about time that local law enforcement officials recognize the seriousness which imperils the lives and property of decent citizens.
>
> "The people who have the responsibility had better throw away their powder puffs and choose weapons strong enough to drive these individuals as far away from this community as possible."

When Mayor Franko heard the governor's "powder puff" remark, he quickly went on the defensive. Claiming that Chief Smolko and Vice Squad Chief George Millovich were capable, he ordered a crackdown "to eliminate all cheating in the city." Franko maintained that the rackets war was not the "entire burden" of Youngstown. Franko declared, "This is a regional problem and the county prosecutor, the county sheriff and officials in the Warren area are equally involved. The 75 bombings did not just happen here, and they did not happen only in the 18 months since I took office. I inherited a bad situation that has been developing since 1944, and I can't be held responsible for everything that I inherited. I have been trying to undo what had developed in the past, but it's a hard job."

Franko continued, "I would like to resolve this problem as much as anyone, but the past is full of failures. Bombings are a vicious crime, and one of the hardest to solve. Even when [former police chief Edward] Allen was here, reputable citizens were bombed in areas where innocent lives were jeopardized, but nothing was solved." The mayor was at a complete loss to explain the wave of violence, which had taken the lives of DeNiro, Sandy Naples and others since his election to office. "Is it someone trying to move in? Is it vindictiveness, or revenge? These are the questions we want to answer and they are not easy. I cannot understand why I must assume the full responsibility. I am the one subject to re-election. I'd be the last one to ask for stuff like this. I have asked the governor for help, and I hope he will eventually send in special agents that will help clear this mess up," he claimed.

Mayor Franko and Chief Smolko were put on the hotseat by the media two days later. Youngstown television station WFMJ interviewed the governor, mayor and police chief on a program called "Spotlight." DiSalle reiterated, in a telephone interview, that it was up to local law enforcement to handle the problem. Meanwhile, Franko and Chief Smolko were jittery and clearly on the defensive. The mayor "complained about harassment, ducked direct questions and contradicted himself many times." Again denying the problem was solely his, he stated he was the target of a "vendetta" by the *Vindicator*. Both Franko and Smolko denied the city was wide open and that vice was flourishing. They said gambling could never be completely eliminated from the city. In a self-serving statement the mayor claimed, "I deny rackets are wide open in the city. I feel the racket charges are being trumped up and are being used as a political weapon against me."

To argue his point about wide-open gambling in the city, station news director William Lindsay said he had bet $2 on a horse and $1 on the bug the previous day at a location three blocks from City Hall.

Smolko, who was appointed chief just nine weeks earlier, stated, "We are making every effort to hold down gambling activities. It would be foolish for me to say I will eradicate gambling. It has been here and always will be here to some degree. But we are doing the best job we know how."

By July 20, Youngstown detectives and vice squad members had questioned more than 30 people and had come up empty. Sources both inside and outside the police department claimed DeNiro wanted to become a legitimate businessman, but his connections to the Mafia prevented this. According to an unnamed police official, DeNiro was murdered by someone close to him in the underworld. "As far as I'm concerned, Vince was murdered by someone who knew him well and knew his habits. It couldn't have been a Mafia job because he was supporting a number of Mafia figures," the official claimed. In support of this theory, he pointed out that DeNiro was giving 70 percent of his $100,000 income from National Cigarette Company, Inc. to mob figures in the Valley. Due to his generosity the question became, why would the Mafia want to kill him?

Still, others theories abounded. One reporter wrote, "Vince was a county and city racket king for years, but had little power in Struthers. About six months ago he lost the county but reportedly was making a comeback there. Why was he picked to die? Was it a local fight with local killers, as old-timers see it? Or was it the 'syndicate's' way of shutting off a man who either got out of line or no longer was useful? Was Pittsburgh trying to wrest control from Cleveland, represented by DeNiro?" Yet another report claimed that DeNiro was "squeezed out," that he was a "representative for one prong of a three-way effort by out-of-town syndicates to absorb the Youngstown district's gambling and related profits." The participants in this "effort" were mobsters from New Kensington, Buffalo and Cleveland who were reputed to be looking for a larger return on their investment. The conclusion was that, "Lesser gangsters, ones who don't get into the public limelight too much, are to handle the local operations."

On July 21, detectives interviewed Edith Magnolia who had flown home from California, where she had driven to visit her brother three weeks earlier. Her statement gave some insight into DeNiro's personal life. Below are some items from her statement:

> "I have known Vince DeNiro since I was twelve years old and going to school. I have been going with him for fifteen years and I have been living with him as man and wife, he provided all my personal needs and everything for the home [551 Loveless Ave].
>
> "We got along fairly well, Vince had a "long arm," he would strike me quite often, most of our arguments were about something unimportant.

> "Vince has not been living at the house since the middle of June, 1961 after my brother came to live with us, Vince gave up his bed to him. Vince and I had a "misunderstanding" in December 1960 and I spent 6 months and two days in the hospital.
>
> "There were times when Vince was broke for a time, and other times he would have lots of money. Sometimes he would have me hold large sums of money for him.
>
> "The last time I saw Vince was at about 3:00 A.M. July 1st, when he came to the house. I left for California that day. One week before this date Vince and I had an argument, it all started over the phone call, I had been in the bathroom and when I came out Vince was on the phone, when he saw me he started to whisper into the phone, I told him he didn't have to do that with me, he became angry and we argued. I told him to get out."

While Magnolia was at her brothers in Stockton, California, DeNiro had flowers sent to her once a week. He made several phone calls to her, but she refused to speak to him. She said the two never discussed business. When he made phone calls she didn't listen and when men came to the house she went to another room. She did state that he received calls at her home from Huntington, West Virginia, Las Vegas, Nevada and New Castle, Pennsylvania.

Magnolia, who later married Tropics Nightclub owner Louis Tiberio, said DeNiro's ritual of changing cars began after the murder of Sandy Naples. She stated that in the last few months Vince appeared to be "very weary looking" and "sometimes he seemed to be foggy, like in a daze."

Vince DeNiro, was buried in Calvary Cemetery, his killing, like every other murder in the Valley since the bombing death of Christ Sofocleous, went unsolved. As for DeNiro's popular restaurant, Cicero's, in June 1963 the Ohio Department of Liquor Control refused to renew the establishment's liquor permit and transfer of stock to Louis DeNiro, due the past reputation of Vince DeNiro. In their ruling the department stated, "The issuing of a stock transfer into the hands of Louis DeNiro...would create an atmosphere attractive to other persons of similar character to James Vincent DeNiro and would be conducive to further disregard of law and order." This soon resulted in the demise of the restaurant on Market Street. Years later the abandoned restaurant became the target of arsonists.

A week after DeNiro's murder, a conflict arose between the sheriff's office and the Youngstown police. Mahoning County Sheriff Ray T. Davis had his men "prowling" the city looking for clues in the gambler's murder. He gave his men orders to "check for houses of prostitution, lottery operations, betting parlors and any other form of vice they can find." One of the men nabbed in the countywide crackdown was Tony Lucci, known as the "dean of the Central Square bookies." Lucci was arrested at Central Billiards after deputies entered and found a quantity of horse race betting slips. When he refused to make a statement he was charged with possession of gambling slips for horse races and suspicion.

Davis called a meeting and invited police personnel from cities throughout Mahoning County to attend. Chief Smolko took exception because Davis extended the invitation to other police officials before informing him. Because of this, Smolko didn't attend the meeting, and refused to allow his officers to attend, claiming, "We will gladly meet with the sheriff when *proper* arrangements are made."

At Sheriff Davis' meeting, which included enforcement officials from ten area departments, the group determined that gambling was behind DeNiro's death. No one at the meeting seemed eager to talk with the press. The *Vindicator* reported, "While no one would comment on the real meat of the meeting, it was reported the officers agreed that the killing boiled down to one of two popular theories – the syndicate killed because it wanted a bigger cut or a local hood killed for control."

The sensational murder of DeNiro led to more unsavory attention, as the city became the focus of an article in *Newsweek* magazine in the national weekly's July 31 issue. Helping to spotlight publicity on the article was the mention of it on NBC-TV's national nightly news broadcast, "The Huntley-Brinkley Report" on July 25. The article reported in part:

> "Youngstown's steel industry may not be as dependably profitable as its gambling industry, but at least everyone knows who's in charge, and if there's an occasional fight for control, it's fought with bloodless proxies, all pretty much out in the open.
>
> "The people who fight for control of Youngstown's gambling industry do it with explosives, and don't announce themselves. By and large, the Cleveland and Pittsburgh syndicates are the principal contenders, but there are wheels within wheels within wheels, and nowadays no one is ever sure where the next bomb will sail in from."

On July 28, John Magourias was questioned by Lieutenant Orlando DiLullo of the sheriff's office. Known as "Johnny the Greek," the ex-convict was paroled in July 1960 from a burglary conviction he was serving in the Ohio Penitentiary. Magourias made headlines during a 1958 trial in which he was charged with the attempted car bombing of Thomas Ciarnello, owner of the Ohio Tavern. Magourias turned himself into the sheriff's department after hearing he was wanted for questioning in the DeNiro's death. He was interrogated and released.

The murder of Vince DeNiro faded from the front pages only to resurface as other Youngstown underworld figures met their demise as the bloody 1960s moved on.

Death of William "Billy" Naples

On July 1, 1962, Youngstown witnessed its third fatal car bombing in four years. William "Billy" Naples, the 34 year-old brother of Sandy Naples, was "virtually ripped to shreds" by an explosion that was said to be more powerful than the one that killed Vince DeNiro. The circumstances in which Billy Naples was killed made it entirely possible that he may have been planting the bomb when it went off. The bombing was the Youngstown district's 78th since 1951.

The criminal record of Billy Naples seemed like minor league compared to that of his older, more infamous brother Sandy. Billy was picked up on the charge of suspicion in the years 1951, 1952, 1958 and 1961. Each time he was released without being charged. The newspapers pointed out that in November 1961 he purchased a federal gambling tax stamp in Ohio and Pennsylvania.

Billy Naples most serious brush with the law occurred on March 19, 1951 when he was arrested for the beating of John Price outside the Center Sandwich Shop. Naples and Stephen "Skin" Bajnok, described as a Naples henchman, were charged with assault with intent to kill. They were both found guilty of assault and battery. Sentenced to six months in the Mahoning County jail, Billy was released on August 10, 1951.

In 1954, Naples was reported to be a business representative of the Vending Machine Employees Council. The business agent of the local was Joseph Blumetti, who was involved in the notorious white slavery ring in Youngstown during the early 1940s.

After the murder of Sandy Naples, Billy and his brothers James and Joseph continued to operate the Center Sandwich Shop. In addition, they were partners with Louis LePoris in the United Music Company, which operated out of the rear of the sandwich shop on Wilson Avenue. The business, according to LePoris, was "the display of cigarette machines, music boxes and bowling machines, most of their business is in the city, some in the county." LePoris had worked in these types of operations since 1941. At that time the business was more lucrative, due to the wide use of slot machines in the Valley. LePoris explained "after the Kefauver investigations, we gave up the illegal boards and turned 'legit.'" Since 1951, he was in and out of work because of the cutthroat business climate. LePoris was happy to have gone into business with Billy. "About a year ago, I got in with Billy Naples. I have no fear of being pushed out of the business; they have to have me. I'm the only man that can repair some of these machines, I make sure of this, and I don't think the Naples would push me out," LePoris explained to police. The business arrangement he had with the brothers called for him and Billy to each get 45 percent of the profits with the remaining 10 percent going to Joey Naples.

It was difficult to determine what the remaining Naples brothers planned to do about avenging Sandy's murder. The subsequent killing of Mike Farah and Vince DeNiro kept them looking over their shoulders during this period. As for Billy, it was said he seldom ventured out alone at night, and when he did it was always with "a very good friend."

One of the friends, who was later identified by Louis LePoris as "D" from the Gaytime Café, was Dominic Moio. The friendship between Billy Naples and Moio began a year earlier after the latter moved to Youngstown from Canton. Moio, who worked as a bartender at the Gaytime, claimed he knew Billy because he serviced the cigarette and jukebox machines at the bar. Over the next twelve months the friendship flourished. Moio and his girlfriend, Angelina Constantino spent a lot of time with Billy and his wife Enez Albanesi. Constantino was the owner of the Gaytime Café, which she sold in June 1962.

On Sunday, July 1, Billy made plans to have dinner with "Dom and Angie." On Sundays Enez had dinner at her mother's house and Billy usually stopped at his mother's. On this day, Billy arrived around 3:00 p.m., Constantino later recalled. He "ate a small portion of spaghetti with her family, two daughters, and Moio."

Billy arrived at his Carlotta Drive home that evening around 7:45, some fifteen minutes after his wife and mother-in-law, Nicolina Albanesi, returned from spending the day at a picnic. Around 9:15 the telephone rang and Billy answered. Enez heard Billy tell the caller to "come on up." Fifteen minutes later, an automobile pulled up and the horn was sounded. Billy walked outside and moments later hollered from the garage that he would be back in half an hour to 45 minutes. At that time he would take Mrs. Albanesi home. Billy's wife was later able to pinpoint the time of departure at 9:30 claiming, "General Electric Theatre was just off the air when Billy left." Enez never knew who called her husband that night or who picked him up.

At the rear of 218 West Madison Avenue was a five-car garage owned by Rosanna Beach. She rented out spaces for $4 a month. Beach had an arrangement with Harry Maller, a resident of West Madison Avenue, to collect the rents due her. Once a month she stopped to pick up the rent money Maller collected for both the garages and a home she owned there. On June 17, a man came to the home of Maller to see if he could rent a space in the garage. He returned three days later and paid the rent; then Maller never saw the man again. A green and white 1955 Pontiac began parking in the rented space. The automobile, which had a dealer plate on it, was later traced to Stark Sports Car, Inc. of Massillon, Ohio. While several neighbors saw the car go in and out of the garage, nobody recalled ever seeing the driver's face. While neighbors remembered seeing different men come up the driveway, none of them fit the description of Billy Naples. Some of the activity with the new occupant occurred during the early hours of the morning, according to Sadie Hoagland, another West Madison Avenue resident.

Shortly before 10:00 p.m. on July 1, the car containing Billy Naples and another man arrived at the West Madison Avenue garage. Billy exited the vehicle and made his way to the first stall of the wooden frame and tile block structure. He was only in there a short time. Located across the street at the corner of Elm Street and West Madison was Youngstown Fire Station #7. Fire Captain George Vesmas was attending to normal fire station business when he heard a tremendous explosion. Vesmas looked at his watch. It was 10:05 and the life of Billy Naples had come to an end.

The *Vindicator* reported:

> "The explosion was terrific and extensive damage resulted to all parts of [Naples] body, except the face, which had a deep gash on the chin and black powder [burns]. Naples' left arm was in shreds, his right shoulder was slashed under the armpit...his left hand and arm was mangled.
>
> "The force of the explosion had driven Naples' body and the front seat back to the rear seat and his head protruded from the shattered rear window. The rear wall of the garage was blasted and knocked flat."

The coroner, Dr. David Belinky, reported that fragments of small wire coil and electric wire were found embedded in Naples chest wall and arms. Belinky stated, "Naples died only of the effects of a terrific explosion."

The garage itself was nearly flattened. The wooden roof was caved in over the demolished automobile. A car parked in the next stall was heavily damaged. As police and fire officials arrived they could see Naples' body nearly twisted around the driver's seat. His head and part of his shoulder were visible under the collapsed car roof. A picture on the front page of the *Vindicator* the next day showed Billy's lifeless arm hanging limply over the side of the automobile.

An unloaded, double-barrel shotgun was blown out of the trunk and found lying on the ground. Police later found a paper bag in the trunk loaded with shotgun shells.

The large crowd of morbid fascinated residents who rushed to the scene hampered police and fire department efforts to get to the site. The newspaper reported that the crowd "came in two waves, those who heard the explosion and those who heard television and radio reports." An estimated 200 to 300 automobiles blocked West Madison Avenue and surrounding streets.

Officers repeatedly had to force onlookers from the area to allow police and crime lab technicians to survey the grounds in and around the garage. Twenty officers were assigned full-time throughout the cleanup effort just to keep the crowd back. Police investigators found themselves competing with the news media in an effort to question witnesses. At one point the police ordered people not to speak with reporters until they were able to complete their investigation at the scene. Officers finally roped off the area, but spectators didn't begin to disperse until after Billy Naples body was removed from the area more than two hours after the explosion.

In addition to fighting the crowds of gawkers and the news people, police needed help in recovering the body. The *Vindicator* reported:

> "A tow-truck was finally brought in and a cable attached to the collapsed roof to lift the heavy wooden section from the torn car. Police and firemen worked for some time before they were able to lift the garage roof and the battered car roof. A piece of 2" x 4" was inserted under the roof to permit the men to work on the car and body.

> "Naples' body was lifted up over the back seat of the car and dropped into a stretcher like a bundle of rags. Police Chief Golden and Dr. David Belinky jumped forward when they saw a pistol clatter to the ground from the torn clothing of the racket figure."

In the initial report filed by police officers they reported seeing James and Joey Naples at the scene, "They both walked up to the car and left immediately after seeing the body." One officer recalled that after viewing the twisted and mangled body of his brother, Joey began to wretch on the driveway. One of the mysteries that evening was how the two Naples brothers found out about Billy so quickly. When questioned, a surly Joey Naples told detectives:

> "I first heard of the bombing from Jimmy, who came to the house and said he had heard of a bombing somewhere. I called Billy's house and Inez (sic) said he wasn't home. Jimmy and I went to St. Elizabeth's Hospital, there was no activity there, we went down to the bombing, we saw Billy there...then we went home."

When police arrived at Billy Naples' home Enez was hysterical and already under the care of a physician. Jimmy Naples was also at the home. He had spoken to Billy's wife earlier and relayed the information about the telephone call to the police.

The two patrolmen who visited the Naples home were ordered to return to find out what kind of clothes Billy was wearing when he left. When they returned they encountered Billy's attorney Joseph O'Neill. The lawyer inquired and then told the officers that Billy was wearing "a green gabardine slack suit, no jacket." At the garage police confirmed Billy was "wearing the green slack suit" with a dark blue jacket and black leather gloves.

The newspapers quickly ran the rumor mill of motives. In reporting Naples' death the *Vindicator* began asking:

> "Why was Billy Naples killed?
>
> "Did he find out who killed his brother Sandy and was out to get revenge when somebody got him first?
>
> "Was he involved in a bank burglary planned for the weekend?
>
> "Was he getting strong again in the rackets at the expense of others who were harassed by police?"

Youngstown Police Chief William R. Golden had his own theory. He claimed the killing wasn't connected to underworld gambling, but rather was "a good possibility of a double-cross or falling out as the result of recent burglaries and safe robberies." The newspaper reported, "One high ranking officer stated that he believes that Billy was 'dressed to kill' and his victim was to be the man who directed the slaying of his brother, Sandy."

That Billy was going out on a "job," out on a kill or out on a burglary is still the popular theory to this day. While it's hard to believe that green gabardine was the standard dress for a mob killer, the key to the theory has always been the infamous "black leather gloves" Billy was wearing that warm July night. Chief Golden later referred to them as "dark leather gloves." By the time the crime lab in Columbus got them they were downgraded to a pair of brown cotton gloves.

A report in the *Vindicator* after the blast stated, "Other police officials believe Naples may have gone to the garage with the unidentified man to set a "booby trap" in the car for one of his partners and accidentally set off the charge of dynamite while he was placing it under the dash board."

The body of Billy Naples was removed to South Side Hospital where the coroner and a pathologist examined it. An official autopsy was not held. The body was then taken, like Sandy's, to the Schiavone Funeral Home for preparation.

The funeral of Billy Naples lacked the pomp and crowds that attended that of Sandy Naples. The Naples family requested that only close friends and family call at the funeral home Monday night where the wake was held with a closed casket. Funeral services were held, just 36 hours after the blast that took Billy's life, at St. Edwards Church. The service was followed by a 40-car procession to Calvary Cemetery. The graveside service was brief due to a rain shower. The two remaining Naples brothers led Billy's wife and sisters from the gravesite.

The police investigation was in full swing. A Monday morning search of the Billy and Enez Naples' home drew a letter of protest from attorney O'Neill who complained that "detectives should have had more respect for the grief of Naples' widow and daughter." During the search police seized three revolvers from a bedroom dresser. In a gun cabinet in the basement police found five rifles and four shot guns, as well as more than 20 boxes of ammunition. One weapon, a Springfield Remington rifle, was reported stolen from a Stambaugh-Thompson store on January 14, 1962. During the robbery 46 rifles and 116 shotguns were taken. Another weapon seized, a Beretta Silver Snipe 12 gauge shotgun, fit the description of another item from the robbery, but the serial number were destroyed. Police said they were able to trace the shotgun that was blown out of the trunk of the death car, a Stevens 12 gauge, to the robbery despite the fact that its serial number had also been removed.

During a Monday afternoon raid at the Center Sandwich Shop police arrested Stephen "Skin" Bajnok. In addition to an arrest for assault with Billy Naples in 1951, Bajnok had a long record of arrests for gambling. The previous December he was fined $1,000 in federal court for "operating gambling without purchasing a $50 federal wagering stamp." When police arrested him at the Wilson Avenue eatery he was in possession of two revolvers and a shotgun. Bajnok was released in time to serve as a pallbearer at Billy's funeral.

With the arrest of Bajnok, Chief Golden suspended all city licenses for the Center Sandwich Shop causing a shut down of the restaurant, which authorities long suspected of being the Naples' bug headquarters. The licenses, the chief said, were suspended until further notice. The chief pointed out that padlocking the eatery required a court order.

On July 3, the day of the funeral, the homes of Jimmy and Irene Naples and Joey and Joan Naples were searched.

In a change from normal police procedure in Youngstown, Chief Golden did not "round up the usual suspects." Golden told reporters the custom of jailing the city's hoodlums for hours would not be adhered to any longer. He said he believed in arresting a person only when there was a reason to. "When we think these characters should be brought in we'll pick them up. They are always available," the chief affirmed. One senior officer echoed the chief's sentiments. He stated that detectives preferred to be "on the trail while it is hot instead of being locked up down here questioning guys who won't tell us anything anyway."

Sadie Hoagland, one of the residents who reported seeing a man in the driveway days before the blast, was asked to come to the police station to review mug shots. She recalled sitting on her front porch around 2:00 o'clock on the morning of June 30. From her seat she observed a "fire-engine read, Corvair, circle the block about ten times." She "tentatively" identified John "Tar Baby" Millovich as the person she saw.

Police questioned James Naples after the funeral. He told detectives he and Billy were never close and that his brother did not confide in him. James claimed he was not connected with the cigarette machine or jukebox business. Detectives were trying to determine who Billy had gone out with the night he was killed and inquired if he was in the habit of going out with "people who he was not well acquainted with." When James replied he would only go out at night with "good friends, those that he could trust," the detectives asked him to identify who those friends might be. James replied he couldn't possibly identify them all because "there would be "300 or 400" names.

Detectives questioned Louis LePoris several times. Much of the questioning involved Billy's relationship with Dominic Moio. LePoris said he had gone with Billy on several occasions to the Gaytime Café, but didn't sit with the two while they discussed business. "I did not like Dom," LePoris admitted. "I don't like 'kidders' and he needled all the time."

The police report covering the detective's interview with Joey Naples on July 5 produced an eye opening statement:

> "Joseph started by telling us that we are not trying to solve any of these killings because we knew who killed Sandy but haven't done anything about it, stating that the shotgun used in Sandy Naples' killing had been traced and that it was stolen by a Lombardi, who is now a Detective or Sergeant on the Canton, Ohio, Police Department, stolen from that department and sold to a "Pimp" named Pete Dellerba, who sold it to George Floria for $20.00. Also stating that Leo Moceri and Ernie LaSalle (Fusco) were in town before the death of Sandy."

Joey told detectives, "We are not friendly with Fats Aiello. We are friendly with Joe Romano, but after Sandy's killing we did not see him anymore." Joey claimed that he and his brother were not having any "serious" problems with the competition in the vending business. He acknowledged that Billy and Moio were "real good friends." When asked about the rumor that Billy was out to avenge the murder of his older brother, Joey simply replied, "If Billy knew who killed Sandy, I'm sure he would tell me or Jimmy."

Dominic Moio became the prime suspect as the person who called Billy and later picked him up. He was questioned a multitude of times by the police, but never confessed to being the man who drove Billy to his death. In his initial interview with detectives on July 6, he claimed he never left the Constantino home after Billy left that Sunday. He was informed of the bombing by Angeline, who heard it on the television, after which he called the Naples' home and spoke to attorney O'Neill.

Detectives looked into the vending machine business to see if there was any recent unrest. Youngstown United Music, operated by the Naples and LePoris, distributed and serviced cigarette machines, jukeboxes and bowling machines to bars, restaurants and other business establishments in Campbell, Struthers and Youngstown. The normal business arrangement had the supplier splitting the profits with the customer on a 50/50 basis. The investigation revealed the following power structure in the vending business in the Valley:

Vendor	Stops
Auto-Matic Refreshment	N/A
Saffron Cigarette Service	600 – 650
National Cigarette Service (DeNiro)	450 – 500
Alexander Music Service	200
Allied Vending	150
Youngstown United Music	40

Detectives were told that the Naples/LePoris operation was "a very small outfit, lucky to have 40 stops and none of them good."

On July 12, a Youngstown police sergeant received a telephone message from an anonymous called: "Tell Lou DeNiro not to start his car." Police were dispatched to check the automobile of Vince DeNiro's brother, but nothing suspicious was found. During an interview with detectives Louis DeNiro claimed he knew of no reason for the threat. He stated that he was friendly with the Naples brothers and relayed a conversation he had with Billy four months earlier. At the Center Sandwich Shop, DeNiro claimed that Billy, "who seemed awfully nervous," said he wanted to "get out" but couldn't because his brothers wouldn't go along.

After his initial interview with police on July 6, Dominic Moio left the area. The detective team of Carmen Bruno and Donald Baker checked with Angie

Constantino and others as to his whereabouts. The detectives went to Ralph's Tavern, the new name of the Gaytime Café, now under the ownership of Ralph Cocucci. The new proprietor told detectives that Moio was in on July 8 and had told him he was leaving the next day for New Jersey and would be gone for a week. Cocucci also mentioned that two days after Moio's visit a man was in asking questions about him.

The detectives then went to a private residence where Moio had rented a "sleeping room." The owner of the home reported that Moio had lived there for three months, but was rarely there during the daytime. She stated that he was definitely not there the day of Billy Naples' death, having moved out his belongings the previous day, which was the last day of the month.

The next stop was back to see Constantino. She explained to them that she had met Moio while she was in the hospital on Mother's Day 1961. The two became friends and he spent most of his time with her, either at the Gaytime Café or at her home. He continued to spend most nights with her even after he rented the "sleeping room." Constantino claimed Moio visited Canton every Monday and returned with sausage and bread. On the night of Billy's death, Angie said she went upstairs to take a nap around 9:30 p.m. and Moio was playing solitaire in the breakfast nook. She awoke when her daughter returned home around 10:45. She said Moio was in the house at that time, but she couldn't say if he had left while she slept. Constantino said two of Moio's friends from Canton were Pat Ferruccio and Lou Christian.

The next day Bruno and Baker interviewed Constantino again. She had spoken to Moio and now appeared nervous and was reluctant to say anything. The detectives reported Angie did say that "after the machinegun was found in the catch basin on Shady Run Road [on June 8], Moio had said Billy is starting to find out about Sandy and later said Billy is talking too much."

Constantino also said that when she was introduced to Moio in the hospital it was by a good friend of the family – Paul Clautti.[3]

Bruno and Baker were still trying to account for Billy Naples' whereabouts between 3:30pm, when he left the Constantino home, and 7:45 when he returned home. The next entry on their report accounted for this time:

> "We went to William Naples girlfriend's home. She states he arrived at her home July 1, 1962, about 3:00 or 3:30 P.M.. He seemed in good spirits. They had a steak dinner about 6:00 P.M. and then sat in the back yard for awhile before he left. He was driving his beige Cadillac. He never talked to her about his business. She had never seen him with a 1955 Pontiac, four door sedan, green in color."

With one mystery cleared up another arose. On July 13 funeral director Joseph Schiavone submitted a voluntary statement to the police:

VOLUNTARY STATEMENT OF JOSEPH SCHIAVONE

About 3:00 A.M. on Sunday, July 1, 1962, I received a call from the South Side Unit of Youngstown Hospital stating that I was requested to remove the body of William Naples. I then called the American Ambulance Co. to pick up the body. At 3:30 A.M. July 1, 1962, The American Ambulance delivered the body of William Naples to my establishment. Upon receipt of the body I noted it was enclosed in a rubber zippered pouch.

Upon examination of the body I noted it still was clothed, however the clothing was shredded and the body was mangled. I then removed the clothing and laid it aside. The clothing remained here for about four or five days in a plastic bag, at which time Dr. David Belinky, Mahoning County Coronor (sic) came to the Funeral Home, looked at the clothing, and requested a sample of each piece of clothing, this I did, handed the samples over to him and he then left. The clothing was dress cloth material either green or brown and had a print pattern.

About 1:00 P.M. Sunday, July 1, 1962, Joseph and James Naples, brothers of the deceased, Mrs. Dominic Tocco, sister, and the widow Mrs. William (Enez) Naples, arrived to make funeral arrangements.

Joseph and James Naples indicated they would like to see the clothing and I then took them to the embalming room where I gave them the clothing. I then left the room. I am not sure what they removed from the clothing. However, in removing the clothing it was apparent something heavy was in the pockets.

Going back to the clothing worn by the deceased, Dr. David Belinky, Mahoning County Coronor ordered the clothing burned the same day he came to the Funeral Home, which was four or five days after we received the body. The reason being that they were offensive and would smell the house out.

On Friday, July 13, 1962 at 3:00 P.M. we received the death certificate of William Naples which indicated no autopsy was made by the coronor.

Two things were apparent from the statement. First, Schiavone's times in the first three paragraphs were off by 24 hours, and second, the coroner had obviously not conducted a "close examination" of the body as the *Vindicator* had reported.

The team of Bruno and Baker met with Joey Naples again on July 16. Joey admitted that Billy and Moio were friends and that it was possible Dominic could have picked up his brother the night he was killed. Joey denied knowing any reason for the killing, but was certain it wasn't because of the numbers business or the barbut game. Joey claimed "they lost their share of the barbut game shortly after Sandy's killing." The detectives asked if Joey was involved in the wounding of Joe Romano, to which he replied, "he hasn't been out after dark since Sandy was killed." Naples refused, however, to submit to a polygraph test.

Before leaving, Joey was asked if Paul "Pinto" Holovatick could have picked

Billy up that night. Joey claimed that Holovatick was not a "close associate of Billy, but was a close friend of his." Holovatick continued to be a close friend of Naples for the next thirty years serving as a trusted aide and bodyguard until the day Joey died.

Dominic Moio was back in town and went to the police station to answer questions on July 16. Moio's story was the same one he had told detectives before. Moio was read a litany of names and asked if he knew any of them. The only person he admitted to knowing "slightly" was Dominic Mallamo.

Another mystery was surfacing, this time it involved one of the people Moio was quizzed about. After Billy's death, detectives and an investigator from the coroner's office arrived at Joey Naples' home around 4:00 in the morning. Joey was not in a pleasant mood and refused to allow the men into his home, he spoke to them on the front porch. During a brief interview, Joey said he had no information that could help them. Naples said he and his brothers "were not involved in any other 'business' but that which everyone knew about, that is the 'Bug,' in a small way, and cigarette machines and jukeboxes." He denied that he and his brothers had anything to do with barbut.

When detectives pressed Joey as to who was behind his brother's death, he stated it could only be the "old fellas." Asked to explain what that meant Joey replied "Mafadan," and then stated that "the younger people in the 'business' would never do anything like this that happened to Billy."

During the July 16 questioning of Moio, when he was asked about various people, detectives gave him first and last names with one exception, "Malfadon," according to the police report. Who was this mysterious "Mafadan" or "Malfadon?" Could they have been referring to Calogero Malfitano? The former mentor of Vince DeNiro was seldom mentioned in the Valley. He died in April 1967.

Moio was held as a material witness and questioned numerous times by investigators. A dapper dresser Moio stated "clothes were his sole luxury...he watched his money and he lived very conservatively...didn't smoke, drink or go out much." At one point Moio was told that police had information that the syndicate was planning to kill him. Moio replied that he had to die sometime and if "they wanted to kill him that was their business."

He denied any knowledge of Billy's killing or that he was with him the night of the explosion. Moio told detectives he "wished he knew who committed it as he would get the person." An investigator from the U.S. Department of Immigration conducted one questioning session, because Moio had admitted to entering the United States as a stowaway. Moio told detectives that Paul Clautti had brought him to Youngstown to meet Angelina Constantino "and another woman to make a match with one of them." This statement could be understood to mean that Moio was hoping to get married in order to stay in the United States.

Police continued to run names past Moio wanting to know who he knew and how he knew them. One of the people he was asked about was George Florea. Moio responded that Florea was no good and that he hated his guts.

On July 19, Bruno and Baker interviewed Paul Clautti. He confirmed some of Moio's statements, but informed the detectives that after he introduced Moio and Constantino, he and Moio "drifted apart." Because Moio was an alleged arsonist, Clautti was questioned about a suspicious fire at the U-Sav Company where he once worked. Clautti denied any connection between Moio and the fire, claiming it was an accident and that the company had lost money due to valuable inventories that were destroyed.

During the four days that police held Moio he was questioned about two brothers named Lombardi who were Canton police officers. Allegations were made that one of the officers had something to do with the stolen shotgun that was used in the Sandy Naples murder. When Moio was interviewed on July 6, he had told detectives, "I know Lombardi, the policeman, also his brother." He claimed, however, that he never had any dealings with them. On July 20, Chief Golden was served with a writ for the release of Moio. Later that day, a jail house informant told police that Moio was worried. He asked the informant if he would call two policemen in Canton. Moio said it was real important that he contact them. When another prisoner was released that day Moio gave him the telephone number of Constantino to call and warn her not to speak to detectives again before he spoke with her.

On July 25, Charles "Cadillac Charlie" Cavallaro appeared for questioning. The first question asked was, "What do you do for a living?"

"I don't do nothing, I'm sick," replied Cavallaro

"Cadillac Charlie" went on to explain that he had "a bad back and a bad heart." He hurt himself in an automobile accident and was living off a second mortgage on his home. Prior to this he worked as a salesman at Hersch Motors selling automobiles.

Cavallaro was asked a litany of questions, all of which he answered "no" to, including "Do you know Dominic Moio?" and "Do you belong to the Mafia?" When asked if he would like to take a lie detector test he replied "no" because of his bad heart.

The *Vindicator* was trying to link the murder of Billy Naples to a war-to-the-death over the barbut game. The newspaper reported:

> "The barbut theory, popular in the City Hall area, notes that Struthers' stranglehold on the Turkish (sic) dice game has been slipping. After Vince DeNiro's murder, barbut moved from its South Ave. home to Struthers where it has bumped about between Walton St. and Youngstown-Poland Road."

The story stated the Struther's crowds were so big that new Trumbull County gambling boss Tony Delsanter wanted to shift the game to Campbell. "Apparently Delsanter's power runs over into Mahoning County. The game has been slowly shifting back across the Mahoning River to a Wilson Ave. location in Campbell. And Naples reportedly was with Delsanter in the push."

The murder of Billy Naples, like that of his brother Sandy, was never solved. There is more than a casual collection of evidence to conclude that Billy accidentally killed himself while planting the bomb. It was never determined who actually rented the garage from Rosanna Beach or who was using the automobile that was parked there. Residents who reported seeing a man there at different times were shown photographs of Billy Naples. They claimed he was not the man they saw. For Billy to be going out on a burglary doesn't make sense based on the fact that he told his wife that he would return within 30 to 45 minutes to take Mrs. Albanesi home. Who wants to upset their mother-in-law? It was reported that the position in which Billy's body was found lent support to the theory that he was "leaning over working under the dashboard" when the blast occurred.

Perhaps the strongest piece of evidence to support this theory was the gloves themselves. On August 9, 1962, the Ohio State Bureau of Criminal Identification & Investigation released its Official Laboratory Report on the examination of the physical evidence found at the scene. The infamous black-leather-turned-brown-cotton gloves bore "traces of automotive type grease stains, such as might be found around an auto engine or machinery."

Survivor - Joseph "Little Joey" Naples

Joseph N. Naples was the youngest of the four Naples brothers. Nicknamed "Little Joey," there have been rumors in the Valley for years that Joey was actually the son of Sandy and raised by Sandy's parents as their own child. Part of this belief was based on the difference in their age; Sandy was 25 years older than Joey. Billy, however, was approximately four and a half years older than his younger brother making the disparity in Sandy and Joey's ages less significant.

The Naples were a close knit family. During the 1950s, Sandy had the Carlotta Drive home built and lived in it with his parents and Joey and his wife Joan. Later Billy moved into a house on Carlotta just a block away.

As Joey grew up he learned the bug business at an early age. He had great teachers. In January 1954, Joey was arrested for possession of bug slips and was fined $613. In November 1961, he was arrested in the sandwich shop by U.S. Treasury Agents who were in the process of conducting raids in 13 different cities. For this offense Joey was fined $1,000 by a federal judge for operating gambling without purchasing the $50 federal wagering stamp.

After Billy's death, raids were conducted at his home, those of James and Joey, and at the sandwich shop. At Billy's home police confiscated a cache of weapons. While a couple were found to have been stolen, the FBI laboratory checked them but found the majority "were clean."

On July 24, another raid was conducted at the Carlotta Drive home where Joey lived. This time police found a secret basement room in the home. Hidden behind a sliding panel police found a large room containing bug slips, rundown sheets (accounting tallies the operators keep showing the daily business the pickup men have done for the day), money, shotguns, rifles and a mink coat. The room had a desk and telephone and was reputed to be the "main headquarters for the Naples' bug bank," now that the sandwich shop was forced to close.

Lieutenant Michael Carney, who was heading the Billy Naples investigation, said he had received information, which he wouldn't reveal his source, then retained a search warrant and moved quickly before "word could reach the Naples clan before we arrived." Joey told Lieutenant Carney that the weapons belonged to Billy and the mink stole belonged to his wife. The coat was kept in the basement "because it was cold down there." Joey was arrested and booked on the new state charge of promoting a numbers game.

A *Vindicator* story claimed, "Joey is the first 'name' bug operator in Youngstown to be booked under the new state statute, aimed at stopping the promotion of the numbers game. The law carried a catchall clause covering persons who act as "bankers" or "vendors" in such operations. The law called for a fine of $500 to $1,000 or a sentence of from one to ten years, or both, upon conviction.

Whether the new law was effective was already in question. In June, five men – George and James Limberopoulos, Nick and Ted Pappas and Pete Skevos – were arrested after an undercover investigation involving Patrolman John Lynch, a rookie member of the police intelligence squad, posed as a numbers player. The key man in the indictment was Peter Skevos. Municipal Judge Martin P. Joyce dismissed eight of nine felony counts against Skevos and then Police Prosecutor William Green declined to prosecute the others, recommending that they be held over to the grand jury.

Joey Naples pled innocent at the arraignment and was released on a $1,000 bond. On September 11, a Mahoning County grand jury returned with an indictment charging him with promoting a numbers game, receiving stolen property, and possession of a machinegun without a permit. Word was leaked to Naples about the indictments and Joey appeared at the county jail with his lawyer, Joseph O'Neill, before 2:00 p.m. hoping to get through the booking and out on bond before having to spend the night in a jail cell. When this plan didn't work Naples simply disappeared for the evening. When deputies went to his home his wife told them he was in Cleveland. Law enforcement officials got the last laugh, however. The next day, Naples was arrested at his home and placed in jail. When O'Neill arrived to bail him out Common Pleas John W. Ford was conveniently away enjoying an extended lunch.

The Mahoning County grand jury indicted Pete Skevos and some of the other operators William Green had requested. Skevos was no where to be found. One source said he had left for Greece; another claimed he went to Colorado. Seven others were indicted for promoting numbers – Carmen Tisone, Anthony "Booze" Gianfrancesco, brothers Nick and Ted Pappas,[4] brothers George and James Limberopoulos and Gus Leamis. Their indictment stemmed from the undercover sting of Patrolman Lynch of the police intelligence unit. His sting work covered seven operations – Federal Billiards, New System Lunch, American Billiards, the Greek Coffee House, Parthenon Bar, and the Sportsman's Club.

The trials that resulted from the indictments of Joey Naples turned into three-ring circus. On Monday, November 5, the first trial, for promoting numbers, got underway in Judge Ford's courtroom. Naples' attorney Joseph O'Neill raised a motion to suppress the evidence that assistant prosecutors Loren E. Van Brocklin and Clyde W. Osborne were planning to present to the jury. The four men met in the judge's chambers where Ford overruled the motion. When the parties returned to the courtroom to begin jury selection someone had already "suppressed" the evidence by stealing it. Despite the fact that a half dozen detectives sat in an attached anteroom waiting to testify, no one saw the removal of bug slips, numbers work sheets, law books and legal documents from the prosecutor's table. Naples was not in the courtroom during the time the motion was being discussed. He divided his time between the bailiff's office and walking the hallways. Three spectators in the courtroom were seated in the back rows of the gallery, no where near the evidence.

While the prosecutors were embarrassed and the defense pleased, the judge was unfazed. He simply dismissed the potential jurors and empanelled a second jury to hear the possession of stolen property case. The day after the bug slip heist, prosecutors announced they had made photographic copies of all the evidence that could be used in place of the originals. Judge Ford set December 3 as the new date for the numbers trial.

The next day the second trial began for Naples on the charges of possessing stolen property – the weapons found in the secret storeroom that were stolen from the Stambaugh-Thompson Company. The evidence consisted of the weapons seized from the secret basement hideaway. County Prosecutor Thomas A. Beil called in a city police officer to guard his storage vault, which was located outside his office and contained the machineguns Naples was charged with "possessing without a permit." The prosecutor claimed he would keep a 24-hour watch on the vault.

Detective Gerald Brace was the first witness to take the stand. He told how he obtained the search warrant and then went to the Carlotta Drive home with Donald Baker and Martin Krohn. Baker, after measuring the exterior and interior came up with a discrepancy of twelve feet. They determined that a concealed area was beneath one of two stairways leading to the basement. Krohn then testified that he found the opening to the secret room by tapping on a pine panel wall beneath the stairway.

The detectives testified Naples, who was present during the search, stated, "You got me. You found it." They said Naples later blamed his brother Jimmy for "not closing the panel properly when he left the den earlier that morning."

Inside the secret room the detectives found, "two gun cabinets on the walls in the room, another wall cabinet in which the pistols and ammunition were located, a desk, chairs and gambling paraphernalia including bug slips, rundown slips, adding machines and a lineman's tap-in telephone system. Later during the investigation some $3,000 to $5,000 was found in a desk drawer."

During the second day of the trial a management official from the Stambaugh-Thompson Company testified that some of the seized weapons were stolen from a company warehouse in January 1962.

On November 7, "Little Joey" took the stand and blamed his brothers – past and present – for the secret room and denied knowing what went on in it. While admitting to doing a "little gambling," he claimed he wasn't a gambler by profession, but rather worked in the excavating business. After his brief appearance the defense rested its case. The next day closing arguments were heard and the jury received the case at 10:30 a.m. At 11:35 a.m. the jury found Naples guilty of receiving stolen property.

After the verdict prosecutors, paranoid after the theft of their numbers case evidence, accompanied the cache of weapons to the Mahoning National Bank, Bystanders and bank employees were startled to see Van Brocklin and Osborne entering the bank each toting a carbine. They assured one bank guard, "Don't worry, we're on your side."

On November 19, the third trial began, again in the courtroom of Judge John Ford. Naples was being tried for possession of a machinegun without a permit. The weapon was actually a carbine, however it was modified to fire in a fully automatic capacity, thereby classifying itself as a machinegun.

On the second day of the trial the prosecution rested its case. The defense's case lasted a total of 36 minutes. Attorneys Joseph O'Neill and Edward L. Williams called but one witness, a gun salesman. The man testified that "anybody" could order an M-1 carbine. On cross-examination the prosecutor asked the witness if "anybody" could order the weapon if it was modified with an adapter that allowed it to fire automatic as well as semi-automatic. The witness replied, "No." Unlike the first trial, Naples did not testify in his own defense.

The judge kept the jury into the evening to hear closing arguments. On the morning of November 21, the jury began its deliberations. After three hours the jury came back with a "not guilty" decision. The stunned prosecutors later found out from members of the jury that they "could not reconcile beyond the question of reasonable doubt that the gun in court was one and the same for sure with that taken by police from the Naples home."

On December 3, the numbers trial, which had its auspicious start a month earlier with the theft of evidence in the courtroom, continued. Lieutenant Donald Baker surprised the court during cross-examination by testifying that police were tipped off that the original bug slips and rundown sheets might be stolen from the police station. Due to the "tip," the police crime lab made several photographic copies of the evidence.

The prosecution rested its case on December 6 with Assistant County Prosecutor Van Brocklin voluntarily taking the stand to describe for the jury "the care normally exercised in protection of court evidence before trial and during court recesses. Defense attorney O'Neill declined to have Naples take the stand despite having no defense witnesses to call.

After closing arguments and instructions from Judge Ford the jury received the case at 4:50 on the afternoon of Thursday, December 7. At 9:30 that night they returned with a guilty verdict. Naples became the first underworld figure in the Valley to be convicted under the new state charge of promoting a numbers game.

On December 17, Judge Ford sentenced Naples to a term of one-to-seven years for receiving stolen goods, and one-to-ten years for promoting a gambling game. He ordered the sentences to be served concurrently. Ford explained that he was sending Joey to prison "not because he was afraid Naples would again participate in criminal acts, but that he feared that he would not be acting in the public good if he were to grant probation." Ford allowed Naples to remain free on bond while his appeal was pending.

The case dragged on until April 1964, when Naples was ordered to prison. On April 21 Naples entered the Ohio Penitentiary to serve his sentence. He was paroled on August 13, 1970.

Murder of "Cadillac Charlie" Cavallaro

Charles Cavallaro was born in Agrigento, Sicily on February 2, 1902. When he was 19 years old Cavallaro stowed away on a ship bound for New Orleans. He arrived on May 1, 1921. There are no records to indicate what Cavallaro did from the date of his arrival until his first arrest on June 28, 1934 in New York City by agents of the Alcohol Tax Unit for violation of internal revenue laws. During his booking, he used the alias Charles DiFrancesco. Cavallaro apparently made no effort to go to trial, perhaps because a check of his background would reveal he was an illegal alien.

Cavallaro was arrested on August 12, 1936, for using a blackjack while committing petite larceny. This time he used a new alias – Joseph Tropicano. Less than two weeks after this arrest, the New York State Tax Unit issued a fugitive warrant and Charles DiFrancesco was a wanted man. On April 4, 1938, nearly four years after his first arrest, the charges were dismissed. On August 20, 1942, the U.S. Treasury Department, from its Buffalo, New York, headquarters, decided DiFrancesco was no longer wanted. The fact that the decision was made in Buffalo may be significant, as that was where Joe DiCarlo called home. There were rumors the two men were associated and that DiCarlo may have been either a friend or mentor to "Cadillac Charlie."

Contrary to some references, Cavallaro was not operating in Youngstown during the mid-1920s. His first recorded presence here was on October 6, 1941, when he was arrested for suspicion. This time he used his correct name at the arraignment. Cavallaro was "investigated" and released the next day. This was followed by two arrests for extortion, just five days apart, in July 1942. The first charge, which occurred in Ashtabula, Ohio, was resolved in January 1943, when Cavallaro agreed to stay out of Ashtabula County. The second charge, in Jefferson, the Ashtabula County seat, was dismissed in February 1943 after restitution was made.

During the mid-1940s, Cavallaro began to build his reputation as a bookmaker in Youngstown. While there is no evidence that he was ever involved in the "bug" business, an incident took place on February 14, 1945, that linked him to the slot machine rackets. On that St. Valentine's Day, a meeting was held in Richmond Heights, then a small township east of Cleveland on the Lake County border. The meeting took place at the Ohio Villa, a nightclub operated by Anthony Milano, a long time Cleveland Mafia figure and a future underboss of the crime family there. The attendees were gambling figures from cities in Northeastern Ohio. Cavallaro was one of two men from the Youngstown area.

Cuyahoga County Deputy Sheriff Mason Nichols was driving by the Highland Road club and noticed a number of large expensive automobiles. He decided to investigate. Nichols walked in on a group of known racketeers from around the state. In the kitchen the chef was grilling up large steaks for the men.

"What's going on boys?" Nichols inquired.

"A funeral," one of the hoods replied.

"Are you planning one?" asked Nichols.

"No, we're just holding a meeting to determine what to do with the club," one of the men responded.

Before leaving, Nichols wrote down the license numbers of several of the automobiles sitting in the parking lot. He later discovered they were issued to underworld figures in Akron, Youngstown, North Lima and Lowellville. Ten days after the Ohio Villa meeting, Cleveland slot machine czar Nathan Weisenberg was murdered on a Cleveland Heights street.

Cavallaro's hangout and headquarters was the Champion Pool Room at 26 South Champion Street where, during the hot summer months, "Cadillac Charlie" literally "hung out" on the sidewalks. So much so, that on August 13, 1946, he was arrested for violation of the sidewalk ordinance. Cavallaro pled guilty in Municipal Court, but the judge suspended his fine of one dollar.

On October 9, 1947, Sheriff Ralph Elser conducted raids at three bookie operations, including the South Champion Street location, where an estimated 175 to 200 bettors had gathered. Deputies were tearing out telephones and communication systems before the patrons realized the place was being raided. Ten men were arrested during the raid, including Cavallaro, but it was Paul D. Crothers who was hit with the big fine of $500. The rest were slapped with $25.

It was during this time that the "Big Three" were taking over the bookie operations in the Valley. "Fats" Aiello, "Moosey" Caputo and Joe DiCarlo had forced all the independent bookmakers to pay protection money to them in order to remain in business. Cavallaro's status in the underworld, from connections to either the Licavoli clan or the Cleveland family, soon made him exempt, as Aiello later testified.

The fact that Cavallaro was becoming one of the city's major bookmakers was confirmed during a trial for "Fats" Aiello in November 1949. Chief Allen told the court that during a private interrogation Aiello told him Cavallaro "was not a partner of ours after the first year. Whether he got tired of paying us 50 percent I do not know."

Allen kept a watchful eye on Cavallaro. When it was reported he was receiving information by telephone from the race wire service at the poolroom, the chief had the phones disconnected by Ohio Bell Telephone Company. Undaunted by Allen's efforts, Cavallaro tapped into the telephone at the Yoho Club, located on the second floor. The chief responded by sending out the vice squad on April 6, 1950, to arrest Cavallaro and two of his associates. At headquarters Cavallaro tried to convince Allen that he sold the poolroom, however, he couldn't produce any documentation to prove it.

Cavallaro was released the next day, but not before a heated argument ensued between Allen and Russell Mock. After the attorney stormed out of the chief's office, reporters asked Allen why Mock was so angry. "Oh, he always gets mad when he comes in here," the chief replied matter-of-factly.

In October 1950, Allen struck again after downtown merchants complained about "idlers and hoodlums" loitering around store entrances and blocking the sidewalks. He sent out vice squad members who arrested and jailed Cavallaro for "violating the city ordinance prohibiting the blocking of sidewalks by loiterers." Cavallaro spent the weekend in the city jail and pled not guilty during his arraignment on Monday. Allen used the opportunity to tell reporters, "Hoods have been chased from corner to corner for sometime, but arrests will be made from now on to show these racketeers we mean business." Despite his not guilty plea, the next day Cavallaro paid his $2 fine and the matter was settled.

In January 1951, Cavallaro was subpoenaed to appear before the Kefauver Committee in Cleveland. Although he was present in the courthouse, he was never called to testify.

The years after the Kefauver Hearings were not kind to "Cadillac Charlie." It began with a condemnation of his headquarters. Describing the buildings around Cavallaro's Champion Pool Room as "dilapidated and unsanitary," and calling them the worst fire trap in the downtown area, the city building inspector ordered them torn down in April 1951. A delighted Chief Allen declared, "We're pleased to see that the inspection department is going to tear these buildings down since it appears to be the only way under existing laws, which entail no jail sentences, to route these chronic criminals from their haunts." This effort was followed by the government hitting Cavallaro with a tax lien for the years 1948 through 1950.

With a new administration taking office in January 1954, Chief Eddie Allen was out, replaced by Paul H. Cress. In his first week as the new chief, Cress called all the top underworld figures in for private conferences to let them know the city would not be "opening up." In reporting the story the *Vindicator*, without any elaboration, referred to Cavallaro as the "reputed Youngstown link with the Detroit Licavoli gang."

Cavallaro's "link" with the Detroit mobsters was unclear, but according to mob historian and author Hank Messick it did exist. In his book The *Private Lives of Public Enemies*, Messick claims that Giovanni Mirabella, a suspect in the July 1930 slaying of Detroit radio broadcaster Jerry Buckley and an indicted participant in the Jackie Kennedy murder, came to Youngstown to hide out. Messick states that Mirabella had "served the Mafia well and deserved reward." In Youngstown, Mirabella took the alias Paul Mangine. He was given a produce concern to operate, but spent little time there. Instead, he dressed well, drove an expensive car, drank like a fiend and "wandered from bookie joint to barbut game in an alcoholic haze."

How could he afford to live that lifestyle? According to Messick, the former chauffeur for "Cadillac Charlie" once told the FBI about a weekly meeting that took place between Mirabella and Cavallaro:

> "They always embraced and kissed each other on the cheek, each cheek, and had a helluva reunion, as if they hadn't seen each other for years. Then Charley would hand over a wad of dough. All the way home he would curse and rave about having to give money to 'short coats and leeches,' but the next week he'd go back and the same thing would happen all over again."

Cavallaro's *famiglia* duties came to an end on April 5, 1955, when the drinking habits of Mirabella-Mangine killed him.

Cavallaro's biggest problem with the authorities began in July 1953, when U.S. Immigration officials initiated deportation proceedings against Cavallaro on charges of being an undesirable alien. An Immigration Department investigator explained that Cavallaro was in the "deportable class" of immigrants outlined in the new McCarran-Walters Immigration Act of 1952 which, among other changes, called for the deportation of undesirable aliens and known racket figures. Cavallaro appeared at the Immigration Bureau's Youngstown office in the Post Office Building and posted a $10,000 bond. During a hearing at the Immigration Department's Buffalo district headquarters, officials recommended that Cavallaro be deported. The matter was then forwarded to Washington D.C. where, on April 19, 1954, it became official that Cavallaro be ordered back to his native land. Cavallaro hired attorney Patrick J. Melillo, who immediately filed an appeal with the Board of Immigration Appeals. (See Appendix E for the chronology of the deportation effort.)

As if his problems with the Immigration Department weren't bad enough, in June 1954, Cavallaro and several other underworld figures were told by Vice Squad leader George Krispli to "get a job or face constant police harassment." Friends suggested Cavallaro get a job working on the Ohio Turnpike near the Route 7 interchange. Cavallaro took the advice – which nearly cost him his life. In August, he was injured in a fall while pouring concrete. Cavallaro was rushed to South Side Hospital where x-rays reportedly showed he broke his back and fractured his leg in five places.

Except for traffic violations, Cavallaro's rap sheet showed no activity for nearly four years. Then on July 15, 1958, Cavallaro was picked up for suspicion and questioned by Krispli during another hoodlum-harassment campaign. Cavallaro told the new "Morals Squad" chieftain that he was now making his living by renting out two dump trucks to local contractors.

On June 30, 1961, Cavallaro was in an automobile accident after he claimed he "lost consciousness" and hit a telephone pole on Roslyn Drive, not far from his home. Cavallaro fractured several ribs and some reports claimed he suffered a heart attack.

Newspaper articles reporting these last two incidents described Cavallaro as a "former 'big time' bookmaker" and "one-time Youngstown vice lord." Was "Cadillac Charlie" a has-been in the Mahoning Valley underworld? When he was interviewed by police after the July 1, 1962, death of Billy Naples he practically cried poverty, stating he had a bad heart, was living off money borrowed from a friend and that he hadn't worked in eight months. He also claimed, "I've been out of the rackets 15 or 16 years."

In October 1947, Cavallaro ended his common-law marriage to Iva Bijoul. Less than six months later he married Helen Biola, an American citizen, 14 years his junior. Cavallaro told his new bride that he had received his nickname from the "shiny" car he bought after his arrival in America. Helen Cavallaro was an attractive and personable woman, devoted to her family. She had two children of her own at the time and later gave Charlie two sons. The family moved to a home at 164 Roslyn Drive, on the city's North Side.

During Charlie's hey-day in the 1950s, he and Helen were invited out often. He once introduced her to singer Vic Damone, who at the time was dating Joe DiCarlo's daughter. A great cook, Helen often prepared dinner for the top hoods in the Youngstown and Warren underworld. However, "the life" had its down side. Charlie didn't want his wife and kids anywhere near his business, where he faced the constant fear of being arrested. Not that this didn't happen at his home. Helen recalled, "There were a number of times that cruisers roared up Roslyn Drive, sirens screaming, and took him to the police station for questioning." Because of this, Cavallaro forbade his family to go downtown for nearly a ten-year period, beginning in 1952. Instead, Charlie did the shopping for the family, purchasing clothes for the children and dresses for both his wife and mother-in-law. Family members didn't seem to mind, as Charlie's tastes were "exquisite and expensive." Cavallaro also handled most of the family's grocery shopping.

Helen described her husband as "always a gentleman." When Charlie ran his bookie operation there were numerous times that women knocked at the door during the day to complain that their husbands had lost their entire paychecks, "betting the ponies." Charlie returned the money to the desperate housewives. When Helen's mother passed away, Charlie suggested that her father come live with them so they could provide him with the proper attention he needed. He passed away in late 1961.

The senseless murders during 1960 and 1961 had taken a toll on Cavallaro. Charlie and Vince DeNiro were close friends. DeNiro and his father were frequent guests at the Cavallaro home where they enjoyed Charlie's homemade wine, which he prepared in his basement. Rumors persisted that it was Cavallaro who stepped in to run DeNiro's operations after his sensational murder.

By this time, however, Charlie had more serious problems to deal with. He had suffered six heart attacks by the end of 1961 and spent considerable time in the hospital. There was little or no income. Cavallaro was still wearing a back brace and was in constant pain from the construction site accident and was having legal trouble getting compensation from the state. His only income was from the Charles Cavallaro Grape Company, but he owed a lot of creditors money. As 1962 arrived, "Cadillac Charlie" was in dire straits. The man who had once owned a "shiny" new Cadillac was reduced to driving a six year-old Ford sedan.

In November 1962, Youngstown earned its most infamous and lasting nickname. The frequent bombings that took place during the 1950s had caused the city to be dubbed "Bombtown." When the bombings turned fatal in the late 1950s and early 1960s, along with the other more conventional killings, the city got its second nickname. Allegedly, a former Youngstown resident, disgusted with the criminal activity which was heightened by the brutal death of Vince DeNiro, sent a letter home addressed to "Murdertown, Ohio." The letter reached Youngstown.

Nine deaths, however, scattered over the past three years in "Murdertown" could not compare to the carnage the city would bear witness to on the morning of November 23, 1962, when Youngstown forever became known as "Crimetown, U.S.A."

On late Wednesday afternoon, November 21, 1962, Cavallaro pulled his 1956 red and white Ford sedan into the Roslyn Drive garage. It was Thanksgiving Eve and Cavallaro was looking forward to spending time with Helen and the children, Allen, 17; Ramona, 15; Charles, Jr. (Chuckie), 12 and Thomas, known as Tommy, 11.

Speculation was that during the late night hours of November 21, or the early morning hours of November 22, someone entered the Cavallaro's garage, located 30 feet behind the home, and planted a bomb in the Ford, wiring it to the ignition. The people behind the planting of the bomb must have been familiar with Cavallaro's routine. On school days "Cadillac Charlie" rose early and drove his four children to school. It was normal for neighborhood children to pile into the Cavallaro car and ride along. Once the bomb was planted, the killers needed to make sure Cavallaro left home on Thanksgiving Day alone. This was accomplished by an unknown individual setting up an appointment with Charlie for Thursday evening. Whether this was arranged by a telephone call on Thanksgiving Day or was discussed the day before will never be known.

On Thanksgiving night, after the family had finished their dinner, a former employee of Cavallaro stopped by for a visit. Helen, a gracious host, warmed up a meal for their guest. After he finished, Helen took the scraps and went outside to place them in the garbage. She noticed that two garbage pails that sat alongside the garage were moved, crushing some of the "yellow mums" near the structure. When she went back inside she "bawled out" Tommy and Chuckie for moving the containers even though both boys denied doing so.

Later that night, Cavallaro told his wife he had "an appointment" to keep. Not wanting him to leave home on this festive holiday evening, Helen "dissuaded" her husband from going out. The family of six spent the evening together. It would be their last.

The next morning, Friday, the children had the day off from school. Both Chuckie and Tommy had a football practice scheduled at Harding Field. "Cadillac Charlie" had business to attend to downtown. A grape merchant, Cavallaro planned to sell a load of grapes and take care of a bill he owed at a wholesale house on Front Street.

Around 11:30, Cavallaro and his two young sons departed the house. In the backyard the boys encountered one of their neighborhood playmates. Asked if he wanted to accompany them to the football field, the youngster took off through the backyards to get permission from his mother. Unable to find her he was on his way back to the Cavallaro home to say he couldn't go along.

The Cavallaros had opened the garage doors and piled into the automobile. Tommy sat beside his father, while Chuckie sat on the right side of the front seat. Chuckie suddenly realized he had left behind the football. He jumped out of the car, raced to his bedroom to retrieve it, and had just stepped back into the garage. Charlie Cavallaro put the key in the ignition and turned it. The ensuing blast was devastating.

The garage was leveled into a heap of rubble. Both doors were blown back toward the house, some 30 feet away, smashing windows in the rear door and cellar entrance. Pieces of bricks and wood were scattered in a 50-foot radius. The blast blew the entire roof off the Ford as well as the hood, and peeled back the metal flooring. The car's front seat landed 15 feet away; one entire side was soaked in blood.

The young friend of the Cavallaro brothers witnessed the explosion. The image of Tommy's hand lying in the driveway was etched forever in the young man's mind. He later suffered nightmares from the carnage he experienced that day.

Helen Cavallaro and her daughter, Ramona, were in the kitchen when the blast occurred. Plaster showered down on them from the kitchen ceiling. Both ran to the back yard. While staring at the horrific destruction they could hear the cries of little Chuckie, spared from a certain death because of the forgotten football, coming from somewhere beneath the rubble.

"Mommy, Mommy! Help me," the tiny voice cried over and over again.

Unable to get to her child, Helen Cavallaro was near hysterics. She ran down the driveway and into the middle of the street screaming at every arriving neighbor, "My kids need me and I can't help them."

One neighbor threw a coat around Mrs. Cavallaro and shouted for others to call the police. Within five minutes police cars, fire trucks and ambulances were on the scene.

Patrolman Andrew Kovac was the first officer to arrive. Helen kept repeating to him, "What do they want, blood, but why the blood of my boy? We have given them everything but blood, and now they have that."

Officer Don Komara, the first officer on the scene at the Naples / Vrancich murder, parked his squad car on Roslyn and headed up the driveway toward the devastation. As he reached the back area, he recalled stepping on something soft. He looked down and to his horror saw the severed hand of Tommy Cavallaro.

Helen told police that the car was parked in the garage since Wednesday afternoon. She sobbed something about Charlie was going to take the kids to get some candy. At that point she became hysterical and the police couldn't get anymore from her. The *Vindicator* reported that Helen barricaded herself in the house. Later, she and Ramona were taken to a neighbor's home. Soon afterward Cavallaro's former attorney, now Youngstown City Law Director, Russell Mock arrived. His reason for meeting with Helen and what transpired was never explained. She soon left in an automobile.

The newspaper also reported that 45 minutes after the explosion an argument began between Police Chief Golden and Coroner Dr. David A. Belinky. In trying to rescue Chuckie, the chief directed his men to remove the bodies of Charles Cavallaro and Tommy. Belinky was upset and complained they should have been left where they were until he arrived.

Chuckie was rushed to St. Elizabeth's Hospital. With emergency room personnel unable to locate his mother they began operating on the boy's severely damaged hip at 1:00 p.m. In addition to the mutilated hip, young Chuckie had multiple cuts and wounds to his face, head, arms, hands and legs. Surgery was required to repair injuries to his face around both eyes. Little Chuckie endured five hours of "delicate surgery" that afternoon and while doctors were confident he would survive, they doubted he would ever walk again. Charles Cavallaro, Jr. remained in the hospital until February 20, 1963.

There was speculation that had Cavallaro kept his "appointment" on Thursday night he might have been the bomb's only victim. Some reasoned the tragedy to the children might have been averted had Helen not insisted that her husband remain at home with his family Thanksgiving night. Helen would suffer dearly.

The reality was that luck had just run out on the underworld killers who used bombs to murder their victims. It was only a coincidence that Mary Higgins, the girlfriend of Christ Sofocleous, and her son weren't in the car with him that fateful morning in 1959. Fate also played a role in the Vince DeNiro bombing in that he arrived at his automobile late enough to miss the crowds that were normally on the sidewalks of the city's "Uptown" section at an earlier hour. Although there was good reason to believe that Billy Naples had accidentally killed himself, there was a very real possibility that one of the other renters of the five-car garage, in which he perished, could have been present at the time the bomb went off. Despite the fact that the only innocent victim in the gang war to-date was Mary Ann Vrancich, it was by the grace of God, not any noble effort by the Youngstown mob, that other innocent people weren't killed or maimed. That streak of luck ended on November 23, 1962, when little Tommy Cavallaro and his brother paid the price.

On Sunday afternoon, 200 people visited the Vaschak Funeral Home where the bodies of Charles Cavallaro and his son Tommy were laid out in closed coffins. The funeral mass was on Monday morning at St. Edwards, where Tommy was a fifth grade student. The hearse bearing the young boy's body arrived at 11:00 a.m. A second hearse containing Charles Cavallaro remained at the funeral home. "Cadillac Charlie's" past caused him to be denied the last rites of the Catholic Church.

As Helen and her two older children, Ramona and Allen entered the church, the grief stricken Mrs. Cavallaro broke down and was assisted by the Reverend Stewart J. Platt, the assistant pastor of the church. Platt's sermon to the mourners that day went beyond just prayers for the young man.

Platt told the mourners, "The blood of this child cries out to God for vengeance, but retribution belongs to God. We believe in His wisdom this death was for a reason. Perhaps it may move the conscience of 175,000 citizens of this city. Have we neglected to vote or misused that vote, contributing possibly to corruption in office? Have we kept silent when we could have helped by giving information to the proper authorities? Not one of us can say we are innocent of the blood of this child. Let us each examine his conscience to determine to what extent he has contributed to the death of this child."

The funeral procession headed down Ohio Avenue where the hearse containing the body of Charles Cavallaro joined it. The procession made its way to Cavalry Cemetery where little Tommy Cavallaro would remain eleven years old forever. The father and son were buried side by side with simple headstones.

A change would come to the Mahoning Valley, but it wasn't initiated by God. Rather it would come from someone who at times thought he was God – J. Edgar Hoover. Before nightfall came to Youngstown on the day of the tragic double murder, Attorney General Robert F. Kennedy ordered Hoover's FBI to conduct a full-scale investigation into the bombing. This marked the first time the FBI officially became involved with an underworld bombing in the Valley. The FBI had stepped in once before when three Steubenville teenagers set off an explosion next to Gus Leamis' South Avenue coffee shop, in order to extort money from the gambler. While that bombing was not connected to the underworld activity in the Valley the FBI got involved because the extortion plot was a violation of federal law. The young men in that case were convicted and to date it was the only bombing in the Valley where the participants were apprehended.

John J. Coneys, the assistant special agent in charge of the Cleveland FBI office, was quick to confirm that federal agents were called in. Coneys pointed out that "the FBI will enter this case on the authority of civil rights legislation passed by Congress recently. Congress authorized the FBI to probe the racial and religious bombings and vandalism, occurring chiefly in the South, on the assumption that explosives used were shipped interstate. This is the same assumption we are going on in the Youngstown situation."

During the days immediately following the bombing the morbid fascinated came in droves to Roslyn Drive to gawk at the damage. A manned police car was kept in the driveway for several days to keep the curious from traveling back to the investigation scene.

The newspaper began immediately to uncover a motive for the bombing. On Sunday, November 25, the *Vindicator* headlines read:

Battle over Barbut Racket
May Be Key to Bomb Deaths

> "While familiar theories of Mafia inner fighting and underworld vendetta continue to be mentioned as possible motives, the barbut angle held top prominence.
> "It applies not only to the Cavallaro slaughter but to the underworld slayings

that preceded it, the gunning down of S. Joseph "Sandy" Naples and the dynamite murders of Vince DeNiro and Billy Naples.

"Police Chief William R. Golden said, 'I honestly believe that barbut is the underlying cause of this killing.'

"He said it was going to be hard to prove, but added, 'my men are working on this theory and we just might be able to come up with something, now that we have the added assistance of other investigations.'"

The newspaper pointed out that William "Billy Sunday" Lantini and Gus Leamis, both linked to the game, were the first to be brought in for questioning. Leamis operated a coffee shop on South Avenue where the barbut operation was run for several years. Lantini oversaw the operation of the game in Campbell, in which "underworld sources" claimed Cavallaro owned an interest. Lantini agreed to take a lie detector test. Questioned about the game Lantini replied, "I just deal it." He admitted to working six days a week at it and that he made approximately $100 a week. For the past three months he was working the game in Campbell for a man named "Brownie... [sounds like Celuberto, wrote the detective]" who operated the game. Lantini said they used the code words "making coffee" to signify they were dealing barbut.

A police informant told detectives that there was a meeting two weeks prior to the bombing on a Saturday at the Caravan Club on 422 in New Castle, Pennsylvania. From police photographs the informant identified Charles Cavallaro, who he stated was referred to as the "boss." Others he recognized were Howard "Waxey" Moore, "Jack the Ripper" Zentko, Richard Dota, Joseph Drago, Joseph "Duke" Mainer, Mario Guerrieri and Al Oponovich. The informant identified Ed Genock as "the big wheel in the rackets in New Castle."

The newspaper speculated that the string of murders in these early years of the decade were tied together by the lust for barbut profits. A *Vindicator* article explained:

"The Leamis joint was the barbut center when Sandy Naples was shot to death with his girlfriend in March 1960. Naples was figured primarily as a bug operator, but there was considerable speculation preceding his death that he had joined a local combine that was aiming to consolidate gambling operations, and the struggle over how the take would be split led to his killing. This theory gained importance three months later when a similar shotgun attempt was made on the life of Joseph Romano...linked very closely to the South Avenue barbut game.

"There was a strong feeling that the Romano shooting was a retaliatory move for Naples' death, one that misfired, but did little to break the struggle because of the intended victim's silence following his recovery. Police sources at the time had linked Romano and Cavallaro in gambling operations. It was also around this time that underworld rumblings began popping up of pressure from a Struthers' gang to take over the barbut game. These grew and reached a climax following the first bombing death related to the rackets, the murder of Vince DeNiro in July 1961. The DeNiro killing saw a shift in the barbut operations from down-

> town Youngstown to Struthers, where two spots were reported flourishing alternately in the lucrative game. It was not a loss that Youngstown operators could be expected to take lightly, and the whispers of the underworld strife continued unabated, with a steady stream of rumors that one or more racket leaders faced extinction. Just two days [before Billy Naples death] the underworld reported barbut shifted again, this time to Campbell, and Cavallaro's name again gained prominence. Naples was said to have had a piece of the Struthers' game but was to have been stronger in the Campbell operation."

It was rumored that the police had amassed a considerable amount of incriminating evidence during their investigation. Even though there was some bragging to the effect that department files contained enough evidence "to blow the roof off," higher-ups in the department claimed the information wasn't good enough to bring charges, let alone convictions. Many now felt that with the FBI taking a more active role that the "break" the Valley was waiting for was surely at hand.

Despite the solid theory the newspaper presented about barbut, which was supported by Chief Golden and many others in the Youngstown Police Department, the next day the *Vindicator* ran another front-page story blaming the warfare on the numbers rackets. Mayor Harry N. Savasten, like his predecessors, pleaded with citizens to quit gambling, especially on the bug. The article pointed out how big the desire to gamble was locally. The report stated, "An indication that the gambling business must be lucrative is the fact that the district now has 19 holders of federal gambling stamps, making Mahoning County the second largest in the gambling business in 47 covered by the Cleveland Internal Revenue Service office."

The death of Tommy Cavallaro was the topic of many church sermons throughout the Valley the Sunday after Thanksgiving. The consensus was that the "resolution of the problems of community life depends upon every citizen accepting personal responsibility and making a corresponding commitment."

The *Vindicator* offices were flooded with letters and telegrams from angry citizens denouncing the bombing in disgust. Attorney General Kennedy's office was receiving similar correspondence. Below is a sampling of the feelings of the citizenry:

> "After 82 unsolved bombings in the Youngstown district, don't you think it's about time to send in the first team?"
>
> "Please help us. Are our children next?"
>
> "When law and order on a local level becomes ineffective the government of the U.S. should declare marshal law. Send us federal marshals to protect our families."

"No matter what your political background – we have a common problem and we need uncommon men to solve that problem."

"Have we no more Hendersons and Allens?"

"The people in this stinking town better wake up!"

Of all the responses perhaps the most creative was a poem by M. R. Garwood:

Racketeer Man
We go in some restaurants
And we go in some dives,
And pour out our dough
Where the racketeer thrives.
We talk of big autos and
Sables and minks,
We haven't the guts to show
Where it stinks.
As long as we aid and assist
Such a clan
Should we really condemn the
Racketeer man?

At police headquarters during Monday morning roll call a letter written by Chief Golden was read to the troops:

> "All officers will redouble their efforts in the enforcement of violations concerning vice. Each individual officer shall make a relentless effort to stamp out any and all corruption that has infested this community. The recent slaying, taking the life of an innocent child, should be incentive enough for all men to make an all-out effort to bring the situation to a just and final conclusion."

On the Monday after Thanksgiving, Edward E. Hargett, the special agent in charge of the Cleveland FBI office, was in Youngstown conferring with Mayor Savasten. Police reported that the Campbell barbut game, which Cavallaro was alleged to have been running with Warren's Anthony "Tony Dope" Delsanter, was ordered shut down by the "boss." Whoever the "boss" was, the police failed to identify him.

For the first time in history it looked like a total law enforcement team effort was taking place in the Mahoning Valley. In addition to the Youngstown Police Department and the FBI, County Sheriff Ray Davis notified both Chief Golden and Edward Hargett that he was assigning full-time undercover men to the case and was prepared to exchange all the information his investigators obtained. In addition, Ohio Governor Michael V. DiSalle empowered James H. Barber, the chief liquor enforcement officer for the Youngstown District, to call in "any state liquor enforcement agent to assist" in the murder probe. Barber was already striking at local cheat spots in the county by calling for public boycotts of the Frontier Club in Struthers, and two Campbell locations – Big Jim's Barbecue and what he called a "bootleg operation" on Gordon Avenue.

Despite these good intentions, petty back fighting soon took center stage. During a taped interview on WFMJ television, Chief Golden told a reporter that, despite the fact bombs were going off in Youngstown, "the illegal activities producing them are taking place outside of the city," out of his jurisdiction.

"There are two known places operating outside the city," the chief claimed. "Reporters know about them."

County Sheriff Davis was quick to respond to the remarks figuring the insinuation was that he was not doing his job. "If he means Campbell and Struthers, why doesn't he say Campbell and Struthers?" asked Davis. "The county is clear, I defy anyone to find gambling in the county."

Davis claimed his men found out about barbut being played in both cities and the operations were raided and closed by the respective police agencies. He then countered that his deputies found numerous incidents of gambling and prostitution going on inside Youngstown.

"We didn't embarrass [Golden] by raiding those places. We informed him about them, and they were closed eventually by Youngstown police."

Chief Golden later stated that his comments were "largely unprepared" and not intended to start a feud with another policing agency.

James Barber of the State Liquor Enforcement office stated that over the weekend "the two Campbell joints had suspended operations as a result of the heat generated by the bombing." He claimed, however, it was business as usual at the Frontier Club in Struthers, where at 4:00 o'clock Saturday morning there were more than 50 cars in the parking lot. This led to a denial by Struthers' Police Chief G. Woodrow Sicafuse, who claimed the cheat spot "has been closed for months."

In addition to the FBI, Attorney General Kennedy also assigned two attorneys from his staff to Youngstown. With the FBI and Justice Department now involved, information from the investigation would be kept a little closer to the vest. Chief Golden quickly announced, "We will not be making any round-by-round reports to the news media." When questioned by reporters, Detective Chief John Terlesky responded that "any information on the investigation would have to come from the FBI."

Youngstown and Mahoning County law enforcement and public officials seemed united in their desire to give their full attention to ridding the Valley of underworld gamblers. The one exception seemed to be the city law director's office. Former defense attorney Russell Mock now held the position. He immediately upheld a ruling from 1956 that the city does not have the authority to offer a reward for the arrest and conviction of those responsible for the Cavallaro murders.

On November 30, one week after the murders, the *Vindicator* reported:

> "Kennedy also heard...from the board of directors of the Youngstown area Chamber of Commerce, who wired that they appreciated the dispatch of the FBI here to supplement the work of local officials and urged that 'these men be kept here until the area situation is corrected.'
>
> "The Health and Welfare Council...passed a resolution calling on all public officials who are charged with the responsibility for law enforcement to wage 'a constant and vigorous war against organized vice in the community until racket rule has been effectively crushed.'
>
> "The resolution...calls on citizens to examine their consciences to see how much they have supported the vice lords, and to aid law enforcement agencies in the investigation."

The one catch to the combined investigation was being able to build a case that clearly violated federal law. Some federal authorities were not optimistic about their chances of accomplishing this. It was understood, however, that all evidence collected by the bureau would be turned over to local authorities for prosecution if a federal violation could not be established.

Special Agent in Charge Ed Hargett, dedicated to the task at hand, confirmed "his men will continue working on the Cavallaro case until it is solved, regardless of the time it takes." He pointed out that "it took the department six years to solve the Brinks' robbery in Massachusetts, emphasizing that they do not leave a case they enter until it is solved."

The FBI announced, "Barbut and other gambling reportedly shut down with the pressure of agents here, and underworld characters have gone underground." The FBI was working round-the-clock on the case and hoping that some citizen would be able to furnish them with assistance. Hargett also revealed that no information had developed from informants, even though they were being offered protection.

Three weeks after the bombing little Chuckie Cavallaro was still recovering. Orthopedic surgeons now believed the young man would walk again. The injured hip was held together with steel pins – muscle, ligaments, bone and tissue all miraculously brought together by the caring surgeons. As the Christmas holiday approached it was Chuckie's wish to spend the day at home with his family. Surgeons were ready to place him in a cast that would allow him to go home. His family and the hospital staff set about the task of making his wish come true.

Two days before Christmas, it was announced that the plans were scuttled due to Blue Cross hospitalization red tape. It was revealed the next day, however, that the family had not moved back to the Roslyn Drive location and the home where they were now residing was not big enough to accommodate Chuckie's hospital bed. The young man spent his Christmas at St. Elizabeth's Hospital surrounded by his mother, brother and sister, aunts and uncles and a loving hospital staff. After an 86-day stay in the hospital, 12 year-old Chuckie Cavallaro[5] walked out of St. Elizabeth's on crutches on February 16, 1963.

The damage to the Cavallaro family wasn't over. Helen was nearly ruined financially. The family lived with Helen's sister until Chuckie could return home. By the time they did creditors were threatening to place liens against the house. The underworld figures who she once cooked delicious meals for were nowhere to be found. They only called to ask for money they claimed Cavallaro owed them. The family was forced to live on peanut butter and jelly sandwiches until the FBI could confirm to the Mahoning County Department of Welfare that Charles Cavallaro had no hidden assets. An insurance policy on the home was cancelled the day after the explosion. A $1,000 insurance policy in Tommy's name was used to purchase cemetery plots.

In an exclusive interview with the Cleveland *Plain Dealer* in 1971, Helen spoke publicly for the first time since the bombing more than eight years earlier. She related how a fortuneteller had "visualized" that there was money hidden in the Roslyn Drive home. "For two months, I took everything apart and found nothing," Helen confessed.

"The neighbors were decent," Helen continued. "When we were most hungry, someone always dropped in with some food." She revealed the family lived on public assistance and food stamps. Many of Chuckie's expensive hospital bills "were written off by kindly doctors and other professionals."

Helen admitted to living a "sheltered" life. She claimed the incident caused her to become mentally ill. By the early 1970s, she suffered from severe arthritis and high blood pressure. Her few outings were to attend church services.

Helen related, you'd think I wouldn't be afraid at night anymore. People say, 'Helen, it's over.' Is it? I hear 'they' think it is because of me, because Tommy died, the FBI is watching this town."

She recalled fondly, "Vince DeNiro's old father was kind. He sold flowers at the cemetery and once, when I was there, he gave me two big pots of white ones for Charlie's grave. I never went back. I didn't want him to think I wanted more free flowers."

Helen Cavallaro passed away in 1987.

Nearly a year passed and law enforcement wasn't any closer to solving the crime than they were on the day of the explosion. FBI Agent Hargett gave the following update on the investigation:

> "We have been continuously investigating the murder of Charles Cavallaro since November 23, 1962, in an effort to determine whether a federal law involving the interstate transportation of explosives was violated. Many facets have been explored and new avenues are being continuously pursued. In this connection we have developed information concerning purely local law violations which have been turned over to the proper authorities for such action as they deem appropriate.

> "In continuing the investigation of the Cavallaro bombing-murder, if further infractions of gambling violations are noted, the information gathered will be turned over to the proper authorities for prosecution."

A grand jury investigation only concluded that "Cadillac Charlie" was trying to move in on a Campbell barbut operation prior to his murder. In May 1967, a Mahoning County Probate Court revealed that Cavallaro's estate totaled a mere $12,552, of which $10,000 was the value of his home and $1,600 was from the accounts receivable of the Charles Cavallaro Grape Company.

One last item concerning the Cavallaro murder came to light on June 10, 1969. On that day the FBI released 13 volumes of conversations recorded by hidden microphone involving Northern New Jersey Mafia boss Samuel "Sam the Plumber" DeCavalcante. In one of the conversations, recorded on February 23, 1963, FBI agents listened as DeCavalcante criticized the method used to booby trap the Cavallaro automobile. The East Coast mobster stated that a hand grenade was used in the killing. The *Vindicator* reported, "The transcript shows that one Mafia member described the results as 'messy' because the child was killed, too, and deplored the use of a hand grenade. He also said the word was out not to use grenades in the future."

Youngstown investigators were curious as to where DeCavalcante got his information. Evidence sent to the Crime Laboratory at the London Prison Farm showed that dynamite was used. A demolition squad from the Ravenna Arsenal, although unable to determine the exact explosive, decided it was most likely ten or more sticks of dynamite. Both considered it highly unlikely that a single hand grenade could have caused that much damage; not to mention the ensuing investigation failed to turn up any shrapnel, which is common with grenades.

Murder of Dominic Moio

Dominic Moio's first illegal act in the United States was entering the country, which he did as a stowaway on May 18, 1923, in Philadelphia. Moio was born in Ferrussano, Reggio Calabria, Italy on December 14, 1901. When he was 22, he boarded a boat in France and headed for Havana, Cuba, in hopes of eventually getting to America. From there, Moio stowed away on a merchant vessel where he claimed he paid crewmembers $200 to help him. After 23 days the ship landed at Philadelphia, where Moio soon found work as a general laborer.

Moio remained in the "City of Brotherly Love" for about four years before moving to Jersey City in 1927. The next year he moved to Detroit where he remained for approximately four and half years. His time in Detroit coincided with the heyday of the Licavoli mob in that city, though, there was never any indication that Moio had connections to the Licavolis there. Moio's later associations in Canton and Youngstown put him opposite the Licavolis and their Cleveland connections.

Moio left Detroit in the early 1930s and went to Canton. In interviews with the Youngstown police after the death of Billy Naples, Moio's memory of his movements changed considerably at times. After insisting to have lived in Canton for nearly 30 years, Moio said that in the late 1930s he moved to California, got married, and had a son named John, who still lived on the West Coast. Moio said he first wife died.

During his years in Canton, Moio worked as a laborer, steel mill employee, plasterman and bartender. Although Moio had a number of arrests in the late 1930s and early 1940s, he avoided indictment. His only conviction came after an August 1939, arrest for conspiring to manufacture alcohol illegally. This involved purchasing five-gallon cans of "white whiskey" and reselling it to bootleggers. Moio served six months at the federal prison facility in Milan, Michigan.

Moio worked in Canton for Pat Ferruccio as a bartender and developed a close friendship with Nick Terse. In the early 1960s, after a bomb was detonated at Terse's home, Moio sat watch outside the house each night from 9:00 p.m. until 2:00 a.m. for "six or seven" months. The only people he encountered during his watch were "a couple of detectives in a car."

In 1961, Moio was indicted for arson after his wallet was found near the recently torched Wadsworth Feed Company in Warren, Ohio. Moio told authorities his pants were stolen from a dry-cleaning shop in Canton, and that his wallet was dropped at the scene of the fire in order to frame him. In 1963, he was cleared of the charges by Trumbull County Common Pleas Judge George H. Birrell in a directed acquittal.

After the car-bombing death of Billy Naples, police suspected Moio was the "friend" who called Naples at his home, picked him up, and drove him to the Madison Avenue garage. During the first interrogation by detectives, Moio was asked about scars on his face and hands. He replied, "I got the [scars] from carburetor explosion ...Frank Amato started the car when I was fooling with the carburetor. Frank's now in Cleveland, Ohio. I haven't seen him since then."

Moio confessed to entering the United States illegally to an official of the immigration service while being questioned as a material witness during the Billy Naples' investigation. Nearly a year later, after Moio returned to Canton, he was charged with being a criminal alien. He was arrested in Canton and arraigned on the charge in Cleveland. During an investigation into his background by the U.S. Immigration and Naturalization Service they discovered convictions that he had failed to mention when being held the year before. He was convicted in August 1928 for "unlawful assault in a menacing manner with a knife," and in September 1946 in Canton "for receiving stolen goods."

During a hearing in February 1963, Moio admitted that he drove Billy Naples to the Madison Avenue garage the night he was killed. He wouldn't say who else was with them that night or what he knew, if anything, about the bomb. Moio refused to answer some 31 questions put to him by Deputy State Fire Marshal

Michael J. Melillo. The state official claimed the refusal constituted general contempt and he requested that Moio be jailed. Melillo's request was upheld by Common Pleas Judge David G. Jenkins, who denied Moio a writ of habeas corpus, which he appealed. Judge Jenkins claimed his action was due to Moio's "blanket refusal to answer questions of the fire marshal, even those not pertinent or non-incriminating, constituted contemptuous action and flaunted the laws of the state and federal government." The Seventh District Court of Appeals, however, ruled in favor of Moio on July 9 stating, "The self-incrimination clause of the Constitution must be accorded liberal construction."

Moio's deportation case was still pending on September 2, 1963. On that day a farmer, living in the Pike Township area of Stark County, noticed a 1961 Oldsmobile parked near an abandoned strip mine. The next night the automobile was still there and the farmer approached to investigate. As he moved closer he detected "a terrible odor" and called the Stark County Sheriff's Department.

When authorities arrived they forced open the trunk of the car and found the scorched and rotting remains of Dominic Moio. Despite the fact the automobile was registered in Moio's name and that Stark County Coroner Gus S. Shaheen stated he had once treated Moio and recognized him by his deformed hand and facial characteristics, it took another 24 hours before positive identification was made. This coming after both Moio's hands were removed at the wrist and sent to the FBI lab in Washington DC for positive fingerprint identification.

Oddly, the first report by the *Vindicator* stated, "The body showed signs of a brutal beating. No bullet wounds have been found." The next day Coroner Shaheen reported different findings. Moio was shot once in the base of the skull; the bullet exited above his left eye. Shaheen said, "The body was not mutilated, as is the case in Mafia killings, and bore no evidence of physical torture." The body was stuffed in the trunk fully clothed and "drenched with a kerosene-like substance" before it was set on fire. The body didn't burn long because the trunk was closed, smothering the fire. Reports said Moio was last seen in Canton around August 26. The coroner believed Moio's body was decomposing for at least a week.

There were three theories advanced by law enforcement and the newspapers for Moio's murder. First, that it was due to his connection to the deaths of Billy Naples, Charles Cavallaro and his son Tommy; second, that it was a revenge murder carried out by people close to Cavallaro; and third, that it was carried out by the people behind Moio because of the death of Tommy Cavallaro and the heat that it brought on by the FBI and law enforcement due to the child's death.

Moio's son, John, arrived from California. Funeral arrangements were handled by the Rossi Funeral Home in Canton. The service and burial were private.

Deputy State Fire Marshal Melillo soon launched an investigation into Moio's death. The first three people subpoenaed were "Fats" Aiello, Ronald Carabbia and Joey Naples. During the investigation in Youngstown, Melillo wouldn't allow counsel for the men to enter the hearing room. It didn't matter anyway because after giving their names and addresses they all invoked their Fifth Amendment rights. Aiello didn't even bother to appear with his lawyer. "I don't need any attorney," the gambler claimed. "I didn't do anything and I have nothing to tell them."

State arson investigators also subpoenaed three Canton men – Louis J. "Bones" Battista, Louis Christian and Pat Ferruccio. They provided the same information the Youngstown mobsters did. In Cleveland, investigators called Angelo A. Amato and his son Angelo J. Amato. The father ran the Amalina Cement & Construction Company, which employed Moio for a short time before his death. While the Amatos reportedly "answered all our questions," according to one state official, no testimony linking anyone to Moio's murder was revealed. One last subpoena was issued to Leo Moceri, now a resident of Northampton Township in Summit County, but it was never served.

"He asked me if I had a search warrant, then I said I was placing him under arrest. He said, 'I'd like to give you and your partner a half-yard.' Novosel said he didn't know that Aiello was offering him a $50 bribe and wondered if he was talking about concrete." – Patrolman Pete Novosel on the stand on April 14, 1962, during the bribery trial of "Fats" Aiello after the gambler tried to bribe him and his partner William Gruver.

14

The Fall of the Valley's "Big 3" – Fats, Moosey and the Wolf

Demise of "Fats" Aiello

Surviving the bombs and bullets of the early 1960s was the Valley's most publicized mobster, Jasper Joseph Aiello. However, "Fats" had his own legal woes and in the end went away to prison after being convicted for his involvement in a highly un-gangster-like activity.

In March 1960, the trial for Aiello, who was charged with passing a bad check for $28,500 the previous year, got underway after attempts at a final repayment plan between the bank and the mobster fell through. The 1960s brought a new style of reporting to the *Vindicator* and instead of being happy to call Aiello a "dapper" rackets figure, they were now describing his attire, which in this case was "a well-cut conservative dark brown, ivy-league business suit with a tan-collared shirt and conservative brown tie."

On March 27, the trial began. Representing Aiello in Judge Frank Battisti's courtroom was attorney Eugene Fox. Loren E. Van Brocklin and Robert O'Linn handled the prosecution. No sooner had the jury been selected that Battisti adjourned court for the day in order for the principles to be present for the bedside deposition of James G. Ruble. The former Union National Bank teller, who was fired after accepting the check from Aiello that bounced, was hospitalized at North Side Hospital after an automobile accident two weeks earlier.

From his bed, Ruble testified that he cashed huge checks before at Aiello's request, some as high as $15,000. Ruble stated, "I never questioned him. They were always good." He then explained the bank has "pages and pages of cases where checks have been cashed and come back marked insufficient funds. It has happened to some of our most respected business and professional men."

Ruble claimed he didn't believe at the time the check was returned, nor did he believe now, that Aiello "had any intention of defrauding the bank." After the return of the check, Ruble went to Aiello's home to inform him. At the same time a smaller check for $1,500 had also bounced. Aiello made good on the smaller check and made arrangements to repay the other.

During testimony the next day, the president of Union National Bank told jurors that Aiello put up life insurance policies as collateral for the $28,500 until he could pay it back, but refused to change the beneficiary on the documents. The banker explained the policies were no good to the bank since they were still in the name of Rose Aiello. Attorney Fox brought out during cross-examination that the only reason Aiello didn't have the beneficiary changed was "because he didn't want his wife to have to come down to sign the papers."

An official from Dollar Savings Bank, where the gambler kept his account in Niles, testified that Aiello "played fast and loose with his checking account, cashing large checks one day and covering them at the last minute a day or so later."

Once the prosecution rested, the defense set out to prove that Aiello wanted to make good on the check and had no intention of defrauding the bank. Aiello took the stand and testified for more than an hour. He told the jury that on several occasions he informed bank tellers, "I'm a little short now, but this money will be there before the check gets there." His explanation as to what happened with the money was that he gave it to a friend to use to "show good faith in a Miami, Florida land deal." The friend was supposed to deposit the money with the Niles bank but left instead for Chicago. "That's the last I heard of him," Aiello stated.

Under cross-examination by Van Brocklin, Aiello claimed he didn't know the owner or location of the Miami property. "I trusted my friend," he told the prosecutor. Aiello stated that, "I've made a living all my life gambling," but admitted he hadn't worked in almost seven years. Van Brocklin asked, "Isn't it a fact you needed that [money] to cover heavy bug hits the weekend of March 27, 1959?" (This was a change from earlier speculation that Aiello had used the money to front a barbut game.)

Aiello replied, "I'm a gambler, not a bookmaker."

On the afternoon of March 30, the jury received the case. After deliberating for four and a half-hours they came back deadlocked at 11 to 1 for acquittal. The one holdout was said to be a woman on the evenly split male/female jury. (In December 1961 the Maryland Casualty Company reached an undisclosed settlement with former teller James Ruble for his part in the fraudulent check case. At that time Aiello had still not made any additional payments and still owed $24,550.)

The *Vindicator*, quick to editorialize about its favorite gangster, called Aiello a "chiseler" and wrote had the jury "decided to return a verdict on the basis of the defendant's record and reputation, he would have been found guilty on the first ballot."

As had happened back in August 1948, when Aiello foolishly told Chief Allen that, "I can't remember having a legitimate job," his words from his latest trial would again come back to haunt him. Less than 48 hours after the jury was dismissed, Aiello was arrested and charged with being a "common gambler" based on his statements during the trial. He pleaded not guilty before Judge Cavalier and posted a $500 bond. The newspaper reported, "The common gambler charge is based on a statute which carries a mandatory jail term and a fine. If convicted Aiello would also have to post a security of $500 for one year, refundable after the defendant proves he has a means of livelihood other than gambling." A state law, which defined a "common gambler," declared that illegal gambling for a livelihood was a crime.

Before Aiello faced trial as a "common gambler," he still had to deal with his *common* armed robbery indictment in Warren. Three and a half years had now passed since the robbery at the Griswold Store on South Park Avenue in Trumbull County. The trial began on May 9 in the courtroom of Judge George H. Birrell. The prosecution's star witness was imprisoned former Warren police officer Richard Stanley.

Stanley testified that he met Aiello at the Purple Cow in March 1955, and that they had several other meetings to discuss "business in Warren." On the night of the robbery, November 30, 1956, Stanley stood watch at the rear of the Griswold Store as Aiello, Ronald Carabbia, James Zimmerman and Willie Napoli entered the back armed and with silk stockings covering their faces. The next day, Stanley testified, Aiello handed him $1,000 in an A & P Supermarket parking lot in Niles.

Convicted for his own participation in the robbery, Stanley was in the Ohio Penitentiary when he received a letter from Warren Police Chief Manley English stating, "I know they are paying your wife $100 a month, but is it worth it?" After receiving the letter Stanley said he decided to cooperate, but denied "being offered any concessions if he turned state's evidence."

Aiello was represented again by Eugene Fox. His testimony was orchestrated not only to help him in this trial, but also with his pending "common gambler" case. Aiello told the court that he met Stanley only twice and both encounters ended in arguments. Aiello claimed his money came from settlements from two automobile accidents and from his "living" from gambling, which he quickly pointed out came from horse racetrack proceeds "where it is legal" to gamble. Aiello stated Stanley's reason to accuse him might have resulted from an attempt by "Fats" to "steal one of his girls." After less than two days of testimony the jury took just one hour to find Aiello not guilty on May 10.

The next day Aiello was all smiles as he paid a speeding fine of $5 and court costs of $8 from a citation he received six days earlier. Handing down the fine was former Aiello attorney, now municipal court judge, Donald Hanni. Aiello declined the judges offer to suspend the $8 if the gambler attended traffic school for two nights.

Before Aiello could be tried on the "common gambler" charge, he was arrested on June 24 for loitering outside his favorite downtown haunt – the Purple

Cow. The arrest came during Mayor Franko's brief cleanup effort following the mob turbulence during the first half of 1960. Aiello was spotted by the mayor and his newly appointed vice squad chief, George Millovich, the law-abiding brother of John "Tar Baby" Millovich, who was arrested with Aiello by the FBI for art theft in 1953.

Frank Watters, in his second day as police chief, said the arrest was an effort to "clean off the sidewalk in front of the Purple Cow," which is literally across the street and half a block west of the police station. Watters told reporters that Aiello would be questioned to see if he has "any legitimate business being on the sidewalk all hours of the day." An irritated Aiello spent 14 hours in the city jail before he was released the next afternoon.

In mid-September 1960, a local businessman announced that Aiello would become the host and business manager of the Colonial Bar at the corner of West Boardman and Hazel Street, directly across from the Hotel Pick-Ohio and the Purple Cow. The bar was in the process of being turned into a swanky new lounge. Now Aiello would have a not only legitimate job, but also a reason to be loitering on the sidewalk of his favorite corner.

On November 30, at 4:30 a.m. a call was received at the Youngstown police station from St. Elizabeth's Hospital that Aiello had driven himself there after being shot through the leg. When police arrived Aiello told them that shortly before 4:00 a.m. he was sitting in the living room of his Wesley Avenue home, on the city's West Side, when he heard a noise outside. Thinking it may be a prowler, he got up to investigate. He then tripped over a rug and shot himself. The slug entered the left thigh muscle toward the inside of the leg below the hip, and exited on the outside of the thigh three inches above the knee. There were powder burns on his pant leg. Detectives checked with Aiello's mother-in-law, who lived at the Wesley Avenue address, but she denied that a shooting took place there. One police officer dismissed the prowler story totally stating, "Aiello hasn't been home by 4:00 a.m. for 20 or 30 years." After that, Aiello changed his story and said the shooting took place at his home on Raccoon Road, in Austin Township, but he refused to give the detectives the address so they could verify his tale. The police soon found more holes in Aiello's story than in his leg.

The next day a new story emerged. Gus Leamis claimed Aiello was shot *outside* his Greek-Syrian Coffee House on South Avenue while getting out of his automobile. Detectives later questioned a "reliable source" who claimed Aiello *was in* the coffee house involved in a game of barbut, "There was a lot of action," he said. "The game broke up when Aiello shot himself." According to the source, Aiello's gun was tucked in his belt, but the hammer was "not down all the way and when Fats brought his arm back to shake the dice, it hit the hammer and the gun went off."

Police officials were pondering what charges they could bring against Aiello in the incident. The first choice was to charge him with carrying a concealed weapon, but police were never able to recover the revolver. A second choice was for filing a false report since he initially claimed the shooting happened at his home.

Meanwhile, many were wondering what happened to the "common gambler" charge from last April. The trouble Aiello had gotten himself into during the bounced check trial, "shooting himself in the foot" by announcing he made his money as a gambler, was forgotten. That is until he really shot himself eight months later. Aiello had demanded a jury trial in the case. The newspaper quoted an unnamed city official who stated, "A jury demand generally is nothing but a delaying tactic used by the attorneys in municipal court. At the worst, it delays the case, but at the best – and as is often the result – this action means the case is forgotten and dies."

The trial was initially set for May 23, until Judge Cavalier moved it to June so he could clear his criminal docket. What transpired next embarrassed city officials. The *Vindicator* reported, "Judge Cavalier said he had forgotten about the case. He said the police prosecutor's office is responsible for prosecuting the charge and has not followed through. He indicated he could take the case after he returns to the criminal bench in January." City Law Director S. S. Fekett claimed he didn't know the case was still pending. On December 5, the city's legal minds got together and, after determining that "a man cannot be convicted on his own uncorroborated testimony," dropped the charges against Aiello of being a "common gambler."

Three days later Aiello was released from St. Elizabeth's. The gambler, "scowling and sullen," was picked up by detectives and taken downtown for questioning. Police brass and prosecutors were still discussing charging Aiello with filing a false report. At the station it was reported that Aiello, "leaning heavily on a cane, nearly collapsed when he was asked to walk around the booking counter...to be finger printed." He was then taken to be grilled again about the shooting.

Aiello's story changed again. He now told detectives he did "not know how he got to the hospital from his home, that he blacked out after the shooting and does not remember what happened until he regained consciousness on the emergency room operating table." Despite Gus Leamis' tale to the contrary, Aiello insisted the shooting took place at his "new home out in the country. It doesn't have a number [address]. I moved there about five days before this accident."

While officials were mulling over their decision on whether to charge Aiello, reporters talked with the gambler as he paced back and forth to "keep up the circulation" in his wounded leg. When asked to make a statement, Aiello snapped, "A statement? What kind of statement, Jack? It was an accident, an accident that's all. I was looking for a burglar at my home." Police Chief Watters, even though detectives had four different versions of the shooting, announced no charges would be filed.

As Aiello hobbled out of the police station he realized that despite his wound he had quite a fortunate year. He was acquitted in one trial, a jury deadlocked in another and in the space of three days charges were dropped in one incident and not filed in another. Yes, 1960 was a good year indeed for the mobster whose only defeat was having to pay $13 for a traffic violation.

On January 17, 1961, Aiello began what might have been his only legitimate job: Host of the remodeled Colonial Bar now called the "A" Lounge. Greeting patrons while "resplendent in an expensive dark suit and tie," Aiello insisted to those who inquired that he was not the owner, just a $100 a week manager. The owner John N. Bombolis, who had spent nearly $100,000 turning the former bar into a modern split-level lounge, with two separate cushioned, oval-shaped bars with cushioned arm rests, deep rose carpeting and imported Italian cherry siding, hoped to gain a return on his investment from a "high-spending clientele."

A reporter noted, "A striking ash blonde in a tight red dress added a decorative touch behind one of the two bars. The 25 year-old divorcee hardly knew how to make drinks. 'She's never worked behind a bar before, but what the hell,' a bartender confided. 'She'll bring in the male trade'. Another blonde, often seen in the company of Aiello was mixing drinks."

The opening night crowd included businessmen, city employees, councilmen, politicians and, of course, several underworld figures.

In March, Trumbull County Prosecutor Lynn B. Griffith, Jr. surprised the Youngstown gambler with his decision to try Aiello for the October 1956 burglarizing of the Rappold Company, a woman's clothing store. Griffith told reporters, "Aiello hadn't expected to see a Trumbull County courtroom again."

Aiello wasn't the only target of Griffith's prosecution. Ronald Carabbia was tried for the Griswold Store holdup and Willie Napoli, arrested January 5 after being a fugitive for two years, was tried for two separate robberies. James Zimmerman, who was convicted the previous summer for a liquor store break-in during July 1958, was serving a one-to-five-year sentence in the Ohio Penitentiary. The last person indicted, Donald "Bull" Jones, pleaded guilty and was awaiting sentencing. Griffith's star witness was former police officer Richard Stanley. The convicted cop's testimony, which earlier had failed to convince jurors of Aiello's guilt, had already helped convict Zimmerman.

Stanley's testimony helped gain his parole in late summer 1960. As the time for the new trials drew near, Griffith was concerned for Stanley's safety and offered to finance a trip for him until he was needed in court to testify. This was apparently prompted by the fact that one of the men charged had "hinted" to Griffith in the prosecutor's office that it could be worth as much as $7,000 for him to forget the pending cases. Griffith didn't reveal who offered the "hint." Stanley declined the trip and an offer of protective custody. Since his release from prison the former police officer was living with his wife, Doris, and her seven year-old daughter Darlene, in the upstairs of a duplex on Chamber Street in Warren.

A few weeks before the first trial was scheduled – the April 3 trial of Ronald Carabbia – Stanley's mother received a telephone call asking where her son lived and what his telephone number was. The Stanleys didn't have a telephone at their home. Doris Stanley, who worked at a little restaurant called the Dog House a block from the couple's home, was told that someone had called the eatery to inquire where she lived.

On Thursday morning, March 23, Paul Jagnow, working for the *Vindicator's* Warren bureau, spoke with Richard Stanley for a half-hour about the upcoming trials. Stanley said he was readying himself to testify against both Aiello and Carabbia, who he claimed to have accompanied on several burglaries and one armed robbery. Jagnow wrote:

> "Stanley was aware of the underworld code and ruefully admitted he had been used as a 'fall guy' for the area burglary gang. Stanley told me that while in prison he'd found God and wished to turn state's evidence against his gangster associates. Stanley revealed he had been offered $15,000 not to testify against Aiello and Carabbia, and hesitantly added, 'That's a lot of money, when unemployed like I am.' I asked him if he planned to accept the bribe and he said with a laugh, 'It's a real tempting offer and he's been thinking it over, but I think I will stick with the prosecutor and testify as planned.'"

Around 7:30 that evening, as Doris was finishing her shift at the Dog House, a neatly dressed man in his mid-40s entered the restaurant. Although he ignored her greeting, he watched her every move. The man took off minutes before Doris left, but as she walked home she felt as if she was being followed. Scared, she ran the short distance to her home and up the back outside stairs. Once inside their four-room dwelling, Doris put Darlene to bed, while her husband watched a television program.

Minutes later, while she was changing her clothes, Doris heard a "light tap" on the window of the back door. Because she was only half dressed, she called to her husband to answer the door. Seconds later she heard two shots fired followed by her daughter screaming, "Daddy, don't die! Daddy, don't die!"

The first bullet struck Richard Stanley in the face, near his nose, and passed completely through his head and exited out the back. The second shot ripped through his right shoulder, and imbedded itself in the doorframe of Darlene's room. The gunmen fled down the stairs and escaped.

Doris found her husband lying in the hallway bleeding profusely. She ran downstairs to the landlord to use the telephone. After phoning the police she ran back upstairs where she found Stanley struggling to breathe. After making a second call to police she returned to find her husband now seated on the couch where he remained until the ambulance arrived.

Stanley was rushed to Trumbull Memorial Hospital but, due to the nature of the head wound, was transferred to St. Elizabeth's. On the trip to Youngstown, a

Warren detective rode with Stanley. The wounded man said he could not identify his attacker as the man fired as soon as he lifted the shade to the door. Once Stanley arrived at St. Elizabeth's doctors worked on him for nearly two hours. By midnight he was listed in "very critical" condition. The next day it was reported that "for the next few days his chances of survival still are 'very doubtful.'"

Police immediately set out to round up all the mobsters Stanley was involved with. Aiello was picked up in downtown Youngstown; Dominic Senzarino was arrested at his home in Struthers; Zimmerman was arrested in Cleveland; Carabbia and Willie Napoli turned themselves in to the Warren police the next day; and Donald "Bull" Jones had just been sentenced the previous day to a term of 8 to 18 years for burglary and was in the Mercer, Pennsylvania jail. Later, Carabbia and Napoli's alibi that they were in Cleveland checked out. Zimmerman was babysitting and Senzarino was watching television at a girlfriend's house.

The morning after the shooting, two 12 year-old junior high school girls were on their way to school near the scene of the attack. One of them let out a cry, "Oh, look at the big gun." She ran over, picked it up and pointed it at her friend. Scared, the friend told her not to point the weapon at her. She then aimed it at the ground and pulled the trigger. At the sound of the shot a neighbor ran out and took the weapon away from the startled young girl and called police. Detectives sent the .45 caliber Remington-Rand Army issue automatic, along with the recovered slugs, to the Bureau of Criminal Investigation.

While several of the men taken in for questioning were released within 24 hours, police kept Aiello for more than three days. Warren police ordered him held at the Niles jail under the watchful eye of Niles Police Chief John Ross. The newspaper reported, "Ross ordered Aiello confined to his cell and given no bullpen freedom like other prisoners. He was released only occasionally to walk to a fountain for a drink of water. As a result, Aiello was sporting a heavy growth of beard. He received the customary fare of four cheese sandwiches daily. On Sunday, like other prisoners, he had hamburgers. Aiello remained cheerful, in spite of the fact that he had no exercise, limited food, no conversation and no reading material."

Aiello apparently used the incident to show that his spirit couldn't be broken. "He was very philosophical about the whole thing," Ross told reporters. "He told me that it was the most rest he's had all his life. He must have been pretty tired."

Once released, Aiello filed a motion to have the charges against him dropped because he was denied the right to a speedy trial. Prosecutor Griffith responded that since his January 1959 indictment, Aiello had never requested a trial. Judge Birrell dismissed the motion. Aiello's scheduled trial date of April 10 was obviously postponed because of the shooting.

Around 5:00 on the morning of April 23, a fight broke out inside the Purple Cow. The disturbance began between six men seated at one table and two men sitting with their wives in a booth. One man from the group of six insulted the wife of amateur boxing champ Frank Lentine, who were both seated in the booth. Lentine started swinging and two policemen seated in the restaurant moved the participants outside. Meanwhile, after two of the remaining men made disparaging remarks about Lentine, Aiello and Charles Carabbia, who were also present, bloodied the two men and then quickly fled the restaurant. Claiming that the drunken brawl was a political plot and that, "These gangsters are against me," Mayor Franko ordered the arrests of Aiello and Carabbia as well as an investigation into why the police didn't arrest the pair in the first place. Both men appeared before Judge Hanni and were released on their own recognizance pending a hearing set for the following month.

The next weekend, Aiello was hauled in for questioning again after the Metropolitan Club, described as a "downtown liquor cheat spot," was raided. Police believed Aiello was the "real operator" of the club and James "Dankers" Petrella, who was arrested during the raid, was managing it for "Fats." Aiello told vice squad interrogators that, "If anyone can prove I'm in anything illegal at this time I'll jump off the roof of City Hall." Aiello admitted to knowing Petrella, but denied any connection to the club. Meanwhile, the embattled Mayor Franko promised to suspend members of the vice squad, including his handpicked leader Nicholas Pavelko, for failing to close the club earlier. Pavelko claimed his inquiries into the club determined it to be a members only social club and that one of his own vice squad men belonged. After its opening, vice squad members reported to him that only "social gathering" was taking place there.

After Richard Stanley recovered from his wounds and was able to testify, the trial of Ronald Carabbia began. Unfortunately for Prosecutor Griffith, the jury acquitted Carabbia. Deciding that any further prosecution would be a waste of the taxpayer's money, and because he was unable to obtain any additional corroborating witnesses, Griffith dropped the charges against Aiello, Napoli and Jones on May 12.

The year 1962 was not a good one for the 48 year-old Aiello. During the previous two years the on-going gang war claimed the lives of former friends and business associates Sandy Naples, Vince DeNiro and Mike Farah. Aiello was beginning to feel the heat. In mid-February, Aiello was nailed with another speeding ticket. Fined $50, Judge Martin P. Joyce suspended $45 when Aiello agreed to attend court school classes on driving.

At the end of the month, the "A" Lounge, where Aiello was drawing a steady paycheck, came under fire from James H. Barber, superintendent of the Youngstown district of the Ohio State Liquor Department's enforcement division. Barber cited the plush lounge because of Aiello's felony convictions in

Springfield, Illinois, from the early 1930s. Barber recited a state law that explained: "The board may suspend or revoke a permit for conviction of the permit holder or his agent of a felony. No person heretofore convicted of any felony shall receive or be permitted to retain any permit, nor shall such person have an interest, direct or indirect, in any permit." Aiello's name was immediately removed from the payroll and he was rumored to have been "laid off," at least temporarily. Prior to a January 1963 hearing on the matter, Barber said he had a notarized statement signed by Bombolis outlining his oral agreement with Aiello. Part of the agreement provided for Aiello to receive ten percent of the profits "if business warrants." At the time of the citation Aiello was receiving $200 a week for his "services." Without providing a reason, the *Vindicator* reported on February 5, 1963, that the board had dismissed two citations against Bombolis and the lounge.

On March 28, Aiello was stopped for speeding, going 41 in a 25mph-speed zone, by Patrolmen Peter Novosel and William E. Gruver. As Aiello reached to get his registration Novosel noticed a bulge beneath his sports coat. The gambler explained to police, "My life has been threatened. I've got the thing that makes all men equal and I'm going to get them before they get me."

Police confiscated the .45 caliber handgun and arrested Aiello for carrying a concealed weapon, suspicion and speeding. The newspaper reported, "The usually dapper hoodlum was unshaven and haggard looking when arrested." At the station Aiello claimed that several months back a woman named Aiello, but not related to him, received an anonymous telephone threat stating, "Your husband Fats is the next to get killed." Despite his protest that he had a right to protect his life and that police had no right to search him without a warrant, Aiello was placed in a cell where he spent the night.

Aiello appeared with his attorney, Eugene Fox, the next day before Judge Hanni. The judge set a preliminary hearing date for April 13. When the apparently superstitious Fox reminded Hanni that it was Friday the 13th, the judge moved it back a day. Aiello was released on a $1,000 bond provided by Mario Guerrieri of the Acme Bonding Company.

On April 9, Aiello was stopped again for speeding, making it his third citation of the year. Ironically he was stopped on the same street by the same police officers, Gruver and Novosel, that had clocked him for speeding on radar less than two weeks earlier.

"Oh no! Not again! Are you guys trying to be funny?" Aiello cried out. The speed-limit-challenged gambler told the officers he wanted a summons "like an ordinary citizen" and to be released to go about his business. Instead, the policemen escorted him to the police station for booking. Aiello was told to post a $25 bond or spend the night in jail again. Since Aiello "reportedly carried little money on his person," he sent a boy to get the money for his release. The next morning, Judge Leskovyansky fined Aiello $50 and again suspended $45 if he agreed to attend classes. In addition, the judge suspended his license for three days.

It should be noted that in the last two arrests, Aiello was not driving his own car. In the April incident he was driving a car which belonged to the wife of an "A" Lounge employee, while the second vehicle belonged to a girlfriend. This was the same practice Vince DeNiro adhered to when his enemies were stalking him.

After Aiello's second speeding arrest in a two-week period, the *Vindicator* published an editorial that for the first time didn't blast the gambler since they started writing about him in 1946. The editorial claimed that the 25-mile speed limit in Marshall Street, where Aiello was stopped twice, "may be a little unrealistic." They concluded, however, that, "In any case, 40 miles is too fast."

Incredibly, just like Aiello's previous court cases the speeding tickets became a long, drawn out affair. Due to the ticketing officer's mix-up, the affidavit describing the violation specified the charge as "reckless driving." Attorney Fox got the police to admit that the speed and conditions Aiello was driving under were not unsafe for weather or road conditions on Marshall Street. In court on April 12, Leskovyansky fined Aiello $50 and suspended his license for 90 days for reckless driving. Fox then objected on the grounds that his client was arrested for speeding, pointing out that Ohio case law supported his contention that reckless driving and speeding "are not identical charges," concluding that his client was being tried for something he was not charged with. Stating that it was the "court's right to pass up superfluous language in affidavits," Leskovyansky overruled Fox's request for a dismissal, but postponed execution of the sentence pending a motion for a new trial.

On Saturday, April 14, the preliminary hearing into the concealed weapons charge was held before Judge Hanni. The arresting officer claimed that after he stopped Aiello and realized he was armed, he "feared for his life." Using the fact that there was a burned out light on the car, he ordered Aiello out to look at it before questioning him about what he had hidden under his coat. "He asked me if I had a search warrant, then I said I was placing him under arrest," Officer Peter Novosel told the judge. "He said, 'I'd like to give you and your partner a half-yard." Novosel said he didn't know what Aiello meant and wondered if he was talking about concrete (half-yard is a slang term for $50).

Mrs. Margaret Aiello then testified that she had received telephone calls for the gambler for the past 15 years even though she wasn't related and had never met him. During October 1961, she received a call and was given the message "You tell Fats that Scardine is going to get him!" Mrs. Aiello said she called the police and informed them about the threat. "I assumed they notified Mr. Aiello," she said. Detectives Gerald Brace and Joseph Zetts investigated the threat and testified that they stopped at the "A" Lounge and informed Aiello of the threat.

Attorney Fox claimed this threat gave his client the reason to carry a concealed weapon. Judge Hanni ruled first that the search by the police officer was a "legitimate procedure" in making the arrest. As to the concealed weapons charge, the judge claimed the motion to dismiss was "out of his jurisdiction in the preliminary hearing." Hanni then turned the matter over for the grand jury to consider action. On May 3, the grand jury indicted Aiello for carrying a concealed weapon.

Moving into 1963, Aiello had more to worry about than just his legal matters. On the evening of January 9, Youngstown police received a telephone call from a woman who stated, "I live in Greenbriar, and they are going to blow up Fats Aiello's home. This is not a crank call." The police immediately notified Austintown officials where Aiello's home was located at 4465 Woodridge Drive. The one-story Cape Cod home was in a new development called Greenbriar. Police set up a vigil to watch Aiello's home and the neighborhood. Detectives notified Aiello of the threat at the "A" Lounge, and he did not return home that night.

On the last day of February 1963, the trial for the concealed weapons charge got underway. Aiello was represented by Eugene Fox in Judge Cavalier's courtroom. The Mahoning County Prosecutor was Clyde W. Osborne. Two witnesses from the preliminary hearing before Judge Hanni were called. Margaret Aiello repeated her telephone message that, "You tell Fats that Scardine is going to get him!" Aiello claimed he had no idea who Scardine was.

Officer Novosel again testified about the bribe, but claimed, "No one took it seriously." He stated that on the way to the police wagon, Aiello said, "You guys will be the death of me," and complained about the "splash this will make in the *Vindicator*."

John Bombolis was questioned by Osborne about Aiello's compensation at the "A" Lounge and about some of the clientele the gambler brought in. Bombolis stated that he never paid Aiello a percentage of the profits because "business did not get that good." The lounge owner claimed the presence of municipal judges Hanni, Joyce and Leskovyansky in the place was "due to Aiello."

The highlight of the trial was the testimony of Aiello. The gambler was questioned about many topics, but mostly regarding the threats made to him. Aiello told the court that after police notified him about the threat made through Margaret Aiello, he walked down the street from the "A" Lounge to police headquarters to see the chief and ask for protection. When informed that the chief was out, he spoke to then vice squad chief George Millovich. According to Aiello, Millovich told him, "We can't protect a guy like you; you'll just have to protect yourself the best way you know how." Aiello then told the jury, "This is the only way [having a gun] I knew how."

During cross-examination, the newspaper reported, "Osborne asked if Aiello had made a statement to be published in a national magazine that he had received a warning bouquet of one dozen white roses indicating that his life was in danger. He denied such a statement or saying that he was not scared."

Aiello was also questioned about his mysterious leg wound in 1960 and yet another version of the shooting was told. This time Aiello denied driving himself to the hospital, but instead was "assisted by a couple of strangers when he passed out." The prosecution had called Gus Leamis as a rebuttal witness, but the proprietor of the Greek Coffee House was a no-show.

On March 1, the jury deliberated for nearly six and half hours before announcing to Judge Cavalier that they were deadlocked. They were reported to be at nine for conviction and three for acquittal. At 9:30 that night, Cavalier dismissed the jury and declared a mistrial. Osborne said he would retry Aiello.

Three days after the trial's conclusion, an insurance man and his wife, living in Austintown, received an interesting telephone message. "Fats is going to get it tonight," the caller advised. The couple immediately notified police, who quickly figured out why the couple had received the call. Their telephone number was the former listing for a Nick Aiello, who had asked that it be discontinued under his name. The next afternoon, "Fats" Aiello was almost in a bragging mood as he told a Youngstown police sergeant having tea at the Dutch House restaurant, "Didn't you know about the last threat I received?" Aiello told him that he was planning to "see the prosecuting attorney [to] get the matter straightened out."

On March 6, Mahoning County sheriff's deputies and city detectives sat down with Aiello. The gambler boasted, "If anyone wants me, tell the yellow dog to contact me and quit bothering innocent people." Detective Chief John Terlesky and Assistant Chief deputy Sheriff Orlando DiLullo were both of the opinion that Aiello was making a big deal of the incident to "magnify the defense" of his carrying a weapon to protect himself in his pending re-trial. For all they knew, Aiello could have placed the threatening call himself.

Nothing seemed to be going right for the Valley's most publicized gambler. During the fall of 1962 Aiello's favorite hangout, the Purple Cow, closed. In early 1963, he lost his job and another hangout, the "A" Lounge, when the IRS closed the plush bar for non-payment of back taxes. Aiello's newest spot was the Dutch House, which had extended its hours to remain open overnight after the closing of the Purple Cow. Now the Dutch House was coming under fire as a new harassment campaign was initiated by the police department.

Under Police Chief William R. Golden, former vice squad leader Dan Maggianetti was made chief of the police Intelligence and Security squad, known as the I & S. Sparked by a number of local robberies, a recent attempted safecracking at the Waterford Park Race Track in Chester, West Virginia, and "numerous complaints ...of known underworld figures hanging about the downtown area in the early hours," Maggianetti responded. On April 9, 1963, Aiello was holding court at the Dutch House along with Dominic Senzarino, Richard Dota and Steve Kandis. Around 3:00 a.m. William E. Gruver, who was present for Aiello's two speeding tickets in the spring of 1962, and his partner, a young officer who made a name for himself in years to come as both Youngstown police chief and Mahoning County sheriff – Randall A. "Duke" Wellington walked in and arrested all four. They were held in jail until their attorneys filed petitions for their release. As the men were leaving the police station one was overheard to say, "They got to keep us in jail all night to tell us to stay out of town?"

Maggianetti explained the I & S's new position to the press. Asserting that the arrests were the beginning of a "harassment program" against local hoodlums he stated, "We have been looking for all hoodlums in the downtown area and other sections of the city to learn what they are doing. They may as well make up their minds to stay in after dark or go to jail." Maggianetti made reference to the "hoodlums" new hangout. "The Dutch House is getting a reputation as a hangout for hoodlums. If the owner doesn't clean them out, we will take action by having his city restaurant and soft drink licenses removed."

The owner of the establishment, Michael Paul, was quick to reply telling reporters, "I'm trying to run a decent place and serve everybody. In fact, the police chief and a lot of policemen eat here every day. When these so-called hoodlums come in here they behave, eat and leave. We can't keep them from coming in. We serve everyone. It's up to the police department to get rid of them."

Twenty-four hours after being arrested, Aiello was in police custody again after running a red light at South Hazel and West Federal Streets. Unable to produce his driver's license, Aiello was arrested again. Ironically, it was the same I & S officers who had arrested him at the Dutch House, Gruver and Wellington.

Aiello posted a $75 bond and was released shortly after 4:00 a.m., and told to return for traffic court later that morning. As was his custom, Judge Leskovyansky lectured all the "erring motorists" as a group before hearing the individual cases. Aiello's name was called first and when the judge realized the gambler was out in the corridor and did not hear his lecture, he became irate. "He belongs in here and not in the hall. If he thinks he will get special privileges, he will when he appears before the court," a sarcastic Leskovyansky bellowed.

Aiello's case was heard last, at which time his attorney apologized profusely stating that his client was waiting for him in the corridor while he was busy in another courtroom. Fox entered a not guilty plea and a hearing date was set. When the time for the hearing came, on April 26, as was his custom, the gambler asked for a trial by jury delaying the case for two months.

On June 17, Aiello pleaded guilty to the "misdemeanor section" of the concealed weapons laws and asked the court for probation. Aiello, who was looking at as much as up to six months in jail, was free to get his affairs in order while Judge Cavalier had George Hadnett, still working as the area's probation officer, review his record.

Before the sentence came down, Aiello decided to withdraw his request for a jury trial for running the red light and pleaded no-contest before Leskovyansky on June 26. The judge fined him $10 and suspended his license for 60 days, granting him permission to drive himself home. The judge dismissed the second charge for driving without a license when Aiello was able to produce a valid license.

Two days later, Aiello found out that he wouldn't need a car for the next 60 days as that was the sentence handed down by Judge Cavalier for the concealed weapons charge. Aiello was ordered jailed immediately. During the sentencing hearing attorney Fox, who requested probation, told the court, "that police urged Aiello to get a legitimate job, and then after he did so, the police and present city administration moved in to ruin John Bombolis, Aiello's employer." Fox also claimed that his client was being discriminated against "because he is a police character and because he has been 'good press' here for years for his gambling and hoodlum activities."

Prosecutor Osborne said that Aiello was "a denizen of the underworld." He stated, "In my estimation this man is primarily responsible as one man can be for the poor reputation Youngstown has had nationally in recent years."

Denying Fox's request for probation, Judge Cavalier suggested that when Aiello is released from prison that he move out of Youngstown "for his own and the community's good."

In a June 30, 1963, editorial, the *Vindicator* took exception to comments made by attorney Fox:

> "We can't be sure what the defense counsel meant by 'good press.' However, we do wish to make it clear at this time that this newspaper can do without the kind of 'good press' created by crime and those who violate laws. This is the kind of news which must be handled when it occurs, but this or any other reputable newspaper would prefer to do without it. The city's reputation had been badly smeared by such news."

Aiello finished his 60-day term and was released on the morning of August 26. It was the longest time the notorious gambler had spent behind bars to date. Few doubted he would heed Judge Cavalier's advice, though, and leave town.

Three weeks later, the Ohio Highway Patrol arrested Aiello after he ran a stop light at Route 422 and North Road. Giving his home address as Wesley Avenue, he was freed after posting a $50 bond. The next day a Trumbull County judge fined him $15 and costs.

It was during this time that Aiello was called to testify by the state arson investigator who was leading the probe into the murder of Dominic Moio.

In his continuing harassment campaign to keep underworld figures off the streets of Youngstown, Maggianetti had Aiello arrested and brought in for questioning on the morning of November 1, 1963. The I & S chief told reporters, "I talked to him myself, and I told him to stay out of the downtown area." Before leaving, after three hours of questioning, Aiello told an officer that he was going to the Common Pleas Court to get an injunction against further police harassment.

The beginning of the end for the gambler began on March 3, 1964 when the Youngstown police announced it had received a request to pick up Aiello from the police department in Warrensville Heights, a small suburb located on the South-east side of Cleveland. Aiello was wanted on a charge of aiding and abetting in an abortion. The Youngstown police said they expected the gambler to appear soon with his attorney although the "racket figure has not been seen in his usual haunts."

As details of the abortion ring, of which Aiello was said to be the "mastermind" were revealed, the gambler stayed in deep hiding – except to emerge and collect another traffic citation. On March 13, Aiello was one of four people indicted by the Cuyahoga County grand jury. Also indicted were Joseph White of Shenango Township near New Castle, Pennsylvania, Abe Kottler and Anna Dominiak from the Cleveland area.

White was charged with performing abortions for $500 each on two Cleveland area women – aged 22 and 26 – both of whom later had to be hospitalized. The women were granted immunity from prosecution. The indictment alleged that Aiello took the women to the Turfside Motor Lodge on Northfield Road in Warrensville Heights where the abortions were performed.

On April 6, Aiello was arrested by two FBI agents as he sat in a restaurant at the Sahara Motel in Cleveland. The agents had gone to the motel on another matter and decided to have lunch there. Earl B. Brown, special agent-in-charge of the Cleveland office, had once interrogated Aiello after one of the many fatal car bombings in the city. The agent recognized the gambler and arrested him without incident. Aiello was taken before a U.S. Commissioner and charged with unlawful flight to avoid prosecution before being released into the hands of the Cuyahoga County sheriff. Taken to the county common pleas court, Aiello pled not guilty and was released on a $5,000 bond.

Aiello had been in hiding since February 29, when he first heard Warrensville Heights police were looking for him. Two days prior to that, he was stopped for making an illegal turn on Market Street. When he failed to appear for a hearing on March 11, Judge Leskovyansky issued a bench warrant for his arrest. Once he posted bail in Cleveland and returned to Youngstown, he was brought before the judge where he pleaded guilty. Leskovyansky suspended his license for five days and fined him $50, then offered to suspend the obligatory $45 if Aiello agreed to attend traffic school for three sessions.

While waiting for the abortion trial to begin, Aiello was called to testify before the Mahoning County grand jury in May 1964, during Prosecutor Clyde Osborne's racket's probe. On May 29, after refusing to answer questions before the grand jury, Judge David Jenkins jailed Aiello. The newspaper reported, "After sentencing Aiello to 10 days for direct contempt in his court," Judge Jenkins ordered Aiello imprisoned "until he performs the order of the court." After spending just four hours in jail, Aiello was released on a $5,000 bond, which was granted by the 7th District Court of Appeals late in the afternoon. On August 3, the same court which set bond for the gambler, overruled Jenkins' 10 day sentence, but ruled that Aiello must "purge" himself of the contempt of grand jury charges or go to jail.

Aiello had more serious problems to be concerned with other than the contempt charge. After numerous delays, the abortion trial finally got underway with jury selection on June 7, 1965, more than a year after the indictment. The next day a Cuyahoga County jury of six men and six women began hearing testimony. Jean Walker, a 23 year-old, who testified that her boyfriend had gotten her pregnant, detailed her ordeal. Five months into her pregnancy Walker finally confronted her boyfriend with the facts. The boyfriend made arrangements for an abortion. On February 20, 1964, Walker and the other women, a 27 year-old identified as Miss White, met at a Cleveland Heights restaurant where they were joined by Anna Dominiak of East Cleveland. Dominiak, who was tried later with Abe Kottler for their roles, introduced the two young ladies to Aiello. The group then left, driven by Aiello, and headed to the Turfside Motor Lodge in Warrensville Heights. Along the way both women were nervous but, Walker testified, Aiello assured them that everything would be all right – they were in the hands of a competent doctor. "Ladies, only one out of a thousand miss. If you girls miss, come back. We won't charge you anything," Walker quoted Aiello.

When they arrived at the hotel, Aiello led them to Room 59 where Joseph White was waiting with a satchel and a "heat sterilizer." White also assured both women that there was nothing to worry about. "In a couple of weeks you will be laughing about this," White told them.

Walker went first and the procedure was performed with both Aiello and the other women watching. When the second procedure was complete, both women were handed an envelope with three pills and instructed to "take them after you abort, could be anytime." Nine days later, Miss White became ill and was hospitalized at Euclid-Glenville Hospital. That same day Walker was admitted to Suburban Community Hospital. One woman was determined to have had a miscarriage the day after the abortion, while the other gave birth to stillborn twins on February 29. Attending physicians reported both incidents to the police. The doctor who treated Miss White testified that the instrument used in her procedure caused an infection to develop.

The Warrensville Heights detective-sergeant who conducted the investigation testified that they tracked down Joseph White from the license number he listed on the register at the motor lodge. While he was being booked, the detective noticed that the signature on the fingerprint card matched the one on the register; a fact later confirmed by a handwriting expert that prosecutors called. While White was being transported back to Warrensville Heights, the detective told the court he admitted to him that he was not a doctor but a lumber salesman.

The detective then stated that the women told him that the man who drove them to the motor lodge was introduced to them as "Fats." Police photographs were shown to the women and they both picked out Aiello's picture.

On Monday, June 14, the prosecution rested its case. The defense was built on the fact that the men were falsely identified by the women. The next day, Aiello took the stand where he denied that he played any part in the abortion – that he never knew the women or their boyfriends, had never been to the Turfside Motor Lodge and had never met Joseph White. In addition, he could not recall where he was that night. White did not take the stand. Aiello was followed by one of the boyfriends who told the court he had never met either of the defendants and had made the arrangements for the abortion through a man named "Pete," whom he paid $500.

Defense attorneys called Abe Kottler to the stand. Accused of helping to have arranged the abortion with Aiello, Kottler invoked his Fifth Amendment rights and refused to answer questions. Two others charged in the case did not answer subpoenas to appear and testify.

Eugene Fox, who was co-counsel with prominent Cleveland attorney Elmer Guiliani, had told the jury in his opening statement that police had pulled Aiello's name "out of a hat." To prove this point, Fox called as their final witness a member of the Cleveland Police Department's record division who testified that their felony files contained 17 individuals with the nickname "Fats." Under cross-examination, however, the officer admitted that only two of the men were white.

After closing arguments, the jury got the case on the afternoon of June 16. After less than three hours of deliberations they returned around 5:30 with a verdict of guilty on both counts. Judge Jackson immediately pronounced sentence on the pair giving them one-to-seven years on each conviction to be served consecutively. Aiello was looking at a stretch of up to 14 years.

On July 10, Jackson denied their motion for a new trial, but continued bond on both men, which he had increased to $10,000 after the convictions. Their next move was to appeal to the district appellate court. Three months later, while the appeal was still being considered, Aiello made news when his gall bladder was removed at St. Elizabeth's.

The appeals process dragged on through all of 1966. In February 1967, after the Cuyahoga County Court of Appeals upheld the lower court's decision, attorney Fox prepared his appeal to the Ohio Supreme Court. The state's highest court heard arguments on May 25. Six days later, the Ohio Supreme Court dismissed the appeals. Fox filed an appeal to the U.S. Supreme Court and asked for a stay of execution pending the outcome. The prosecution opposed the stay and the judge concurred. On July 13, Aiello and White entered the Ohio Penitentiary to begin their sentences.

Aiello was in prison just three months before Fox filed a motion to have his sentence reduced to just a single term of one-to-seven years. Judge Jackson heard arguments on October 17. Aiello was an ill man and suffered several heart attacks while incarcerated. After serving less than two years he was paroled on May 1, 1969.

After his release from prison Aiello kept a low profile. The heart attacks had slowed the aging gambler, who was still a relatively young man. Over the next few years he worked as an inspector for the American Concrete Company. During the early hours of Sunday morning, December 14, 1975, the 62 year-old Aiello suffered another heart attack at his Woodridge Avenue home. Rushed to St. Elizabeth's Hospital, Aiello was pronounced dead at 4:00 a.m.

Demise of "Moosey" Caputo

In November 1943, Dominic "Moosey" Caputo's son was mentioned in the newspaper when it was revealed that his father was given a Thanksgiving furlough to spend with the family since the son was inducted into the service. Seventeen years later John J. Caputo was making his own news. John, known as Jackie, was sent to a military academy during his unruly teen years. Described as a "good-hearted kid," his problems, like that of his Uncle Frank were initiated when he was drinking. In Girard, on November 20, 1960, John Caputo and a companion entered a bar after having driven their vehicle off the road. A police officer arrived to investigate the incident and was told the two men had entered a bar just a short distance away. When the officer went in he found Caputo and his companion drunk and fighting – he arrested both of them. After they were searched police found football pools, horse race betting tickets and more than $1,000. On December 3, Caputo pled guilty to all charges. He was fined $50 for possession of gambling devices, $10 for resisting arrest and $5 for creating a disturbance.

By early 1963, the Tri State Social Club, which Moosey was associated with during the late 1950s, changed its name to the Jockey Club. On February 16, FBI agents raided the casino and arrested eleven men, including Dominic Caputo. Agents broke down the doors and, in addition to the arrests, seized slot machines, roulette wheels, dice and blackjack tables, and a large amount of cash. Four days later, a total of 13 people were indicted by a federal grand jury in Wheeling and charged with "traveling interstate for purposes of operating a gambling casino." All pled not guilty at arraignment.[6]

Although Caputo requested a non-jury trial, Federal Judge Charles Paul, Jr. denied it and the case was scheduled to be heard on Monday, April 1. On the first day of trial, 10 of the 13 defendants were freed after charges against them were dropped. Five were released when Judge Paul ordered a directed verdict of acquittal after a defense motion, which claimed "the government had failed to prove a complicated technicality in federal law regarding the defendant's residency." The second group of five had charges against them dismissed, "after government lawyers said they were unable to prove the defendants had knowledge of certain facts pertinent to the charges."

The three remaining defendants were Caputo, Charles F. Teemer, the owner of the Jockey Club, and Joseph Pecora, who managed the club in Teemer's absence. Caputo was not mentioned as being in management or ownership of the club. The prosecutor in his opening statement called Caputo a "boxman," and stating he deposited money in an East Liverpool bank in Teemer's name. The charges were reduced to three counts accusing the men of "conspiracy, and intent to violate a federal statute governing interstate travel to promote, manage and establish a gambling establishment." In his opening statement defense attorney Gilbert Bachman conceded that gambling took place at the Jockey Club in violation of West Virginia law, however, it did not violate federal law.

Testimony got underway with two FBI agents from the Pittsburgh office telling jurors they had made eight trips the Jockey Club and witnessed "free parking, free hat-checking, free whiskey and other enticements to attract gamblers."

After the government rested its case on Tuesday afternoon, Judge Paul ordered an acquittal for Joseph Pecora stating that charges had failed to be proven. Charges of conspiracy against the other two were also dropped. The defense then began their case and called only one witness – Charles Teemer. The defendant testified that he had owned the Jockey Club for four and a half years and was aware of new federal laws passed in September 1961. He claimed he had a meeting about the new statutes with a local attorney. "We discussed the law in general and came to the conclusion the main issue in the new law was residency," Teemer told the jury. After that meeting he gathered his 65 employees and announced they would have to live in West Virginia in order to work at the Jockey Club. Caputo had already presented the court with an affidavit proving his residency in the state. Teemer concluded with, "I thought I was 100 percent within the federal law," and stated that, as his employee, Caputo "did only what he was told," which was to deposit the clubs checks.

In their closing arguments, prosecutors described Caputo as Teemer's "loyal and trusted employee" as he acted as doorman at the club "with X-ray eyes who could see if a man had money in his pockets." The jury deliberated just two hours before coming back with a verdict of acquittal for both men. While Caputo and Teemer were all smiles, the judge was anything but elated as he delivered a "public dressing down" of federal officials. The *Vindicator* reported:

> "Judge Charles F. Paul, Jr. stated, 'Before you seek and obtain an indictment by a federal grand jury be satisfied of the following:
> 1. That you understand what the federal law is.
> 2. That a violation of the federal law, as opposed to the state law, has occurred.
> 3. That you have enough evidence ...to at least carry the case to the jury.

Judge Paul claimed that had those rules been followed the defendants would not have been indicted and federal law enforcement agencies would not have been embarrassed by the action he was compelled to take. The only victory the government could claim was the pending destruction of $20,000 worth of gambling equipment.

Caputo was free and clear of legal problems for a week. He then appeared in a Weirton, West Virginia, court where he was fined $50 by a magistrate on a state gambling charge of being the "doorkeeper" at the Jockey Club in connection with the February 16 raid.

Caputo's April 1963, fine was the last time any news appeared about him in the local newspapers. He returned to Hollywood, Florida, where in the late 1960s Margaret became stricken with leukemia. Caputo spent the last twelve years of Margaret's life caring for her until she passed away around 1981. Caputo then lived with a son in Stuart, Florida until his death at the ripe old age of 90 on June 13, 1993.

Demise of "Joe the Wolf" DiCarlo

On June 14 and 15, 1960, Senate hearings were held in Washington D.C. Officially called the "Hearings before the Subcommittee On Antitrust And Monopoly," the newspapers referred to them as the "Kefauver Boxing Scandals" or the "Kefauver Anti-monopoly Subcommittee Hearings." Part of the testimony covered the infamous Apalachin Summit. James P. McShane, a subcommittee staff member gave testimony on DiCarlo and his connections to John C. Montana[7] and other Buffalo attendees to the meeting, of which Montana was an arrested participant. McShane reported, "An investigating agency also has informed us that Montana was very closely associated with DiCarlo in Buffalo. DiCarlo at that time was affiliated with the labor and union rackets. DiCarlo was a power in Buffalo politics and the subcommittee information is that he backed and advised Montana in his political moves."

On June 16, the *Buffalo Courier-Express* reported more of McShane's testimony to the subcommittee:

> "'In 1934,' he testified, 'Joe DiCarlo was characterized by a Buffalo police chief as Buffalo's Public Enemy No. 1. He and his brother, Sam DiCarlo, controlled the pinball operations in Buffalo in the early 1930s. The DiCarlo brothers, with John Torrolone (sic), Philip Mangano, Joseph Calafata and Sam Pieri, were the Buffalo representatives of the Detroit Purple Gang.'
>
> "'Sam Pieri, a brother-in-law of the DiCarlos, has a criminal record which reflects over 40 arrests.'
>
> "'And in closing,' the witness concluded, 'it is interesting to note that DiCarlo was observed with Frank Carbo at Eddy Coco's murder trial in Miami in 1953.'"

It was at Eddie Coco's[8] murder trial that DiCarlo was spotted by Dan Sullivan of the Greater Miami Crime Commission and arrested shortly afterward. Frank "Frankie" Carbo, a onetime member of the notorious Murder, Inc. gang and involved in the West Coast murder of Harry "Big Greenie Greenberg" Gottesman in November 1939 with Benjamin "Bugsy" Siegel, was long associated with the Lucchese Family and the underworld hold on professional boxing as a promoter. Boxing was the main topic of these hearings at which Carbo was described, "as someone whose evil influence extended to fighters, managers, and promoters throughout the country." At the time of the hearings, Carbo was incarcerated, serving a two-year term for managing boxers in New York without a license.

The key witness to testify at these hearings was Jake "the Raging Bull" LaMotta, the former middleweight boxing champ. He told Senate investigators that he was offered $100,000 to throw a fight to Youngstown boxer Tony Janiro on June 6, 1947. LaMotta declined the offer and won a decision over the local fighter in Madison Square Garden.

Later that year, LaMotta said he was again offered $100,000 to "take a dive" against another fighter, Billy Fox. This time LaMotta said he rejected the money, but agreed to throw the fight in exchange for a guaranteed shot at the middleweight title. LaMotta lost on a fourth-round technical knockout to Fox on November 14, 1947, in Madison Square Garden. LaMotta then got his title shot, beating champ Marcel Cerdan in Detroit in 1949, but claimed he had to pay $20,000 for the opportunity.

Based on the information provided by LaMotta, the Senate committee investigators immediately began looking for DiCarlo in Miami as the man who offered $100,000 for Janiro to win. Locally it was reported that in the mid-1940s, "DiCarlo and Janiro often were seen together in a Youngstown restaurant where Tony idled away some of his off-training hours and where DiCarlo met with his gambling lieutenants and hangers-on." A reporter tracked down Janiro in New York City. The 33 year-old was now retired from the ring, married with a son, and working as a stagehand in the city. Janiro was questioned about LaMotta's testimony.

"I can't believe it," he replied.

When asked about his relationship with DiCarlo, Janiro responded, "I knew him, but not too well. I saw him once or twice in New York, not in Youngstown. I hardly remember talking to him." The reporter then inquired if he had ever been offered a bribe. Janiro answered, "That bribe stuff's movie picture stuff. My hands are clean, I was never approached."

Just days after the revelations in Washington, D.C. the *Courier-Express* published a rather scurrilous article about DiCarlo. It began, "Evidence is accumulating here that Joe DiCarlo, Buffalo's erstwhile public enemy No. 1 has fallen on lean days. Once he was feared by Buffalo, Youngstown and Miami Beach mobsters as the 'Boss,' the 'wolf' or the 'muscle' but those in the know say that in recent years crime definitely has not paid off for Joe."

The article claimed that further evidence of DiCarlo's financial fall came in his inability to pay off the $5,000 fine from his 1924 conviction until 1957. While many believed this was just a stalling attempt by DiCarlo, it is unusual that he took it to the extent that colleagues such as John "Johnny King" Angersola and Mike Coppola had to be dragged into court with him because of it.

Another item cited was an embarrassing incident in 1955 when Cleveland mob heavyweight Frank Brancato,[9] a former hitman for the Mayfield Road Mob, was called before a House committee to testify. In 1948, DiCarlo backed the wrong team when the Cleveland Indians beat the Boston Braves in the World Series. Brancato vouched for DiCarlo to a Cleveland bookie who extended the gambler $16,000 credit. "I told the bookie that Joe was all right, so the bookmaker extended him credit for the $16,000. And Joe hasn't paid it yet..." Brancato claimed DiCarlo welshed on the bet.

In Miami, following LaMotta's testimony, after searching for DiCarlo for two and half months, federal marshals found him on September 1 playing hearts at the Mid-Town Social Club in central Miami. He was handed a subpoena and ordered to appear before the committee. DiCarlo's first date to be questioned, October 18, was postponed at the request of a former president of the international boxing association, who was scheduled to be a "key" witness. When the committee reconvened on December 5, DiCarlo was told that he would not be called to testify, but that he remained under subpoena to be called at a later date.

On December 14, 1960, DiCarlo was arrested, along with 38 others, during gambling raids ordered by the Florida attorney general's office and conducted at four locations in Miami and Miami Beach. All of the men were charged with "vagrancy for being present at a gambling establishment." Arrested with DiCarlo at the Mid-Town Social Club were John Angersola and another man described as the "bookmaking wire boss" of Dade County. As the raiders entered the club, someone inside turned off the lights, but they were quickly switched back on. With that DiCarlo bellowed, "What are you trying to do – run up the light bill on this private club?" DiCarlo posted a $250 bond and was released. On February 14, 1961, DiCarlo was fined $100, but claimed he would appeal.

After an absence of eleven years, DiCarlo returned to the Valley on August 26, 1962 amid the bloody turmoil that had taken hold here. DiCarlo moved into a home on Roosevelt Drive in Liberty Township, just outside the Youngstown city limits, that was formerly occupied by the late Vincent Innocenzi and his paramour, and then Philip "Fleegle" Mainer, who was in the Allegheny County workhouse serving a sentence for a burglary conviction. It was reported that, "Rumors began several months ago that DiCarlo was asked to come into the city to see if he could "cut in" on any of the rackets."

On September 13, DiCarlo appeared at police headquarters in Youngstown with Eugene Fox, the mouthpiece of "Fats" Aiello. After being questioned for more than two hours by Vice Squad Lieutenant Michael P. Carney, DiCarlo was allowed to leave. During the session, DiCarlo disclosed that he had rented the Liberty Township house and "might stay a couple of months and visit with friends." With him were Elsie and his two grandchildren. The proud grandfather explained that his daughter in Buffalo was experiencing "domestic problems," and that he might enroll the older child in school here. Vincinetta's marriage appeared to be in shambles after John Johnson's imprisonment in June 1961. He was sentenced to two years in a federal penitentiary for his role in a mail fraud involving worthless oil leases. The Buffalo newspapers were referring to Vincinetta as the "estranged wife." Eventually the couple divorced.

DiCarlo told Carney that he had operated a restaurant in Florida, but recently sold it. Unemployed, he had no immediate plans to look for a job. At the end of his visit, he planned to return to Florida. DiCarlo could shed no light on any of the underworld killings that had recently rocked the Valley. Without offering any names, the *Vindicator* reported, "Grumblings from the underworld already indicate the local racket leaders are unhappy about DiCarlo's reappearance. Reports began circulating that DiCarlo will be told to leave immediately or face trouble."

In late September 1963, the country's first major mob turncoat, Joseph Valachi, gave testimony before a Senate Investigating Subcommittee. Valachi revealed many facts, some believed supplied to him by his FBI handlers, which unlocked Mafia secrets dating back to the 1920s. Valachi's incredible testimony revealed the creation of the five New York City crime families for the first time. Valachi told the subcommittee that Stefano Magaddino was the boss of the Buffalo-Toronto based crime family.

The following month, during additional hearings in Washington D.C., Lieutenant Michael A. Amico, of the Buffalo Police Department Intelligence Bureau, produced a chart for the committee that showed Magaddino as the "boss of the entire western New York area as well as the Ohio Valley area." In this "empire of organized crime," DiCarlo was listed as the "subordinate boss" of the Mahoning Valley.

The following is from the "Hearings Before The Subcommittee On Investigations," from October 1963:

> "Mr. Amico: We also have in the chart Youngstown, Ohio; and I don't mean to depict that as a big threat, but presently in Youngstown we have Joe DiCarlo, very close associate of Magaddino, Montana, and others on our particular chart.
>
> "Joe DiCarlo was quite a menace to Buffalo's Police Department some 10 or 15 or 20 years ago. He was a big man then and he ruled in a violent manner, and since has left for other places, gone down to Florida. He returned to Buffalo a short time and he is presently in Youngstown, Ohio.
>
> "The Chairman: You still regard him as a big man in the syndicate, do you?
>
> "Mr. Amico: In the syndicate; he still has influence in the syndicate and he still has a lot to say."

On October 17, a day after the Senate hearing, an angry Youngstown Police Chief William Golden let it be known he was going to give the lieutenant from the Buffalo intelligence bureau a little history lesson. "There is no one in Youngstown under DiCarlo's control. He controls nothing here and there is no crime boss in Youngstown. I will inform him DiCarlo is not a boss here and that he has not been for some time. DiCarlo came here under the [Mayor] Ralph W. O'Neill administration in the late 1940s. He was forced out of town by the Charles P. Henderson administration and former Police Chief Edward J. Allen. DiCarlo has not been seen in the Youngstown area for several months. There has been a continued program of harassment against all hoodlums and racket figures. We will slap him in jail if he so much as steps into the city," Golden boasted. A week later Golden's letter was reported in the *Buffalo Evening News.*

Since his interview with Youngstown police, more than a year earlier, DiCarlo was rarely seen in the area. Elsie DiCarlo was reported to still be living in the Liberty Township home, but her husband was said to be spending his time between visits in Buffalo.

DiCarlo's last newsworthy item in the Valley came during Mahoning County Prosecutor Clyde Osborne's grand jury investigation during the fall of 1963. Deputies served his subpoena to Elsie at the Liberty Township home. The summons called for DiCarlo to be there on December 1. He did not put in an appearance.

In October 1965 DiCarlo was involved in an automobile accident in Williamsville, New York. The collision left him with eight broken ribs and a charge of driving without a license, which was later dropped. Elsie DiCarlo, his wife of 41 years died on January 17, 1966. DiCarlo then moved into a suite at the Executive Towers.

In *Mob Nemesis*, former FBI Agent Joseph E. Griffin discusses the 1967 arrest of DiCarlo in Buffalo:

> "In early May 1967 I received a telephone call from my informant who said that Joe Todaro Sr. was sponsoring a 'stag party,' which was to be held at Panaro's Snowballs Lounge in Buffalo on May 8, 1967. The informant reported that an illegal craps game would be set up in the basement of the lounge. My informant also said that virtually the entire membership of the Magaddino crime family planned to attend this event."

Griffin contacted the head of the Buffalo Police Department's gambling squad, who had the authority to conduct a liquor inspection of the restaurant. If the mobsters were indeed there they could be arrested "on charges of consorting with each other as known criminals." The plan was for the FBI to "tag along" and afterwards be able to "display to the community evidence that organized crime did in fact exist."

A combined force of federal state and local law enforcement officials began their surveillance at 7:00.p.m. that night. They waited until 10:15 before entering and announcing that they were conducting a liquor inspection. On the first floor of the restaurant dozens of "legitimate people," including judges and businessmen were seated. But downstairs all of the mobsters had congregated including DiCarlo. When Griffin's men couldn't find several of the "key" Mafia people they had witnessed entering the lounge they grew suspicious of a wine cellar that had several padlocks on it. When the owner was ordered to unlock it seven ranking mobsters were found inside sipping wine. Police arrested 36 known underworld figures that night, practically the entire upper echelon of the Buffalo Family with the exception of boss Stefano Magaddino.[10] Several days after the raid charges of consorting were dismissed. Joe Todaro, Sr. filed a lawsuit charging discrimination "against persons of Italian extraction." A judge dismissed the suit. The lounge later lost its liquor license and closed.

After the raid, a *Courier-Express* article reported that DiCarlo's "main occupation, according to one informed source who asked not to be identified, is loan-collecting for underworld clients. The source said that recalcitrant debtors frequently respond to a plan for payment from DiCarlo."

Under the leadership of Stefano Magaddino the Buffalo Mafia was said to have been one of the most stable families in the nation, free of internal strife. That came to an end on November 28, 1968, when the FBI raided the home of Magaddino's son Peter. In searching the house, agents uncovered $500,000 hidden in a trunk. Magaddino told the troops in December 1967 there was no "Christmas bonus" because the "take" that year was inadequate. This revelation caused immediate dissention in the family and it was rumored that Magaddino retired in 1969. The *Courier-Express* reported that, "Members of the Buffalo mob...decided to bring the matter before the commission at a pre-arranged conference in New York City. For Magaddino it was pure disgrace – a justified revolt within his family – and when the commission finally decided the matter in 1969, the Buffalo group was allowed to withdraw from 'Don' Stefano's control and begin operations as a separate entity. Under the commission ruling 'Don' Stefano would be allowed to keep all his enterprises, outside Buffalo, but not be permitted to expand his holdings."

In a February 11, 1973, article the *Courier-Express* wrote:

> "Another step reported by mob sources was the elevation of Joseph DiCarlo to the rank of consiglieri or counselor, a decision seen as an attempt to smooth the break with 'Don' Stefano.
>
> "DiCarlo, sources say, was chosen also because of his alleged close-in ties with mobsters throughout the country, his ability to negotiate on behalf of the family through those connections and his selection by former Magaddino underboss, Pieri, as the watchdog over his (Pieri's) holdings throughout the balance of his prison term.

> "DiCarlo, now aging and a mere shadow of the man local police termed Buffalo's Public Enemy No. 1, is said, however, to hold the respect of local mobsters, who reportedly seek his counsel regularly in matters involving dealings with other mob families."

One year later, after Sam Pieri's release from prison, the newspaper reported that he had launched a campaign to take control of the family from Magaddino, indicating that the aged mob boss was in control all along. The battle for leadership was short-lived. On July 19, 1974, the 82 year-old Magaddino succumbed to a heart attack. The next day it was reported that Pieri was filling the "Don's" boots.

In March 1975, DiCarlo's name surfaced during a highly publicized gambling probe. The 73 year-old was hardly a factor in the investigation. A younger generation of mobsters had moved in and were the focus of law enforcement officials.

DiCarlo's last public scrutiny crime came in August 1978, when he was identified as a participant in a meeting held at the Auburn Correctional Facility during an Italian-American Festival. DiCarlo was listed as a "special invited" guest at the prison. It was believed that the meeting took place to discuss an ongoing mob war in Rochester, New York.

On October 10, 1980, DiCarlo died at the Hamlin Terrace Nursing Home in Buffalo. The newspapers said the 80 year-old died after a lengthy illness. Despite his long criminal record, DiCarlo was allowed a funeral mass in the Catholic Church.

Section IV Notes

1.Victor Riesel, a nationally known columnist and radio commentator who specialized in labor affairs, was the victim of Mafia violence on April 5, 1956, when an assailant threw sulfuric acid in his face and blinded him. The attack took place around 3:00 a.m. outside of Lindy's Restaurant on Broadway in New York City. Abraham Telvi, a 22 year-old who threw the liquid, was believed to have come to Youngstown with his girlfriend Olga Dela Cruz after the attack. When Telvi realized all the attention the incident was generating he began to demand more than the $1,175 he received and quickly headed back to New York. On July 28, Telvi was shot to death on the Lower East Side of Manhattan. On August 17, FBI agents arrested George and Della Moore of Youngstown as material witnesses in the investigation. The belief was they had harbored Telvi and Dela Cruz. Labor racketeer John "Johnny Dio" Dioguardi, who was behind the plot with six others, was indicted by a federal grand jury. After three defendants were tried, convicted and sent to prison, it was believed that at least two would flip and testify against Dioguardi. The two were threatened in their prison cells and refused to testify for the government. On May 27, 1957, the charges against Dioguardi were dismissed. Riesel continued his career as a syndicated columnist for years. His column was carried by the Youngstown *Vindicator.*

2 Detective Chief William W. Reed was a 50-year veteran of the Youngstown Police Department. He joined the force on September 1, 1911. He was promoted to sergeant in 1918 and ten years later made detective. On September 16, 1937, Reed was promoted to detective chief. In 1960, a new city ordinance passed setting a retirement age of 65 for police and firemen. Reed challenged the law in court and lost at both the municipal and appeals court level. In the fall of 1961, Reed became ill while waiting for the Ohio Supreme Court to make a ruling. In April 1962, the state supreme court ruled the law invalid. Reed, still ill, was hoping to return to the department before a scheduled July retirement date. But Reed's health was not improving. On the morning of June 2, he took his life in the bathroom of his West Warren Avenue home. Reed was 76 years old.

3 Paul Clautti's name has also appeared as Calautti. But Clautti is the name used on the autopsy report and on his headstone.

4 It was unclear if Nick and Ted Pappas were brothers. Two *Vindicator* ar-

ticles claimed they weren't related a third said they were. Nick Pappas had a number of arrests between 1956 and 1963, mostly for possession of lottery slips, suspicion and promoting a numbers game. On November 11, 1958, he took a shot at Gus Leamis and got off with firing a weapon within city limits. Nick Pappas' milieu was the American Billiards poolroom at 261 East Federal Street, where he was arrested a number of times. Ted and Nick Pappas pleaded not guilty to the gambling counts from the undercover operation in September 1962. During a trial in March 1963, Ted Pappas was found guilty of promoting a numbers game, Nick Pappas had already pleaded guilty to four counts. Common Pleas Judge Sidney M. Rigelhaupt sentenced them each to one to ten year prison terms. A year later the Ohio Supreme Court refused to review Ted Pappas' case. On April 27, 1964, the two men arrived at the Ohio Penitentiary in Columbus to begin their sentences

5 On March 30, 1969, Chuckie Cavallaro, now 19 years old, broke into a Pepsi Cola machine at the Self Serve Laundry at 2208 Market Street. He and an accomplice stole two cans of Pepsi and $14. Cavallaro was arrested the same day. On April 17, he was found guilty in Municipal Court. He was sentenced to five days in the city jail and placed on probation for six months. The irony of this is that his father, during an almost 30-year criminal career, spent only two nights in jail.

6 The 12 men arraigned with Dominic "Moosey" Caputo from the February 16, 1963, Jockey Club raid in Chester, West Virginia were reported as:

Louis Anzelone	25	Pittsburgh, PA
Sidney Baum	54	McKeesport, PA
Paul Bellow	50	Steubenville, OH
Domenic Bieuo	66	Pittsburgh, PA
Joseph Pecora	43	Pittsburgh
Joseph Rizzo	54	Glassport, PA
Peter Short	57	White Oak, PA
Abraham Silverhart	56	Pittsburgh, PA
Michael Simera	40	Steubenville, OH
Joseph Tamburro	40	Steubenville, OH
Charles F. Teemer	62	Hollywood, FL
Alex Zrinyi, Jr.		Steubenville, OH

All the men were arrested the night of the raid except Teemer and Bellow.

7 John C. Montana and DiCarlo had known each other since the early 1920s. In 1956, Montana received the "Man of the Year" award from the city of Buffalo. The annual presentation was made by the Erie Club and sponsored by the Buffalo Police Department. On November 14, 1957, Montana was arrested in Apalachin, New York during the infamous meeting there. His excuse for being there, according to police, was that he had automobile trouble on his way to Pennsylvania and stopped there with Anthony Magaddino, the brother of Buffalo Mafia boss Stefano Magaddino.

8 Ettore "Eddie" Coco was described as a close friend of mob-backed boxing promoter Frankie Carbo. His rap sheet showed 13 arrests including murder, rape and felony assault. On February 21, 1951, he shot and killed a car-washer/ parking lot attendant named Johnny Smith after an early morning argument. While out on bail, Coco was reportedly running a floating crap game in New York City that was earning $10,000 a night. DiCarlo attended his murder trial in December 1953. Coco was convicted and given life in prison, but did not begin his sentence until May 5, 1955, after all appeals had failed. According to the New York Police Department's Intelligence Division, Coco served as Acting Boss of the Lucchese family from Thomas Lucchese's death in July 1967 until September of that year. He died in December 1991.

9 Frank Brancato was alleged to have been one of the gunmen in Cleveland's most notorious Prohibition killings during the Lonardo-Porrello War. On February 25, 1932, Raymond and Rosario Porrello and Dominic Gueli were killed and Joseph Damanti was wounded in a cigar store during the middle of the afternoon. Brancato was wounded in the stomach in the return fire. He remained a top figure in the Cleveland Mafia until his death of natural causes on December 17, 1973.

10 According to Joseph Griffin in Mob Nemesis the key mobsters arrested were:

Joseph DiCarlo – former LCN leader in Youngstown, Ohio
Frederico Randaccio – Magaddino underboss
Roy Carlisi – Magaddino capo and brother of Chicago LCN boss Sam Carlisi
James V. LaDuca – LCN member and son-in-law of Stefano Magaddino
Joseph Fino – Magaddino capo and future LCN boss in Buffalo
Daniel "Boots" Sansanese, Sr. – Magaddino capo and future Buffalo underboss
Pasquale Natarelli – Magaddino capo

Sam "The Frenchman" Frangiamore – Magaddino capo
John Cammilleri – Magaddino capo (murdered on May 8, 1974)
Joseph "Leadpipe Joe" Todaro, Sr. – future Buffalo LCN boss
Victor Randaccio – LCN member and boss of Local 210 of the Laborers' International Union of North America

Section V

End of an Era

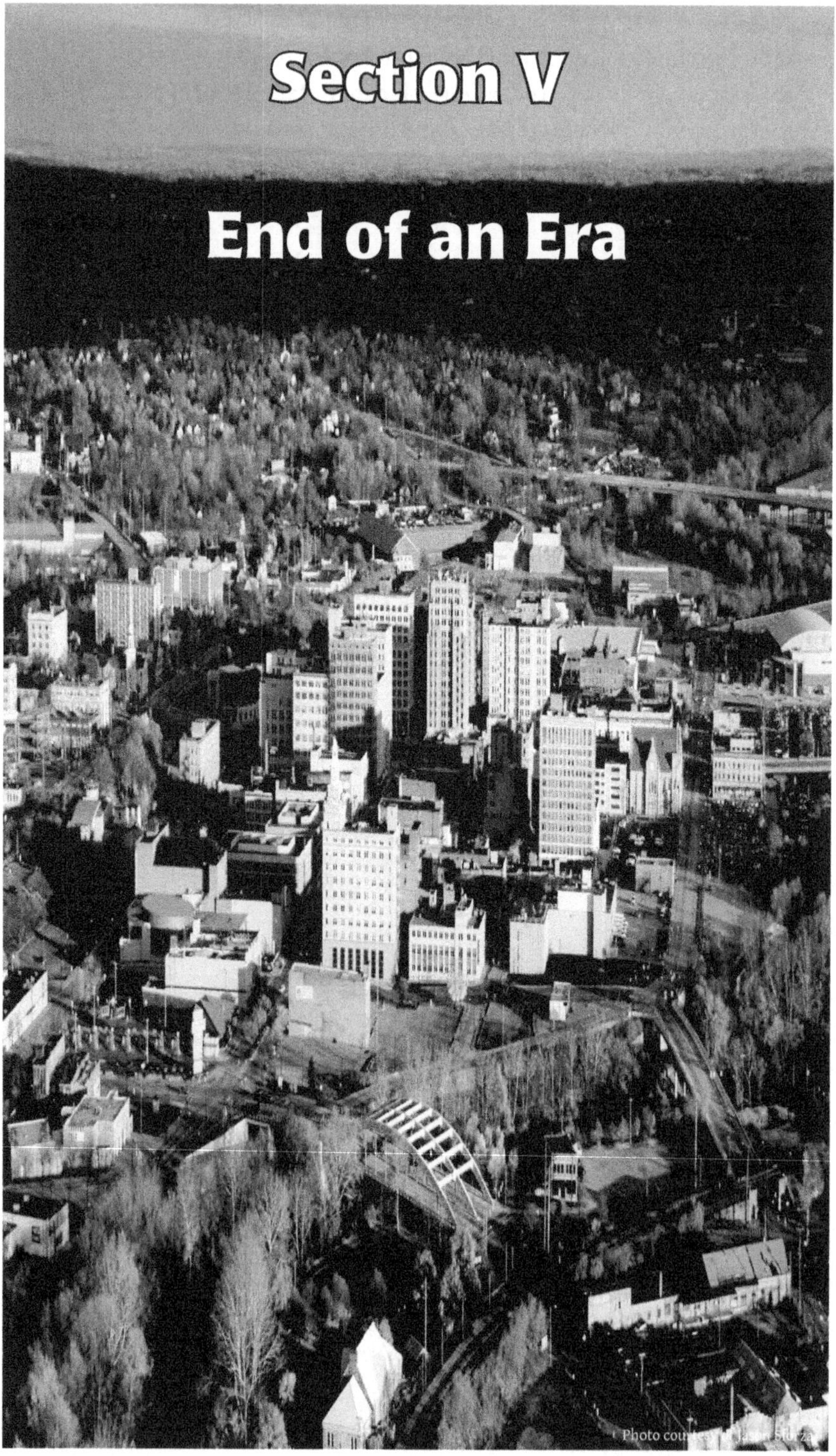

Photo courtesy of Jason Sforza

"These men had grown up in a terrible moral environment and in a city which did not care, and in a business which would have been legitimate in any other place. I don't think your honor wants to hold these men responsible for all the acts of many other men down the years. You speak of public clamor in Youngstown, but there was no public clamor until a boy was killed. The killing of the father didn't matter. That was just like the other bombings to which Youngstown paid no attention." – Attorney Dan W. Duffy speaking on behalf of the Alexander brothers and Carabbia brothers during their sentencing for Federal tax charges on June 25, 1964.

15

The Usual Suspects

Joe Alexander

Joseph Frederick Alexander was born in Youngstown on August 15, 1913. His parents were of Greek descent. Educated in the local school system, he graduated from East High School in 1931. Alexander was arrested for the first time on September 7, 1934 for illegal possession of liquor. A life as a career criminal did not appear to be on the horizon for him. He was employed by the Youngstown Neon Sign Company, where he advanced to the position of secretary-treasurer in 1937. That same year he was a candidate to unseat Innocenzo Vagnozzi as Second Ward Councilman in the Democratic Primary. Alexander ran on the platform of "concerted efforts for improvements of the Second Ward and cooperation with other councilmen to maintain Youngstown on a plane with other large cities."

Losing the election put a halt to his political ambitions. It apparently put a stop to his ambitions to continue as a law-abiding citizen also. The next time he was reported about in the newspapers was after an arrest on January 1, 1945, on charges of "possessing illegal liquor for sale and exhibiting gambling devices." Alexander was operating the BSA Club at 321 West Federal Street when deputy sheriffs under the command of Sheriff Ralph E. Elser decided to demolish the place. The *Vindicator* reported after the raid, "Not a chair was left in a single piece." Alexander and his bartender, Ralph Gaudio, were each fined $100 and court costs.

In January 1946, Alexander formed the Center Amusement Company, with Sandy Naples and Pinky Walsh, at the corner of Center Street and Wilson Avenue. For years the location served at the headquarters for the Naples brothers "bug" activity (See chapter 11).

In the late 1940s, Alexander got involved in the ownership and distribution of pinball machines, also known as marble boards. In April 1949, a hint of corruption made front-page news after Mayor Lloyd Culler of Washingtonville (located south of Youngstown, just over the Columbiana County line), "threw the book at him." The problem began when new Mahoning County Sheriff Paul J. Langley went into Washingtonville, stopped at a filling station and ordered a pinball machine removed. Three days later Alexander replaced the machine with one of his own. When told about the sheriff's order, Alexander replied, "You won't have to worry about this stuff. No one else can put 'em in, but our boards are okay."

When the matter was brought to Mayor Culler's attention, he ordered Alexander arrested. In mayor's court, Culler found Alexander guilty of distributing gambling devices. Before he sentenced him, Culler placed four calls to Sheriff Langley's office for an explanation, but was ignored. Culler then slapped Alexander with a $500 fine and declared, "When Sheriff Paul J. Langley orders one marble board out and lets others in I won't stand for it. Neither the sheriff nor any of his 'friends' are going to employ gangster tactics to muscle in here."

A *Vindicator* reporter immediately contacted the sheriff's office and had no trouble getting through to Langley. Apprised of the mayor's comments the sheriff lashed out, "I want you to publish that and I will be up there so God damned fast and sue you that it won't be funny. I've given the OK to no one. Everyone is going around with that excuse but I have ordered all slots and gambling equipment of all kinds out of the county. I was in Washingtonville and I was all over the county. Who is Alexander, anyway?"

By early August 1949, the *Vindicator* proclaimed that gambling, outside of Youngstown in Mahoning County, was wide-open again and that slot machines were spread throughout. Supplying the one-armed bandits was the Woodworth Novelty Company on New Springfield Road. It was alleged that this new operation was run by Alexander and Joseph "Red" Giordano, who was waiting appeal on a burglary conviction in the Rocco Marino home break-in. The company was supplying slot machines to The Coliseum in Wickliffe and a brand new gambling joint known as the Green Village, located on Mahoning Avenue, a half-mile from Lake Milton.

On August 8, a front-page article touted the grand opening of the new gambling den. The article reported that the new "emporium" was owned by Joe DiCarlo, but now stated Alexander was "not connected" to the Woodworth Novelty Company, the slot machine supplier (Alexander later claimed that he was only a "mechanic" for the company). The story went on to compare the new gambling operation to Trumbull County's infamous Jungle Inn, which by the end of that week was raided and closed forever.

On December 9, Alexander and eight others were arrested when the vice squad raided a suspected house of prostitution at 18 Hanley Avenue. Vice Squad Chief Dan Maggianetti said Alexander was a frequent visitor to the house. Police Chief Edward J. Allen may have ordered the arrest as part of his hoodlum harassment campaign. Alexander was released the next day, but not before Allen let Washingtonville Mayor Culler know he was holding him. Culler issued a warrant for Alexander's arrest because he had not completed payment of the fine he was assessed back in April. A friend picked up Alexander from the Youngstown police station and rushed him to Washingtonville to pay another installment on the fine to avoid being jailed again.

Alexander stayed out of trouble for nearly ten months. On September 15, 1950, a $6,400 load of steel was hijacked while on its way from Republic Steel Company in Warren to the Truscon Steel Company. The truck driver, an accomplice in the scheme, turned the load over to the hijackers for $1,000 at West Madison and West Federal Streets. By late September, Youngstown police had four men, including Philip "Fleegle" Mainer, under arrest. Police wanted to question Alexander. When they couldn't locate him they went to the home of his stepmother, arrested his brother Nicholas and confiscated 32 slot machines and 14 pinball machines, which were allegedly there for repairs. The next day Joe Alexander turned himself in to police for questioning. Alexander was bound over to the grand jury for the hijacking.

On February 6, 1951, the defendants pled guilty before Judge Erskine Maiden, Jr. In a strange twist, Youngstown Manufacturing Company, the buyer of the stolen shipment, discovered that Truscon Company was the actual purchaser of the load and contacted Republic Steel to come and recover it. Maiden ordered the defendants to pay restitution to Youngstown Manufacturing Company. Alexander's share was $750 and he was placed on probation until October 1952.

In July 1953, Alexander was ordered by the court to pay Buddy Fares, publisher of *The Youngstowner*, a weekly nightclub and entertainment pamphlet, $690 for a past due note dated March 1, 1947, for equipment ordered by the Center Amusement Company.

During the mid-1950s, Alexander turned his full attention to the Alexander Distributing Company (also referred to as the Alexander Music Company). Some stories state the company was around as early as 1931; however, Alexander was only graduating from high school that year. There was also a question of what Alexander's role in the company really was. There was speculation he was merely a front man for Sandy Naples. Others believed Vince DeNiro was involved. The newspaper portrayed Alexander as a part-owner without suggesting who the other owners might be. Over the years Alexander's brothers Elias and Nicholas were involved in managing the concern.

Alexander Distributing Company was responsible for putting coin operated devices in taverns, restaurants and poolrooms in the valley. These devices consisted of pinball machines (marble boards), music boxes (jukeboxes), bowling machines as well as cigarette machines. Due to an Ohio Supreme Court ruling that defined many of these machines as games of chance, the pinball machines were deemed gambling devices making them illegal. This didn't stop their placement in as many establishments as possible. Bar and restaurant owners could enhance their income by several hundred dollars a month depending on how many machines were on the premises. Patrons were dropping dimes in record numbers into the machines. The play was significant enough to cause bank tellers to realize the demand for dimes.

By 1956, because of enforcement of the pinball ordinance by Youngstown police, most of the boards were installed in places outside the city. A normal split of the profits from the machines was 60 percent to the supplier and 40 percent to the proprietor.

With the profits from the company, Alexander opened the Sands Lounge & Restaurant in Austintown. The $25,000 building permit was taken out on August 27, 1958, by Nicholas Alexander. The building contractor was B & B Construction Company, Inc. The Sands was described as one of the swankiest nightclubs in the area, possessing a luxurious cocktail lounge and spacious banquet room. As with Alexander Distributing Company, the Sands was rumored to have both Naples' and DeNiro's financial backing.

The 1960s brought a series of hardships to Alexander's operations. A week after the murder of Sandy Naples, a bomb was detonated at the side of the Sands Lounge causing slight damage. Law enforcement saw it as a warning to Alexander. Before the month was out Music Systems Inc. of Cleveland sued Alexander for non-payment of parts and equipment he purchased for machine repairs. In court, Alexander lost and was ordered to pay $7,700. In February 1961, Mahoning County Prosecutor Thomas Beil ordered all pinball machines located outside of the city of Youngstown removed where municipal ordinances disallowed them.

The Sands Lounge was sold to a business group from Columbiana County in October 1961. The key figure in the buying group was William C. Lodge, described as a prominent attorney and a "buddy of Youngstown underworld characters." In addition to the Sands Lounge, Lodge was also rumored to have been a part owner of DeNiro's restaurant, Cicero's, around the time of Vince's demise. Lodge was said to have kept an enlarged color photo of DeNiro in his home.

On November 22, 1961, one month after purchasing the Sands Lounge, Lodge drove to Youngstown and picked up Alexander. The two then drove back to Lodge's Columbiana home, arriving about 10:30 a.m. Something was bothering Lodge that morning, causing him to consume a half-bottle of liquor. While Lodge's two year-old son and his maid waited with Alexander downstairs, the attorney went upstairs, pulled out a legal document and wrote, "Bury me from Fry" on one of the pages and signed it "Bill." Lodge then took a .38 revolver from a shoulder holster he was wearing and sent a bullet crashing through his forehead. At the time, the 36 year-old lawyer was under indictment by the Columbiana County grand jury for arranging perjured testimony in a divorce case in Lisbon, Ohio. Police discovered that "Fry" was the name of a funeral home Lodge wished to have handle his remains.

Joe Alexander suffered his biggest blow in June 1963, when he and his two brothers were indicted by a Federal grand jury in Cleveland for multiple income tax violations. The indictments were part of the government's full court press on underworld figures in the Mahoning Valley after the bombing murder of Charles Cavallaro and his son Tommy in November 1962.

The Alexander brothers were charged with filing false partnership returns for Alexander Distributing Company in 1957 and 1958. The government also accused the brothers of inducing customers to keep false records of cash receipts from the machines in their establishments. The brothers pleaded not guilty and were released on $2,500 bonds. The federal case hinged on a coin-operated gaming device tax on pinball machines. The machines in question were located in Struthers' establishments controlled by the Carabbia family, of which four members – Ronald, Orland and Charlie and his wife, Dorothy – were also indicted.

On May 12, 1964, all three Alexander brothers pled guilty to one conspiracy charge each. At the sentencing on June 25 in Cleveland before Federal Judge Ben Green, attorney Dan W. Duffy spoke on behalf of the Alexander and Carabbia brothers. He gave the following impassioned plea:

> "These men had grown up in terrible moral environment and in a city which did not care, and in a business which would have been legitimate in any other place.
>
> "The moral climate was so bad that even when the newspaper and a committee for civic pride, both editorially and through advertisements, attacked the mayor, the citizens still elected him by a big majority.
>
> "Your honor, these men were born in this environment. I don't think your honor wants to hold these men responsible for all the acts of many other men down the years.
>
> "You speak of public clamor in Youngstown, but there was no public clamor until a boy was killed. The killing of the father didn't matter. That was just like the other bombings to which Youngstown paid no attention."

In discussing Joseph Alexander, Duffy described him as "a church member, a family man, charity-minded and a good person whom people respect." The attorney pointed out that Joseph kept the family business together while his brothers served this country during World War II. Joseph received two years and Elias one year; both received $5,000 fines. Nicholas, who was charged with perjury during the investigation, was fined $5,000 and placed on a year's probation. Elias Alexander served nine months of his sentence and was released. Joseph did 14 months, serving the last two at an "honor camp" in Allenwood, Pennsylvania. He was released in August 1965.

Joseph Alexander lived to the ripe old age of 84, passing away on November 5, 1997, at St. Elizabeth's Hospital after suffering a heart attack. The old adage, "the apple doesn't fall far from the tree," referring to children following in their father's footsteps, didn't apply to the Alexander children. Three of his four children – two sons and a daughter – became respected doctors.

"Little Joe" Blumetti

In the years after his conviction for white slavery charges and lying on a Selective Service statement, which earned him a six-year prison term, Joseph Thomas Blumetti climbed the ranks of Youngstown's labor rackets – with a little help from his friends.

Known to friends and acquaintances as "Joe Blue" and "Little Joe," Blumetti was the handpicked president and business agent of Local 410 of the Vending Machine Employee's Union by William Presser of Cleveland, the president of the Ohio Conference of Teamsters and the Teamsters Joint Council No. 41. In this capacity, Blumetti explained, his role was to make sure "my men don't lose any commissions due to the displacement of jukeboxes from their locations."

In September 1952, Blumetti was questioned by Chief Allen after the creosote acid bombings at the homes of Dominic Delbone and Paul Duritza. Allen, who called Blumetti an "ex-pimp," was battling city council and took this opportunity to level a blast at both union terrorists and local politicians. The chief declared, "So long as gangsters are secure in the knowledge that they have political figures and forces ready to front for them in whatever way they can, just so long will the community witness intermittent terrorism of the sort that injures wives of decent citizens and mothers of small babies. Whenever and wherever public officials use the power of the people to protect this scum, they are nothing more than political rocks whose undersides help to spawn, nourish and conceal from public view the slimy creatures whose activities cannot survive the light of day."

On November 10, 1954, Blumetti appeared before the House Subcommittee investigating racketeering to answer questions about recent unrest in the jukebox industry. Preceding him on the stand that day was William Presser, who spent most of his testimony invoking his Fifth Amendment rights. Blumetti was questioned about his criminal record, which in addition to white slavery included arrests for counterfeiting and draft dodging. He assured committee members, "I have been going straight ever since I got out of the Penitentiary." But when it came to answering questions about his finances, he took Presser's cue and pled the Fifth. This infuriated panel members who were interested in finding out why, through the first nine months of 1954, Blumetti's salary was $5,251 while his expenses were $6,197.

Before the session got underway there was some question as to whether Ohio Senator George H. Bender was the right man to chair the hearings. Bender knew Bill Presser and had received support from the Teamsters in his campaigns. Bender scoffed at the criticism stating, "I wouldn't know a racketeer if I met one." Nothing ever became of the Senate committee's investigation of the "Ohio juke box conspiracy." Bender adjourned them on November 10, after just two days, and they were never reconvened. Cleveland author James Neff cleared up this mystery in his book *Mobbed Up*. Neff wrote, "Years later, Bill Presser freely admitted to close friends that he and the union had spent a small fortune buying off Bender. Among other things, Bender 'went to Cuba and came back a wealthy man,' Bill told a high-ranking Teamsters official."

During this time, Blumetti tried to expand his role in the local labor industry. In 1954, Kathryn Klee, the top official of the Dry Cleaners & Dye Workers Union, passed away. Blumetti moved in and took over the position, apparently without the knowledge of the rank and file. An August 30, 1956, *Vindicator* article revealed, "Most dry cleaning workers here frankly don't know how Blumetti took over after Miss Klee's death. Blumetti was not elected. He told some executives in the dry cleaning and laundry businesses that he was 'appointed' to the business agent post." Others believed Blumetti's connections with Bill Presser and Cleveland labor rackets' figures brothers Alfred "Babe" and Anthony Salupo had something to do with Blumetti's quiet advance. Blumetti's involvement there was short-lived as a merger of the Laundry Workers and Dry Cleaners provided new leadership in the union.

In October 1957, Blumetti was one of six delegates from Youngstown Local 377 of the Teamster's Union to travel to Miami, Florida, to elect James R. Hoffa to succeed Dave Beck as president of the International Teamster's union. The other delegates were John J. Angelo, Abe Schwartz, Robert W. Higham, Frank Zangara and Thomas J. Farello. In reporting Blumetti's presence in Miami, the *Vindicator* made sure to expose his past, entitling the article, "White Slaver Joe Blumetti Is Delegate." They described his connection to Local 377 as obscure, but that he was known to be "one of the chief lieutenants" of Presser.

Blumetti announced his plans to seek election as a trustee of Local 377 in July 1958. The 5,000 member Local was controlled at the time by John Angelo. As election time drew near the *Vindicator* reported, "Union sources say the fight is between Angelo and Blumetti. Angelo no longer is Presser's fair-haired boy. Blumetti is out to take over from Angelo." The newspaper also revealed that Blumetti's assistant in the Machine Service Employees Union was William "Billy" Naples.

As the election, scheduled for September 27, drew near, sides were being drawn and the campaign was getting bitter. The slate of candidates were: Robert Higham, business agent and president, Thomas Farello, business agent and vice president; and Abe Schwartz, business agent and trustee. All three were reputed to be in the Blumetti camp. On the Angelo side were Harold Kauffman, business agent and recording secretary, John Ferguson, business agent; and John Povne, business agent. A seventh man, Frank Zangara, was said to go "either way – wherever the strength was."

Supporters of Angelo claimed Blumetti had no right to hold office. They argued that according to the national constitution, "a member must have worked at the trade at least two years before he is eligible for office." Blumetti had never worked as a truck driver, he was appointed by Bill Presser.

Five days before the election, three members of Local 377 went to Washington D.C. to lodge their complaint about Blumetti's eligibility for office. At the same time, the executive secretary of the Board of Monitors said the panel voted to recommend to Hoffa that the election be postponed.

That night in Youngstown, a meeting of the executive board took place at union headquarters on Rayen Avenue. The meeting began with a heated exchange between the two opposing factions over the presence of a *Vindicator* reporter. The Blumetti faction wanted him to leave, while the Angelo backers welcomed his presence. After a brief huddle by officers the reporter was ordered to leave by Robert Higham.

The union battle raged on until December 3, 1958, when a membership meeting, held at Eagles Hall, was disrupted as factions argued over the presence of police security guards and reporters. The dispute ended when Blumetti and his followers walked out of the meeting. "Joe Blue" called a press conference and announced he was resigning as local business agent.

One of the reasons Blumetti gave for his retirement was that he was dropping out due to the "adverse publicity" that his family had to endure since his candidacy over the summer. Another reason, he claimed, were the misleading rumors that he was taking over the union for Presser. Many believed that his resignation was due to his pending appearance before the McClellan Committee, scheduled for the next day in Washington D.C., where he was subpoenaed to testify about underworld infiltration in the coin machine industry. Blumetti vehemently denied that the hearing had anything to do with his decision. He later released a printed statement regarding his alleged takeover of the union; in which he declared, "there is only one man attempting to take over Local 377 and that man is John J. Angelo."

John Angelo was asked to comment on his rival's sudden departure from the union. He replied, "Blumetti's resignation comes as a surprise to me. His resignation will, of course, be accepted." Angelo and his backers went further than just accepting the resignation. Higham, the president, had recently turned over the chair to Thomas Farello, due to a "mysterious" illness. Farello left the meeting when the Blumetti faction walked out. Like sharks in a feeding frenzy, Angelo and his supporters used the opportunity to pass a resolution reducing the salaries of all the officers in Blumetti's faction by 44 percent and cut their expense accounts in half. The proposed resolution stated that the cuts were intended as punishment to Blumetti's supporters for blocking the "best wishes of the union rank-and-file membership." They then relieved Higham of his presidency and most of his powers. The Angelo faction finished by reassigning Farello to the freight division and removing him as business agent of Ashtabula County. Credit cards of the men were confiscated and a union automobile used by Farello to travel on union business between Ashtabula and Youngstown was taken away.

Farello, speaking at a news conference afterward, declared that all business passed in his absence was illegal because he had adjourned the meeting after the bickering over the presence of outsiders. Angelo claimed the meeting was not adjourned because it had never been put to a vote.[1]

The day after Blumetti's walkout, he was scheduled to appear before Senator John McClellan's Rackets Committee to answer the questions of committee counsel Robert F. Kennedy. There was a mistake in the issuance of cancellation notices and Blumetti received one when he shouldn't have and did not travel to Washington D.C. Blumetti was then ordered to appear on December 8. At that time he used his Fifth Amendment right 47 times before the committee, refusing to answer any questions about his criminal past. When the committee's chief counsel, Robert Kennedy decided to hold a hearing in Cleveland during mid-1959, Blumetti was conveniently in Florida.

Blumetti was never a factor in Youngstown's labor unions again. For the next 20 years he served as a business agent and union official for the Teamsters Union's health and welfare fund, operating out of the Chicago office.

In 1970, after a grand jury investigation of labor racketeering in Northern Ohio, "Joe Blue" was indicted along with Bill Presser and Louis "Babe" Triscaro. Blumetti was charged with embezzling $2,217 in union funds.

During his later life, Blumetti lived in Canfield on Indian Run Road. In the early 1980s he was diagnosed with cancer. His wife, Doris had remained by his side all these years. On February 6, 1981, he died in North Side Hospital. Blumetti was 67.

John Burnich

John Burnich, Jr. led a charmed life...for a bug man. Arrested for suspicion on August 18, 1945, he was not arrested again for nearly 16 years, even though he was considered one of the top numbers men in Youngstown. That's not to say he didn't spend any time at the police station. Between the bombings and his federal gambling tax stamp purchases, he became a regular there.

Burnich, known as Barney or J.B. to his friends and family, was born in Youngstown on January 25, 1920. His education ended in his junior year at Rayen High School. In August 1941, he married Catherine Terlecky. For 59 days in 1942, Burnich served his country as a Marine until he was given a medical discharge. Returning to Youngstown, he went back to a job as assistant to the foreman at the General Fireproofing Company, where he was employed from 1940 to 1945.

In the late 1940s, Burnich obtained an interest in his in-laws business, Terlecky's Appliance Company. Burnich was given the title of vice president. He also owned half interest in Johnnie's Grocery Store, named for his father, at 1157 West Rayen Avenue. During the early 1950s, he had an interest in the Highway Driving Range, a golf range in Hubbard. In addition, he operated four poolrooms in the area.

Burnich made his debut in the *Vindicator* when it was announced on February 13, 1954, that he and fellow Austintown Township resident Joseph "Crow" Romanchuk purchased a federal gambling tax stamp together. Romanchuk and Burnich were life-long friends. "Crow" was employed as a salesman at Terlecky's Appliance and was once the Third Ward Democratic precinct committeeman.

In May 1954, Johnnie's Grocery Store was bombed. That summer Burnich was called in and grilled by investigators after the July bombing at the home of Jack Sulligan (see chapter 12). During the interrogation, Burnich, while admitting he played the numbers, denied he ever ran a bug bank and hadn't written numbers in ten years. When asked about the bombing of the store, he played down the incident stating, "If you say it was bombed, I don't know, the windows were just knocked out."

Despite the recent bombing and intense scrutiny by the vice squad, when the new listing of tax stamp purchasers was released on July 2, Burnich and Romanchuk were on it, this time showing Canfield as their home address. Again on November 18, 1955, Burnich was one of four federal gambling tax stamp holders (as reported the previous day in the *Vindicator*), who claimed they had suspended their gambling operations when questioned by Vice Squad Chief George Krispli.

In November 1956, after the second bombing at the home of Jack Sulligan, Burnich was again one of several suspects the police wanted to question. Burnich arrived at police headquarters on the morning of November 26, saying he had heard police wanted to see him. He claimed he was with his family in Florida over the recent Thanksgiving holiday. The newspaper pointed out, that although questioned, Burnich was not "officially booked." It was reported Burnich agreed to take a lie-detector test, but there was no confirmation that he had and he left the station after offering nothing to help the investigation.

Despite the intensified police effort, and the seemingly incessant bombing activity, Burnich continued to be viewed by police as one of the district's busiest lottery operators. In March 1957, he was again on the list of gamblers who purchased the tax stamp. A March 24 *Vindicator* article, claimed area gamblers, who had purchased the stamp, had paid revenue tax on nearly $3 million of income.

When the continuing bug warfare turned deadly in the early 1960s, Burnich was questioned after the murders of Sandy Naples and Mary Ann Vrancich. After the murder of Vince DeNiro in July 1961, Burnich was arrested on suspicion and held for questioning.

On January 19, 1962, Burnich was picked up at Johnnie's Grocery Store and brought in for questioning by Dan Maggianetti, chief of the Intelligence & Security Division, previously known as the Vice Squad and the Morals Squad. Burnich was questioned about his recent purchase of yet another federal gambling tax stamp and released.

A little over a month later, on February 23, Maggianetti gave his men orders to arrest Burnich. A warrant was sworn out charging him with being a "common gambler." Maggianetti's explanation was that the city had an ordinance against gambling. Since Burnich was holding a gambling stamp, and reported income regularly to the IRS, he was in violation of the ordinance. When Maggianetti was asked if he was going to haul in all the tax stamp purchasers, he replied, "They'd better look out. I'm not going to let up on them."

Burnish pled not guilty before Municipal Judge Martin P. Joyce and was released on a $100 bond. Maggianetti was hoping to use the arrest as a test case against local gamblers. When the case came to trial on March 1, however, Judge Leskovyansky, "citing technicalities in the little-used city ordinance," dismissed the charges. The judge claimed that the city failed to prove that Burnich was "a known gambler," despite his income statements filed with the IRS indicating just that. In his ruling Leskovyansky stated, "Justice was served today because I heard the case in its entirety. I could have ended the matter sooner. The city ordinance is improperly written and in my opinion, unconstitutional. Where do the city fathers get off classifying a gambler as a criminal? Under this ordinance, a Las Vegas casino operator could be arrested just visiting Youngstown."

In late 1963, Burnich sold the property on which Johnnie's Grocery Store was located to the city. A total of seven pieces of property were purchased from Burnich for the River Bend Urban Renewal project for $53,650, bringing him a profit of $14,650. The notorious grocery store was then razed. Today it is the site of East Dominion Gas Company.

Police and FBI agents, whose presence was increased after the bombing deaths of Charles Cavallaro and his son, were keeping an eye on Burnich figuring he was looking for a new place to open his bug bank. Burnich purchased a home at 704 Fairmont Avenue through the Federal Housing Authority. He rented it to Leroy Anderson, his wife Jacqueline and Abraham Fletcher. Back when he operated Johnnie's Grocery the same three people lived in a house that Burnich owned next door to the store. It too was sold to the city for the urban renewal project.

On July 24, 1964, ten law enforcement officers, including investigators for the county prosecutor, deputy sheriffs and an FBI agent, raided the Fairmont Avenue home shortly after 2:00 in the afternoon. The FBI agent signed the affidavit and obtained the search warrant from Common Pleas Judge David G. Jenkins. According to the *Vindicator*, "The affidavit, based on observations of an FBI agent, indicated that gambling paraphernalia used in illegal operations, horse bet slips, and numbers operations might be found at the home along with receipts. It also stated that 'on several occasions' Burnich admitted to the FBI that he operated the bug at the home."

Inside the home at the time of the raid were Burnich and Leroy Anderson. The newspaper reported, "The loot included a sizable amount of bug slips, adding machine tapes, records of pick-up men and writers, notations of their commissions and amounts they owed the bank." The raiders were confident they "scored" a direct hit on Burnich's lottery bank.

Neither Burnich nor Anderson were arrested, but they were held until the search was completed. Burnich told the raiders the house was his and the reason he was there was to negotiate the sale of the home to Anderson. A few days later, the newspaper announced, "Evidence seized...will be sent to the FBI laboratories in Washington for study and reports received will be presented to the Mahoning County grand jury." For some unexplained reason, nothing ever became of the case. What transpired, however, might have been enough to scare Burnich into going straight.

John Burnich was convicted only once. That was for failing to talk to a grand jury during the late fall of 1963. He was jailed for contempt and later sentenced to ten days in the county jail and fined $500. The decision was appealed and the Seventh District Court of Appeals reversed the ruling. In November 1965, the U.S. Supreme Court refused to review the reversal.

In November 1973, Burnich was honored with a plaque from the local chapter of the National Multiple Sclerosis Society for his "outstanding leadership in fund raising" for the chapter's annual awards dinner. Burnich was long active as a director of the Multiple Sclerosis Society. In January 1975, he donated the first $1,000 in establishing a reward fund for the safe return of a local 14 year-old who was missing. During the 1970s, Burnich turned his talents to the real estate market. In July 1978, as an associate of Fairway Realty, he was named Realtor of the Year.

Burnich died on November 14, 1994, at the age of 74. His family requested that contributions be made to the Multiple Sclerosis Society.

DeNiro Brothers Trial

In December 1963, during a Justice Department probe of organized crime and racketeering in the Valley, initiated over two years earlier by United States Attorney General Robert F. Kennedy, a federal grand jury began looking into the "extensive legitimate holdings" of the late Vince DeNiro. Treasury agents, ordered into the Valley just after the gambler's death, had already investigated DeNiro's Las Vegas interests. Called to testify before the grand jury in Cleveland were Dominic Frank, who was listed as the owner of the building in which Cicero's operated; Chauncey "Pat" Riley, DeNiro's former income tax accountant; James Modarelli, who was with Vince the night he was killed; Joseph Catoline, a relative; William Coleman, a former manager of Cicero's; Andrew Marino, a brother of Roy "Happy" Marino; and Edward and Helen Cochrane, who were with DeNiro when Cicero's opened and helped with some of the remodeling at the restaurant.

Led by chief government counsel, attorney William S. Lynch, the Justice Department was looking at what the gambler left behind at the time of his death. On April 14, 1964, after an intensive investigation into Vince's estate, a federal grand jury began hearing evidence by calling his legal, tax and financial advisers. At the time it was rumored DeNiro had left behind an estate valued at $700,000 to $1,000,000. No will was filed or estate probated in Mahoning County court.

On April 22, brothers Louis J., Michael and Frank J. DeNiro Jr. were indicted on three counts each, charging they defrauded the government of over $111,000 in inheritance tax from Vince DeNiro's "racket built empire." Government prosecutors claimed that the three began their scheme to defraud the government at Cicero's restaurant "before the rubble was cleared from the bomb that killed" their brother.

Count one of the indictment charged that the three brothers took from Vince, "$50,000 in cash; 20,000 shares of stock in Continental Tobacco Company; stock in and ownership of the National Cigarette Service, Valley Land Company, Cicero's and the Sans Souci Club in Las Vegas." A time line of the various fraudulent activities reveals:

July 17, 1961 – Louis and Michael met at Cicero's and "caused preparation of so-called option to purchase agreements back-dated to January 30 and purporting to show contracts of that date for sale of stock in Cicero's." The three brothers obtained the signatures of Dominic Frank and Helen Cochrane, partners in the restaurant, on the option agreements.

July 1961 (after the 17th) – Frank contacted the manager of the Union National Bank, the Uptown branch, to discuss a $25,000 deposit made by Vince.

August 1961 – Louis discussed a loan with the head of the old Century Food Stores, which Vince had made.

August 1961 – Louis and Frank brought papers to Attorney Robert Tatman's office and "caused stock certificates to be prepared purporting to represent ownership of the National Cigarette Service and caused minutes of the board of directors of Valley Land Co. to be prepared and back-dated to various dates prior to July 17."

September 1961 – Louis visited Las Vegas where Vince had held ownership in the Sans Souci Hotel and casino.

October 13, 1961 – Frank filed a false corporate tax return for Valley Land Company.

April 19, 1962 – Louis denied to government agents that Vince had left behind any real estate or that he was in possession of any property belonging to the DeNiro estate.

August 1962 – Frank and Michael denied to government agents that they were holding "directly or indirectly" any property belonging to Vince.

November 20, 1962 – Louis denied to government agents that Vince had any proprietary interest in Cicero's, Valley Land or National Cigarette Service at the time of his death.

March 1963 – Frank and Michael denied they were in possession of any property, which rightfully belonged to Vince.

March 11, 1963 – Michael told government agents that he paid Edward Cochrane $10,000 for interest in the Valley Land Co.

April 16, 1963 – Louis told government agents that Vince had signed a stock certificate and rider for 20,000 shares of Continental Tobacco to transfer Vince's stock rights to Louis.

August 19, 1963 – in Cincinnati, all three brothers denied to IRS agents that Vince left any estate and that they had received property that belonged to Vince.

The indictment charged that the three brothers "conspired to defraud the government by impeding lawful government functions of the IRS, by attempting to avoid estate taxes, by making false statements and by aiding and abetting in preparation of fraudulent statements and documents."

Over 13 months passed before the trial got underway. On Monday, May 24, 1965, attorneys Sam Karam and James Carroll, representing the three brothers, argued that Vince DeNiro had no personal estate and worked for National Cigarette Service, which was owned and operated by his brothers. The brothers elected to have the case heard without a jury. Although the trial was held in Cleveland, it had a distinct Youngstown flavor as the U.S. District Judge hearing the case was Frank J. Battisti.

During the first day of testimony, the prosecution questioned William Griffith, the manager of Union National Bank. The banker testified that Vince DeNiro had opened an account under the name of T. J. Rogers and between January and March 1961 had deposited $280,000; all except $76,000 was withdrawn by March 24. Griffith also testified that DeNiro had once handed him $25,000 to hold without crediting it to any account. After his death the money was turned over to National Cigarette Service.

Jules Aron, the former head of Century Foods, testified that once while dining at Cicero's he mentioned to DeNiro that he needed $25,000 for a business transaction. DeNiro left and returned 30 minutes later with 500 $50 bills. Aron placed the money in a safe deposit box and gave DeNiro a dated check to hold. Later, after DeNiro's death, his brother Louis discovered the check and brought it to Aron's attention. Aron retrieved the original $25,000 and returned it to Louis.

On the second day of trial, Edward Cochrane told an interesting story of his financial dealings with DeNiro. Cochrane testified that he had known Vince for five years and was hired to renovate the Dry Men's Social Club in Coitsville. Soon afterward, DeNiro invested $20,000 in Cochrane's Valley Land Company. The construction concern built duplexes in Struthers as income property. In the late 1950s, Cochrane invested $35,000 in the Sans Souci in Las Vegas. He held 35,000 shares of his own and 195,000 of Vince's shares, which were under the Cochrane name. When Vince opened Cicero's in 1959, Cochrane was responsible for the remodeling work. His then wife Helen and Dominic Frank were listed as owners of the restaurant. Later, Frank's $20,000 interest was purchased by Cochrane and one of Vince's brothers. Cochrane said he sold his interest in Cicero's to Vince for $42,000.

On the day of Vince's death, Cochrane met with the brothers around noon to discuss "how the restaurant was held." Later that night, paperwork was brought to his house to be signed by Helen. The defense claimed that the documents were dated January 30, 1961. Cochrane testified, "That was the first I ever heard of this agreement." He claimed he had no deal with the brothers before Vince's death. Cochrane said that the night his wife signed the papers he received a portion of the $20,000 he was due for his shares in cash.

Cochrane said Vince told him that he had dropped $250,000 into the Sans Souci casino operation, but "there is no use crying about it: we'll just have to make it up." Apparently this wasn't the only money pit in which Vince had invested. The *Vindicator* reported, "Cochrane spoke of another loser, Cicero's Restaurant. Cochrane said it took $200,000 to open the spot and that he furnished $74,000 of this sum, Dominic Frank $20,000 and Vince the rest. Asked how they shared the profits, Cochrane said there was no profits, but 'Vince and I supported the losses.'"

Under cross-examination by Sam Karam, Cochrane said the 195,000 shares of stock in his name belonging to Vince stayed in his name until several months later when a trip was made to Las Vegas by Louis DeNiro, attorney Robert Tatman and himself; after Vince's death. Cochrane testified that Andrew Marino had $100,000 worth of stock in the Sans Souci.

Testifying on the third day was Cochrane's ex-wife Helen. She corroborated all her former husband's testimony. As he had stated, she signed the Cicero's paperwork late on the night of July 17, 1961.

Also testifying this day was Andrew Marino, the former automobile dealer now involved in commercial real estate. Marino told the court that he had known DeNiro since Vince was an 11 year-old. In later years he "negotiated" bank loans to the gambler of $25,000, $30,000, $50,000 and $60,000. Most of the loans were made to the National Cigarette Service and Frank and Louis DeNiro were the signers. Shortly after Vince's death Marino returned from a trip to San Francisco. He met with Frank and Louis to discuss a $60,000 loan the two had signed for. The men went to the Union National Bank to discuss a check and were told by a bank official there that they were "being investigated."

During the Thursday afternoon session, Mary DeNiro, Vince's former wife, took the stand. She testified that in 1959, at Vince's request, she took out an additional $10,000 mortgage on her home and signed the check over to the Cochranes. She said she didn't ask Vince what it was for because she knew he wouldn't tell her. Vince "engineered" the transaction to make it appear that Mary DeNiro was purchasing shares of Valley Land Co. After Vince's death, at Frank DeNiro, Jr's request, Mary signed the minute's book of the corporation. "I had no reason to question Frank," she explained. When questioned by Karam, Mary said there was no bitterness between her and Vince since their divorce in 1950. She stated, "Vince never told me anything about his business. He never discussed his holdings."

That same afternoon Victor Kosa and David Williams, a Canfield furniture dealer testified. Kosa stated that while working on Cicero's he was paid by check by Cochrane and in cash by DeNiro. In January 1959, Kosa was given $2,000 by Vince to be paid to Williams, who was supplying the furniture. After Vince's death, Kosa told Louis DeNiro he was still owed a large sum of money. Kosa testified that Louis told him, "If Vince promised to take care of you, you will be taken care of." Kosa concluded by saying he was still due nearly $6,500.

Williams told the court that Vince and Kosa had visited his store and that the latter had selected the patterns for the restaurant. He claimed DeNiro was concerned about the price. Williams testified Dominic Frank signed for the order and that he later had to file a lien against Cicero's to collect his money.

Dominic Frank had purchased Burton's Grille from the estate of Tom Burton, the original owner. Frank, who was at one time associated with DeNiro at the Dry Men's Social Club, was the holder of the liquor permit at Cicero's. In February 1960, he said he was paid $20,000 by Ed Cochrane and Frank DeNiro, Jr. for his share of the restaurant and was supposed to get an additional $5,000, which he never received. On the day Vince died he said he signed paperwork dated January 30, giving National Cigarette Service an option to buy half interest in Cicero's.

On Friday morning, May 28, former DeNiro brothers' attorney, now mayor of Poland, Ohio, Robert Tatman testified. When asked how he came to represent the DeNiros, Tatman responded he was asked to "take over the National Cigarette Service client because the firm was going to be examined by the Internal Revenue Service and the other attorney did not have time to handle it." Tatman said that on instructions from Louis DeNiro he prepared three "dated" documents related to Cicero's and the National Cigarette Service. He said he was told by Louis that the "transactions covered were completed early that year, and he wanted to have something on paper to show for them."

When questioned about stock certificates Louis brought to Tatman's office in a shoebox after Vince's death, the attorney stated, "One was made out to a Mike Dota from Colonial Farm, White Sulpher Springs, West Virginia." A bankbook, with a small savings account, was also in Dota's name. Tatman said that Michael DeNiro explained that Dota was an alias his brother Vince used. When Tatman said they would have to probate Vince's estate, Louis called and made arrangements to have the shoebox and its contents picked up.

Tatman was followed to the stand Friday morning by an IRS official from the Cleveland office, who testified that he had conducted a search of records since 1952 and could find no returns filed by Vince DeNiro under gift or estate taxes.

Closing out testimony that first week, Edith Magnolia, Vince's longtime girlfriend took the stand. She testified that after hearing of Vince's death she immediately returned from a trip to California and met with the DeNiro family at their Lincoln Park Drive home. Magnolia said Vince's mother asked her if James Modarelli was holding any money that belonged to her son. Michael DeNiro also asked her if she had any papers belonging to Vince. The day after the funeral she was asked by Vince's mother, "Where is the $63,000?" Magnolia answered that she didn't know what she was talking about. At this point Mrs. DeNiro repeated, "Where is it?"

As the second week of testimony began, the government questioned accountants, appraisers, realtors and brokers to present a clearer picture of Vince DeNiro's holdings at the time of his death. The duplexes owned by Valley Land Company were worth in excess of $500,000, while Cicero's was valued at a little over $100,000. One of the government's last witnesses was Nicholas Tweel, a former associate of Teamsters union boss James R. Hoffa. Tweel was at one time the president of Continental Tobacco Company and the year before was acquitted in a jury tampering case in Tennessee involving Hoffa. Tweel was called to testify about the signature on a stock transfer showing that 20,000 shares of Continental Tobacco Co. stock went to Louis DeNiro.

On June 4 the government rested its case. Attorneys for the DeNiro brothers filed a motion for a directed acquittal. Judge Battisti said it was necessary for briefs to be filed and further arguments heard before the acquittal motion could be ruled on. At this point the defense announced it would rest its case without calling a single witness.

It was August 23 before the trial reconvened. At that time Battisti denied defense counsel's motion for acquittal and final arguments were heard. Prosecutor Lynch argued "that the action of the brothers in gathering property of their slain brother, Vince, and distributing it among themselves was a fraud on the rightful heirs and an invasion of estate taxes. The rightful heirs are Vince's two teenage daughters who live with their mother, Vince's former wife."

The next day Judge Battisti found the three brothers guilty on two of the three counts. Michael, Frank, Jr. and Louis were convicted of "conspiring to take over the assets to evade the estate tax on DeNiro's widespread holdings and willfully evading payment of the estate taxes." The last count of making a false report to an IRS agent was dismissed. The maximum penalty for each count was a five-year prison sentence and/or a $5,000 fine. Each brother was looking at up to ten years in prison and a $10,000 fine. The judge delayed sentencing until a probation report could be made. The brothers remained free on bond.

On October 15, 1965, the day of sentencing, Judge Battisti went easy on Michael and Frank, Jr. fining them $1,000 and giving them two years probation each. Then, after calling Louis the "ringleader," he ordered him to the custody of the U.S. attorney general for three years, with the first 90 days to be spent in the Cuyahoga County jail and the balance on probation, and fined him $3,000. The newspaper reported Battisti told Louis, the youngest of the three brothers, "I believe you led your brothers in this crime" and are guilty of "despicable conduct." According to the judge, the plus factors in Louis' probation report "are that this is his first offense, that he cares for his aged parents and that he has supported his brother's widow and paid for the education of his brother's children." Speaking of Michael and Frank, Jr., the judge stated, "I am aware that they do not share equal guilt with their brother, Louis. Also they have not had previous brushes with the law."

Given the opportunity to speak before sentencing, Frank, Jr. stated, "I feel I am not guilty. I feel because our name is DeNiro and we are from Youngstown that we got indicted." Michael meanwhile criticized the *Vindicator* claiming the newspaper "has been picking on [Vince] since he died. They should let him rest in peace."

The judge ordered a stay of sentence pending defense counsel's appeal to the Sixth Circuit Court of Appeals in Cincinnati. Two and a half years later the Appellate Court upheld the convictions in a decision handed down on April 17, 1968. On the eve of the third anniversary of their sentencing, the U.S. Supreme Court rejected the brother's appeal. The sentences began in November 1968.

In April 1969, the IRS filed seven notices of federal tax liens totaling $1,188,000 for unpaid taxes against the estate of Vince DeNiro. The liens tied up any property in DeNiro's estate and made it subject to seizure by the government. One of the properties tied up by the liens was Cicero's. On July 23, a spectacular fire engulfed the restaurant causing $75,000 in damage and slightly injured two firemen. The newspaper reported that, "The interior and most of its contents were virtually a complete loss. The roof caved in and steel joists crumpled from the intense heat. Outer walls were left standing." The estimated $15,000 loss in contents was not insured. At the time, two local businessmen were in the process of purchasing the business from the DeNiro brothers. As of the early 2000s the building houses an adult video store.

In late September 1969, the liens were released after a settlement with the IRS. An attorney for the brothers announced that, "the entire $1,188,000 figure was not paid, but a settlement was agreed upon." The attorney refused to reveal the settlement figure, but when asked if it was substantial replied, "On a sum this large, most any settlement might seem substantial."

Incredibly, tax problems continued to plaque the DeNiro family for the next 15 years. In 1974, the three brothers filed suit in federal court claiming that National Cigarette Service and Valley Land Company made an overpayment in 1969 of Vince DeNiro's estate taxes totaling $105,000. In August 1977, the Appellate Court ruled that neither the brothers nor the IRS were entitled to the money, which must be returned to the estate even though it had not yet been probated. In July 1979, U.S. District Court Judge Robert B. Krupansky, empowered the IRS to collect the money. Finally in October 1984, the Sixth U.S. Circuit Court of Appeals ruled that the 1969 payment was legitimate.

Casino DeVincent

On the afternoon of February 12, 1946, citizens of Youngstown crowded around East Federal Street to witness a bizarre sight. Picketing in front of the Regent Pool Room was 34 year-old U.S. Army veteran Casino DeVincent in full uniform.

DeVincent was an employee of the Ohio Works of the Carnegie-Illinois Steel Corporation before entering the Army in June 1941. He served 39 months in Europe before his discharge on November 16, 1945. Returning to Youngstown he went back to work at the steel plant. With his wartime earnings DeVincent began betting on the horses at the Regent Pool Room and a few other locations in the city. The veteran steadily lost his money until his losses totaled $5,500, of which $4,000 ended up in the hands of the bookies from the Regent.

Whether or not the bookies cheated DeVincent is unknown, he never spoke about it. What he did do was make a sign:

I Lost All Of My
Army Savings
at the

Regent Pool Room
Gambling Parlor

Where Are The Police?

They Will Take Other Soldiers
If Not Stopped

He then began picketing outside the Regent Pool Room. His presence caused the operators to discontinue releasing racing results that afternoon. DeVincent vowed to return and picket for two hours each day, until something was done about his money.

Police were alerted by a caller who claimed there was a shooting at the poolroom. When Vice Squad Chief Frank Bognar and his men arrived at Champion and East Federal Streets they found their way blocked by the crowd, which was sympathetic to DeVincent's plight.

Bognar found his way through the crowd, entered the poolroom and arrested William J. Dounchie for operating a gambling place. Bognar's men thought that while they were in the area they would swoop down on some other locations. With the story of DeVincent's demonstration going around, the police found all the places they checked closed.

Police took DeVincent in for questioning, fearing the swelling crowd might riot. The former soldier told his interrogators, "If they [the police] keep the places closed, I'll put my sign away...and if they open up again I'll bring it out." A group of youths "organized as Youngstown Veterans of World War II" arrived at the police station in a riotous mood. DeVincent was released to his attorney Kedgwin Powell, a former Youngstown police chief. Outside the station Powell told the crowd, "Be quiet and everything will be taken care of." He then turned to DeVincent and advised, "Return to your picket post."

DeVincent in speaking with reporters stated that he had threatened the operators of the Regent with a lawsuit if his money was not returned. "They talked pretty rough in trying to convince me not to do it," he said. "All these gambling places should be closed because it is apparent that these gamblers never did a day's work in their lives."

There were no more reports of DeVincent picketing the poolroom, and no confirmation that his money was ever returned. On July 24, however, DeVincent left home and was reported missing. Family members said the veteran had left town before, but never without telling someone where he was going. DeVincent was never seen or heard from again.

Zollie Engel

Described as the last of the independent bookmakers in Youngstown, until falling under the thumb of the Valley's Big 3 – Aiello, Caputo and DiCarlo – during their takeover of the bookmaking business, Zollie Engel was said to be genial until it came to troublesome neighbors. Engel got into the bookmaking profession in the late 1930s and was successful through his subscribership to the race wire service, which provided horse race results from every major track in the country.

During the vice crackdown after the bombing of Youngstown Police Sergeant William Davis' home on April 20, 1942, the vice squad under new squad leader Andrew Przelomski was making it tough on the area bookies. The service from the race wire was cut off locally by police. In July, vice squad members suspected that the "roly-poly" Engel was receiving wire service information from an out of town source. On the morning of July 25, vice squad officers raided his operation at the Pick-Out News Stand at 1307 Market Street, next door to Louis Tiberio's Tropics Night Club near Myrtle Avenue. Engel was arrested and officers recovered racing forms, betting sheets and a set of ear phones, apparently used in the receiving of wire service information. Two days later, Engel pleaded not guilty at his arraignment before Judge Harry C. Hoffman. When the case came to trial on September 2, Engel pleaded guilty and was fined $25 and costs.

On March 15, 1943, the vice squad again raided Engel's Market Street location, seizing racing forms and betting slips. Five men were found on the premises wagering on horses. Engel was arrested and held overnight before being released on bond the next morning. Engel went right back to the Pick-Out News Stand to begin business again in open defiance of both Special Prosecutor Simon Leis, who was in the process of bringing down the lottery houses and anything else in his way, and Sergeant William Davis, who was back in charge of the vice squad.

Incensed by Engel's arrogance, Davis led a raiding party over to Market Street less than six hours after Zollie's release. The *Vindicator* described the set up Davis and his raiders walked in to:

> "Engel was in a small booth at one side of the room, just behind a plywood partition which shuts off view from the street. He was listening to a telephone over which racing results were being given. As the results came in, Engel announced them over a loud-speaking system and the results were posted on a board."

Confronting Davis, Engel stated, "You can't do this to me."

Davis glared at the bookie and retorted, "You're not going to tell me what I can do."

With that, Davis' men produced an axe and a sledgehammer and went to work. In minutes tables, chairs and a horse race result board lay on the floor reduced to kindling. Six patrons of the newsstand, which featured nary a newspaper nor magazine, watched the spectacle before being carted off to the city jail where they were questioned by Leis' investigator and released.

On March 24, Engel appeared before Municipal Judge Robert Nevin, where he pleaded guilty to two charges – unlawful possession of gambling equipment and operating a place of gambling. The fines totaled $1,000, which the judge reduced to $250, and a 30-day jail sentence was suspended. Nevin warned Engel that if he violated a city or state gambling law in the next two years, the sentence and the balance of the fines would be imposed. Zollie informed the judge that he was through with the "bookie business."

An August 27, 1946, *Vindicator* article stated that Engel "never considered a 'big operator'...has operated without interference since March 1943." That ended the previous day when Mahoning County Sheriff Ralph Elser and a raiding crew were on a city and county drive against vice. The newspaper reported that the raid "came at the height of the afternoon traffic rush. Motorists parked double, and even triple to watch the action at the horse race betting 'joint' which Engel has only recently remodeled." Thirty patrons were in the Market Street establishment when Elser and ten deputies arrived at 5:00 p.m.

Engel was taken before Justice of the Peace Bert Rosensteel and charged with keeping a place where gambling is permitted. Zollie pleaded guilty and was fined $500 and costs. Incredibly, Engel was back in business the next afternoon.

In the fall of 1946, Thomas J. Herbert, the Republican nominee for governor of Ohio, attacked incumbent Frank Lausche claiming that, "gambling is flourishing unmolested in Ohio and particularly in Mahoning County." Lausche responded by demanding that state lawmakers give him the authority to remove county sheriffs "who failed to enforce the law."

When asked for his comment to the political rhetoric, Sheriff Elser replied, "I have nothing to say, but if I do, it'll be good, I guarantee you."

Instead, Elser's actions spoke louder than his words and resulted in raids on October 9 at three bookie joints in the city; 26 South Champion Street, run by "Cadillac Charlie" Cavallaro; 1307 Market Street, operated by Engel; and the Regent Poolroom at 26 East Federal Street, where Rocky Polito was in charge.

The *Vindicator* described the action:

> "Raiders smashed result boards, jerked telephones out and confiscated them, tore public address systems from the walls and brought them into the county jail. Form sheets and other equipment were packed into boxes and hauled to Elser's office.
>
> "Engel's place was left a shambles by sledgehammer-wielding deputies."

At Engel's place, camouflaged as a radio repair shop, Zollie escaped through a side door when the raiders arrived. The deputies later admitted they didn't guard the door because during a previous raid, when it was the Pick-Out News Stand, the door led to an apartment on the second floor. It had now been "remodeled for escape purposes." Upset over Engel's flight, Elser announced he would get a warrant for him. Shortly after that, Engel appeared at the county jail in the company of his lawyer David Shermer.

Despite another pulverized operation, Engel quickly returned to business at his Market Street address. He was soon facing a different kind of problem. The triumvirate of "Fats" Aiello, "Moosey" Caputo and Joe "the Wolf" DiCarlo were now taking over and providing "protection" to the Valley's bookmakers – at a price. Most of the bookies knuckled under to the pressure, especially since the trio was backed by Mafia muscle coming from another prominent force, the Mafia families of Buffalo, Cleveland and Detroit.

The takeover began around 1945-1946, and by 1947 Zollie Engel was one of the few independents left in the business. By June 1947, Engel was reportedly on the hot seat. A newspaper article claimed Caputo had delivered the word "to close Engel's place because Engel refused to play ball with the downtown[2] boys." The *Vindicator* made the following comments on Engel's current status:

◊ The gambling "bosses" in the city object to the treatment accorded to some customers by Engel.

◊ Engel has long professed disassociation with the gambling rings, which have dominated the city's bookie shops since the old independents were put in the back seat and members of a closed and carefully organized ring took over.

◊ Engel is known to have remarked on several occasions that he wanted nothing to do with downtown operations, but wished to remain in business strictly for himself.

◊ Whether Engel will be forced to join the syndicate along with other old-timers in the bookie business is a question.

Things came to a head for Zollie during the early morning hours of June 30, when a large plate glass window and his front door were smashed by a vandal. Engel quickly had the broken window and the door replaced. At 4:00 the next morning the newly replaced window and door were destroyed, along with a second plate glass window. Although squad cars were reported on Market Street in front of Engel's location, no report of the vandalism was filed at the police station. Police Chief William J. Cleary and Detective Chief William Reed told reporters they had heard nothing of the incident.

When Cleary inquired as to why there was no report of the incident, he was told that two squad cars made the investigation and each one thought the other would write the report. Vice Squad Chief Frank Bognar ordered Engel to close his operation and keep it closed permanently.

In these last months of the administration of Ralph O'Neill, gambling seemed to run wide open in the town. Nothing made that clearer than the way the Engel operation was handled. Within two weeks, Zollie was operating again, apparently having "signed on" with Caputo et al. The *Vindicator*, when pointing this out, stated that Bognar who had ordered it closed, did nothing about the "8 to 10 big operators downtown." In fact, the newspaper stated that Engel's operation was the only bookie joint the vice squad had closed "or even visited officially" since August 30, 1946, nearly a year earlier.

As the November 4 election drew nearer, Republican Charles F. Henderson battered incumbent O'Neill with his "Smash Racket Rule" campaign, pointing out nine bookie joints in the city that the O'Neill administration allowed to operate freely. Two years after Henderson won office, his new chief Eddie Allen had "Fats' Aiello in court on a suspicious person charge and used the opportunity to expose publicly the "muscling in" that the "Big-3" triumvirate had accomplished. Names of the former independent bookies who were brought "into the fold" were Zollie Engel, Phil Rose, Dutch Manley, Joe Melek, Frank Carey and for a short while Charles Cavallaro.

Engel next made the news in May 1951, when he was arrested for assaulting his 61 year-old next door neighbor. At the time of his arrest, the newspaper claimed that "the former smalltime bookmaker is said to have had several brawls with neighbors near his home at 21 Woodview Avenue," in Boardman. In this case, it was reported that Engel was picked up after the neighbor Paul Foster filed an affidavit. Engel and Foster had a number of disputes over the boundaries of their yards until a fence was erected. On May 28, Engel saw Foster on his property trimming the hedges which had reached over the fence. The newspaper reported, "After an argument and an exchange of blows, the former bookie struck Foster with a wire support for wreaths. A doctor's report showed Foster partially disabled for six weeks."

Brought to the police station, Engel was "arraigned by telephone" when it was found that Common Pleas Judge John Ford had left for the day. The newspaper didn't mention what Engel was doing for employment but stated the "former smalltime bookmaker" pulled $300 from his pocket to make his own bail. On August 4, Engel pleaded guilty to assault and battery and was fined $200 and sentenced to 90 days in jail. The sentence was suspended, pending "good behavior."

Zollie Engel last made the news in October 1963, when the *Vindicator* reported that a Federal grand jury in Cleveland had subpoenaed him to appear. A wire service reported that Engel's name was called, but Federal sources said he was not on the list of people to be questioned.

Engel remained in the Youngstown area, where he died in June 1984.

Buddy Fares

Bud J. "Buddy" Fares was a colorful and controversial figure in Youngstown. Born in Lebanon in 1909, Fares came to America as part of a large family (ten children) at a young age. The family first settled in Trenton, New Jersey, before moving to Youngstown in 1924.

In grade school at Sacred Heart and high school at South High, Fares gained a reputation as a superb athlete. He built his own backyard gym and worked out at the Idora Park Beach to build a body that earned him the reputation as "Youngstown's outstanding strong man." Pictures of Fares posing in bathing trunks appeared in bodybuilding magazines around the country and made him an international celebrity during the early 1930s. Fares turned to the popular sport of wrestling and racked up 304 wins without a defeat.

From the mid-1930s until his death Fares was never far from some publicized event:

◊ 1937 filed suit against the city claiming that the establishment of a boxing commission in the city was unconstitutional, that it was run as a "dictatorship," and that he was unfairly dismissed as a member of it.

◊ 1938 filed a law suit against the *Vindicator* charging that sports editor Frank "Doc" Ward libeled him in a commentary regarding his suspension by the boxing commission. The $100,000 suit ended when Judge JHC Lyon ordered a directed verdict.

◊ 1949 two young people drowned – Beverly Adler, 18 and Eugene Procopio, 21 – when Fares lost control of a motorboat on Lake Milton. Fares, the victims and two others – Mary Helen Adler and Joseph Ronci (the younger brother of Nello Ronci) – were thrown out of the boat when Fares failed to negotiate a sharp turn 100 yards from shore.

◊ 1952 had his brother Thomas indicted after an argument involving the removal of a float from his Lake Milton property.

◊ 1953 arrested and indicted for criminal libel for comments he made in his weekly publication, *The Youngstowner*, which accused Chief Edward Allen and members of his vice squad of being in an "alliance" with local underworld figures.

◊ 1953 his home at 633 Almyra Avenue, Youngstown was the target of a 3:00 a.m. dynamite explosion on December 10, which destroyed a porch railing, broke two large windows, damaged the porch floor and destroyed the front door and a storm door. Damage was estimated at $500.

◊ 1953 won a suit against Joseph Alexander after suing for non-payment of a 1947 loan made to him for equipment purchased for the Center Amusement Company.

◊ 1960 indicted for failure to file tax returns for the years 1957 through 1959.

◊ 1964 appointed Mahoning County Civil Defense Director by county commissioners.

◊ 1964 arrested for possession of obscene films. Two rolls of 8-mm. film were found in the trunk of Fares' county car, used in his civil defense work. Fares claimed he was "framed." Three months later Judge Martin P. Joyce cleared him of any wrongdoing.

In addition to his work on *The Youngstowner* and as Civil Defense Director, Fares had a varied career. He spent 15 years with the U.S. Post Office, was a sales supervisor for Randolph Hearst Publications, a sales manager for the Leisy Brewing Company, president of Fares Ice Cream Cone Company, served as an auditor, investigator and enforcement officer for the Ohio Public Utilities Commission, performed public relations work and was a free-lance writer.

One of Fares' talents was speechmaking. He led the Youngstown Toastmaster's Club and won trophies for speechmaking at the local, state and national level. He also helped conduct local classes in the art.

On April 9, 1974, Fares was making a late afternoon drive through Mill Creek Park. He suffered an apparent heart attack and his automobile went off the road ending up on a hillside. He was rushed to South Side Hospital where he was pronounced dead. Fares was 64 years old.

"Booze" Gianfrancesco

Anthony P. Gianfrancesco was known in the Youngstown area as "Booze." There was no explanation, at least not in the newspapers or police records, as to where the nickname came from. It may have come from his rap sheet, which showed three arrests for liquor violations. If that were the case, however, they could have nicknamed him "Bugs" for the 15 arrests for policy related infractions or "Traffic" for the 14 vehicle related marks on his record, all between 1941 and 1962.

Gianfrancesco was born on April 30, 1922. His first arrest came when he was just 19 years old. On March 2, 1941, he was arrested for suspicion and released. He was arrested seven times between November 1941 and September 1946; twice for possession of lottery slips, once for disturbance and four times for reckless driving. Perhaps the last five incidents involved "booze." Despite these early arrests, Gianfrancesco found time to serve his country as a member of the Navy. After the war he became a lifetime member of the Italian-American War Veterans

On February 13, 1948, while working as a bug writer for Louis Tiberio, Gianfrancesco was arrested for possession of betting slips. Before Judge Frank Anzellotti he was fined $500, of which $400 was suspended, and placed on two years probation. Five days later he was arrested for the same crime. This time he demanded a jury trial. When he came before Anzellotti again on February 28, 1949, he was arrested for a liquor violation and for possession of football pools. Gianfrancesco appeared in court to drop his request for a jury trial and pleaded guilty on all three charges. He was fined $559 and his probation extended another two years. Before the year 1949 was over, Gianfrancesco was arrested twice more for possession of lottery tickets.

On January 5, 1951, vice squad officers arrested Gianfrancesco at Market Street and Myrtle Avenue after finding 30 policy slips on him. "Booze" was on his way to setting a record for the most arrests for possession of lottery slips in the Valley. As was becoming his modus operandi, Gianfrancesco demanded a jury trial and would then plead guilty before the trial date and take his $500 fine.

With Gianfrancesco's wallet a little lighter after these fines, he could sometimes be found bartending at Tiberio's Tropics Night Club. It was here that his next arrest occurred on April Fools' Day 1951. Two state liquor agents walked in and ordered a shot of whiskey. They then arrested Gianfrancesco for serving liquor after the Sunday morning closing time. He gave his name as Anthony Ross and his address as the nightclub's. In reporting the arrest, the newspaper referred to him as the "oft-nabbed" bug man.

In court eleven days later, Gianfrancesco was fined $50. He appealed with a defense that he was not an employee of the Tropics and had merely stopped behind the bar in the absence of the regular bartender to help out. More than a year later, on May 1, 1952, Common Pleas Judge John W. Powers wasn't buying it and he fined "Booze" $50 for serving the booze.

It was nearly three years before Gianfrancesco was arrested again on bug charges. On February 1, 1954, vice squad members nabbed two veterans of the policy rackets. Sam Zappi was arrested for the eleventh time, while Gianfrancesco suffered his seventh policy-related apprehension. "Booze" was stopped by police at the intersection of Market Street and Woodland Avenue. In his automobile the officers found bug slips and lottery books in a hidden compartment behind a fake clock in the dashboard. Gianfrancesco pleaded not guilty and asked for a jury trial.

On March 24, 1954, police again stopped Gianfrancesco's automobile on Market Street and discovered two policy pads on the front seat. A search of the car revealed four bug slips hidden in the upholstery. When questioned by Vice Squad Chief George Krispli, he admitted to picking up the bug slips but refused to reveal for whom he was working. Gianfrancesco pleaded innocent before Judge Franko and had his $1,000 bond from his previous arrest continued. On April 3, "Booze" waived his jury trial and was fined a total of $500 for both charges.

The following month Gianfrancesco was arrested by Mahoning County officials for possession of lottery slips. The county vice squad chief and a deputy sheriff stopped his vehicle on Market Street and found 25 bug slips. On May 23, "Booze" broke his old record of being arrested twice in five days when he was arrested for the second time in two days. It was the same two county officials who stopped him and found bug slips in a secret dashboard compartment.

Gianfrancesco remained free of lottery arrests for the next eight years. Then on August 17, 1962, he was stopped in the parking lot of the Atlantic Mills Thrift Center on Belmont Avenue after police saw him stuffing lottery slips in a crack in the front seat of his car. By now laws were passed to make it tougher on the policy operators and "Booze" was charged with "promoting a numbers game" and was indicted by the county grand jury. Provisions under a new state law allowed judges to place convicted defendants in the penitentiary. Gianfrancesco's case was the second to be tried under the new law. In December 1962, Joey Naples was convicted and sentenced to a term of one to ten years in the Ohio Penitentiary.

The case went to trial on February 13, 1963, and Gianfrancesco was represented by Edward L. Williams and Jack W. Nybell. The case was prosecuted by Assistant County Prosecutor Loren E. Van Brocklin before Judge Sidney Rigelhaupt, who was trying his first criminal case on the common pleas bench. Defense counsel filed a motion to suppress the evidence claiming it was obtained illegally. The motion was overruled and Gianfrancesco's defense was now that the slips weren't his.

When the arresting officer took the stand he was asked by Nybell to describe Gianfrancesco's role in Youngstown's policy rackets. The officer replied, "I'd say he is one of the main cogs in the wheel; not just an ordinary pickup man."

Gianfrancesco did not testify and the defense did not put any witnesses on the stand. After a two-day trial the jury deliberated five hours before finding "Booze" guilty as charged. On February 25, Gianfrancesco stood in front of Judge Rigelhaupt for sentencing. Attorney Nybell spoke before the court and admitted to knowing Gianfrancesco "all his life." Constantly referring to his client as "Booze," Nybell described his friend as a "small fry" in the business and gave the following impassioned plea:

> "Let's be honest about this thing, Judge. The numbers traffic is in existence and the extent that it exists is the result of collusion between the police...and people who run around and tell you anything else are idiots and distort the known facts.
>
> "There is such a thing, your honor, as taking a pinch and that's the case where the policeman for reasons of his own, for either the newspaper, or for the purpose of satisfying the captain or some superior, has to make an arrest, at a particular time, and they need to have somebody to be arrested.
>
> "So the fellow makes a pinch, takes a $5 bill. In one case that I know of and in other cases, the price might be $10, $20, $25, $50, and he goes and stands on the corner, sits in a car at some pre-arranged place and waits for the policeman that comes to arrest him with the slips and money and takes him down before the magistrate. He is fined $25 and the newspaperman gets his story and the policeman has his arrest and I suppose the general public thought that the numbers traffic was being disposed of.
>
> "I don't know if anybody was fooled or merely wanted to be fooled and I don't think they really cared, your honor. But at any rate that's the circumstances, your honor, under which those arrests were compiled. I think you can ask any policeman or any so-called hoodlum or any guy in the rackets in Youngstown."

Nybell was far from through; he tried to justify Gianfrancesco's role in the policy racket by adding that "Booze" was involved in numbers for years and that the "neighborhood bug man arrived with the same regularity and was looked on with the same respect as the mail man or the milk man."

As far as a legitimate job, Nybell claimed Gianfrancesco was out of work for the past 17 months after losing his job because of a difference in politics, having worked as a truck driver for the city street and water departments. The attorney's appeal touched on Gianfrancesco's ethnicity as he pleaded with Rigelhaupt for probation because "with Governor [James] Rhodes in office, there will be a new pardon and parole board and it will be prejudiced against 'Booze' because of his long last name, his manner of speech and because he comes from Youngstown, which has had so much adverse publicity as a crime and racket town." Nybell then pulled out all the stops when he sought sympathy from the judge by revealing that his client was now separated from his wife and was trying to support five children, aged 10 to 20 years old.

When Police Chief William Golden was informed of Nybell's courtroom dramatics, including the "rigged arrests" statement, he countered, "I certainly don't know of any such arrangement and if I did, I would not stand for it. I would fire any policeman who ever made such a deal and I certainly mean this."

Golden made the understatement that Nybell was simply trying to "create an air of sympathy in court." Still, the chief declared, "Let him file an affidavit against any man in the department and if there is any truth to it, we'll take action and bring it before a grand jury."

Prosecutor Van Brocklin also saw the plea for sympathy and told the court the prosecutor's office was vehemently opposed to probation. Judge Rigelhaupt was not impressed by the defense attorney's diatribe. He declared that Gianfrancesco's past record, with numbers arrests dating back to 1942, made it "impossible" for him to grant probation. He then sentenced "Booze" to serve one to ten years in the penitentiary.

Nybell immediately filed a motion with the Seventh District Court of Appeals. Bond was set at $5,000 and Gianfrancesco was free while the conviction was appealed and he prepared for his next trial.

Just 49 days after his August 17 arrest, Youngstown police arrested Gianfrancesco and four others for selling lottery tickets near North Side Hospital. The men were turned over to Trumbull County officials to be tried in that jurisdiction. The men were charged under the new state felony statute. The other four men pleaded guilty and were sentenced to 30 days in jail and fined $500, but "Booze," as usual, demanded his day in court.

The trial got underway with jury selection in the courtroom of Trumbull County Common Pleas Judge William M. McLain on June 4, 1963. Again Nybell represented Gianfrancesco. Dan Maggianetti and five officers from the Intelligence & Security Squad, including William Gruver and Randall Wellington, testified to the arrests made back on October 5, 1962.

Unlike the previous trial, Gianfrancesco took the stand this time and was questioned for 90 minutes. He admitted that he was at the North Side Hospital facility, but was only there to collect money from the sale of a set of automobile tires he had sold. After the jury deliberated for five and a half hours they returned with a verdict of guilty. On June 8, Gianfrancesco was sentenced to a term of one to ten years in prison and fined $500.

Nearly two years passed before Gianfrancesco entered prison. Nybell appealed the case claiming the search of his client's automobile was illegal. In late November, the Seventh District Court of Appeals upheld the decision. In March 1964, the Ohio Supreme Court refused to review the case. The following month, Judge Rigelhaupt ordered the arrest of Gianfrancesco after the newspaper reported he was missing for "some time." When the bonding company was notified to produce Gianfrancesco or forfeit the bond, Gianfrancesco suddenly reappeared and his attorney filed for a stay of sentence.

In May 1964, the U.S. Supreme Court approved the stay and Gianfrancesco was released on a $5,000 bond. The following month the state supreme court again rejected his appeal.

While Gianfrancesco was still out on bond, he was charged with the attempted rape of Barbara Femia, an "exotic dancer" on July 10. The next day Femia announced she wanted to drop the charges. On July 19, Femia failed to appear in court and the charges were dismissed.

On December 8, the U.S. Supreme Court refused to review Gianfrancesco's case. After one final appeal Gianfrancesco turned himself in on March 9, 1965. "Booze" was housed at the Marion Correctional Institution, from where he was released on December 1, 1966. From 1969 to 1975 "Booze" was a constant target of the FBI. He was swept up in a raid in late November 1969, which targeted area bookmakers at 60 locations. In April 1970, he was one of 20 gambling figures secretly indicted in Cleveland by a special federal grand jury investigating organized crime in northeastern Ohio. That November, he pleaded guilty to a conspiracy charge for conducting interstate gambling. When he came up for sentencing in U.S. District Court in Cleveland he was fined $2,000.

On November 18, 1971, the FBI raided 22 area gambling joints. Gianfrancesco, who was still on federal probation from his May 1971 sentencing, was fined $1,000 after pleading guilty to another gambling conspiracy charge. In July 1975, he was arrested for failing to pay more than half of the fine imposed over four years earlier. During a hearing before a federal judge in Akron, Gianfrancesco told the court that his only income came from working at Standard Motors and Ravenwood Motors in Youngstown. The judge responded by extending the terms of Gianfrancesco's probation by another two years.

Three months later, Gianfrancesco was indicted by a federal grand jury in Cleveland for lying to the Akron judge after information was presented to them by the U.S. Department of Justice's Organized Crime and Racketeering Strike

Force that Gianfrancesco was involved in bookmaking activities with Nello Ronci during 1974. On December 19, 1975, Gianfrancesco and Nello Ronci were indicted with eleven other gamblers and charged with federal gambling and conspiracy violations. Convicted on May 23, 1977, Gianfrancesca was given an eight month sentence.

By the mid-1970s Gianfrancesco's criminal career was at an end. He spent his last years in Youngstown working for the Mahoning County Nursing Home. In the early 1980s, Gianfrancesco got married and relocated to Ligonier, Pennsylvania, where he spent the last 23 years of his life. He died on August 13, 2005, of respiratory failure at the age of 83.

Red Giordano & the Marino Fur Theft

Rocco E. "Rocky" Marino was the brother of Roy "Happy" Marino. While Rocco appeared to be a legitimate businessman, he was never far from controversy. In 1924, he received a franchise to operate the Checker Taxi Cabs in the city. Later that year, he took over the Yellow Cab business when that franchise failed. He was remotely connected to bookmaking operations and the pin ball machine business in Youngstown. Marino, however, and his beautiful wife Marguerite were also involved in charitable work in the city. Each summer they held an annual picnic for crippled and blind children.

With the profits from his business Marino invested in restaurants, nightclubs and taverns both in Youngstown and in Miami Beach, Florida, where the couple had a second home. By the 1960s, Marino was running a successful chain of restaurants known as Doghouse, Inc. Both Marino and his wife died in south Florida, Marguerite in Miami Beach in January 1986, and Rocco in Miami in October 1989.

On New Years' Eve 1947, Marino and his wife were entertaining friends at their Supper Club. Rocco and Marguerite sent their 17 year-old son home early to turn off the Christmas tree lights, which were left on. When he arrived at 2:45 a.m., he found the home ransacked.

During the wee hours of this first day of 1948, thieves broke into the home at 136 Broadway and stole furs and jewelry valued at $16,000. From the home, which was next door to recently defeated Mayor Ralph O'Neill, burglars got a silver blue mink coat and a gray stone marten stole worth $5,000 apiece. In addition, jewelry valued at $6,000 was taken. For some reason, silver, said to be worth thousands of dollars, was untouched. With few leads, other than it was a "professional job" the investigation quickly fizzled out.

On February 21, Detroit police followed gambler Max Stern and a companion to Willow Run Airport. The Detroit FBI had received a tip that two men, flying in from Cleveland, had stolen furs in their possession. At the airport police arrested the two Detroit men along with Joseph "Red" Giordano and Anthony "Tony

Dope" Delsanter. Giordano, who was living at the Youngstown Hotel for the past two years, told police he was arrested twice in New Kensington, Pennsylvania, but outside of that he apparently had no record.[3] Delsanter, from the Little Italy section of Cleveland, had quite an extensive record going back to his early twenties when he was friends with Aladena "Jimmy the Weasel" Fratianno. Delsanter once served a nine-year term in the Ohio Penitentiary for robbery.

Police found in Giordano's possession a silver blue mink coat and a gray stone marten stole. Giordano was carrying a bag containing the furs. In the car was a matching carrying case, which contained a .38 revolver with extra ammunition. He claimed the case was not his.

Two days later, it was reported that the furs were the ones taken from the Marino residence on New Years' Day. The Marinos were vacationing in Florida, but plans were announced that their daughter and a furrier from Cleveland, where they purchased the furs, would travel to Detroit to identify them. After arrival, the two identified the coats, through serial numbers stamped into the expensive pelts, as belonging to Marguerite. The daughter also revealed that since it was reported that she was going to Detroit she received a number of threatening phone calls.

On February 26, Delsanter, Giordano and Stern appeared in Federal court where they were officially charged with violating the national stolen property act. All three pleaded not guilty and were returned to jail under $25,000 bonds. Five days later, a bond hearing was held. A federal prosecutor asked that the bonds be continued because witnesses were being threatened. The judge, instead, reduced the bonds of all three – Delsanter and Stern to $20,000, and Giordano to $10,000.

The trial of the three men did not take place until April 1949. During the trial Delsanter was acquitted on a directed verdict. On April 28, a federal jury deliberated 90 minutes before it found Giordano and Stern guilty. On July 14, both men were sentenced to four years in Federal prison, but were released on bond pending appeal.

While the appeal was pending, Giordano returned to Youngstown and continued his nefarious activities. In August 1949, he was tied to Joe DiCarlo and Joseph Alexander in the Green Village nightclub and ownership of the Woodworth Novelty Company.

On December 11, the Sixth Circuit Court of Appeals granted Giordano and Stern a new trial. The decision was based on the finding of the concealed handgun. Giordano was not charged with carrying a concealed weapon, because police could not say it was in his possession at the time of his arrest. An assistant U.S. attorney, however, mentioned the finding of the weapon and the appeals court found that grounds for reversal of the conviction.

On October 3, 1951, Giordano and Stern were again found guilty of the fur theft and again sentenced to four years in federal prison...and again remained free while appeals were pending. Incredibly, on May 25, 1953, the two were granted yet another trial after the same appeals court sent the case back to the district court because the judge's instructions limited the jury's ability to consider the value of the furs. Originally estimated at a value of $10,000 the two coats were now said to be worth $7,995. I can find no record of another court trial in the records of the *Vindicator* on this case.

It was reported that Giordano returned to New Kensington, where he worked for Pittsburgh Mafia heavyweight Kelly Mannarino. On July 14, 1961, he was one of six men sentenced to federal prison for trying to smuggle guns and ammunition, stolen from a Canton, Ohio, armory and placed aboard a small plane in Morgantown, West Virginia, headed to Fidel Castro's Cuban rebels back 1958. Giordano was sentenced to three years.

Giordano died in April 1974.

Green Acres Casino Robbery

By Friday, September 17, 1948, a new gambling joint known as the Green Acres casino, located at 150 Broad Street in Struthers, was reportedly in operation from ten to thirty days. Underworld names associated with the club were Joe DiCarlo and Frank Budak. Around 4:00 this Friday morning, five masked bandits entered and one of them announced, "This is a stickup." There were approximately 250 patrons present, who were ordered to line up against the walls, along with club employees. While three of the bandits kept everyone covered, the other two methodically searched the pockets of the patrons taking money, wallets, rings and anything else of value – the total haul was estimated at $25,000 to $30,000 (this estimate was later reduced to $8,000 to $10,000). One of the alleged robbery victims was Joe DiCarlo, who, witnesses said, turned over an expensive diamond ring to the bandits. Then all the money left behind at the chuck-o-luck, roulette, and dice tables was collected. The robbery was reminiscent of the Mounds Club robbery in Lake County in September 1947, where an alleged $500,000 was taken.

When the robbers completed their work they headed for a door leading to the outside where three vehicles were waiting. Before all could escape one of the casino's guards, stationed in a wire cage above the entrance, opened fire with a revolver, emptying it at the fleeing intruders. When the gunfire began, the patrons dove to the floor to escape any stray bullets. The guard later claimed he "winged" three of the bandits. One eyewitness account said one of the robbers fell to the floor and crawled to the door where his accomplices helped him to the cars.

When the shooting was over, the patrons crowded to the exits and poured out into the street, many looking for taxis to get them out of the area. In all the excitement, no one took time to call the Struther's police to report the incident.

Instead, the bolting patrons told cab drivers what happened and by sunrise the story of the robbery was the talk of the town, seemingly being discussed everywhere with the exception of Struthers police headquarters.

Around midnight that Friday, a 25 year-old hood, who had already collected an impressive rap sheet, was brought into Emergency Clinic Hospital in Cleveland by a younger brother. Hospital personnel notified Cleveland police and Inspector Frank W. Story arrived and identified the wounded man as Julius Anthony Petro.[4] Doctors were treating him for wounds in the right chest and right arm. When Story questioned him, Petro claimed he was shot "accidentally while out drinking with the boys." When police received conflicting stories from Petro's family, they decided to investigate further. One of the things Julius Petro told police was that he was treated earlier by another doctor, whom he refused to name, claiming the physician had removed the bullet that had entered his chest. Doctors at the Emergency Clinic Hospital discovered otherwise, the bullet was still in Petro.

On Saturday, Struthers police questioned John Sanko, whose position at the casino was not clear. One report said he identified himself to police as the owner, another claimed he was merely a bartender. Sanko was no stranger to police. His rap sheet started when he was just eleven years old after breaking the door seals on several Baltimore & Ohio Railroad cars. On November 17, 1933, Sanko was stopped on the street while carrying money stolen from a service station. He slugged his captor and broke free while the officer was requesting help at a police call box. The officer fired a warning shot and when Sanko didn't stop he was shot twice in the back. Sanko did two and half years in the Ohio Penitentiary and returned for a year and half after violating parole. In 1938, he was sentenced to 10 to 25 years after an armed robbery in Warren. His sentence was commuted by Governor John W. Bricker in January 1945, and Sanko was released a year later. Sanko became a close associate of Frank Budak and managed his activities when Budak served a prison term for tax evasion. Sanko was currently working for Budak at the Poland Country Club, where a federal slot machine license was listed in his name.

After Cleveland police heard about the Green Acres robbery, they contacted Struthers officials about the mysterious shooting of Petro. Struthers Police Chief Neil Gordon, Captain Woodrow Sicafuse and a patrolman escorted Sanko to Cleveland to see if he could identify Petro as one of the bandits.

In the prison ward of City Hospital, where Petro was moved, Sanko said he could not identify the wounded man. Wearing a patch over his right eye, Sanko explained to police that one of the robbers hit him with the butt of his revolver, knocking him unconscious. He also declared that none of the casino guards were armed, so it must have been a "gun-toting patron" who opened fire on the escaping bandits. This statement obviously clashed with those given by eyewitnesses. The next day Sanko was charged with being the keeper of a gambling casino.

The Struthers police investigation revealed that the building that housed the Green Acres was owned in part by Helen Tablack, the wife of State Representative George D. Tablack, who was known as the "Little Caesar" of Struthers' First Ward. In addition to the Green Acres, the building housed the Town Tavern and three apartments on the second floor. When asked who the Green Acres portion was leased to, George Tablack replied, "I don't recall the name."

By Sunday, none of the patrons had filed police reports regarding their losses. Struther's Police Chief Gordon pointed out that the victims of the Mounds Club robbery also declined to make reports until they realized they could not collect on insurance claims without a formal police report being filed.

Currently free on a $2,500 bond on a charge of robbing a café on Superior Avenue in Cleveland, Petro's bond was quickly raised to $25,000 by a common pleas judge at the request of prosecutors. On September 20, City Hospital physicians planned on surgically removing the bullet from Petro's chest. Removing the bullet and hoping that the gun that fired it would be recovered was the only chance police had to tie Petro to the robbery. No other slugs were recovered from the club. Petro, who was sitting up and reading in his hospital bed, became agitated when the attendants entered his room. Petro foiled their surgery plans when his condition improved to the point that the removal of the bullet was not necessary. On September 28, Petro was released from City Hospital with the slug still in him. He was taken to the county jail where he posted his $25,000 bond and left on a stretcher headed for his home and bed rest.

That same day, Sam Jerry Monachino, an alleged accomplice of Petro in both the Mounds Club and Green Acres robberies, tried to sell a three-and-a-quarter-carat diamond ring for $1,000. At 1:10 the next morning he left his Cleveland home after telling his wife, Margaret he was going to purchase a newspaper, despite not having a cent on him. A few minutes later, Margaret heard him yell, "Honey! Honey! Help!" Despite being eight months pregnant Margaret Monachino, a former nightclub singer, ran to her husband's aid. She arrived just as a gunman was firing the last of six slugs into her prone husband as he lay in the gutter. The gunman pulled the lapel of his coat over his face, aimed the gun at Margaret and dry-fired the revolver three more times before running to a waiting automobile. Police believed that the ring Monachino had tried to pawn the day before was the one taken from Joe DiCarlo. Investigators theorized that Monachino was set up by a man wanting to purchase the ring.

An autopsy showed Monachino had ten wounds causing police to conclude that at least two men were involved in the killing. Hours after the shooting, a Smith & Wesson .38 revolver was recovered from the tree lawn of Newton D. Baker III, the son of the former mayor and Secretary of War under President Wilson. Police traced the gun and found that it was sold by the factory to a sporting goods store in Springfield, Illinois, before being purchased by a man who gave a fictitious Youngstown address. On October 6, a second Smith & Wesson .38 revolver was found by a doctor in the neighborhood of the killing. Police traced its sale from the factory, to a gunsmith in Sandusky, and then to a dealer in Youngstown where a man named "Legs" purchased it. Youngstown Police Chief Eddie Allen later claimed an employee of the Jungle Inn purchased one of the guns.

While in Cleveland attempting to purchase tickets to a World Series game, police arrested Joe DiCarlo on October 6 at the Hollenden Hotel. He was questioned about the Green Acres robbery and the murder of Monachino before being released. He denied any ring was stolen.

William Lantini

Known to many as "Billy Sunday," this Youngstown bootlegger and gambler was no clergyman. Born William Vito Lantini on January 1, 1899 (some records list 1898) in Trapani Paceo, Italy, he had his brush with the law on May 30, 1921, when he was arrested as Vito DeManco for armed robbery in Detroit. On October 5, 1937, he was arrested in Cleveland for operating a still and sentenced to a year and a day in federal prison.

During World War II, the United States went to a system of gasoline rationing to help with the war effort. This practice created a black market for counterfeit and stolen gasoline ration coupons throughout the country. Underworld figures in every city became involved in the racket; the most notable was Carlo Gambino in New York City, then a capo in the crime family run by Vincent Mangano. Involved in policing the ration stamps were investigators from the Office of Price Administration, known as the OPA.

In early 1944, the OPA became aware of a ring operating in the Mahoning Valley that was receiving counterfeit stamps from Cleveland and Detroit. Outside of the activity in the Motor City, the Youngstown district was cited as the worst in the Mid-West when it came to illegal activity in the gas-rationing field. Seventy-seven gasoline dealers were cited for violations of OPA regulations and 40 dealers were suspended.

In March, an OPA investigator, posing as a filling station attendant, arrested Anthony Longo and Mike Pavliga, from whom 800 gallons of counterfeit coupons were confiscated. Days later, four more were arrested – William Lantini, Nicholas "Shine" Jardine, Dominic DeSantis and Roland "Lunch" DeSantis. Lantini and Jardine were arrested in a Market Street tavern, where they were caught with counterfeit coupons for 30,000 gallons, worth about $1,200.

With the maximum penalty for possessing or transferring counterfeit coupons a year in prison and a $10,000 fine, both men were looking at stiff sentences. After several preliminary hearings, on April 5, on the recommendation of the Assistant U.S. attorney in Cleveland, the charges against Lantini and Jardine were suddenly dismissed without explanation. The next year Jardine was convicted on another gas coupon counterfeiting charge and was sent to a federal prison for ten months.

Outside of traffic violations and the seemingly obligatory "suspicious person" arrests in connection with the 1950s bombing epidemic, Lantini was off the front pages until April 23, 1959. Around 4:00 a.m. that morning he was arrested after sheriff's deputies checked on the activity at a new pool room, said to be operated by Vince DeNiro – A & A Billiards on North Meridian Road. Lantini was reported to be involved in a dice game, where $350 was found on the table. Two days later Roland "Lunch" DeSantis "took the rap" and was fined $150. Lantini wasn't charged.

In April of the following year, at the same location now known as the B & B Billiards Club, U.S. Treasury agents paid a visit. The Treasury Agency was in the process of a crack down on 51 cities in 23 states looking for violators of the federal gambling tax stamp. When they arrived, in the late afternoon, Lantini was outside enjoying the sunshine. The six agents searched the premises and while they found dice, cards, crap tables, money boxes, poker chips and a chuck-a-luck cage, they didn't find any signs of bookmaking, which was the only charge for which they could arrest Lantini. Ironically, the one thing they didn't find in the billiards club was a billiards table.

Lantini spoke to the agent-in-charge and said he was the proprietor of the club. He even admitted that he made his living from taking cuts from the poker and dice games. Lantini had no gambling stamp, but since there were no federal violations "Billy Sunday" was released after a long interrogation. The discouraged agents said they would alert the local authorities, "If they wish to discuss what we found."

During the early 1960s, Lantini's name was associated with the barbut game that some believed to be behind the deadly murder spree that was gripping the city. He was hauled in a number of times, charged as a suspicious person. Lantini was questioned extensively after the bombing murder of Charles Cavallaro that resulted in the tragic death of his son. During the grand jury investigation that followed, he was cited for contempt for not answering questions and sentenced to two days in jail and fined; the Seventh District Court of Appeals later reversed the contempt charges.

Lantini worked as a bartender at the Capital Bar until the mid-1960s. Around this time he was diagnosed with cancer, which he fought for the last few years of his life. On New Year's Day 1968, Lantini succumbed to his illness at St. Elizabeth's Hospital. He was 69 years old.

Gus Leamis / Greek-Syrian Coffee House

"Gus" Leamis had his first arrest in Youngstown on April 11, 1945, when he was 45 years old – or thereabouts. His Youngstown police arrest card shows three different dates of birth. His obituary stated he was born on August 13,

1900, in Rhodes, Greece, and that relatives spelled the name Liamis (between the newspapers and the police files, his first name appears as Custas, Costos and Constant; while his last name was Leamas, Leames and Leamis). The first arrest was for having an open container of alcohol in a public place. No one accused Leamis of having a drinking problem, but by 1956 he had additional arrests for public drunkenness, open container violations, drunk and disorderliness, as well as larceny, suspicion, interfering with an officer, assault and battery.

Leamis' first gambling arrest came on August 5, 1954, on a night when the police raided seven suspected policy headquarters, but jailed only two men. Leamis was apprehended at his headquarters, the Greek-Syrian Coffee House at 28 South Avenue. Perhaps the fact that Leamis had lottery tickets in his pocket, along with $800 in cash, led to him being singled out for arrest. Vice Squad Chief George Krispli announced the raids were carried out because the "bug" operators were "getting a little bold."

On November 23, 1956, shortly after the second bombing of Mahoning County Democratic Chairman Jack Sulligan's home, police made a citywide sweep arresting 12 men for questioning. When they entered Leamis' South Avenue office, around 11:45 that morning, he was carrying 57 bug slips and $440 in cash. Leamis was charged with possession of numbers slips and carrying on a lottery game. The other men were released.

Leamis was tried before Judge Franko on December 19, 1956. Vice Squad Chief Krispli testified that the slips found in Leamis' possession were in different handwriting and had different lottery station numbers printed on them. This proved, according to City Prosecutor Irwin Kretzer, that Leamis was either a pickup man for the operation or served as the man to whom the numbers slips were turned in. "Either way," Kretzer declared, "it proves Leamis was an important part of a numbers racket in Youngstown, even if it doesn't mean he was the head of it." The prosecutor pointed out that Leamis produced no witnesses to testify to his innocence and failed to take the stand himself. "We've never had a more clear-cut case here," Kretzer added.

Franko didn't see it that way. He ruled the city had failed to prove anything except simple possession of the slips. Instead of Leamis being found guilty of operating a numbers game, he was found guilty of possessing betting slips and fined $100.

Leamis was arrested for assault and battery in August 1957. The victim was Temeus Zaronias, a 70 year-old South Avenue man. Two men held Zaronias in the coffeehouse while Leamis pummeled him. At trial Zaronias told Judge Robert Nevin that he "had a change of heart," and did not wish to prosecute. This apparently infuriated Nevin, who dismissed the charge but then ordered Zaronias to pay court costs.

On November 11, 1958, Leamis was dealing pinochle in the Coffee House when Nick John Pappas, an oft-arrested bug writer, called for a new set of cards to be used. Leamis refused and Pappas stormed out angry. Soon afterward, Leamis was summoned to take a phone call across the street at the Parthenon Bar, his telephone having been removed on the orders of Chief Cress the previous March. After taking the phone call, Leamis was crossing South Avenue to return to the Coffee House when Pappas fired a shot at him with a .32. The bullet missed and police soon arrived. They found the gun hidden in a drawer behind the bar in the Parthenon and arrested Pappas. The next day, before a generous Judge Franko, instead of being charged with attempted murder, Pappas pled guilty to a charge of discharging a firearm within the city limits. His fine of $100 was suspended after he agreed to stay away from South Avenue for 90 days. Leamis and Pappas must have made amends since the latter was found in the Coffee Shop on August 7, 1962, during a raid.

In 1960, Leamis was arrested twice for suspicion and released. In September, he was questioned about the shooting of "Fats" Aiello. The Valley's most recognized hood allegedly shot himself accidentally in the leg and gave police several stories as to how it happened. The most accepted one was that he shot himself while rolling dice at a barbut game in Leamis' Greek-Syrian Coffee House. Leamis countered saying Aiello's "accident" occurred when he was in the parking lot getting out of his car.

On the night of March 22, 1961, Leamis was standing in front of the Marathon Bar at 26 South Avenue with a friend. The man, said to be a "bug" pickup man associated with Vince DeNiro, was arrested. Leamis, seemingly passed over by the officers, protested the arrest. "You'll be sorry for making that arrest," Leamis warned. The angry officers responded by searching Leamis and found a .38 snub-nosed revolver. The coffeehouse operator was taken to jail and charged with carrying a concealed weapon. Nick Pavelko, the vice squad chief, reported Leamis said he carried the gun for his own protection. Pavelko reported, "He is a businessman and he had a good bit of money on him which he said he collected from several persons. Leamis is getting ready to take a trip to Greece and he is carrying a gun to protect himself from possible hold ups." Leamis faced Municipal Judge Don Hanni on May 8. Hanni fined Leamis $50 and took away the gun.

On January 5, 1962, Captain Joseph Lepo and Lieutenant Thomas Baker checked the Greek-Syrian Coffee House just after 12:30 .a.m. While they found no gambling, they still chased out 20 patrons and ordered Leamis to close. Lepo was reprimanded by Chief Golden for his actions.

The bombing epidemic was more than a decade old when one of the more bizarre incidents occurred involving Leamis and his coffeehouse. Shortly after 1:00 a.m. on February 11, 1962, a bomb went off causing slight damage to the Cleveland Hotel on East Boardman Street and the Marathon Bar on South Avenue. No damage occurred to the Greek-Syrian Coffee House. A few days later, Leamis received a letter in the mail demanding $4,000 for protection. The note stated that if he went to the authorities the coffeehouse would be "leveled." Leamis took the letter to the Youngstown police, who immediately contacted the FBI.

The letter directed Leamis to be at Mike's Place, a bar located on Route 7 in Stratton, Ohio, along the Ohio River north of Steubenville. An FBI agent, posing as Leamis, went to the bar at 8:00 p.m., the time designated in the letter. A phone call was made to the bar asking for a "Mr. Smith." The agent took the call and was directed to go to a location five miles south of Stratton in Toronto, Ohio, and told to drop the package near a designated street sign on a lonely stretch of road known as Outer Drive. The agent found the spot alongside the 45-foot steep riverbank, dropped the package around 8:25, and returned to Mike's Place as directed.

About an hour later, three men in a 1959 station wagon arrived to get the package. The FBI moved in and arrested them. To their surprise, the extortionists turned out to be two 17 year-old high school boys, Charles T. Oxley and John H. Brewer, and 20 year-old John A. Reducha, an ex-marine, all from Steubenville. When questioned, the youths said they picked Youngstown for their "shakedown" because of the rash of unsolved bombings. They selected the Greek-Syrian Coffee House as a target because "it had gambling joint written all over it." The young men were bound over to the U.S. District Court in Cleveland on $20,000 bonds each. The conviction of the three young men was one of the few bombings ever to be solved in the area.

The FBI got a second surprise when they searched the Oxley property. In a dilapidated barn at the rear of the property, agents found buried five boxes of explosives, including two cartons containing 155 plastic bombs, and three boxes containing 1,000 rolls of detonating cord. The youths stole the material from local mining firms along the Ohio River. A search of Oxley's bedroom uncovered blasting caps, homemade black-powder bombs and a .22 handgun. When the three were sentenced in Cleveland on April 17, the judge placed them in a Federal prison camp for an indeterminate amount of time.

On June 19, 1962, police officers, including William Gruver, arrested Leamis at his South Avenue coffeehouse on a charge of possessing numbers slips and conducting a lottery. The charges were later reduced to a misdemeanor and Leamis got off with a $200 fine.

During County Prosecutor Clyde Osborne's Special grand jury investigation, a year after the Cavallaro murders, Leamis refused to answer any questions, including whether or not he could speak English. He was jailed for contempt and fined $250 in August 1964.

By the mid-60s Leamis' name disappeared from the newspapers. In January 1968, he made $18,450 when he sold the property on which the Greek-Syrian Coffee House was located to the Youngstown Board of Control for urban renewal. In 1982, Leamis retired to Clearwater, Florida where he died on February 18, 1986, at the age of 85.

Leo "Dutch" Manley

Leo J. "Dutch" Manley was born in Youngstown on November 14, 1896. His father was one of the first funeral directors in the city, operating the E.J. Manley Undertaking & Livery Service in Central Square.

During the early 1940s, he ran Manley's News Agency at 15 Commerce Street. If Manley was distributing news it was only known by him. A look inside from the front of the store revealed no newspapers, magazines or any other saleable merchandise. In fact, all that could be seen, according to one report were "a soft drink dispenser, a wheel chair, an empty show case, an old refrigerator and a couple of straight chairs."

On April 14, 1942, Manley was arrested during one of the raids conducted by Youngstown Police Sergeant William Davis and charged with running a bookie operation. In court, Manley was found guilty by Judge Robert Nevin on May 28 and fined $500. His attorney immediately filed an appeal.

Manley was in his News Agency on the evening of September 25, 1942, when he was robbed of $1,300. Manley was on the phone to police as the man escaped in a waiting taxicab. Minutes later, Patrolman William H. Armstrong spotted the vehicle and ordered the cab to stop on Market Street. The officer, with less than a year on the job, wrestled the suspect to the ground and sprayed him with mace. Arrested was John Keenan,[5] who was out on parole. In 1931, he assaulted a man by beating him over the head with a revolver. During the attack the gun accidentally went off and hit Keenan's accomplice right between the eyes killing him instantly. He was found guilty of second degree murder and sentenced to 7 to 20 years in the Ohio Penitentiary. He was paroled after spending less than five years in the Western Penitentiary in Pittsburgh, although his parole didn't expire until 1952.

Keenan was still in custody for the News Agency robbery when he filed a lawsuit against Manley on January 29, 1943, for $2,107 to recover horse race betting losses he claimed he had incurred. According to Keenan's petition, he placed wagers totaling $2,282 during August and September 1942, but received just $175 in winnings. In his suit, he named Dollar Savings Bank & Trust, who owned the property where the News Agency was located, as a co-conspirator. Keenan claimed the bank "knew or should have known" what Manley was doing there.

In early February 1943, Keenan went on trial for armed robbery. Defense counsel, Kedgwin Powell served as defense counsel. His contention was a) Keenan wasn't armed when he went in, that he found the gun inside the News Agency, b) that his client was merely taking back money lost in bets, and c) that "a man can't be guilty in taking his own money from a gang of thieves."

The state's key witness was Manley, who boasted on the stand that a Youngstown police officer escorted him from his place of business to the bank each day to deposit between $1,500 and $2,500. During cross-examination by Powell the following exchange took place:

> Powell: When did the policeman come to get you?
> Manley: Oh, whenever the races were over for the day. I think as a taxpayer I have that right.
> Powell: How much did you pay the policeman?
> Manley: That's irrelevant.
> Powell: Have you ever studied law, Mr. Manley?

Showing utter disregard for the gambling laws, Manley explained his business as "accepting wagers on sporting events. Persons come into my place and wager on the horse they think might win the race. If the horse wins, I pay them up to 15 to 1, with my money. If they lose I keep the money." Manley testified that he had never seen Keenan prior to the robbery. He claimed he was no longer involved in bookmaking – since last month.

Manley then went into detail about how he recorded his bets. He stated he kept the wagers on a slip and then transferred them a week later onto a ledger that included the bettor's initials, the amount of the bet and whether or not the house paid off. Attorney Powell asked that he identify the persons listed as the bettors. Judge John W. Ford interjected that the records were confidential. Powell cried out incredulously, "They can't be confidential when it's illegal!"

On February 6, Keenan took the stand. He was immediately questioned about the gun. A police officer had already testified that Keenan had confessed that he stole the gun from an automobile, and clerks at Manley's News Agency told the court that no weapon was kept on the premises. Still, Keenan stated that he took the gun from a drawer at Manley's operation. He told the court that he had deliberated a long time before going to Manley to recover the money he lost on horse races. Keenan stated the bets he placed were kept in a black notebook, which mysteriously disappeared after his arrest.

In his closing statement, Powell argued that the defendant had the right to take back the money he lost to Manley by any means, because he lost it illegally. Ohio law did allow a person to recover money lost through gambling – which was shown through cases at the Jungle Inn – but by filing a civil suit. Powell made an impassioned plea to the jury to return Keenan to his wife and little boy. Keenan's 4 year-old son was present in the courtroom throughout the trial and rested his head on his father's arm during Powell's closing. Powell drew tears from the eyes of onlookers when he talked about his own sons serving their country and asked what the racketeers had ever done in defense of America. When the prosecution delivered their closing, they simply asked the jury to return a verdict based on the law and the evidence, not on sympathy.

On Monday, February 8, a jury of one man and eleven women found Keenan not guilty after deliberating less than two hours. The jury apparently believed

Keenan's story that he was not armed when he entered the News Agency, despite the police officer's testimony. Perhaps expecting a loss, none of the prosecuting attorneys were on hand when the verdict was read. After the verdict, Keenan was returned to the county jail to await a determination on whether he had violated his parole.

The trial seems to have been the high point in Manley's career. He died on May 26, 1969, at North Side Hospital, three weeks after being admitted for emphysema. Manley was 72 years old.

Joseph Melek

In the big Lottery House indictments of 1943, Joe Melek was a significant enough figure to warrant an arrest. When it came time, however, to settle his debt to society, state investigators called him a "small fry operator."

Melek appeared in court on October 6, 1943, the day Frank Budak was sentenced to six months and fined $3,510 after pleading guilty to heading the Campbell House lottery operations. Melek followed Budak, appearing before Judge Adrian Newcomb. Melek, indicted as a bookie, pled guilty and was fined $1,000 and given two 30-day jail sentences – both of which were suspended, pending good behavior for one year.

In the wake of the Lottery House indictments, things were quiet for Youngstown's bookies. Vice raids were directed at illegal liquor joints, dice games and brothels. Some 27 months had passed since the last raid on a bookie joint in the downtown area was conducted on June 4, 1944, by Sheriff Elser at Melek's 43 Club, located at 43 Central Square. When the next raid occurred, August 29, 1946, it was again "small fry operator" Joe Melek's 43 Club. The Youngstown Vice Squad, led by Frank Bognar swooped down on the club and another operation at 4:55 in the afternoon as dozens of betting patrons and onlookers watched the action. The club was on the second floor, where nearly 70 bettors were following the horse race action. Melek was not at the club, or escaped, when the raiders arrived, and a subordinate was hauled before Judge Nevin and fined $200.

When Charles Henderson was campaigning in 1947, he named Melek's 43 Club as one of the gambling locations that were allowed to run openly. Henderson linked the "small fry" to Joe DiCarlo and "Fats" Aiello. Just weeks before the November elections, a fire nearly destroyed the 43 Club after breaking out in the gambling room.

Melek then moved his operations to the basement of a private club located on North Meridian Road. When this was raided, by state liquor agents, Melek moved into the Old Barn. Located on South Avenue, the Old Barn was a hot spot for dancers who enjoyed the 1940's version of the "oldies." Later, the building housed a skating rink. In September 1949, it was being operated as a telephone service bookie joint with Melek and his brother-in-law in charge. When new

Mahoning County Sheriff Paul J. Langley and his men arrived on the afternoon of September 9, Melek pulled another disappearing act just like he had three years earlier. Again it was a subordinate who found himself in court getting fined.

Perhaps at this point Melek wised up. Since January 1948, Chief Eddie Allen was leading a crusade against bookies and the race wire service; it was all but extinct in Youngstown and the chief was looking to make it that way throughout the county. That may have been Melek's cue to seek another line of work. Because of his past, Melek was one of several Youngstown individuals subpoenaed to appear before the Kefauver Committee in January 1951. While it was unlikely that he would have actually been called, Melek ducked the subpoena and was later ordered arrested.

Melek died on March 16, 1998, in Youngstown at the age of 93.

"Dankers" Petrella

James Vincent "Dankers" Petrella's arrest record at the Youngstown police station takes up four entire cards, with two of them double-spaced. On them are 14 arrests for suspicion and an alarming 22 entries involving driving, including 11 for reckless driving or automobile accidents, and five for speeding. There are a total of 48 entries on his record, which doesn't include arrests outside of Youngstown. The cards show 12 different home addresses.

Petrella, who was born on December 9, 1927, had his first arrest in Youngstown on May 13, 1944, when he was 17 years old. Between reckless driving arrests he found time to serve in the Army during World War II and got married during June 1950. In April 1950, he had his first gambling arrest when he was charged for possession of lottery tickets. He was fined the normal $500, with $400 suspended.

In October 1954, Petrella, Mike Walley and Peter Nasse opened the RCA Club at 1689 Poland Avenue. Considered a "cheat joint" by the police, the club featured a pool table and was open from 1:00 a.m. to 4:00 a.m. When vice squad officers began showing up too often to check on activities, the hours changed from 4:00 a.m. to 7:00 a.m.

Chief Paul Cress had city inspectors check the premises in order to find building code violations in hopes of closing the club. When only minor infractions were found, Cress began stationing men inside the club. On February 23, 1955, Petrella filed an injunction claiming that for several weeks club members were deprived of their right of free assembly due to the police presence on the premises for eight to ten hours every night. The injunction requested that Cress and his officers be restrained from "trespassing, taking up property, intimidating, coercing, oppressing or otherwise interfering with the premises and activities" of the RCA Club.

When the court action failed, the club closed and Petrella was literally out on the street. In May 1955, plainclothes officers were assigned to the corner of West Boardman and Hazel Street to keep hoodlums from congregating on the sidewalk and street corner outside the Purple Cow. On July 13, Petrella and Walley were arrested for loitering there. They were released after being held for ten hours and given a warning from Cress and Krispli not to be caught there again.

On September 20, officers watched as Petrella parked his automobile on Medina Avenue. They walked over to check his vehicle and spotted nearly 3,000 college football betting tickets on the floor. Petrella was arrested and charged with possession of pool tickets for gambling. After pleading innocent before Judge Cavalier, he was released after posting a $1,000 bond. Represented by attorney Eugene Fox, Petrella, following the normal hoodlum procedure, demanded a jury trial to delay the process as long as possible. In the end he paid a $50 fine.

On November 3, 1956, Petrella left the Family Wine Shop, an alleged bug operation run by Vince DeNiro, which was managed by Petrella's wife. Three vice squad members, including Peter Novosel, followed Petrella to Covington and Scott Streets where they found him in possession of a large number of lottery slips. Petrella attempted to run away, but was quickly apprehended. He was charged with operating a game of chance and possession of lottery tickets. He pleaded not guilty before Judge Cavalier and was released on a $2,000 bond.

The trial was delayed until March 1957, as attorney Fox tried in vain to have the more serious charge of operating a game of chance dismissed, which Judge Franko was refusing to grant. During the second week of March, Franko finally heard the motion. At the end of Fox's argument, and thinking the attorney had completed his case, Franko denied the motion and found Petrella guilty of both counts.

Fox had to convince the judge that he had only completed his motion, not his case. On March 14, Franko allowed Fox to present his case, during which he produced additional evidence. Petrella took the stand and told the judge that he had left the wine shop to drive an injured customer home. The customer handed him an envelope when he was dropped off and asked Petrella to deliver it to a man waiting at Covington and Scott Streets. He claimed he didn't know what was in the envelope. After hearing all the testimony, Franko found Petrella guilty of possessing the lottery slips, but declared there was no evidence of him operating a game of chance. He then fined Petrella $500.

During the bombing war that spanned the entire decade of the 1950s, Petrella was picked up for questioning a number of times. The first time was in November 1956, after the second bombing at the home of Jack Sulligan. As the investigation continued, police brought pressure on as many of the numbers men as they could find. On April 10, 1957, a police crackdown netted Petrella, Louis DeLuca, William Lantini, Calogero Malfitano, Sam Zappi and four others.

On May 13, 1957, Petrella began work as manager of the Sportsman's Tavern on Belmont Avenue. He was hired by the bar's owner, Mary Mogus, who lived in a suite above the bar. After the completion of his second day of work, Petrella was leaving the bar around 3:00 a.m. with Louis DeLuca, described as an employee. As the two men crossed the darkened parking lot toward their automobile a voice called out to them. The men stopped to see who shouted at them. Suddenly a blast from a shotgun rang out and pellets hit Petrella in the legs below the knee. Trumbull County deputies were called and took Petrella to St. Elizabeth's Hospital. Later that morning, *Vindicator* reporters questioned Mary Mogus about the shooting. Despite the fact that her open bedroom window looked over the parking area, she claimed she had not heard anything.

Despite all the recent violence, which authorities ascribed to the Valley's bug activity, the theory offered by law enforcement was that the shooting was over pinball operations at the Sportman's Tavern. The rumor was that Petrella had refused to accept syndicate-owned pinball machines inside the bar. Just what "syndicate" authorities were referring to was not revealed and there was no help coming from Petrella. After his release from the hospital a day later, he informed Trumbull County deputies he had no idea who would want to shoot him, or why.

Petrella quickly recovered from his wounds and was not heard from again until he was seen racing out of DeNiro's Dry Men's Social Club just before deputies padlocked the place (See Chapter 11).

On July 16, 1958, Petrella was hauled in during another "harassment" campaign by the police. He was picked up while dining at the BBQ Restaurant on West Federal Street. Joining him in this latest round were Fats Aiello, Charles Cavallaro, Vince DeNiro and Tony Greco.

The day after the December 15, 1960, murder of "Big John" Schuller, Petrella and Joseph Joyce were picked up and held for questioning after leaving the home of Philip Kimla, the last person to see Schuller alive. Petrella said they were there only to offer support to Kimla's wife while her husband was being held as a material witness.

In April 1961, a new "cheat spot" named the Metropolitan Club opened at 19 Fifth Avenue. When informed about the operation, Mayor Franko ordered Nicholas Pavelko, his new vice squad chief, to close it and keep it closed. Around 4:00 a.m. Sunday morning, April 30, state liquor agents raided the bar. Assisting them were Youngstown police officers, not members of the vice squad. It was reported that no vice squad vehicles were on duty that Saturday night and Sunday morning.

The state liquor agent in charge, later reported that the people inside were tipped off just minutes before they arrived. Drinks were ordered cleared from the bar, any gambling activity was quickly ended and approximately 50 customers were told to put their coats on and leave. Inside the second floor club, John Josephs rushed downstairs and locked the door just as the raiders arrived. When no one responded to the agents pounding on the door, they broke a glass to unlock it and raced up the stairs. They found many of the patrons, with their coats on, ready to leave. Raiders seized 36 bottles of liquor and six cases on beer, but no gambling equipment.

Arrested were "Dankers" Petrella, charged with "keeping a place where illegal liquor is sold," and Josephs, charged with hindering police. On Monday morning both men pled not guilty. Petrella was released on a $500 bond; Josephs' was set at $525.

Mayor Franko was furious that state liquor agents came and raided a place he had specifically ordered closed. He threatened to suspend the officers responsible. Among several excuses offered by Pavelko was that he thought the Metropolitan was only a social club and even had a vice squad man as a member.

The vice squad chief tried in vain to link the club's ownership to "Fats" Aiello. City officials moved quickly to padlock the Metropolitan Club. Named as defendants in the padlock case were Dominic Marino, listed as the owner of the building; Frank Miladore, the club's president; Nick Petrella, the custodian of the club; and James Petrella and John Josephs – but no "Fats" Aiello. The closing and padlocking of the club took place on May 11. Two weeks later, Petrella was fined $100 and Josephs $200 for their activities at the Metropolitan Club on the morning of the raid. Nearly two years later a warrant was issued for Petrella's arrest for not having paid the fine.

On January 29, 1963, Petrella was stopped by Liberty Township police officers and arrested for having a concealed weapon, driving with an expired license and using fictitious plates. Petrella gave police an address on Jefferson Street as his residence. A follow up revealed Petrella, who was using that address for years, had not lived there since 1947. At a preliminary hearing, he pleaded not guilty to the charges and was released on a $1,000 bond. Two days later, he was arrested by Youngstown police during a crackdown on drivers with delinquent parking tickets. Petrella had 13 unpaid tickets for which he paid a $13 fine and was released. As far as the Liberty Township arrest, the driving with fictitious plates charge was dismissed; he was found guilty in Girard Municipal Court for driving without a valid license and fined $50; but was found not guilty in the same court on the gun charge.

On August 25, 1975, Petrella was charged with hindering a police investigation. Petrella was at the Schenley Tavern around 3:45 a.m. the previous morning, well after the 2:30 legal closing time. Police arrived and when one officer attempted to confiscate a drink from the bar, Petrella and bar owner Peter Manos grabbed if from him. Vice Squad officers and other police soon arrived and took the two into custody. Inside the bar at the time of the arrest was Peter Manos' brother, U.S. Magistrate Nicholas Manos, whose law partner was Carmen Policy. The jurist "demanded" that his name not appear in the incident report.

The arrested men pled not guilty before Municipal Judge Frank X. Kryzan, the former mayor, and were released on $500 bonds. On September 11, Municipal Judge Lloyd R. Haynes, the former vice squad officer whose home was bombed back in April 1957, fined Peter Manos $500, but suspended $400 on condition that the bar owner not commit another after-hours offense for a year. The prosecutor asked the judge to dismiss the charge against Petrella, deciding he had not committed a crime. Haynes concurred.

In the mid-1970s Petrella was involved in the used automobile business as a salesman. It was not long before he tired of this and became involved in the most elaborate criminal act of his career.

On September 21, 1978, Petrella, Dominic DelSignore, his brother William DelSignore, Sr. and Gary M. DelSignore, William's son, were arraigned in federal court charged with offering to fix cases in Mahoning and Trumbull Counties. The plot involved Osvaldo "Pete" Giordano, who was facing trials in two different counties. In July, Liberty Township detectives arrested him for burglarizing a building and wounding a man. In Boardman, Giordano was facing felony and misdemeanor charges for assaulting a Liberty Township officer and a Boardman detective. Giordano was facing sure jail time and a heavy fine. The four defendants then approached Giordano, claiming they could fix the cases in both counties; Petrella declaring he would handle the fix in the Trumbull County case through his "contacts."

Giordano went to Liberty Township detectives and informed them of the offer; they in turn told the FBI. Agents fronted Giordano $7,000 to make the deal and then wired him to get it all on tape. The four men were then taken into custody, arraigned and released on $15,000 bonds. An FBI spokesman claimed the arrests were, "part of the continuing effort by the FBI to target those individuals involved with organized crime, political corruption and bribery in the white-collar area." The men were to be charged with violation of the Hobbs Act, described as "a many faceted law that makes it a federal crime to illegally influence or offer to influence a court."

The four men were officially indicted by a federal grand jury on January 3, 1979. Don Hanni was hired to represent the four defendants. He filed a motion in the U.S. District Court in Cleveland to have the charges dismissed, which Federal Judge William K. Thomas granted. The judge ruled there was "insufficient basis for federal jurisdiction," in the case. Assistant U.S. Attorney John S. Pyle declared that "the case is by no means a dead issue," and it was quickly turned over to the local authorities.

On July 6, the Mahoning County grand jury indicted Petrella and the others for "theft by deception." It was decided that the defendants had no real connections through who to carry out their offer and were merely extorting money from Giordano with false promises. Less than two weeks later, the case was transferred from the common pleas court to the municipal court. Where the men were once faced with penalties of 20 years in federal prison and a $10,000 fine, they were now looking at a maximum sentence of six months in the county jail and a $1,000 fine.

In early September, on the advice of Hanni, Petrella and the DelSignore brothers pleaded no-contest, while the charges against Gary DelSignore were dismissed. The three men immediately asked for probation instead of jail time. Instead, Judge Haynes sentenced then to the maximum, but left the door open for "shock probation."

The trio entered the county jail on October 29. Three days later Petrella was admitted to St. Elizabeth's Hospital with the explanation that he was "experiencing some kind of attack." After nearly two weeks in the hospital, Petrella was returned to the county jail. Judge Haynes received a note from Petrella's doctor stating that if his patient remained in lockup, it "may aggravate" is condition and "lead to further deterioration." What this condition was and what was deteriorating remained a mystery. Incredibly, the next day, November 14, Judge Haynes released all three prisoners after they had spent just 15 days of a six-month sentence behind bars. After payment of the fine, Petrella was placed on probation for two years.

Ten months later, Petrella and his brother Nick were implicated in the running of a gambling operation at the Girard Brotherhood Club. The club was formed so "members can fraternize, relax and enjoy social activities with one another." The charter said the club would, "encourage the relationship of various ethnic and cultural ideas, especially Italian and southern European, so that they may be preserved for their children and to encourage Americanism along with the ethnic background of various members."

The club, which had the blessing of Girard Mayor Joseph Melfi, and was operated by William Nail, a Melfi supporter, was raided by the FBI on September 12, 1980. Nick Petrella and his wife were responsible for the initial purchase of the club and then selling it to Nail. During the raid agents confiscated an envelope addressed to "J. Dankers" inside the club.

The last entry on Petrella's Youngstown rap sheet was dated March 24, 1988, when the FBI charged him with distribution of cocaine. He was placed on probation for three years, spending the first four months in a halfway house on Market Street.

On January 12, 1997, "Dankers" Petrella passed away at his home on Brandon Avenue at the age of 69.

Purple Cow

The Purple Cow opened for business in 1939 after the Albert Pick Hotel Company purchased the Ohio Hotel at the corner of Hazel and West Boardman Streets. Although located within a stone's throw of the Youngstown Police Department, the coffee shop / restaurant became infamous as a hangout for the city's underworld element. Most nights the hoods sipped coffee inside or congregated outside on the corner, laughing and telling "war stories." Its history was highlighted by the December 1946 shooting there of Anthony Bova by "Fats" Aiello.

During his hoodlum harassment campaign, the action phase of Mayor Charles Henderson's "Smash Rackets Rule," the Purple Cow was an easy target of Chief Edward Allen in his search for criminals to toss into jail. Long after Allen was replaced as Youngstown chief of police, the Purple Cow continued to serve as the preferred restaurant for "Fats" Aiello and others of his ilk to meet for coffee and meals. In March 1955, new police chief Paul H. Cress began a concerted effort to keep the hoodlums out of the hotel dining room, or harass them when they patronized the place, by assigning plainclothesmen to the restaurant around-the-clock to keep track of the mobsters that hung out there.

Cress ordered his men to "keep these punks on the run. If there is one thing the underworld fears most, it is to see a policeman sitting in a certain spot day after day taking notes on his activities. They don't want anyone, including policemen, to know what they do or with whom they associate." At the same time, the chief voiced his opinion about the places his own men frequented concerned about them fraternizing with known hoods. Cress stated there are a number of places for his officers to go for a cup of coffee without having to stop at such places as the Purple Cow and the Center Sandwich Shop.

Cress told his men that if they must enter these places they must "take notes on who is in the place, whom he [the hood] is with and how long he stays.

"With enough information on the activities of these punks, maybe we can file charges against them as suspicious persons without the means of earning an honest living, or, through constant harassment, drive them from these hangouts and off the streets."

Cress assigned certain officers to begin hanging out at these places to see who showed up. When informed of the new assignments of these officers, Aiello remarked, "Why doesn't he have officers out looking for burglars, thieves and rapists instead of wasting their time spying on men drinking coffee and not bothering anybody?" At the Purple Cow, it was reported that a hotel official spoke to some of the underworld guests and suggested they go elsewhere.

Some policemen didn't like the idea of falling in the cross-hairs of their fellow officers. "We are doing our jobs the best we can, but what's the difference where we drink coffee as long as we pay the bill," one complained.

A few days after Christmas 1957, the Purple Cow was closed after a fire began in a ventilator shaft in the kitchen. Five fire companies had the blaze under control within 30 minutes; damage was estimated at $5,000. This was the eleventh fire in as many years at the hotel, and the fourth at the Purple Cow. In January 1946, a fire at the restaurant caused $15,000 damage.

In late April 1961, another highly publicized fight, with Aiello and Struthers hood Charlie Carabbia taking on two East Liverpool men, resulted in the suspension of Police Captain Stephen Birich for not intervening in the brawl. Disgusted with the response to this incident by the *Vindicator* and local politicians, Hotel Pick-Ohio manager Roger S. Jacobson lashed out. "I have been manager of the Pick-Ohio seven years and this is the first time we have had what you would really call a fight. According to the politicians and the *Vindicator*, it is implied that we have a fight every night. In my opinion, the incident made for good political fodder and that's what was made of it.

"The public seems to think that the Purple Cow is only a hangout for our hoodlum element in the community. This is not true. We have many, fine respectable people eat in the restaurant regularly. We do not solicit business from the bad elements in our community. I wish there was a way we could eliminate their patronage. We are a public eating place and must serve everyone. Of course we could close the place, but we feel we are a legitimate business and under such circumstances should not have to close our doors.

"In my opinion, the Youngstown area is going to continue to have this problem of a bad element until we, the citizens, sincerely want it differently."

The last straw came on October 7, 1962, when Dominic "Junior" Senzarino got into a "bloody" fight with a Cleveland man ending in the arrest of both. New hotel manager Trevett A. Wilson, Jr. announced ten days later, that the restaurant would close by the end of the month. He cited a "business decline" and the "undesirable element that loitered in and around the Purple Cow" as factors in determining his decision. He called a "complete shutdown" the only solution to the problem.

At 7:00 p.m. on Halloween night 1962, the Purple Cow, the downtown landmark restaurant which was opened 24 hours a day, seven days a week for the past 23 years, closed forever. A rumor that a "sit-in" demonstration was going to be held caused Wilson to close the restaurant three hours earlier than planned. Several of the workers were transferred to the hotel's dining room, others were let go.

The *Vindicator* wrote, "Downtown loiterers and others accustomed to going to the 'Cow' at any hour of the day for coffee and a bite to eat, already were beginning to grieve the restaurant's passing. Quietly gazing at the restaurant's familiar 'Purple Cow' neon sign, now dark, one man said, 'It doesn't seem right somehow. It just isn't the same.'"

After sitting idle for a year and a half, Wilson announced on April 4, 1964, that the former Purple Cow would be reopened as a meeting room in the hotel. Today the old Hotel Pick-Ohio is operated by the Youngstown Metropolitan Housing Authority catering to the needs of the elderly and troubled.

Nello Ronci / William Campanizzi Incident

Nello A. Ronci was born in Strait, Pennsylvania,[6] on July 25, 1921. By the late 1930s, he and a couple of his brothers – Joseph and Reno – were living in

Youngstown. At 6-foot-1 inches tall and 228 pounds, Ronci was one of the bigger underworld figures in the Mahoning Valley. With his jet-black hair, dark complexion, and snarling stare he was also one of the more frightening looking members. Although he listed his occupation as a "checker" for Truscon Steel Company, Ronci was seldom employed in anything legitimate.

Ronci's rap sheet began with two charges of reckless driving in 1941. On the second one, the day after Christmas, he was fined $25 and had his license suspended for 30 days by Judge Peter Mulholland.

On March 18, 1951, Ronci was arrested by four police officers, including then Patrolman George Krispli, on suspicion of passing a counterfeit $10 bill at a Sunoco station on Hubbard Road. He was questioned and held for two days before he was released. No charges were filed. A year later, in March 1952, he was arrested for assault and battery. The case was dismissed by Judge Nevin when the complainant failed to appear in court.

On September 25, 1954, Trumbull County Sheriff T. Herbert Thomas and five deputies raided the Midway Restaurant on the Hubbard-Youngstown Road (Route 7) just north of the Mahoning County line. As the officers rushed through two entrances at 3:00 a.m., they found 16 men huddled around a dice table playing barbut. The raiders seized cards, dice, money and lottery slips before carting off the men to jail. Later that morning, Ronci was charged with operating a gambling place. The fact that Ronci was operating the barbut game, where it was estimated that $5,000 exchanged hands nightly, gives some indication of Nello's standing in the Mahoning Valley underworld. At the arraignment he and the others, including his brother Reno, appeared before Municipal Judge James A. Ravella, where they pleaded not guilty. Ronci was released on a $300 bond, while the rest were set at $100.

Records showed the restaurant was owned by James Longo, an elected Hubbard Township constable. The job must have paid well. The constable reportedly owned Longo's Beverage Center, Longo's Tavern and Longo's Restaurant – all located in Hubbard. The Midway Restaurant was located outside Hubbard. When the deputies visited the Longo home, they were informed he was on a fishing trip in Canada and not expected home until the following week.

Ronci's next brush with the law came on October 12, 1955. Vice squad officers stopped his automobile at 6:40 in the morning and discovered 60 football pool tickets hidden in the jacket pocket of the front seat. On St. Valentine's Day, 1956, Ronci pled guilty before Judge Cavalier, who fined him $75.

One of the big news stories in the spring of 1958 was that Ronci and Youngstown Police Patrolman William C. Campanizzi were under investigation in Mercer County, Pennsylvania, for their alleged participation in "a police-operated crooked crap game" in Farrell. The investigation came to light on May 13, when the *Vindicator* reported that Mercer County District Attorney John Q. Stranahan met with Mayor Frank X. Kryzan and Police Chief Paul Cress to request the cooperation of Campanizzi in their probe, and that he be ordered to honor a subpoena to testify before a grand jury. The subject of the probe was a stag party, one of a series sponsored by the Fraternal Order of Police – Shenango Valley Lodge 34, which was held at the Polish Home in Farrell on April 16. The sponsors sold about 300 tickets and more than 200 men attended, including local businessman, county officials and "representatives of local governments." Stranahan told the Youngstown officials that Campanizzi was positively identified "by a large number of witnesses" as being at the game.

Campanizzi was born in 1920, and grew up on the East Side of Youngstown. After working in the steel mills he joined the Army in 1943. When he returned home, he was appointed to the police department in 1946. In 1954, shortly after Kryzan took office, Campanizzi was named to the vice squad. He also put in time with the detective bureau, the narcotics squad and the Morals Squad. The *Vindicator* reported that Campanizzi was a relative of Ronci; it turned out that Nello was a cousin of the officer's wife. The newspaper stated the two were "close buddies and toured area stags, concentrating on dice games." It was clear the newspaper was trying to show the officer was involved with illegal activity. To make their point they posted a picture of Campanizzi's "beautiful dwelling" on the front-page, stating that he had taken out an $8,500 mortgage on a police officer's salary.

Already in trouble for his role in the dice game at the stag, was Farrell Police Chief Albert L. Timparo. Stranahan pointed out that the game was a serious infraction, not only because it was sponsored by police in violation of the law, but also because it was a crooked game. The *Vindicator* stated, "Stranahan began the investigation last month after it was reported that three 'sharpies,' said to have been from Youngstown, used loaded dice in a game. Reports were out that one of the men won $3,000 before claims were made that the dice were loaded. Campanizzi reportedly uncovered a pair of crooked dice early in the game and the owner was ejected from the hall. Later on, another Youngstown man yelled out, 'That Youngstown vice squad guy is a thief' and threatened to punch him."

Stranahan had requested that Campanizzi be at the May 13 meeting. Cress called the home and asked Mrs. Campanizzi to instruct her husband to come to the station, but he did not respond. A controversy arose when Detective Sam Schiavi, of the Morals Squad, and City Council President Anthony B. Flask visited the mayor's office later that afternoon. There was immediate speculation that the two were trying to shield Campanizzi, an accusation that the men vehemently denied.

Two days later it was now unclear if Stranahan had even met with the mayor. Kryzan claimed that Stranahan "never came directly to him" to seek cooperation in getting Campanizzi to testify. He claimed that politics were behind the incident in Farrell. "Everyone in Mercer County knows it's a political matter aimed at embarrassing a Democratic mayor there." As far as the alleged meeting, the *Vindicator* now reported that Kryzan said Stranahan "went to the police station and said 'he had a friend at the newspaper,' using this as a 'hammer' to get cooperation of local officials.

"'If he were really interested in getting our help,' Kryzan said, 'he would not have asked for it through the newspaper but come to me directly.'"

"He added, 'We are not in any way shielding or helping Campanizzi or not cooperating, and if Mr. Stranahan sincerely wants cooperation we're certainly happy to have him come to our office and discuss his problem.'

"Stranahan said...that none of Kryzan's charges is true. He said he went to Chief Cress, who is a duly appointed representative of the mayor.

"'I will not comment further because I am not interested in what the mayor of Youngstown says about the case,' Stranahan added."

When Cress spoke to Campanizzi about the accusations, the officer told the chief he was not there. In fact, Campanizzi was supposed to be working and was marked "on duty" by the shift supervisor that night.

On May 15, Stranahan formally presented a certificate to Mahoning County Prosecutor Thomas Beil requesting that Campanizzi and Ronci appear on June 2 before the Mercer County grand jury investigating the crap game at the stag party. A hearing was held before Common Pleas Judge Harold B. Doyle. Appearing before the judge was Mercer County Sheriff Joseph R. Knowles, who stated he saw Campanizzi shooting dice at the stag party and that his own investigation revealed that the officer knew who initiated the game. Doyle ruled that Campanizzi and Ronci were material witnesses to the dice game. Doyle refused to allow either man put into custody or ask them to post an appearance bond. Instead, he took the word of the men, and that of their attorneys, that they would appear. Stranahan declared that they weren't accusing the men of any crime; they just wanted them as material witnesses. Doyle then stated that as part of his official ruling the men would have complete immunity to arrest or the serving of criminal and civil summonses while they were in Pennsylvania. William A. Ambrose, however, the former county prosecutor who was representing Campanizzi, firmly stated that he would instruct both men to stand behind the Fifth Amendment and not answer any questions.

Days before the grand jury appearance, Ronci and his wife, Margaret, got into a scuffle at St. Elizabeth's Hospital. The incident began after Ronci visited a 47 year-old woman who was a patient there. Whether she was a love interest of the gambler wasn't speculated on in the newspaper. Margaret surprised him there and after an argument in a wing on the second floor blows were struck. Mrs. Ronci had bruises on her face and head, as well as a slight concussion. No charges were filed. In January 1961, Margaret Ronci filed for divorce on the grounds of extreme cruelty.

On June 3, 1958, Campanizzi and Ronci appeared before the Mercer County grand jury, along with 21 other witnesses. The grand jury proceedings were held in secret and initially there was no indication as to whether the two men cooperated. Ambrose later told reporters that when Campanizzi returned home, he phoned and said, "Everything went fine."

Two days later, the grand jury indicted Farrell Police Chief Albert Timparo on charges of "establishing a gambling place." Campanizzi and Ronci were asked to testify at the upcoming trial. It was then brought out that both "cooperated" in the grand jury investigation and, at the time, said they would appear at the trial if needed. After this announcement, Chief Cress said that Campanizzi might face disciplinary action if his testimony revealed he attended the stag party after claiming he was on duty.

To insure the pair's appearance, Stranahan requested an order demanding their presence as material witnesses. The court order, announced by Judge Doyle, stated that Campanizzi and Ronci would be granted immunity and protection from arrest.

On June 10, the trial of Farrell Chief Timparo began in Mercer. Campanizzi was the second witness called. The officer told the court that he met Ronci at a restaurant around 10:00 o'clock on the night of April 16. Ronci "asked me to go with him to an affair in Farrell," he explained. At the door to the stag party he was charged a $5 entrance fee because he had no ticket. Later, "they refunded me my money before I left and were quite apologetic about charging a brother police officer," he stated.

"I was standing there with Ronci when the doorman (a Farrell policeman) told Nello he would have to leave. The officer said someone told him Ronci was a sharpie," Campanizzi said. Ronci left the gaming room without incident and entered the adjoining dining room. Ronci later testified that he was barred from the dice table because, "I was a stranger."

Campanizzi related to the court an incident at the dice table where a man won $160. Someone at the table called out, "Let me see those dice, something is wrong." Campanizzi said he picked up the dice, and threw them to the man who wanted to see them. The shooter grabbed the dice, made a gesture as if to throw them out of the room, then grabbed his money and left. A neighbor who lived next door to the Poland Home later testified he found "a pair of crooked dice" the next morning while mowing his lawn.

After the incident with the dice Campanizzi stated, "Then Timparo came over and we were introduced. I complained as to why Nello was being ejected. The chief said there was a complaint that Nello was a sharpie and that he invited only the best people. Timparo also said he was in charge of the stag. At this point I told Timparo that it seemed to me he had a couple of sharpies there."

Campanizzi was put through a tough cross-examination, which brought Stranahan to his feet a number of times calling out objections. It's interesting to note that neither the defense counsel nor prosecution questioned Campanizzi on the fact that the Youngstown police duty roster showed him "on duty" from 8:00 p.m. on the night of April 16 until 4:00 a.m. the next day.

After hearing of Campanizzi's testimony, that he was indeed in attendance at the stag, Cress softened his tone. He stated no disciplinary action would be taken until he discussed the Morals Squad officer's testimony with Stranahan. "I don't know what he said before the grand jury or what he said at the trial...I want to check with Stranahan to see if he told different stories or gave the same account in open court before I make any move. I'd be a fool to do anything now. I'll wait until it's over and Stranahan contacts me." Meanwhile, rumors were still rampant that Campanizzi would get off easy because of political pressure on Kryzan.

When the prosecution ended its case, defense counsel presented 17 witnesses on Chief Timparo's behalf, mostly character witnesses who also attended the stag. One of the witnesses, William Stratter was well acquainted with Ronci. He testified to Nello's reputation and said the he was barred from crap games at Yankee Lake, a small resort near Brookfield in Trumbull County. Stratter explained that he was associated with Ronci for five years at area dice games. "Years ago," the witness stated, "he had [a game] every Friday morning."

During cross-examination the following exchange took place:

> Stratter: Ronci doesn't go into a game to lose.
> Stranahan: He's a skinner, isn't he?
> Stratter: He's a crook.
> Stranahan: Darn right he is.

Many of the character witnesses were office holders or former office holders, and some prominent local businessmen from Farrell, all with glowing words for Timparo. They testified that what ever games were going on were sociable ones. Every witness was asked if they saw any "rake" coming from the gambling activities, meaning was anyone taking a cut of the pot for operating the game. Every witness denied seeing anything of that nature. Most claimed Timparo remained in the kitchen most of the evening.

After the hearing, Timparo was found innocent of "establishing a gambling place." A full report of the hearing and Campanizzi's testimony was forwarded to Chief Cress. On June 23, Campanizzi and Patrolman Walter Cegan, who covered for him, were suspended from the police department – Campanizzi for 30 days, Cegan for 15 – and removed from the Morals Squad. Both were moved to new assignments at the end of their suspensions.

On August 8, 1959, Ronci was picked up by Youngstown police after a local businessman reported he lost $27,000, during what he claimed was a crooked dice game at Squaw Creek Country Club in Trumbull County. The night of gambling followed an afternoon round of golf sponsored by the Youngstown Chamber of Commerce. Ronci was identified as one of the gamblers that Mahoning County Prosecutor Beil wanted to question. The gamblers allowed the businessman, unidentified by the newspaper, to continue to ring up loses by making verbal bets knowing he ran a profitable business. The *Vindicator* reported, "It was learned that one of the pro crapshooters made 35 straight 'passes' with the dice, a feat almost unheard of without the benefit of crooked dice."

Ronci was actually arrested outside the Purple Cow around 1:00 a.m. because of another unrelated gambling complaint made against him that same night. Police were tipped that Nello was at the General Fireproofing Hall, where a retirement party was being held. One of the partygoers called police and said Ronci, "just did not look right and may have come to start a dice game." Ronci left the hall and was spotted by Sergeant Thomas Baker. Ronci was released 12 hours later without being charged.

By now Ronci had a reputation in the Mahoning Valley of being a "cheater" and had a hard time trying to find a game to start. Many believed this was the reason Ronci tried to ply his trade in Erie during the spring of 1960. Ronci was working his crooked dice routine in this lakeside Pennsylvania city with three accomplices – Joseph Margiotta, Arthur Horn and Robert McLaughlin. Around the beginning of May, Sergeant Chester Wizikowski, of the Erie Police Department, reported that the men took $3,500 from local players at a game. He kept an eye out for them figuring they would return for more. On the night of May 28, his hunch proved correct.

A stag party was going on at the same hall. Wizikowski received a phone call from a player at the hall informing the sergeant that some dice sharpies were trying to take the players. Wizikowski recognized the men as soon as he entered. When Ronci was pointed out to him he went to apprehend him, but Nello took off. Margiotta, who witnessed the incident, quickly disappeared, leaving Horn and McLaughlin to be captured.

A search of the men uncovered a motel key. Wizikowski went to the room and searched it. Hidden behind a bed he found an expensive case full of crooked dice. The case had four large grooves to hold the dice. "It was the prettiest piece of phony gambling equipment I have ever seen," Wizikowski stated, "and I've been on the force for many years. The dice in that case could match any dice used in any game in the country. They even had sandpaper to file the corners down."

Wizikowski called the station and had radio dispatch warn other police in the area to be on the lookout for Ronci and Margiotta. Ironically, as Wizikowski was heading back to the station he came across the two. As the sergeant was pulling their car over, one of the men began throwing dice out the window. A patrolman found 20 sets of dice scattered along the road near where the car was stopped. At one point Wizikowski was forced to draw his revolver when Ronci made a motion as if to flee. Ronci then shouted at his captor, "Let me talk to you, let me talk to you."

Margiotta, who was an alleged gambler and bug dealer in Youngstown, was listed as proprietor of the Tasty Sandwich Shop in Brier Hill, once the alleged bug headquarters of Frank Fetchet. While he was being interrogated, one of the detectives remarked about the fancy dice case and joked they were "going to burn the case." Margiotta cried out, "Don't put a match to that case, those dice are worth five grand."

The four men were charged with being "common gamblers" before Alderman Michael Kinecki, an Erie magistrate. The next morning they were released on a $1,000 bond. After several delays the men were formally arraigned on June 24. Attorneys for the defendants declared the state had insufficient evidence to warrant conviction on the charges, claiming police never saw the men using the crooked dice at the benefit stag, nor did they find dice or cards on their person when they were searched.

Assistant Erie County District Attorney Richard Agresti countered that possession of crooked dice was sufficient enough evidence that the men were gamblers. He claimed other evidence – the trip to Erie, the renting of a motel room for one night, and their presence at the stag party – was strong enough to prove the men came to the city as professional gamblers. At the end of the brief hearing, their arraignment was continued for a third time. On June 22, yet another continuance was asked for by the state. Agresti requested the delay reporting that the prosecutor, who was attending a convention of district attorneys, wanted additional time to study the case.

On August 4, the men were held to the Erie County grand jury, who listened to testimony during the September session. On September 9, all four were indicted by the grand jurors on the charge of being common gamblers. When the trial began eleven days later, the *Vindicator* reported that the defendants "have been under pressure of their legal counsel to plead guilty rather than stand trial." When Ronci balked, defense attorney Lindley McClelland approached District Attorney Herbert Johnson, Jr. and proposed that Horn and McLaughlin plead guilty, if the prosecutor dropped the charges against Ronci and Margiotta. Johnson, who saw Ronci and Margiotta as the ringleaders, proposed the exact opposite. This proposal was rejected.

Testimony began on September 21, before Judge Samuel Roberts. After a one-day break for the Jewish holiday Rosh Hashanah, testimony was completed on September 23, without the defense calling a single witness. McClelland asked for Roberts to dismiss the charges stating that under Pennsylvania law, "possession of dice does not constitute a crime." With the motion denied, McClelland attacked Sergeant Wizikowski in his closing. He told jurors, "There were 30 persons shooting dice when he entered the East Side club. Why didn't he arrest the gamblers instead of the non-participants? Is that fair play?"

The jury apparently saw it as "fair play" as they found all four men guilty. McClelland announced immediately that he would file a motion for a new trial and Judge Roberts delayed the sentencing. The attorney filed the motion based on the fact that mere possession of dice does not a lawbreaker make.

More than four months passed before the men were sentenced. On February 13, 1961, Ronci and Margiotta were fined $500 each; Horn and McLaughlin received $300 fines. The four were placed on a one-year probation, the terms of which stated that any time the men entered Erie County they had to report to the police department or county probation office.

On June 18, 1963, members of the Intelligence & Security Squad, including Randall Wellington and William Gruver, raided Ronci's home at 1892 Chapel Hill Drive. The officers found more than $1,000 in cash, a $900 check and gambling paraphernalia consisting of a wooden case and two cigar boxes containing more than 100 pair of dice, a chuck-a-luck device, a dice layout cloth, a tape recorder with horse race results and two adding machines. Ronci was arrested on charges of possessing gambling equipment. In Nello's home were Carl "Lucky" Venzeio and Attelio "New York Jack" Veltri, both were booked suspicion, questioned and released.

On July 10, the trial began before Municipal Judge Martin P. Joyce, who was hearing the case without a jury. The trial was conducted under strange circumstances, being continued seemingly after just two hours of testimony each time and then reconvening a week or so later. No explanation for these recesses was given. Ronci's attorney Frank P. Anzellotti, Sr., a former municipal judge, filed a motion for the suppression of the evidence claiming the search was illegal because the officers didn't have sufficient evidence to obtain the warrant and that the warrant did not specify the items that were to be confiscated.

On the first day, Joyce allowed some testimony to be heard before recessing the trial until July 19. On that date, Officer William Gruver was called to the stand. He testified as to how the squad kept watch of the Ronci residence from May 1 until the date of the raid on June 18. During this time Nello was visited by "several notorious figures." Gruver described the dice seized at the home, he found dice of various sizes and shapes, many with odd numbers and holes drilled in them. Many were stamped with names of "flourishing Las Vegas night spots."

When the trial resumed on July 30, Ronci took the stand for a memorable cross-examination. Under questioning from Assistant City Prosecutor Joseph Maxim, Ronci was asked why Carl Venzeio was at his home so often. Nello replied that "Lucky" was "just a friend who does errands for me sometimes." Ronci related that when he ordered things from stores, "'Lucky' delivers them." Maxim asked why Ronci didn't retrieve the items himself; he had plenty of time on his hands. To which Ronci replied, "I don't feel like getting them myself."

When Maxim asked about the defendant's occupation, Ronci replied that he was a salesman, but was unemployed for the last two years. When the prosecutor asked what he sold, Nello replied, "I try to sell anything I can." Maxim requested to know how much he earned during the past week. Ronci answered, "I don't know."

Ronci was then questioned about the $1,000 that was found hidden under his couch. Nello explained that he was saving the money to give to his new wife Adele, so she could buy a rug. (In December 1965, Adele filed for divorce under the same claim Margaret had, extreme cruelty.) Maxim next questioned Ronci's need for two telephones in the home. Nello stated that one was for a roomer who had once lived there. He admitted that the roomer moved out two years earlier.

Throughout the cross-examination, Maxim felt the need to remind Ronci that he was under oath and needed to answer all the questions truthfully. Before Maxim completed his questioning, Joyce called another recess to the trial.

When the trial resumed on August 16, Maxim completed his cross of Ronci. The prosecutor questioned him again about being a salesman. Nello explained that he purchased a vendor's license in March 1952. He stated that he had the gambling devices in his home because this is what he sold for a living. Ronci said he believed his vendor's license authorized such sales.

When Ronci testimony was complete, Maxim called a rebuttal witness, an employee of the county auditor's office. She testified that Ronci's license was cancelled by the state back in June 1954. The hearing finally completed, Joyce announced he would make his ruling on August 23.

On that day, Joyce began by denying Anzellotti's latest motions. He ruled that "in the light of Ronci's reputation as a gambler, the articles in Ronci's possession constitute a crime." Joyce found Ronci guilty of possessing gambling devices and fined him $500 and court costs. The *Vindicator* reported, "Judge Joyce ordered the destruction of the loaded dice, about 50 pair of good dice, chuck-o-luck shakers and layout cloths and a table, but allowed the return of a tape recorder and tape with a recording of a horse race and a vendor's license."

Nello Ronci's criminal activities continued throughout the 1960s and into the 1970s and 1980s. He passed away at the age of 83 on January 26, 2005.

Philip Rose

Philip Rose was one of the few Jewish mobsters to operate in Mahoning County. Born in Russia in 1909, he came to Youngstown with his parents at the age of two. His first arrest occurred in Jersey City, New Jersey, in December 1943, when he was arrested for illegal possession of a weapon. In 1949, he was arrested in Washingtonville after trying to work out a deal with city officials to install slot machines in local bars.

In 1949, Chief Allen identified Rose, who used the alias "Phil Ross," as one of the local bookmakers that was paying a 50 percent tribute to the Aiello-Caputo-DiCarlo combine. Rose faded from view over the next decade.

On Halloween 1959, Rose charged in an affidavit that Frank Franko, then candidate for mayor against Edward J. Gilronan, was receiving financing from a man who had bombed his neighbor to embarrass him. At the time, Rose was named by Franko's campaign as a bookmaker contributing to Gilronan's campaign chest. Rose, who had already donated $1,000 towards Franko's campaign, demanded the money back and received it.

On July 5, 1961, Rose was at work when he began to complain about pain in his arm. Rushed to St. Elizabeth's Hospital by a friend, Rose suffered a massive heart attack and died that afternoon.

"Little Pete" Skevos

Although he used the alias "Pete Pitakos" and was called "Little Pete" by his friends, Peter Skevos was best known as the operator of the Parthenon Bar at 21 South Avenue during the mid-1950s in Youngstown.

Before arriving in Youngstown, Skevos had a record in Indianapolis where he was arrested on July 27, 1937, on a charge of assault and battery with intent to kill. His first arrest in Youngstown came on December 11, 1941. Using the name Pitakos, he was arrested for operating a gambling den and fined $5.

At 54 years of age, "Little Pete" might have seemed a bit old to be getting started in the bug business. His first policy arrest came on February 1, 1948, when Vice Sergeant Dan Maggianetti and two patrolmen arrested Skevos at a Greek coffeehouse he ran at 102 South Avenue. The officers found five lottery books and several bug slips in his possession.

Skevos was listed as "an active lottery operator and suspected top man of a 'bug' bank in the East End" in police department records. His coffeehouse at the corner of South Avenue and Boardman Street was the frequent target of vice squad scrutiny. Once his Parthenon Bar was in operation, he came under surveillance after a barbut game was reported being played there. In January 1955, the Parthenon Bar was one of ten locations the administration threatened to padlock for alleged violations.

Skevos made the front page on May 8, 1955, after he arrived at St. Elizabeth's Hospital with a gunshot wound to his right leg. "Little Pete" told hospital personnel and police that it was "just an accident," the same type of "accident" that would befall "Fats" Aiello in November 1960. He claimed he was visiting a friend on Fifth Avenue around 1:30 in the afternoon and while removing a .32 automatic from under his coat it fell to the floor and discharged leaving a hole in his leg. The friend called a taxi, which transported Skevos to the hospital. Police immediately suspected the shooting was a result of increased "bug" activity in the city. A check of records revealed Skevos had no permit for the gun.

The next day, Detective Chief William Reed announced that the shooting of Skevos was accidental and not the result of a bug feud. Skevos told the investigating officers that he carried the weapon for protection, but refused to elaborate on whom he needed protection from. The police must have felt sorry for

"Little Pete" because they decided not to file charges against him for carrying a concealed weapon.

On October 17, 1956, Skevos was on the front page again for another shooting. This time he was the one pulling the trigger. Three men were drinking in the Parthenon Bar and by 1:15 a.m. had had their fill. When a waitress began to sing the men chimed in. An argument ensued and Skevos ordered the men to stop singing and to leave. They apparently didn't move fast enough for "Little Pete," because he fired twice as they made their way out the door. One man was wounded in the abdomen, the other in the wrist, while the third man was struck over the right eye with the butt of the gun by the mad Greek. The two gunshot victims were taken to South Side Hospital and the third to jail. Skevos soon joined him.

The next day Skevos pleaded not guilty to two counts of shooting with intent to wound, and assault and battery before Municipal Judge Forrest Cavalier. He was released on a $1,100 bond. Within four days, both of the shooting victims were arrested on disturbance complaints filed by Skevos.

On December 28, Skevos was fined $75 and court costs and placed on a year's probation by the very generous Municipal Judge Frank Franko. The judge was so charitable, in fact, that on his own volition he reduced the felony charge of shooting with intent to wound down to a misdemeanor assault and battery charge.

Articles written about the shooting incident described Skevos as the "former" operator of a lottery syndicate. The "former" title was removed on March 21, 1958, when "Little Pete" was arrested after police found five bug slips and a dream book[7] under a soda pop case behind a counter at Cosmo's Coffee House at 23 South Avenue. Skevos pleaded not guilty to possessing gambling slips before Municipal Judge Robert Nevin and was released on a $1,000 bond. During a hearing on April 8, Skevos' attorney demanded a jury trial.

Nearly a year later, on March 18, 1959, the case was heard. The attorney then withdrew his request for a jury trial and it was Judge Cavalier's turn to be generous to Skevos. After reviewing the evidence Cavalier responded, "I think there are other factors concerned before disposing of the matter. First the slips bear the date of [March 18], referring to the date they were written. The arrest was made on the 21st. Second, the premises was repeatedly searched in the past and when the officers came in and asked permission to search, he gave them permission. The slips were three days old and he denies, through his attorney, he had controlled possession of them.

"It is not reasonable to believe he was foolish enough to hide the slips and then let someone find them. I don't think he would be that dumb. He is too sharp an individual to do such a thing. The city has failed to prove he possessed the slips and I find him not guilty."

Except for being questioned in the general roundup after the murder of Sandy Naples and his girlfriend, Skevos was out of the news until June 1962, when he was arrested for possessing bug slips at the 23 South Avenue address, which was now known as the Norwood Athletic & Political Club. As officers of the new Intelligence and Security division entered, Skevos ran to the window and tossed out six lottery slips. Again Skevos pleaded innocent and was released on a $1,000 bond.

It looked as if there was no limit to the generosity of the municipal judges. This time it was Martin Joyce who was questioning Skevos' innocence. At a July 6, hearing he told the city prosecutor "there is some doubt in my mind as to whether or not you have proven this man a numbers promoter." Although he was in possession of the lottery slips, the judge claimed the city had not proven Skevos was actually promoting the game. Joyce must have had a change of heart because he ended up fining Skevos $500 and gave him a suspended 30-day jail sentence. He placed Skevos on probation for one year, but dismissed eight other counts against him.

In the meantime, City Prosecutor William Green decided to secretly indict Skevos and eight others on September 11, 1962. Skevos was charged with nine counts in the indictment. When it came time to arrest him Skevos was no where to be found. It was reported that the 69 year-old had gone to Greece.

Skevos never returned to the Mahoning Valley. On June 18, 1965, County Prosecutor Clyde Osborne dropped the charges against "Little Pete" after family members produced a letter that confirmed Skevos died in his native Greece on November 27, 1963.

Louis Tiberio / Tropics Night Club

Louis T. Tiberio was a lottery agent who was known for operating the Tropics Night Club at 1305 Market Street. He ran the club as a co-owner with his brother Lee until 1956, when he took full ownership. He was born on August 25, 1913 (some sources show 1914). His first pinch, for possession of lottery slips, came two days after his 23rd birthday in 1937. This was followed by an additional 13 arrests, before his 25th birthday, all on the same charge.

As a young man in the lottery business, Tiberio first began working for the Big House, the most successful of the lottery houses. When he realized the tremendous profits that could be made, he branched out on his own, only to find that without protection, as the number of arrests showed, he couldn't operate. He then went to work for Dominic Mallamo's South Side Lottery House. He soon found out that this operation wasn't immune from arrests and police raids. Rumors abounded that the police favored the Big House operators, while raiding everyone else in town.

Tiberio stayed out of trouble during the war years. The next time he was heard from was during the murder trial of Jimmy Munsene in Warren. Tiberio provided the alibi for hitman Thomas Viola, claiming he was at the Tropics the night he allegedly murdered the Warren underworld figure at his Prime Steak House restaurant. The jury didn't believe him, and Viola was convicted of the murder. A few weeks after his court appearance, on May 31, 1946, two men were arrested in a room above the Tropics and charged with illegal possession of liquor for sale. Tiberio claimed that the rooms above his establishment were a separate operation known as the "230 Club" in which he wasn't involved.

In the years that followed the famous 1943 indictment of the Lottery House operators, Tiberio felt safe about going out on his own again. It proved to be a business with a lot of overhead. Employing his own stable of lottery agents, in February 1948, Tiberio was in court bailing out his fourth bug writer in less than three weeks. This latest arrest was of Anthony "Booze" Gianfrancesco, who was found with seven numbers slips in his possession. He denied that he was connected with Tiberio, but it was the Tropics' owner who had to bail him out. By now Tiberio was running out of $50 bills and was forced to pay the remainder of the $500 bond with one-dollar bills. Gianfrancesco pleaded guilty before Judge Frank Anzellotti and was fined $500, of which $400 was suspended on the condition he refrain from gambling activities for two years.

Gianfrancesco couldn't refrain from gambling for two weeks. Just four days later, he was arrested by Sergeant Charles Bush while walking on Marion Avenue near Market Street with 22 "bug" slips in his possession. Tiberio was incensed when he appeared at police headquarters to shell out another $500 bond. Turning to a *Vindicator* reporter, Tiberio exclaimed, "It's going to be rough on somebody!"

That "somebody" turned out to be Tiberio. The next day the *Vindicator* seized on Tiberio's comment and editorialized. They pointed out that under the new administration of Mayor Charles Henderson things were going to change. They concluded, "They can show him [Tiberio] that 'crime does not pay' and that Mayor Henderson's drive on rackets really is going to be 'rough on somebody,' namely, Mr. Tiberio."

The new administration did not take kindly to Tiberio's remarks feeling that they were directed at them. Sergeant Bush went out to the Tropics to see Tiberio, but was told he was not available. Other officers called to ask for an explanation of his remark. Next, squad cars began to make regular stops in the neighborhood where the Tropics was located. Just 28 hours after Gianfrancesco's arrest, Vice Squad Officers George Maxim and William Turnbull, accompanied by Policewoman Theresa Gillespie, raided the nightclub. They arrested barmaid Mary Cimmento after finding four "bug" slips, a run-down tape, an adding machine ribbon, and a notebook in her purse. While admitting ownership of the purse, which was found in a drawer behind the bar, Cimmento claimed she "had no idea how the lottery slips got in there." Tiberio chose not to go to the station and bail Miss Cimmento out, thus avoiding the possibility of uttering another stupid comment.

On February 20, Chief Allen requested that Tiberio come to headquarters for a "heart to heart." In the chief's office, Tiberio claimed the *Vindicator* reporter misquoted him. He said he meant to say, "It's going to be rough on the pocket book." In the past month, Tiberio doled out $2,500 for bond money, $300 in fines and was looking at an additional $900 in fines for Gianfrancesco alone. After the private discussion, Allen told reporters that Tiberio said, "I'm getting out of the rackets and intend to stay out."

If 1948, was a financial disaster for Tiberio, the early months of 1949 were a personal disaster. On January 7, his father, Lee Tiberio, Sr., died of a cerebral hemorrhage at St. Elizabeth's Hospital at the age of 62. The elder Tiberio had a successful career as a road contractor and was retired. Around this time Helen Tiberio, Louis's wife, filed for divorce claiming infidelity and gross neglect.

Sometime after his promise to stay out of trouble, Tiberio temporarily changed the name of the nightclub from the Tropics to the Red Dragon. In June 1949, Tiberio was arrested for receiving stolen property – a refrigerator and a freezer. The items were part of a $9,000 heist on December 21, 1948, from the Fisher-Gilder Cartage & Storage Company at 574 Mahoning Avenue. Tiberio, after spending the night in jail, was released on a $2,000 bond. On June 16, the grand jury named Tiberio in two separate indictments; one included his brother-in-law Anthony Fortunato. Both men pleaded not guilty.

On January 4, 1950, Tiberio was arrested by Youngstown police on a warrant sworn out by a Warren television store after a check he issued for $100 bounced. The charges were dismissed in Warren Municipal Court when the proprietor failed to pursue the matter.

Before the month was out, Tiberio was back in jail for possession of lottery slips; it was his 15th and final arrest on numbers charges. On January 28, he was arrested by Vice Squad Officer William Turnbull while sitting in an automobile outside the Youngstown Foundry & Machine Company on Poland Avenue. As the officer approached, Tiberio tried to get rid of the slips. Two days later, he pleaded not guilty and was released on a $500 bond. On the day Tiberio was to be tried, a 23 year-old man came to court and "took the rap" for him. Judge Anzellotti, as was the norm, fined him $500, but suspended $400, and put the young man on a year's probation.

Around this time, Tiberio changed the name of his nightclub back to the Tropics. On April 2, 1951, the *Vindicator* reported that state liquor agents made a number of visits around the city, including the Tropics, and several arrests were made. Inside the Market Street club the agents arrested "Booze" Gianfrancesco after he served them a shot of whiskey after closing hour. After the "visits,"

Chief Allen requested that the state liquor board begin to revoke the permits of chronic violators.

In discussing the Tropics with the media, Allen revealed that Joe DiCarlo, Charles Cavallaro and others had met there prior to the Kefauver Hearings in Cleveland "to talk things over." Since these two men were initiated Mafia members, one has to wonder how this reflected on Tiberio; with the pair holding him in such high regard that they met at his nightclub for such a sensitive meeting.

During August 1951, Tiberio, who had a history of traffic violations (15 in Youngstown), had his license suspended for 30 days by Judge Nevin after being clocked at 50 miles-per-hour in Mill Creek Park.

In May 1952, Tiberio got into a new kind of legal trouble. Two New York City music publishing firms filed suit against him and the Tropics Night Club for allowing unlicensed public performances for profit of the songs "Oh Lady Be Good," and "Don't Take Your Love from Me." The infringement suits were filed in Federal Court in Cleveland and in October the firms were awarded $250 apiece in damages, as well as court costs and attorney fees.

The next year, the government filed tax liens against Tiberio for income and cabaret taxes dating back to 1949. Before the year was out, vice squad officers arrested Tiberio at the Tropics after they entered and found three youths in a booth in the bar. When the case was heard before Judge Cavalier in January 1954, he found Tiberio not guilty, claiming that "the prosecution failed to establish that the defendant had allowed or permitted minors to enter his establishment. The proof indicates he was unaware of their presence."

On March 8, 1958, burglars broke into Tiberio's home at 49 Elva Avenue and stole $2,700 in currency, $500 in government bonds, jewelry, a .45 automatic and a case of whiskey. Louis's brother Gilbert discovered the home ransacked. Exactly a year-to-the-day later vandals broke into the Tropics Musical Bar and destroyed 40 bottles of liquor by smashing them on the floor. Tiberio denied that he had any problems in recent months. Incredibly, burglars broke into Tiberio's home two years later on March 6, 1961. By now he had moved to a new home on Woodview Avenue in Boardman. This time thieves kicked in two doors and ransacked the house, making off with $400 in cash, two sets of diamond studded cuff-links valued at $800, new clothes and liquor.

On June 18, 1963, a small bomb exploded alongside the Coutris Restaurant, a small all-night diner connected to the Tropics and leased to Steven Coutris by Tiberio. The explosion, just before 2:00 a.m. caused minor damage, leaving some flash burns along the side of the building. The restaurant was reputed to be patronized by "Fats" Aiello. The *Vindicator* reported it was the first bombing since the one that killed Charles Cavallaro and his son in November 1962. Police Chief William R. Golden didn't see it that way. "There was no attempt to destroy property or injure anyone. It was just a prank committed by someone to cause a commotion," the chief argued.

Tiberio believed the same thing, he told police it was probably "kids" that were responsible. As far as the speculation that Tiberio was the target of a bomb plot, the club owner stated, "Everyone knows where I live. They know I live alone and they could get me at anytime. Why would they try something down here at the bar?" Six weeks later on August 8, someone placed a firecracker on the windowsill at Tiberio's home in Boardman. The explosion, just after midnight, broke a pane of glass but nothing more. A witness spotted a man racing across Tiberio's lawn, but due to a dense fog was unable to identify whether he escaped on foot or in a vehicle. An investigating officer commented, "Someone is warning Tiberio about something."

Throughout the early and mid-1960s, Tiberio battled the Ohio Liquor Control Board over selling liquor after closing time, Sunday consumption, or selling to minors. Some charges were dismissed, some were fought, and on another occasion the Tropics had its liquor license suspended for a while.

In September 1969, Tiberio won a lawsuit emanating out of the Tobin-Shade insurance fraud of the late 1950s. Common Pleas Judge Clyde Osborne ruled that Tiberio had cashed a check issued by Tobin in good faith for a local doctor. The physician had asked Tiberio to cash the insurance check over the weekend when banks were closed because he needed the money to purchase a new automobile. Tiberio recovered nearly $2,300.

In January 1971, the Tropics Musical Bar became the first establishment in Youngstown to receive a D-6 liquor permit, allowing it to sale alcoholic beverages on Sunday. During the next decade Tiberio seemed to leave the business end in the hands of his wife. Tiberio married Edith Magnolia, the former girlfriend of Vince DeNiro, in the mid-1960s. By the late 1970s, Edith Tiberio was operating the Mansion, the former Colonial House located near DeNiro's old restaurant Cicero's. She also took over the management of the Limelighter Lounge, another Uptown District night spot.

Louis Tiberio passed away on March 23, 1997, at the age of 83. His wife Edith died on November 25, 2010; she was 87.

Carmen Tisone / Tesone's Tavern

Born on February 13, 1917, Carmen Eugene Tisone was one of six brothers and sisters born to James and Michelena Tisone. In 1933, James opened Tesone's Tavern at 1810 Wilson Avenue. In May 1937, when Carmen was 20 years old, his father was robbed and murdered by bandits outside the café (See Chapter 3).

Carmen's sister Ruby married a man named Policy. The couple had a son and named him after Carmen. Tisone helped raise the young man. Years later Carmen Policy obtained a law degree and earned a reputation as a "mob attorney" in the Youngstown area. A friend of Edward DeBartolo, Jr., Carmen moved west when "Eddie" DeBartolo purchased the San Francisco 49ers NFL football team.

Policy became president and general manager of the team. After four Super Bowls, Policy moved to Cleveland where he served as president of the Cleveland Browns for owner Al Lerner when that fabled franchise rejoined the National Football League in 1999. He left that position in May 2004.

In 1940, Tisone was arrested for operating an illegal still near North Jackson. The conviction came back to haunt him in the 1960s. During the Second World War, Tisone served in Europe as a soldier in the U.S. Army. Captured and held as a prisoner of war by the Germans, Tisone was awarded the Purple Heart after his release.

Returning to Youngstown after the war, Tisone became involved in the operation of Tesone's Tavern with his brother Joseph. The two were co-owners until Joseph's death in February 1962. In 1948, Carmen married Mary Magdalene Chismar. The couple had three children.

On May 3, 1959, just like fellow tavern owner Louis Tiberio, Carmen Tisone's home was broken into and burglarized. He reported to police that he was robbed of $3,000 in cash. Two days later, with the exception of $15, all of the money was returned. Mary Tisone found the money on the front porch wrapped inside a copy of the *Vindicator* dated April 17, 1957.

The return of the stolen money would seemingly be the last piece of good luck the Tisones enjoyed for a long time. On Saturday, February 25, 1961, state liquor agents, operating out of the Canton office, conducted a raid at Tesone's Tavern. Responding to a citizen's complaint, they arrived around 3:30 p.m. to coincide with the time that the horse betting would be heaviest on the southern tracks. The undercover agents ordered beers, placed bets with marked money and then waited. The result? As one agent put it, "We hit the jackpot this time. This is one of the largest operations I have seen in some time." A review of the betting records kept at the bar indicated Tisone was handling $3,000 a day.

Since the agents didn't have power of arrest, they could only seize the betting slips covering their own wagers and the marked money they used. In addition to the horse race betting, the agents noted that Tisone was collecting bug bets and accepting bets on basketball games. During a brief chat with the agents, Tisone admitted that he did not possess a federal gambling tax stamp. Word spread quickly about the raid and as the agents moved on to additional targets they found the alleged betting sites quiet.

A few days later information obtained from the raid was turned over to the Internal Revenue Service to determine if that agency wanted to prosecute the tavern for failure to have a federal gambling stamp. Meanwhile, the Ohio Board of Liquor Control filed charges against Tisone for allowing gambling on a premises where a liquor permit was granted. After two hearings scheduled in Columbus were delayed, the Tisone brothers finally met with the board on June 2. While "technically denying" the specific charge, they admitted to a violation of the liquor law. Instead of putting up a formal defense, they asked for leniency.

When the board met to decide a punishment for the Tisones, they split 2 – 2 and nothing was done.

On the afternoon of August 2, 1962, Sergeant Dan Maggianetti and Intelligence and Security Officers raided Tesone's Tavern. Tisone was arrested and charged with operating a numbers game. During the raid police officers found policy slips hidden under Tisone's shirt. The next day, police tacked on an additional charge for possession of horse race betting slips. Tisone was re-arrested and his bond increased to $2,000. The raid followed the death of Billy Naples by one month. At that time, Youngstown revoked all the city licenses at the Center Sandwich Shop, which was located one door west of Tesone's Tavern. Tisone couldn't help but pick up some extra business. With the latest raid, Maggianetti declared he would lift all of the Tisone's licenses and ask that the telephone be removed.

Before the month was out, Carmen found himself in trouble due to his conviction for running a still near North Jackson 22 years earlier. On December 8, 1952, Tisone was cited for making a false statement on a renewal for his liquor license. The incident remained dormant. He had answered "no" on the application when it asked, "if he or anyone else associated with the tavern was ever convicted of a felony." On August 24, 1962, state liquor agents filed a new citation against Tisone, charging him with lying on the application. Five days after this latest incident, Tisone filed an application with the Ohio Department of Liquor Control to transfer the tavern's liquor permit to their sister Helen Ann George.

On September 14, 1962, some 15 months after Tisone asked the state for leniency, the liquor board handed down a 21-day suspension, which was to go into effect six days later. This was followed by a decision of the Ohio Board of Liquor Control on November 5, to revoke the liquor license citing the "false material statement" and possession of gambling devices – horse betting and bug slips. Tisone appealed the ruling. On February 7, 1963, the board denied the appeal.

Tisone faced another problem on January 25, 1963, when he was arrested by Patrolmen Randall Wellington and William Gruver on charges that the tavern had no food on the premises to be served, a violation of the state's Liquor Control Act.

The situation was about to get worse for Tisone. In mid-March, he went on trial before Common Pleas Judge Sidney Rigelhaupt charged under the new state law for promoting a number's game, stemming from the August raid. The new law carried with it a possible prison term. Among the state's witnesses called by Assistant Mahoning County Prosecutor Loren E. Van Brocklin were two patrolmen and a liquor enforcement agent. On the stand, Patrolman Andrew Kovac described the current set up of numbers banks, listing Tisone as one of the key operators. Officer Clarence Sexton's testimony was particularly damaging, as he told the court how Tisone pleaded with the officer to give him a break, promising to "quit the business for a break." Tisone cried that he would lose his liquor license if he were arrested.

On March 19, the case went to a jury of eight men and four women without Tisone taking the stand or the defense calling a single witness. At 10:05 p.m., after deliberating for less than three hours, the jury returned a guilty verdict. Judge Rigelhaupt delayed sentencing as defense filed a motion for a new trial. Tisone was released on a continuing $2,000 bond.

Six days later, Rigelhaupt threw the book at Tisone. He denied his motion for a new trial; he denied a motion for probation; he sentenced Tisone from one to ten years in the penitentiary; and he denied a stay of sentence pending the filing of an appeal. Tisone's counsel, Avetis G. Darvanan was able to get the Seventh District Court of Appeals to allow a bond pending appeal. The next day, the same court granted a stay of sentence.

While Tisone was appealing his first license revocation and his jail sentence, he was hit with a second revocation. On July 23, Officers Wellington and Gruver[8] testified in Columbus at a liquor board hearing, that Tesone's Tavern had no food to serve when they entered back in January. After the hearing, the Ohio Board of Liquor Control ordered a second revocation to be effective August 28.

On October 22, the Seventh District Court of Appeals upheld Tisone's lower court conviction. Attorney Darvanan claimed there was an illegal search and seizure among other things. In writing the opinion for the three-judge panel, Appellate Judge Paul W. Brown stated:

> "The search in this case was reasonable and in all respects lawful, no right of privacy was unlawfully invaded. Due process was carefully observed. The police officers involved should be commended for diligence."

Darvanan immediately announced plans to appeal to the Ohio Supreme Court. On March 25, 1964, after an appeal that again claimed an improper warrant and search, the Ohio Supreme Court ruled that Tisone "had presented no debatable constitutional question in his plea that he was arrested during an illegal search." A second attempt to appeal to the higher court was also rejected. The court, however, granted another stay of sentence to allow Tisone time to appeal to the U.S. Supreme Court. On the day this second stay expired, the U.S. Supreme Court granted an indefinite stay until it decided whether or not it would hear the case.

Nine months went by before the U.S. Supreme Court made a decision. On January 20, 1965, the Steel Valley News reported, "The Supreme Court, in a terse telegram to Mahoning County Prosecutor Clyde W. Osborne said the appeal was dismissed 'for want of jurisdiction.'"

It was just a matter of weeks before Tisone was off to prison. He still had three revocation orders, held up by restraining orders from the Franklin County (Columbus) Common Pleas Court:

◊ December 8, 1953, making a false statement on a renewal for a liquor license. Failing to list a prior felony conviction. This lay dormant until October 1962, and the permit was to be revoked effective November 15, 1962.

◊ August 2, 1962, gambling violations – horse betting and lottery slips found on Tisone's person and premises. The permit was to be revoked as of November 15, 1962.

◊ January 25, 1963, not serving food or meeting minimum food requirements. Permit to be revoked as of August 28, 1963.

After the U.S. Supreme Court's rejection, Darvanan filed a second motion that was denied on March 15, 1965. Two days later, Judge Rigelhaupt issued a bench warrant for Tisone's arrest and he was picked up and taken to the Mahoning County Jail. On March 19, exactly two years after he was convicted on state numbers charges, Tisone entered the Ohio Penitentiary to begin a one to ten year sentence. On March 31, 1966, after just one year and 13 days, Tisone was released from prison. Tisone stayed out of trouble for the next ten years. On September 21, 1976, he was arrested for a gaming violation and was fined $15.

In early 1989, Tisone fell ill. On August 16, at the age of 72, he died at home of complications from a stroke.

Variety News Stand

One of the most popular locations to place horse race bets and play the bug during the latter half of the 1950s in downtown Youngstown was the Variety News Stand, located at 26 East Boardman Street. The 24-hour newsstand sold newspapers, magazines and books – some material described as "rather spicy." The store supplemented its income by selling fruit, cigars, cigarettes and cold beverages. In addition, it owned a permit for carryout sales of beer and wine.

The Variety News Stand's operators were Anthony J. "Tony" Greco and James V. Ricciuti, in whose name the carryout license for beer and wine appeared. Law enforcement authorities, however, had pegged the newsstand as one of the bug pickup stations under the control of Vince DeNiro.

The newsstand first came to the public's attention on February 21, 1955, after Police Chief Paul Cress solicited the Ohio Bell Telephone Company to discontinue service due to gambling activity. Cress stated, "Horse bets and numbers are being taken by telephone and then phoned into a bank outside the city." Despite the fact police knew it catered to horse race bettors and policy players, it was never raided nor had its customers harassed. The telephone company responded by notifying Greco and Ricciuti that services to a pay phone, a private phone and extension would be cut off in three days. On the morning of February 26, workmen removed the telephones without incident.

At different intervals during the 1950s, the *Vindicator* conducted "surveys" of the bug activity going on in the city revealing selling locations that operated openly. On August 26, 1956, the newspaper announced the result of its fifth "survey." The report called the increased activity at the Variety News Stand the "most spectacular," pointing out that the operation was taking place just a block and a half from City Hall. The article stated, "Observers saw business and professional men, who would be presumed to have little or no interest in the bug take part in the betting." Also pointed out, was the fact that the newsstand did not hand out receipt slips, that the players relied solely on trusting Greco and Ricciuti.

After the results of the latest "survey," police increased their surveillance of the newsstand. Two raids were conducted in October with arrests made. When the first case came to trial, Judge Forest Cavalier decided there wasn't sufficient evidence of guilt. In the second, which followed an October 16 arrest during which Anthony "Tony" Lucci was found with a pocket full of bug slips, the defendant demanded a jury trial, but the case never saw a courtroom. Police, however, used this arrest to request a cancellation of the newsstand's beer and wine carryout permit.

On February 28, 1957, one day after another *Vindicator* "survey," Vice Squad Chief George Krispli and Officer Andrew Kovac entered the Variety News Stand at 7:20 in the morning. They watched as Tony Greco relieved himself of a .38 revolver and shoulder holster. They seized the weapon and searched Greco finding $1,300 in his pockets. A search of the premises came up empty as far as lottery tickets, but a number of dream books, which were considered unlawful gambling equipment, were discovered.

Greco told the officers he had the money on him to pay magazine distributors and other vendors. He claimed he was armed due to the large amount of cash he was carrying. Krispli called the prosecutor's office to confer about the arrest. They advised him to charge Greco with carrying a concealed weapon, until other charges could be determined. While still in the store the telephone rang. Thinking it might be someone wanting to place a bet, Krispli answered. To his astonishment, an unidentified voice on the other end, apparently aware of what was going on in the store, inquired, "Is it important that this man be booked?"

By the time Greco was arraigned, he was charged with having a concealed weapon and possession of gambling equipment – the dream books. He pleaded not guilty and asked for a jury trial. On March 16, Greco withdrew his request for a jury trial and was tried by Municipal Judge Frank Franko. The judge found him not guilty on both counts. Franko explained, "I acquitted him on the weapons charge...because a man has a right to keep a weapon in his place of business." As for the dream books, although a city ordinance defined them as "gambling paraphernalia," the judge declared, "Anyone who believes in dream books is superstitious – it's a hoax."

The police kept up their vigilance and on April 12, 1957, another raid was conducted. This time Officer Kovac and two state liquor men entered the newsstand and found four "freshly written" bug slips tossed behind a door. James Ricciuti was arrested and charged with possessing lottery slips. He pleaded not guilty and was released by Judge Franko on a $1,000 bond.

In addition to having to face charges in municipal court, Ricciuti's case went before the Ohio Board of Liquor Control in mid-July and through his attorney he pled guilty to possession of the lottery slips. On July 17, the Variety News Stand had its carryout beer and wine permit suspended for 14 days effective August 1. While on suspension First Assistant City Law Director Frank Battisti filed petitions to have padlocks placed on the newsstand and the Family Wine Shop at 901 West Federal Street, which the authorities also claimed was also a DeNiro lottery operation.

After reviewing the petition, Judge Erskine Maiden, Jr. issued a temporary restraining order, but forbade any gambling from going on at the newsstand. The notoriety of the Variety News Stand, in addition to the pending padlock order, resulted in Renner Realty Company, the owner of the building which housed the newsstand, to issue an evacuation order notifying Ricciuti he was to be out by August 31. Ricciuti promised the realty firm that no more gambling "of any kind" would take place again in the building.

On September 16, an eviction hearing was held before Municipal Judge Robert Nevin. The judge ordered a writ of eviction to be issued on September 23, giving Ricciuti until October 3 to vacate the premises. Nevin also ordered Ricciuti to pay back-rent totaling $200.

On October 3, Krispli found the front door locked and the windows soaped-over when he checked the newsstand. Ricciuti had removed out his furniture and inventory and was hoping to move to a new location on Market Street. He had not made good on the back rent. Greco had relocated to Park Dry Cleaning at 21 South Champion Street where, according to police, he was already booking horse race bets.

Both Ricciuti and Greco ran into problems in their new endeavors. First, Krispli refused to okay a permit to allow Ricciuti to transfer his liquor permit to the new location known as the News Center at 1313 Market Street. Krispli received some unexpected help from the Youngstown Board of Education, which opposed the transfer because the News Center was located within 500 feet of Williamson Elementary School. The tag-team effort from the duo of Krispli and the Board of Education resulted in the State Liquor Control department denying the license transfer in February 1958.

As for Greco, Krispli kept sending his vice squad officers over to Champion Street to keep an eye on the horse race bookie. Greco complained that police surveillance had "ruined his dry cleaning business."

James Ricciuti died in October 1970. Anthony Greco died in October 1981 at the age of 75. Today the area where the Variety News Stand was located is a parking lot.

Vona / Walley Affair

Sam Vona and Michael Walley grew up together on the city's East Side (some reports claim they were cousins). In addition to a life-long friendship, the two shared something else – long rap sheets. By Vona's own admission he was arrested "50 to 75 times." Walley's crimes took up four police cards at the Youngstown Police Department.

Walley was born Michael Lavaglia. Two of his brothers, Lee and Nick, also used the name Walley. (A check of the list of purchasers of the $50 federal gambling tax stamp shows a Joseph Walley and Nick Lavaglia.) Mike's first arrest came in 1942 for assaulting a woman.

Vona, who was born in Scottsdale, Pennsylvania, in May 1925, moved to Youngstown as a youngster and attended East High School. During World War II, he served in the Marine Corp as a member of the 9th Battalion, 3rd Division. While a marine he won the corps' light-heavyweight boxing title. Police records show that after being picked up for suspicion in 1944, he was arrested the next year after being AWOL from military duty.

On September 11, 1956, Vona and John Magourias (See Chapter 12) broke into the Public Market on East Federal Street and stole $334 worth of merchandise, which they later sold to a Himrod Avenue merchant. Magourias pleaded guilty and was sent to the Ohio Penitentiary, while Vona was granted a term of two years' probation by Common Pleas Judge John W. Ford.

Around 3:45 on the morning of March 13, 1959, James Durkin, a resident of 1123 McHenry Street was awakened by a knock at his door. He answered to find a bleeding man with gunshot wounds of the forehead, jaw and left shoulder. The wounded man asked Durkin to call an ambulance. He then advised him, "In the event I die, tell them Sam Vona shot me."

An ambulance quickly arrived and transported Michael Walley to St. Elizabeth's Hospital, where he was reported to be in serious condition after surgery. When questioned by police, Walley said that around 2:30 that morning, Vona picked him up at the East Side Civics Club at Albert and McHenry Streets. Instead of taking Walley for a cup of coffee as he had promised, Vona drove him around for a while and then Walley asked him to take him to the Arco Club back on Albert Street, where he had parked his car. As Vona drove near North Garland Avenue and McHenry Street, he suddenly stopped the car and told Walley, "I have to kill you, you double-crosser." With that he fired three times at Walley, who then slumped down in the seat and pretended to be dead. Vona pulled him out of the automobile and dragged him into a snow-covered field. "He held his hand over my mouth for about a minute and then left," Walley stated.

Despite Walley's accusations, police didn't go to the Vona home until some four hours later, a time lapse that was never explained. Police found Vona's car parked in front of his East Boston Avenue home. For some reason, Vona made no effort to hide the vehicle...or even attempt to clean it. In addition to the bloodstains, police found two bullet holes in the front seat. Vona was taken to police headquarters where he refused to answer questions on advice of counsel – attorney Don Hanni. The police officer who woke Vona noticed that he had "fresh scratches" on his face. When he asked about them Vona told him they came from an argument with his wife, Dolores.

Vona's decision not to talk sent the rumor mill into action. It was soon reported that Walley lost $7,000 while gambling in Trumbull County and that a portion of the money was not his. An anonymous caller told the *Vindicator* that "Walley has been using doctored dice in games and other gambling in the basement of a pizza shop next door to the East Side Civics Club."

On St. Patrick's Day, 1959, Vona was arraigned on a charge of shooting with intent to kill. He pled not guilty and was later released after posting a $5,000 bond. That same day it was reported that Walley claimed he was shot after he "refused to go with Vona to pull a burglary because Vona needed money."

In May, Vona's case was bound over to the grand jury, which indicted him the following month. He again pleaded not guilty, this time before Common Pleas Judge Frank J. Battisti. Instead of Battisti handling the trial, Judge Ford, who had placed Vona on probation for the Public Market burglary, took the case. Despite the fact that this was Vona's second arrest since the probation was granted, he was still free to walk the streets.

On September 23, a jury of six men and six women were sworn in to decide the case. Attorney Jack Nybell represented Vona against Assistant County Prosecutor Clyde Osborne. One of the state's witnesses was a detective, who testified that Vona agreed to a paraffin test at police headquarters, which concluded that his right hand had recently fired a gun.

The trial was marked by heated exchanges between Osborne and Nybell. During Walley's testimony Osborne asked if he had a police record. Nybell interrupted, calling out "About three pages," as he waved the sheets in the air. Osborne waved back with three sheets of his own. "I'll trade you," he quipped. He was holding a copy of Vona's police record.

Walley testified that he was arrested eleven times for possession of bug slips, but was never convicted of a felony. Under cross-examination Nybell hoped to embarrass Walley by bringing up the assault charge from 1942. Nybell pointed out that the girl was a juvenile and that Walley had sex with her. His strategy fell apart, however, when Osborne asked on re-direct, "Who was with you?"

"Sam Vona and Ben Guerrieri," Walley answered.

Walley described the events of the night of the shooting, how he was picked up, driven around, shot and then dumped in a field. During cross-examination,

Nybell questioned him about his relationship with Vona, indicating that there was some "bad blood." It came out that during Walley's divorce from his first wife, Vona's wife Dolores testified against Walley during the trial. Walley denied Nybell's accusation that he had once tried to run down Dolores with his car. Later, Walley's second wife took the stand and stated that Vona had once come to the house, gun in hand, looking for her husband.

Another witness called by the state was a barmaid. Vona was not a drinker, but the barmaid testified that Vona came into the Central Bar on Hubbard Road several hours before the shooting and ordered three double-shots.

On the afternoon of September 24, Sam Vona took the stand. Everyone believed the defense was going to present an alibi defense – that Vona was home asleep at the time of the shooting. Instead, Vona surprised everyone in the courtroom. Earlier he had walked in with Dolores, his attractive blonde wife, who took a seat with him at the defense table. Once on the stand, Vona told the jury he had waited nine years to get revenge against Walley for "bad mouthing" his wife. He admitted to having the shots at the Central Bar, but claimed they were to "help cure a cold."

Nybell asked his client about his participation in the theft of coffee, bananas and other goods from the Public Market with John Magourias. The attorney asked him, "What did you get out of the burglary?" Now it was Osborne's turn to interrupt. He called out, "Probation." This resulted in laughter in the courtroom and an irate response from Nybell.

Vona related that after picking up Walley, he drove around as he questioned him about the insults he had made about Dolores. At one point, Vona said, Walley referred to Dolores with some "vile and offensive" remarks and Vona said he responded by slugging him in the face.

It was here that the story got bizarre. Vona claimed Walley pulled a gun and that the two fought over its possession. Under Nybell's questioning, Vona "intimated" that during the struggle Walley shot himself three times.

Under cross-examination Vona stated it was possible that he had gotten hold of the gun in the car and pulled the trigger. He offered, "Maybe I did. I don't know." After the shots were fired, Vona said he got scared. He pulled Walley out of the car and left him for dead in the snow-covered field. Vona stated he thought about calling the police, but decided to wait until morning. He admitted he was only thinking of himself.

The court was spellbound when Osborne had Vona participate in a demonstration to show how the shooting occurred. When it was apparent it couldn't have happened the way Vona described, Osborne asked, "Did you deliberately shoot Mike Walley to save your own skin?"

Vona answered, "It might have happened that way, I don't know."

When asked why he hadn't told this story before, Vona calmly answered, "I'm under oath now."

On September 26, after two hours of deliberations, the jury found Vona guilty of a reduced charge of assault and battery. The jurors were never presented with the weapon, but even more puzzling to them was the real motive.

Two days later, Judge Ford sentenced Vona to a term of six months in the county jail for the assault and battery conviction, but ordered it served concurrently with a stiffer one-to-fifteen-year sentence in the Ohio Penitentiary for violating his probation for the Public Market burglary. After two years in prison, Vona was released from the Marion Correctional Institute on September 28, 1961.

In his later life Vona served for nearly three decades as a union official for Teamster Local No. 377. Vona died on January 4, 2002 at the age of 76. Michael Walley passed away on December 9, 1988 at Northside Hospital where he was suffering from a heart ailment. He was 65 years old.

Pinky" Walsh

John Thomas Walsh was born in Youngstown on July 14, 1902. While he was always known as "Pinky," there was never a public explanation as to where the nickname came from.

In 1934, Walsh received a one to fifteen year sentence in the Ohio Penitentiary for entering a restaurant at 131 West Federal Street and breaking open a safe. Returning to Youngstown after his sentence, he worked as a card dealer at a south-side coffeehouse and at "Black Sam's" on East Federal Street. His first gambling arrest came on August 22, 1942, when vice squad officers apprehended him for possession of gambling equipment, "rundown sheets" used for horse race betting, in a basement on West Commerce Street.

During the early 1940s Walsh became associated with Jerry Pascarella in gambling and slot machines (see chapter 7). The two were arrested during a gambling raid on January 31, 1944, at a coffeehouse at the corner of South Avenue and Boardman Street. Walsh was convicted and fined $200. In the months to come, Walsh seemed to back away from the brash, young Pascarella, who disappeared in May 1945.

Walsh kept a low profile after the disappearance of Pascarella and stayed out of the public eye until January 1946. It was revealed at this time that he was one of three men involved in the purchase of a property at Center Street and Wilson Avenue, which became notorious as the Center Street Sandwich Shop and the headquarters of Sandy Naples. Walsh was a partner in the ownership of this property with Naples and Joseph Alexander (see chapter 8).

In August 1949, Walsh was a suspect in an attempted burglary at Duffy's Tavern at 1384 Belmont Avenue. Walsh and another man were apparently scared off while they trying to break open a safe. He and his accomplice were seen by a police officer driving away from the tavern. Walsh was arrested after police captured a suspected lookout. When booked, he used his middle name Thomas, and then pleaded not guilty at arraignment before Judge Nevin, who set bond at $5,000. After a two-day preliminary hearing, in which attorney John Hooker claimed that any connection between his clients and the crime was purely circumstantial, the men were bound over to the grand jury, which failed to indict.

In June 1951, Walsh was involved with Sandy Naples in the ill-fated robbery at the home of Joseph Jennings, Jr. in Niles (see chapter 11). Both got off with a slap on the wrist – a $50 fine for pleading guilty to be a suspicious person.

On April 8, 1954, Walsh and John Keenan (see entry on Dutch Manley) were arrested by a rookie patrolman in Farrell, Pennsylvania, while attempting to break into the Italian Social Club Home on Spearman Avenue around 3:00 a.m. After hearing pounding noises while passing the social club, Officer Ernest Saunders walked to the rear of the building and surprised the men as they were trying to break open a door with a crowbar. Saunders ordered the pair to put up their hands and then fired two rounds into the air from his service revolver to get the attention of passersby in order to get help. When this failed, he simply marched the two culprits at gunpoint to the Farrell Police Station a block and a half away.

The two men were arraigned on charges of attempted burglary, possession of burglary tools and violating the uniform firearms acts – in a valise Saunders found a loaded .32 automatic and burglary tools. The case was dragged out for over a year until April 18, 1955, when both men were sentenced in Mercer County Court to 12 months in the Allegheny County Workhouse. On May 10, 1955, Patrolman Saunders was honored by the Youngstown Crime Clinic during the organization's Crime Prevention Day. The officer was awarded a certificate for meritorious service and $200 by Common Pleas Judge David Jenkins.

On November 18, after serving seven months of a twelve-month sentence, Keenan and Walsh were paroled. Facing an angry judge who made it clear he was reluctant to grant the parole, the pair was told, "We don't want you back in Pennsylvania, we don't want you back in this county and we don't want you back in this court."

On January 3, 1958, Walsh was arrested with Joseph "Little Joey" Naples after the kidnapping of an obstetrician and the violent home invasion of a wealthy retired businessman at 1010 Colonial Drive. On the day after New Year's, two men abducted Dr. Jordan Dentscheff around 8:45 in the evening as he alighted from a car at his Gypsy Lane apartment. The doctor was beaten and forced to lie on the floor of the back seat. The men drove away and later picked up a third man on their way to the mansion of Benjamin Friedkin on Colonial Drive. Friedkin was the former president of an aluminum products firm, who made $10 million when he sold his company to a Texas conglomerate.

Once at the home, nine people were held captive while a daughter of the Friedkins hid in an upstairs bedroom closet. Though the robbery seemed well planned, the intruders left behind thousands of dollars in cash and jewelry, while making off with $1,000 in cash and a $1,500 silver mink stole. The daring holdup followed a pattern of robberies that had taken place over the prior two years.

At 6:00 the next morning, Walsh was arrested at his home and Joey Naples was apprehended at the home of his brother Sandy. Despite the fact that one of the bandits was unmasked the whole time, none of the eight victims to view police lineups said they could identify Walsh or Naples as one of the holdup men. Both were soon released.

After the murder of Sandy Naples, for which Walsh was held for three days, Pinky seemed to stay out of trouble. Although in his 60s, Walsh became a structural ironworker and a member of Local 207. He helped build Southern Park Mall. Walsh was married to Mary Patrick for 28 years. The couple had two children, including a son who became an attorney. On October 14, 1969, at the age of 67, Walsh had a heart attack at his home. He was pronounced dead at North Side Hospital.

Woodworth Novelty

On Sunday, August 7, 1949, the *Vindicator* announced in a front-page story that Woodworth Novelty Company was supplying slot machines to The Coliseum in Wickliffe and the brand new Green Village casino at Lake Milton. The new gambling den was a remodeled house, camouflaged to look like a gasoline station. Rumors claimed the Green Village was the operation of Joe DiCarlo, while Joseph "Red" Giordano, Joseph Alexander and Frank Yockman were said to be linked to it.

This shocking revelation initiated a wave of indignation among citizens of Beaver Township, located south of Youngstown in Mahoning County. The result of which was the irate inhabitants banding together to run the gamblers out of town.

The newspaper first announced that Woodworth Novelty was run by Joe Giordano and Joe Alexander. They quickly backed down about the involvement of the latter. On Tuesday night, about 50 residents met with Beaver Township trustees and demanded action. Spearheading the response was new Beaver Township Justice of the Peace Richard Bauman. During the meeting residents voiced the following opinions recorded by the *Vindicator:*

◊ They won't tolerate gambling devices

◊ They won't let Woodworth continue to be a headquarters for a gambling syndicate because if Sheriff Paul J. Langley won't run racketeers out of the county he'll have to put them in some other township.

◊ They won't have hoodlums hanging around the area.

◊ They won't give the sheriff another chance to refuse their requests that he enforce anti-gambling laws.

Residents confessed that they should have reacted sooner. They recalled seeing expensive automobiles and trucks arriving at the company and slot machines being removed. Some openly admitted they called Sheriff Paul J. Langley and informed him of the activity. Others residents were already aware of some of the problems. One told of seeing a young newsboy spend his entire week's collection money in a slot machine at a local dairy. Another complained about the "riffraff" that sometimes congregated outside the Woodworth Novelty store. "Once they get a foothold they would be hard to move out," the man warned.

A local pastor offered, "We are in the business of saving souls and are challenged by the moral conditions set up by a thing like this. All they need is an entering wedge. Let's keep gambling out," he implored.

One of the final speakers was former County Sheriff Ralph Elser. "If the sheriff won't rid our township of gambling, we can do it ourselves with a couple of good constables and a good squire," he declared.

At the end of the night Bauman presented a resolution that was unanimously approved by the board of trustees:

> "Whereas unfavorable publicity has been given to the Woodworth community and Beaver Township in general, and public testimony of slot machines, pinboard machines and punchboards having been given before township trustees:
>
> "Be it therefore resolved that all such gambling devices within the boundaries of this township are condemned as illegal and that the proprietors of such establishments having such gambling devices be served with a written copy of this resolution, condemning such devices, by the duly elected constable of this township, that the proprietors of such establishments here are hereby given five days within which to comply with the Ohio law or further action shall be taken by duly elected and / or appointed officers of Beaver Township."

Instead of addressing the Beaver Township problem, Sheriff Langley instead became involved in a battle of one-upmanship with Chief Eddie Allen. Despite all the success Allen was achieving in Youngstown, Langley decided to conduct a number of raids there, seemingly to rub it in the chief's face.

When questioned about the slots business in Beaver Township, Langley claimed he didn't know if there were any slot machines in the county. He then declared, "We will take care of them when we get to them. The city [Youngstown] is part of the county and we are going to cleanup the stinking mess. Today I am going to show who is the sheriff of this county."

The Youngstown raids, the first conducted by Langley since February, were at downtown locations in which there was constant activity – the Federal Pool

Room and the Tasty Sandwich Shoppe. At the South Avenue Café, Langley's men arrested Pete Skevos, the same man they had arrested back in February. Despite almost daily scrutiny and raids by Allen's men Langley felt the need to conduct his own raids.

Allen wrote a response to Langley, which was reprinted on the front-page of the *Vindicator*. The newspaper didn't think much of Langley's efforts, reporting that the arrests were of "small fries." The letter said, in part:

> "We are pleased that the sheriff's office is still enthusiastic about helping us to mop up the residue of the gambling gentry in the city.
>
> "We were beginning to fear that due to the press of all their work in the county, they (sheriff and deputies) would be too busy and we would lose the assistance of the sheriff and his men.
>
> "We realize, of course, that on occasions there may be some law violations in the county, and we cannot insist that they devote all of their time and talents to help the city alone.
>
> "The sheriff has the power to invest our men with county-wide authority, and we would be glad to attempt to repay him for his altruistic assistance to us."

In his closing Allen took time to get in a shot at city council, which refused all efforts of the Henderson administration to amend the bug ordinance to include jail time in the sentencing:

> "We hope that, because these punks are merely assessed small fines, that he (Langley) will not become discouraged but will be as persistent and persevering as he can be in our mutual endeavors to eradicate them from the city."

On Wednesday night, Langley and his men raided the Green Village at Milton Lake. Inside at the time were just seven patrons and one employee, who were arrested on charges of possessing gambling equipment.

After the raid on the Green Village, Langley and his men went to the Woodworth Novelty Company around 12:30 p.m. but reported he found no signs of gambling. After announcing the night's activities to reporters, Langley took a moment to take pot shots at Chief Allen and former Sheriff Elser. He scoffed at Allen's "mop up the residue" remark, claiming the Federal Pool Room was taking in $4,000 daily. As for the former sheriff, Langley stated, "Let Elser reminisce on his 14 years of office and think over the mistakes he has made."

The hoopla over the Woodworth Novelty Company came to a close on August 23 during a meeting called to review the results of Beaver Township's anti-gambling crusade. Sheriff Langley was in attendance to defend his actions...or non-actions.

Langley opened with a sarcastic remark, which did nothing to endear him to his audience. "I'm glad to see you people were able to leave your homes tonight, glad that you are not afraid of these supposed mobsters who burn your homes and harm your children," the arrogant sheriff quipped.

The residents of the township were grateful that the *Vindicator* exposed the Green Village and the Woodworth Novelty Company for their illegal activities. Langley chose to attack the *Vindicator.* "You God-fearing people are being made tools by a vicious mob of poison-pen people who profess to be newspaper people," Langley told them. The sheriff claimed the newspaper's position was solely for political gain – what gain that was he never explained.

Meanwhile, the *Vindicator's* efforts were praised by most of the 108 residents present. In the end, the citizens of Beaver Township were rewarded with the announcement that the landlord of the Woodworth Novelty Company property had ordered the gamblers to vacate the premises by August 31.

Sam Zappi

On April 18, 1949, Samuel "Patsy" Zappi was stopped while driving his car on South Forest Avenue. While he was being questioned, Vice Squad Sergeant Clayton Geise saw several bug slips stashed under the dashboard. This was Zappi's third bug arrest in less than a year. He was apprehended in May and June 1948. Each time he pleaded guilty and was fined $50, as was the case this time.

Zappi didn't fare as well in his next encounter. On November 16, he led plainclothes officers on a chase from the East End Bridge to Penn Avenue. Along the way he tossed 118 policy slips out the window. This time, instead of the usual $50 slap on the wrist, Judge Powers leveled the maximum fine of $500.

On January 6, 1953, the newspaper reported that Zappi was one of eight Youngstown residents to obtain a federal gambling tax stamp. Zappi purchased the $50 stamp with Joseph Walley. At the time the two men claimed they had plans to "begin operations" in September. Chief Eddie Allen responded by hauling in as many of the tax stamp holders as his men could find, and then interrogating them for hours.

Zappi responded to this police harassment by announcing he was quitting the bug business. Police had little reason to believe him and on May 7, he was arrested after officers found him with nine policy tickets in his possession on Himrod Avenue. A few days later, Zappi pleaded guilty before Judge Cavalier. The judge fined him $500, but suspended $200, and placed him on probation for six months.

Arrest number seven for Zappi came on the morning of August 4, 1953, when officers followed Zappi into a service station on Himrod Avenue and retrieved five bug slips inside a newspaper he tossed into a garbage can. This time Zappi decided to fight the charge. On August 25, Judge Cavalier dismissed the charges after the arresting officers failed to appear in court.

Zappi faced new charges, playing a game chance, when he, Mike Walley and another man were busted for shooting craps on the afternoon of September 28, 1953. Although vice squad officers called it a "floating crap game" and claimed they had received dozens of complaints, Judge Powers decided it was only a "small game" and fined each man $5, then suspended it.

Zappi received the same treatment on a different charge from Judge Franko. On January 13, 1954, he was arrested after crashing a stop sign at Andrews Avenue and the McGuffey Street Bridge. Summoned to appear before Judge Nevin on January 19, Zappi instead showed up three days earlier in Judge Franko's court. The controversial judge fined Zappi $5 and costs then suspended both. Two months later, Franko's generosity toward traffic violators was front-page news. There were accusations that the judge had "fixed" at least 100 violations.

February 1, 1954, found Zappi again inside the station house after yet another bug arrest. This time vice squad officers, including William Campanizzi, found policy slips in the door panel of Zappi's automobile. Less than two weeks later, he was again listed in the newspaper as a purchaser of the federal gambling tax stamp. This time it was in association with Mike Walley's brother Nick Lavaglio. When Zappi was hauled in this time, he told Vice Squad Chief Krispli that he was retired from the gambling business and was working as a railroad brakeman. The next day, February 19, Zappi appeared before Judge Franko on the possession charge. Unimpressed with his new career path, the judge fined him $500. Despite his alleged retirement, when the new list of federal gambling tax stamp holders was released in July, his name again appeared.

During Sandy Naples' highly publicized trial (See Chapter 11) in July 1954, for "promoting a game of chance," Zappi was one of 14 convicted numbers operators called by the state to testify. The gist of Zappi's testimony was that although his fines and court costs were paid by the "racket bosses," he had no idea who they were. While he admitted he had picked up bug slips, he wasn't sure to whom he had delivered them. He was sure, however, that he "never had any direct or individual business connections with Sandy Naples."

By the mid-1950s, when the bombing epidemic hit the policy rackets, Zappi was a regular when it came to hauling numbers men in for questioning. He also remained free from arrest for nearly a year and a half. Then on June 28, 1955, vice squad officers found him on Hine Street with a pocket full of bug slips. He pleaded not guilty and was released on a $1,000 bond. Two weeks later, he pleaded guilty before Judge Nevin and was again hit with a $500 fine.

On November 17, 1955, when the government again released the list of federal gambling tax stamp purchasers, Zappi and Nick (Walley) Lavaglio were again on the list. The next day both men told Vice Squad Chief Krispli that they suspended their operations. Some wondered if it was true this time, since Zappi was able to avoid arrest for quite some time. When the next stamp purchasers, however, were announced the following March, Zappi and Lavaglio were still on the list.

In April 1957, word reached the vice squad that Zappi was in the bug business again. Officers went to his home, where they found four policy tickets in a drawer in his buffet. Zappi was arrested, but freed just a half-hour later after posting a $1,000 bond. Less than three hours later, police stopped him as he drove over the East End Bridge. When he was unable to prove ownership of the car, he was held for three hours until his wife appeared at headquarters with the owner-registration document. Since Zappi was operating out of his home, George Krispli contacted the Ohio Bell Telephone Company and asked that service be discontinued. Before the month was over Zappi was out $500, the fine for his latest arrest, and a home telephone.

After this last incident, Zappi apparently decided he had had enough. He and his wife moved to Miami, Florida. Zappi remained there for three years before coming back to Youngstown, shortly after the murder of Sandy Naples. Zappi attempted to open his own bug bank and bookie service and was operating out of a home at 448 Lansing Avenue, which was owned by Frank Lucarell, an employee of General Fireproofing Company.

On Friday afternoon, April 22, 1960, members of the Morals Squad, the former vice squad, arrived at the Lansing Avenue address after receiving a tip about the new operation. Officers found policy tickets and horse race betting slips on the kitchen table and arrested Zappi. Lucarell, when questioned by police, claimed the only reason Zappi was at his house was to visit a family member. Zappi initially told his interrogators that he was staying at an Avondale Avenue address. City records showed the home as that of Angelo Mosco, another General Fireproofing employee. Zappi finally gave a Florida address where his wife was residing.

Morals Squad Chief Lieutenant Frank Waters told reporters, "We found among other things an adding machine and run-down tapes, which usually means a bank." He described the operation as "just getting started," and that it looked like Zappi was running the operation himself and "not fronting for bigger gambling kingpins."

After a couple of delays, including the usual demand of a jury trial, Zappi appeared in court on June 17, and pleaded guilty. He was fined $500.

It was Zappi's last arrest in Youngstown, as well as the last report of any of his activities by the *Vindicator*. Zappi returned to Florida. He died in Fort Lauderdale in September 1995, at the age of 77.

"Jack the Ripper" Zentko

Despite his auspicious introduction to organized crime in Youngstown – having a savage beating administered to him by Sandy Naples and other friends of "Fats" Aiello – John Paul Zentko made a comeback and was a noted underworld personality until his suicide in 1993. Despite his colorful nickname, there was never any explanation as to how it originated.

Zentko may lead all the Youngstown hoods in the category of arrests for "suspicion." He had a total of 24. Five of those were on his rap sheet – along with arrests for petit larceny, non-support and vehicle violations – before the fateful

New Year's Eve beating took place. After the attack outside the Purple Cow (see chapter 8), Zentko and Anthony J. Bova, alias Lou Bogash, were sought by police. Zentko was arrested ten days later by the "mayor's special investigators," who were assigned to the highly publicized case. Zentko scored points with his assailants when he refused to testify against them and even denied that Aiello had fired at him and Bova.

With a number of Youngstown police on friendly terms with Aiello, Zentko found himself the target of constant police harassment for months. In July 1947, officers threw him in jail for 24 hours simply for parking on the wrong side of the street.

In February 1947, Zentko made his way back into the good graces of the underworld. The newspaper had taken to calling people who bailed out arrested bug men "angels." On February 25, Zentko paid a $500 bond for the release of Ralph Gaudio, an alleged bug runner for Lou Tiberio. It was a busy month for Tiberio, owner of the Tropics Night Club. He had twice paid a bond for the release of "Booze" Gianfrancesco.

On March 11, 1952, Zentko, now described by the newspapers as a "henchman" of Sandy Naples, was stopped for speeding by police in Moreland Hills, a wealthy suburb southeast of Cleveland. When officers searched the automobile they found a mink coat wrapped in a bed sheet in the rear. Zentko and his companion, Joseph "Stubby" Galioto, were arrested and held while Youngstown authorities were notified. The two were turned over to Youngstown detectives. When questioned, Zentko told the officers that the coat, valued at $1,000, belonged to "one of his wives," from whom he was separated seven years earlier. He was still riding around with it in his car. Police, however, determined the coat was brand new and had never been worn. Since the labels were missing, police were sure it was stolen.

Police had a mystery on their hands. They were unable to connect the coat to any recent robberies. In mid-February there was a theft at the Strouss-Hirshburg Company. Police put Zentko in a lineup, but employees of the downtown department store were not able to identify him. Police wanted to question Zentko's ex-wife, but were unable to locate her. For most of the 1950s, Zentko's address was given in the newspapers as the Edison Hotel; police found no sign he was living with anyone there. Zentko and Galioto were released on March 14, and their attorney S.S. Fekette immediately filed suit for the return of the mink coat. After legal documents were filed, the Youngstown police turned the coat over to the sheriff's department for an appraisal to be determined and bond set. Fifteen days after the arrest and discovery of the mink in Moreland Hills, the coat was returned to Zentko by county deputies.

Zentko and Galioto returned to Moreland Hills on March 21, where Zentko pleaded guilty to reckless driving and was fined $200 and costs. On the return trip to Youngstown, Galioto, who was driving, was stopped for speeding on

Route 224 in Portage County. When deputies found no identification on them the two were taken to the Portage County jail in Ravenna. They were both questioned and released.

Four months later Zentko, who seemed to have no problem finding trouble, made the news again after being caught in a love triangle. On Friday, July 25, at 1:30 a.m., Zentko and Mrs. Dorothy Inman arrived at the latter's home on East Florida Avenue. Waiting for them was Charlotte Zentko, "Jack the Ripper's" wife. The two married women slugged it out in the living room of the Inman home, overturning furnisher and smashing whatever wasn't nailed down. Police arrived and struggled to separate the women as Charlotte spewed a barrage of profanity. Mrs. Zentko seemed to be worse for wear as she was treated for bruises of the head, ankle and arm at South Side Hospital.

Zentko and his wife were arrested and charged with disturbing the peace. Both pleaded not guilty and were released by Municipal Judge Cavalier on Monday on $200 bonds. While in jail over the weekend, Zentko hired Fekette to represent his wife. Charlotte was in no mood to speak with the attorney claiming, "What do I need a lawyer for, anyway?" Chief Allen refused to let Fekette see her. The attorney responded by swearing out an affidavit charging Allen with refusing to allow him to see his client. Fekette threatened to have the chief arrested. On August 22, Judge Cavalier fined Charlotte $25 and costs after she pleaded guilty to disturbing the peace. On the recommendation of the prosecutor, charges against John Zentko were dropped.

The harassment against Zentko continued. On September 7, 1952, he was arrested while standing on the sidewalk outside Naples' Center Sandwich Shop as Sandy sat inside and watched. When questioned, the two arresting officers said they didn't know why Zentko was picked up, they were just acting on orders from squad leader Lieutenant Dan Maggianetti.

Zentko was back in the news on January 9, 1953, when he was injured in an automobile accident. He was in a vehicle driven by Hartley Moore, the holder of a federal gambling tax stamp operating out of the Dixie Tavern on Glenwood Avenue. Moore failed to negotiate a bend on West Federal Street and slammed into a utility pool. Both men were taken to South Side Hospital.

Less than two months later, Zentko and his wife Charlotte were arrested on a warrant issued by a Pittsburgh alderman. Charlotte was wanted as a fugitive from justice and Zentko for aiding her. The next day, Pittsburgh authorities came to retrieve Charlotte and asked the police to release Zentko. She was taken to Pittsburgh where she was charged with "suspicion of prostitution."

On October 22, 1956, Zentko was in a car driven by Joey Naples when they arrived at 318 East Boardman Street, a known bug pickup station. Naples exited the vehicle and went inside. Patrolman John Kohut and Pete Novosel were keeping an eye on the place. They approached the automobile, flashed their badges and ordered Zentko to get out. Zentko refused to open the door claiming,

"That's not enough," obviously stalling for time. Novosel, a no-nonsense officer, threatened to shoot out the tires. Zentko then backed the car to the curb, all the while blowing the horn to warn Naples. He then opened the door. Inside the automobile the officers found a bag containing $53, three adding machine tapes and more than 90 lottery slips. Just then Naples walked out and told Zentko, "I made the call," just before both men were arrested.

Prosecutors charged the two under the state statute of carrying on a game of chance and added a municipal charge of possessing lottery slips. When the case came to trial in December, Judge Franko dismissed the state charges against Naples for insufficient evidence after attorney Fekette argued the city failed to prove the defendant had custody of the slips.

On December 19, Franko found Zentko guilty on the city charge of possessing lottery slips and fined him $250 and dismissed the state charge. Franko then found Naples not guilty of the city charges, since the arresting officers never saw the bag in Naples' hands. Franko then took a shot at city prosecutors, especially Assistant John Leskovyansky, declaring, "These cases were very carelessly handled by the prosecutor's office. Let's be fair: the warrants in these cases were issued before the affidavits were ever executed by Vice Squad Chief George Krispli, placing me in a difficult position in presenting a decision."

Sometime in late 1959, Zentko began dating Broadway singer and comedienne Martha Raye. In early December, rumors abounded that the two were actually married. A publicist for the performer told reporters the marriage was "quite impossible." While he acknowledged the two were dating, he claimed Raye was seeing "two or three other fellows, too."

It seemed as if Zentko would never live down the incident outside the Purple Cow that fateful New Years' Eve 1947. Nearly every article that his name appeared in seemed to refer to the night he took a beating at the hands of Naples and Aiello. Perhaps this is what led to him changing his name to Lane during the 1960s.

At twenty minutes past midnight on St. Valentine's Day, 1962, a squad of police officers, including Andrew Kovac, entered the A-Lounge at the corner of Boardman and South Hazel Streets where they hauled out Zentko / Lane and Dominic Senzarino. It was part of a new police harassment campaign, which Maggianetti explained as a drive to "rid the city's all-night spots of the hangers-on, who are responsible for recent burglaries and gambling activities." The two men were held overnight despite the efforts of their attorney to free them. The next morning Senzarino was charged with being a suspicious person. Zentko / Lane was released without being charged at 11:30 a.m.

On October 9, 1962, one of the most "tremendous" explosions in the Valley's history destroyed the home of bail bondsman Mario Guerrieri. The huge, 14-room dwelling on Fifth Avenue was in the process of being renovated after a "mysterious" fire gutted the home during December 1961. Guerrieri was in Pittsburgh on business when his wife notified him about the destruction. Around 4:00 that morning, Guerrieri arrived at the seen with Zentko / Lane to view the damage. The two were quickly taken into custody, but not before Guerrieri was seen tears, declaring he had no insurance to cover the loss.

Also taken into custody around the same time were Carl Venzeio, Frank Lentine, Dominic Senzarino and Joseph Walley. All were questioned by Detective Chief John Terlesky. Police were also on the lookout for Dominic Moio. After the December fire, it was reported that "hoodlums" were being used to work on the home. Some claimed these were clients of Guerrieri's who still owed him money. Moio was one of the "hoodlums" and was said to have completed the plastering work.

"Zentko / Lane was questioned and released and a few hours later picked up again. Guerrieri was held and questioned for ten hours, claiming he had no idea as to who could have planted the bomb or why. The next day, a city condemnation order was issued to raze the home. Guerrieri consented.

Seven years passed before Zentko / Lane was in the news again. During the early hours of November 25, 1969, an argument and scuffle took place outside Satan's Inferno at 22 Fifth Avenue. It ended in gunfire with two brothers being wounded and another man stabbed in the arm. After gathering information at the scene, police went to Zentko / Lane's home at 2123 South Avenue and arrested him for the assault. Two young women with him at the time were also arrested after police found marijuana in the place. During a hearing on December 22, the judge dismissed the marijuana charge against the women, ruling that it had not been "properly obtained." On July 6, 1970, Zentko / Lane was bound over to the grand jury on a charge of assault with a deadly weapon. He was eventually fined $3,000.

Zentko / Lane remained out of trouble for the last 24 years of his life. In the summer of 1993 Lane became ill. On Friday, August 20, he left his home without telling family members where he was going. The family filed a "missing persons" report the next day. On Sunday afternoon, Lane was found dead in Mill Creek Park with a bullet in his head. Beside the body was a .38 revolver. The coroner ruled his death a suicide. Zentko / Lane was 73 years old.

Section V Notes

1 John J. Angelo was the most recognized figure in the labor unions in the history of Youngstown. From 1947 until 1972, Angelo was constantly in the public eye, mostly as Secretary-Treasurer of Teamster's Local 377. Angelo died while vacationing in Las Vegas in August 1981.

2 Zollie Engel's operation at 1307 Market Street was considered on the city's South Side, while other "bookie joints" ran inside the downtown area.

3 If Joseph "Red" Giordano seemed anxious to explain his record to Detroit police he had good reason. There was a second Joseph Giordano from Youngstown who was a career criminal. On July 24, 1947, hours before he was to be sentenced to a long term as a habitual criminal, he and another inmate sawed their way out of the Mahoning County jail. He was captured in Cleveland on March 17, 1948, while participating in a burglary on West 25th Street. Police searched him and placed him in a patrol wagon with another suspect. As the wagon drove near Lutheran Hospital on West 25th Giordano pulled a German Luger. The hood had a blue belt wrapped around his waist and the gun was tied to it and allowed to dangle between his legs. The cops missed it during their normal search. Giordano poked the gun through a vent into the cab and ordered the driver, Nelson Belcher to pull over and park. As soon as he did Giordano opened fire. Belcher was wounded in the groin. Three shots fired at his partner, Julius Murer, missed the mark and both men tumbled out of the vehicle. Unfortunately for Giordano, he was still locked in the wagon. Murer crawled to the back of the wagon, stuck his revolver through a window and wildly fired all six rounds. Giordano, wounded in the arm, dropped his weapon. His accomplice was wounded in the leg. All three wounded men were taken to Cleveland City Hospital.

When he recovered, Giordano was later taken to the London Prison Farm to begin a 25-year sentence. By April 1958, it was reported that Giordano was denied freedom 17 times. One year later Giordano was paroled. Authorities in Cleveland wanted him tried on an 11 year-old indictment for the shooting of Officer Belcher. The judge dismissed the charge claiming Giordano was deprived of his constitutional right to a speedy trial.

4 Julius Anthony Petro had a long criminal record in the Northeast Ohio area. Convicted of the 1946 murder of Theodore "Bobby" Knaus, a robbery accomplice whom Petro didn't want to split the proceeds with, he spent 19 months on death row before a second trial ended in acquittal. He was released from the Ohio Penitentiary less than 90 days before the Green Acres casino robbery in Struthers. In 1952, he was convicted of robbing a Warren bank cashier

and sentenced to 25 years in Leavenworth. Petro was released after serving 13 years and moved to California, where he worked for former Clevelander James "Jimmy the Weasel" Fratianno. One of the people Petro worked with was Ray Ferritto of Erie, Pennsylvania. Ferritto and others thought Petro was a "violent nuisance." On January 10, 1969, Petro was murdered while sitting in a car at Los Angeles International Airport. In November 1977, Ferritto was indicted for the car-bomb murder of Cleveland gangster Danny Greene, in which Ronald Carabbia of Struthers was an accomplice. When Ferritto realized he was a target of the Cleveland Mafia, who had hired him to kill Greene, he became a government witness. In making his deal with the government he confessed to the murder of Julius Petro.

5 John Keenan's other crimes included the kidnapping of Ralph K. Jones of New Castle, Pennsylvania, on March 16, 1949. Keenan robbed Jones of $2,485 when he walked out of the Gully Bank. Keenan was also a suspect in the murder of a Pittsburgh man. In April 1951, he was arrested for a shooting in the Allegheny Sportsmen's Club. He was acquitted two months later. In 1955, Keenan served seven months for an attempted robbery in Farrell, Pennsylvania with "Pinky" Walsh (see Walsh entry).

6 This is the Pennsylvania town that appears on Nello Ronci's rap sheet as his place of birth. No city by that name appears in Pennsylvania today. The closest match is a Strait Creek, near the town of Nelson not far from the New York / Pennsylvania border.

7 Dream books analyzed the dreams of the bug players and assigned a three-digit number to visions within the dream. Dream books were published weekly and monthly. In June 1938, the *Vindicator* ran a seven-part series on gambling in the Valley. The series had the following to say about the use of dream books:

"The dream book is by far the most widely used of the "dope" publications. In these fantastic booklets the player is sure to find the answer to his dream and with it the lucky number – though usually there are several.

"An example...A bug addict dreamed he took a motor trip to Canada during his vacation, visiting among other places, the nursery of...quintuplets.

"Consulting one of the many dream books, he learned his dream involved a large number of "bug" selections.

"[The dream book advised him] If he dreams about an auto...he should play 572. If he dreams about a baby he should play 112; children, 212; nursery, 715... etc."

8 Before joining the Youngstown Police Department, William E. Gruver

served in the Merchant Marine (European Theatre / Atlantic War Zone 1944) and the U.S. Naval Construction Force (the Navy Seabees) in the Pacific Theatre during World War II. Returning to Youngstown after the war, he attended pre-cadet police school before becoming a member of the police force under Chief Eddie Allen in December 1951. Beginning as a beat patrolman, Gruver worked many duties, such as wagon man, radio operator, squad car, and traffic. In 1962, he became a member of the vice squad where he partnered with Randall "Duke" Wellington. In 1963 Gruver and Wellington were pursuing a suspect when he abandoned his moving automobile. The vehicle struck Gruver, sending his to Southside Hospital. Gruver left the department in 1966. He joined the Federal U.S. Marshal Service in 1971, and worked protecting Federal witnesses. Some of the more notable people Gruver ran into in this capacity were Joe Barboza, Meyer Lansky and men involved in the French Connection drug smuggling ring. From 1992 to 1998 Gruver worked security at South Side and later North Side Hospital. In the mid-2000s, nearing the age of 80, Gruver was back with his old partner, "Duke" Wellington. The former Youngstown Chief of Police served as Mahoning County Sheriff, the only man to serve in both capacities, from August 1999 to January 2013. While working at the county jail delivering subpoenas and organizing the property room and archive records, Gruver was diagnosed with cancer. Despite his condition he continued to serve almost until the time of his death in August 2008.

Appendix A

Names and Descriptions of "Fats" Aiello As Reported in the Vindicator

No mobster in the history of the Mahoning Valley was written about as often as Joseph Jasper "Fats" Aiello. Beginning with the pronunciation of his last name (A-Leo, as opposed to the traditional I-Yel-Lo), to the misnomer of his nickname ("Fats" weighed in at 137 pounds) his name and description appeared in different formats for four decades as evidenced by the following information printed on the pages of the *Vindicator*.

12-31-1946	"Fats" Aiello	widely known gambler
01-03-1947	J. J. "Fats" Aiello	gambling joint operator, alleged shooter
01-04-1947	Joe Joseph Aiello	gun-toting Youngstown gambler
02-18-1947	Joe Joseph "Fats" Aiello	local gun-toting gambler
03-09-1947	Joe Joseph "Fats" Aiello	pistol packing gambler
09-14-1947	Joseph "Fats" Aiello	Y'town gambler and underworld character
08-04-1948	Joseph J. "Fats" Aiello	prominent racketeer
12-03-1948	Jasper Joseph "Fats" Aiello	Youngstown racketeer
11-10-1949	Joseph J. "Fats" Aiello	petty racketeer
04-06-1950	Jasper J. "Fats" Aiello	local racketeer
01-10-1951	Jasper J. "Fats" Aiello	former small-time racketeer
01-14-1951	Jasper J. "Fats" Aiello	small-time Youngstown racketeer
10-16-1951	J. "Fats" Aiello	racketeer
11-28-1952	J. Joseph "Fats" Aiello	local racketeer
12-10-1952	Joseph Jasper "Fats" Aiello	erstwhile gambler and racket figure
04-06-1953	Jasper Joseph "Fats" Aiello	Y'town underworld figure and gambler
07-20-1955	Joseph Jasper "Fats" Aiello	underworld character and petty racketeer
11-11-1955	J. J. (Fats) Aiello	well-known gambler
01-16-1957	Joseph J. (Fats) Aiello	widely known area racket figure
05-11-1957	Joseph Jasper (Fats) Aiello	racketeer and cigarette service operator
05-26-1959	Joseph Jasper "Fats" Aiello	Youngstown hoodlum and racketeer
04-12-1960	J. Joseph (Fats) Aiello	Youngstown racket figure
05-10-1960	Joseph (Fats) Aiello	self-described gambler and lady's man
11-30-1960	Joseph Jasper (Fats) Aiello	notorious common gambler and racketeer

04-24-1961	J. Jasper (Fats) Aiello	racketeer turned tavern host
02-27-1962	Joseph "Fats" Aiello	manager and host
01-10-1963	Joseph Jasper (Fats) Aiello	petty racket figure
05-05-1963	Joseph Jasper "Fats" Aiello	felon
03-02-1963	J. Jasper (Fats) Aiello	Youngstown gambler and police character
06-17-1963	Joseph Jasper (Fats) Aiello	hoodlum and admitted professional gambler
03-13-1964	Joseph Jasper (Fats) Aiello	Youngstown underworld character
06-17-1965	Joseph (Fats) Aiello	Youngstown rackets kingpin
10-13-1965	Joseph Jasper (Fats) Aiello	convicted abortionist
12-15-1975	Joseph J. Jasper (Fats) Aiello	self-styled glamour boy of the racket crowd

Appendix B

Federal Gambling Tax Stamp Purchasers As Reported by the *Vindicator*

(The spelling of the names may not be the same from year to year)

December 5, 1951

Sullivan S. Cretella	Girard	Hartley P. Moore	North Lima
Henry N. Madeline	Hubbard	Albert DeCapito	Warren
Mary Smith	Hubbard	Louis DeCapito	Warren
Willie Baker	Lowellville	Guy DiCenso	Warren
Fuerino Berardinelli	Lowellville	Christ Morris	Warren
Vincent J. DeNiro	Lowellville	Adolph F. Schaers	Warren

July 31, 1952

Joseph A. Fasnelli	Niles	Joseph J. Beshara	Youngstown
David Fredericka	Niles	Peter J. Fetchet	Youngstown
Anthony Naples	Niles	Sandy Naples	Youngstown
John P. O'Hara	Struthers	Roosevelt Rivers	Youngstown

August 2, 1952
(Supplement to the July listing)

John Cella	Niles	James Jennings	Niles
Al DeChristofaro	Niles	Mike Naples	Niles
Gene DeChristofaro	Niles	Alex Trimbur	Niles
Spero G. Gulgas	Niles		

January 6, 1953

Alex Alexander	Youngstown	Roosevelt Rivers	Youngstown
Joseph J. Beshara	Youngstown	John Surianoudis	Youngstown
Nick Markovis	Youngstown	Joseph Walley	Youngstown
Sandy Naples	Youngstown	Sam Zappi	Youngstown

June 23, 1953

John Petrakos	Youngstown	Sandy Naples	Youngstown
Annie White	Youngstown	Alfred Catoline	Youngstown

Joseph J. Beshara	Youngstown	Arthur Masko	Youngstown
Cunnie Hartfield	Youngstown	Roosevelt Rivers	Youngstown
Leona Posey	Youngstown	Sam Zappi	Youngstown
Joseph Walley	Youngstown		

February 13, 1954

John Burnich, Jr.	Austin Township	John Sweetko	Campbell
Joseph Romanchuk	Austin Township	George S. Tzakka	Campbell
Nick Lavaglio	Boardman	Mike Turak	Campbell
Sam Zappi	Boardman	V. Vasilages	Campbell
Nick Andrew	Campbell	Richard Williams	Campbell
F. Carandonis	Campbell	Laura McJunkin (1)	Ellsworth
Jacob Eidelman	Campbell	Vince J. DeNiro	Lowellville
Christos Georgion	Campbell	Sandy Naples (2)	Struthers
Ben Heyman	Campbell	John P. O'Hara	Struthers
Joseph Jones	Campbell	John M. Salvatori (3)	Struthers
Joseph Koza	Campbell	R.W. Brown	Youngstown
Vincent Koza	Campbell	Louis Ciminelli	Youngstown
Paul Majirsky	Campbell	Joseph Fezzuogho	Youngstown
Michael Pacek	Campbell	John Petrakos	Youngstown
Ben Salvator	Campbell		

(1) Ellsworth, a community located on Route 224 southwest of Youngstown, was the smallest location in the northeast Ohio district to be issued a Federal gambling stamp.

(2) Naples used the address 185 Como Street in Struthers. Anthony G. Vitale, the owner of the property, claimed Naples was his brother-in-law and lived there. Naples' sister later gave a signed statement to the mayor of Struthers denying that Sandy lived there.

(3) The address given by Salvatori proved to be fictitious.

July 2, 1954

John Burnish, Jr.	Canfield	Howard Winfield	Niles
Joseph Romanchuk	Canfield	Nick Papalos (4)	Warren
John Cella	Niles	John Burnish Jr.	Youngstown
Al DeChristofaro	Niles	Vincent J. DeNiro (5)	Youngstown
Gene DeChristofaro	Niles	Peter J. Fetchet	Youngstown
Harold Flynn	Niles	Nick Lavaglio	Youngstown
Spero G. Gulgas	Niles	Joe D. Naples (5)	Youngstown

Anthony Naples	Niles	Sandy Naples (5)	Youngstown
Mike Naples	Niles	Sam Zappi	Youngstown
Alex Trinbur	Niles		

(4) Nick Papalos was identified as an associate of Anthony "Tony Dope" Delsanter

(5) All three were added to the listing on August 4, 1954. The *Vindicator* had reported earlier that "top racketeers could purchase their federal stamps later to avoid publicity that usually accompanies announcement of a new list."

July 7, 1956

John Carantonis	Campbell	Spero G. Gulgas	Niles
Christos Georgion	Campbell	Anthony Naples	Niles
Ben Heyman	Campbell	Mike Naples	Niles
James M. Lemonis	Campbell	Alex Timbur	Niles
Laura M. McJunkin	Ellsworth	Nick Papalas	Niles
John Cella	Niles	George Battles	Youngstown
Al DeChristofaro	Niles	Joe D. Naples	Youngstown
Gene DeChristofaro	Niles	Sandy Naples	Youngstown

March 24, 1957

John Carantonis	Campbell	Spero G. Gulgas	Niles
Christos Georgiou	Campbell	Michael J. Malvasi	Niles
Ben Heyman	Campbell	Anthony Naples	Niles
James M. Lemonis	Campbell	Mike Naples	Niles
John Sweetko	Campbell	Alex Trinbur	Niles
Laura M. McJunkin	Ellsworth	Howard C. Winfield	Niles
Peter J. Fetchet	Liberty Township	John P. O'Hara	Struthers
John Cella	Niles	Nick Papalas	Warren
James Dean	Niles	George Battles	Youngstown
Al DeChristofaro	Niles	John Burnich, Jr.	Youngstown
Gene DeChristofaro	Niles	Vince DeNiro	Youngstown
Anthony DeJerolme	Niles	Nick Lavaglio	Youngstown
John Fasanelli	Niles	Joe D. Naples	Youngstown
Harold Flynn	Niles	Sandy Naples	Youngstown
William A. Gray	Niles	Sam Zappi	Youngstown

August 12, 1958

John Carantonis	Campbell	Joseph Koza	Campbell

Stanley Cerech	Campbell	George Tzakka	Campbell
Tony Chirakos	Campbell	John Sweetko	Campbell
Ben Heyman	Campbell	Joseph A. Fasanelli	Niles

August 4, 1962

John Carantonis	Campbell	Ronald Carabbia	Struthers
Anthony Chirakos	Campbell	Michael Grbachway	Struthers
Chris Konton	Campbell	John O'Hara	Struthers
James Lemonis	Campbell	David J. Coman	Youngstown
Charles Nardolli	Campbell	Costas "Gus" Leamis	Youngstown
George Tzakka	Campbell	William Naples (6)	Youngstown
Stephen Almasy	Struthers		

(6) By the time the list was published William "Billy" Naples had been killed.

August 19, 1963

John Carantonis	Campbell	Carmen J. Perfette	Niles
Anthony Chirakos	Campbell	David J. Coman	Youngstown
James Lemonis	Campbell	Joseph Naples, Jr.	Youngstown
Charles Nardelli	Campbell	Theodore I. Rivers	Youngstown
George S. Tzakka	Campbell		

Appendix C

List of Youngstown Area Bombings During the 1950s

10-03-1951 – Croatian Fraternal Union Club on Route 422
12-15-1951 – Croatian Fraternal Union Club on Route 422
02-14-1952 – Croatian Fraternal Union Club on Route 422
03-06-1952 – Garage of attorney Frank Mastriana, 4030 Hudson Drive
03-11-1952 – M. DeBartolo Construction Company, 216 Alexander Street
04-29-1952 – Automobile of Hubbard Mayor Joseph Baldine, Newton Falls
08-16-1952 – Porch of Valentino Milton, 407 West Marion Avenue
09-02-1952 – Acid bomb at home of Dominic R. Delbone, 264 North Watt Street
09-02-1952 – Acid bomb at home of Paul Duritza, 145 South Bruce Street
02-05-1953 – Home of John Robinson, Trumbull Avenue, Hubbard Township
03-14-1953 – Cab of truck in garage of the Central Trucking Co., Niles-Cortland Rd.
03-19-1953 – Garage and truck at Central Trucking Co., Niles-Cortland Rd.
03-20-1953 – State Road Shopping Center in Cuyahoga Falls, being built by M. DeBartolo Construction Company
03-30-1953 – Home of F. P. DeNiro, 116 Lincoln Park Drive
04-16-1953 – Home of F. P. DeNiro, 116 Lincoln Park Drive
06-19-1953 – Golden Gate Restaurant on Route 422, north of Warren
07-07-1953 – Dump truck at home of Nelson Brutz, 404 Lincoln Avenue, Niles
12-10-1953 – Home of Bud J. Fares, 633 Almyra Avenue
02-13-1954 – Home of Paul P. Marr, 130 Ridgeway, Struthers
03-28-1954 – Stink bomb at Tauro Dump Truck Service and Marino Coal Co., 226 Pratt Street, Niles
04-03-1954 – Home of Frank Fetchet, 2044 Felicia Avenue
04-24-1954 – Towne Plaza Shopping Center in Massillon owned by William Cafaro
05-12-1954 – Home of Roland Leibert, 156 Wilson Avenue, Niles
05-13-1954 – Stink bomb at home of Raymond White, 245 Gypsy Lane
05-14-1954 – Towne Plaza Shopping Center in Massillon owned by William Cafaro
05-23-1954 – Tauro Dump Truck Service and Marino Coal Co., 226 Pratt St., Niles
05-25-1954 – Union Distributing Co., 1141 S. State St., Girard owned by An thony Flask, Jr.
05-28-1954 – Johnnie's Grocery, 1157 West Rayen Avenue, owned by J. Burnich

06-11-1954 – Jennings plant of Canada Dry Bottling Co., 2680 Youngstown Rd., Warren
07-17-1954 – Home of Jack Sulligan, 1966 Smithfield Street
07-31-1954 – In home under construction for truck driver Paul Brown, Niles
08-02-1954 – Automobile of Elman Burnett, 338 Park Avenue, New Castle, PA
08-03-1954 – On Denver Drive near Route 90, Poland
08-28-1954 – Circella Grocery Store at 2047 Jacobs Road
09-24-1954 – Garage of Joseph "Jugg" and Sam "Hobo" Sanfrey, Warren
10-22-1954 – Home of Julius Benson, 26 Sycamore Street
10-26-1954 – Entrance to Sunrise Confectionery, 1601 McGuffey Road
10-26-1954 – Three stores at State Road Plaza, Inc. in Cuyahoga Falls, owned by M. DeBartolo Construction Company
10-29-1954 – Windows in Warren Richey Elementary School, East High Ave / Early Rd
12-27-1954 – Windows and sign at State Street Tavern, 186 State Street, Struthers
01-28-1955 – Home of Paul Kurosky, 831 North Garland Avenue
08-09-1955 – Unexploded stick of dynamite found on porch of Joseph "Shorty" Bardinello, 491 Catalina Avenue
08-14-1955 – Found in automobile of Thomas Ciarniello, owner of the Ohio Tavern, 1525 Hubbard Road, Trumbull County, failed to explode
11-06-1955 – Steel City Club, 2123 Belmont Avenue
04-02-1956 – Oak Street School, New Castle, Pa.
04-02-1956 – Stink bomb at home of George Sledge, 142 North Fruit Street
04-16-1956 – Hillcrest Sportsman's Club, 138 Walton Street, Struthers
08-01-1956 – Frank's Food Market, 3305 South Avenue
08-18-1956 – Home of Peter Fetchet, 3496 Fifth Avenue, Liberty Township
11-05-1956 – Truck at Martin Brothers Trucking Co., Bessemer, Pa.
11-09-1956 – Stink bomb at home of John S. Basista, 843 East Boston Avenue
11-19-1956 – Home of Jack Sulligan, 1966 Smithfield Street
03-16-1957 – In home under construction for Sandy Naples, 605 Carlotta Drive
04-06-1957 – Home of Charles Bowers, 3522 Dover Road
05-06-1957 – Alleged cheat spot rented by Lawrence Breckenridge, Liberty Rd., Warren, owned by the Mathie Real Estate Company
08-13-1957 – Home of Detective Lloyd Haynes, 3049 McGuffey Road
01-22-1958 – Auto occupied by John Schuller, Michael Fedchina and Edward Tabus, parked at the rear of the American-Croatian Citizens Club, 1639 Poland Ave
01-29-1958 – Simon Street Metal Shop, 730 South Avenue
01-30-1958 – Youngstown Boat Supply, 2209 Mahoning Avenue

Appendix D

Interrogation of Detective Lloyd Haynes August 16, 1957

Sadly most of the police department records prior to 1960 have been destroyed. One that survived was the bombing of Detective Lloyd Hayne's home. The information contained in an interview of Haynes by Lieutenant George Maxim and Detective Edward Przelomski may be one of the few records in existence where the ties between the Mafia and Sandy Naples and Vince DeNiro are discussed. This, of course, is assuming that what was relayed to Haynes is true.

Two days after the Haynes' bombing Mayor Kryzan met with Przelomski and told him that Haynes had come to his office and stated that he wanted to take a polygraph test and that afterwards he wanted the mayor to release a statement to the media that he was cleared of any knowledge of who bombed his home. According to Kryzan, Haynes was in fear for his life and the lives of family members since the report he turned in on April 9 regarding the 422 Club.

At 2:35 that afternoon Maxim and Przelomski went to Haynes' South Hazel Street law office to interview him. What follows is the report filed by the two officers, minus typographical errors, on August 16.

"Lloyd Haynes informed us that he was ordered by Vice Squad Chief, George Krispli to make an investigation of the bombing of the home [Charles Bowers] on Dover Road. He stated that he was making this investigation and interviewed J. B. Burnich, and Burnich stated, 'Blackhands or Whitehands, I am not paying nothing.'

"He stated that he interviewed Sandy Naples and Sandy Naples mentioned the Mafia and stated that he would not give them anything. He stated that Sandy Naples informed him that Charlie Cavallaro bombed his (Sandy's) home, but he could not prove it, but when he does, he will kill him, he will not need the police to take care of the matter.

"He stated that he interviewed Louis (Lulu) Marian, who had been fired from the 422 Club, and Marian told him not to fool with it, it was too big for him, and as a result of his interview with Louis Marian, he wrote the report of April 9, 1957.

"Lloyd Haynes stated that on August 14, 1957 he and Patrolman Robert Berry went out to see if they could get some information concerning the bombing of Haynes' home. He stated that they were in Haynes' personal car and drove out Market Street and at Indianola Avenue at about 10:00pm he noticed Vince DeNiro on the street and Vince DeNiro came over to the car. Lloyd Haynes stated that he pulled out his gun and talked to Vince. He stated that DeNiro stated that

'I've been expecting you to look for me, I have talked to three or four friends, and we are sorry it happened. I would not do anything like that it would put the heat on me and I am about out of business now.' Haynes stated that he told DeNiro that if DeNiro did not do it himself, he knows who did it and he was going to hold him responsible for it. He stated that DeNiro informed him he was going to find out who did it and let Haynes know, he then left and went into the Colonial House on Market Street.

"Lloyd Haynes stated that after DeNiro left, he and Berry went to the Center Sandwich Shop, Center Street and Sandy Naples was there. They took Sandy Naples in the back and talked to him. He stated that Sandy Naples stated, 'I know that you are not involved in anything, but they have funny ways of doing things and do what they wish to do.' He stated that Vince DeNiro is in their hands and can't do anything with them or to them. Haynes stated that Sandy Naples stated that the purpose of this all is because he won't pay and several of them will not pay the SB's [author's assumption that he means sons of bitches] anything. He stated that Sandy Naples informed him that he will die before he will pay them. He said that he has a man in his house 24 hours a day with a shotgun. He informed Haynes that he will find out for him who put the bomb at his house and when he does then he will know who bombed Sandy's house.

"Haynes stated that after he and Berry left the Center Sandwich Shop they went to the Flamingo Club, Campbell, Ohio. He stated that he had talked to Calvin Menyard (Campbell Bug Man) owner of the Flamingo Club, on the telephone and he had informed him that he would find out who bombed his home. He stated that they arrived at the Flamingo Club and talked to Menyard and Menyard informed him that Mike Romeo of Campbell bombed Haynes' home.

"Haynes stated that he wanted to know how Menyard knew this information and Menyard informed him that Vince DeNiro was down to see Menyard and informed him that Haynes was out to see DeNiro and he (Haynes) was in a bad mood. Haynes stated that Menyard told him that Vince DeNiro told Menyard that Romeo bombed Haynes' home. Also that all bug men would have to get together and fight the 'boys' even if it takes a war. He said that one man cannot do it alone.

"Haynes informed us that he had forgotten to tell us something that he and DeNiro talked about when they were on Market Street and Indianola Avenue. He stated that DeNiro informed him that his theory was wrong, the people you think did it did not do it, they are my friends. Lieutenant Maxim asked him how did DeNiro know what and whom he was referring to and Haynes stated that he believes that DeNiro was referring to the report that he had turned in. [Since the report wasn't publicized it would be interesting to know how DeNiro knew about it.]

"Lieutenant Maxine asked Haynes what his opinions were as to why his home was bombed and he stated that his opinions were that (1) it was common knowledge that he had an inside in politics in Youngstown. (2) That he was putting his nose in 'their' business. (3) That they want to put pressure on in Youngstown for some reason.

"Lieutenant Maxim asked Haynes concerning his dealings with Sandy Naples and he asked Maxim to check and find out the truth, and that is that his dealings with Sandy Naples were sanctioned by George Krispli for him to get information from Sandy Naples reference the bombings.

"Lieutenant Maxim informed Haynes that he had some questions that he wanted to ask Haynes and told him that they would be personal and he wanted him to tell the truth about the questions. Haynes agreed that he would tell the truth and informed Maxim that he has enemies who spread stories about him.

"Did Sandy Naples aid you financially to obtain a college education?

"Are you involved in the house of prostitution at 113 John Street?

"Are you involved in the house of prostitution on Gerwig Avenue in reference the Britt deal?

"Are you involved in the Sunday Liquor Sales deal?

"Haynes denied that he was involved in any of the above listed matters and explained his knowledge and association of the matters.

"The matter of the lie detector test was brought up and Haynes stated that he wanted to take the test and wanted Mayor Kryzan to release the news release stating that Haynes had no knowledge of who bombed his home. Haynes promised to come in and said that he did not think that he wanted to have an out of town operator conduct the test stating that it was alright with him if Lieutenant Maxim conducted the test. It was left that the test would be taken on August 16. Haynes promised to cooperate with the bomb squad in all matters and the interview was concluded, at 4:40pm."

Appendix E

Chronology of Charles Cavallaro's Deportation Battle (Vindicator November 23, 1962)

May 1, 1921 – Date on which Cavallaro claimed he entered the United States as a stowaway. Cavallaro tried to establish an entry date before July 11924, in order to be eligible to submit an application for a "record of legal entry" which can be granted by the service (the "service" refers to the Immigration and Naturalization Service) to persons of good moral character. The service states it has proof Cavallaro was in the Italian army in 1921 and could not have entered the United States until after the 1924 cut-off date.

March 1935 – The service issues a deportation warrant against Cavallaro on grounds of illegal entry, but cannot find him.

October 27, 1947 – According to service records, he terminates his common-law marriage to Iva Bijoul.

April 13, 1948 – Cavallaro marries Helen Biola, an American citizen.

July 22, 1953 - US Immigration officials initiated proceedings to deport Cavallaro on a charge of being an undesirable alien. An Immigration Department investigator states that Cavallaro is in the "deportable class" of immigrants outlined in the new McCarran-Walters Immigration Act of 1952, which, among other changes, called for the deportation of undesirable aliens and known racket figures. Cavallaro appeared at the Immigration Bureau's Youngstown office in the Post Office Building and posted a $10,000 bond.

April 19, 1954 – A special inquiry officer of the service holds the first hearing in the Cavallaro case and orders him deported. Cavallaro files an application to "create a record of lawful admission."

June 28, 1954 – The Board of Immigration Appeals postpones action on Cavallaro's appeal until the Immigration Service disposed of the application for record of lawful admission. Cavallaro was injured in an accident in the autumn of 1954 and the hearing on the application was not held until May 18, 1955.

July 10, 1956 – The application for record of lawful entry is denied by a hearing officer in Cleveland.

April 10, 1957 – The Board of Immigration Appeals finally orders Cavallaro deported.

April 26, 1957 – Cavallaro files a petition for review of the case in the U.S. District Court in Cleveland.

January 22, 1958 – The petition for review is dismissed.

January 23, 1958 – Cavallaro wins a stay of the deportation order pending appeal to the Sixth Circuit Court of Appeals.

February 18, 1959 – The Court of Appeals upholds the deportation order. Cavallaro wins a new stay pending appeal to the U.S. Supreme Court, but this appeal in never filed.

May 21, 1959 – Cavallaro files a second application for a record of lawful admission.

July 13, 1960 – The second application is denied by the director of the Cleveland office of the Immigration Service. The regional commissioner of the service, however, orders the denial withdrawn to permit Cavallaro to submit additional evidence to show he was employed in the U.S. before 1924.

October 25, 1962 – The Board of Immigration Appeals granted a motion permitting withdrawal of the deportation order pending the new hearing in Cleveland on the additional evidence.

Cavallaro was killed before the Cleveland hearing takes place.

Bibliography

Newspapers:

Akron Beacon Journal
Arizona Daily Star
Ashtabula Star-Beacon
Buffalo Commercial
Buffalo Courier-Express
Buffalo Daily Courier
Buffalo Evening News
Buffalo Evening Times
Buffalo Express
Buffalo Morning Express
Buffalo Times
Chicago Daily Tribune
Cleveland News
Cleveland Plain Dealer
Cleveland Press
Jefferson Gazette
Miami Daily News
Miami News
New York Daily News
New York Times
Newton Falls Herald
Niagara Gazette
Niagara Falls Gazette
Steel Valley News
Toledo Blade
Tucson Daily Citizen
Warren Tribune Chronicle
Youngstown Telegram
Youngstown Vindicator

Government Publications:

Third Interim Report of the Special Committee to Investigate Organized Crime in Interstate Commerce – May 1, 1951.

Tax Court Of The United States – Anthony Delsanter, et al., Petitioners, v. Commissioner of Internal Revenue, Respondent – July 18, 1957..

State of New York Executive Department, Office of the Commissioner of Investigation: Report on the Activities and Associations of Persons Identified as Present at the Residence of Joseph Barbara, Sr., at Apalachin, New York, on November 14, 1957, and the Reasons for their Presence – April 23, 1958..

Hearings before The Subcommittee on Antitrust and Monopoly of the Committee on the Judiciary United States Senate, Part 1, Jacob "Jake" La Motta, June 14 and 15, 1960.

Hearings before the Permanent Subcommittee on Investigations of the Committee on Government Operations United States Senate, Part 2, October 10, 11, 15 and 16, 1963.

Hearings before the Permanent Subcommittee on the Investigations of the Committee on Governmental Affairs United States Senate One Hundredth Congress Second Session, October 11, 15, 21, 22, 29, 1988 (aka Organized Crime: 25 Years After Valachi).

Books:

Allen, Edward J. *Merchants of Menace: The Mafia: A Study of Organized Crime* 1962. Charles C. Thomas. Publisher.

Cook, Fred J.. *The Secret Rulers: Criminal Syndicates and How They Control the U.S. Underworld.* 1966. Duell, Sloan and Pearce.

D'Amato, Grace Anselmo. *Chance of a Lifetime.* 2001. Down The Shore Publishing.

Demaris, Ovid. *The Last Mafiosi.* 1981. Times Books.

Griffin, Joseph E. with Don DeNevi. *Mob Nemesis: How the FBI Crippled Organized Crime.* 2002. Prometheus Books.

Illman, Harry R.. *Unholy Toledo.* 1985. Polemic Press Publications .

Jenkins, William D.. *Steel Valley Klan: The Ku Klux Klan in Ohio's Mahoning Valley.* 1990. The Kent State University Press.

Kavieff, Paul R.. *The Violent Years: Prohibition and the Detroit Mobs.* 2001. Barricade Books.

King, Jeffrey S.. *The Life and Death of Pretty Boy Floyd.* 1998. The Kent State University Press.

Messick, Hank. *The Silent Syndicate.* 1967. The MacMillan Company.

Messick, Hank and Joseph L. Nellis. *The Private Lives of Public Enemies.* 1973. Peter H. Wyden, Inc.

Messick, Hank and Burt Goldblatt. *The Only Game In Town.* 1976. Thomas Y. Crowell Company.

Morton, James. *Gangland International* 1998. Little, Brown and Company.

Porrello, Rick. *The Rise and Fall of the Cleveland Mafia: Corn Sugar and Blood.* 1995 – Barricade Books, Inc..

Purvis, Melvin. *American Agent.* 1936. Doubleday, Doran & Co., Inc. .

Reid, Ed. *Mafia.* 1952. Random House.

Unger, Robert. *Union Station Massacre.* 1997. Andrews McMeel Publishing .

Youngstown Vindicator. *These Hundred Years: A Chronicle of the Twentieth Century as Recorded in the Pages of The Youngstown Vindicator.* 2000. The Vindicator Printing Company.

Index

Note to reader, the Index does not include names or places from the Appendices or the Chapter End Notes.